NO SPACE BETWEEN BERGOGLIO AND RATZINGER:

SO CLOSE IN APOSTASY, SO FAR FROM CATHOLIC TRUTH

by Thomas A. Droleskey, Ph.D.

Table of Contents

Introduction

Every day seems to bring news of outrageous comments and actions from the man most people in the world, Catholics and non-Catholics alike, believe is a true and legitimate Successor of Saint Peter, Jorge Mario Bergoglio. Many "conservative" and traditionally-minded Catholics within the structures of what they think is the Catholic Church believe that these aberrations are something new, that they have nothing to do with the "teachings" of the "Second" Vatican Council and the "magisterium" of the conciliar "popes."

Some "conservative" and traditionally-minded Catholics know that the man masquerading as "Pope Francis" teaches heresy and has endorsed a laissez-faire approach of dealing with hardened sinners who have no intention of quitting their lives of sin. Grasping at straws in order to avoid coming to the conclusion that the See of Peter is vacant, some of these Catholics have used what the late Monsignor Joseph Clifford Fenton called a "shoddy minimism" to provide blatant heretics and apostates with fig leaves of respectability and legitimacy as "officials" of the Catholic Church.

In doing so, however, Catholics who have created and sustained a cottage industry, one in which there is much money to be made, by the way, of criticizing a man they believe is a true and legitimate Successor of Saint Peter stand condemned by the words of Pope Leo XIII in *Epistola Tua*, June 17, 1885, and *Est Sane Molestum*, December 17, 1888, that forbid such criticism of a reigning Sovereign Pontiff. Thus far, though, these Catholics have chosen to ignore these apostolic letters, which Pope Leo XIII had inserted into the *Acta Apostolicae Sedis* to make it part of the binding teaching of the Catholic Church although it was merely a reiteration of basic Catholic principles that had been taught from time immemorial.

Yet other traditionally-minded Catholics of the "resist while recognize" mentality condemned by Pope Pius VI in Auctorem Fidei, August 28, 1794, ninety-one years before Pope Leo XIII's Epistola Tua, have been attempting to cling to the belief that that Jorge Mario Bergoglio's predecessor, Joseph Alois Ratzinger/Benedict XVI, is still the putative Vicar of Christ. Such fantasizing must necessarily ignore the fact that the supposed "restorer of tradition" from Germany, who was under suspicion of heresy by the Holy Office during the last years of the pontificate of Pope Pius XII, was a progenitor of the conciliar revolution that has devastated the vineyard of Our Blessed Lord and Saviour Jesus Christ.

The truth is, of course, that there is no theological "space" of any substance between the retired Joseph Alois Ratzinger/Benedict XVI and his successor, Jorge Mario Bergoglio/Francis. The differences that exist between these two Modernists center around matters of style and emphasis, not on substance. Ratzinger/Benedict's style was formal and intellectual. Bergoglio/Francis is the self-styled "street priest" who relishes in the vulgar, the profane and the unconventional, freed at last to do as he pleases without any external constraints being imposed upon him by authorities in Rome.

Ratzinger tried to "prove" a "continuity" existed between the immutable teaching of the Catholic Church and what he says is an "apparent" discontinuity represented by the teaching of the "Second" Vatican Council. Bergoglio simply does not care about proving any such thing, proving Ratzinger's own philosophically absurd and dogmatically condemned "hermeneutic of continuity" that the former "pontiff" used to relativize the teaching of our true popes can be used against the conciliar "popes" by their successors. After all, why should Ratzinger's interpretation of the "Second" Vatican Council be the definitive one if the teaching of our true popes are said to have become "obsolete in the particulars they contained" after having served their purpose "at the time"?

The problem, however, is not with the style or even the particular teaching of the conciliar "popes." No, the problem facing us is a false religion, conciliarism, that treats the articles contained in the Sacred Deposit of Faith as subject to Modernism's "evolution of dogma" whereby every aspect of the Holy Faith can be "redefined" in "new" and "innovative" ways to bring it "up-to-date" with the supposed "needs" of the mythical entity known as "modern man."

The purpose of this book, therefore, is to demonstrate the complete theological closeness of Joseph Alois Ratzinger/Benedict XVI with his successor, Jorge Mario Bergoglio/Francis. The former was a guiding force of the conciliar revolution at its inception; the latter is a true so of the revolution who is intent on removing all remaining bastions of Catholicism in the conciliar structures that have, he believes and has told us endless numbers of times, "caged the Holy Spirit" from effecting what he dares to call "God's surprises" in what is said to be the Catholic Church.

This book is not an apologia in defense of the principles underlying the Catholic teaching that a heretic cannot be a true and legitimate Successor of Saint Peter. Although Chapter Fifteen of this book explains that the Catholic Church is indeed perpetually immune from error and heresy, there are many others far more qualified than this author who have laid out the case for sedevacantism in a number of learned articles and books.

It is this author's intention to demonstrate to the reader the differences between the teaching of the Catholic Church and that of her counterfeit ape, the conciliar church, by presenting evidence from the words and actions of Joseph Alois Ratzinger and Jorge Mario Bergoglio themselves. No one who has a shred of intellectual honesty can claim that these two men possess the Catholic Faith as It has been handed down us from the Apostles, who received It from Our Lord Himself, and protected infallibly by the Third Person of the Most Blessed Trinity, God the Holy Ghost, from all error and falsehood.

As Pope Leo XIII noted in *A Review of His Pontificate*, March 19, 1902:

> In the Catholic Church Christianity is Incarnate. It identifies Itself with that perfect, spiritual, and, in its own order, sovereign society, which is the Mystical Body of Jesus Christ and which has for Its visible head the Roman Pontiff, successor of the Prince of the Apostles. It is the continuation of the mission of the Savior, the daughter and the heiress of His Redemption. It has preached the Gospel, and has defended it at the price of Its blood, and strong in the Divine assistance and of that immortality which has been promised it, **It makes no terms with error but remains faithful to the commands which it has received, to carry the doctrine of Jesus Christ to the uttermost limits of the world and to the end of time, and to protect it in its inviolable integrity**. (Pope Leo XIII, A Review of His Pontificate, March 19, 1902.)

No terms with error means precisely that, no terms with error. The Catholic Church is the spotless, virginal mystical spouse of her Divine Founder, Invisible Head and Mystical Bridegroom, Our Blessed Lord and Saviour Jesus Christ. It is impossible for error of any kind to be associated with the Catholic Church. Impossible.

As the lords of conciliarism have specialized in little else other than error, however, it has been necessary to reemphasize various points several times in this book. Although one reading this book from cover to cover may find the documentation that is repeated several times to be redundant, the purpose of doing this is to provide readers with information in the context of a particular subject without forcing them to refer to an earlier chapter. Repetition is the mother of learning, and this author has always striven to repeat points as it is the tendency of more than a few readers to forget what they had read earlier in an article or a book such as this one.

Readers will come to whatever conclusions they desire to draw from the evidence presented in the pages that follow. Believing Catholics, though, do have an obligation to adhere to the truth once they have come to accept it as such, and it is the hope of this author that at least a few people who have not done so thus far will be given pause to do so now.

Entrusting all in this time of apostasy and betrayal to the Blessed Virgin Mary as the consecrated slaves of her Divine Son, Christ the King, through her own Sorrowful and Immaculate Heart, may we pray as many Rosaries each day as our state-in-life permits. We must also embrace the penances of the moment, which may include estrangement from close relatives and friends and former acquaintances, with joy and gratitude for having been chosen by God from all eternity to bear the crosses we find in our daily lives in this challenging time of ours.

The final victory belongs to Christ the King through the Immaculate Heart of Mary.

Our Lady herself told us in the Cova da Iria near Fatima, Portugal, that her Immaculate Heart will triumph in the end.

It is simply our task to plant a few seeds, unworthy though we may be and mindful of our need to make reparation for our own sins and those of the whole world, for this triumph.

What are we waiting for?

Vivat Christus Rex!

Viva Cristo Rey!

Thomas A. Droleskey, Ph.D.

Publisher-Editor

www.Christorchaos.com

Chapter One

Complete Agreement Concerning the "Enduring Validity" of Judaism

One of the most absurd developments in the past nearly nine years now is the extent to which former critics of Joseph "Cardinal" Ratzinger attempted to transform him into a veritable "restorer of Tradition" once he, as "Benedict XVI," had met at Castel Gandolfo with Bishop Bernard Fellay, the Superior General of the Society of Saint Pius X, on August 29, 2005, the Feast of the Beheading of Saint John the Baptist, and especially after the issuance of *Summorum Pontificum* on July 7, 2007.

The effort to transform a man who was termed by one prominent "resist while recognize" movement writer an "ecclesial termite" and mocked as "our only friend in the Vatican" into an opponent of the very conciliar revolution he helped to design and impose upon the "Second" Vatican Council is beneath contempt as it was nothing other than a supposedly "strategic" exercise in intellectual dishonesty designed to keep traditionally-minded Catholics from examining the truthfulness of the following statement of the late Mario Francesco "Cardinal" Pompedda in February of 2005:

> **It is true that the canonical doctrine states that the see would be vacant in the case of heresy**. ... But in regard to all else, I think what is applicable is what judgment regulates human acts. And the act of will, namely a resignation or capacity to govern or not govern, is a human act. (**Cardinal Says Pope Could Govern Even If Unable to Speak**, Zenit, February 8, 2005; see also see also Gregorius's **The Chair is Still Empty**.)

The effort to transform the one-time "ecclesial termite" into a "restorer of Tradition" and, at the present time, into a supposed counterpoint to the allegedly more "progressive" Jorge Mario Bergoglio has had to overlook the now retired "pontiff's" expressly stated desire to use *Summorum Pontificum* as a means of "pacifying the spirits" of those who were "attached" to the 1961/1962 Missal that had been promulgated by Angelo Roncalli/John XXIII and was in effect in the counterfeit church of conciliarism for precisely three years before being replaced by Giovanni Montini/Paul VI's *Ordo Missae* on Sunday, November 29, 1964:

> **Leading men and women to God, to the God Who speaks in the Bible**: this is the supreme and fundamental priority of the Church and of the Successor of Peter at the present time. A logical consequence of this is that we must have at heart the unity of all believers. Their disunity, their disagreement among themselves, calls into question the credibility of their talk of God. **Hence the effort to promote a common witness by Christians to their faith - ecumenism - is part of the supreme priority**. Added to this is the need for all those who believe in God to join in seeking peace, to attempt to draw closer to one another, and to journey together, even with their differing images of God, towards the source of Light - this is inter-religious dialogue. Whoever proclaims that God is Love 'to the end' has to bear witness to love: in loving devotion to the suffering, in the rejection of hatred and enmity - this is the social dimension of the Christian faith, of which I spoke in the Encyclical 'Deus caritas est'.

"So if the arduous task of working for faith, hope and love in the world is presently (and, in various ways, always) the Church's real priority, then part of this is also made up of acts of reconciliation, small and not so small. That the quiet gesture of extending a hand gave rise to a huge uproar, and thus became exactly the opposite of a gesture of reconciliation, is a fact which we must accept. But I ask now: Was it, and is it, truly wrong in this case to meet half-way the brother who 'has something against you' and to seek reconciliation? **Should not civil society also try to forestall forms of extremism and to incorporate their eventual adherents - to the extent possible - in the great currents shaping social life, and thus avoid their being segregated, with all its consequences? Can it be completely mistaken to work to break down obstinacy and narrowness, and to make space for what is positive and retrievable for the whole**? I myself saw, in the years after 1988, how the return of communities which had been separated from Rome changed their interior attitudes; I saw how returning to the bigger and broader Church enabled them to **move beyond one-sided positions and broke down rigidity so that positive energies could emerge for the whole**. Can we be totally indifferent about a community which has 491 priests, 215 seminarians, 6 seminaries, 88 schools, 2 university-level institutes, 117 religious brothers, 164 religious sisters and thousands of lay faithful? Should we casually let them drift farther from the Church? I think for example of the 491 priests. We cannot know how mixed their motives may be. All the same, I do not think that they would have chosen the priesthood if, **alongside various distorted and unhealthy elements**, they did not have a love for Christ and a desire to proclaim Him and, with Him, the living God. Can we simply exclude them, as representatives of a radical fringe, from our pursuit of reconciliation and unity? What would then become of them?

"Certainly, for some time now, and once again on this specific occasion, we have heard from some representatives of that community many **unpleasant things - arrogance and presumptuousness, an obsession with one-sided positions**, etc. Yet to tell the truth, I must add that I have also received a number of touching testimonials of gratitude which clearly showed an openness of heart. But should not the great Church also allow herself to be generous in the knowledge of her great breadth, in the knowledge of the promise made to her? Should not we, as good educators, **also be capable of overlooking various faults and making every effort to open up broader vistas**? And should we not admit that some unpleasant things have also emerged in Church circles? At times one gets the impression that our society needs to have at least one group to which no tolerance may be shown; which one can easily attack and hate. And should someone dare to approach them - in this case the Pope - he too loses any right to tolerance; he too can be treated hatefully, without misgiving or restraint. (**Letter to the Bishops of the Catholic Church concerning the remission of the excommunication of the four Bishops consecrated by Archbishop Lefebvre, March 10, 2009**.)

Fr Federico Lombardi, S.J., Director of the Holy See Press Office: *What do you say to those who, in France, fear that the "Motu proprio'* Summorum Pontificum *signals a step backwards from the great insights of the Second Vatican Council? How can you reassure them?*

Benedict XVI: Their fear is unfounded, for this "Motu Proprio' ***is merely an act of tolerance, with a pastoral aim, for those people who were brought up with this liturgy, who love it, are familiar with it and want to live with this liturgy***. They form a small group, because this presupposes a schooling in Latin, a training in a certain culture. Yet for these people, to have the love and tolerance to let them live with this liturgy seems to me a normal requirement of the faith and pastoral concern of any Bishop of our Church. There is no opposition between the liturgy renewed by the Second Vatican Council and this liturgy.

On each day [of the Council], the Council Fathers celebrated Mass in accordance with the ancient rite and, at the same time, they conceived of a natural development for the liturgy within the whole of this century, for the liturgy is a living reality that develops but, in its development, retains its identity. Thus, there are certainly different accents, but nevertheless [there remains] a fundamental identity that excludes a contradiction, an opposition between the renewed liturgy and the previous liturgy. In any case, I believe that there is an opportunity for the enrichment of both parties. **On the one hand the friends of the old liturgy can and must know the new saints, the new prefaces of the liturgy, etc.... On the other, the new liturgy places greater emphasis on common participation, but it is not merely an assembly of a certain community, but rather always an act of the universal Church in communion with all believers of all times, and an act of worship. In this sense, it seems to me that there is a mutual enrichment, and it is clear that the renewed liturgy is the ordinary liturgy of our time.** (**Interview of the Holy Father during the flight to France, September 12, 2008**.)

Liturgical worship is the supreme expression of priestly and episcopal life, just as it is of catechetical teaching. Your duty to sanctify the faithful people, dear Brothers, is indispensable for the growth of the Church. In the *Motu Proprio "Summorum Pontificum"*, I was led to set out the conditions in which this duty is to be exercised, with regard to the possibility of using the missal of Blessed John XXIII (1962) in addition to that of Pope Paul VI (1970). **Some fruits of these new arrangements have already been seen, and I hope that, thanks be to God, the necessary pacification of spirits is already taking place. I am aware of your difficulties, but I do not doubt that, within a reasonable time, you can find solutions satisfactory for all, lest the seamless tunic of Christ be further torn. Everyone has a place in the Church. Every person, without exception, should be able to feel at home, and never rejected. God, who loves all men and women and wishes none to be lost, entrusts us with this mission by appointing us shepherds of his sheep. We can only thank him for the honour and the trust that he has placed in us. Let us therefore strive always to be servants of unity!** (**Meeting with the French Bishops in the *Hemicycle Sainte-Bernadette*, Lourdes, 14 September 2008**.)

Only the willfully blind in the Motu blogosphere could ignore Ratzinger/Benedict's frank discussion of the reason he issued *Summorum Pontificum*. Ratzinger/Benedict was not personally devoted to the Immemorial Mass of Tradition as it enshrined a Faith that was counter to the alleged "needs" of his mythical "modern man." He desired there to be a "synthesis" between the Missal of Pope Saint Pius V and that of the very unblessed Giovanni Montini/**Paul The Sick.**

Yet it is that the "strategists" in the "resist while recognize" movement chose to ignore their "restorer of Tradition's" multiple defections from the Catholic Faith during his 2,873 days as the universal public face of apostasy that were summarized (mind you, only summarized) on February 13, 2013, in **Mister Asteroid Is Looking Pretty Good Right About Now**. The omissions of fact from their newspapers and websites were glaring as they knew that their "pope's" defections from the Faith, which were identical to the ones for which they had criticized Karol Wojtyla/John Paul II with relentless fury, were indefensible.

Jorge Mario Bergoglio is only a cruder, more vulgar, profane and visceral popularizer of the conciliar revolution than the supposedly "erudite" Hegelian, Joseph Ratzinger/Benedict XVI. Most, although not all, of the differences between the two are matters of style and emphasis, not substance, as each man is but a total creature of the conciliar revolution. Ratzinger/Benedict was one of its progenitors. Bergoglio is its child and current propagator.

Consider the fact that Ratzinger/Benedict committed Mortal Sins against the First Commandment every time he put into question or has denied a dogma of the Faith or praised a false religion or entered into a temple of false worship. He did so every time he has staged the Protestant and Judeo-Masonic *Novus Ordo* liturgical service.

Anyone who denies that entering into and treating with respect places of false worship without seeking the unconditional conversion of those who adhere to the devils worshiped therein is a Mortal Sin is intellectually dishonest or bereft of the *sensus Catholicus* (thereby lacking any knowledge of the necessity of defending the honor and glory and majesty of the Most Blessed Trinity) or is a coward who is afraid to speak to the truth of the Faith for one reason or another.

God will not be mocked. The God of Revelation does not want members of the Catholic Church, no less those who believe themselves to be bishops and priests, to give even the slightest degree of credibility to any false religion. The God of Revelation, which consists of Sacred Scripture and Sacred (Apostolic) Tradition, hates each and every false religion. He has no respect for false religions, which have the power to save no one and are instruments of disorder in souls and thus of disorder and chaos within nations. Those who show respect for false religions by esteeming their symbols and praising their nonexistent "ability" to contribute to the "betterment" of nations and the world are themselves enemies of God as they find themselves condemned by these very words of Our Blessed Lord and Saviour Jesus Christ Himself:

> **But he that shall scandalize one of these little ones that believe in me, it were better for him that a millstone should be hanged about his neck, and that he should be drowned in the depth of the sea.** Woe to the world because of scandals. For it must needs be that scandals come: but nevertheless woe to that man by whom the scandal cometh. And if thy hand, or thy foot scandalize thee, cut it off, and cast it from thee. It is better for thee to go into life maimed or lame, than having two hands or two feet, to be cast into everlasting fire. And if thy eye scandalize thee, pluck it out, and cast it from thee. It is better for thee having one eye to enter into life, than having two eyes to be cast into hell fire. See that you despise not one of these little ones: for I say to you, that their angels in heaven always see the face of my Father who is in heaven. (Matthew 18: 6-10.)

Yet it is to most Catholics that those of us who reject the legitimacy of these spiritual robber barons are considered to be a source of scandal! Amazing irrationality and illogic.

The true scandal is that the former head of the counterfeit church of conciliarism could enter into Talmudic synagogues and listen without complaint to a Talmudic hymn speaking of the "waiting" for the Messiah as he, the putative Successor of Saint Peter, is treated as an inferior.

The true scandal is that the former head of the counterfeit church of conciliarism took off his shoes and entered Mohammedan mosques, even going so far once as to assume the Mohammedan "prayer" position as he turns in the direction of Mecca in Istanbul, Turkey, on November 30, 2006. His successor, Jorge Mario Bergoglio, turned in the direction of Mecca and "prayed" next to a Mohammedan imam in the Mosque of the Sultan Ahmed in Istanbul, Turkey, on Saturday, November 29, 2014, the Vigil of the Feast of Saint Andrew and the Commemoration of Saint Saturninus.

Bergoglio boasted of having "prayed" in what is known as the "Blue Mosque":

> Vatican City, Nov 29, 2014 / 06:04 am (CNA/EWTN News).- During Pope Francis' visit to Istanbul's Blue Mosque, he paused for a moment of prayer alongside Ankara's Grand Mufti **– a moment of "interreligious dialogue" which mirrored that of his predecessor**.
>
> **"When they were under the Dome, the Pope insisted: 'not only must we praise and glorify him, but we must adore him,'"** Vatican spokesman Fr. Federico Lombardi S.J. told journalists Nov. 29. **"Therefore it is reasonable to qualify this moment of silence a moment of silent adoration."**
>
> **"(It was) a beautiful moment of interreligious dialogue, and it the exact same thing happened in 2006 with Pope Benedict, it was exactly the same**."
>
> Fr. Lombardi offered his statement to the head of the Holy See Press Office association of journalists by telephone. The message was then relayed to the journalists present in the press center in Istanbul.
>
> Pope Francis' visit to the historic Sultan Ahmet Mosque, known as the "Blue Mosque" due to the blue tiles covering the inside, marks the third time a Pope has ever gone inside, the first being St. John Paul II in 1979.
>
> In his statement, Fr. Lombardi said that upon his arrival, the Roman Pontiff was greeted in the Mosque's garden by a group of 50-60 people coming from different Christian communities – including Latin, Coptic, Syro and Armenian – as well as their bishops.
>
> President of the Turkish Episcopal Conference Bishop Smirme Franceschini offered a welcoming address before the Pope went inside.
>
> The Bishop of Rome was accompanied into the mosque by Ankara's Grand Mufti

Mehmet Görmez and two imam. After entering, the Grand Mufti explained to the Pope some verses from the Quran in which Niqab spoke of Zachariah, the birth of John the Baptist, of Elizabeth and Mary.

Once the Grand Mufti finished speaking, he and the Pope "took a moment of silence, a silent adoration (and) **the Pope said twice to the Muftì: we must adore God**," Fr. Lombardi said.

It was a true moment of interreligious dialogue, he observed, noting that afterward the Grand Mufti cited more verses of the Quran which refer to God as a God of love and justice.

Fr. Lombardi recalled how the Mufti said to Pope Francis that "**'on that we are agreed.' And the Pope said: 'Yes, on that we are agreed.' It was also a beautiful moment of dialogue.**"

After leaving the Mosque the Roman Pontiff went to visit the nearby Hagia Sofia, which is a former Greek Orthodox patriarchal basilica that was later turned into an imperial mosque, and is now a museum.

While inside Pope Francis signed the museum's Golden Book, writing in Greek "St. Sofia, Holy Wisdom of God," and cited a passage in Latin from psalm 84 that says "How lovely is thy dwelling place, O LORD of hosts!" (**Bergoglio's prayer at Blue Mosque 'exactly the same' as Ratzinger's**. Also see the post at **Novus Ordo Watch Wire**.)

During a televised moment of silent prayer in Istanbul's Blue Mosque Nov. 29, alongside the city's grand mufti, "I prayed for Turkey, I prayed for the mufti, I prayed for myself because I need it, and I prayed above all for the peace and an end to war." (**Jorge's Press Confab**.)

It was in 1948 that The Holy Office, which was headed at the time by none other than Pope Pius XII, reiterated the Catholic Church's complete ban on Catholics participating in the services of false religions or "praying" within their temples that had been reaffirmed by Pope Pius XI *Mortalium Animos*, January 6, 1928:

Mixed gatherings of non-Catholics with Catholics have been reportedly held in various places, where things pertaining to the Faith have been discussed against the prescriptions of the Sacred Canons and without previous permission of the Holy See. Therefore all are reminded that according to the norm of Canon 1325 § 3 laypeople as well as clerics both secular and regular are forbidden to attend these gatherings without the aforesaid permission. It is however much less licit for Catholics to summon and institute such kind of gatherings. Let therefore Ordinaries urge all to serve these prescriptions accurately.

These are to be observed with even stronger force of law when it comes to gatherings called "ecumenical", which laypeople and clerics may not attend at all without previous consent of the Holy See.

> **Moreover, since acts of mixed worship have also been posed not rarely both within and without the aforesaid gatherings, all are once more warned that any communication in sacred affairs is totally forbidden according to the norm of Canons 1258 and 731, § 2.**
>
> Given at Rome, at the premises of the Holy Office, on June 5th 1948. (This was translated by those who run *Novus Ordo Watch*. **See** The Holy Office's 1948 Canonical Warning against Ecumenical Gatherings.)

Jorge Mario Bergoglio, acting in complete "continuity" with his conciliar predecessors, believes that such statements were erroneous because men sought to "cage" God the Holy Ghost. The origins of Jorge's "spirits," of course, are diabolical as he projects into God his own imaginings of what He *really* teaches in spite of all past "errors." Bergoglio placed himself outside of the pale of Holy Mother Church long before his "election" six hundred twenty-nine days ago, that is, on Wednesday, March 13, 2013.

No, those those who recognize that a man who has defected from the Catholic Faith cannot serve as an official in the Catholic Church are not the ones given "scandal" at this time.

The conciliar "popes" and their "bishops" are the ones who have been and continue to be the source of the *true* scandals in this time of apostasy and betrayal, and on this score Joseph Alois Ratzinger/Benedict is of one Modernist mind and apostate heart with Jorge Mario Bergoglio.

Remember, the former head of the counterfeit church of conciliarism referred in August of 2007 to a mountain in Japan, Mount Hiei, upon which the Tendei sect of Buddhism worship their devils, as "sacred."

The true scandal is that Giovanni Enrico Antonio Maria Montini/Paul VI, Karol Josef Wojtyla/John Paul II, Joseph Alois Ratzinger/Benedict XVI and Jorge Mario Bergoglio/Francis have chosen repeatedly to ignore the following words of Sacred Scripture, written under the inspiration of the Third Person of the Most Blessed Trinity, God the Holy Ghost, as he esteems the symbols and even the essential "goodness" of false religions:

> Or, that the idol is any thing? But the things which the heathens sacrifice, they sacrifice to devils, and not to God. And I would not that you should be made partakers with devils.
>
> You cannot drink the chalice of the Lord, and the chalice of devils: you cannot be partakers of the table of the Lord, and of the table of devils. Do we provoke the Lord to jealousy? Are we stronger than he? (1 Cor. 10: 19-22.)

Those who turned a blind eye to Ratzinger/Benedict's multiple defections from the Catholic Faith during his 2,873 days in office knew that these things are true.

Some even know that the Protestant and Judeo-Masonic *Novus Ordo* liturgical service is evil.

They know that the nature of dogmatic truth cannot be explained away by the absurd and dogmatically condemned thesis contained in Ratzinger/Benedict's "hermeneutic of continuity and discontinuity."

They know that the conciliar "popes" have abandoned the Catholic Church's mission to seek with urgency the unconditional conversion of all men to her maternal bosom. They know that Our Blessed Lord and Saviour Jesus Christ is meant to reign as the King over men and over nations.

Most of those who consider themselves to be the "gatekeepers" of traditionalism, however, were content to keep their mouths shut about the apostasies and sacrileges and blasphemies that they saw emanating from Ratzinger/Benedict in order not to "jeopardize" *Summorum Pontificum.*

Things are supposedly "different" now that Jorge Mario Bergoglio, whom some of the same "gatekeepers" who kept their mouths shut about Ratzinger/Benedict after having criticized him during his twenty-three and one-half year tenure as Wojtyla/John Paul II's prefect of the so-called Congregation for the Doctrine of the Faith, has "wounded" *Summorum Pontificum* and has engaged in the same kind of "papal" extravaganza liturgies as had the "canonized" Polish "pope" had pioneered from October 16, 1978, to April 1 or 2 (depending upon which date he actually died), 2005.

Some, such as "Father" Paul Kramer, have concluded that Bergoglio's open heresy about the "permanent validity" of the Mosaic Covenant makes him a false claimant to the Throne of Saint Peter while believing that Ratzinger/Benedict, who believed and professed publicly, both by words and symbolic gestures, the exact same heresy that is "orthodox" conciliar doctrine, was "forced" to resign the conciliar "papacy," making Ratzinger/Benedict still the "legitimate" conciliar "pontiff." Such must be the absolute, patent absurdities that result when those who cannot bear to admit that the "crazies" who adhere to sedevacantism might be correct and that they, the sedevacantists, are not the problem facing the Church Militant in this time of apostasy and betrayal.

The Two-Headed "Pope Monster" and the Jews

It is to try to discredit this delusional belief that this series of articles, published in January of 2014, has been placed into book form. There are many areas of absolute convergence between Joseph Alois Ratzinger/Benedict XVI and Jorge Mario Bergoglio. The first of these areas deals with the heresies held by both men about Talmudic Judaism and its "enduring validity."

Jorge Mario Bergoglio's most open heresy about the Jews was contained in *Evangelii Gaudium*, November 26, 2013, although he has said and done many other things, including reading "prayers" from the blasphemous Talmud and keeping a Kosher kitchen while entertaining his rabbi friends, including his pro-abortion and pro-perversity comrade from Argentina, Abraham Skorka. Bergoglio is an identical twin to Joseph Ratzinger/Benedict XVI concerning the "validity" of Talmudic Judaism.

This is what Jorge Mario Bergoglio wrote in *Evangelii Gaudium*:

> 247. **We hold the Jewish people in special regard because their covenant with God has never been revoked, for "the gifts and the call of God are irrevocable" (*Rom* 11:29). The Church, which shares with Jews an important part of the sacred Scriptures, looks upon the people of the covenant and their faith as one of the sacred roots of her own Christian identity (cf. *Rom* 11:16-18). As Christians, we cannot consider Judaism as a foreign religion; nor do we include the Jews among those called to turn from idols and to serve the true God (cf. *1 Thes* 1:9). With them, we believe in the one God who acts in history, and with them we accept his revealed word.**
>
> 248. Dialogue and friendship with the children of Israel are part of the life of Jesus' disciples. The friendship which has grown between us makes us bitterly and sincerely regret the terrible persecutions which they have endured, and continue to endure, especially those that have involved Christians.
>
> 249. God **continues to work among the people of the Old Covenant and to bring forth treasures of wisdom which flow from their encounter with his word. For this reason, the Church also is enriched when she receives the values of Judaism. While it is true that certain Christian beliefs are unacceptable to Judaism, and that the Church cannot refrain from proclaiming Jesus as Lord and Messiah, there exists as well a rich complementarity which allows us to read the texts of the Hebrew Scriptures together and to help one another to mine the riches of God's word. We can also share many ethical convictions and a common concern for justice and the development of peoples.** (Jorge Mario Bergoglio, *Evangelii Gaudium*, November 26, 2013. See **Jorge and Oscar's False Gospel of False Joy, part one**.)

Here is but a sampling of *some* of Joseph Ratzinger's statements that are premised upon an acceptance of the same heresy:

> It is of course possible to read the Old Testament so that it is not directed toward Christ; it does not point quite unequivocally to Christ. And if Jews cannot see the promises as being fulfilled in him, this is not just ill will on their part, but genuinely because of the obscurity of the texts and the tension in the relationship between these texts and the figure of Jesus. Jesus brings a new meaning to these texts – yet it is he who first gives them their proper coherence and relevance and significance. **There are perfectly good reasons, then, for denying that the Old Testament refers to Christ and for saying, No, that is not what he said. And there are also good reasons for referring it to him – that is what the dispute between Jews and Christians is about.** (Joseph "Cardinal" Ratzinger, *God and the World*, p. 209.)
>
> In its work, the Biblical Commission could not ignore the contemporary context, where the shock of the Shoah has put the whole question under a new light. Two main problems are posed: Can Christians, after all that has happened, still claim in good conscience to be the legitimate heirs of Israel's Bible? Have they the right to propose a Christian interpretation of this Bible, or should they not instead, respectfully and humbly, renounce any claim that, in the light of what has happened, must look like a usurpation? The second question follows from the first: In its presentation of the Jews and the Jewish people, has not the New

Testament itself contributed to creating a hostility towards the Jewish people that provided a support for the ideology of those who wished to destroy Israel? The Commission set about addressing those two questions. It is clear that a Christian rejection of the Old Testament would not only put an end to Christianity itself as indicated above, but, in addition, would prevent the fostering of positive relations between Christians and Jews, precisely because they would lack common ground. **In the light of what has happened, what ought to emerge now is a new respect for the Jewish interpretation of the Old Testament. On this subject, the Document says two things. First it declares that "the Jewish reading of the Bible is a possible one, in continuity with the Jewish Scriptures of the Second Temple period, a reading analogous to the Christian reading, which developed in parallel fashion" (no. 22). It adds that Christians can learn a great deal from a Jewish exegesis practised for more than 2000 years; in return, Christians may hope that Jews can profit from Christian exegetical research (ibid.). I think this analysis will prove useful for the pursuit of Judeo-Christian dialogue, as well as for the interior formation of Christian consciousness.** (Joseph "Cardinal" Ratzinger, Preface to The Jewish People and Their Scriptures in the Christian Bible.)

It is clear that this commitment to expressing a specific truth in a new way demands new thinking on this truth and a new and vital relationship with it; it is also clear that new words can only develop if they come from an informed understanding of the truth expressed, and on the other hand, that a reflection on faith also requires that this faith be lived. In this regard, the programme that Pope John XXIII proposed was extremely demanding, indeed, just as the synthesis of fidelity and dynamic is demanding.. . .

Thirdly, linked more generally to this was the problem of religious tolerance - a question that required a new definition of the relationship between the Christian faith and the world religions. **In particular, before the recent crimes of the Nazi regime and, in general, with a retrospective look at a long and difficult history, it was necessary to evaluate and define in a new way the relationship between the Church and the faith of Israel.** (Christmas greetings to the Members of the Roman Curia and Prelature, December 22, 2005)

To the religious leaders present this afternoon, **I wish to say that the particular contribution of religions to the quest for peace lies primarily in the wholehearted, united search for God**. Ours is the task of proclaiming and witnessing that the Almighty is present and knowable even when he seems hidden from our sight, that he acts in our world for our good, and that a society's future is marked with hope when it resonates in harmony with his divine order. It is God's dynamic presence that draws hearts together and ensures unity. In fact, the ultimate foundation of unity among persons lies in the perfect oneness and universality of God, who created man and woman in his image and likeness in order to draw us into his own divine life so that all may be one. ("Pope" Benedict XVI, **Courtesy visit to the President of the State of Israel at the presidential palace in Jerusalem, May 11, 2009**.)

When he came among you for the first time, as a Christian and as Pope, my Venerable Predecessor John Paul II, almost 24 years ago, wanted to make a decisive contribution to strengthening the good relations between our two communities, so as to overcome every misconception and prejudice. My visit forms a part of the journey already begun, to confirm and deepen it. With sentiments of heartfelt appreciation, I come among you to express to you the esteem and the affection which the Bishop and the Church of Rome, as well as the entire Catholic Church, have towards this Community and all Jewish communities around the world.

2. The teaching of the Second Vatican Council has represented for Catholics a clear landmark to which constant reference is made in our attitude and our relations with the Jewish people, marking a new and significant stage. The Council gave a strong impetus to our irrevocable commitment to pursue the path of dialogue, fraternity and friendship, a journey which has been deepened and developed in the last forty years, through important steps and significant gestures. Among them, I should mention once again the historic visit by my Venerable Predecessor to this Synagogue on 13 April 1986, the numerous meetings he had with Jewish representatives, both here in Rome and during his Apostolic Visits throughout the world, the Jubilee Pilgrimage which he made to the Holy Land in the year 2000, the various documents of the Holy See which, following the Second Vatican Council's Declaration Nostra Aetate, have made helpful contributions to the increasingly close relations between Catholics and Jews. I too, in the course of my Pontificate, have wanted to demonstrate my closeness to and my affection for the people of the Covenant. I cherish in my heart each moment of the pilgrimage that I had the joy of making to the Holy Land in May of last year, along with the memories of numerous meetings with Jewish Communities and Organizations, in particular my visits to the Synagogues of Cologne and New York.

Furthermore, the Church has not failed to deplore the failings of her sons and daughters, begging forgiveness for all that could in any way have contributed to the scourge of anti-Semitism and anti-Judaism (cf. Commission for Religious Relations with the Jews, We Remember: A Reflection on the Shoah, 16 March 1998). May these wounds be healed forever! The heartfelt prayer which Pope John Paul II offered at the Western Wall on 26 March 2000 comes back to my mind, and it calls forth a profound echo in our hearts: "**God of our Fathers, you chose Abraham and his descendants to bring your Name to the nations: we are deeply saddened by the behaviour of those who in the course of history have caused these children of yours to suffer, and asking your forgiveness we wish to commit ourselves to genuine brotherhood with the people of the Covenant.**" (**Ratzinger at Rome synagogue: 'May these wounds be healed forever!'**)

9. **Christians and Jews share to a great extent a common spiritual patrimony, they pray to the same Lord,** they have the same roots, and yet they often remain unknown to each other. It is our duty, in response to God's call, to strive to keep open the space for dialogue, for reciprocal respect, for growth in friendship, for a common witness in the face of the challenges of our time, which invite us to cooperate for the good of humanity in this world created by God, the **Omnipotent and Merciful**. (**Ratzinger/Benedict at Rome synagogue: 'May these wounds be healed forever!'**)

There is no space between Ratzinger and Bergoglio on the matter of the "enduring nature" of the Mosaic Covenant.

Indeed, much was made in late-2013 of the following photograph showing Israeli Prime Minister Benjamin Netanyahu handing a menorah to Jorge Mario Bergoglio in the Vatican in December of 2013:

To this, good readers, I say the following: SO WHAT?

The one-time "ecclesial termite" (see **Ratzinger Personally Consecrates Neo-Modernist Bishop**) turned "restorer of Tradition" received a menorah at the John Paul II Cultural Center in Washington, District of Columbia, on Thursday, April 17, 2008:

> "David Michaels, director of intercommunal affairs at B'nai B'rith International, the oldest Jewish humanitarian organization, presented the pope with a silver menorah, symbolizing the validity of God's covenant of peace." (**USCCB Papal Visit Site | Pope Meets Interreligious Leaders, Says Dialogue Discovers Truth**.)

Ratzinger/Benedict also received a "shofar" from the Talmudists at the synagogue in Cologne, Germany, that he visited on Friday, August 19, 2005:

At the Cologne synagogue: prayer with the Jews, August 19, 2005:

August 27, 2007: Joseph Ratzinger/Benedict bestowed "papal" knighthood upon the pro-abortion, pro-perversity Rabbi Leon Klenicki. (see Continuing to Knight Infidels).

Rabbi Leon Klenicki, ADL Interfaith Affairs Director Emeritus and Pope Benedict XVI at one of their many meetings

Ratzinger/Benedict at the Park East Synagogue, New York, New York, Friday, April 18, 2008.

Ratzinger/Benedict also placed the following "nondenominational prayer" in the Western (Wailing) Wall in Jerusalem on May 12, 2009:

> God of all the ages, on my visit to Jerusalem, the "City of Peace", spiritual home to Jews, Christians and Muslims alike, I bring before you the joys, the hopes and the aspirations, the trials, the suffering and the pain of all your people throughout the world.
>
> God of Abraham, Isaac and Jacob, hear the cry of the afflicted, the fearful, the bereft; send your peace upon this Holy Land, upon the Middle East, upon the entire human family; stir the hearts of all who call upon your name, to walk humbly in the path of justice and compassion.
>
> "The Lord is good to those who wait for him, to the soul that seeks him" (Lam 3:25)! (Prayer at the Western Wall, May 12, 2009; one will note, of course, that there is not one reference to Our Blessed Lord and Saviour Jesus Christ.)

What's that about a picture being worth a thousand words?

The former conciliar "pontiff" also sat as an inferior at the Rome Synagogue on Sunday, January 17, 2010, with a menorah towering over him:

Rome Synagogue, Sunday, January 17, 2010.

It was a little over a year after the visit to the Rome Synagogue that Ratzinger/Benedict issued *Jesus of Nazareth: Holy Week: From the Entrance into Jerusalem to the Resurrection*, which contained the following piece of apostasy concerning "Israel's mission:"

> **In this regard, the question of Israel's mission has always been present in the background. We realize today with horror how many misunderstandings with grave consequences have weighed down our history. Yet a new reflection can acknowledge that the beginnings of a correct understanding have always been there, waiting to be rediscovered, however deep in the shadows**. (Joseph Ratzinger/Benedict XVI, *Jesus of Nazareth: Holy Week: From the Entrance into Jerusalem to the Resurrection*. San Francisco, California: Ignatius Press, 2011, p. 44.)

Ratzinger/Benedict was saying here, whether or not he realized it, that the Third Person of the Most Blessed Trinity, God the Holy Ghost kept a "correct understanding" of "Israel's mission" deep in the shadows until he helped to "rediscover" this "true meaning" in order to bring it to the world's attention.

Ratzinger/Benedict's long held belief about "Israel's mission" is also a rejection of the guidance that God the Holy Ghost gave to Pope Pius XII when he wrote the following in *Mystici Corporis*, June 29, 1943:

> 28.That He completed His work on the gibbet of the Cross is the unanimous teaching of the holy Fathers who assert that the Church was born from the side of our Savior on the Cross like a new Eve, mother of all the living. [28] "And it is now," says the great St. Ambrose, speaking of the pierced side of Christ, "that it is built, it is now that it is formed, it is now that is .... molded, it is now that it is created . . . Now it is that arises a spiritual house, a holy priesthood." [29] One who reverently examines this venerable teaching will easily discover the reasons on which it is based.
>
> 29.**And first of all, by the death of our Redeemer, the New Testament took the place of the Old Law which had been abolished; then the Law of Christ together with its mysteries, enactments, institutions, and sacred rites was ratified for the whole world in the blood of Jesus Christ**. For, while our Divine Savior was preaching in a restricted area -- He was not sent but to the sheep that were lost of the house of Israel [30] -the Law and the Gospel were together in force; [31] **but on the gibbet of his death Jesus made void the Law with its decrees, [32] fastened the handwriting of the Old Testament to the Cross, [33] establishing the New Testament in His blood shed for the whole human race. [34] "To such an extent, then," says St. Leo the Great, speaking of the Cross of our Lord, "was there effected a transfer from the Law to the Gospel, from the Synagogue to the Church, from many sacrifices to one Victim, that, as our Lord expired, that mystical veil which shut off the innermost part of the temple and its sacred secret was rent violently from top to bottom**." [35]
>
> 30. **On the Cross then the Old Law died, soon to be buried and to be a bearer of death, [36] in order to give way to the New Testament of which Christ had chosen the Apostles as qualified ministers**; [37] and although He had been constituted the Head of

> the whole human family in the womb of the Blessed Virgin, it is by the power of the Cross that our Savior exercises fully the office itself of Head in His Church. "For it was through His triumph on the Cross," according to the teaching of the Angelic and Common Doctor, "that He won power and dominion over the gentiles"; [38] by that same victory He increased the immense treasure of graces, which, as He reigns in glory in heaven, He lavishes continually on His mortal members. It was by His blood shed on the Cross that God's anger was averted and that all the heavenly gifts, especially the spiritual graces of the New and Eternal Testament, could then flow from the fountains of our Savior for the salvation of men, of the faithful above all; it was on the tree of the Cross, finally, that He entered into possession of His Church, that is, of all the members of His Mystical Body; for they would not have been united to this Mystical Body. (Pope Pius XII, *Mystici Corporis*, June 29, 1943.)

As noted in **To Be Loved by the Jews** in 2011 (and in countless other articles on my **www.Christorchaos.com** website, including **Saint Vincent Ferrer and Anti-Saint Vincent Ferrers**), Ratzinger/Benedict believes that the crimes committed by the agents of Adolf Hitler's Third Reich against adherents of the Talmud, crimes that were made possible by the overthrow of the Social Reign of Christ the King in Europe wrought by the Protestant Revolution and the subsequent rise of the naturalism of Judeo-Masonry that sought to replace the influence of Holy Mother Church with the religious indifferentism and pluralism of the modern civil state, made it necessary to "evaluate and define in a new way" what he believes is the Catholic Church's relationship with "the Faith of Israel," and it was in that "evaluation" process that Ratzinger/Benedict, among others, "discovered" that the "answer" had been there all along.

The conciliar "popes" have indeed gone to great efforts to be loved by the Jews, whose false religion is not of God, demonstrating that they, the conciliar "popes" cannot possibly love God as He has revealed Himself to us exclusively through His true Church that he founded upon the Rock of Peter, the Pope. This effort to be liked and respected and understood by the Jews, who are not of God, has been justified in an effort to oppose "secularism," a contention that is preposterous as it is the very forces of Judeo-Masonry that have resulted in the anti-Incarnational, religiously indifferentist civil state of modernity that has been a vessel out of which has flowed every poison of naturalism imaginable.

There is simply no "space" whatsoever between Ratzinger and Bergoglio on the matter of the "validity" of the Talmudic religion.

To wit, Jorge Mario Bergoglio continues to commit, objectively speaking, one Mortal Sin after another by praying Talmudic prayers, which, of course, just happen to deny the Sacred Divinity of Our Blessed Lord and Saviour Jesus Christ, with his favorite pro-abortion, pro-perversity rabbi, Abraham Skorka, including the ones he prayed with Skorka at the Casa Santa Marta inside the walls of the Occupied Vatican on the West Bank of the Tiber, during the rabbi's recent stay there:

> *(JNS.org)* Argentine Rabbi Abraham Skorka made history when he spent several days in the Vatican living together with Pope Francis I over the Sukkot holiday.

> "I eat with him at breakfast, lunch and dinner every day. He cares for me, and controls everything regarding my food to makes sure it is all kosher, and according to my religious tradition," Skorka told the Italian daily *La Stampa*, which covers Vatican affairs.
>
> "These are festive days, and I have to say certain prayers at meals and, I expand the last prayer and translate it. He accompanies me together with the others at table—his secretaries and a bishop, and they all say 'Amen' at the end," Skorka said.
>
> According to Skorka, who is rector of the Latin American Rabbinic Seminary, his friendship with Pope Francis began in 1997 when Francis, known at the time as Jorge Mario Bergoglio, became Coadjutor Archbishop of Buenos Aires. Skorka said that while their close friendship might be shocking to some, he believes that "history is made more by action than by political reasoning."
>
> "We hold to different traditions, but we are creating a dialogue that has not existed for centuries. Both of us believe that God has something to do with our friendship and with what we are doing," he said.
>
> Skorka also revealed that he is planning to travel to Israel with Pope Francis next year.
>
> "I dream of embracing him at the Kotel, or Wailing Wall, and I will accompany him to Bethlehem, in the Palestinian territories. His presence can help a lot at this moment when the peace talks are starting again," Skorka said. (**Antipope Francis I, Argentine rabbi make history by spending Sukkot together**.)

Jorge Mario Bergoglio is so respectful of Talmudic sensibilities that he even hid his pectoral cross (which is not his to wear as he is not a true bishop) beneath his fascia (the white sash that goes around a pope's white cassock) when he addressed the two chief rabbis of Jerusalem on Monday, May 26, 2014, the Feast of Saint Philip Neri and the Commemoration of Pope Saint Eleutherius:

> **Mutual understanding of our spiritual heritage, appreciation for what we have in common and respect in matters on which we disagree: all these can help to guide us to a closer relationship, an intention which we put in God's hands. Together, we can make a great contribution to the cause of peace**; together, we can bear witness, in this rapidly changing world, to the perennial importance of the divine plan of creation; together, we can firmly oppose every form of anti-Semitism and all other forms of discrimination. May the Lord help us to walk with confidence and strength in his ways. Shalom! (**Courtesy Visit to Caiphas and Annas at Heichal Shlomo Center in Jerusalem**.)

Although there were some rumblings to be found among a few professional Talmudic victimologists about the symbolism of Bergoglio's touching his head against the Israeli version of the Berlin Wall that separates the Palestinian Authority from Irsael while he was in the Palestinian Authority on Sunday, May 25, 2014, the Fifth Sunday after Easter and the Commemoration of Popes Saint Gregory VII and Saint Urban I (see **A slap in the face**), Jorge Mario Bergoglio made all manner of symbolic gestures to show his love and appreciation for "the people of the Covenant," including, as noted just above, removing his pectoral cross:

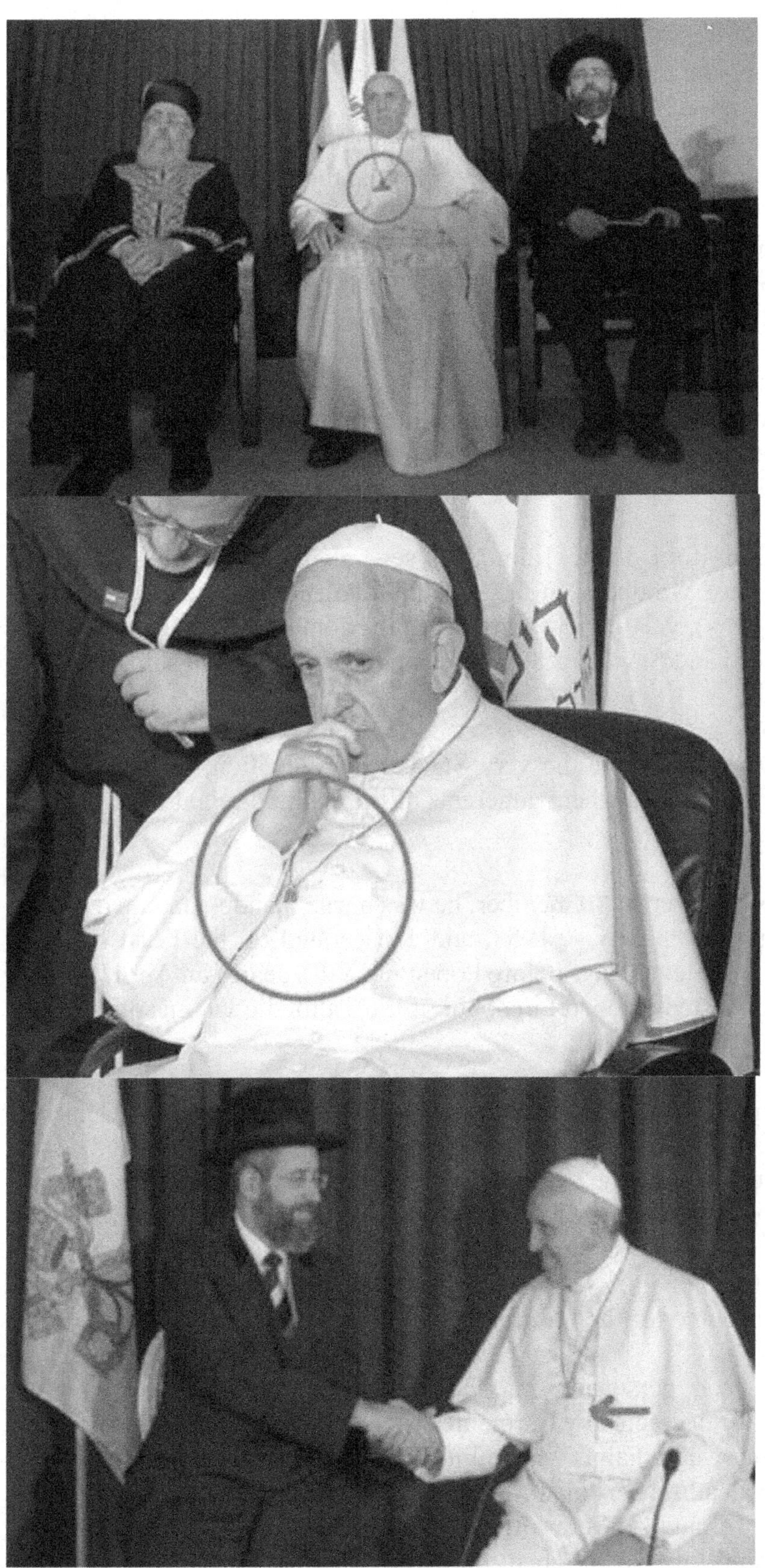

(As found at **Novus Ordo Watch Wire**. There is also excellent information and commentary at **Call Me Jorge**)

Gestures such as these are not lost on the rabbis, who will let the politicians vent their spleens over the "incident" at the Israeli version of the Berlin Wall. The rabbis are very pleased to see a putative Catholic "pope" hide the very instrument of human salvation that they hate with an indescribable ferocity of passion. This is why some Talmudic rabbis recognize that they have never had a better friend than Jorge Mario Bergoglio (see **Jorge most open Modernist to Jews in history, rabbi says**), who has lit menorahs in Argentina, "prayed" from the blasphemous Talmud and has hidden his pectoral cross before, doing so just four months ago as he hosted some Talmudic pals from Argentina for a "Kosher" lunch at the Casa Santa Marta whose "purity" was supervised by a local rabbi in Rome.

Moreover, Jorge Mario Bergoglio is not the first of the conciliar "pontiffs" to hide his pectoral cross when in the presence of Talmudists. Karol Wojtyla/John Paul II, excuse me, "Saint John Paul II," did this several times.

Yes, "Saint John Paul II," who ran afoul of the Talmudists several times, including when he received then Austrian President Kurt Waldheim in the Apostolic Palace on June 26, 1987 (see **John Paul Holds Waldehim Meeting**), was a great appeaser of the contemporary enemies of the Sacred Divinity of Our Blessed Lord and Saviour Jesus Christ and His Social Kingship over men and their nations in his own right.

Wojtyla/John Paul II went so far as to remove the very Sign of our salvation, the Sign of the Cross, at various times and in various places where adherents of the Talmud might have or were in fact offended.

The false "pontiff" removed his pectoral cross (remember, he was a true bishop appointed by our last true pope thus far, Pope Pius XII on July 4, 1958, and consecrated on the Feast of Saint Wenceslaus, September 28, 1958, just eleven days before Pope Pius XII's death) on April 7, 1994, at the Paul VI Audience Hall as he hosted a concert in honor of the Talmudic victims of the Nazi regime.

He did more than that, however: he removed a crucifix from the Paul VI Audience Hall. This has nothing to do with fidelity to the Christ King, who won our salvation for us on the wood of the Holy Cross. That concert was "the first time the Chief Rabbi of Rome was invited to co-officiate at a public function in the Vatican, the first time a Jewish cantor sang at the Vatican, and the first time the Vatican choir sang a Hebrew text in performance" (**The Vatican, the Holocaust, and the Jews: 1945-2000**, a Talmudic source for this; see also: **Chronicle – *The New York Times*** and **Yom Hashoah**, another Talmudic source for the "concert").

Wojtyla/John Paul II also intervened personally in 1998 when Talmudists expressed their opposition to a large cross that had been erected by Carmelite sisters in Poland near the Auschwitz concentration camp and death center where Father Maximilian Kolbe, the great apostle of the City of Mary Immaculate, was put to death. The Polish "pope" requested that the Carmelite nuns remove the large cross because the Talmudists were "offended" by it. So what? Catholics are never afraid to lift high the standard of the Holy Cross. Then again, the conciliar "popes" had expelled themselves from the Catholic Faith long before their apparent "elections."

Not to be outdone by the man he called his "boss," the late John "Cardinal" O'Connor, the conciliar "archbishop" of New York from March 19, 1984, to May 3, 2000, never offended the Talmudists. Not once. Ever.

O'Connor even spoke approvingly of the decision of a Catholic man, Stephen Dubner, to convert to Talmudism:

> But like many a Jewish son before him, he couldn't separate from his mother. He wanted her approval. He presented his problem to Cardinal O'Connor, who artfully contrived a theological olive branch: **"Tell your mother that you have tried to study this, that you have prayed about it, this is not just a revolt or a rejection, this is not a dismissal of what you don't understand — that this is where you think God wants you to be, an informed Jew**." (BOOKS OF THE TIMES; Words Upon the Heart, Heard at Last)

"Cardinal" O'Connor told an interviewer for the American Broadcasting Company's *Nightline* television program that "God is smiling on all of this" when recalling his conversation with Stephen Dubner. Oh, by the way, the wonderful people at *Nightline* televised the interview on the evening of December 25, 1997.

O'Connor also told a B'Nai Brith meeting in early-1998 that Judaism and Catholicism were meant to "coexist side by side" until the end of time. "This is what my boss (John Paul II) teaches, and I work for my boss." The original citation for this came from a newspaper article that I cited in the printed pages of *Christ or Chaos*. There is also an allusion to this address in a reminiscence of O'Connor provided by the late pro-abortion "papal" "knight," Rabbi Leon Klenicki, in *Full of Grace: An Oral Biography of John Cardinal O'Connor*, edited by Terry Golway:

> Once we invited him to talk at one of the Anti-Defamation League dinners. He was there to help present a booklet we had put out. During his speech, he told a story about how he once went to a Reform synagogue and he was the only one there with a yarmulke. Several Reform rabbis who were there looked at each other–I think they couldn't believe it–but everybody was laughing. The Cardinal had a serious point, too. **Later that night, he said that he was in pain because there are Jews who do not want to exercise their Judaism because of assimilation or other reasons. It is their duty to practice their faith, he said, to prove that God exists and to refute the Holocaust. He sounded very much like a rabbi when he spoke. The crowd was all around him afterwards, shaking his hand and embracing him. I told him if he ever needed a job I knew a congregation that could use him**. (**Page 148** of **Full of Grace: An Oral Biography of John Cardinal O'Connor**.)

In our own time, of course, even Jorge Mario Bergoglio has been outdone by the man whose star has faded in conciliar circles in the last fourteen months (see **Dolan Faces New Reality in the Era of Jorge**), Timothy Michael Dolan, the former "cheesehead" conciliar "archbishop" of Milwaukee, Wisconsin, who has been the conciliar "archbishop" of New York since April 15, 2009. Dolan said the following on February 23, 2013, when addressing the pro-abortion, pro-perversity Lincoln Square Synagogue in the Borough of Manhattan of the City of New York, New

York, that played an instrumental role in the "formation" of a certain Elena Kagan, who has been an associate justice of the Supreme Court of the United States of America since August 7, 2010:

Shabbat Shalom!

Thank you so much for your generous invitation and warm welcome. What an honor and a joy to be with you here at the historic and renowned Lincoln Square Synagogue.

Long have I been aware of the prominence of this community, as, during my graduate studies at the Catholic University of America, our course in American Religious History featured attention to Modern Orthodox Judaism, its flagship synagogue here, and the foundational efforts of Rabbi Shlomo Riskin.

Now what a privilege it is to be a part of the celebration of welcome as we thank God for this splendid new sanctuary! As your psalms pray, "Unless the Lord builds the house, they labor in vain who toil!" So, praise God:

I'd say "Alleluia" but I can't because for us Catholics it's our penitential season of Lent, and we can't say that "A-word" until Easter!

Can I get a little personal here? Today is the fourth anniversary of my appointment by Pope Benedict XVI as archbishop of New York.

Four happy years…and the Jewish community of New York is one of the big reasons why. From the start you have welcomed and embraced me. I love you; I respect you; I need you; I thank you.

Tomorrow, the second Sunday of Lent, we always have the Gospel account of what we call the Transfiguration of Jesus on Mount Tabor. There, the Jewish fisherman, the Jewish first pope, St. Peter, said to Jesus, **"It is good for us to be here**."

Those words I make my own this morning.

I also appreciate the encouragement this visit gives me in my efforts to repair and restore another historic house of prayer and worship, Saint Patrick's Cathedral. Don't worry: I'm not going to ask for money—while recognizing what a tradition that is in both of our religions—although I do happen to have some pledge cards on me!

This beautiful occasion this morning might be a providential occasion to celebrate as well the common values we as Jews and Catholics deeply cherish. Can I mention just two?

One would be the high importance of the Sabbath: you begin with sundown on Friday and go through Saturday; we start with sundown on Saturday and go through Sunday.

We both do it with humble obedience to the Lord's command, following His own example of rest after the labor of creation, don't we?

I propose that our fidelity to the Sabbath is good for us, and good for the world.

It's good for us as we individually, and as a religious community, need worship, prayer, and fellowship to keep our spirits focused and our faith fervent.

A wise mentor once told me, "Science teaches us that the earth is not the center of the universe. Faith teaches me that neither am I."

God and others come first. The weekly reminder of the Sabbath.

I suppose that's the message to be found in the startling decision of Pope Benedict XVI to leave the Chair of St. Peter. It's not about an office, the pomp, the prominence, the prestige, the Holy Father hints, but about Jesus and His Church. It's really all about God.

That's what you and I profess every Sabbath! That's good for us; that's good for our culture.

Two, we both value love and service. Just ten days ago, on Ash Wednesday, as we began our forty days of fervent prayer, penance, and acts of charity in preparation for our high holy days, the fifty thousand folks who came through Saint Patrick's Cathedral, heard the words of your prophet, Isaiah.

"This is the worship and fasting that I wish: releasing those bound unjustly, untying the thongs of the yoke; setting free the oppressed, breaking every yoke; sharing your bread with the hungry, sheltering the oppressed and the homeless; clothing the naked when you see them, and not turning your back on your own."

Jesus won't let me brag about such work that we as Catholics do, since, on that same day, Ash Wednesday, He told us in the Gospel that our good works should be done in secret.

But, I sure can congratulate you for the radiant love, service, and works of charity and justice you do! We're all impressed by your effective food and clothing drives, your Red Cross blood drives, your community outreach and weekly bags of bread to the West Side Campaign Against Hunger. And we sure appreciated the partnership of the UJA with Catholic Charities in the Feeding Our Neighbors Campaign three weeks ago.

Blessed Mother Teresa of Calcutta observed, "There's a word for faith without love, and that word is a sham."

And Bl. John Paul II, who so loved you, remarked, "Men and women today learn much more from witness than from words."

God bless you, Lincoln Square Synagogue, for the radiant witness of your love which make genuine the words of praise we express on the sabbath! (**The Gospel in the Digital Age**. For the dissection of this, see **"You're Not Supposed To Do This"**).

What Bergoglio did in Jerusalem in front of Caiphas and Annas on May 26, 2014, was just standard issue conciliarism: never preach Our Blessed Lord and Saviour Jesus Christ and Him Crucified to the Jews. Never.

To use a term coined by none other than Vladimir I. Lenin, the conciliar "popes," including Wojtyla/John Paul II, Ratzinger/Benedict and Bergoglio/Francis, have been "useful idiots" to the Talmudists and Zionists as they know that they can count on a conciliar "pope" to denounce any Catholic who dares to speak in traditionally Catholic terms about Judaism or its contemporary manifestation, Talmudism. And it is indeed a telling commentary on the state of apostasy and betrayal in which we find ourselves at this time that the Talmudists know orthodox Catholic doctrine better than perhaps ninety-five cent of Catholics alive today, and they want to make sure that it stays that way. Bergoglio does them great favors by bashing fully believing Catholics time and time again at the Casa Santa Marta.

Quite in contrast to the two-headed "pope monster," Father Fahey wrote the following in *The Kingship of Christ and the Conversion of the Jewish Nation*:

> As I was not able to bring out this book when it was originally written, it has been laid aside for years. In the meantime, the need for setting forth the full doctrine of the Kingship of Christ has been forcibly brought home to me by the confusion created in minds owing to the use of the term "Anti-Semitism." The Hitlerite naturalistic or anti-supernatural régime in Germany gave to the world the odious spectacle of a display of Anti-Semitism, that is, of hatred of the Jewish Nation. Yet all the propaganda about that display of Anti-Semitism should not have made Catholics forget the existence of age-long Jewish Naturalism or Anti-Supernaturalism. Forgetfulness of the disorder of Jewish Naturalistic opposition to Christ the King is keeping Catholics blind to the danger that is arising from the clever extension of the term "Anti-Semitism," with all its war-connotation in the minds of the unthinking, to include any form of opposition to the Jewish Nation's naturalistic aims. **For the leaders of the Jewish Nation, to stand for the rights of Christ the King is logically to be "anti-Semitic**."
>
> In March, 1917, Pope Benedict XV wrote to the Archbishop of Tours: "**In the midst of the present upheavals, it is important to repeat to men that by her divine institution the Catholic Church is the only ark of salvation for the human race . . . . Accordingly, it is more seasonable than ever to teach . . . that the truth which liberates, not only individuals, but societies, is supernatural truth in all its fulness and in all its purity, without attenuation, diminution or compromise: in a word, exactly as Our Lord Jesus Christ delivered it to the world**." These sublime words of the Vicar of Christ have nerved me to do all in my power to set forth the opposition of every form of Naturalism, including Jewish Naturalism, to the supernatural Reign of Christ the King. In addition, for over twenty years I have been offering the Holy Sacrifice of the Mass every year, on the Feasts of the Resurrection, Corpus Christi, SS. Peter and Paul and the Assumption of Our Blessed Mother, for the acceptance by the Jewish Nation of the Divine Plan for order. Thus I have been striving to follow the example of our Divine Master. Blessed Pius X insists that **"though Jesus was kind to those who had gone astray, and to sinners, He did not respect their erroneous convictions, however sincere they appeared to be." The need**

> **of combining firmness in the proclamation of the integral truth with loving charity towards those in error is insisted on, even more emphatically, by Pope Pius XI: "Comprehending and merciful charity towards the erring," he writes, "and even towards the contemptuous, does not mean and can not mean that you renounce in any way the proclaiming of, the insisting on, and the courageous defence of the truth and its free and unhindered application to the realities about you. The first and obvious duty the priest owes to the world about him is service to the truth, the whole truth, the unmasking and refutation of error in whatever form or disguise it conceals itself**."
>
> A day will come when the Jewish Nation will cease to oppose order and will turn in sorrow and repentance to Him Whom they rejected before Pilate. That will be a glorious triumph for the Immaculate Heart of Our Blessed Mother. **Until that day dawns, however, their naturalistic opposition to the True Supernatural Order of the world must be exposed and combated**. (Father Denis Fahey, Foreword, *The Kingship of Christ and the Conversion of the Jewish Nation.*)

This is our duty as Catholics.

We are not to support the lords of conciliarism who want to be loved by the Jews, who are of this world and are thus not of God.

We are not to support the witting or unwitting dupes of naturalism in the blathering world of talk radio and cable television.

We are to stand for the rights of Christ the King openly and unapologetically without fear of the consequences as we pray very fervently for the conversion of those who adhere to the Talmud and as we bear ourselves kindly toward those of their number who God's Holy Providence places in our paths, providing them with truly blessed Green Scapulars as we pray "Immaculate Heart of Mary, pray for us now and at the hour of our death" for each of them by name without fail every day. God wills the good of all men, the ultimate expression of which is the salvation of their immortal souls as members of the Catholic Church. It is not an act of true Charity to reaffirm one in a false religion by acts of omission or commission. Indeed, it is a dereliction of our duties as Catholics not to perform the Spiritual Works of Mercy for those who are in the grip of the devil though they may not realize it themselves.

We must remember, however, that the Pharisees of Our Lord's day did not act on their own. Our own sins, having transcended time, played a large role in motivating them to act as they did in hating the very One Who had created them and was about to redeem them so that they could be sanctified as members of His Catholic Church. We play the part of those very same Pharisees whenever we turn away from Our Lord and His true Church by means of sinful thoughts, words, desires and deeds. We play the part of the adherents of the Talmud today when we refuse to speak as Catholics in public life and when we plunge headlong in the traps of naturalism posed by the devil as we spend time listening to the babbling inanities of naturalists rather than praying more Rosaries as Our Lady requested of Jacinta and Francisco Marto and Lucia dos Santos ninety-four years ago now.

Dom Prosper Gueranger, O.S.B., emphasized this point in his reflection on the Feast of the Seven Dolors of Our Lady in Passion Week:

> How many there are, who once drank at the vein of living waters, and afterwards turned away to seek to quench their thirst in the muddy waters of the world, which can only make them thirst the more! **Let them tremble at the punishment that came upon the Jews; for, unless they return to the Lord their God, they must fall into those devouring and eternal flames, where even a drop of water is refused. Jesus, by the mouth of His prophet, tells the Jews that the day of affliction shall overtake them; and when, later on, He comes to them Himself, He forewarns them, that the tribulation which is to fall on Jerusalem, in punishment for her deicide, shall be so great that such hath not been from the beginning of the world until now, neither shall be.(2)-{St. Matt. xxiv. 21} But if God so rigorously avenged the Blood of His Son against a city that was so long a place of the habitation of His glory, and against a people that He had preferred to all others, will He spare the sinner who, in spite of the Church's entreaties, continues obstinate in his evil ways**? Jerusalem had filled up the measure of her iniquities; we, also have a measure of sin, beyond which the justice of God will not permit us to go. Let us sin no more: let us fill up that other measure, the measure of good works. Let us pray for those sinners who are to pass these days of grace without being converted; let us pray that this divine Blood, which is to be so generously given to them, but which they are about again to trample upon, may again spare them. (**Reflections for the Fifth Friday of Lent**)

As Our Lord told Saint Margaret Mary Alacoque, it is the sins of *Catholics* that grieve His Most Sacred Heart as much as did the rejection of His own people during His Passion and Death as we, the members of His Catholic Church, have turned away so frequently from the supernatural helps that He gives us through the loving hands of His Most Blessed Mother, she who is the Mediatrix of All Graces:

> Consider that it was no less afflicting and sad for Jesus Christ **to see the ingratitude of the majority of the faithful, who would have only coldness and indifference for Him in the Sacrament of His love.** He saw the little esteem, nay, even the contempt with which they would treat this greatest proof of His love. He saw that no matter what He might do to be loved by the faithful, even dwelling always amongst them in the Blessed Eucharist, neither this excess of His love, nor His benefits, nor His very presence would be capable of making the greater part of them love Him or would prevent them from forgetting Him. He saw that those churches in which He was to be sacramentally present would be left for most of the time without adorers. He saw what little reverence, nay, what disrespect would be shown in His presence. He saw clearly how the greater part of His followers, **who spend long hours in vain amusement and useless visits and complete idleness, would rarely find a quarter of an hour to spend before Him in the Blessed Sacrament. He knew how many others would visit Him only under compulsion and without either devotion or reverence. And finally, He saw the very small number who would eagerly visit Him and devoutly adore Him. He saw clearly that the greater number take no more notice of Him than if He were not really present in the Blessed Sacrament or than if He were a person of no consequence.**

> The harsh treatment which He received from the Jews, Gentiles and heretics was indeed very painful to Him, but they were His open enemies. But could we ever have thought it possible that those who recognize His benefits, that those who make profession of being faithful to Him, that His own children should not only be insensible to His benefits and in no way touched with compassion at the sight of the grief caused by such contempt, but that they should treat Him with contempt by their irreverences and sacrileges? Our Saviour might well say: "If pagans and Turks and infidels had treated Me so, I might have endured it." "For if my enemy had reviled me, I would verily have borne it". (Ps. 54:13), but that Christians, Catholics whom I have not only redeemed, but have fed and nourished with my Body and Blood, should have nothing but contempt for Me, that they should treat Me with ingratitude, is too much. "But thou a man of one mind, my guide and my familiar: who didst take sweetmeats together with me!" (Ps. 54: 14-15)
>
> What must be the sentiments of this most generous and tender Heart of Jesus which has so loved men, and which finds in the hearts of those men only coldness and contempt? "I am become a reproach among my enemies." (Ps. 30: 12). If after exposing Myself to the contempt and hatred of My enemies in the midst of the outrages which I suffer, I could at least find a large number of faithful friends who would console Me! But it is quite the contrary: "They that saw me without fled from me." (Ps. 30:12) The greater number, seeing that I have disguised Myself under the feeble appearance of bread in order to have the pleasure of dwelling among men, abandon Me and forget Me as a person who has no place in their hearts, "I am forgotten as one dead from the heart." (Ps. 30:13) (Father John Croiset, *The Devotion to the Sacred Heart of Jesus*, republished by TAN Books and Publishers.)

If we are faithful to the revelations of the Most Sacred Heart given by Our Blessed Lord and Saviour Jesus Christ to such mystics as Saint Gertrude the Great and Saint John Eudes and to Saint Margaret Mary Alacoque, then we can be confident that these great saints will intercede for us from Heaven so that we can imitate their complete self-surrender to the Sacred Heart of Jesus as we, who have been given the privilege to live after Our Lord sent His Most Blessed Mother to the Cova da Iria in Fatima, Portugal, to establish devotion her Sorrowful and Immaculate Heart, attempt to lead all souls, including adherents of the Talmud, to the font of Divine Mercy through the Immaculate Heart of Mary out of which It was formed and to which It is perfectly united.

We are loved by the Most Sacred Heart of Jesus. As clients of the Sorrowful and Immaculate Heart of Mary, out of which that Heart of all hearts was formed, may it be the singular longing of our own hearts to be content with this all-encompassing, matchless love of Love Incarnate rather than compromise on any point of the Holy Faith at any time for any reason, no less to do so to be loved by the Jews, that is to be part of a world that is in the grip of the devil.

May these words of Pope Leo the Great, whose feast we celebrate today, inspire us to oppose conciliarism's false accommodation to the spirit of Modernity and to the "goodness" of false religions lest we condemn ourselves by refusing to do so with holy fervor:

> **But it is vain for them to adopt the name of catholic, as they do not oppose these blasphemies: they must believe them, if they can listen so patiently to such words.**

(Pope Saint Leo the Great, Epistle XIV, To Anastasius, Bishop of Thessalonica, **St. Leo the Great | Letters 1-59**)

No one has anything to gain, humanly speaking, by recognizing that the conciliar "popes" are apostates and their liturgical rites are sacramentally barren and offensive to God and their doctrines have been condemned repeatedly by the authority of the Catholic Church. Yes, it is good to suffer for one's sins. It is necessary to do so in order to save one's soul. One does not embrace the truth in order *to* suffer, though, as that suffering will find him in due course.

Sedevacantists compose only a handful of mostly warring tribes. They are not the problem facing Holy Mother Church in this time of apostasy and betrayal. Just take a look at the evidence presented above if you believe that I am mistaken.

All the more reason, of course, to flee from everything to do with conciliarism and its false shepherds. If we can't see that the public esteeming of the symbols and places of "worship" of false religions is offensive to God and can in no way lead to any kind of authentic restoration of the "Catholic" Church, then it is perhaps necessary to recall these words of Saint Teresa of Avila in her Foundations:

> "Know this: **it is by very little breaches of regularity that the devil succeeds in introducing the greatest abuses. May you never end up saying: 'This is nothing, this is an exaggeration**.'" (Saint Teresa of Avila, Foundations, Chapter Twenty-nine)

We turn, as always to Our Lady, who holds us in the crossing of her arms and in the folds of her mantle. We must, as the consecrated slaves of her Divine Son, Our Blessed Lord and Saviour Jesus Christ, through her Sorrowful and Immaculate Heart, pray as many Rosaries each day as our states-in-life permit, trusting that we might be able to plant a few seeds for the Triumph of that same Immaculate Heart.

We may not see until eternity, please God and by the graces He sends to us through the loving hands of His Most Blessed Mother, the fruit of the seeds we plant by means of our prayers and penances and sacrifices, given unto the Most Sacred Heart of Jesus through the Immaculate Heart of Mary. We must remain confident, however, that Our Blessed Lord and Saviour Jesus Christ wants us, as unworthy as we are, to try to plant a few seeds so that more and more Catholics in the conciliar structures, both "priests" and laity alike, will recognize that it is indeed a sin to stand by as He is blasphemed by Modernists, that He--and His true priesthood--are to be found in the catacombs where no concessions at all are made to conciliarism or its wolves, whether their names be Roncalli or Montini or Luciani or Wojtyla or Ratzinger or Bergoglio, in shepherds' clothing.

Chapter Two

Believing that Unbelievers Who Do Good Please God

We live in a world of "false opposites," which are used by the adversary to distract the masses with false conflicts between various gradations of Judeo-Masonic naturalism in order to keep them spinning their wheels endlessly in the belief that they are "making progress" either to advance or to retard certain evils.

The farce that is American electoral politics and public policy decision-making is awash in false conflicts that fill the coffers of various advocacy groups that thrive on fundraising schemes to "fight" this or that battle of the moment. The ratings of talk show hosts on television and radio depend upon endless conflict between the false opposites of the naturalist "right" and the naturalist "left" as listeners and callers dream great dreams of "restoring America" by returning to the very anti-Incarnational principles that are responsible for our inevitable decline into the abyss.

There are three types of blindness at work in all of this, all of which are inter-related.

First, there is, of course, the blindness wrought by Modernity, itself the product of the Protestant Revolution's assault on the Divine plan that God Himself instituted to effect man's return to Him through the Catholic Church. Men and women live their entire lives steeped in the consequences of the Protestant Revolt: the rejection of the Social Reign of Christ the King (institutionalizing the heresy of the separation of Church and State, thereby "liberating" men from a due and docile submission to the Deposit of Faith as it has been entrusted by Our Blessed Lord and Saviour Jesus Christ exclusively to the Catholic Church, which has the authority, exercised judiciously and only after the exhausting of her Indirect Power of teaching and preaching and exhortation, to interpose herself with civil authorities when they propose to do or have in fact done things contrary to the good of souls), semi-Pelagianism (the belief that we are more or less self-redemptive, that we more or less stir up graces within ourselves, that we do not need belief in, access to or cooperation with Sanctifying Grace to be virtuous, that social order does not depend upon men being in a state of Sanctifying Grace), naturalism (the reduction of the affairs of personal and social life to the merely natural level with no thought of Divine Revelation or the necessity of keeping in mind at all times the eternal good of souls), and religious indifferentism (the belief that it does not make any difference what religion, if any, one believes in as long as one is a "good" person). This blindness has been deepened by the rise of Judeo-Masonry, which added an element of overt anti-Incarnationalism into the formation of the Modern civil state, and by the rise of an endless series of naturalistic political philosophies and ideologies that propose to "solve" social problems that have their remote cause in Original Sin and their proximate cause in the overthrow of the Social Reign of Christ the King.

Second, there is the blindness wrought by Americanism's accommodation to the principles of Modernity, as expressed in the Declaration of Independence and in the Constitution of the United States of America. Most, although certainly far from all, of the American bishops of the Nineteenth and Twentieth Centuries believed that the First Amendment to that Constitution permitted Catholics the "freedom" to practice their religion openly after over two decades of oppression in those European countries under the domination of Protestants, especially The Netherlands, England and Ireland.

As I have noted in hundreds of articles, these bishops fell into a diabolical trap: the devil, having raised up bloodthirsty Protestants who persecuted Catholics in Europe, raised up "nice" and "tolerant" Protestants in the United States of America in order to lull Catholics to sleep, to convince them that there was no need to convert the nation to the Social Reign of Christ the King, that everything about the founding of the pluralistic and religiously indifferentist United States of America was more or less compatible with the Catholic Faith.

Third, there is the blindness wrought by conciliarism's formal embrace of Americanism, especially by *Dignitatis Humanae*, December 7, 1965, and by the words and deeds of Karol Wojtyla/John Paul II, Joseph Ratzinger/Benedict XVI and Jorge Mario Bergoglio/Francis, which have confirmed the accommodations of Catholics in the United States of America in their embrace of the false foundations of Judeo-Masonic civil state of Modernity.

Thus it is that Americanism paved the way for the "Second" Vatican Council's embrace of "religious liberty" and for the false "pontiffs" of the counterfeit church of conciliarism, especially Karol Wojtyla/John Paul II and Joseph Ratzinger/Benedict XVI, to endorse the heresy of the "separation of Church and State" in the name of a "healthy secularity." It is not enough, as the false "pontiffs" have said repeatedly, for the Catholic Church to have a "say" in a pluralistic nation, itself the product of the Protestant Revolt and the rise of Judeo-Masonry. She must be recognized as the true religion.

Yes, the Church acknowledges the reality of situations such as those that exist in the United States of America, using the "freedom" of pluralism that exists here to sanctify her children and to exhort them to try to do their best to influence the course of public policy as best they can without compromising the Faith or acknowledging the false principles upon which their political system is based. Fine. The *Catholic* Church does not *accept* such a situation as the *ideal*. She never stops exhorting her children to pray and to plant the seeds for the conversion of their nations to the true Faith. She does not accept false, anti-Incarnational, religiously indifferentist, naturalistic and semi-Pelagian principles as the foundations of either personal or social order.

Pope Pius IX, writing in *Quanta Cura*, December 8, 1864, put the matter this way:

> But, although we have not omitted often to proscribe and reprobate the chief errors of this kind, yet the cause of the Catholic Church, and the salvation of souls entrusted to us by God, and the welfare of human society itself, altogether demand that we again stir up your pastoral solicitude to exterminate other evil opinions, which spring forth from the said errors as from a fountain. Which false and perverse opinions are on that ground the more to be detested, because they chiefly tend to this, that that salutary influence be impeded and (even) removed, which the Catholic Church, according to the institution and command of her Divine Author, should freely exercise even to the end of the world -- not only over private individuals, but over nations, peoples, and their sovereign princes; and (tend also) to take away that mutual fellowship and concord of counsels between Church and State which has ever proved itself propitious and salutary, both for religious and civil interests.

> For you well know, venerable brethren, that at this time men are found not a few who, applying to civil society the impious and absurd principle of "naturalism," as they call it, dare to teach that "the best constitution of public society and (also) civil progress altogether require that human society be conducted and governed without regard being had to religion any more than if it did not exist; or, at least, without any distinction being made between the true religion and false ones." And, against the doctrine of Scripture, of the Church, and of the Holy Fathers, they do not hesitate to assert that "that is the best condition of civil society, in which no duty is recognized, as attached to the civil power, of restraining by enacted penalties, offenders against the Catholic religion, except so far as public peace may require." **From which totally false idea of social government they do not fear to foster that erroneous opinion, most fatal in its effects on the Catholic Church and the salvation of souls, called by Our Predecessor, Gregory XVI, an "insanity," viz., that "liberty of conscience and worship is each man's personal right, which ought to be legally proclaimed and asserted in every rightly constituted society; and that a right resides in the citizens to an absolute liberty, which should be restrained by no authority whether ecclesiastical or civil, whereby they may be able openly and publicly to manifest and declare any of their ideas whatever, either by word of mouth, by the press, or in any other way."** But, while they rashly affirm this, they do not think and consider that they are preaching "liberty of perdition;" **and that "if human arguments are always allowed free room for discussion, there will never be wanting men who will dare to resist truth, and to trust in the flowing speech of human wisdom; whereas we know, from the very teaching of our Lord Jesus Christ, how carefully Christian faith and wisdom should avoid this most injurious babbling."**
>
> And, since where religion has been removed from civil society, and the doctrine and authority of divine revelation repudiated, the genuine notion itself of justice and human right is darkened and lost, and the place of true justice and legitimate right is supplied by material force, thence it appears why it is that some, utterly neglecting and disregarding the surest principles of sound reason, dare to proclaim that "the people's will, manifested by what is called public opinion or in some other way, constitutes a supreme law, free from all divine and human control; and that in the political order accomplished facts, from the very circumstance that they are accomplished, have the force of right." **But who, does not see and clearly perceive that human society, when set loose from the bonds of religion and true justice, can have, in truth, no other end than the purpose of obtaining and amassing wealth, and that (society under such circumstances) follows no other law in its actions, except the unchastened desire of ministering to its own pleasure and interests**? (Pope Pius IX, *Quanta Cura*, December 8, 1864.)

Heedless of these prophetic words, many Catholics, including those who are fully traditional, permit themselves to be drawn into the utter madness of the "left" and the "right" without realizing that we are in the death throes of a world founded upon the overthrow of the Social Reign of Christ the King wrought by the Protestant Revolution and institutionalized by the varied forces of Judeo-Masonry in the centuries thereafter. Thus it is that one phony "battle" after another is fought while the careerists of the "right" do everything they can to ape the statists of the "left" in order to find some "winning" strategy to acquire and retain power.

Readers of this site will understand that the devil has raised up false opposites on the "left" in politics to make those on the "right" seem "good" by way of comparison even though both believe in the same naturalistic, anti-Incarnational errors of Modernity and refuse to accept the truth that Catholicism is the one and only foundation of personal and social order.

Yet it is that what Gilbert Keith Chesterton wrote ninety years ago is as true today as it was in 1924:

> The whole modern world has divided itself into Conservatives and Progressives. The business of Progressives is to go on making mistakes. The business of the Conservatives is to prevent the mistakes from being corrected. (Gilbert Keith Chesterton, *Illustrated London News*, April 19, 1924.)

Similarly, the devil has raised up false opposites of "ultra-progressives" in the counterfeit church of conciliarism, to make alleged "conservatives" or "moderates" seem heroic by way of comparison even though both accept the fundamental revolutionary premises of conciliarism (the new ecclesiology, false ecumenism, religious liberty, separation of Church and State, inter-religious "prayer" services, attacks on the nature of dogmatic truth, a liturgy that is abhorrent in the sight of true God, the Most Blessed Trinity).

In this regard, of course, as I have noted many times since the "election" of Jorge Mario Bergoglio on March 13, 2013, Joseph Ratzinger/Benedict XVI is a Girondist or Menshevik (moderate) revolutionary to Jorge Mario Bergoglio's Jacobin or Bolshevik brand of radical revolutionary. The differences between the two are mostly, although not exclusively, on matters of style and emphasis, something that was noted in chapter one of this book, which featured the two headed "pope" monster's common heretical views about the "enduring validity" of the Mosaic Covenant.

This chapter focuses on the fact that the former universal public face of apostasy and his successor, the ever humble and pious Jorge Mario Bergoglio, who has taken over an entire floor of the Casa Santa Marta, share heretical positions concerning the salvation of those who do not believe in God or who do not believe in the Sacred Divinity of Our Blessed Lord and Saviour Jesus Christ.

Jorge Mario Bergoglio, masquerading at this time as "Pope Francis," has been quite adamant that "we will meet" unbelievers "there" as long as they "do good:"

> "Instead," the Pope continued, "the Lord has created us in His image and likeness, and has given us this commandment in the depths of our heart: do good and do not do evil":
>
> "The Lord has redeemed all of us, all of us, with the Blood of Christ: all of us, not just Catholics. Everyone! 'Father, the atheists?' Even the atheists. Everyone! And this Blood makes us children of God of the first class! We are created children in the likeness of God and the Blood of Christ has redeemed us all! And we all have a duty to do good. **And this commandment for everyone to do good, I think, is a beautiful path towards peace. If we, each doing our own part, if we do good to others, if we meet there, doing good, and we go slowly, gently, little by little, we will make that culture of encounter: we**

need that so much. We must meet one another doing good. 'But I don't believe, Father, I am an atheist!' But do good: we will meet one another there."

"Doing good" the Pope explained, is not a matter of faith: "It is a duty, it is an identity card that our Father has given to all of us, because He has made us in His image and likeness. And He does good, always." (**Culture of encounter is the foundation of peace**.)

(Vatican Radio) Does God forgive non-believers? Does absolute truth exist? And is God merely a creation of the human mind?

In a lengthy letter to the former editor of the Italian daily 'La Repubblica', Eugenio Scalfari, Pope Francis shares reflections on these three questions and urges all non-believers to engage with Christians in an open and sincere conversation.

In the letter published on Wednesday, the Pope laments the impasse that has grown up over the centuries with those who see Christianity as 'dark and superstitious,' in opposition to the 'light of reason'.

Quoting from the recent encyclical 'Lumen Fidei', the Pope stresses that, on the contrary, faith must never be intransigent or arrogant, but rather humble and able to grow in relationship with others.

Responding to the three questions posed by the Italian journalist and writer, the Pope says the key issue for non-believers is that of "obeying their consciences" when faced with choices of good or evil. God's mercy, he stresses, "has no limits" for those who seek him with a sincere and contrite heart.

Reflecting on the question of absolute truth, Pope Francis says he prefers to describe the truth in terms of a dynamic relationship between each Christian and Jesus, who said, 'I am the way, the truth and the life'. The truth of God's love, the Pope insists, is not subjective, **but it is only experienced and expressed as a journey, a living relationship with each one of us, in our different social and cultural contexts**.

Thirdly, Pope Francis considers the question of God as a creation of the human mind, who will thus disappear when human beings cease to exist on earth. In my experience, he says - and in that of so many other Christians past and present – God is not merely an idea but is a "Reality" of infinite goodness and mercy, revealed to us through his son, Jesus of Nazareth.

Reflecting on the originality of the Christian faith in relations to other religions, the Pope stresses the role of Jesus who renders us all sons and daughters of God, therefore also brothers and sisters to each other. **Our arduous task, he says, is that of communicating God's love to all, not in a superior way, but rather through service to all people especially those on the margins of our societies**.

Finally the Pope spoke of his deep respect and friendship for people of Jewish faith –

especially those with whom he worked so closely in his native Argentina. Reflecting on the terrible experience of the Shoah, he said, we can never be grateful enough to the Jews who maintained their faith in God, thus teaching us too to remain always open to his infinite love. (Antipope's letter to non-believers in Italian paper La Repubblica.)

257. **As believers, we also feel close to those who do not consider themselves part of any religious tradition, yet sincerely seek the truth, goodness and beauty which we believe have their highest expression and source in God. We consider them as precious allies in the commitment to defending human dignity, in building peaceful coexistence between peoples and in protecting creation. A special place of encounter is offered by new Areopagi such as the Court of the Gentiles, where "believers and non-believers are able to engage in dialogue about fundamental issues of ethics, art and science, and about the search for transcendence**". [204] This too is a path to peace in our troubled world.

258. Starting from certain social issues of great importance for the future of humanity, I have tried to make explicit once again the inescapable social dimension of the Gospel message and to encourage all Christians to demonstrate it by their words, attitudes and deeds. (Jorge Mario Bergoglio, *Evangelii Gaudium*, November 26, 2013.)

Although Bergoglio grabbed headlines with these statements, they are pure boilerplate conciliarism.

Consider, for example, the following excerpt of a sermon given fifty years ago, way back in 1964, by a priest who fancied himself as a theologian and is seen by many in the Motu world as a scion of orthodoxy and a "restorer of tradition:"

...Everything we believe about God, and everything we know about man, prevents us from accepting that beyond the limits of the Church there is no more salvation, that up to the time of Christ all men were subject to the fate of eternal damnation. We are no longer ready and able to think that our neighbor, who is a decent and respectable man and in many ways better than we are, should be eternally damned simply because he is not a Catholic. We are no longer ready, no longer willing, to think that eternal corruption should be inflicted on people in Asia, in Africa, or wherever it may be, merely on account of their not having "Catholic" marked in their passport.

Actually, a great deal of thought had been devoted in theology, both before and after Ignatius, to the question of how people, without even knowing it, in some way belonged to the Church and to Christ and could thus be saved nevertheless. And still today, a great deal of perspicacity is used in such reflections.

Yet if we are honest, we will have to admit that this is not our problem at all. The question we have to face is not that of whether other people can be saved and how. We are convinced that God is able to do this with or without our theories, with or without our perspicacity, and that we do not need to help him do it with our

cogitations. The question that really troubles us is not in the least concerned with whether and how God manages to save others.

The question that torments us is, much rather, that of why it is still actually necessary for us to carry out the whole ministry of the Christian faith—why, if there are so many other ways to heaven and to salvation, should it still be demanded of us that we bear, day by day, the whole burden of ecclesiastical dogma and ecclesiastical ethics?And with that, we are once more confronted, though from a different approach, with the same question we raised yesterday in conversation with God and with which we parted: What actually is the Christian reality, the real substance of Christianity that goes beyond mere moralism? What is that special thing in Christianity that not only justifies but compels us to be and live as Christians?

It became clear enough to us, yesterday, that there is no answer to this that will resolve every contradiction into incontrovertible, unambivalent truth with scientific clarity. Assent to the hiddenness of God is an essential part of the movement of the spirit that we call "faith." And one more preliminary consideration is requisite. If we are raising the question of the basis and meaning of our life as Christians, as it emerged for us just now, then this can easily conceal a sidelong glance at what we suppose to be the easier and more comfortable life of other people, who will "also" get to heaven. We are too much like the workers taken on in the first hour whom the Lord talks about in his parable of the workers in the vineyard (Mt 20:1-6). When they realized that the day's wage of one denarius could be much more easily earned, they could no longer see why they had sweated all day. Yet how could they really have been certain that it was so much more comfortable to be out of work than to work? And why was it that they were happy with their wages only on the condition that other people were worse off than they were? But the parable is not there on account of those workers at that time; it is there for our sake. For in our raising questions about the "why" of Christianity, we are doing just what those workers did. We are assuming that spiritual "unemployment"—a life without faith or prayer—is more pleasant than spiritual service. Yet how do we know that?

We are staring at the trials of everyday Christianity and forgetting on that account that faith is not just a burden that weighs us down; it is at the same time a light that brings us counsel, gives us a path to follow, and gives us meaning. We are seeing in the Church only the exterior order that limits our freedom and thereby overlooking the fact that she is our spiritual home, which shields us, keeps us safe in life and in death. We are seeing only our own burden and forgetting that other people also have burdens, even if we know nothing of them. And above all, what a strange attitude that actually is, when we no longer find Christian service worthwhile if the denarius of salvation may be obtained even without it! It seems as if we want to be rewarded, not just with our own salvation, but most especially with other people's damnation—just like the workers hired in the first hour. That is very human, but the Lord's parable is particularly meant to make us quite aware of how profoundly un-Christian it is at the same time. Anyone who looks on the loss of salvation for others as the condition, as it were, on which he serves Christ will in the end only be able to turn away grumbling, because that kind of reward is contrary to the loving-kindness of God. (**Catholic Church and Salvation**.)

Yes, those words belong to none other than Father Joseph Ratzinger. These words are vintage Ratzinger. Vintage.

Ratzinger the Rationalist, the man whose war on the very nature of dogmatic truth that is nothing other than direct warfare of the very nature of God Himself and of the Sacred Deposit of Faith that He has entrusted exclusively to His true Church, could not accept that an infallible teaching promulgated by Pope Eugene IV at the Council of Florence, February 4, 1442, whose Fathers met under the infallible guidance and protection of the Third Person of the Most Blessed Trinity, God the Holy Ghost, still bound the Catholic Church after the passage of over 522 years:

> **It** [the Holy Roman Church] **firmly believes, professes, and teaches that the matter pertaining to the law of the Old Testament, of the Mosaic law, which are divided into ceremonies, sacred rites, sacrifices, and sacraments, because they were established to signify something in the future, although they were suited to the divine worship at that time, after our Lord's coming had been signified by them, ceased, and the sacraments of the New Testament began; and that whoever, even after the passion, placed hope in these matters of the law and submitted himself to them as necessary for salvation, as if faith in Christ could not save without them, sinned mortally. Yet it does not deny that after the passion of Christ up to the promulgation of the Gospel they could have been observed until they were believed to be in no way necessary for salvation; but after the promulgation of the Gospel it asserts that they cannot be observed without the loss of eternal salvation. All, therefore, who after that time observe circumcision and the Sabbath and the other requirements of the law, it declares alien to the Christian faith and not in the least fit to participate in eternal salvation, unless someday they recover from these errors**. Therefore, it commands all who glory in the name of Christian, at whatever time, before or after baptism, to cease entirely from circumcision, since, whether or not one places hope in it, it cannot be observed at all without the loss of eternal salvation. Regarding children, indeed, because of danger of death, which can often take place, when no help can be brought to them by another remedy than through the sacrament of baptism, through which they are snatched from the domination of the Devil and adopted among the sons of God, it advises that holy baptism ought not to be deferred for forty or eighty days, or any time according to the observance of certain people, but it should be conferred as soon as it can be done conveniently, but so that, when danger of death is imminent, they be baptized in the form of the Church, early without delay, even by a layman or woman, if a priest should be lacking, just as is contained more fully in the decree of the Armenians. . . .
>
> **It firmly believes, professes, and proclaims that those not living within the Catholic Church, not only pagans, but also Jews and heretics and schismatics cannot become participants in eternal life, but will depart "into everlasting fire which was prepared for the devil and his angels" [Matt. 25:41], unless before the end of life the same have been added to the flock; and that the unity of the ecclesiastical body is so strong that only to those remaining in it are the sacraments of the Church of benefit for salvation, and do fastings, almsgiving, and other functions of piety and exercises of Christian service produce eternal reward, and that no one, whatever almsgiving he has practiced, even if he has shed blood for the name of Christ, can be saved, unless he**

> **has remained in the bosom and unity of the Catholic Church**. (Pope Eugene IV, *Cantate Domino*, Council of Florence, February 4, 1442.)

Ratzinger, who was mentored in large measure by the Hegelian exponent of the "new theology" that was condemned Pope Pius XII in *Humani Generis*, August 12, 1950, Father Hans Urs von Balthasar, demonstrated very clearly his support for the heresy of universal salvation back in 1964, doing so by means of projecting his own rationalist beliefs about God and His teaching rather than accepting with docility and humility the irreformable teaching stated in *Cantate Domino*.

Ratzinger's heretical beliefs, stated fifty years ago now, are as one with the heretical beliefs of Jorge Mario Bergoglio, nine years, eight months his junior, who was then teaching philosophy and literature, who, like Ratzinger, believes in the old Modernist heresy that he calls "faith" springs from within a person's being.

This is what Bergoglio published in *Lumen Fidei*, most of which, of course, had been written by Ratzinger/Benedict:

> **Because faith is a way, it also has to do with the lives of those men and women who, though not believers, nonetheless desire to believe and continue to seek. To the extent that they are sincerely open to love and set out with whatever light they can find, they are already, even without knowing it, on the path leading to faith. They strive to act as if God existed, at times because they realize how important he is for finding a sure compass for our life in common or because they experience a desire for light amid darkness, but also because in perceiving life's grandeur and beauty they intuit that the presence of God would make it all the more beautiful.** Saint Irenaeus of Lyons tells how Abraham, before hearing God's voice, had already sought him "in the ardent desire of his heart" and "went throughout the whole world, asking himself where God was to be found", until "God had pity on him who, all alone, had sought him in silence". **Anyone who sets off on the path of doing good to others is already drawing near to God, is already sustained by his help, for it is characteristic of the divine light to brighten our eyes whenever we walk towards the fullness of love**. (Jorge Mario Bergoglio/Francis, *Lumen Fidei*, July 5, 2013.)

Saint Irenaeus does not look favorably upon how he is being brought forth as yet another in the long line of witnesses used by the conciliar revolutionaries to distort their teaching so as to make them, in effect, **perjured witnesses in behalf of conciliarism**.

For the truth of the matter is that the passage from *Lumen Fidei* cited just above, which is in perfect accord with the writings of Father Joseph Ratzinger and his speeches and allocutions of "Pope Benedict XVI," is a perfect example of the immanence used by Modernists that was condemned by Pope Saint Pius X in *Pascendi Dominci Gregis*, September 8, 1907, all of Bergoglio's protestations to the contrary notwithstanding:

> **7. But it is not solely by objective arguments that the non-believer may be disposed to faith. There are also those that are subjective, and for this purpose the modernist apologists return to the doctrine of immanence. They endeavor, in fact, to persuade**

their non-believer that down in the very depths of his nature and his life lie hidden the need and the desire for some religion, and this not a religion of any kind, but the specific religion known as Catholicism, which, they say, is absolutely postulated by the perfect development of life. And here again We have grave reason to complain that there are Catholics who, while rejecting immanence as a doctrine, employ it as a method of apologetics, and who do this so imprudently that they seem to admit, not merely a capacity and a suitability for the supernatural, such as has at all times been emphasized, within due limits, by Catholic apologists, but that there is in human nature a true and rigorous need for the supernatural order. Truth to tell, it is only the moderate Modernists who make this appeal to an exigency for the Catholic religion. As for the others, who might be called integralists, they would show to the non-believer, **as hidden in his being, the very germ which Christ Himself had in His consciousness, and which He transmitted to mankind**. Such, Venerable Brethren, is a summary description of the apologetic method of the Modernists, in perfect harmony with their doctrines -- **methods and doctrines replete with errors, made not for edification but for destruction, not for the making of Catholics but for the seduction of those who are Catholics into heresy; and tending to the utter subversion of all religion**. (Pope Saint Pius X, *Pascendi Dominci Gregis*, September 8, 1907.)

Thus stands condemned one of the principle cornerstones of the conciliar revolutionaries to justify their kind words and messages of "feast day" greetings to non-Catholics as "believers" even though they do not believe all that Our Blessed Lord and Saviour Jesus Christ taught in the Sacred Deposit of Faith as He has entrusted It to the eternal safekeeping and infallible explication of His Catholic Church and/or reject His Sacred Divinity or even the existence of God altogether.

Thus stands condemned efforts on the part of Karol Wojtyla/John Paul II, advanced at both the "Second" Vatican Council," and during his 9,666 days as the head of the counterfeit church of conciliarism, and of Joseph Ratzinger/Benedict XVI and Jorge Mario Bergoglio/Francis to approach atheists without seeking with urgency their unconditional conversion to the true Faith.

Thus stands condemned the very cornerstone of conciliarism and everything it embodies: the new ecclesiology, false ecumenism, "inter-religious "dialogue" and "prayer services," "religious liberty" and the late Father Karl Rahner's "Anonymous Christian."

Yes, you see, the devil lacks creativity. He is simply repackaging the same old Modernist methodologies in the persons of the supposedly erudite Joseph Alois Ratzinger, and of the "friendly," "ever-humble," "simple" and "devout" Jorge Mario Bergoglio/Francis.

It was almost exactly forty-one years to the day after his sermon in 1964 that "Pope" Benedict XVI revisited his heresy in a general audience speech given on Wednesday, November 30, 2005:

Dear Brothers and Sisters,

1. On this first Wednesday of Advent, a liturgical season of silence, watchfulness and prayer in preparation for Christmas, let us meditate on Psalm 137[136], whose first words in the Latin version became famous: *Super flumina Babylonis.* The text evokes the tragedy

lived by the Jewish people during the destruction of Jerusalem in about 586 B.C., and their subsequent and consequent exile in Babylon. We have before us a national hymn of sorrow, marked by a curt nostalgia for what has been lost.

This heartfelt invocation to the Lord to free his faithful from slavery in Babylon also expresses clearly the sentiments of hope and expectation of salvation with which we have begun our journey through Advent.

The background to the first part of the Psalm (cf. vv. 1-4) is the land of exile with its rivers and streams, indeed, the same that irrigated the Babylonian plain to which the Jews had been deported. It is, as it were, a symbolic foreshadowing of the extermination camps to which the Jewish people - in the century we have just left behind us - were taken in an abominable operation of death that continues to be an indelible disgrace in the history of humanity.

The second part of the Psalm (cf. vv. 5-6) is instead pervaded by the loving memory of Zion, the city lost but still alive in the exiles' hearts.

2. The hand, tongue, palate, voice and tears are included in the Psalmist's words. The hand is indispensable to the harp-player: but it is already paralyzed (cf. v. 5) by grief, also because the harps are hung up on the poplars.

The tongue is essential to the singer, but now it is stuck to the palate (cf. v. 6). In vain do the Babylonian captors "ask... for songs..., songs... of joy" (v. 3). "Zion's songs" are "song[s] of the Lord" (vv. 3-4), not folk songs to be performed. Only through a people's liturgy and freedom can they rise to Heaven.

3. **God, who is the ultimate judge of history, will also know how to understand and accept, in accordance with his justice, the cry of victims, over and above the tones of bitterness that sometimes colours them.**

Let us entrust ourselves to St Augustine for a further meditation on our Psalm. The great Father of the Church introduces a surprising and very timely note: he knows that there are also people among the inhabitants of Babylon who are committed to peace and to the good of the community, although they do not share the biblical faith; the hope of the Eternal City to which we aspire is unknown to them. **Within them they have a spark of desire for the unknown, for the greater, for the transcendent: for true redemption.**

And Augustine says that even among the persecutors, **among the non-believers, there are people who possess this spark, with a sort of faith or hope, as far as is possible for them in the circumstances in which they live. With this faith, even in an unknown reality, they are truly on their way towards the true Jerusalem, towards Christ.**

And with this openness of hope, Augustine also warns the "Babylonians" - as he calls them -, those who do not know Christ or even God and yet desire the unknown, the eternal, and he warns us too, not to focus merely on the material things of the present but to persevere on the journey to God. It is also only with this greater hope that we will be able to transform this world in the right way. St Augustine says so in these words:

"If we are citizens of Jerusalem... and must live in this land, in the confusion of this world and in this Babylon where we do not dwell as citizens but are held prisoner, then we should not just sing what the Psalm says but we should also live it: something that is done with a profound, heartfelt aspiration, a full and religious yearning for the eternal city".

And he adds with regard to the "earthly city called Babylon", that it "has in it people who, prompted by love for it, work to guarantee it peace - temporal peace - nourishing in their hearts no other hope, indeed, by placing in this one all their joy, without any other intention. And we see them making every effort to be useful to earthly society."

"Now, if they strive to do these tasks with a pure conscience, God, having predestined them to be citizens of Jerusalem, will not let them perish within Babylon: this is on condition, however, that while living in Babylon, they do not thirst for ambition, short-lived magnificence or vexing arrogance.... He sees their enslavement and will show them that other city for which they must truly long and towards which they must direct their every effort" (*Esposizioni sui Salmi,* 136, 1-2: *Nuova Biblioteca Agostiniana,* XXVIII, Rome, 1977, pp. 397, 399).

And let us pray to the Lord that in all of us this desire, this openness to God, will be reawakened, and that even those who do not know Christ may be touched by his love so that we are all together on the pilgrimage to the definitive City, and that the light of this City may appear also in our time and in our world. (**30 November 2005, *Psalm 137[136]: 1-6 - If I forget you, Jerusalem*.**)

The Zenit propaganda agency headlined its news story concerning this general audience talk as follow: **Nonbelievers Too Can Be Saved**, a headline that caused all manner of "conservatives" within the structures of the counterfeit church of conciliarism to do all kinds of intellectual gymnastics to try to save the "orthodoxy" of Wojtyla/John Paul II's alleged "defender of the faith." Try as they might have done so, however, the spin doctors in 2005 were as delusional then as are those who are spinning mightily for Bergoglio now.

Moreover, Ratzinger, as was his wont, deconstructed and misrepresented the teaching of Saint Augustine, something that Pope Leo XIII made clear when condemning the reliance upon natural virtue and natural goodness by adherents of the heresy of Americanism:

Can it be that those men illustrious for sanctity, whom the Church distinguishes and openly pays homage to, were deficient, came short in the order of nature and its endowments, because they excelled in Christian strength? And although it be allowed at times to wonder at acts worthy of admiration which are the outcome of natural virtue-is there anyone at all endowed simply with an outfit of natural virtue? Is there any one not tried by mental anxiety, and this in no light degree? Yet ever to master such, as also to preserve in its entirety the law of the natural order, requires an assistance from on high. **These single notable acts to which we have alluded will frequently upon a closer**

> **investigation be found to exhibit the appearance rather than the reality of virtue. Grant that it is virtue, unless we would "run in vain" and be unmindful of that eternal bliss which a good God in his mercy has destined for us, of what avail are natural virtues unless seconded by the gift of divine grace**? Hence St. Augustine well says: "Wonderful is the strength, and swift the course, but outside the true path." **For as the nature of man, owing to the primal fault, is inclined to evil and dishonor, yet by the help of grace is raised up, is borne along with a new greatness and strength, so, too, virtue, which is not the product of nature alone, but of grace also, is made fruitful unto everlasting life and takes on a more strong and abiding character**. (Pope Leo XIII, *Testem Benevolentiae Nostrae*, January 22, 1899.)

Saint Thomas Aquinas taught us in his *Summa Theologica* that unbelievers do not merit anything before God for their good works and thus cannot please Him:

> Objection 1. It would seem that each act of an unbeliever is a sin. Because a gloss on Romans 14:23, "All that is not of faith is sin," says: "The whole life of unbelievers is a sin." Now the life of unbelievers consists of their actions. Therefore every action of an unbeliever is a sin.
>
> Objection 2. Further, faith directs the intention. Now there can be no good save what comes from a right intention. Therefore, among unbelievers, no action can be good.
>
> Objection 3. Further, when that which precedes is corrupted, that which follows is corrupted also. Now an act of faith precedes the acts of all the virtues. Therefore, since there is no act of faith in unbelievers, they can do no good work, but sin in every action of theirs.
>
> On the contrary, It is said of Cornelius, while yet an unbeliever (Acts 10:4-31), that his alms were acceptable to God. Therefore not every action of an unbeliever is a sin, but some of his actions are good.
>
> I answer that, As stated above (I-II, 85, 2,4) mortal sin takes away sanctifying grace, but does not wholly corrupt the good of nature. **Since therefore, unbelief is a mortal sin, unbelievers are without grace indeed, yet some good of nature remains in them.** ***Consequently it is evident that unbelievers cannot do those good works which proceed from grace, viz. meritorious works; yet they can, to a certain extent, do those good works for which the good of nature suffices.***
>
> Hence it does not follow that they sin in everything they do; but whenever they do anything out of their unbelief, then they sin. For even as one who has the faith, can commit an actual sin, venial or even mortal, which he does not refer to the end of faith, so too, an unbeliever can do a good deed in a matter which he does not refer to the end of his unbelief.
>
> Reply to Objection 1. The words quoted must be taken to mean either that the life of unbelievers cannot be sinless, since without faith no sin is taken away, or that whatever

they do out of unbelief, is a sin. Hence the same authority adds: "Because every one that lives or acts according to his unbelief, sins grievously."

Reply to Objection 2. Faith directs the intention with regard to the supernatural last end: but even the light of natural reason can direct the intention in respect of a connatural good.

Reply to Objection 3. Unbelief does not so wholly destroy natural reason in unbelievers, but that some knowledge of the truth remains in them, whereby they are able to do deeds that are generically good. With regard, however, to Cornelius, it is to be observed that he was not an unbeliever, else his works would not have been acceptable to God, **whom none can please without faith. Now he had implicit faith, as the truth of the Gospel was not yet made manifest: hence Peter was sent to him to give him fuller instruction in the faith**. (Saint Thomas Aquinas, *Summa Theologica*, Question 10, Article 4.)

Here is one final example from the false "pontificate" of Ratzinger/Benedict, taken from his address at Assisi III, October 27, 2011, proving yet again that there is no space on matters of substance between himself and his successor as the universal public face of apostasy:

In addition to the two phenomena of religion and anti-religion, a further basic orientation is found in the growing world of agnosticism: people to whom the gift of faith has not been given, but who are nevertheless on the lookout for truth, searching for God. Such people do not simply assert: “There is no God”. They suffer from his absence and yet are inwardly making their way towards him, inasmuch as they seek truth and goodness. They are “pilgrims of truth, pilgrims of peace”. They ask questions of both sides. They take away from militant atheists the false certainty by which these claim to know that there is no God and they invite them to leave polemics aside and to become seekers who do not give up hope in the existence of truth and in the possibility and necessity of living by it. But they also challenge the followers of religions not to consider God as their own property, as if he belonged to them, in such a way that they feel vindicated in using force against others. These people are seeking the truth, they are seeking the true God, whose image is frequently concealed in the religions because of the ways in which they are often practised. Their inability to find God is partly the responsibility of believers with a limited or even falsified image of God. So all their struggling and questioning is in part an appeal to believers to purify their faith, so that God, the true God, becomes accessible. **Therefore I have consciously invited delegates of this third group to our meeting in Assisi, which does not simply bring together representatives of religious institutions. Rather it is a case of being together on a journey towards truth, a case of taking a decisive stand for human dignity and a case of common engagement for peace against every form of destructive force. Finally I would like to assure you that the Catholic Church will not let up in her fight against violence, in her commitment for peace in the world. We are animated by the common desire to be “pilgrims of truth, pilgrims of peace”**. (**Day of reflection, dialogue, and prayer for peace and justice in the world *"Pilgrims of Truth, Pilgrims of Peace"*: Address of the Ratzinger/Benedict, Assisi, 27 October 2011**.)

Unbelievers can challenge "the followers of religion." There is nothing lacking in the Divine Constitution of Holy Mother Church to instruct us on any point. Those who do not believe or who doubt in the existence of God are objects of prayer for their conversion. They make no contribution to the world other than add to the confusion prophesied by Popes Gregory XVI and Pius IX would be the case when men live in a world of unfettered "freedom of conscience" and "freedom of speech" and "freedom of the press" and "religious freedom:"

> This shameful font of indifferentism gives rise to that absurd and erroneous proposition which claims that liberty of conscience must be maintained for everyone. It spreads ruin in sacred and civil affairs, though some repeat over and over again with the greatest impudence that some advantage accrues to religion from it. "**But the death of the soul is worse than freedom of error," as Augustine was wont to say. When all restraints are removed by which men are kept on the narrow path of truth, their nature, which is already inclined to evil, propels them to ruin. Then truly "the bottomless pit" is open from which John saw smoke ascending which obscured the sun, and out of which locusts flew forth to devastate the earth. Thence comes transformation of minds, corruption of youths, contempt of sacred things and holy laws -- in other words, a pestilence more deadly to the state than any other. Experience shows, even from earliest times, that cities renowned for wealth, dominion, and glory perished as a result of this single evil, namely immoderate freedom of opinion, license of free speech, and desire for novelty**. (Pope Gregory XVI, *Mirari Vos*, August 15, 1832.)

The madness represented by Ratzinger/Benedict's speech in 2011 is compounded when one considers the fact that he actually believed that he was "teaching" the "leaders of the world's religions," most of whom actually represent a very tiny sliver of people on the face of this earth as there is no central authority for any of the Eastern "religions" and Protestantism is divided into a welter of warring camps (as is Orthodoxy). Mohammedans have different branches. So do the Talmudists. Ratzinger/Benedict actually believed that his "teaching" will help the "leaders of the world's religions" to be better informed as to how to use their own false religions to prevent violence and thus to build up "peace," which he has defined on numerous occasions to be the "coexistence" of the "world's religions," ignoring the fact that false religions of their nature are violent assaults against the Most Blessed Trinity and the entirety of Divine Revelation, all the while permitting themselves to be "challenged" by unbelievers as they are "pilgrims of truth, pilgrims of peace" just as much as are "believers."

No, those who believe that Joseph Ratzinger still *is* "Pope Benedict XVI" because they think that he was "forced" to resign the conciliar Petrine Ministry are blind to the truth that their "restorer of tradition" is in absolute harmony with his successor, "Pope Francis," on most matters of theological substance. Furthermore, of course, these delusional people have to reckon with the fact that Joseph Ratzinger had nothing to "resign" from as he, a true priest, has never been a bishop or a cardinal, no less a true and legitimate Successor of Saint Peter. He is a Modernist. He is a heretic. So is Jorge Mario Bergoglio.

The path to Heaven is not to be found by exalting atheists or followers of false religions who "do good."

No, men, whether acting individually or collectively, deceive themselves if they think that they can make the world a "better" place absent a profound devotion to Our Lady's Most Holy Rosary.

Our Lady told us in the Cova da Iria near Fatima, Portugal, nearly ninety-seven years ago now that we must pray the Rosary to console the good God and to make reparation for our sins as we pray for the conversion of poor sinners and for the faithful fulfillment of her Fatima Message. This is a work of the Mercy of the Divine Redeemer, Who is giving us every chance to repent and convert. Why do men still persist in their obstinate refusal to take Our Lady's Fatima Message seriously and to organize Rosary processions and rallies to counter the naturalism of the day and to serve as valiant champions of Christ the King?

The devil knows the importance of the Our Lady's Fatima Message, which is Heaven's Peace Plan. He attacks Our Lady of Fatima at every turn, having used the lords of the counterfeit church of conciliarism, including but not limited to Joseph Ratzinger/Benedict XVI, Tarcisio Bertone and Angelo Sodano, to deconstruct, misrepresent and distort the Third Secret of Fatima and to cast doubt as well upon Our Lady's actual, physical apparition in the Cova da Iria (see **We Must Accept What Rationalists Reject**, **Relativizing Our Lady's Rosary and Her Fatima Message** and **On Full Display: The Modernist Mind**).

It cannot be this way with us. We need to petition Our Lady in humility through her Most Holy Rosary to help us to get home to Heaven as we ***recognize and reject*** conciliarism for what it is: a diabolically-planned and executed campaign to prepare Catholics and non-Catholics for Antichrist.

Chapter Three

Trying to Find Distinctions Among Heretics

Laughable and pathetic.

Those are the only two adjectives that can describe the "outrage" that was expressed by many traditionally-minded Catholics attached to the structures of the counterfeit church of conciliarism about the "cardinals" named by Jorge Mario Bergoglio's in early-2014 because those men were not "Ratzingerian."

Yes, laughable and pathetic.

This is laughable as to judge the doctrinal orthodoxy of putative "bishops" and "archbishops" by a "Ratzingerian" standard is to say that such men adhere to Joseph Ratzinger/Benedict XVI's philosophically absurd "hermeneutic of continuity" that is nothing other than a re-labeling of Modernism's "evolution of dogma" that had been condemned by the [First] Vatican Council on April 24, 1870, thirty-seven years before Pope Pius X did so in *Pascendi Dominci Gregis*, September 8, 1907. Those who do not believe this should consult the material referenced in the next chapter as the incontrovertible evidence that condemns Ratzinger/Benedict"s "hermeneutic," which is the same as Karol Wojtyla/John Paul II's "living tradition."

Whatever difference exists between the "cardinals" created by Ratzinger/Benedict between 2006 and 2012 and those created by Bergoglio, a layman, on February 22, 2014, the Feast of the Chair of Saint Peter in Antioch, centers around the rate by which the conciliar revolution is to be advanced and how it can be "justified" in light of Catholic Tradition, which is *in se* a patently absurd, time-wasting proposition. The "Ratzingerians" believe in the idiocy of the "hermeneutic of continuity" while Bergoglio's "boyz in scarlet," shall we say, believe in what is called the Bologna School of Rupture.

One is supposed to ignore the simple fact that both the Ratzingerians and the Bergoglio "boyz in scarlet" reject the binding nature of dogmatic truth, albeit by different means, and support each of the principle foundational building-blocks of conciliarism: the new ecclesiology, false ecumenism, religious "dialogue," "inter-religious prayer services," religious liberty, separation of Church and State, novel interpretations of Sacred Scripture, pastoral "outreaches" to those steeped in lives of unrepentant sin who have no intention of reforming their lives, feminism, environmentalism, Theistic evolutionism, statism, collectivism, redistributionism, episcopal collegiality and the "necessity" of the "liturgical reform" represented by Giovanni Montini/Paul VI's Protestant and Judeo-Masonic *Novus Ordo* liturgical service.

This is, of course, very similar to the simple fact concerning the entirely false nature of the supposed "opposition" between the naturalist "left" and the naturalist "right" that is premised upon a mutually unquestioned acceptance of the false, naturalistic, Judeo-Masonic, anti-Incarnational, religiously indifferentist and Pelagian principles of the modern civil state. Cheerleaders of the "left" and the "right" in the insane world of "instant reactions" that is "Twitterverse," as it is called, do not care to see the simple truth that the only substantial differences between the naturalist "left" and the naturalist "right" revolve around the degree to which the civil state will control our lives and how wealth can be expanded. The "left" believes in total statism and state-sponsored redistribution of wealth. The "right" believes in a "moderate" degree of statism and the "virtues" of the private market place, although many of its adherents are not above stacking the deck in favor of corporations whose executives are their own personal donors.

There is really no substantial difference between the Ratzingerian "cardinals" and Bergoglio's "boyz in scarlet," something that can be demonstrated very amply by reminding readers of just a selected sampling of the identities of the now retired Ratzinger/Benedict's own appointees to the conciliar college of non-cardinals:

Ratzinger's "Consistory" of March 24, 2006:

1. William Levada, Ratzinger's protege and hand-picked successor as the conciliar prefect of the Congregation for the Destruction, Deformation and Deconstruction of the Catholic Faith. Please see **Generating Controversy and Negative Press** and **Rescind the Appointment at Once,** both of which were written in my "resist and recognize days in 2005; **Anathematized by His Own Words**, **No Need to be in Limbo Any Longer**, **Piracy, Conciliar Style**, **Red Carpet For A Modernist**, **Words Really Do Matter** and **Short And To The Catholic Point**, **Apostates Reprimanding Apostates**. Levada is the man who, as the conciliar "archbishop" of Portland, Oregon, once told the late Father Eugene Heidt, whom he suspended for offering the Immemorial Mass of Tradition without "permission," that Transubstantiation is a "long and difficult word" and "that we don't use it any more" (see **Invincible or Inculpable**) and issued an eight-page **Doctrinal Assessment of the Leadership Conference of Women Religious**.
2. Sean Patrick O'Malley, O.F.M., Cap. He is, of course, one of Jorge Mario Bergoglio's own **Commissars**, whose nefarious warfare against the Catholic Faith has been examined on this site many times: (See **Another Victim of Americanism, Behold The Free Rein Given to Error, Behold The Free Rein Given to Error, Unfortunate Enough to Be A Baby, Beacon of Social Justice?; Spotlight On The Ordinary, What's Good For Teddy Is Good For Benny; Sean O'Malley: Coward and Hypocrite: More Rationalizations and Distortions, Peeking into the Old Conciliar Fowler's Lair, part two, It Has Come To This: Viva Chick Fil-A, Not Viva Cristo Rey**, **Vast Is The Damage**, **BLAAAAAABBBBERMOUTHS!**, **Antichrist's Liturgical Presiders**, **Whirlwinds Of Spiritual Destruction**, **No Crime Is Worse Than Deicide**.)

Ratzinger's Consistory of November 24, 2007:

1. Odilo Pedro Scherer, an apostate from Brazil whose aides were openly campaigning for him to be elected as the universal public face of apostasy in late-February and early-March of 2013 (see **BLAAAAAABBBBERMOUTHS!**).
2. Daniel DiNardo, whose warfare against the Catholic Faith has been documented on this site several times. Please see: **A Little Something for Everyone, BLAAAAAABBBBERMOUTHS, Blackbirds Of A Feather Do Stick Together, Don't They?**, **Professional Courtesy**, **Forever Preserving False "Traditions"**.)

3. Sean Brady, who was permitted to remain as the conciliar Primate of Ireland after all of the documentation proving his involvement in the covering up of priest/presbyter abuse cases to the point of his retirement on September 8, 2014, the Feast of the Nativity of the Blessed Virgin Mary. Ratzinger/Benedict did not remove him when all of the evidence of Brady's crimes became public. Bergoglio let Brady continue in office until his mandatory retirement, which occurred when he turned seventy-five years of age on August 16, 2014, and became effective when Bergoglio accepted Brady's resignation thirteen days later.

Ratzinger's Consistory of November 20, 2010:

1. Raymond Leo Burke. Although not in favor with Jorge Mario Bergoglio, who is exiling him to be the head of the Sovereign Military Order of Malta, the former conciliar "archbishop" of St. Louis, Missouri, where he tried to seize a privately owned church that is now independent yet committed to the conciliar revolution (see **It's All About the Money**, which was written five months before jumping off the "resist while recognize" ship), and the former bishop" of La Crosse, Wisconsin, where he permitted a man to form a community of women religious after he had undergone surgery to mutilate his body and "become" a woman, is nevertheless a revolutionary despite his supposedly "traditional" predilections. See **"Cardinals" Burke and Canizares, Meet The Council of Trent**.
2. Kurt Koch, the man who has been the Vatican's new Walter Kasper since July 1, 2010. See **Does The Defense of Truth Matter To You?**, **Happy Vesakh, No, I Mean, Happy Diwali, Oops, Let's Try Again**, **Bearing "Fruits" From Hell Itself**, **Bergoglio, Pride and Joy of the Everyman Religion**, **Francis The Impure**, **Can Anyone Spell A-P-O-S-T-A-S-Y?**, **Yer Durn Tootin'**, **Processing Along The Path To Antichrist**, **Showing Us The Value Of A Conciliar Consecration**, **Francis The Illusionist, Part Two**, **Propagating Only What His Boss Believes and Teaches, part two**, **Continuously Denying The Catholic Faith**, **Forever Preserving False "Traditions"**, **Control The Language, Control The Perception**, **Saint Vincent Ferrer and Anti-Saint Vincent Ferrer**.
3. Gianfranco Ravasi, who tried to assuage the anger of Talmudists following Ratzinger/Benedict's "revised" Good Friday Prayer for the Jews back in 2008. See **The Great Charade**, **Into the Deep Freezer, All for Fear of the Jews**, **Many Acts of Evil Demand Many Acts of Reparation**, **On The Terms Of The Enemies Of Christ The King**, **Blackbirds Of A Feather Do Stick Together, Don't They?**.
4. Donald Wuerl, whose warfare against the Fath, which has included the promotion of the lavender agenda and his refusal to deny pro-abortion Catholics in public life what purports to be Holy Communion in the Protestant and Judeo-Masonic *Novus Ordo* liturgical service, has been documented on this site several times in the past. See **Promoting "Dialogue" Over "Dogmatism"**, **Naughty, Naughty, Nancy**, **Giving Unto Caesar What Belongs To God Alone**, **Latin and the Lector Babe**, **BLAAAAAABBBBERMOUTHS!**, **Destroying Vestiges Of A Forbidden Faith**, **Still Hunkered Down In Mindanao**, **Perhaps Judas Was the First to Sing "A Kiss is Just a Kiss"**. See also Mrs. Randy Engel's **Wuerl's appointment cause for concern?** and **Mother's Watch**'s critique of Wuerl's sponsorship of an explicit program of classroom instruction in matters pertaining to the Sixth and Ninth Commandments, *Growing in Love*.

Ratzinger's Consistory of February 18, 2012

1. João Bráz de Aviz, the defender of feminist communities of women religious in the counterfeit church of conciliarism. See **Francis The Feminist**, **Francis Says ¡Viva la Revolución!, part two**, **Memo From Patrolman Ed Nicholson to Jorge Mario Bergoglio: SHUT UP!**)
2. Timothy Michael Dolan, which means, of course, there is no need to say anymore other than what I have said already in: **Timmy's In The Well (Of Americanism, That Is)**, **Making Everyone Happy Except God**, **Unhappy Is The "Happy" "Bishop"**, **Whatever You Want**, **Ominous Offenders Offending Ominously**, **Memo To David Axelrod And Other Social Engineers**, **John Carroll's Caesar**, **Victims of Compromise**, **Taking A Figure Of Antichrist At His Worthless Words**, **Prisoners Of Their Own Apostasy**, **Timothy Dolan, Meet Timothy Dolan (And Friends)**, **Still Celebrating Half A Century Of Apostasy**, **Candidate For Man Of The Year?**, **From John Carroll To James Gibbons To Timothy Dolan**, **To Help The Children**, **Fake, Phony, Sanctimonious Fraud**, **Happy As A Stuffed Clam With Himself**, **Impossible To Fight Moral Evils With Blasphemy And Error**, **Still Trying to Make Everyone Happy Except God Himself**, **Just Another Ordinary Outrage Permitted by a Conciliar "Ordinary"** and **Forty Years of Emboldening, Appeasing, and Enabling Killers, part two**, **You're Not Supposed To Do This"**, **Francis And Other Judases Abound In Holy Week**, **Auditioning To Be The Next Universal Face of Apostasy**, **Professional Courtesy**, **Fortnight Of Fraud Update**, **Just Another Jolly Thug**, **Memo To Timothy Michael Dolan: Catholics Never Say "We Used To Say"**, **Rocketing To The Very Depths Of Hell**, **"We Want To Be With You"**.
3. Rainer Woelki, a defender of the lavender agenda and other evils. See **Rationalizing The Work of Rationalists**, **"Blessed" Paul The Sick**, **Crushed By The Weight Of Error, Part Two**, **Francis The Blind**.

Mind you, this is only a very, very partial listing of the ninety conciliar revolutionaries who were appointed to the conciliar college of "cardinals" by Joseph Ratzinger/Benedict, leaving aside entirely his last consistory, which was held on November 24, 2012 (see **Apostates Given the Scarlet Hat by Joseph Ratzinger/Benedict XVI**). Those pining for "Ratzingerian 'cardinals'" in the wake of Jorge Mario Bergoglio's elevation of nineteen Modernists on February 22, 2014, the Feast of the Chair of Saint Peter in Antioch, were as delusional as one Alexander Emmanuel Rodriguez was when he contended that he was a victim of Federal arbitrator Fredric Horowitz, the late Michael Weiner, the former executive director of the Major League Baseball Players Association, then Major League Baseball Commissioner Alan H. "Bud" Selig, and the entire front office, medical staff, ushers, grounds keepers, ticket takers and ushers who work for the incarnation of all evil in the world, the New York Yankees.

Additionally, the deluded people who winced in the face of Jorge Mario Bergoglio's "cardinals" forgot an inconvenient little fact: Joseph Ratzinger/Benedict XVI had appointed most, although not all, of them to the positions they held at the time Jorge elevated to the conciliar "college of cardinals."

Facts are troublesome things, aren't they?

Here is a list of the nineteen men whom Jorge Mario Bergoglio elevated to the conciliar college of "cardinals" on February 22, 2014, replete with a brief history about them as found on the Vatican website:

PIETRO PAROLIN
Part of the Holy See's diplomatic corps since 1986, he was Apostolic Nuncio in Venezuela between 2009 and 2013, when Pope Francis nominated him Vatican **Secretary of State**.

LORENZO BALDISSERI
Previously Apostolic Nuncio in Brazil, where he welcomed Pope Benedict XVI on his visit in 2007, he was Secretary of the Congregation of Bishops from January 2012 until nominated **Secretary General of the Synod of Bishops** by Pope Francis in September 2013.

GERHARD LUDWIG MÜLLER
Having graduated in philosophy and theology, he was professor of Dogmatic Theology at the Catholic Ludwig-Maximilians-Universität in Munich (Germany) between 1986 and 2002, travelling as visiting professor to universities worldwide. In 2012 Pope Benedict XVI nominated him **Prefect of the Congregation for the Doctrine of the Faith**, President of the Pontifical Commission "Ecclesia Dei", President of the Pontifical Biblical Commission and President of the International Theological Commission.

BENIAMINO STELLA
Part of the Holy See's diplomatic corps since 1970, he was previously Apostolic Nuncio in Cuba and Colombia, and was nominated **Prefect of the Congregation for the Clergy** by Pope Francis in September 2013.

VINCENT GERARD NICHOLS
Master of Arts in Theology and previously Secretary General of the Catholic Bishops' Conference of England and Wales, he was Metropolitan Archbishop of Birmingham (UK) between 2000 and 2009, when Pope Benedict XVI nominated him **Metropolitan Archbishop of Westminster (UK)**.

LEOPOLDO JOSÉ BRENES SOLÓRZANO
He obtained his Licentiate of Sacred Theology at the Pontifical Lateran University in Rome (Italy) and was nominated **Metropolitan Archbishop of Managua (Nicaragua)** by Pope John Paul II in March 2005.

GÉRALD CYPRIEN LACROIX, I.S.P.X.
Part of the "Institut Séculier Pie X" since 1975, he has been both Secretary General and Director General of the institute, as well as Director General of its centre for spiritual formation "Maison du Renouveau". He was nominated **Metropolitan Archbishop of Québec (Canada)** by Pope Benedict XVI in February 2011.

JEAN-PIERRE KUTWA

Doctor of Philosophy in Biblical Theology and previously Metropolitan Archbishop of Gagnoa (Ivory Coast), he was nominated **Metropolitan Archbishop of Abidjan (Ivory Coast)** in May 2006.

ORANI JOÃO TEMPESTA, O. CIST.
A member of the Cistercian Order since 1969, he was Prior of the São Bernardo monastery in São José do Rio Pardo (Brazil) from 1984 until the monastery became an abbey in 1996, when he was elected its first Abbot. Previously President of Brazil's National Commission for Culture, Education and Social Communications, he was nominated **Metropolitan Archbishop of São Sebastião do Rio de Janeiro (Brazil)** in February 2009, in which capacity he welcomed Pope Francis on his visit in July 2013.

GUALTIERO BASSETTI
He was previously a member of the Episcopal Commission of the Italian Episcopal Conference for the Clergy and Consecrated Life, and a member of the Managing Board of the Catholic Committee for Cultural Collaboration with Orthodox Churches of the Byzantine tradition and Eastern Orthodox Churches. He is currently Vice-President of the Italian Episcopal Conference for Central Italy, and **Archbishop of Perugia-Città della Pieve (Italy)**.

MARIO AURELIO PIOLI
Having graduated as Doctor of Philosophy in Theology from the Pontifical Catholic University of Argentina, he was appointed there as professor of Ecclesiastical History in 1980. He is currently President of the Episcopal Commission for Catholic Education and of the Episcopal Commission for Ministries with the Argentinian Episcopal Conference, and was nominated **Metropolitan Archbishop of Buenos Aires (Argentina)** by Pope Francis in March 2013.

ANDREW YEOM SOO-JUNG
Archbishop of Seoul (South Korea) since May 2012, he previously occupied a series of senior administrative posts within parishes and seminaries across South Korea.

RICCARDO EZZATI ANDRELLO, S.D.B.
A member of the Salesians of Don Bosco since 1966, he worked with the Salesian Society in parishes and educational institutions all over Chile. Previously Metropolitan Archbishop of Concepción (Chile), he was nominated **Metropolitan Archbishop of Santiago (Chile)** in December 2010.

PHILIPPE NAKELLENTUBA OUEDRAOGO
Previously a member of the Congregation for the Evangelization of Peoples, he was nominated **Metropolitan Archbishop of Ouadraogo (Burkina Faso)** by Pope Benedict XVI in May 2009.

ORLANDO QUEVEDO, O.M.I.
Already a member of the Missionary Oblates of Mary Immaculate, he graduated in Pedagogy from the University of Santo Tomas in Manila (Philippines). He was appointed

first Bishop of Kidapawan (Philippines) when the diocese was created in November 1982, and nominated **Metropolitan Archbishop of Cotabato (Philippines)** by Pope John Paul II in 1998.

CHIBLY LANGLOIS
Nominated **Bishop of Les Cayes (Haiti)** by Pope Benedict XVI in August 2011, he was previously professor of Pastoral Theology at the Grand Séminaire Notre-Dame in Port-au-Prince (Haiti) and professor at the Diocesan Institute for Human Education and Promotion in Jacmel (Haiti).

At the same time, Pope Francis will join to the members of the College of Cardinals three Archbishops Emeriti, distinguished for their service to the Holy See and to the Church:

LORIS FRANCESCO CAPOVILLA
A qualified journalist and former editor of a diocesan weekly magazine in Venice (Italy), he was secretary to Angelo Giuseppe Roncalli, later Pope John XXIII, first in Venice and then in the Vatican. He was **Pontifical Delegate for the Shrine of the Holy House of Loreto (Italy)** from 1971 until his retirement in 1988. At 98 years old, he is the third oldest archbishop in the world and will be the oldest member of the College of Cardinals.

SEBASTIÁN AGUILAR, C.M.F.
A member of the Missionary Sons of the Immaculate Heart of Mary and previously Bishop of León (Spain), he is **Archbishop Emeritus of Pamplona (Spain)**, where he served from 1993 until his retirement in 2007.

KELVIN EDWARD FELIX
Having graduated as Doctor of Philosophy in Sociology from the University of Bradford (UK) in 1970, he was professor of Sociology at the University of the West Indies at Saint Augustine (Trinidad and Tobago) for many years. Previously President of the Caribbean Conference of Churches, President of the Antilles Episcopal Conference, member of the Pontifical Council for the Family and member of the Pontifical Council for Inter-religious Dialogue, he is **Archbishop Emeritus of Castries (Saint Lucia)**, where he led the diocese from his appointment in 1981 until his retirement in 2008. (**A closer look at the newest apostates who will soon be a wearin' the scarlet**.)

Remember, Pietro Parolin helped to pave the way for Joseph Ratzinger/Benedict XVI's "reconciliation" with the heretical and schismatic "Chinese Patriotic Association" (see **Red China: Still A Workshop For The New Ecclesiology**, **Conciliarism's Weapons of Mass Destruction, part three**, **Francis The Impure**, **They Have Been Doing Something Different For Fifty-Five Years**). He has also shown himself to be very friendly to the likes of Barack Hussein Obama/Barry Soetoro, differing with him only on what he termed as "bioethical issues" (see **Respect Those Who Break the First Commandment?**). Ratzinger/Benedict had great "faith" in Pietro Parolin?

Vincent Nichols?

Do you really need to know more about Ratzinger/Benedict's hand-picked appointee to be the conciliar "archbishop" of Westminster?

Well, go read the following: **Not Worth A Truckload Full Of Plugged Nickels**, **Benedict And His Boys Are Far Cries From Saint Patrick**, **Jorge Says Party Hearty**, **Francis The Anti-Campion**, **Defaming The English Martyrs**, **Francis Rallies The Forces Of Antichrist**, **Where Does One Begin? part three**.

Reinhard Marx?

Well, other than being Ratzinger/Benedict's hand-picked appointee as the conciliar "archbishop" of his own native country's Munich and Freising that he once headed between March 24, 1977, prior to being promoted by Karol Wojtyla/John Paul to the Congregation for the Deformation, Destruction and Deconstruction of the Catholic Faith in November of 1981, Commissar Marx had the following to say a few months ago that should remind those "pining for Benedict" the way that delusional "conservatives" are pining for the statist war monger named George Walker Bush that they live in a world full of delusion:

> (Munich) The Archbishop of Munich and Freising, Cardinal Reinhard Marx**, has proclaimed Christianity without hell and purgatory, only with more paradise, so to speak, a Christian spa.** Cardinal Marx belongs to the eight-member Cardinal advisory which Pope Francis appointed on 13 April to advise him on the management of the Church. Cardinal Marx represents Europe. Marx is also the Chairman of the Commission of the Bishops' Conferences of the European Union (COMECE) and in the spring of 2014 a contender for the presidency of the German Bishops' Conference.
>
> Cardinal Reinhard Marx held a spiritual talk on 9 November in Erding, Bavaria, a spiritual talk on "Resurrection". Here, the Cardinal tried to explain the Christian doctrine of resurrection: "Every person is a unique, eternal thought of God, who must be thought of to the end and can not disintegrate into nothingness." And further: "If God wanted everyone from all eternity and love, your everything can't be over in death".
>
> But then the Cardinal faltered. The Christian belief in the resurrection depends, says Archbishop Marx, **"that we believe God is possible."** God's existence only as a "possibility"? As the Archdiocese of Munich and Freising himself puts it, the Cardinal continued by saying, if you trust the words of Christ, "**Then the hope is justified that our death opens a gate to something indestructible**."
>
> Today, said the Cardinal, many have a "cramped relationship" to death and the belief in the resurrection has become "weak". "We need to see everything, to touch everything, to understand it." The Church must oppose to that "strong rites and symbols" laying out the coffin in the church, such as at a Requiem for a deceased. Children also should not deter you from confrontation with death, for example, the sight of a deceased person, but must enable them to encounter them and accompany them in this. "Therefore, the Church, and we can witness to that, that at death a change takes place and we are not before a cold

> nothingness," Marx said. The practice of the Church must make the hope of the resurrection visible, reports the Archbishop.
>
> The resurrection, says the Cardinal, that God gives us the assurance that He will transform and lead us with His help to the end, **"but without moralizing and without a hell of torture, imprisonment and a burning oven". The Church caused this with pictures like that of purgatory and hell, fear of death. Not only that, the Church must "repent" for this scaremongering images that a malicious invention will be obvious to Catholics,** said Cardinal Marx. In the Cardinal's words, "**and for that we need to repent**." And you wonder where the Cardinal actually lives. After half a century of the abolition of the sign of hell, the problem is not the belief that there is a hell, but that many Christians no longer believe in the existence of hell and purgatory.
>
> Finally, the Cardinal proffered a logical conclusion to universal salvation: Because Jesus went about not to enumerate sins, but to pledge every man to healing and salvation. "**The Church must completely drive out fear**," emphasized Cardinal Marx. To imagine what would come after death, the person needs images, **"but this must be images of confidence, hope, images and help to continue on, even if they can not give us a definitive answer**." What the Archbishop did was give the impression that the Church has not allowed in its two thousand year history, a great show to salvation, redemption and salvation of souls. (**Commissar Marx Corrects Our Lord and Abolishes Hell and Purgatory**. See also **Jorge Says Party Hearty, part two**.)

Marx, who is one of Jorge Mario Bergoglio's Commissars, also disparaged traditionally-minded Catholics in the conciliar structures when he said the following:

> "According to the Prelate, Benedict XVI is a theologian who 'has never stopped being curious about and admiring everything God made.' In the same way, he stressed, man must continue to discover the Gospel as the novelty by antonomasia: 'The traditionalists venerate the old, they are guardians of a museum. **We must not, however, guard the richness in a museum; we must not look for a restoration, but instead for a rebirth, for a renewal of the faith and Catholic life, a renewal of the Church as a whole and of each individual.' The Catholic faith is 'the greatest adventure of the human spirit, but it is also demanding and wants to take us farther**.'" (As found at: **Reinhard Marx's Museum**. See also **Let's Look At Life Outside Of The "Museum"**).

Gerhard Ludwig Muller, another hand-picked Ratzinger/Benedict appointee, may not be in much favor with Bergoglio. However, he is nevertheless a complete apostate who has denied the Perpetual Virginity of the Blessed Virgin Mary (see **Deft? Daft Is More Like It, part two**, **Deft? Daft Is More Like It, part three**, **Does The Defense of Catholic Truth Matter To *You*?**, **When Will The Madness End?, part one** and **Memo To Bishop Fellay: Ratzinger/Benedict Really, Really, Really, Really, Really Loves Gerhard Ludwig Muller**), something that did not faze Ratzinger/Benedict in the slightest as he has used his own clever devices to do this as well.

Lorenzo Baldisseri?

"Cardinal" Baldiserri helped to steer the 2014 "extraordinary synod of bishops on the family" to further the revolutionary goals of the man who elevated him to the conciliar "college of cardinals," namely, Jorge Mario Bergolgio, who chose to make Baldiserri the executive secretary of the "Synod of Bishops," thereby transferring him from the same position in the Congregation for the Bishops in conciliar captivity. Oh, the "pope" who had appointed Baldiseri to the latter position was none other than Joseph Alois Ratzinger/Benedict XVI.

Thus it is that those who had attempted to find "space" between Bergoglio's non-cardinals and Ratzinger/Benedict's should have known all along that there was virtually none to be found.

What the Argentine Apostate *is* doing, however, is to send a clear signal that the program he outlined in *Evangelii Gaudium*, November 26, 2013 (see **Jorge and Oscar's False Gospel of False Joy, part one**, **Jorge and Oscar's False Gospel of False Joy, part two**, **Jorge and Oscar's False Gospel of False Joy, part three**, **Jorge and Oscar's False Gospel of False Joy, part four**, **Jorge and Oscar's False Gospel of False Joy, part five**, **Jorge and Oscar's False Gospel of False Joy, part six** and **Jorge and Oscar's False Gospel of False Joy, part seven**), is his framework for taking the conciliar revolution to its ultimate conclusion. The whole point of his recently concluded "extraordinary synod of 'bishops' on the family" was to universalize an abandonment of Catholic teaching on matters pertaining to the Sixth and Ninth Commandments in the name of a false concept of "mercy."

By choosing the men that he did to be members of the conciliar college of non-cardinals, Bergoglio was explaining that he wanted men after his own Jacobin heart, that is, men who are willing to put aside "doctrine" in order to show "mercy" and to focus on the "needs" of this world rather than on eternity. All matters of doctrine and fixed pastoral praxis based upon it are subject to re-examination and re-evaluation in light of alleged "pastoral necessities."

Whether or not those "pining for Benedict" realize it, this is simply the ultimate conclusion of the revolution their man from Bavaria helped to engineer as a *peritus* (expert) at the "Second" Vatican Council fifty years ago. Although Ratzinger/Benedict thought that he could control the course of the revolution, that control was bound to end as soon as he left the conciliar "papacy" on February 28, 2013. There is nothing fixed, nothing stable about Modernism. That is, why should Bergoglio consider Ratzinger an authority when the latter believed he could ignore the binding pronouncements against Modernism made by Pope Saint Pius X in *Lamentabili Sane Exitu*, July 3, 1907, *Pascendi Dominici Gregis*, September 8, 1907, *Praestantia Scripturae*, November 18, 1907, and *The Oath Against Modernism*, September 1, 1910?

Indeed, heresy of its very nature must give rise to further "innovations" in the name of "progress" and, in the case of Bergoglio, false mercy and false charity and false joy. The counterfeit church of conciliarism is being transformed more and more into an ape of the heretical and schismatic Anglican sect, whose non-bishops decide matters of "doctrine" by means of "votes" and who are always open to "adapting" the binding precepts of the Divine Positive Law and the Natural Law to the alleged exigencies of the "real world" as it is said to exist. Sterile sacramental rites must lead to the abandonment of all semblance of Christian faith, resulting in a pantheism that is a poorly disguised worship of man himself.

Keep praying your Rosaries. Believe me, this is all going to get worse and worse in human terms. We must simply do our part to offer up the trials of the present moment as the consecrated slaves of Our Blessed Lord and and Saviour Jesus Christ through the Sorrowful and Immaculate Heart of Mary, ever confident that that same Immaculate Heart of Mary will triumph in the end.

Chapter Four

Joseph Ratzinger's Condemned Views on Dogmatic Evolution

Joseph Ratzinger/Benedict XVI gave his "papal" imprimatur to his own version of dogmatic evolution in his infamous Christmas address to the conciliar curia on December 22, 2005:

> "It is precisely in this combination of continuity and discontinuity at different levels that the very nature of true reform consists. **In this process of innovation in continuity we must learn to understand more practically than before that the Church's decisions on contingent matters - for example, certain practical forms of liberalism or a free interpretation of the Bible - should necessarily be contingent themselves, precisely because they refer to a specific reality that is changeable in itself. *It was necessary to learn* to recognize that in these decisions it is only the principles that express the permanent aspect, since they remain as an undercurrent, motivating decisions from within.**
>
> **On the other hand, not so permanent are the practical forms that depend on the historical situation and are therefore subject to change.**" (Christmas greetings to the Members of the Roman Curia and Prelature, December 22, 2005

For Ratzinger/Benedict to be correct about this, of course, the Third Person of the Most Blessed Trinity, God the Holy Ghost, not only hid this "knowledge" that had to be "learned," but He permitted a solemn dogmatic council, the [First] Vatican Council, to falsely condemn the whole concept of viewing dogmatic statements in light of the historical circumstances in which they written. This means that, *ipso facto*, the Catholic Church has no infallibility whatsoever and that God the Holy Ghost misdirected the Fathers of the [First] Vatican Council and that the true popes who reiterated the condemnation were themselves mistaken.

The passages below show how thoroughly consistent Father and "Cardinal" Ratzinger was in his support of dogmatic evolution prior to becoming "Pope" Benedict XVI on April 19, 2005:

> **1971**: "In theses 10-12, the difficult problem of the relationship between language and thought is debated, which in post-conciliar discussions was the immediate departure point of the dispute.
>
> **The identity of the Christian substance as such, the Christian 'thing' was not directly ... censured, but it was pointed out that no formula, no matter how valid and indispensable it may have been in its time, can fully express the thought mentioned in it and declare it unequivocally forever, since language is constantly in movement and the content of its meaning changes.**" (Fr. Ratzinger: Dogmatic formulas must always change.)
>
> **1990**: "The text [of the document Instruction on the Theologian's Ecclesial Vocation] also presents the various types of bonds that rise from the different degrees of magisterial teaching. **It affirms - perhaps for the first time with this clarity - that there are**

decisions of the magisterium that cannot be the last word on the matter as such, but are, in a substantial fixation of the problem, above all an expression of pastoral prudence, a kind of provisional disposition. The nucleus remains valid, but the particulars, which the circumstances of the times influenced, may need further correction.

In this regard, one may think of the declarations of Popes in the last century [19th century] about religious liberty, as well as the anti-Modernist decisions at the beginning of this century, above all, the decisions of the Biblical Commission of the time [on evolutionism]. As a cry of alarm in the face of hasty and superficial adaptations, they will remain fully justified. A personage such as Johann Baptist Metz said, for example, that the Church's anti-Modernist decisions render the great service of preserving her from falling into the liberal-bourgeois world. But in the details of the determinations they contain, they became obsolete after having fulfilled their pastoral mission at their proper time."

(Joseph Ratzinger, "Instruction on the Theologian's Ecclesial Vocation," published with the title "Rinnovato dialogo fra Magistero e Teologia," in L'Osservatore Romano, June 27, 1990, p. 6, cited at **Card. Ratzinger: The teachings of the Popes against Modernism are obsolete**)

The Catholic Church, guided infallibly by God the Holy Ghost, Who is immutable because He is God, has consistently condemned what Ratzinger/Benedict labels as the "hermeneutic of continuity":

- For the doctrine of the faith which God has revealed is put forward
  - not as some philosophical discovery capable of being perfected by human intelligence,
  - but as a divine deposit committed to the spouse of Christ to be faithfully protected and infallibly promulgated.
- Hence, too, **that meaning of the sacred dogmas is ever to be maintained which has once been declared by holy mother church, and there must never be any abandonment of this sense under the pretext or in the name of a more profound understanding.**

God cannot deny himself, nor can truth ever be in opposition to truth.

The appearance of this kind of specious contradiction is chiefly due to the fact that either: the dogmas of faith a**re not understood and explained in accordance with the mind of the church, or unsound views are mistaken for the conclusions of reason**.

Therefore we define that every assertion contrary to the truth of enlightened faith is totally false. . . .

3. **If anyone says that it is possible that at some time, given the advancement of knowledge, a sense may be assigned to the dogmas propounded by the church which is different from that which the church has understood and understands: let him be anathema**.

And so in the performance of our supreme pastoral office, we beseech for the love of Jesus Christ and we command, by the authority of him who is also our God and saviour, all faithful Christians, especially those in authority or who have the duty of teaching, that they contribute their zeal and labour to the warding off and elimination of these errors from the church and to the spreading of the light of the pure faith.

But since it is not enough to avoid the contamination of heresy unless those errors are carefully shunned which approach it in greater or less degree, we warn all of their duty to observe the constitutions and decrees in which such wrong opinions, though not expressly mentioned in this document, have been banned and forbidden by this holy see. (Pope Pius IX, Vatican Council, Session III, Dogmatic Constitution on the Catholic Faith, Chapter 4, On Faith and Reason, April 24, 1870. **SESSION 3 : 24 April 1**.)

Pope Saint Pius X reaffirmed this condemnation in *Pascendi Dominici Gregis*, September 8, 1907:

> Hence it is quite impossible [the Modernists assert] to maintain that they [dogmatic statements] absolutely contain the truth: **for, in so far as they are symbols, they are the images of truth, and so must be adapted to the religious sense in its relation to man; and as instruments, they are the vehicles of truth, and must therefore in their turn be adapted to man in his relation to the religious sense. But the object of the religious sense, as something contained in the absolute, possesses an infinite variety of aspects, of which now one, now another, may present itself. In like manner he who believes can avail himself of varying conditions. Consequently, the formulas which we call dogma must be subject to these vicissitudes, and are, therefore, liable to change. Thus the way is open to the intrinsic evolution of dogma. Here we have an immense structure of sophisms which ruin and wreck all religion**. (Pope Saint Pius X, *Pascendi Dominici Gregis*, September 8, 1907.)

This condemnation was reaffirmed in *Praestantia Scripturae*, November 18, 1907:

> After mature examination and the most diligent deliberations the Pontifical Biblical Commission has happily given certain decisions of a very useful kind for the proper promotion and direction on safe lines of Biblical studies. **But we observe that some persons, unduly prone to opinions and methods tainted by pernicious novelties and excessively devoted to the principle of false liberty, which is really immoderate license and in sacred studies proves itself to be a most insidious and a fruitful source of the worst evils against the purity of the faith, have not received and do not receive these decisions with the proper obedience.**

> Wherefore we find it necessary to declare and to expressly prescribe, and by this our act we do declare and decree that all are bound in conscience to submit to the decisions of the Biblical Commission relating to doctrine, which have been given in the past and which shall be given in the future, in the same way as to the decrees of the Roman congregations approved by the Pontiff; nor can all those escape the note of disobedience or temerity, and consequently of grave sin, who in speech or writing contradict such decisions, and this besides the scandal they give and the other reasons for which they may be responsible before God for other temerities and errors which generally go with such contradictions.
>
> **Moreover, in order to check the daily increasing audacity of many modernists who are endeavoring by all kinds of sophistry and devices to detract from the force and efficacy not only of the decree "Lamentabili sane exitu" (the so-called Syllabus), issued by our order by the Holy Roman and Universal Inquisition on July 3 of the present year, but also of our encyclical letters "Pascendi dominici gregis" given on September 8 of this same year**, we do by our apostolic authority repeat and confirm both that decree of the Supreme Sacred Congregation and those encyclical letters of ours, **adding the penalty of excommunication against their contradictors, and this we declare and decree that should anybody, which may God forbid, be so rash as to defend any one of the propositions, opinions or teachings condemned in these documents he falls, ipso facto, under the censure contained under the chapter "Docentes" of the constitution "Apostolicae Sedis," which is the first among the excommunications latae sententiae, simply reserved to the Roman Pontiff. This excommunication is to be understood as salvis poenis, which may be incurred by those who have violated in any way the said documents, as propagators and defenders of heresies, when their propositions, opinions and teachings are heretical, as has happened more than once in the case of the adversaries of both these documents, especially when they advocate the errors of the modernists that is, the synthesis of all heresies.** (Pope Saint Pius X, Praestantia Scripturae, November 18, 1907.)

Pope Saint Pius X finally required priests and seminary professors and seminarians who had received Minor Orders to take *The Oath Against Modernism*, which was issued on September 1, 1910, and contains the following important passages:

> Fourthly, **I sincerely hold that the doctrine of faith was handed down to us from the apostles through the orthodox Fathers in exactly the same meaning and always in the same purport. Therefore, I entirely reject the heretical misrepresentation that dogmas evolve and change from one meaning to another different from the one which the Church held previously**. . . .
>
> Finally, I declare that I am completely opposed to the error of the modernists who hold that there is nothing divine in sacred tradition; or what is far worse, say that there is, but in a pantheistic sense, with the result that there would remain nothing but this plain simple fact-one to be put on a par with the ordinary facts of history-the fact, namely, that a group of men by their own labor, skill, and talent have continued through subsequent ages a school begun by Christ and his apostles. I firmly hold, then, and shall hold to my dying breath the belief of the Fathers in the charism of truth, which certainly is, was, and always will be in

> the succession of the episcopacy from the apostles. The purpose of this is, then, **not that dogma may be tailored according to what seems better and more suited to the culture of each age; rather, that the absolute and immutable truth preached by the apostles from the beginning may never be believed to be different, may never be understood in any other way.**
>
> I promise that I shall keep all these articles faithfully, entirely, and sincerely, and guard them inviolate, in no way deviating from them in teaching or in any way in word or in writing. Thus I promise, this I swear, so help me God. (*The Oath Against Modernism*, September 1, 1910.)

Undaunted, however, Modernists were still trying to promote dogmatic evolution under the banner of the "New Theology" in whose bosom seminarian Joseph Alois Ratzinger was nurtured with such assiduous care by the likes of the late Father Hans Urs von Balthasar and others.

Pope Pius XII condemned the "New Theology's" repackaging of dogmatic evolution by the use of supposedly clever semantic devices. This is how he condemned such repackaging as found in *Humani Generis*, August 12, 1950:

> **Moreover they assert that when Catholic doctrine has been reduced to this condition, a way will be found to satisfy modern needs, that will permit of dogma being expressed also by the concepts of modern philosophy**, whether of immanentism or idealism or existentialism or any other system. **Some more audacious affirm that this can and must be done, because they hold that the mysteries of faith are never expressed by truly adequate concepts but only by approximate and ever changeable notions, in which the truth is to some extent expressed, but is necessarily distorted. Wherefore they do not consider it absurd, but altogether necessary, that theology should substitute new concepts in place of the old ones in keeping with the various philosophies which in the course of time it uses as its instruments, so that it should give human expression to divine truths in various ways which are even somewhat opposed, but still equivalent**, as they say. They add that the history of dogmas consists in the reporting of the various forms in which revealed truth has been clothed, forms that have succeeded one another in accordance with the different teachings and opinions that have arisen over the course of the centuries. (Pope Pius XII, *Humani Generis*, August 12, 1950.)

Joseph Alois Ratzinger stands condemned for adhering to and propagating his philosophically absurd and dogmatically condemned "hermeneutic of continuity." He placed himself outside of the pale of Holy Mother Church long ago as one falls from the Faith if he fails to adhere to even one article of the Holy Faith. Joseph Ratzinger fails to adhere to multiple articles of the Holy Faith. Only one such defect, however, causes one to fall from the Faith and thus to be incapable of holding any kind of ecclesiastical office within Holy Mother Church legitimately.

The fact that some of our latter day Modernists by way of the "new theology" that was condemned by Pope Pius XII in *Humani Generis*, August 12, 1950, hold to some tenets of the Faith, although, truth be told, it is not infrequently the case that what appears to be belief in a tenet of Faith on the part of conciliarists is simply appearance and not reality, does not mean that they are members of the Catholic Church. The latter day apostles of Modernism by way of the "new theology" in the counterfeit church of conciliarism have a compulsion to "redefine" the Faith and to express It thereafter in ambiguous terms that are designed to confuse people into believing them to be profound thinkers who have to be correct because they appear to be "so intellectual." They are outside of the Holy Faith.

Here is a review of why this is so:

> On this day preachers praise the virtue of the Canaanite woman in various ways. For myself, I will treat of faith, showing you what it is. I will attempt to show the relationship between what I have to say to you with what occurred in the Gospel between Our Lord and the Canaanite woman [Matt. 15: 21-28.] In this way you will learn the qualities that faith should have.
>
> When the Saviour said: Woman, how great is your faith, was it because the woman's faith was greater than ours? Certainly not as regards its object, because faith has for its object the truths revealed by God or the Church, and it is nothing else but an adhesion of our understanding to these truths, which it finds both beautiful and good. Consequently, it comes to believe them, and the will comes to love them. For just as goodness is the object of the will, beauty is that of the understanding. In our day-to-day life, goodness is coveted through our sense appetites and beauty is loved through our eyes. In our spiritual life, it happens in the same way in regard to the truths of the faith. These truths are good, sweet, and true, and are not only loved and desired by the will, but are also valued by the understanding because of the beauty it finds in them. They are beautiful because they are true; for beauty is never without truth, nor truth without beauty. Moreover, beautiful things which are not true are not really beautiful either. They are false and deceitful.
>
> Now the truths of the faith, being true indeed, are loved because of the beauty of this truth, which is the object of the understanding. I say loved, for although the will has goodness for the direct object of its love, nevertheless when the beauty of revealed truths is represented to it by the understanding, it also discovers goodness there, and loves this goodness and beauty of the mysteries of our faith. In order to have great faith, the understanding must perceive the beauty of this faith. For this reason when Our Lord desires to draw some creature to knowledge of the truth (1 Tim. 2: 4) he always reveals its beauty to him. The understanding, feeling itself drawn or captivated by it, communicates this truth to the will, which accordingly loves it for the goodness and beauty it recognizes there. Finally, the love that these two powers have for revealed truths prompts the person to forsake everything in order to believe them and embrace them. This is done spiritually. All this helps to explain how faith can be said to be nothing else but an adhesion of the understanding and will to divine truths.
>
> **With reference to its object, faith cannot be greater for some truths than for others. Nor can it be less with regard to the number of truths to be believed. For we must all believe the very same thing, both as to the object of faith as well as to the number of truths. All are equal in this because everyone must believe all the truths of faith--both**

> **those which God Himself has directly revealed, as well as those he has revealed through His Church. Thus, I must believe as much as you and you as much as I, and all other Christians similarly. He who does not believe all these mysteries is not Catholic and therefore will never enter Paradise**. (Saint Francis de Sales, *The Sermons of Saint Francis de Sales for Lent Given in 1622*, republished by TAN Books and Publishers for the Visitation Monastery of Frederick, Maryland, in 1987, pp. 34-37.)
>
> The Church, founded on these principles and mindful of her office, has done nothing with greater zeal and endeavour than she has displayed in guarding the integrity of the faith. **Hence she regarded as rebels and expelled from the ranks of her children all who held beliefs on any point of doctrine different from her own**. The Arians, the Montanists, the Novatians, the Quartodecimans, the Eutychians, **did not certainly reject all Catholic doctrine: they abandoned only a certain portion of it. Still who does not know that they were declared heretics and banished from the bosom of the Church**? In like manner were condemned all authors of heretical tenets who followed them in subsequent ages. "**There can be nothing more dangerous than those heretics who admit nearly the whole cycle of doctrine, and yet by one word, as with a drop of poison, infect the real and simple faith taught by our Lord and handed down by Apostolic tradition**" (Auctor Tract. de Fide Orthodoxa contra Arianos).
>
> The practice of the Church has always been the same, as is shown by the unanimous teaching of the Fathers, **who were wont to hold as outside Catholic communion, and alien to the Church, whoever would recede in the least degree from any point of doctrine proposed by her authoritative Magisterium**. Epiphanius, Augustine, Theodore :, drew up a long list of the heresies of their times. St. Augustine notes that other heresies may spring up, **to a single one of which, should any one give his assent, he is by the very fact cut off from Catholic unity. "No one who merely disbelieves in all (these heresies) can for that reason regard himself as a Catholic or call himself one. For there may be or may arise some other heresies, which are not set out in this work of ours, and, if any one holds to one single one of these he is not a Catholic**" (S. Augustinus, De Haeresibus, n. 88). (Pope Leo XIII, *Satis Cognitum*, June 29, 1896.)

Pope Benedict *XV* completely rejected any notion of a Catholic who could deny some of the truths of the Faith (say, religious liberty and the condemnation of the separation of Church and State) and remain a believer in the Catholic Faith:

> **Such is the nature of Catholicism that it does not admit of more or less, but must be held as a whole or as a whole rejected: 'This is the Catholic Faith, which unless a man believe faithfully and firmly, he cannot be saved' (Athanasian Creed). There is no need of adding any qualifying terms to the profession of Catholicism: it is quite enough for each one to proclaim 'Christian is my name and Catholic my surname,' only let him endeavor to be in reality what he calls himself**.
>
> Besides, the Church demands from those who have devoted themselves to furthering her interests, something very different from the dwelling upon profitless questions; she demands that they should devote the whole of their energy to preserve the faith intact and unsullied

> by any breath of error, and follow most closely him whom Christ has appointed to be the guardian and interpreter of the truth. There are to be found today, and in no small numbers, men, of whom the Apostle says that: "having itching ears, they will not endure sound doctrine: but according to their own desires they will heap up to themselves teachers, and will indeed turn away their hearing from the truth, but will be turned unto fables" (II Tim. iv. 34). Infatuated and carried away by a lofty idea of the human intellect, by which God's good gift has certainly made incredible progress in the study of nature, confident in their own judgment, and contemptuous of the authority of the Church, they have reached such a degree of rashness as not to hesitate to measure by the standard of their own mind even the hidden things of God and all that God has revealed to men. Hence arose the monstrous errors of "Modernism," which Our Predecessor rightly declared to be "the synthesis of all heresies," and solemnly condemned. We hereby renew that condemnation in all its fulness, Venerable Brethren, and as the plague is not yet entirely stamped out, but lurks here and there in hidden places, We exhort all to be carefully here and there in hidden places, We exhort all to be carefully on their guard against any contagion of the evil, to which we may apply the words Job used in other circumstances: "It is a fire that devoureth even to destruction, and rooteth up all things that spring" (Job xxxi. 12). Nor do We merely desire that Catholics should shrink from the errors of Modernism, but also from the tendencies of what is called the spirit of Modernism. **Those who are infected by that spirit develop a keen dislike for all that savours of antiquity and become eager searchers after novelties in everything: in the way in which they carry out religious functions, in the ruling of Catholic institutions, and even in private exercises of piety. Therefore it is Our will that the law of our forefathers should still be held sacred: "Let there be no innovation; keep to what has been handed down." In matters of faith that must be inviolably adhered to as the law; it may however also serve as a guide even in matters subject to change, but even in such cases the rule would hold: "Old things, but in a new way**." (Pope Benedict XV, *Ad Beatissimi Apostolorum*, November 1, 1914.)

Pope Pius XI, writing in *Mortalium Animos*, January 6, 1928, also rejected any notion of a distinction between "fundamental" and allegedly "non-fundamental" doctrines of the Catholic Faith:

> **Besides this, in connection with things which must be believed, it is nowise licit to use that distinction which some have seen fit to introduce between those articles of faith which are fundamental and those which are not fundamental, as they say, as if the former are to be accepted by all, while the latter may be left to the free assent of the faithful**: for the supernatural virtue of faith has a formal cause, namely the authority of God revealing, and this is patient of no such distinction. For this reason it is that all who are truly Christ's believe, for example, the Conception of the Mother of God without stain of original sin with the same faith as they believe the mystery of the August Trinity, and the Incarnation of our Lord just as they do the infallible teaching authority of the Roman Pontiff, according to the sense in which it was defined by the Ecumenical Council of the Vatican. Are these truths not equally certain, or not equally to be believed, because the Church has solemnly sanctioned and defined them, some in one age and some in another, even in those times immediately before our own? Has not God revealed them all? For the teaching authority of the Church, which in the divine wisdom was constituted on earth in order that revealed

doctrines might remain intact for ever, and that they might be brought with ease and security to the knowledge of men, and which is daily exercised through the Roman Pontiff and the Bishops who are in communion with him, has also the office of defining, when it sees fit, any truth with solemn rites and decrees, whenever this is necessary either to oppose the errors or the attacks of heretics, or more clearly and in greater detail to stamp the minds of the faithful with the articles of sacred doctrine which have been explained. But in the use of this extraordinary teaching authority no newly invented matter is brought in, nor is anything new added to the number of those truths which are at least implicitly contained in the deposit of Revelation, divinely handed down to the Church: only those which are made clear which perhaps may still seem obscure to some, or that which some have previously called into question is declared to be of faith. (Pope Pius XI, *Mortalium Animos*, January 6, 1928.)

Conciliarism is not Catholicism.

It is impossible for the Catholic Church, she who is the Mystical Bride of her Divine Founder, Invisible Head and Mystical Bridegroom, Our Blessed Lord and Saviour Jesus Christ, to be stained by any kind of error, no less out-and-out heresy:

> As for the rest, We greatly deplore the fact that, where the ravings of human reason extend, there is somebody who studies new things and strives to know more than is necessary, against the advice of the apostle. **There you will find someone who is overconfident in seeking the truth outside the Catholic Church, in which it can be found without even a light tarnish of error. Therefore, the Church is called, and is indeed, a pillar and foundation of truth**. You correctly understand, venerable brothers, that We speak here also of that erroneous philosophical system which was recently brought in and is clearly to be condemned. **This system, which comes from the contemptible and unrestrained desire for innovation, does not seek truth where it stands in the received and holy apostolic inheritance. Rather, other empty doctrines, futile and uncertain doctrines not approved by the Church, are adopted. Only the most conceited men wrongly think that these teachings can sustain and support that truth**. (Pope Gregory XVI, *Singulari Nos*, May 25, 1834.)
>
> Just as Christianity cannot penetrate into the soul without making it better, so it cannot enter into public life without establishing order. With the idea of a God Who governs all, Who is infinitely Wise, Good, and Just, the idea of duty seizes upon the consciences of men. It assuages sorrow, it calms hatred, it engenders heroes. If it has transformed pagan society--and that transformation was a veritable resurrection--for barbarism disappeared in proportion as Christianity extended its sway, so, after the terrible shocks which unbelief has given to the world in our days, it will be able to put that world again on the true road, and bring back to order the States and peoples of modern times. **But the return of Christianity will not be efficacious and complete if it does not restore the world to a sincere love of the one Holy Catholic and Apostolic Church. In the Catholic Church Christianity is Incarnate**. It identifies Itself with that perfect, spiritual, and, in its own order, sovereign society, which is the Mystical Body of Jesus Christ and which has for Its visible head the Roman Pontiff, successor of the Prince of the Apostles. It is the continuation of the mission of the Savior, the daughter and the heiress of His Redemption.

It has preached the Gospel, and has defended it at the price of Its blood, and strong in the Divine assistance and of that immortality which has been promised it, **It makes no terms with error but remains faithful to the commands which it has received, to carry the doctrine of Jesus Christ to the uttermost limits of the world and to the end of time, and to protect it in its inviolable integrit**y. Legitimate dispenser of the teachings of the Gospel it does not reveal itself only as the consoler and Redeemer of souls, but It is still more the internal source of justice and charity, and the propagator as well as the guardian of true liberty, and of that equality which alone is possible here below. In applying the doctrine of its Divine Founder, It maintains a wise equilibrium and marks the true limits between the rights and privileges of society. The equality which it proclaims does not destroy the distinction between the different social classes. It keeps them intact, as nature itself demands, in order to oppose the anarchy of reason emancipated from Faith, and abandoned to its own devices. The liberty which it gives in no wise conflicts with the rights of truth, because those rights are superior to the demands of liberty. Not does it infringe upon the rights of justice, because those rights are superior to the claims of mere numbers or power. Nor does it assail the rights of God because they are superior to the rights of humanity. (Pope Leo XIII, *A Review of His Pontificate*, March 19, 1902.)

10. So, Venerable Brethren, it is clear why this Apostolic See has never allowed its subjects to take part in the assemblies of non-Catholics: for the union of Christians can only be promoted by promoting the return to the one true Church of Christ of those who are separated from it, for in the past they have unhappily left it. To the one true Church of Christ, we say, which is visible to all, and which is to remain, according to the will of its Author, exactly the same as He instituted it. **During the lapse of centuries, the mystical Spouse of Christ has never been contaminated, nor can she ever in the future be contaminated, as Cyprian bears witness: "The Bride of Christ cannot be made false to her Spouse: she is incorrupt and modest. She knows but one dwelling, she guards the sanctity of the nuptial chamber chastely and modestly." The same holy Martyr with good reason marveled exceedingly that anyone could believe that "this unity in the Church which arises from a divine foundation, and which is knit together by heavenly sacraments, could be rent and torn asunder by the force of contrary wills."** For since the mystical body of Christ, in the same manner as His physical body, is one, compacted and fitly joined together, it were foolish and out of place to say that the mystical body is made up of members which are disunited and scattered abroad: whosoever therefore is not united with the body is no member of it, neither is he in communion with Christ its head. (Pope Pius XI, *Mortalium Animos*, January 6, 1928.)

For the teaching authority of the Church, which in the divine wisdom was constituted on earth in order that revealed doctrines might remain intact for ever, and that they might be brought with ease and security to the knowledge of men, and which is daily exercised through the Roman Pontiff and the Bishops who are in communion with him, has also the office of defining, when it sees fit, any truth with solemn rites and decrees, whenever this is necessary either to oppose the errors or the attacks of heretics, or more clearly and in greater detail to stamp the minds of the faithful with the articles of sacred doctrine which have been explained. (Pope Pius XI, *Mortalium Animos*, January 6, 1928.)

Please note that Pope Gregory XVI wrote that the truth can be found in the Catholic Church without "**even a slight tarnish of error**."

Please note that Pope Leo XIII stressed that the Catholic Church "**makes no terms with error but remains faithful to the command which it has received, to carry the doctrine of Jesus Christ to the uttermost limits of the world and to the end of time, and to protect it in its inviolable integrity**."

Please note that that Pope Pius XI explained that the Catholic Church brings forth her teaching "**with ease and security to the knowledge of men**."

Anyone who says that this has been done by the counterfeit church of conciliarism, which has made its "reconciliation" with the false principles of Modernity that leave no room for the confessionally Catholic civil state and the Social Reign of Christ the King, is not thinking too clearly (and that is as about as charitably as I can put the matter) or is being, perhaps more accurately, intellectually dishonest. If the conciliar church has brought forth its teaching "with ease and security to the knowledge of men," why is there such disagreement even between the "progressive" conciliarists and "conservative" conciliarists concerning the proper "interpretation" of the "Second" Vatican Council and its aftermath? Or does this depend upon what one means by "ease and security"?

No, the Catholic Church has never endorsed error in any of her official documents and we have never seen anything like the apostasies, blasphemies and sacrileges that have characterized the the "magisterium" of the conciliar "popes" in the past fifty-four years now.

In the midst of this "operation of error" that abounds in the midst of the counterfeit church of conciliarism, we need to ask Our Lady to help us remain with our true bishops and true priests who make no concessions to conciliarism. Any shepherd who does not warn his faithful to stay completely and totally away from the conciliar wolves is exposing them to the deceits of the devil represented by likes of Joseph Ratzinger/Benedict XVI and Jorge Mario Bergoglio and their henchmen who live in a fantasyland of their own making.

Our Lady's Immaculate Heart will indeed triumph in the end.

Chapter Five
Destroying the Truth of Tradition at "Vatican II"

The current universal public face of apostasy, Jorge Mario Bergoglio, is a product of both the texts and the larger "spirit" of the "Second" Vatican Council. His predecessor, Joseph Alois Ratzinger/Benedict XVI, was one of its progenitors and chief apologists.

As noted in the preceding chapter, the attack on the nature of dogmatic truth that has been at the essence of the Ratzinger/Benedict's life work laid the foundation for a new theology for a new religion. That foundation, however, had antecedent roots in the United States of America long before the beginning of the "Second" Vatican Council on October 11, 1962, the Feast of the Divine Maternity of the Blessed Virgin Mary.

The attack on the nature of dogmatic truth and on Sacred Tradition as one of the two sources of Divine Revelation at the "Second" Vatican Council escaped the attention of most Catholics in the world.

Indeed, most American Catholics were so busy with their own lives and the affairs of current events during the Cold War and the escalation of the Vietnam War under the man, Lyndon Johnson, who had promised to send not one more American boy to fight Asian wars (he kept that promise as he sent more than 55,000 American boys to their deaths in a war that was not fought to be won), that they were relatively unaware of everything taking place at the "Second" Vatican Council.

The irony of this is that it was several American bishops, led by the likes of Francis Cardinal Spellman; John Cardinal Dearden, whose Archdiocese of Detroit became a breeding ground of revolutionary cells such as "Call for Action" and a central axis for the lavender brigade in the Midwest; Richard "Cardinal" Cushing; Joseph "Cardinal" Ritter, the Archbishop of St. Louis, Missouri; and the American who is considered perhaps even more influential than the powerhouses just named, Albert "Cardinal" Meyer, the Archbishop of Chicago, who died from a brain tumor on April 9, 1965, who helped to institutionalize Americanist concepts of religious liberty, separation of Church and State and tradition into the texts of the "Second" Vatican Council. The "Second" Vatican Council is really the triumph of Americanism, which was even in its nascent years in the early-Nineteenth Century a prophetic harbinger of full-blown Modernism in all of its hideous aspects.

The now retired conciliar "archbishop" of Chicago, Illinois, Francis "Cardinal" George, who was the first false "archbishop" in the Archdiocese of Chicago's history as both John "Cardinal" Cody and Joseph "Cardinal" Bernardin before George were true bishops, was not one of those Catholics who was unaware of what was taking place at the "Second" Vatican Council. Indeed, he was studying for the priesthood for the Oblates of Mary Immaculate and ordained to the priesthood on December 21, 1963, the Feast of Saint Thomas the Apostle. George was well-educated. He knew full-well what was happening at the "Second" Vatican Council.

Yet it is that the supposedly "conservative" Ratzingerian, Francis George, is "puzzled" by the direction that Jorge Mario Bergoglio/Francis is taking what most people in world believe to be the Catholic Church:

> "He says wonderful things," Cardinal George said about Francis in an interview on Sunday, "but he doesn't put them together all the time, so you're left at times puzzling over what his intention is. What he says is clear enough, but what does he want us to do?"
>
> Cardinal George, who is 77 and being treated for cancer, remains a voting cardinal until age 80 and says he would like to travel to Rome to see Francis: "I'd like to sit down with him and say, Holy Father, first of all, thank you for letting me retire. And could I ask you a few questions about your intentions?" (**U.S. Bishops Struggle to Follow Lead of Francis**.)

Jorge says "wonderful things"?

Puzzled by Jorge's intentions?

There is nothing puzzling at all about where the Argentine Apostate is leading his false church. Jorge Mario Bergoglio is simply taking the counterfeit church of conciliarism to the only end result that could come out of the "Second" Vatican Council: the One World Ecumenical Church of Apostasy.

Perhaps more to the point, Jorge Mario Bergoglio is taking the counterfeit church of conciliarism where the Americanist bishops of the Nineteenth Century, including Bishop John England, an Irish native who was the first Bishop of Charleston, South Carolina, the diocese in which Joseph Bernardin was ordained a priest on April 26, 1952, one hundred ten years after England's death, John Ireland of Saint Paul, Minnesota, James Cardinal Gibbons of Baltimore, Maryland, Peter Kenrick of St. Louis, Missouri, and his brother, Francis Kenrick of Baltimore, Maryland (after having served in Philadelphia, Pennsylvania), and, among others, John Lancaster Spalding of Peoria, Illinois, had long desired. The Americanist bishops desired to make an accommodation with the world as a matter of principle, not as a concession to the actual circumstances in which Catholics found themselves in the modern world.

Pope Leo XIII prophetically noted the following in *Testem Benevolentiae Nostrae*, January 22, 1899:

> For it [an adherence to the condemned precepts of Americanism] **would give rise to the suspicion that there are among you some who conceive of and desire the Church in America to be different from what it is in the rest of the world**. (Pope Leo XIII, Apostolical Letter to James Cardinal Gibbons, *Testem Benevolentiae Nostrae*, January 22, 1899.)

The Roman Curia under Pope Leo XIII did not invent a "phantom heresy." Its members were well aware that Father Isaac Thomas Hecker and others, including Bishop John Keane of Richmond, Virginia (and the first rector of an Americanist stronghold, The Catholic University of America), were promoting a church different from what is in the rest of the world:

"**American Catholicism**" is not, in the thought of is promoters, **a way of thinking and of practicing Catholicism solely in the contingent and changing things that would be common to the United States, in accordance with the particular conditions that are found on American soil. If this had been so, we would not have believed it incumbent upon us to be concerned with it.**

No, their pretension is to speak to the entire universe: "**The ear of the world is open to our thinking, if we know what to say to them**," Msgr. [Bishop of Richmond, John] Keane had written to the Congress of Brussels. And in fact they are speaking, and their word has not been without echo upon each part of France. **If, at least, they had not put into the ear of the world anything other than what the Church leaves to our free discussion; but, no, as we shall see, we shall come to understand that their words are more or less imposed upon that which belongs to the very fundamentals of the Catholic faith.**

The Abbot Klein had said in the preface he gave to **The Life of Fr. Hecker**: "His [Fr. Hecker's] unique and original work is to have shown the profound harmonies joining the new state of the human spirit to the true Christianity." "**The American ideas that he recommended are, he knew, those which GOD wanted all civilized people of our time to be at home with** ..."

"The times are solemn," Msgr. Ireland had said, in his discourse, The Church and the Age. "At such an epoch of history ... the desire to know is intense ... **The ambition of the spirit, fired up by the marvelous success in every field of human knowledge ... The human heart lets itself go to the strangest ideals ... Something new! Such is the ordered word of humanity, and to renew all things is its firm resolution.**

"The moment is opportune for men of talent and character among the children of the Church of God. **Today the routine of old times is dead; today the ordinary means lead to the decrepitude of the aged; the crisis demands something new, something extraordinary; and it is upon this condition that the Church shall record the greatest of victories in the greatest of historical ages**" (Discourse given in the Cathedral of Baltimore, October 18, 1893, on the occasion of the 25th Anniversary of the Episcopal consecration of Cardinal Gibbons.) (*Monsignor Henri Delassus, Americanism and the Anti-Christian Conspiracy*, available from Catholic Action Resource Center, pp. 9-10.)

Without disparaging the roles played by Spellman, Dearden, Cushing and Ritter in behalf of the new ecclesiology, false ecumenism, religious liberty and a "new relationship" with Talmudism, Meyer provided the intellectual muscle behind the heretical decree on Divine Revelation, *Dei Verbum*, which was issued on November 18, 1965, the Feast of the Dedication of the Basilicas of Saints John and Paul. "Cardinal" Meyer proved to be very instrumental in helping to give new life and a new name to the Modernist precept of the "evolution of dogma" that had been condemned by the [First] Vatican Council on April 24, 1870, Pope Saint Pius X in Pascendi *Dominci Gregis*, September 8, 1907, *Praestantia Scripturae*, November 18, 1907, and *The Oath Against Modernism*, September 1, 1910, and by Pope Pius XII in *Humani Generis*, August 12, 1950. "Cardinal" Meyer made so bold as to refer to the concept of "living tradition," a phrase that would be adopted by another heretic at the "Second" Vatican Council, Karol Josef Wojtyla, as his own.

Here are brief excerpts from two of "Cardinal" Meyer's interventions in support of the "Second" Vatican Council's revamped schema on Divine Revelation as found in an article by Father Francis J. Sullivan, S.J., "Catholic Tradition and Traditions," which was included Michael J. Lacey and Francis Oakley, editors, *The Crisis of Authority in Catholic Modernity*, a book that was published in 2011:

> What I have to say in this brief intervention has to do specially with chapter 2, paragraph 8, of our schema. The whole of chapter 2 pleases me very much, and in particular the way in which paragraph 8 shows that tradition is living, is dynamic, is total, is dynamic, that is, it consists not only in doctrinal propositions, but also of the worship and practice of the whole Church. . . . However, this paragraph, if I have understood it correctly. . . . presents the life and the worship of the Church only in its positive aspect. As I understand it, tradition, in this paragraph, extends beyond the limits of infallible magisterium. If this interpretation is correct, then this tradition is subject to the limits and the failings of the pilgrim Church, which is a Church of sinners, that knows divine things "indistinctly, as in a mirror." The history of the Church offers multiple proofs of such failings, for example, the fact that the theological doctrine of the Resurrection of Christ was for a long time obscured, that piety was non-liturgical, that Sacred Scripture was neglected, and other like things. Consequently, this paragraph needs to be completed by adding words about these failings that are always possible in this life, and by proposing remedies for them. I therefore suggestion to the Fathers the following formula. . . . "However, that living progress does not make progress always and in every respect. For when the Church ponders divine things in its pilgrim state, in some respects it can fail, and it does in fact fail. For this reason it carries Sacred Scripture in itself as a perpetual norm, so that it can unceasingly correct and perfect itself by conforming its life to this norm." (As found in an article by Father Francis A. Sullivan, S.J., "Catholic Tradition and Traditions. Michael J. Lacey and Francis Oakley, editors, *The Crisis of Authority in Catholic Modernity*, Oxford University Press, 2011, p. 114. (See The Crisis of Authority in Catholic Modernity.)

This quotation above contains excerpts from two inventions made by Albert "Cardinal" Meyer, Archbishop of Chicago, Illinois, during the third session of the "Second" Vatican Council in 1964. The first was made on September 30, 1964, the Feast of Saint Jerome, and the second was made on October 5, 1964. Taken together, of course, one can see that "Cardinal" Meyer was advancing a view of a "living tradition" that was nothing other than Modernism's "evolution of dogma." It is this condemned Modernist precept that is at the foundation of the process of theological, liturgical, moral and pastoral degeneration that has accelerated apace during the past twenty months since the "election" of Jorge Mario Bergoglio.

Even though Meyer's proposal was not adopted at the "Second" Vatican Council, his intervention nevertheless carried the day theologically just as it is the case that the dissenting justice on the Supreme Court of the United States of America can become the basis of jurisprudence accepted as legitimate by law school professors and even by future Supreme Court justices themselves.

The book that contained the combined excerpts of Albert "Cardinal" Meyer's two inventions on the text of chapter two, paragraph eight of the scheme on Divine Revelation at the "Second"

Vatican Council also included a comment made on Meyer's remarks made by a theology professor in the late-1960s:

> Article 8. . . . is an attempt to a widely expressed need for a clear and positive account of what is meant by tradition. The first section points out the total nature of tradition: primarily it means the many-layered yet one presence of the mystery of Christ throughout all the ages; it means the totality of the presence of Christ in this world. . . . Teaching, life and worship are named as the three ways in which tradition is handed on. It has a place not only in the explicitly traditional statements of Church doctrine, but in the unstated—and often unstatable—elements of the whole service of the Christian worship of God and the life of the Church. This is the basis of the final comprehensive formulation of tradition as the "perpetuation," the constant continuation and making present of everything that the Church is, of everything that it believes. Tradition is identified, and is thus defined, with the being the life of the Church. The danger that lurks in this statement . . . had been pointed out by Cardinal Meyer in an important speech on 30 September 1964: not everything that exists in the Church must for that reason be a legitimate tradition: in other words, not every tradition that arises in the Church, is a true celebration and keeping of the mystery of Christ. There is a distorting, as well as a legitimate, tradition. . . . Consequently, tradition must not only be considered affirmatively, but also critically; we have Scripture as criterion for this indispensable criticism of tradition, and tradition must therefore always be related back to it and measured by it. . . . It is to be regretted that the suggestion made by the American Cardinal was not, in fact, taken up. . . . On this point Vatican II has unfortunately not make any progress, but has more or less ignored the whole question of the criticism of tradition. There is, in fact, no explicit mention of the possibility of distorting tradition . . . which means that a most important side of the problem of tradition, as shown by the history of the Church—has been overlooked. (As found in an article by Father Francis A. Sullivan, S.J., "Catholic Tradition and Traditions. Michael J. Lacey and Francis Oakley, editors, *The Crisis of Authority in Catholic Modernity*, Oxford University Press, 2011, pp. 114-115. (See **The Crisis of Authority in Catholic Modernity**.)

There is thus no need for Francis "Cardinal" George, O.M.I., to be "puzzled" in the slightest by where Jorge Mario Bergoglio, the current star of the counterfeit church of conciliarism's *Masquerade Party*, is leading Catholics. He is leading along the path to the One World Ecumenical Church that is the one and only logical end-result of the principles enshrined in the documents of the "Second" Vatican Council and of the interpretation and application of those principles by the conciliar "popes," who have used Albert "Cardinal" Meyer's "living tradition" as the means to justify wholesale contradictions between conciliar teachings and the immutable truths contained in the Sacred Deposit of Faith.

For his part, Albert "Cardinal" Meyer was advancing a restrictive view of the infallibility of the Universal Ordinary Magisterium of the Catholic Church that was premised upon the belief that it, the magisterium, can and has failed to understand Tradition properly.

There is a quite an irony here as even though the resist while recognize crowd would never admit it, the fact remains that they share the same restrictive view of the Universal Ordinary Magisterium as that advanced by "Cardinal" Meyer fifty years ago now.

Meyer's contention, of course, was blasphemous as, for example, the Council of Trent, which stated dogmatically that Divine Revelation consists of Sacred Scripture and Sacred (Apostolic) Tradition, met under the Divine guidance and infallible protection of the Third Person of the Most Blessed Trinity, God the Holy Ghost.

Similarly, the [First] Vatican Council, which condemned what became known as the "evolution of dogma," met under the same Divine guidance and infallible protection of the same God the Holy Ghost.

To assert, therefore, that there needed to be admission of the possibility of a failure to understand tradition properly is to deny the very Divine Constitution of Holy Mother Church and to make it possible for there be a "religion" without stable dogmas, liturgical rites or pastoral practices.

Moreover, both the late "Cardinal" Meyer and the very much alive former theology professor use the Scripture as the normative means for the interpretation of tradition when Holy Mother Church herself used *Tradition* to prove the canonicity of the books of the New Testament. The Apostles taught *orally* before a single word of the New Testament was written under the Divine inspiration of God the Holy Ghost.

As noted before, however, it had been some of the Americanist bishops of the Nineteenth Century who paved the way for the many of the "doctrines" of the "Second" Vatican Council and the "magisterium" of the conciliar "popes," including on the necessity of a "living tradition" that requires a "reconciliation" with the principles of Modernity.

Archbishop John Ireland, the Bishop and (starting in 1888) the Archbishop of Saint Paul, Minnesota, from July 31, 1884, to May 25, 1918, preached in the Cathedral of Mary our Queen in Baltimore Maryland, on October 18, 1893, on the occasion of the twenty-fifth anniversary of the episcopal consecration of James Cardinal Gibbons, Ireland's co-conspirator in the creation of a new "faith," American Catholicism, which served as one of the prototypes for the "new faith" and the "new theology" and the "new liturgy" and the "new way of 'defining' doctrine" provided to "humanity" and the "age" by the counterfeit church of conciliarism. Here is but a brief excerpt to demonstrate the Americanist anticipation of what the theology professor quoted above noted in *Principles of Catholic Theology* as an "official reconciliation" with the new principles of the era inaugurated in 1789:

> What! the Church of the living God, the Church of ten thousand victories over pagans and barbarians, over false philosophies and heresies, over defiant kings and unruly peoples–the great, freedom-loving, philanthropic, truth-giving Catholic Church–**this Church afraid of the nineteenth century! afraid of any century! not seeing in the nineteenth the fervent ebullitions of noblest sentiments, the germinations of her own Christlike plantings; this Church not eager for the fray, not precipitating herself with force irresistible upon this modern world to claim it, to love it, to foster and admire or to correct and cure, to own it for Christ, and with her impetuous arm to lift it to the very summit of its highest aspirations, to which only the Church's aid this panting, hoping, despairing world can ever reach! Far, far from Catholics be the chilling, fatal, un-Catholic thought**!

> **I preach the new, the most glorious crusade. Church and age! Unite them in the name of humanity, in the name of God.**
>
> **Church and age! Bring them into close contact; they pulsate alike; *the God of humanity works in one,* the God of supernatural revelations works in the other–in both the self-same God. . .**
>
> It is an age of social battlings for justice to all men, for the right of all men to live in the frugal comfort becoming rational creatures, to all of whom birth in the world gives them title of a sufficiency of the things of the world. Very well; is not this sudden revolution which has come upon men in the plea for social justice and social comfort the loud outburst of the cry which has ever been going forth from the bosom of the Church since the words were spoken by the Founder: "Seek first the king of God and His justice, and all things else should be added unto you"? It is not sufficiently made public that the principles underlying the social movement of the times in all its legitimate demands are the principles constantly taught in Catholic theological schools, as, for instance, this chief one proclaimed by the Cardinal Manning, to the horror of the aristocratic England, that in case of extreme need of food all goods become common property. **Catholics have of late been so accustomed to lock up their teachings in temple and seminary that when the same teachings appear in active evolution upon the broad sea of humanity they do not recognize them; they even fear and disown them**.
>
> It is an age of material progress, of inventions, of the subjugation of nature's forces to the service of man, of the building up of the man over all irrational creatures. Does Church in these things condemn the age? It is her doctrines that the earth was given to man that he dominates over it. Progress of every kind the Church blesses; **for progress along the lines of all human activities and human uses is the divine ordering,--stagnation and inactivity calling down from God reprobation, as we learn from the parable of the talents**. (Archbishop John Ireland, A Sermon of the Twenty-fifth Anniversary of the Episcopal Consecration of His Eminence James Cardinal Gibbons, Archbishop of Baltimore. Full text found in *The Voice of the Church*, a book published by the Bishops of the United States of America in 1899, pp. 103-113. We were given this book by a friend of ours who believed that it would be of use in my work. It is a treasure of Americanism mixed in with various articles that are authentically Catholic. In other words, it was very representative of the state of confusion that existed in the minds of Catholics in the United States of America at the end of the Nineteenth Century, a state of confusion that has now been spread worldwide as a result of conciliarism's embrace of "the age.")

Archbishop John Ireland's voice echoed throughout the four sessions of the "Second" Vatican Council, and it helped to produce the likes of men such as Albert "Cardinal" Meyer and Joseph Ratzinger/Benedict XVI and Jorge Mario Bergoglio/Francis, who has long condemned the "locking up" of what he thinks is Catholic teaching in temples and seminaries.

Father Gerald Fogarty, S.J., commented favorably upon the work of these Americanist bishops as having produced the environment in which Albert "Cardinal" Meyer had cut his theological eyeteeth:

> The Constitution on Revelation had not introduced something new for the American Church, but in fact had returned to the teaching on tradition of the early nineteenth century. Yet, there were still problems. While Scripture and Tradition were now seen as a single source of Revelation, and while there were instructions to exegetes for the interpretation of Scripture, there were no similar norms given for the interpretation of Tradition. John England in the 1820s had made the distinction that the Epistle to the Hebrews was inspired even if it was not written by Paul. He thus did not feel obliged to adhere to the literal interpretation of the magisterium of Trent in attributing the letter to Paul. At the beginning of the century, Edward Dyer sought to defend Francis Gigot against charges of deviating from the common teaching of the Church in regard to the Mosaic authorship of the Pentateuch. At Vatican II, among the Americans, only Cardinal Meyer seems to have seen the danger of an uncritical acceptance of Tradition, although he focused primarily on practice and devotion. As the lessons of the debates over Church and State and of the repression of biblical scholarship during the Modernist crisis remind us, however, not everything that the Church has taught, that is not all of tradition, is on the same level of authority. **In these post-conciliar years, the doctrine of tradition is perhaps still developing and will need a close link with the reemergence of episcopal collegiality before it will again have the full dynamic sense it had over a century ago. To do this, it may be necessary for the Church to encourage theologians and others to study tradition in order to determine what is doctrine to be preserved and what is historically conditioned.** (Father Gerald Fogarty, S.J., **Theology of Tradition in the American Church**.)

Yes, according to the likes of apologists for the "Second" Vatican Council and the "magisterium of the conciliar "popes" tradition is "historically conditioned" and "still developing" in order to determine "what is doctrine to be preserved and what is "historically conditioned."

Father Francis Sullivan, S.J., explained that there was a remarkable similarity between the points about Tradition that had been made by Albert "Cardinal" Meyer, Father Joseph Alois Ratzinger and the report of the so-called "Faith and Order Commission" of the pro-abortion, pro-perversity, pro-contraception supporter of one world governance, the World Council of Churches, which was a sorry history of supporting Communist regimes around the world:

> In his commentary on the way the question of tradition was handled at Vatican II, Ratzinger made a positive reference to the same way this question had been treated by the Faith and Order Commission of the World Council of Churches in a conference that took place in Montreal in July of 1963, between the first and second sessions of Vatican II. It is illuminating to see how the report of that conference anticipated the question raised by Meyer and Ratzinger about the need to distinguish between authentic and inauthentic traditions. The report began by distinguishing between different meanings of the word tradition. 'We speak of the *Tradition* (with a capital T), *tradition* (with a small t), and *traditions*. By the *Tradition* is meant the Gospel itself, transmitted from generation to generation in and by the Church itself. Christ himself present in the life of the Church. By *tradition* is meant the traditionary process. The term traditions is meant in two senses, to indicate both the diversity of forms of expression and also what we call confessional traditions, for instance what we call the Lutheran tradition or the Reformed tradition.

The report gave a fuller explanation of what it meant by the Tradition in a passage that Ratzinger quoted with approval in his commentary on *Dei Verbum.* There the Faith and Order Commission had said: "Thus we can cay that we exist as Christians by the Tradition of the Gospel (the *paradosis* of the *kerygma*) testified in Scirpture, transmitted in and by the Church, through the power of the Holy Spirit. Tradition taken in this sense is actualized in the preaching of the Word, in the administration of the Sacraments and worship, in Christian teaching and theology, and in mission and witness to Christ by the lives of the members of the Church.

The report went on to speak of traditions and of their evaluations. It said:

> "But this tradition which is the work of the Holy Spirit is embodied in traditions (in the two senses of the word, both as referring to diversity in forms of expression, and in the sense of separate communions). The traditions in Christian history are distinct from, and yet connect to, the Tradition. They are the expressions and manifestations in diverse historical forms of the one truth and reality which is Christ. The evaluation of the traditions poses serious problems. For some, questions such as these are raised. It is possible to determine more precisely what the content of the one Tradition is, and by what means? Do all traditions which claim to be Christian contain the Tradition? How can we distinguish traditions embodying the true Tradition and merely human traditions? Where do we find the genuine Tradition, and where impoverished tradition or even distortion of Tradition? Tradition can be a faithful transmission of the Gospel, but also a distortion of it. In this ambiguity the seriousness of the problem of tradition is indicated. These questions imply a search for a criterion. This has been the main concern of the Church from the beginning."

There is a remarkable agreement between the point that Cardinal Meyer raised in his intervention at the Second Vatican Council, the commentary that Joseph Ratzinger wrote on chapter 2 of *Dei Verbum*, and the report of the Faith and Order Commission of the World Council of Churches. All three agree on the necessity of distinguishing between *Tradition*, as the whole mystery of Christ as it has been handed on in the teaching, life, and worship of the Church, and *traditions*, which are the particular beliefs and practices in which that mystery has been embodied in the ongoing life of the church. Obviously, such beliefs and practices must have a venerable history and be widely shared to be justified as "traditions." But the problem is, whether the venerable history and wide diffusion of a particular tradition necessarily means that this is an authentic rather than a distorting tradition; in other words, whether it is a genuine embodiment of divine *Tradition* or merely human tradition. (Father Francis A. Sullivan, S.J., Catholic Tradition and Traditions. Michael J. Lacey and Francis Oakley, editors, *The Crisis of Authority in Catholic Modernity*, Oxford University Press, 2011, pp. 114-115. See **The Crisis of Authority in Catholic Modernity**.)

Joseph Alois Ratzinger/Benedict XVI and Jorge Mario Bergoglio are joined at the hip in the heretical belief that Protestant sects and Orthodox churches have valid missions from God to serve Him and to teaching, sanctify and govern souls in His Holy Name.

Joseph Alois Ratzinger/Benedict XVI and Jorge Mario Bergoglio are joined at the hip in the heretical belief that Protestants have "traditions" that come from God and are worthy of veneration.

Joseph Alois Ratzinger/Benedict XVI and Jorge Mario Bergoglio are joined at the hip in believing that the very existence and longevity of Protestant sects and Orthodox churches provide proof that God has positively willed them into existence.

Ratzinger/Benedict and Bergoglio/Francis have followed the "traditions," if you will, of "Blessed" Giovanni Battista Enrico Antonio Maria Montini/Paul VI and "Saint" Karol Josef Wojtyla/John Paul II in treating Protestant "ministers" as valid clergymen and of treating their false places of worship as being places where God is glorified rather than profaned and blasphemed. These conciliar apostates believe that Protestant liturgical rites have "elements" of true sanctification and that the Catholic Church has something to "learn" from Protestant theologians and Scripture "scholars." Ratzinger/Benedict and Bergoglio/Francis have cited such "theologians" and "scholars." Both Modernists have attempted to give joint "blessings" with Protestant ministers, each of whom is a layman, and Orthodox bishops.

Ratzinger and Bergoglio each believes that the Catholic Church has "corrupted" both the "authentic" teaching of Our Blessed Lord and Saviour Jesus Christ by the "filter" of the Scholasticism of Saint Thomas Aquinas, which is why they believe the Gospel and the Fathers of the Church must be read anew, thus following the "example" set by the Protestants and the Orthodox.

This how Ratzinger/Benedict put the matter when he spoke before the Lutherans in Erfrurt, Germany, in the formerly Catholic convent of the Augustinians:

> As I begin to speak, I would like first of all to say how deeply grateful I am that we are able to come together. I am particularly grateful to you, my dear brother, Pastor Schneider, for receiving me and for the words with which you have welcomed me here among you. You have opened your heart and openly expressed a truly shared faith, a longing for unity. And we are also glad, for I believe that this session, our meetings here, are also being celebrated as the feast of our shared faith. **Moreover, I would like to express my thanks to all of you for your gift in making it possible for us to speak with one another as Christians here, in this historic plac**e.
>
> As the Bishop of Rome, it is deeply moving for me to be meeting you here in the ancient Augustinian convent in Erfurt. As we have just heard, this is where Luther studied theology. This is where he was ordained a priest. Against his father's wishes, he did not continue the study of Law, but instead he studied theology and set off on the path towards priesthood in the Order of Saint Augustine. And on this path, he was not simply concerned with this or that. **What constantly exercised him was the question of God, the deep passion and driving force of his whole life's journey. "How do I receive the grace of God?": this question struck him in the heart and lay at the foundation of all his theological searching and inner struggle. For Luther theology was no mere academic pursuit, but the struggle for oneself, which in turn was a struggle for and with God**.

"How do I receive the grace of God?" The fact that this question was the driving force of his whole life never ceases to make a deep impression on me. For who is actually concerned about this today – even among Christians? What does the question of God mean in our lives? In our preaching? Most people today, even Christians, set out from the presupposition that God is not fundamentally interested in our sins and virtues. He knows that we are all mere flesh. And insofar as people believe in an afterlife and a divine judgement at all, nearly everyone presumes for all practical purposes that God is bound to be magnanimous and that ultimately he mercifully overlooks our small failings. The question no longer troubles us. But are they really so small, our failings? Is not the world laid waste through the corruption of the great, but also of the small, who think only of their own advantage? Is it not laid waste through the power of drugs, which thrives on the one hand on greed and avarice, and on the other hand on the craving for pleasure of those who become addicted? Is the world not threatened by the growing readiness to use violence, frequently masking itself with claims to religious motivation? Could hunger and poverty so devastate parts of the world if love for God and godly love of neighbour – of his creatures, of men and women – were more alive in us? I could go on. No, evil is no small matter. **Were we truly to place God at the centre of our lives, it could not be so powerful. The question: what is God's position towards me, where do I stand before God? – Luther's burning question must once more, doubtless in a new form, become our question too, not an academic question, but a real one. In my view, this is the first summons we should attend to in our encounter with Martin Luther**.

Another important point: God, the one God, creator of heaven and earth, is no mere philosophical hypothesis regarding the origins of the universe. This God has a face, and he has spoken to us. He became one of us in the man Jesus Christ – who is both true God and true man. **Luther's thinking, his whole spirituality, was thoroughly Christocentric: "What promotes Christ's cause" was for Luther the decisive hermeneutical criterion for the exegesis of sacred Scripture. This presupposes, however, that Christ is at the heart of our spirituality and that love for him, living in communion with him, is what guides our life**. (Meeting with representatives of the German Evangelical Church Council in the Chapter Hall of the Augustinian Convent Erfurt, Germany, September 23, 2011.)

This was nothing new for Ratzinger/Benedict, who had written the following in *Principles of Catholic Theology* twenty-nine years previously:

In many respects, a decision about the role of the Fathers seems, in fact, to have been reached today. But, since it is more unfavorable than favorable to a greater reliance upon them, it does nothing to lead us out of our present aporia. For, in the debate about what constitutes greater fidelity to the Church of the Fathers, Luther's historical instinct is clearly proving itself right. We are fairly certain today that, while the Fathers were not Roman Catholic as the thirteenth or nineteenth century would have understood the term, they were nonetheless "Catholic", and their Catholicism extended to the very canon of the New Testament itself. With this assessment, paradoxically, the Fathers have lost ground on both side of the argument because, in the controversy about the fundamental basis for understanding Scripture, there is nothing more to be proved or disproved by reference to

> them. But neither have they become totally unimportant in the domain, for, even after the relativization they have suffered in the process we have described, the differences between the Catholicism of an Augustine and a Thomas Aquinas, or even between that of a Cardinal Manning and a Cyprian, still opens a broad field of theological investigation. Granted, only one side can consider them its own Fathers, and the proof of continuity, which once led directly back to them, seems no longer worth the effort for a concept of history and faith that sees continuity as made possible and communicated in terms of discontinuity.
>
> Nevertheless, a fact is emerging from these reflections that can guide us in our search for an answer. For we must admit, on the one hand, that, even for Catholic theology, the so-called Fathers of the Church have, for a long time, been "Fathers" only in an indirect sense, whereas the real "Father" of the form that ultimately dominated nineteenth century theology was Thomas Aquinas, with his classic systematization of the thirteenth century doctrina media, which, it must be added, was in its turn based on the "authority" of the Fathers. (Joseph Ratzinger, *Principles of Catholic Theology*, pp. 141-142.)

Although Jorge Mario Bergoglio has shown his impatience with such things as "doctrine" in favor of a false gospel of a false mercy and a false charity on many occasions, his belief in a "pure Gospel," that is, one that is unfettered by the "chains" of "disjointed doctrines" and adherence to various "human" formulae, is pure Protestantism writ large.

This is what Bergoglio said to "Father" Antonio Spadoro, S.J., in September of 2013:

> "The dogmatic and moral teachings of the church are not all equivalent. The church's pastoral ministry cannot be obsessed with the transmission of a disjointed multitude of doctrines to be imposed insistently. Proclamation in a missionary style focuses on the essentials, on the necessary things: this is also what fascinates and attracts more, what makes the heart burn, as it did for the disciples at Emmaus. We have to find a new balance; otherwise even the moral edifice of the church is likely to fall like a house of cards, losing the freshness and fragrance of the Gospel. The proposal of the Gospel must be more simple, profound, radiant. It is from this proposition that the moral consequences then flow. (**A Big Heart Open to God**.)

"Little things" such as doctrine must be swept aside by Jorge Mario Bergoglio without any intellectual "difficulty" as his predecessor, who lives in a world of paradox and contradiction, had experienced when explaining there is no rupture, only "continuity" in conciliar "doctrines," such as false ecumenism, that treat of non-Catholic Christians as having legitimate "traditions" in "churches" that have been willed positively by God into existence.

Bergoglio expressed the belief in 2009 that the man who had defeated him in the conciliar conclave four years before after the death of Karol Wojtyla/John Paul II was wrong to have established an ordinariate for Anglo-Catholics as this was not a necessity.

This is what Bergoglio said to an Anglican friend of his following the release of Joseph Ratzinger/Benedict XVI's **Anglicanorum Coetibus**, November 9, 2009, which established an ordinariate for Anglicans seeking to switch decks on the One World Ecumenical Church to what presents itself to them as the Catholic Church:

> The new Pope has reportedly said the **Church universal needs Anglicans and that the Ordinariate is "quite unnecessary"**.
>
> In a note released after the election of the first ever pontiff from Latin America, the Anglican Bishop of Argentina and former Primate of the Anglican Church of the Southern Cone, the Rt Revd Greg Venables said Cardinal Jorge Bergoglio was "an inspired choice".
>
> "Many are asking me what is really like. He is much more of a Christian, Christ centered and Spirit filled, than a mere churchman. He believes the Bible as it is written.
>
> "I have been with him on many occasions and he always makes me sit next to him and **invariably makes me take part and often do what he as Cardinal should have done. He is consistently humble and wise, outstandingly gifted yet a common man**. He is no fool and speaks out very quietly yet clearly when necessary."
>
> Bp Venables added that in a conversation with Cardinal Bergoglio, now Pope Francis, **the latter made it clear that he values the place of Anglicans in the Church universal**.
>
> **"He called me to have breakfast with him one morning and told me very clearly that the Ordinariate was quite unnecessary and that the Church needs us as Anglicans**.
>
> The former Primate of the Anglican Communion's Iglesia Anglicana del Cono Sur de America added, "**I consider this to be an inspired appointment not because he is a close and personal friend, but because of who he is In Christ. Pray for him**." (Anglican Communion News Service: "The Church universal needs Anglicans"-- Francis the Head Citizen of the One World Ecumenical Church.)

The Catholic Church *needs* Anglicans to remain as Anglicans?

The English and Irish Martyrs Died for This?

Jorge Mario Bergoglio really believes that the Catholic Church has persecuted Protestants, thereby preventing them from exercising their "religious freedom," a heresy that flowed over time as a direct result of the Protestant Revolution that was inspired by the devil from its inception to take souls out of the Catholic Church and to sow the seeds for moral and social chaos to prepare the world for the coming of Antichrist. As what he thinks is the Catholic Church was too slow to accept the "truth" of religious liberty, it is necessary for him to give an apology to his friend Giovanni Trettino, who is the evangelical counterpart of his pals Justin Welby, Abraham Skorka, Bartholomew I and Omar Abboud, "privately" even though he has stated his beliefs both publicly and privately many times in the past.

Jorge Mario Bergoglio really believes that the Catholic Church has persecuted Protestants from exercising their "religious freedom," a heresy that flowed over time as a direct result of the Protestant Revolution that was inspired by the devil from its inception to take souls out of the Catholic Church and to sow the seeds for moral and social chaos to prepare the world for the coming of Antichrist. As to why Bergoglio thinks is the Catholic Church was too slow to accept the "truth" of religious liberty, it was necessary for him to give an apology to his friend Giovanni Trettino, who is an Italian Protestant preacher who serves as an "evangelical" to his pals "Archbishop" Justin Welby, Rabbi Abraham Skorka, Greek Orthodox Patriarch Bartholomew I and Mohammedan Omar Abboud, "privately" even though he has stated his beliefs both publicly and privately many times in the past.

This is nothing other than an insidious attempt to put a "papal" imprimatur on continued acts of apostasy while giving any stuffy "minders" of his in the Vatican who are concerned about what passes for orthodox conciliarism an out to say to "conservatives" in the conciliar structures that none of this matters, that it's all "unofficial." Not in the eyes of the true God of Divine Revelation, and it should not be in the eyes of any Cathlolic as Jorge Mario Bergoglio defames the martyrs who died at the hands of the Protestants, including the English and Irish Martyrs, Saint Fidelis Sigmaringen and the Martyrs of Gorkum, and the efforts of Saint Francis de Sales and countless of others to convert Calvinists back to the true Church. Morever, Jorge's comcept of universal salvation is such that the entire missionary work of Holy Mother Church from the time of Pentecost Sunday is rendered as a complete waste of time and effort and of the martyrs' blood.

So much for Pope Pius XII's words in *Mystici Corporis*, June 29, 1943:

> **Actually only those are to be included as members of the Church who have been baptized and profess the true faith, and who have not been so unfortunate as to separate themselves from the unity of the Body, or been excluded by legitimate authority for grave faults committed**. "For in one spirit" says the Apostle, "were we all baptized into one Body, whether Jews or Gentiles, whether bond or free." As therefore in the true Christian community there is only one Body, one Spirit, one Lord, and one Baptism, so there can be only one faith. **And therefore, if a man refuse to hear the Church, let him be considered - so the Lord commands - as a heathen and a publican. It follows that those who are divided in faith or government cannot be living in the unity of such a Body, nor can they be living the life of its one Divine Spirit**. (Pope Pius XII, *Mystici Corporis*, June 29, 1943.)

Thus it is that Jorge Mario Bergoglio is only bringing to fruition the One World Ecumenical Church whose foundations were laid by the likes of Albert "Cardinal" Meyer and Father Joseph Alois Ratzinger fifty years ago as each sought to deconstruct the whole meaning of Sacred Tradition in order to bring it more into accord with the "thought" of the members of the World Council of Churches, whose "work" was praised repeatedly by "Pope" Benedict XVI.

The now-retired head of the counterfeit church of conciliarism said the following to Dr. Samuel Kobia, who was then the General Secretary of the World Council of Churches, on January 25, 2008, the Feast of the Conversion of Saint Paul the Apostle:

I am pleased to greet all of you who are gathered for the Ninth General Assembly of the World Council of Churches being held in Porto Alegre to reflect on the theme: *God in your grace, transform the world.* In a special way I greet the General Secretary, Dr Samuel Kobia, Archbishop Dadeus Grings, the Bishops of the Catholic Church in Brazil and all those who have worked for the realization of this important event. To all of you I express my heartfelt good wishes in the words of Saint Paul to the Romans: "*Grace to you and peace from God our Father and the Lord Jesus Christ"(Rom* 1:7).

Mindful of our shared baptismal faith in the Triune God, the Catholic Church and the World Council of Churches seek ways to cooperate ever more effectively in the task of witnessing to God's divine love. After forty years of fruitful collaboration, we look forward to continuing this journey of hope and promise, as we intensify our endeavours towards reaching that day when Christians are united in proclaiming the Gospel message of salvation to all. As we together make this journey, we must be open to the signs of divine Providence and the inspiration of the Holy Spirit, for we know that "the holy objective of reconciling all Christians in the unity of the one and the only Church of Christ transcends human powers and gifts" *(Unitatis Redintegratio,* 24). Our trust therefore is solely in the prayer of Christ himself: "Holy Father, keep them in thy name, which thou hast given me, that they may be one, even as we are one" *(Jn* 17: 11).

During this General Assembly thousands of Christians join in this same prayer for unity. As we ask *God in his grace* to *transform the world,* we pray that he will bless our ecumenical dialogue with the progress we so ardently desire.

Assuring you of my spiritual closeness and reaffirming the **Catholic Church's intention to continue a solid partnership with the World Council of Churches in its important contribution to the ecumenical movement**, I invoke God's abundant blessings of peace and joy upon all of you. (**Benedict XVI's greets to Dr. Samuel Kobia** .)

No, there is no "space" between Bergoglio and Ratzinger when it comes to undermining Catholic truth, starting with the whole nature of dogmatic truth itself.

Here is a reminder of how the former theology professor, who shifted residences within the confines of the walls of the Occupied Vatican on the West Bank of the Tiber River in 2013, has been able to disparage "past" teaching by claiming that it was "conditioned" by the historical circumstances in which it was formulated:

1971: "In theses 10-12, the difficult problem of the relationship between language and thought is debated, which in post-conciliar discussions was the immediate departure point of the dispute.

The identity of the Christian substance as such, the Christian 'thing' was not directly ... censured, but it was pointed out that no formula, no matter how valid and indispensable it may have been in its time, can fully express the thought mentioned in it and declare it unequivocally forever, since language is constantly in movement and

> **the content of its meaning changes.**" (Fr. Ratzinger: Dogmatic formulas must always change.)
>
> **1990**: "The text [of the document Instruction on the Theologian's Ecclesial Vocation] also presents the various types of bonds that rise from the different degrees of magisterial teaching. **It affirms - perhaps for the first time with this clarity - that there are decisions of the magisterium that cannot be the last word on the matter as such, but are, in a substantial fixation of the problem, above all an expression of pastoral prudence, a kind of provisional disposition. The nucleus remains valid, but the particulars, which the circumstances of the times influenced, may need further correction.**
>
> **In this regard, one may think of the declarations of Popes in the last century [19th century] about religious liberty, as well as the anti-Modernist decisions at the beginning of this century, above all, the decisions of the Biblical Commission of the time [on evolutionism]. As a cry of alarm in the face of hasty and superficial adaptations, they will remain fully justified. A personage such as Johann Baptist Metz said, for example, that the Church's anti-Modernist decisions render the great service of preserving her from falling into the liberal-bourgeois world. But in the details of the determinations they contain, they became obsolete after having fulfilled their pastoral mission at their proper time.**"
>
> (Joseph Ratzinger, "Instruction on the Theologian's Ecclesial Vocation," published with the title "Rinnovato dialogo fra Magistero e Teologia," in L'Osservatore Romano, June 27, 1990, p. 6, cited at Card. Ratzinger: The teachings of the Popes against Modernism are obsolete)

As noted earlier, Pope Pius IX and the Fathers of the [First] Vatican Council condemned such views on April 24, 1870, a condemnation that was taken up anew by Pope Saint Pius X in *Pascendi Dominici Gregis*, September 8, 1907:

> Hence it is quite impossible [the Modernists assert] to maintain that they [dogmatic statements] absolutely contain the truth: **for, in so far as they are symbols, they are the images of truth, and so must be adapted to the religious sense in its relation to man; and as instruments, they are the vehicles of truth, and must therefore in their turn be adapted to man in his relation to the religious sense. But the object of the religious sense, as something contained in the absolute, possesses an infinite variety of aspects, of which now one, now another, may present itself. In like manner he who believes can avail himself of varying conditions. Consequently, the formulas which we call dogma must be subject to these vicissitudes, and are, therefore, liable to change. Thus the way is open to the intrinsic evolution of dogma. Here we have an immense structure of sophisms which ruin and wreck all religion**. (Pope Saint Pius X, *Pascendi Dominici Gregis*, September 8, 1907.)

Behold a false religion, conciliarism, which is built on an edifice of sophisms that have indeed ruined and wrecked the average Catholic's understanding of the Holy Faith. This edifice of sophisms has produced such instability and uncertainty in the counterfeit church of conciliarism that Joseph Ratzinger/Benedict XVI's interpretation of the "Second" Vatican Council can be swept away by the next by using the exact same "hermeneutic" that he been used to sweep away the immutable teaching of the Catholic Church in order to justify the new ecclesiology, episcopal collegiality, false ecumenism, religious liberty, separation of Church and State, condemned interpretations of Sacred Scripture according to an unfettered use of the historical-critical method of modern Scriptural exegesis and, of course, ever-changing liturgical rites and pastoral practices.

Chapter Six
Complete Twins on False Ecumenism

Madness reigns supreme in the insane world in which the counterfeit church of conciliarism. Just complete and utter madness.

The madness is so profound that one traditionally-minded presbyter whose "wisdom" was quoted on a Motu Mania website wrote in early-2014 that Joseph Ratzinger/Benedict XVI was "the greatest Supreme Pontiff since Benedict XIV." Meaning no disrespect to this unfortunate man, this is complete and total madness.

Joseph Ratzinger/Benedict was the "greatest Supreme Pontiff since Benedict XIV"?

An apostate who esteemed the symbols of false religions with his own priestly hands was "great" in the eyes of the true God of Divine Revelation, "greater" than Popes Gregory XVI, Pius IX, Leo XIII and St. Pius X?

A man who entered into synagogues and mosques while treating them as "sacred" places and being content to be treated as an inferior by his infidel hosts was as "great" as Pope Benedict XIV, a Supreme Pontiff who wrote the following about Talmudists in his Bull *A Quo Primum*, June 14, 1751, as he warned against the pernicious influences of Jews living near Catholics in Poland while at the same inveighing against all violence directed against Jews as had been done by Radulph the Monk in the Twelfth Century:

> We esteem the glorious memory of Polish martyrs, confessors, virgins and holy men; their exemplary lives are recorded in the holy annals of the Church. We also recall the many successful councils and synods which gloriously defeated the Lutherans who tried tenaciously, using a variety of methods, to establish a foothold and welcome in this kingdom. At that time indeed the great council of Piotrkow met under Our great predecessor and fellow citizen Gregory XIII, with prelate Lippomano, bishop of Verona and Apostolic nuncio, as its president. **To the great glory of God it prohibited the principle of freedom of conscience; adherents of this principle were seeking to introduce and establish it in Poland. Another threat to Christians has been the influence of Jewish faithlessness; this influence was strong because Christians and Jews were living in the same cities and towns. However their influence was minimized because the Polish bishops did all they could to aid the Poles in their resistance to the Jews. What the bishops did is recorded in the large tome which contains the constitutions of the synods of the province of Gniezno. These facts establish most clearly and plainly the great glory which the Polish nation has won for its zeal in preserving the holy religion embraced by its ancestors so many ages before**.
>
> 2. In regard to the matter of the Jews We must express our concern, which causes Us to cry aloud: "the best color has been changed." Our credible experts in Polish affairs and the citizens of Poland itself who communicated with Us have informed Us that the number of Jews in that country has greatly increased. **In fact, some cities and towns which had been predominantly Christian are now practically devoid of Christians**.

The Jews have so replaced the Christians that some parishes are about to lose their ministers because their revenue has dwindled so drastically. **Because the Jews control businesses selling liquor and even wine, they are therefore allowed to supervise the collection of public revenues. They have also gained control of inns, bankrupt estates, villages and public land by means of which they have subjugated poor Christian farmers. The Jews are cruel taskmasters, not only working the farmers harshly and forcing them to carry excessive loads, but also whipping them for punishment. So it has come about that those poor farmers are the subjects of the Jews, submissive to their will and power. Furthermore, although the power to punish lies with the Christian official, he must comply with the commands of the Jews and inflict the punishments they desire. If he doesn't, he would lose his post. Therefore the tyrannical orders of the Jews have to be carried out**.

3. In addition to the harm done to Christians in these regards, other unreasonable matters can result in even greater loss and danger. The most serious is that some households of the great have employed a Jew as "Superintendent-of-the-Household"; in this capacity, they not only administer domestic and economic matters, but they also ceaselessly exhibit and flaunt authority over the Christians they are living with. It is now even commonplace for Christians and Jews to intermingle anywhere. **But what is even less comprehensible is that Jews fearlessly keep Christians of both sexes in their houses as their domestics, bound to their service. Furthermore, by means of their particular practice of commerce, they amass a great store of money and then by an exorbitant rate of interest utterly destroy the wealth and inheritance of Christians. Even if they borrow money from Christians at heavy and undue interest with their synagogues as surety, it is obvious to anyone who thinks about it that they do so to employ the money borrowed from Christians in their commercial dealings; this enables them to make enough profit to pay the agreed interest and simultaneously increase their own store. At the same time, they gain as many defenders of their synagogues and themselves as they have creditor**s.

4. The famous monk, Radulph, inspired long ago by an excess of zeal, was so inflamed against the Jews that he traversed Germany and France in the twelfth century and, by preaching against the Jews as the enemies of our holy religion, incited Christians to destroy them. This resulted in the deaths of a very large number of Jews. What must we think his deeds or thoughts would be if he were now alive and saw what was happening in Poland? But the great St. Bernard opposed this immoderate and maddened zeal of Radulph, and wrote to the clergy and people of eastern France: **"The Jews are not to be persecuted: they are not to be slaughtered: they are not even to be driven out. Examine the divine writings concerning them. We read in the psalm a new kind of prophecy concerning the Jews: God has shown me, says the Church, on the subject of my enemies, not to slay them in case they should ever forget my people. Alive, however, they are eminent reminders for us of the Lord's suffering. On this account they are scattered through all lands in order that they may be witnesses to Our redemption while they pay the just penalties for so great a crime**" (epistle 363). And he writes this to Henry, Archbishop of Mainz: "**Doesn't the Church every day triumph more fully over the Jews in convicting or converting them than if once and for all she destroyed them with the**

edge of the sword: Surely it is not in vain that the Church has established the universal prayer which is offered up for the faithless Jews from the rising of the sun to its setting, that the Lord God may remove the veil from their hearts, that they may be rescued from their darkness into the light of truth. For unless it hoped that those who do not believe would believe, it would obviously be futile and empty to pray for them." (epistle 365).

5. Peter, abbot of Cluny, likewise wrote against Radulph to King Louis of France, and urged him not to allow the destruction of the Jews. **But at the same time he encouraged him to punish their excesses and to strip them of the property they had taken from Christians or had acquired by usury; he should then devote the value of this to the use and benefit of holy religion, as may be seen in the Annals of Venerable Cardinal Baronius** (1146). In this matter, as in all others, We adopt the same norm of action as did the Roman Pontiffs who were Our venerable predecessors. Alexander III forbade Christians under heavy penalties to accept permanent domestic service under Jews. **"Let them not continually devote themselves to the service of Jews for a wage**." He sets out the reason for this in the decretal *Ad haec, de Judaeis*. "**Because Jewish ways do not harmonize in any way with ours and they could easily turn the minds of the simple to their own superstitions and faithlessness through continual intercourse and unceasing acquaintance**." Innocent III, after saying that Jews were being received by Christians into their cities, warns that the method and condition of this reception should guard against their repaying the benefit with evildoing. "**They on being admitted to our acquaintance in a spirit of mercy, repay us, the popular proverb says, as the mouse in the wallet, the snake in the lap and fire in the bosom usually repay their host**." The same Pope stated that it was fitting for Jews to serve Christians rather than vice versa and added: "**Let not the sons of the free woman be servants of the sons of the handmaid; but as servants rejected by their lord for whose death they evilly conspired, let them realize that the result of this deed is to make them servants of those whom Christ's death made free**," as we read in his decretal *Etsi Judaeos*. Likewise in the decretal *Cum sit nimis* under the same heading *de Judaeis, et Saracenis*, he forbids the promotion of Jews to public office: **"forbidding Jews to be promoted to public offices since in such circumstances they may be very dangerous to Christians." Innocent IV, also, in writing to St. Louis, King of France, who intended to drive the Jews beyond the boundaries of his kingdom, approves of this plan since the Jews gave very little heed to the regulations made by the Apostolic See in their regard: "Since We strive with all Our heart for the salvation of souls, We grant you full power by the authority of this letter to expel the Jews, particularly since We have learned that they do not obey the said statutes issued by this See against them**" (Raynaldus, Annals, A.D. 1253, no. 34).

6. But if it is asked what matters the Apostolic See forbids to Jews living in the same cities as Christians, We will say that all those activities which are now allowed in Poland are forbidden; these We recounted above. There is no need of much reading to understand that this is the clear truth of the matter. It is enough to peruse decretals with the heading *de Judaeis, et Saracenis*; the constitutions of Our predecessors, the Roman Pontiffs Nicholas IV, Paul IV, St. Pius V, Gregory XIII and Clement VIII are readily available in the Roman Bullarium. To understand these matters most clearly, Venerable Brothers, you do not even

need to read those. You will recall the statutes and prescripts of the synods of your predecessors; they always entered in their constitutions every measure concerning the Jews which was sanctioned and ordained by the Roman Pontiffs.

7. The essence of the difficulty, however, is that either the sanctions of the synods are forgotten or they are not put into effect. To you then, Venerable Brothers, passes the task of renewing those sanctions. The nature of your office requires that you carefully encourage their implementation. In this matter begin with the clergy, as is fair and reasonable. These will have to show others the right way to act, and light the way for the rest by their example. For in God's mercy, We hope that the good example of the clergy will lead the straying laity back to the straight path. **You will be able to give these orders and commands easily and confidently, in that neither your property nor your privileges are hired to Jews; furthermore you do no business with them and you neither lend them money nor borrow from them. Thus, you will be free from and unaffected by all dealings with them**.

8. The sacred canons, prescribe that in the most important cases, such as the present, censures should be imposed upon the recalcitrant; and that those cases which bode danger and ruin to religion should be reckoned as reserved cases in which only the bishop can give absolution. The Council of Trent considered your jurisdiction when it affirmed your right to reserve cases. It did not restrict such cases to public crimes only, but extended them to include more notorious and serious cases, provided they were not purely internal. But we have often said that some cases should be considered more notorious and serious. These are cases, to which men are more prone, which are a danger both to ecclesiastical discipline and to the salvation of the souls which have been entrusted to your episcopal care. We have discussed these at length in Our treatise *On the diocesan synod*, Book 5, 5.

9. In this matter We will help as much as possible. If you have to proceed against ecclesiastics exempt from your jurisdiction, you will doubtless encounter additional difficulties. Therefore We are giving Our Venerable Brother Archbishop Nicaenus, Our Nuncio there, a mandate appropriate for this business, in order that he may supply for you the necessary means from the powers entrusted to him. At the same time We promise you that when the situation arises, We will cooperate energetically and effectively with those whose combined authority and power are appropriate to remove this stain of shame from Poland. But first Venerable Brothers, ask aid from God, the source of all things. From Him beg help for Us and this Apostolic See. And while We embrace you in the fullness of charity, We lovingly impart to you, Our brothers, and to the flocks entrusted to your care, Our Apostolic Blessing. (Pope Benedict XIV, *A Quo Primum*, June 14, 1751.)

This is just a little different spirit than that exhibited by the supposedly "greatest Supreme Pontiff" since Pope Benedict XIV.

Imagine the hubris that it takes for a man who thinks himself to be a priest of the Holy Catholic Church to contend that a man who heralded the text of *Gaudium et Spes*, December 7, 1965, as a "countersyllabus" to Pope Pius IX's *The Syllabus of Errors*, December 8, 1864, and who endorsed, albeit by his own slogan, the Modernist principle of the "evolution of dogma" that had been condemned by the same Pope Pius IX at the [First] Vatican Council on April 24, 1870, and by Pope Saint Pius X in *Pascendi Dominci Gregis*, September 8, 1907, and *The Oath Against Modernism*, September 1, 1910, and by Pope Pius XII in *Humani Generis*, August 12, 1950 (see Chapter Three, supra).

Yes, madness reigns supreme in the minds of those who seek to reconcile the work of Antichrist himself, conciliarism, with Catholicism. Complete and utter madness.

There is, of course, absolutely no space between the supposedly "greatest Supreme Pontiff since Benedict XIV" and his supposedly more revolutionary successor, Jorge Mario Bergoglio, on matters of theological substance, including that of false ecumenism itself.

Although there is much evidence to support the Siamese Twin nature of the two-headed "pope" monster's closeness in all that pertains to false ecumenism, all one needs to do is to compare "Pope Francis's" address to an "ecumenical group" from Finland with one given by "Pope Benedict XVI" in January of 2011:

Jorge Mario Bergoglio, Friday, January 17, 2014, the Feast of Saint Antony of the Desert:

> "Grace to you and peace from God our Father and the Lord Jesus Christ" (*Rom* 1:7). I offer you a very warm welcome, as my Predecessors, Blessed John Paul II and Benedict XVI, have done for over twenty-five years, as I receive your ecumenical delegations on the occasion of the Feast of Saint Henry, Patron of Finland.
>
> Writing to the members of the community of Corinth, marked by divisions, Saint Paul asked: "Is Christ divided?" (*1 Cor* 1:13). This question has been chosen as the theme for the Week of Prayer for Christian Unity, which we begin tomorrow. **Today that same question is being asked of us. Ignoring voices which no longer recognize the full and visible unity of the Church as an achievable goal, we are urged not to grow weary of our ecumenical efforts, but to remain faithful to the petition which the Lord Jesus made to the Father: that "all may be one"** (*Jn* 17:21).
>
> In our day, ecumenism and relationships between Christians are changing significantly. This is due above all to the fact that we profess our faith within a society and a culture increasingly less concerned with God and all that involves the transcendental dimension of life. We see this especially in Europe, but not only here.
>
> **For this reason, our witness has to be centred on the core of our faith: the proclamation of God's love made known in Christ his Son. This gives us a great opportunity to grow in communion and unity by promoting that spiritual ecumenism which flows directly from the commandment of love given by Jesus to his disciples.** The Second Vatican Council itself alluded to it in these words: "Change of heart and holiness of life, along with public and private prayer for the unity of Christians, should be regarded as the soul of the whole ecumenical movement, and can rightly be called spiritual ecumenism" (*Unitatis Redintegratio*, 8). **Ecumenism is a spiritual process, one which**

takes place in faithful obedience to the Father, in fulfilment of the will of Christ and under the guidance of the Holy Spirit.

So let us constantly implore the help of God's grace and the enlightenment of the Holy Spirit, **who leads us to the fullness of truth, the source of reconciliation and communion**.

Renewing my warm welcome, I gladly invoke God's blessings on you, on all the Christians of Finland and on the nation. (**To an ecumenical delegation from Finland for the Feast of Saint Henry, 17 January 2014**.)

Joseph Ratzinger/Benedict XVI, January 15, 2011, the **Feast of Saint Paul the Hermit and Saint Maurus the Abbot**:

I welcome you with great joy on the occasion of your annual ecumenical pilgrimage to Rome to celebrate the Feast of St Henry, Patron of your beloved land. Every year, during this period, your traditional pilgrimage testifies to the sincere, friendly and helpful relations which have been established between Lutherans and Catholics, as well as in general between all the Christians in your Country.

Even though we have not yet achieved the objective of the ecumenical movement, namely full unity of faith, through dialogue many elements of agreement and closeness have matured which strengthen our general desire to do the will of our Lord Jesus Christ: "that they may all be one" (Jn 17:21). One result recently obtained that deserves attention was the conclusive report on the theme of justification in the life of the Church. This report was prepared by a group centred on Nordic Catholic-Lutheran dialogue in Finland and Sweden, that met last year.

In theology and in faith everything is linked together, and thus a common deeper understanding of the justification will help us to understand together the nature of the Church better and, as you mentioned, the episcopal ministry. Thus it will also help us to find the unity of the Church in a concrete form and thereby to be more capable, as you observed, to explain the faith to all people of today who ask each other about it and to make it more comprehensible to them so that they see that he is the answer, that Christ is the Redeemer for us all.**Thus our hope remains alive that, under the guidance of the Holy Spirit, many people involved in the ecumenical field, competent and aware, will contribute to the realization of this important ecumenical task and, always guided by the Holy Spirit, will be able to forge ahead**.

Having said this, it is implied that the efficacy of our efforts cannot come solely from study and discussion, but above all depend on our constant prayer, on our life in conformity with the will of God, **because ecumenicism is not our work but rather a fruit of God's action**.

At the same time, we are all conscious of the fact that in recent years the ecumenical path, from certain points of view, has become more difficult and certainly more demanding.

> Questions will be asked concerning the ecumenical method and the breakthroughs of past years will be mentioned, as well as the uncertainty of the future, and the problems of our time with faith in general. In this light, your annual pilgrimage to Rome for the Feast of St Henry is an important event, a sign and an encouragement for our ecumenical efforts, for our certainty that we must walk together and that Christ is the way for humanity.
>
> Your pilgrimage helps us to look back with joy at what has been achieved so far and to look to the future with the desire to take on a task full of faith and responsibility. **On the occasion of your visit, we all wish to reinforce our certainty of the fact that the Holy Spirit, who reawakens us, accompanies us and to this day has made the ecumenical movement fruitful, may continue in this way also in the future.**
>
> I firmly hope that your visit to Rome will strengthen the future collaboration of Lutherans and Catholics, yes, between all the Christians in Finland. Looking forward to the upcoming **Week of Prayer for Christian Unity** let us pray that the spirit of truth will lead us to even greater love and brotherhood. May God grant you his rich Blessing in newly begun year. (**To an Ecumenical Delegation from Finland on the occasion of the feast of Saint Henry, Patron of Finland, January 15, 2011**.)

Where is the "space" between Ratzinger and Bergoglio here?

Obviously, there is no "space" as each man's blasphemy against the Third Person of the Most Holy Trinity, God the Holy Ghost, and heresy against the Divine Constitution of Holy Mother Church stand naked for all who have the intellectual honesty to see and to accept. The conciliarist doctrine to which each of the conciliar "popes," including Ratzinger and Bergoglio, has subscribed, comes from one source only: the devil himself, he who is the author of each and every false religion on the face of this earth.

Pope Pius XI had this to say about Ratzinger's and Bergoglio's misuse of the prayer of Our Blessed Lord and Saviour Jesus Christ at the Last Supper, "that they may all be one:"

> And here it seems opportune to expound and to refute a certain false opinion, on which this whole question, as well as that complex movement by which non-Catholics seek to bring about the union of the Christian churches depends. For authors who favor this view are accustomed, times almost without number, to bring forward these words of Christ: **"That they all may be one.... And there shall be one fold and one shepherd,"**[14] **with this signification however: that Christ Jesus merely expressed a desire and prayer, which still lacks its fulfillment. For they are of the opinion that the unity of faith and government**, which is a note of the one true Church of Christ, has hardly up to the present time existed, and does not to-day exist. They consider that this unity may indeed be desired and that it may even be one day attained through the instrumentality of wills directed to a common end, but that meanwhile it can only be regarded as mere ideal. They add that the Church in itself, or of its nature, is divided into sections; that is to say, that it is made up of several churches or distinct communities, which still remain separate, and although having certain articles of doctrine in common, nevertheless disagree concerning the remainder; that these all enjoy the same rights; and that the Church was one and unique from, at the

most, the apostolic age until the first Ecumenical Councils. Controversies therefore, they say, and longstanding differences of opinion which keep asunder till the present day the members of the Christian family, must be entirely put aside, and from the remaining doctrines a common form of faith drawn up and proposed for belief, and in the profession of which all may not only know but feel that they are brothers. **The manifold churches or communities, if united in some kind of universal federation, would then be in a position to oppose strongly and with success the progress of irreligion. This, Venerable Brethren, is what is commonly said. There are some, indeed, who recognize and affirm that Protestantism, as they call it, has rejected, with a great lack of consideration, certain articles of faith and some external ceremonies, which are, in fact, pleasing and useful, and which the Roman Church still retains**. They soon, however, go on to say that that Church also has erred, and corrupted the original religion by adding and proposing for belief certain doctrines which are not only alien to the Gospel, but even repugnant to it. Among the chief of these they number that which concerns the primacy of jurisdiction, which was granted to Peter and to his successors in the See of Rome. Among them there indeed are some, though few, who grant to the Roman Pontiff a primacy of honor or even a certain jurisdiction or power, but this, however, they consider not to arise from the divine law but from the consent of the faithful. Others again, even go so far as to wish the Pontiff Himself to preside over their motley, so to say, assemblies. But, all the same, although many non-Catholics may be found who loudly preach fraternal communion in Christ Jesus, yet you will find none at all to whom it ever occurs to submit to and obey the Vicar of Jesus Christ either in His capacity as a teacher or as a governor. Meanwhile they affirm that they would willingly treat with the Church of Rome, but on equal terms, that is as equals with an equal: but even if they could so act, it does not seem open to doubt that any pact into which they might enter would not compel them to turn from those opinions which are still the reason why they err and stray from the one fold of Christ. (Pope Pius XI, *Mortalium Animos*, January 6, 1928.)

There is only one path for those outside of the Catholic Church to convert unconditionally to the her maternal bosom. Period. There is no need for "dialogue" and to offer up blasphemous prayers to God the Holy Ghost for a "unity" that exists entirely in the Catholic Church. Those who do not belong to the Catholic Church do not have a "share" in some kind of mythical "ecclesial communion" with her. Pope Pius XII made this very clear in *Mystici Corporis Christi*, June 29, 1943:

Actually only those are to be included as members of the Church who have been baptized and profess the true faith, and who have not been so unfortunate as to separate themselves from the unity of the Body, or been excluded by legitimate authority for grave faults committed. "For in one spirit" says the Apostle, "were we all baptized into one Body, whether Jews or Gentiles, whether bond or free." As therefore in the true Christian community there is only one Body, one Spirit, one Lord, and one Baptism, so there can be only one faith. **And therefore, if a man refuse to hear the Church, let him be considered - so the Lord commands - as a heathen and a publican. It follows that those who are divided in faith or government cannot be living in the unity of such a Body, nor can they be living the life of its one Divine Spirit**. (Pope Pius XII, *Mystici Corporis*, June 29, 1943.)

Those who are not members of the Catholic Faith have absolutely no mission from the true God of Divine Revelation, the Most Blessed Trinity, to serve Him, no less to serve Him as instruments of "evangelization" and "sanctification." Adherents of heretical and schismatic Protestant sects do not have true sacraments and they--along with the heretical and schismatic Orthodox, who have true sacraments--do not have the Catholic Faith to teach, meaning that they are agents of Antichrist, not of Christ the King.

Pope Leo XIII made it clear in *Satis Cognitum*, June 29, 1896, that unity exists whole and entire in the Catholic Church, which unites her members with agreement of minds and wills on all that pertains to Faith and Morals:

> **Agreement and union of minds is the necessary foundation of this perfect concord amongst men, from which concurrence of wills and similarity of action are the natural results**. Wherefore, in His divine wisdom, He ordained in His Church Unity of Faith; a virtue which is the first of those bonds which unite man to God, and whence we receive the name of the faithful - "one Lord, one faith, one baptism" (Eph. iv., 5). That is, as there is one Lord and one baptism, so should all Christians, without exception, have but one faith. And so the Apostle **St. Paul not merely begs, but entreats and implores Christians to be all of the same mind, and to avoid difference of opinions: "I beseech you, brethren, by the name of our Lord Jesus Christ, that you all speak the same thing, and that there be no schisms amongst you, and that you be perfect in the same mind and in the same judgment**" (I Cor. i., 10). ***Such passages certainly need no interpreter; they speak clearly enough for themselves.*** Besides, all who profess Christianity allow that there can be but one faith. **It is of the greatest importance and indeed of absolute necessity, as to which many are deceived, that the nature and character of this unity should be recognized. And, as We have already stated, this is not to be ascertained by conjecture, but by the certain knowledge of what was done; that is by seeking for and ascertaining what kind of unity in faith has been commanded by Jesus Christ.** (Pope Leo XIII, *Satis Cognitum*, June 29, 1896.)

Joseph Ratzinger/Benedict XVI and Jorge Mario Bergoglio/Francis are absolutely united in the heresy that it is necessary to "search" for a unity that exists solely in the Catholic Church. The eighty-seven-year-old Modernist from Bavaria and the nearly seventy-eight-year-old from Buenos Aires, Argentina, are blood brothers in heresy by rejecting the necessity of seeking with urgency the unconditional conversion of non-Catholics to the bosom of Holy Mother Church, meaning that they both believe that those outside of the Catholic Church are not in peril of eternal loss.

Rather than being agents of "mercy" and "tolerance" as they suppose themselves to be, both Ratzinger and Bergoglio are actually the worst enemies of non-Catholics as they are content to leave them in false religions that have no power to save their souls and by reaffirming them that they have a "mission" to combat a secularism that is the direct and inevitable result of the revolution began when Father Martin Luther posted his ninety-five theses on the door of Castle Church in Wittenberg, Germany, on October 31, 1517.

Joseph Ratzinger/Benedict XVI and Jorge Mario Bergoglio/"Francis" are also as one when it comes to the praise of "spiritual ecumenism" that was near and dear to the Modernist heart of Karol Wojtyla/John Paul II, known as “Saint John Paul II” to those in the mad world of conciliarism.

Here is just a sampling of what Ratzinger/Benedict has said about spiritual ecumenism and its chief proponent, the late Abbe Paul Couturier of the Order of Saint Irenaeus:

> Thank you, dear Brother Alois, for your warm words, full of affection.
>
> Dear young people, dear pilgrims of trust, welcome to Rome! You have come in great numbers, from all over Europe and from other continents, to pray at the tombs of the holy Apostles Peter and Paul. In fact, in this city both shed their blood for Christ. The faith that motivated these two great apostles of Christ is the same that compelled you to start out on this journey. During the year that is about to begin, you are proposing to uncover the well springs of trust in God in order to live it in your everyday life. It gladdens me that in this way, you have embraced the aims of the Year of Faith which began in October.
>
> This is the fourth European meeting to be held in Rome. On this occasion, I would like to repeat the words my predecessor, John Paul II to young people during your third Meeting in Rome: "The Pope feels deeply committed together with you all on this pilgrimage of trust on earth ... I too am called to be a pilgrim of trust in the name of Christ". (30 December 1987).
>
> Just over seventy years ago, Brother Roger established the Taizé Community. Thousands of young people from all over the world continue to go there to seek meaning for their lives. The Brothers welcome them to share in their prayer and provide them with an opportunity to experience a personal relationship with God. It was to support these young people on their journey to Christ that Brother Roger had the idea of starting a “pilgrimage of trust on earth”. A tireless witness to the Gospel of peace and reconciliation, ardently committed to an ecumenism of holiness, **Brother Roger encouraged all those who passed through Taizé to become seekers of communion. We should listen in our hearts to his spiritually lived ecumenism, and let ourselves be guided by his witness towards an ecumenism which is truly interiorized and spiritualized**. Following his example, may all of you be bearers of this message of unity. I assure you of the irrevocable commitment of the Catholic Church to continue seeking the paths of reconciliation leading to the visible unity of Christians. And so this evening I greet with special affection those among you who are Orthodox or Protestants. **(Ratzinger to *Taizé youth*: Be bearers of Christian unity.)**
>
> The father of spiritual ecumenism, Paul Couturier, spoke in this regard of an "invisible cloister" which unites within its walls those souls inflamed with love for Christ and his Church. I am convinced that if more and more people unite themselves interiorly to the Lord's prayer "that all may be one" (Jn 17: 21), then this prayer, made in the Name of Jesus, will not go unheard (cf. Jn 14: 13; 15: 7, 16, etc.).

> With the help that comes from on high, we will also find practical solutions to the different questions which remain open, and in the end our desire for unity will come to fulfilment, whenever and however the Lord wills.
>
> Now let us all go along this path in the awareness that walking together is a form of unity. Let us thank God for this and pray that he will continue to guide us all. (**Ecumenical meeting at the Archbishopric of Cologne: *Address*, August 19, 2005**.)

The "father" of "spiritual ecumenism," Abbe Paul Couturier, was a disciple of the quintessential theological evolutionist himself, the late Father Pierre Teilhard de Chardin, S.J., something that a website devoted to his nefarious work, condemned by Pope Pius XI in *Mortalium Animos*, January 6, 1928, makes very clear:

> **A third influence on Couturier was Teilhard de Chardin. Both men were scientists, and Teilhard's vision of the unity of creation and humanity expressed in the unity of Christ and the life of the Church appealed both scientifically and spiritually to Couturier**. A reasoned consequence for him was that the unity of Christians was the sign for the unity of humanity, and that praying for the sanctification of Jews, Muslims and Hindus, among many others, could not fail but to lead to a new spiritual understanding of God where Christ could at last be recognised and understood. Couturier felt this keenly as he was partly Jewish and had been raised among Muslims in North Africa. It is worth noting that among Couturier's voluminous correspondents were Jews, Muslims, and Hindus, as well as every kind of Christian, all caught up in the Abbé's spirit of prayer, realising the significance and dimensions of prayer for the unity of Christians. Coincidentally, years later Mother Theresa spoke of the considerable number of Muslims who volunteered and worked at her house in Calcutta: 'If you are a Christian, I want to make you a better Christian - if you are a Muslim, I want to make you a better Muslim'. It cannot be denied that what those Muslims were seeing in Mother Theresa was Jesus Christ himself, just as the Abbe attracted so many to prayer across previously unbridgeable divides by his humility, penitence, and joyful charity in the peace of Christ.
>
> 2003-2004 also marks the 50th Anniversary of the launch of the Week of Prayer in Morocco as an act of charity and prayer among the people of Islam, a significant milestone in the experiences of today as much as then. (**The Abbé Paul Couturier and Spiritual Ecumenism**)

No, there is no "space" between Joseph Ratzinger/Benedict XVI and Jorge Mario Bergoglio/Francis on any matter of false ecumenism.

Unfortunately for them, both now and at the time when each must face the Particular Judgment, there is a wide gulf between them and the teaching of the Catholic Church as enunciated clearly by our true popes:

> It is for this reason that so many who do not share 'the communion and the truth of the Catholic Church' must make use of the occasion of the Council, by the means of the Catholic Church, which received in Her bosom their ancestors, proposes [further]

demonstration of profound unity and of firm vital force; hear the requirements [demands] of her heart, they must engage themselves to leave this state that does not guarantee for them the security of salvation. **She does not hesitate to raise to the Lord of mercy most fervent prayers to tear down of the walls of division, to dissipate the haze of errors, and lead them back within holy Mother Church, where their Ancestors found salutary pastures of life; where, in an exclusive way, is conserved and transmitted whole the doctrine of Jesus Christ and wherein is dispensed the mysteries of heavenly grace**.

It is therefore by force of the right of Our supreme Apostolic ministry, entrusted to us by the same Christ the Lord, which, having to carry out with [supreme] participation all the duties of the good Shepherd and to follow and embrace with paternal love all the men of the world, we send this Letter of Ours to all the Christians from whom **We are separated, with which we exhort them warmly and beseech them with insistence to hasten to return to the one fold of Christ; we desire in fact from the depths of the heart their salvation in Christ Jesus**, *and we fear having to render an account one day to Him, Our Judge, if, through some possibility, we have not pointed out and prepared the way for them to attain eternal salvation. In all Our prayers and supplications, with thankfulness, day and night we never omit to ask for them, with humble insistence, from the eternal Shepherd of souls the abundance of goods and heavenly graces*. And since, if also, we fulfill in the earth the office of vicar, with all our heart we await with open arms the return of the wayward sons to the Catholic Church, in order to receive them with infinite fondness into the house of the Heavenly Father and to enrich them with its inexhaustible treasures. By our greatest wish for the return to the truth and the communion with the Catholic Church, upon which depends not only the salvation of all of them, but above all also of the whole Christian society: the entire world in fact cannot enjoy true peace if it is not of one fold and one shepherd. (Pope Pius IX, *Iam Vos Omnes*, September 13, 1868.)

Weigh carefully in your minds and before God the nature of Our request. It is not for any human motive, but impelled by Divine Charity and a desire for the salvation of all, that We advise the reconciliation and union with the Church of Rome; and **We mean a perfect and complete union, such as could not subsist in any way if nothing else was brought about but a certain kind of agreement in the Tenets of Belief and an intercourse of Fraternal love. The True Union between Christians is that which Jesus Christ, the Author of the Church, instituted and desired, and which consists in a Unity of Faith and Unity of Government**. (Pope Leo XIII, *Praeclara Gratulationis Publicae*, June 20, 1894.)

So, Venerable Brethren, it is clear why this Apostolic See has never allowed its subjects to take part in the assemblies of non-Catholics: **for the union of Christians can only be promoted by promoting the return to the one true Church of Christ of those who are separated from it, for in the past they have unhappily left it. To the one true Church of Christ, we say, which is visible to all, and which is to remain, according to the will of its Author, exactly the same as He instituted it. During the lapse of centuries, the mystical Spouse of Christ has never been contaminated, nor can she ever in the future be contaminated, as Cyprian bears witness: "The Bride of Christ cannot be made false to her Spouse: she is incorrupt and modest. She knows but one dwelling, she**

> **guards the sanctity of the nuptial chamber chastely and modestly.**" The same holy Martyr with good reason marveled exceedingly that anyone could believe that "this unity in the Church which arises from a divine foundation, and which is knit together by heavenly sacraments, could be rent and torn asunder by the force of contrary wills." For since the mystical body of Christ, in the same manner as His physical body, is one, compacted and fitly joined together, it were foolish and out of place to say that the mystical body is made up of members which are disunited and scattered abroad: whosoever therefore is not united with the body is no member of it, neither is he in communion with Christ its head. (Pope Pius XI, *Mortalium Animos*, January 6, 1928.)

Quite a gulf between the two headed "pope" monster and Popes Pius IX, Leo XIII and Pius XI. Quite a gulf.

The examples provided above have indeed shown the public face of what most people in the world think is Catholicism, thereby deceiving the souls of Catholics and non-Catholics alike, reaffirming billions of souls outside of the bosom of Holy Mother Church into believing that there is absolutely no need for them to even consider converting to the Catholic Faith before they die. Did not Our Blessed Lord and Saviour Jesus Christ shed every single drop of His Most Precious Blood to redeem these poor people?

How is it any act of fidelity to Him, Christ the King, to make it appear to them that God is pleased with their false religions and their false liturgies?

Where is the precedent for this in the history of the Catholic Church.

Where?

Where is this callous disregard for the salvation of souls to be found prior to October 28, 1958?

Where?

This is all--every single last bit of it--without any precedent in the history of the Catholic Church. Although anti-sedevacantists like to disparage the canonical teaching of the Church, reiterated by a conciliar "cardinal," Mario Francesco Pompedda, shortly before John Paul II's death on April 1 or 2, 2005, by noting that a papal vacancy of half a century is without precedent and that it is to defy the teaching of the [First] Vatican Council that Saint Peter has perpetual successors to assert that this is so (see **An Objection to Sedevacantism: 'Perpetual Successors' to Peter**). Well, my friends, none of what has been documented above is without any kind of precedent in the history of the Church. And to continue to indemnify the conciliar "popes" as legitimate successors of Saint Peter is to assert that the Catholic Church can give us defective liturgies or liturgies that can can give rise to unprecedented acts of impiety and sacrilege and that popes can teach error when they are not defining a doctrine ex cathedra. This is simply not so.

No one can be forced to "see" the truth of our situation for what it is, that the conciliar revolutionaries are not Catholic and that they belong to a counterfeit church bereft of Holy Orders and of the graces that flow therefrom. That any of our true bishops and priests, among so many others, who have seen things clearly in the past forty years, right in the midst of a most diabolically clever use of the media to convey images of Catholicism and Catholicity, is the working of the graces won for us by the shedding of every single drop of the Most Precious Blood of Our Blessed Lord and Saviour Jesus Christ and that flowed into their hearts and souls through the loving hands of Our Lady, the Mediatrix of All Graces. We must remember that it is very easy to go "back," to refuse to "kick against the goad," to "conform" to what the "mainstream" believes is "respectable" and "prudent."

All the more reason, of course, to flee from everything to do with conciliarism and its false shepherds. If we can't see that the public esteeming of the symbols and places of "worship" of false religions is offensive to God and can in no way lead to any kind of authentic restoration of the "Catholic" Church, then it is perhaps necessary to recall these words of Saint Teresa of Avila in her Foundations:

> "Know this: **it is by very little breaches of regularity that the devil succeeds in introducing the greatest abuses. May you never end up saying: 'This is nothing, this is an exaggeration**.'" (Saint Teresa of Avila, Foundations, Chapter Twenty-nine)

We turn, as always, to Our Lady, who holds us in the crossing of her arms and in the folds of her mantle. We must, as the consecrated slaves of her Divine Son, Our Blessed Lord and Saviour Jesus Christ, through her Sorrowful and Immaculate Heart, pray as many Rosaries each day as our states-in-life permit, trusting that we might be able to plant a few seeds for the Triumph of that same Immaculate Heart.

We may not see until eternity, please God and by the graces He sends to us through the loving hands of His Most Blessed Mother, the fruit of the seeds we plant by means of our prayers and penances and sacrifices, given unto the Most Sacred Heart of Jesus through the Immaculate Heart of Mary. We must remain confident, however, that Our Blessed Lord and Saviour Jesus Christ wants us, as unworthy as we are, to try to plant a few seeds so that more and more Catholics in the conciliar structures, both "priests" and laity alike, will recognize that it is indeed a sin to stand by as He is blasphemed by Modernists, that He--and His true priesthood--are to be found in the catacombs where no concessions at all are made to conciliarism or its wolves in shepherds' clothing.

Chapter Seven
Not So Orthodox With the Orthodox

Apart from the many ways by which he blasphemed the honor and majesty and glory of the Most Blessed Trinity during his 2,784 days as the universal public face of apostasy, Joseph Ratzinger/Benedict XVI regularly blasphemed many of the Fathers and the Doctors of Holy Mother Church by attempting to make them witnesses in behalf of conciliarism and its multiple defections from the Holy Faith (see **Attempting to Coerce Perjury**), a "novelty" that Jorge Mario Bergoglio has maintained and perfected as a "tradition" in his own twisted right.

Notably, Joseph Ratzinger/Benedict XVI blasphemed the thirteen million martyrs of the first centuries of the Church by claiming on December 22, 2005, that they died as "martyrs for religious liberty." The first martyrs died as martyrs for the Catholic Faith precisely because they refused to acknowledge false religions or to place them on a level of equality with the one and only true religion, Catholicism, revealed by the true God of Divine Revelation. As has been noted in other chapters of this book, Jorge Mario Bergoglio has continued his predecessor's penchant for distorting, misrepresenting and contradicting the truths of the Catholic Faith, making short work of genuine history as he does so.

Joseph Ratzinger/Benedict XVI also blasphemed the memory of the English Martyrs, each and every single one of whom refused to give any credence to the liturgical books of the false Anglican "Church" that he, Ratzinger/Benedict, accepted as legitimate even though they were declared heretical by Pope Saint Pius V in *Regnans in Excelsis,* March 5, 1570 (see **Defaming The English Martyrs** and **Still Defaming The English Martyrs**), and that Pope Leo XIII's *Apostolicae Curae*, September 15, 1896, declared to be null and void. Jorge Mario Bergoglio really believes that Justin Welby, the layman posing as the "archbishop" of Canterbury in the heretical and schismatic Anglican sect, is a "bishop" and has a mission from Christ the King to serve souls in His Holy Name.

Joseph Ratzinger/Benedict XVI has dared to spit in the face of God by claiming in a Talmudic synagogue that Christians and Jews "pray to the same Lord," showing himself to be bereft of the Catholic Faith (see **Saint Peter and Anti-Peter**), thereby mocking a mockery of the work begun by the first pope, Saint Peter, on this very day as he preached to the Jews to seek with urgency their unconditional conversion to the Catholic Faith. Jorge Mario Bergoglio has gone so far as to actually pray from the blasphemous Talmud, something that is itself an act of apostasy (see **No Space Between Ratzinger and Bergoglio, part one**).

One of Ratzinger/Benedict's greatest specialties, however, was his distortion of genuine history in order to effect a "communion" with the Orthodox that is premised upon a belief that the doctrine of Papal Primacy was understood "differently" in the First Millennium that it was by the the time of the [First] Vatican Council.

Ratzinger/Benedict has given his own very personal expression of support for this long held view of his in a general audience address two years ago, thereby placing his own "papal" stamp on that which is nothing other than a complete and total distortion of the history of the papacy in the First Millennium of the Church. Readers will see in a moment that "Pope" Benedict XVI's views are identical to those of Joseph "Cardinal" Ratzinger, views that have migrated from his own *Principles of Catholic Theology* (published in 1982) to the "unofficial" **The Ravenna Document**, October 13, 2007:

> Turning then to refer specifically to "the study of a crucial theme in dialogue between Catholic and Orthodox: 'the role of the Bishop of Rome in the communion of the Church in the first millennium'", a study which will subsequently "also extend to the second millennium", the Holy Father recalled how he had asked Catholics to pray "for this delicate dialogue which is so essential for the entire ecumenical movement". (**CONTINUE TO PRAY FOR THE UNITY OF ALL CHRISTIANS**; this link may no longer work. it was a Vatican Information Service report on a general audience address of Ratzinger/Benedict.)

> After all, Cardinal Humbert of Silva Candida, in the same bull in which he excommunicated the Patriarch Michael Cerularius and thus inaugurated the schism between East and West, designated the Emperor and the people of Constantinople as "very Christian and orthodox", although their concept of the Roman primary was certainly far less different from that of Cerularius than from that, let us say, of the First Vatican Council. **In other words, Rome must not require more from the East with respect to the doctrine of primacy than had been formulated and was lived in the first millennium**. (Joseph Ratzinger, *Principles of Catholic Theology*, pp. 198-199)

> It remains for the question of the role of the bishop of Rome in the communion of all the Churches to be studied in greater depth. What is the specific function of the bishop of the "first see" in an ecclesiology of koinonia and in view of what we have said on conciliarity and authority in the present text? **How should the teaching of the first and second Vatican councils on the universal primacy be understood and lived in the light of the ecclesial practice of the first millennium**? These are crucial questions for our dialogue and for our hopes of restoring full communion between us.

> We, the members of the Joint International Commission for the Theological Dialogue between the Roman Catholic Church and the Orthodox Church, are convinced that the above statement on ecclesial communion, conciliarity and authority represents positive and significant progress in our dialogue, and that it provides a firm basis for **future discussion of the question of primacy at the universal level in the Church**. **We are conscious that many difficult questions remain to be clarified, but we hope that, sustained by the prayer of Jesus "That they may all be one** … so that the world may believe" (Jn 17, 21), and in obedience to the Holy Spirit, we can build upon the agreement already reached. Reaffirming and confessing "one Lord, one faith, one baptism" (Eph 4, 5), we give glory to God the Holy Trinity, Father, Son and Holy Spirit, who has gathered us together. (**The Ravenna Document**)

Future discussion of "primacy at the universal level in the Church"?

Difficult questions remain to be clarified?

The Third Person of the Most Blessed Trinity, God the Holy Ghost, needs to help to reach "an agreement" on Papal Primacy?

Apostasy.

Yet it is that this apostasy is shared entirely by Jorge Mario Bergoglio:

> Russia's Metropolitan Hilarion Alfeyev and Pope Francis met yesterday morning on the occasion of the presentation of the late Sergei Averintsev's book "Word of God and word of man". Yesterday the high representative of the Patriarchate of Moscow confirmed how quickly Orthodox faithful in Russia are picking up and interpreting the signals that are being sent out by the current Bishop of Rome. The presentation of Averintsev's book took place at the Russian centre for science and culture in Rome.
>
> The Patriarchate of Moscow's "foreign affairs minister" spoke about the great Russian philosopher who died in Vienna in February 2004 and looked into ways in which ecumenical dialogue between the Catholic and Orthodox Churches could be re-tuned in the years to come.
>
> In the post-Soviet years, the great Christian scholar Averincev had already foreseen the fatal failure of an idea of Christian unity which he defined as "political" or "ideological". That is, unity in Christianity described by many adjectives - conservative, liberal and so on – a unity that follows world rules and tends to grow out of an opposition towards someone or something, the unity of a "religion without faith, without belief"," Hilarion explained. The Metropolitan quoted Averintsev to stress that common paths are only possible if there is unity in "Christian Christianity". **This unity is possible when one remains faithful to the Sacraments and the dynamics of the Christians faith, despite all differences. The unity of those who see every word of the Creed as an expression of their own faith**."
>
> This is just as valid today. Real Christian unity cannot be distorted, with unity being formed out of opposition or motivated by "ideological, pragmatic or propagandistic" elements. Eastern and Western Churches "which have their roots in Apostolic Christianity" "have the very special mission of testifying "Christian Christianity" together, "professing the truth of the Cross together." "**But his joint confession will only be fruitful if we learn to see one another not as adversaries, as we did during the crusades, nor as rivals, as often happens today, but as workers who work together in the Lord's vineyard." When "we can learn to value the differences that distinguish our various religious traditions and stop looking for external uniformity.**"
>
> In his message, Hilarion sees the basic element of shared apostolic faith as a propelling factor of today's and tomorrow's ecumenical path. It is a "**return to the sources**" which can be developed also thanks to Pope Francis' work. The Russian Metropolitan eloquently concluded his speech by extensively quoting two points made by the current Bishop of Rome. The first quotation was of the words pronounced by Pope Francis on the return flight from Rio after World Youth Day, referring to Dostoevskij and the Orthodox Churches: "In the Orthodox Churches, they have retained that pristine liturgy, which is so beautiful. We

have lost some of the sense of adoration. The Orthodox preserved it; they praise God, they adore God, they sing, time does not matter."

The second quotation by Francis which Hilarion referred to and emphasised, was a passage from the Pope's interview with Italian Jesuit journal Civiltà Cattolica. Hilarion quoted the bit where the Bishop of Rome wanted **"to learn" from the Orthodox Church about "the meaning of Episcopal collegiality and the tradition of synodality**."

A shared reflection on how the Church was governed in the early centuries "will bear fruit in due time," Pope Francis said in the interview quoted by Hilarion. "In ecumenical relations it is important not only to know each other better, but also to recognize what the Spirit has sown in the other as a gift for us," the Pope said.

The extensive review of the institute of the Synod of Bishops, which Francis ordered, is a concrete sign of his willingness to recognise what the Holy Spirit sewed along the path of the Orthodox Churches as a gift for the Catholic Church. **This means ecumenical dialogue can venture down new and unknown paths, away from the tedious ritualistic ceremonies between the two Churches**. (Metropolitan Hilarion on Francis and "Christian Christianity". See the appendix below for a list of ways in which the Orthodox defect from Catholic doctrine.)

"Christian Christianity"?

Well, that means putting aside divisive little things such as doctrine despite all of the mutual assurances to the contrary given by Bergoglio and his ecumaniacal partners such as the forty-seven year-old Hilarion, who is the Russian Orthodox equivalent of the now retired Walter Kasper and his successor, Kurt Koch, as the "President" of the "Pontifical" Council for Promoting the Unity of Christians.

Yes, we have been down this road before. Many times before.

Jorge Mario Bergoglio himself greeted the Greek Orthodox Patriarch, Bartholomew, as follows on Friday, June 28, 2013, the Feast of Saint Irenaeus and the Vigil of the Feast of Saints Peter and Paul:

> I am particularly pleased to greet you with a warm welcome to the Church of Rome, which is celebrating its patron saints Peter and Paul. Your presence in this circumstance is a sign of the deep bond that unites the Church of Constantinople and the Church of Rome in faith, hope and love. **The beautiful custom, which began in 1969, of exchanging delegations between our Churches for their patronal feast days, is for me a source of great joy: fraternal encounter is an essential part of the journey towards unity**. I would like to express my heartfelt gratitude to Your Holiness Bartholomew I and the Holy Synod of the Ecumenical Patriarchate, who wanted to once again send a high level delegation. I remember with fraternal affection the gesture of exquisite attention shown to me by Your Holiness Bartholomew, when you honored me with your presence at the celebration of **the**

> **beginning of my ministry as Bishop of Rome**. I am also very grateful to Your Eminence, for your participation in this event and I am happy to see you again on this occasion.
>
> **The search for unity among Christians is an urgency which, today more than ever, we cannot ignore.** In our world, hungry and thirsty for truth, love, hope, peace and unity, it is important for our own witness, to be finally able to announce with one voice the good news of the Gospel and to celebrate the Divine Mysteries of the new life in Christ! We know very well that unity is primarily a gift from God for which we must pray without ceasing, but we all have the task of preparing the conditions, of cultivating the soil of the heart, so that this extraordinary grace can be received.
>
> A fundamental contribution to the search for full communion between Catholics and Orthodox is offered by the Joint International Commission for Theological Dialogue, co-chaired by Your Eminence, Metropolitan Ioannis, and by my venerable brother Cardinal Kurt Koch. I sincerely thank you for your valuable and tireless commitment. **This Commission has already produced many common texts and is now studying the delicate issue of theological and ecclesiological relationship between primacy and synodality in the life of the Church. It is significant that today we are able to reflect together, in truth and love, on these issues, starting with what we have in common, but without hiding that which still separates us. This is not merely a theoretical exercise, but one of getting to know each other's traditions in order to understand, and sometimes also to learn from them. I refer for example to the reflection of the Catholic Church on the meaning of episcopal collegiality, and the tradition of synodality, so typical of the Orthodox Churches**. I am confident that the effort of shared reflection, so complex and laborious, will bear fruit in due time. I am comforted to know that Catholics and Orthodox share the same conception of dialogue that does not seek a theological minimalism on which to reach a compromise, but rather is based on the deepening of the one truth that Christ has given to His Church, which we never cease to understand better as we are moved by the Holy Spirit. For this, we should not be afraid of encounter and of true dialogue. It does not take us away from the truth, but rather, through an exchange of gifts, it leads us, under the guidance of the Spirit of truth, to the whole truth (cf. Jn 16:13). (**Francis the Flexible to Orthodox delegation from Ecumenical Patriarchate**.)

As demonstrated earlier in this chapter, each of these bits of apostasy is in perfect continuity with the Modernist mind and heart of Joseph Ratzinger/Benedict XVI, who gave his own personal expression of support for the supposedly "unofficial" *The Ravenna Document*, which was issued by the Joint International Commission for Theological Dialogue on October 13, 2007, on a number of occasions, thereby placing his "papal" seal of approval on the document and providing an "official" expression of the views on the primacy of the "Petrine Ministry" in light of how it was supposedly exercised in the First Millennium before the Greek Schism of 1054. There is no space between Ratzinger and Bergoglio on the matter of "communion" with the Orthodox. None whatsoever.

Pope Leo XIII dealt with the two-headed "pope" monster's false assertions about the alleged "synodality" of the First Millennium in *Praeclara Gratulationis Publicae*, June 20, 1894:

First of all, then, We cast an affectionate look upon the East, from whence in the beginning came forth the salvation of the world. Yes, and the yearning desire of Our heart bids us conceive and hope that the day is not far distant when the Eastern Churches, so illustrious in their ancient faith and glorious past, will return to the fold they have abandoned. We hope it all the more, that the distance separating them from Us is not so great: nay, with some few exceptions, we agree so entirely on other heads that, in defense of the Catholic Faith, we often have recourse to reasons and testimony borrowed from the teaching, the Rites, and Customs of the East.

The Principal subject of contention is the Primacy of the Roman Pontiff. **But let them look back to the early years of their existence, let them consider the sentiments entertained by their forefathers, and examine what the oldest Traditions testify, and it will, indeed, become evident to them that Christ's Divine Utterance, Thou art Peter, and upon this rock I will build My Church, has undoubtedly been realized in the Roman Pontiffs. Many of these latter in the first gates of the Church were chosen from the East, and foremost among them Anacletus, Evaristus, Anicetus, Eleutherius, Zosimus, and Agatho; and of these a great number, after Governing the Church in Wisdom and Sanctity, Consecrated their Ministry with the shedding of their blood. The time, the reasons, the promoters of the unfortunate division, are well known. Before the day when man separated what God had joined together, the name of the Apostolic See was held in Reverence by all the nations of the Christian world: and the East, like the West, agreed without hesitation in its obedience to the Pontiff of Rome, as the Legitimate Successor of St. Peter, and, therefore, the Vicar of Christ here on earth**.

And, accordingly, if we refer to the beginning of the dissension, **we shall see that Photius himself was careful to send his advocates to Rome on the matters that concerned him; and Pope Nicholas I sent his Legates to Constantinople from the Eternal City, without the slightest opposition, "in order to examine the case of Ignatius the Patriarch with all diligence, and to bring back to the Apostolic See a full and accurate report"; so that the history of the whole negotiation is a manifest Confirmation of the Primacy of the Roman See with which the dissension then began. Finally, in two great Councils, the second of Lyons and that of Florence, Latins and Greeks, as is notorious, easily agreed, and all unanimously proclaimed as Dogma the Supreme Power of the Roman Pontiffs**.

We have recalled those things intentionally, for they constitute an invitation to peace and reconciliation; and with all the more reason that in Our own days it would seem as if there were a more conciliatory spirit towards Catholics on the part of the Eastern Churches, and even some degree of kindly feeling. To mention an instance, those sentiments were lately made manifest when some of Our faithful travelled to the East on a Holy Enterprise, and received so many proofs of courtesy and good-will.

Therefore, Our mouth is open to you, to you all of Greek or other Oriental Rites who are separated from the Catholic Church, We earnestly desire that each and every one of you should meditate upon the words, so full of gravity and love, addressed by Bessarion to your forefathers: "What answer shall we give to God when He comes to ask why we have separated from our Brethren: to Him Who, to unite us and bring us into One Fold, came down from Heaven, was Incarnate, and was Crucified? What will our defense be in the eyes of posterity? Oh, my Venerable Fathers, we must not suffer this to be, we must not entertain this thought, we must not thus so ill provide for ourselves and for our Brethren."

Weigh carefully in your minds and before God the nature of Our request. It is not for any human motive, but impelled by Divine Charity and a desire for the salvation of all, that **We advise the reconciliation and union with the Church of Rome; and We mean a perfect and complete union, such as could not subsist in any way if nothing else was brought about but a certain kind of agreement in the Tenets of Belief and an intercourse of Fraternal love. The True Union between Christians is that which Jesus Christ, the Author of the Church, instituted and desired, and which consists in a Unity of Faith and Unity of Government.**

Nor is there any reason for you to fear on that account that We or any of Our Successors will ever diminish your rights, the privileges of your Patriarchs, or the established Ritual of any one of your Churches. It has been and always will be the intent and Tradition of the Apostolic See, to make a large allowance, in all that is right and good, for the primitive Traditions and special customs of every nation. On the contrary, if you re-establish Union with Us, you will see how, by God's bounty, the glory and dignity of your Churches will be remarkably increased.

May God, then, in His goodness, hear the Prayer that you yourselves address to Him: "Make the schisms of the Churches cease," and "Assemble those who are dispersed, bring back those who err, and unite them to Thy Holy Catholic and Apostolic Church." May you thus return to that one Holy Faith which has been handed down both to Us and to you from time immemorial; which your forefathers preserved untainted, and which was enhanced by the rival splendor of the Virtues, the great genius, and the sublime learning of St. Athanasius and St. Basil, St. Gregory of Nazianzum and St. John Chrysostom, the two Saints who bore the name of Cyril, and so many other great men whose glory belongs as a common inheritance to the East and to the West. (Pope Leo XIII, *Praeclara Gratulationis Publicae*, June 20, 1894. See also the excellent discussion of the the history of what led up to the Greek Schism that is contained in Fathers Francisco and Dominic Radecki's **Tumultuous Times.**)

Ratzinger and Bergoglio have distorted history to suit their perverted purposes of effecting a false "communion" with the Orthodox. Those in the Motu world, especially those who believe in "resignationism," must suspend all pretense of rationality to contend that their man "Benedict" is more "orthodox" than the "bad" Bergoglio. Each man is more [Greek] Orthodox than Catholic. Indeed, neither man is a Catholic as they defect from numerous points of Catholic doctrine, placing them outside of the Catholic Faith.

Ratzinger issued a joint statement with the Greek Orthodox Patriarch, Bartholomew I, on November 30, 2006, that referred to their "responsibility as Pastors in the Church of Christ" while Bergoglio referred to Bartholomew as "my brother" last year:

> This fraternal encounter which brings us together, Pope Benedict XVI of Rome and Ecumenical Patriarch Bartholomew I, is God's work, and in a certain sense his gift. We give thanks to the Author of all that is good, who allows us once again, in prayer and in dialogue, to express the joy we feel as brothers and to renew our commitment to move towards full communion. **This commitment comes from the Lord's will and from our responsibility as Pastors in the Church of Christ**. May our meeting be a sign and an encouragement for us to share the same sentiments and the same attitudes of fraternity, cooperation and communion in charity and truth. The Holy Spirit will help us to prepare the great day of the re-establishment of full unity, whenever and however God wills it. Then we shall truly be able to rejoice and be glad. (**Common declaration by Benedict XVI and Patriarch Bartholomew I, November 30, 2006**.)
>
> First of all I thank my **Brother Andrew** [Bartholomew I] very much for what he said. Thank you very much! Thank you!
>
> It is a cause for particular joy to meet today with you, delegates of the Orthodox churches, the Oriental Orthodox churches and ecclesial communities of the West. Thank you for having wanted to take part in the celebration that has marked the beginning of my Ministry as Bishop of Rome and successor of Peter.
>
> Yesterday morning, during Holy Mass, through your persons I recognized as spiritually present the communities that you represent. In this manifestation of faith, I seemed to experience in an even more urgent way the prayer for unity among believers in Christ and together to see somehow foreshadowed that full realization, which depends on the plan of God and on our loyal collaboration. (**Address to Representative of the Schismatic and Heretical Orthodox Churches, Protesant sects, Talmudists, Mohammedans and Other Infidels, Masons and Pantheists**.)
>
> **Tornielli**: This coming January marks the 50th anniversary of Paul VI's historic visit to the Holy Land. Will you go?
>
> **Bergoglio**: "Christmas always makes us think of Bethlehem, and Bethlehem is a precise point in the Holy Land where Jesus lived. On Christmas night, I think above all with the Christians who live there, of those who are in difficulty, of the many people who have had to leave that land because of various problems. But Bethlehem is still Bethlehem. God arrived at a specific time in a specific land; that is where God's tenderness and grace appeared. We cannot think of Christmas without thinking of the Holy land. Fifty years ago, **Paul VI had the courage to go out and go there and this marked the beginning of the era of papal journeys. I would also like to go there, to meet my brother Bartholomew, the Patriarch of Constantinople, and commemorate this 50th anniversary with him, renewing that embrace which took place between Pope**

> **Montini and Athenagoras in Jerusalem, in 1964. We are preparing for this.**" (**Never Be Afraid of Tenderness**)

No heretic/schismatic has any "pastoral ministry" to fulfill in the "Church of Christ" as the Church of Christ is the Catholic Church and none other, something that applies as much to the conciliar "popes" as to the "ecumenical patriarchs" of the Greek Orthodox Church.

Jorge Mario Bergoglio put his own "signature" on relations to the Orthodox as he bowed to Patriarch Bartholmew I as he attended a Greek Orthdox Divine Liturgy of Saint John Chrysostom in the Patriarch Church of Saint George in Istanbul, Turkey on Sunday, November 30, 2014, the First Sunday of Advent, starting off by stating that he had "participated" in many Greek Orthodox liturgies when he was the conciliar "archbishop" of Buenos Aires, Argentina, from 1998 to 2013:

> When I was the Archbishop of Buenos Aires, I often took part in the celebration of the Divine Liturgy of the Orthodox communities there. Today, the Lord has given me the singular grace to be present in this Patriarchal Church of Saint George for the celebration of the Feast of the holy Apostle Andrew, the first-called, the brother of Saint Peter, and the Patron Saint of the Ecumenical Patriarchate.
>
> Meeting each other, seeing each other face to face, exchanging the embrace of peace, and praying for each other, are all essential aspects of our journey towards the restoration of full communion. All of this precedes and always accompanies that other essential aspect of this journey, namely, theological dialogue. An authentic dialogue is, in every case, an encounter between persons with a name, a face, a past, and not merely a meeting of ideas. (**Divine Liturgy in the Patriarchal Church of St. George**.)

As a true son of the conciliar revolution, the lay Jesuit from Argentina, Jorge Mario Bergoglio, has participated in the Divine Liturgy of various Orthodox communities when he was the conciliar "archbishop" of Buenos Aires, Argentina, from 1998 to 2013. This is simply normal for the man. It is part of what he believes, erroneously, of course, that the Catholic Church professes as the God the Holy Ghost has been "uncaged" to blow as He will to help Catholics and non-Catholics find a "path to unity," to "full communion."

An excellent article that appeared in *The Latin Mass: A Journal of Catholic Culture*, twelve years ago now explained the many different condemnations of "ecumenical prayer" that had been issued by the Holy Office from 1622 to 1939. The article concluded as follows:

> To summarize, we may recall that the Holy Office said that it is not so much a matter of whether schismatic worship contains anything objectionable to the Faith; rather, the problem is the very participation in worship with schismatics. By participating in schismatic and heretical worship, one is giving exterior signs of segregation and disapproval. Any participation in liturgical actions would constitute a sign of unity with those who are not in union with the Church. By coming together with them in unity of prayer, in unity of cult, in unity of veneration and worship, Catholics would offer worship with perverse schismatic and heretical ministers. **In effect, the Holy Office said that it is by the very coming together with them and joining one's prayer and worship to theirs that one is**

participating in worship of those who reject the Catholic Church. To participate with those who reject the Faith was therefore forbidden, since there is a danger of perversion and loss of the Catholic faith. There is the very danger of participating in a heretical or schismatic rite, since the participation manifests a sign of disunity from the Church. Participation in heretical or schismatic worship is an occasion of scandal and by participating in their worship, one confirms schismatics and heretics in their errors. The Holy Office therefore observed that the Council of Carthage forbade praying and singing with heretics and that participation in schismatic and heretic worship is "universally prohibited by natural and divine law...[about which] no one has the power to dispense...[and with respect to this participation] nothing excuses." (The Holy Office on Worship with Non-Catholics from 1622 to 1939 by Craig Allan.)

Guess what?

The conciliar "popes" have been doing precisely what our true popes and the Holy Office have condemned, a condemnation that dates back to apostolical times, something that Bishop George Hay had noted at the beginning of the Eighteenth Century, and has its roots in Sacred Scripture itself. Although there may be a "hermeneutic of continuity" at work between Bergoglio and his predecessors, those who have worn the Shoes of the Antichrist are in abject discontinuity from the truths of the Catholic Faith.

Bergoglio then repeated the distortions of the history of the Catholic Church that have been made in the past twenty years by the likes of Karol Josef Wojtyla/John Paul II, Joseph Alois Ratzinger/Benedict XVI and Walter Kasper:

> It is not by chance that the path of reconciliation and peace between Catholics and Orthodox was, in some way, ushered in by an encounter, by an embrace between our venerable predecessors, Ecumenical Patriarch Athenagoras and Pope Paul VI, which took place fifty years ago in Jerusalem. Your Holiness and I wished to commemorate that moment when we met recently in the same city where our Lord Jesus Christ died and rose.
>
> By happy coincidence, my visit falls a few days after the fiftieth anniversary of the promulgation of *Unitatis Redintegratio*, the Second Vatican Council's Decree on Christian Unity. This is a fundamental document which opened new avenues for encounter between Catholics and their brothers and sisters of other Churches and ecclesial communities.
>
> In particular, in that Decree the Catholic Church acknowledges that the Orthodox Churches "possess true sacraments, above all – by apostolic succession – the priesthood and the Eucharist, whereby they are still joined to us in closest intimacy" (15). The Decree goes on to state that in order to guard faithfully the fullness of the Christian tradition and to bring to fulfilment the reconciliation of Eastern and Western Christians, it is of the greatest importance to preserve and support the rich patrimony of the Eastern Churches. This regards not only their liturgical and spiritual traditions, but also their canonical disciplines, sanctioned as they are by the Fathers and by Councils, which regulate the lives of these Churches (cf. 15-16).

I believe that it is important to reaffirm respect for this principle as an essential condition, accepted by both, for the restoration of full communion, which does not signify the submission of one to the other, or assimilation. Rather, it means welcoming all the gifts that God has given to each, thus demonstrating to the entire world the great mystery of salvation accomplished by Christ the Lord through the Holy Spirit. I want to assure each one of you here that, to reach the desired goal of full unity, the Catholic Church does not intend to impose any conditions except that of the shared profession of faith. **Further, I would add that we are ready to seek together, in light of Scriptural teaching and the experience of the first millennium, the ways in which we can guarantee the needed unity of the Church in the present circumstances. The one thing that the Catholic Church desires, and that I seek as Bishop of Rome, "the Church which presides in charity", is communion with the Orthodox Churches. Such communion will always be the fruit of that love which "has been poured into our hearts through the Holy Spirit who has been given to us" (cf. *Rom* 5:5), a fraternal love which expresses the spiritual and transcendent bond which unites us as disciples of the Lord.** (Divine Liturgy in the Patriarchal Church of St. George.)

This old canard owes its proximate origins to none other than that "restorer of tradition," Joseph Ratzinger/Benedict XVI, who helped to convince his superior at the time, "Saint John Paul II," to write about such a "restoration" of how popes "presided" in" charity in communion *with* the Eastern churches, which means that, according to the conciliar reveolutionaries, those popes did not excercise Papal Primacy *over* the Eastern churches in the First Millennium. As noted earlier in this chapter, Pope Leo XIII put the lie to this distortion of history in *Praeclara Gratulationis Publicae*, June 29, 1884.

Yes, one must believe in everything taught by Holy Mother Church as it has been defined and understood from time immemorial or he is simply not a Catholic.

Who says so?

Well, perhaps it would be good to take a look at the following sources:

With reference to its object, faith cannot be greater for some truths than for others. Nor can it be less with regard to the number of truths to be believed. For we must all believe the very same thing, both as to the object of faith as well as to the number of truths. All are equal in this because everyone must believe all the truths of faith--both those which God Himself has directly revealed, as well as those he has revealed through His Church. Thus, I must believe as much as you and you as much as I, and all other Christians similarly. He who does not believe all these mysteries is not Catholic and therefore will never enter Paradise. (Saint Francis de Sales, *The Sermons of Saint Francis de Sales for Lent Given in 1622*, republished by TAN Books and Publishers for the Visitation Monastery of Frederick, Maryland, in 1987, pp. 34-37.)

The Church, founded on these principles and mindful of her office, has done nothing with greater zeal and endeavour than she has displayed in guarding the integrity of the faith. **Hence she regarded as rebels and expelled from the ranks of her children all**

> **who held beliefs on any point of doctrine different from her own**. The Arians, the Montanists, the Novatians, the Quartodecimans, the Eutychians, **did not certainly reject all Catholic doctrine: they abandoned only a certain portion of it. Still who does not know that they were declared heretics and banished from the bosom of the Church**? In like manner were condemned all authors of heretical tenets who followed them in subsequent ages. "**There can be nothing more dangerous than those heretics who admit nearly the whole cycle of doctrine, and yet by one word, as with a drop of poison, infect the real and simple faith taught by our Lord and handed down by Apostolic tradition**" (Auctor Tract. de Fide Orthodoxa contra Arianos).
>
> The practice of the Church has always been the same, as is shown by the unanimous teaching of the Fathers, **who were wont to hold as outside Catholic communion, and alien to the Church, whoever would recede in the least degree from any point of doctrine proposed by her authoritative Magisterium**. Epiphanius, Augustine, Theodore drew up a long list of the heresies of their times. St. Augustine notes that other heresies may spring up, **to a single one of which, should any one give his assent, he is by the very fact cut off from Catholic unity. "No one who merely disbelieves in all (these heresies) can for that reason regard himself as a Catholic or call himself one. For there may be or may arise some other heresies, which are not set out in this work of ours, and, if any one holds to one single one of these he is not a Catholic**" (S. Augustinus, De Haeresibus, n. 88). (Pope Leo XIII, *Satis Cognitum*, June 29, 1896.)
>
> Actually **only those are to be included as members of the Church who have been baptized and profess the true faith, and who have not been so unfortunate as to separate themselves from the unity of the Body, or been excluded by legitimate authority for grave faults committed**. "For in one spirit" says the Apostle, "were we all baptized into one Body, whether Jews or Gentiles, whether bond or free." As therefore in the true Christian community there is only one Body, one Spirit, one Lord, and one Baptism, so there can be only one faith. **And therefore, if a man refuse to hear the Church, let him be considered - so the Lord commands - as a heathen and a publican. It follows that those who are divided in faith or government cannot be living in the unity of such a Body, nor can they be living the life of its one Divine Spirit**. (Pope Pius XII, *Mystici Corporis*, June 29, 1943.)

In order to justify their defections from the Catholic Faith, Ratzinger/Benedict and Jorge Mario Bergoglio/Francis have given Catholics and non-Catholics alike a distorted view of history and in order to make it as though the new ecclesiology's concept of the "church as communion" has replaced the perennial teaching of the Catholic Church that there is no "Christian Church" outside of her. She is the one and sole embodiment of Christianity. The schismatic and heretical sects of Orthodoxy may have true sacraments because they possess true apostolic succession and have liturgical rites that were used, at least for the most part, long before the Greek Schism of 1054. They do not have the Catholic Faith. Only those who adhere to the totality of the Deposit of Faith and are in full communion with a true and legitimate Successor of Saint Peter possess the Catholic Faith:

> **Agreement and union of minds is the necessary foundation of this perfect concord amongst men, from which concurrence of wills and similarity of action are the natural results.** Wherefore, in His divine wisdom, He ordained in His Church Unity of Faith; a virtue which is the first of those bonds which unite man to God, and whence we receive the name of the faithful - "one Lord, one faith, one baptism" (Eph. iv., 5). That is, as there is one Lord and one baptism, so should all Christians, without exception, have but one faith. And so the Apostle St. Paul not merely begs, but entreats and implores Christians to be all of the same mind, and to avoid difference of opinions: "**I beseech you, brethren, by the name of our Lord Jesus Christ, that you all speak the same thing, and that there be no schisms amongst you, and that you be perfect in the same mind and in the same judgment**" (I Cor. i., 10). Such passages certainly need no interpreter; they speak clearly enough for themselves. **Besides, all who profess Christianity allow that there can be but one faith. It is of the greatest importance and indeed of absolute necessity, as to which many are deceived, that the nature and character of this unity should be recognized. And, as We have already stated, this is not to be ascertained by conjecture, but by the certain knowledge of what was done; that is by seeking for and ascertaining what kind of unity in faith has been commanded by Jesus Christ**. (Pope Leo XIII, *Satis Cognitum*, June 29, 1896.)

Neither Ratzinger or Bergoglio believe that "believers" have to agree on everything taught by the Catholic Church. It is enough for there to be that nebulous "Christian Christianity" referred to by Bergoglio seven months ago now.

The Orthodox hold a particular appeal to Joseph Ratzinger/Benedict XVI and Jorge Mario Bergoglio as "Greek theology" is said to go back to "original sources" without the supposed distorted "filter" of the Scholasticism of Saint Thomas Aquinas that the two-headed "pope" monster contends has corrupted both the meaning of Sacred Scripture and the writing of the early Church Fathers.

Pope Pius XII made short work of this "re-reading" of "original sources" without relying upon the Scholasticism of Saint Thomas Aquinas that was used by the Fathers of the Council of Florence, the Council of Trent and the [First] Vatican Council.

The following passages from Pope Pius XII's *Humani Generis*, August 12, 1950, describe--and condemn--the entirety of the intellectual work of Joseph Ratzinger/Benedict XVI and his successor, Jorge Mario Bergoglio/Francis. Both Ratzinger and Bergoglio have used "vague notions" and outright heresies to appeal for "unity" with the schismatic and heretical Orthodox churches without forcing them to accept the dogmatic pronouncements of the Second Millennium that were made without their "participation" and that were "distorted" by Scholasticism as a result:

> Hence to neglect, or to reject, or to devalue so many and such great resources which have been conceived, expressed and perfected so often by the age-old work of men endowed with no common talent and holiness, working under the vigilant supervision of the holy magisterium and with the light and leadership of the Holy Ghost in order to state the truths of the faith ever more accurately, to do this so that these things may be replaced by conjectural notions and by some formless and unstable tenets of a new philosophy, tenets

which, like the flowers of the field, are in existence today and die tomorrow; this is supreme imprudence and something that would make dogma itself a reed shaken by the wind. The contempt for terms and notions habitually used by scholastic theologians leads of itself to the weakening of what they call speculative theology, a discipline which these men consider devoid of true certitude because it is based on theological reasoning.

Unfortunately these advocates of novelty easily pass from despising scholastic theology to the neglect of and even contempt for the Teaching Authority of the Church itself, which gives such authoritative approval to scholastic theology. This Teaching Authority is represented by them as a hindrance to progress and an obstacle in the way of science. Some non-Catholics consider it as an unjust restraint preventing some more qualified theologians from reforming their subject. And although this sacred Office of Teacher in matters of faith and morals must be the proximate and universal criterion of truth for all theologians, since to it has been entrusted by Christ Our Lord the whole deposit of faith --**Sacred Scripture and divine Tradition -- to be preserved, guarded and interpreted, still the duty that is incumbent on the faithful to flee also those errors which more or less approach heresy, and accordingly "to keep also the constitutions and decrees by which such evil opinions are proscribed and forbidden by the Holy See," is sometimes as little known as if it did not exist. What is expounded in the Encyclical Letters of the Roman Pontiffs concerning the nature and constitution of the Church, is deliberately and habitually neglected by some with the idea of giving force to a certain vague notion which they profess to have found in the ancient Fathers, especially the Greeks. The Popes, they assert, do not wish to pass judgment on what is a matter of dispute among theologians, so recourse must be had to the early sources, and the recent constitutions and decrees of the Teaching Church must be explained from the writings of the ancients.** (Pope Pius XII, *Humani Generis*, August 12, 1950.)

Thus stand condemned both Joseph Ratzinger/Benedict XVI and Jorge Mario Bergoglio/Francis insofar as their willingness to do anything other than seek the unconditional conversion of the Orthodox to the Catholic Church, outside of which there is no salvation and without which there is no true social order.

Resignationism, anyone?

Utter, delusional nonsense.

There is no "space" between Joseph Ratzinger and Jorge Mario Bergoglio.

Obviously, we must, as always, spend time in prayer before Our Lord's Real Presence in the Most Blessed Sacrament and pray as many Rosaries each day as our states-in-life permit, using the shield of Our Lady's Brown Scapular of Mount Carmel and the weapon of her Rosary to protect us from the contagion of apostasy and betrayal that is all around us. We must also, of course, make reparation for our own many sins by offering up all of our prayers and sufferings and sacrifices and humiliations and penances and mortifications and fastings to the Most Sacred Heart of Jesus through the Sorrowful and Immaculate Heart of Mary.

The final victory belongs to the Immaculate Heart of Mary. We must pray to her, the Spouse of God the Holy Ghost, to help us to cooperate with the Seven Gifts and the Twelve Fruits of the Holy Ghost so that we can be instruments, unworthy though we may be, of planting the seeds for the restoration of Holy Mother Church and of the Social Reign of Christ the King so that everyone in the whole world will exclaim with hearts consecrated to the Most Sacred Heart of Jesus through the Sorrowful and Immaculate Heart of Mary:

Vivat Christus Rex! *Viva Cristo Rey*!

Chapter Appendix
Various Ways in Which the Orthodox Defect From the Deposit of Faith Entrusted to the Catholic Church

1. Papal Primacy.

2. Papal Infallibility.

3. The doctrine of Original Sin as defined dogmatically by the Catholic Church. The ambiguous doctrine of the Orthodox was noted by Pope Pius VI in *Auctorem Fidei*, August 28, 1794, when discussing the Greek rejection of Limbo that is, of course, shared by Joseph Ratzinger/Benedict XVI:

Very few Greek Fathers dealt with the destiny of infants who die without Baptism because there was no controversy about this issue in the East. Furthermore, they had a different view of the present condition of humanity. **For the Greek Fathers, as the consequence of Adam's sin, human beings inherited corruption, possibility, and mortality, from which they could be restored by a process of deification made possible through the redemptive work of Christ. The idea of an inheritance of sin or guilt - common in Western tradition - was foreign to this perspective, since in their view sin could only be a free, personal act**.

This is what the Orthodox still believe, which makes them fit "partners" for "ecumenical dialogue" with Ratzinger/Benedict, who has told us in his own murky way that he is of one mind with them on the matter of Original Sin, which he called in 1995 an "imprecise" term (!). Here is a statement on Original Sin from the Orthodox Church in America:

> With regard to original sin, the difference between Orthodox Christianity and the West may be outlined as follows:
>
> In the Orthodox Faith, the term "original sin" refers to the "first" sin of Adam and Eve. As a result of this sin, humanity bears the "consequences" of sin, the chief of which is death. Here the word "original" may be seen as synonymous with "first." Hence, the "original sin" refers to the "first sin" in much the same way as "original chair" refers to the "first chair."
>
> In the West, humanity likewise bears the "consequences" of the "original sin" of Adam and Eve. However, the West also understands that humanity is likewise "guilty" of the sin

> of Adam and Eve. The term "Original Sin" here refers to the condition into which humanity is born, a condition in which guilt as well as consequence is involved.
>
> In the Orthodox Christian understanding, while humanity does bear the consequences of the original, or first, sin, humanity does not bear the personal guilt associated with this sin. Adam and Eve are guilty of their willful action; we bear the consequences, chief of which is death.
>
> One might look at all of this in a completely different light. Imagine, if you will, that one of your close relatives was a mass murderer. He committed many serious crimes for which he was found guilty and perhaps even admitted his guilt publicly. You, as his or her son or brother or cousin, may very well bear the consequences of his action - people may shy away from you or say, "Watch out for him - he comes from a family of mass murderers." Your name may be tainted, or you may face some other forms of discrimination as a consequence of your relative's sin. You, however, are not personally guilty of his or her sin.
>
> There are some within Orthodoxy who approach a westernized view of sin, primarily after the 17th and 18th centuries due to a variety of westernizing influences particularly in Ukraine and Russia after the time of Peter Mohyla. These influences have from time to time colored explanations of the Orthodox Faith which are in many respects lacking. (Orthodox Church in America, Questions and Answers on **Original Sin**)

This is not Catholic doctrine. This matter cannot be "bridged" by concerts of music composed by Russians.

4. The Filioque, that God the Holy Ghost proceeds from both the Father and the Son.

5. The doctrine of Purgatory as defined by the authority of the Catholic Church.

6. The doctrine of Our Lady's Immaculate Conception as defined by the authority of the Catholic Church.

7. The doctrine of Our Lady's Assumption body and soul into Heaven as defined by the authority of the Catholic Church.

8. The doctrine of the indissolubility of a sacramentally valid, ratified and consummated marriage; the Orthodox hold that a person can marry up to three times following two divorces. Here is the Orthodox "consensus" (as there is no ultimate ecclesiastical authority within Orthodoxy to decide doctrinal matters) on the issue:

> Marriage is one of the sacraments of the Orthodox Church. Orthodox Christians who marry must marry in the Church in order to be in sacramental communion with the Church. According to the Church canons, an Orthodox who marries outside the Church may not receive Holy Communion and may not serve as a sponsor, i.e. a Godparent at a Baptism, or as a sponsor at a Wedding. Certain marriages are prohibited by canon law, such as a

marriage between first and second cousins, or between a Godparent and a Godchild. The first marriage of a man and a woman is honored by the Church with a richly symbolic service that eloquently speaks to everyone regarding the married state. The form of the service calls upon God to unite the couple through the prayer of the priest or bishop officiating.

The church will permit up to, but not more than, three marriages for any Orthodox Christian. If both partners are entering a second or third marriage, another form of the marriage ceremony is conducted, much more subdued and penitential in character. Marriages end either through the death of one of the partners or through ecclesiastical recognition of divorce. The Church grants "ecclesiastical divorces" on the basis of the exception given by Christ to his general prohibition of the practice. The Church has frequently deplored the rise of divorce and generally sees divorce as a tragic failure. Yet, the Orthodox Church also recognizes that sometimes the spiritual well-being of Christians caught in a broken and essentially nonexistent marriage justifies a divorce, with the right of one or both of the partners to remarry. Each parish priest is required to do all he can to help couples resolve their differences. If they cannot, and they obtain a civil divorce, they may apply for an ecclesiastical divorce in some jurisdictions of the Orthodox Church. In others, the judgment is left to the parish priest when and if a civilly divorced person seeks to remarry.

Those Orthodox jurisdictions which issue ecclesiastical divorces require a thorough evaluation of the situation, and the appearance of the civilly divorced couple before a local ecclesiastical court, where another investigation is made. Only after an ecclesiastical divorce is issued by the presiding bishop can they apply for an ecclesiastical license to remarry.

Though the Church would prefer that all Orthodox Christians would marry Orthodox Christians, it does not insist on it in practice. Out of its concern for the spiritual welfare of members who wish to marry a non-Orthodox Christian, the Church will conduct a "mixed marriage." For this purpose, a "non-Orthodox Christian" is a member of the Roman Catholic Church, or one of the many Protestant Churches which believe in and baptize in the name of the Holy Trinity. This means that such mixed marriages may be performed in the Orthodox Church. However, the Orthodox Church does not perform marriages between Orthodox Christians and persons belonging to other religions, such as Islam, Judaism, Buddhism, Hinduism, or any sectarian and cult group, such as Christian Science, Mormonism, or the followers of Rev. Moon. (**The Stand of the Orthodox Church on Controversial Issues**.)

9. The absolute prohibition against the use of any form of contraception whatsoever. This is from the website of the Greek Orthodox Church in America:

General agreement exists among Orthodox writers on the following two points:

1. since at least one of the purposes of marriage is the birth of children, a couple acts immorally when it consistently uses contraceptive methods to avoid the birth of any children, if there are not extenuating circumstances;
2. contraception is also immoral when used to encourage the practice of fornication and adultery.

Less agreement exists among Eastern Orthodox authors on the issue of contraception within marriage for the spacing of children or for the limitation of the number of children. Some authors take a negative view and count any use of contraceptive methods within or outside of marriage as immoral (Papacostas, pp. 13-18; Gabriel Dionysiatou). These authors tend to emphasize as the primary and almost exclusive purpose of marriage the birth of children and their upbringing. They tend to consider any other exercise of the sexual function as the submission of this holy act to unworthy purposes, i.e., pleasure-seeking, passion, and bodily gratification, which are held to be inappropriate for the Christian growing in spiritual perfection. These teachers hold that the only alternative is sexual abstinence in marriage, which, though difficult, is both desirable and possible through the aid of the grace of God. It must be noted also that, for these writers, abortion and contraception are closely tied together, and often little or no distinction is made between the two. Further, it is hard to discern in their writings any difference in judgment between those who use contraceptive methods so as to have no children and those who use them to space and limit the number of children.

Other Orthodox writers have challenged this view by seriously questioning the Orthodoxy of the exclusive and all-controlling role of the procreative purpose of marriage (Zaphiris; Constantelos, 1975). Some note the inconsistency of the advocacy of sexual continence in marriage with the scriptural teaching that one of the purposes of marriage is to permit the ethical fulfillment of sexual drives, so as to avoid fornication and adultery (1 Cor. 7:1-7). Most authors, however, emphasize the sacramental nature of marriage and its place within the framework of Christian anthropology, seeing the sexual relationship of husband and wife as one aspect of the mutual growth of the couple in love and unity. T**his approach readily adapts itself to an ethical position that would not only permit but also enjoin sexual relationships of husband and wife for their own sake as expressions of mutual love. Such a view clearly would support the use of contraceptive practices for the purpose of spacing and limiting children so as to permit greater freedom of the couple in the expression of their mutual love**. (**For the Health of Body and Soul: An Eastern Orthodox Introduction to Bioethics**.)

These are not minor matters. And this all going to be "bridged" by means of appeals to the "heart"? Preposterous.

A mutual dislike of Scholasticism and a desire to "re-read" the Church Fathers without the "filter" provided by Saint Thomas Aquinas links Joseph Ratzinger/Benedict XVI's "New Theology" and the ambiguous doctrinal views of the Orthodox. I explored this in an article seventeen months ago now:

The following passages from Pope Pius XII's *Humani Generis*, August 12, 1950, describe--and condemn--the entirety of the intellectual work of Joseph Ratzinger/Benedict XVI. Joseph Ratzinger/Benedict XVI is using his "vague notions" and outright heresies to appeal for "unity" with the schismatic and heretical Orthodox churches without forcing them to accept the dogmatic pronouncements of the Second Millennium that were made without their "participation" and that were "distorted" by Scholasticism as a result:

> **Hence to neglect, or to reject, or to devalue so many and such great resources which have been conceived, expressed and perfected so often by the age-old work of men endowed with no common talent and holiness, working under the vigilant supervision of the holy magisterium and with the light and leadership of the Holy Ghost in order to state the truths of the faith ever more accurately, to do this so that these things may be replaced by conjectural notions and by some formless and unstable tenets of a new philosophy, tenets which, like the flowers of the field, are in existence today and die tomorrow; this is supreme imprudence and something that would make dogma itself a reed shaken by the wind. The contempt for terms and notions habitually used by scholastic theologians leads of itself to the weakening of what they call speculative theology, a discipline which these men consider devoid of true certitude because it is based on theological reasoning.**
>
> **Unfortunately these advocates of novelty easily pass from despising scholastic theology to the neglect of and even contempt for the Teaching Authority of the Church itself, which gives such authoritative approval to scholastic theology**. This Teaching Authority is represented by them as a hindrance to progress and an obstacle in the way of science. Some non Catholics consider it as an unjust restraint preventing some more qualified theologians from reforming their subject. And although this sacred Office of Teacher in matters of faith and morals must be the proximate and universal criterion of truth for all theologians, since to it has been entrusted by Christ Our Lord the whole deposit of faith -- **Sacred Scripture and divine Tradition -- to be preserved, guarded and interpreted, still the duty that is incumbent on the faithful to flee also those errors which more or less approach heresy, and accordingly "to keep also the constitutions and decrees by which such evil opinions are proscribed and forbidden by the Holy See," is sometimes as little known as if it did not exist. What is expounded in the Encyclical Letters of the Roman Pontiffs concerning the nature and constitution of the Church, is deliberately and habitually neglected by some with the idea of giving force to a certain vague notion which they profess to have found in the ancient Fathers, especially the Greeks. The Popes, they assert, do not wish to pass judgment on what is a matter of dispute among theologians, so recourse must be had to the early sources, and the recent constitutions and decrees of the Teaching Church must be explained from the writings of the ancients.** (Pope Pius XII, *Humani Generis*, August 12, 1950.)

Such is not the foundation of any kind of true reconciliation between the Orthodox and the *Catholic* Church, admitting that the counterfeit church of conciliarism can indeed "live" with these differences in the name of a false notion of "unity" and "love."

Chapter Eight

"Papal" Undermining of Belief in Papal Primacy and Purgatory

As propagators and disciples of a false religion, conciliarism, the "popes" of the counterfeit church of conciliarism have undermined belief in practically every tenet of the Sacred Deposit of Faith. The doctrinal, liturgical, moral and pastoral revolutions they have wrought and whose "evolution" they have overseen have produced several generations of Catholics who are not only ignorant of the true teaching and worship of the Catholic Church, but are positively hostile to it when someone attempts to discuss this with them.

The conciliar "popes," each of whom has been an egalitarian imbued with the ethos of both Protestantism and Judeo-Masonry, have undermined the doctrine of Papal Primacy in a number of ways.

Giovanni Battista Enrico Antonio Maria Montini/Paul VI, whom a conciliar presbyter in my acquaintance in the 1980s termed "Paul the Sick" and "Paolo Sicko," took off his papal tiara in November of 1963, laying it on the altar of the Basilica of Saint Peter as a manifestation of the conciliar "papacy's" surrender of any claim to temporal authority. This, of course, was nothing other than a complete mockery of the Social Reign of Christ the King and the very monarchical nature of the papacy itself.

Interestingly, the tiara which Antipope Montini wore for a little over four months was revolutionary in itself as it was made for him in an "art deco" style by the Archdiocese of Milan prior to the conclave that "elected" him on June 21, 1963, thus differing dramatically from the papal tiaras wore by Popes Pius IX through Pius XII and the first in the line of conciliar false "popes," Angelo Roncalli/John XXIII.

Montini/Paul VI also genuflected before the heretical and schismatic patriarch of the Greek Orthodox Church, Athenagoras I, on December 5, 1963, when the two met in Istanbul, Turkey, thus signifying, at least in a de facto sense, that Athenagoras was equal, if not superior, in authority of a putative Sovereign Pontiff of the Catholic Church.

As the counterfeit church of conciliarism is full of contradiction and paradox, however, Montini/Paul VI, who was "beatified" by Jorge Mario Bergoglio on Sunday, October 19, 2014, the Nineteenth Sunday after Pentecost, decreed the following in *Romano Pontifici Eligendo*, October 1, 1975:

> 92. Finally, the Pontiff will be crowned by the Senior Cardinal Deacon, and, within an appropriate time, will take possession of the Patriarchal Archbasilica of the Lateran, according to the ritual prescribed. (Giovanni Enrico Battista Antonio Mario Montini/Paul VI, *Romano Pontifici Eligendo*, October 1, 1975.)

Montini's successor in the line of conciliar "popes," Albino Luciani, caused quite a stir when he refused to follow the terms of his predecessor's *Romano Pontifici Eligendo* and chose not be crowned when he was "installed" with a pallium as the third conciliar "pope" on Sunday,

September 3, 1978. Thus was born another conciliar "tradition" that was followed by the conciliar Archbishop of Krakow, Poland, Karol Josef Wojtyla/John Paul II, when he was "installed" with the pallium on Sunday, October 22, 1978, six days after his "election" as the fourth conciliar "pope." This "tradition" has, of course been continued by Joseph Alois Ratzinger and Jorge Mario Bergoglio.

Perhaps inspired by Ratzinger, his handpicked prefect of the so-called Congregation for the Doctrine of the Faith, Karol Wojtyla/John Paul II became the first conciliar "pope" to speak of a "rethinking" of the "Petrine Ministry" after over twenty years of the little "papal" acts that whittled away at the notion of the papacy as a monarchy.

Wojtyla/John Paul II wrote the following in *Ut Unum Sint*, May 25, 1995, a heretical document that is the antithesis of Pope Pius XI's *Mortalium Animos*, January 6, 1928:

> Whatever relates to the unity of all Christian communities clearly forms part of the concerns of the primacy. As Bishop of Rome I am fully aware, as I have reaffirmed in the present Encyclical Letter, that Christ ardently desires the full and visible communion of all those Communities in which, by virtue of God's faithfulness, his Spirit dwells. I am convinced that I have a particular responsibility in this regard, above all in acknowledging the ecumenical aspirations of the majority of the Christian Communities and in heeding the request made of me to find a way of exercising the primacy which, while in no way renouncing what is essential to its mission, is nonetheless open to a new situation. **For a whole millennium Christians were united in "a brotherly fraternal communion of faith and sacramental life ... If disagreements in belief and discipline arose among them, the Roman See acted by common consent as moderator"**.
>
> **In this way the primacy exercised its office of unity. When addressing the Ecumenical Patriarch His Holiness Dimitrios I, I acknowledged my awareness that "for a great variety of reasons, and against the will of all concerned, what should have been a service sometimes manifested itself in a very different light. But ... it is out of a desire to obey the will of Christ truly that I recognize that as Bishop of Rome I am called to exercise that ministry ... I insistently pray the Holy Spirit to shine his light upon us, enlightening all the Pastors and theologians of our Churches, that we may seek—together, of course—the forms in which this ministry may accomplish a service of love recognized by all concerned"**.
>
> **This is an immense task, which we cannot refuse and which I cannot carry out by myself. Could not the real but imperfect communion existing between us persuade Church leaders and their theologians to engage with me in a patient and fraternal dialogue on this subject, a dialogue in which, leaving useless controversies behind, we could listen to one another, keeping before us only the will of Christ for his Church and allowing ourselves to be deeply moved by his plea "that they may all be one ... so that the world may believe that you have sent me"** (*Jn* 17:21)? (Karol Wojtyla/John Paul II, *Ut Unum Sint*, May 25, 1995.)

This is a theme, developed first by the then Joseph "Cardinal" Ratzinger in *Principles of Catholic Theology*, that became a hallmark of the "Saint John Paul II" "Petrine Ministry" for the following decade prior to his death on Friday, April 1, 2005 (or, according to the official Vatican line, Saturday, April 2, 2005). None other than the President of the "Pontifical" Council for Promoting Christian Unity, the now-retired but nevertheless active Walter "Cardinal" Kasper, elaborated on it when addressing Anglicans in England on May 24, 2003:

> It was Pope John Paul II who opened the door to future discussion on this subject. In his encyclical *Ut Unum Sint* (1995) he extended an invitation to a fraternal dialogue on **how to exercise the Petrine ministry in a way that is more acceptable to non-Catholic Christians. It was a source of pleasure for us that among others the Anglican community officially responded to this invitation. The Pontifical Council for Christian Unity gathered the many responses, analyzed the data, and sent its conclusions to the churches that had responded. We hope in this way to have initiated a second phase of a dialogue that will be decisive for the future of the ecumenical approach**.
>
> Nobody could reasonably expect that we could from the outset reach a phase of consensus; but what we have reached is not negligible. It has become evident that a new atmosphere and a new climate exist. In our globalized world situation the biblical testimonies on Peter and the Petrine tradition of Rome **are read with new eyes because in this new context the question of a ministry of universal unity, a common reference point and a common voice of the universal church, becomes urgent. Old polemical formulas stand at odds with this urgency; fraternal relations have become the norm.** Extensive research has been undertaken that has highlighted the different traditions between East and West already in the first millennium, and has traced the development in understanding and in practice of the Petrine ministry throughout the centuries. **As well, the historical conditionality of the dogma of the First Vatican Council (1869-70), which must be distinguished from its remaining obligatory content, has become clear. This historical development did not come to an end with the two Vatican Councils, but goes on, and so also in the future the Petrine ministry has to be exercised in line with the changing needs of the Church**.
>
> **These insights have led to a re-interpretation of the dogma of the Roman primacy**. This does not at all mean that there are still not enormous problems in terms of what such a ministry of unity should look like, how it should be administered, whether and to what degree it should have jurisdiction and whether under certain circumstances it could make infallible statements in order to guarantee the unity of the Church and at the same time the legitimate plurality of local churches. But there is at least a wide consensus about the common central problem, which all churches have to solve: how the three dimensions, highlighted already by the Lima documents on Baptism, Eucharist and Ministry (1982), namely unity through primacy, collegiality through synodality, and communality of all the faithful and their spiritual gifts, can be brought into a convincing synthesis. (**A Vision of Christian Unity for the Next Generation**.)

Ratzinger's resignation (and, yes, boys and girls, he *did* resign) from the conciliar "Petrine Ministry," which was announced on Monday, February 11, 2013, the Feast of the Apparition of

Our Lady of Lourdes, and became effective at 8:00 p.m., Rome time, on Thursday, February 28, 2013, was meant to establish a precedent that would be followed by the future universal public faces of apostasy (aka conciliar "popes").

None other than Jorge Mario Bergoglio/Francis, who has referred to his now-deceased "convergence theology" Anglican friend Tony Palmer as his "brother bishop," said in one of his endless series of interviews that his predecessor, Ratzinger/Benedict, had established an "institution" with his resignation:

> "I will do what the Lord tells me to do. Pray and try to follow God's will. Benedict XVI no longer had the strength and honestly, as a man of faith, humble as he is, he took this decision. **Seventy years ago, Popes Emeritus didn't exist. What will happen with Popes Emeritus? We need to look at Benedict XVI as an institution, he opened a door, that of the Popes Emeritus. The door is open, whether there will be others, only God knows. I believe that if a bishop of Rome feels he is losing his strength, he must ask himself the same questions Pope Benedict XVI did**." (**Interview Number I've Lost Count of the Number**.)

I predicted that conciliar "papal" resignations would become institutionalized when I wrote the following on February 14, 2013:

> Moreover, as noted two days ago in **Mister Asteroid Is Looking Pretty Good Right About Now**, Ratzinger/Benedict's resignation sets what will be considered as a mandatory precedent for all future executive directors of the Occupy Vatican Movement. And if God does not intervene to put an end the chastisement represented by the apostasies, blasphemies and sacrileges of conciliarism, the "papal" resignation might even lead to calls for "papal" "term limits" and for "re-election" by the conciliar college of colleges over four or eight years. After all, wouldn't this be in line with the "episcopal collegiality" that false "pontiff" praised yesterday as he termed this deviation from the Holy Faith to be an essential part of his new ecclesiology? (**Living In Fantasyland To The Very End, part one**.)

As has been noted in my articles in the past, however, the Ratzinger-Wojtyla-Kasper-Bergoglio contention about how the papacy functioned in the First Millennium is false.

Pope Leo XIII explained this very succinctly in *Praeclara Gratulationis Publicae*, June 29, 1894:

> First of all, then, We cast an affectionate look upon the East, from whence in the beginning came forth the salvation of the world. Yes, and the yearning desire of Our heart bids us conceive and hope that the day is not far distant when the Eastern Churches, so illustrious in their ancient faith and glorious past, will return to the fold they have abandoned. We hope it all the more, that the distance separating them from Us is not so great: nay, with some few exceptions, we agree so entirely on other heads that, in defense of the Catholic Faith, we often have recourse to reasons and testimony borrowed from the teaching, the Rites, and Customs of the East.

The Principal subject of contention is the Primacy of the Roman Pontiff. **But let them look back to the early years of their existence, let them consider the sentiments entertained by their forefathers, and examine what the oldest Traditions testify, and it will, indeed, become evident to them that Christ's Divine Utterance, Thou art Peter, and upon this rock I will build My Church, has undoubtedly been realized in the Roman Pontiffs. Many of these latter in the first gates of the Church were chosen from the East, and foremost among them Anacletus, Evaristus, Anicetus, Eleutherius, Zosimus, and Agatho**; and of these a great number, after Governing the Church in Wisdom and Sanctity, Consecrated their Ministry with the shedding of their blood. The time, the reasons, the promoters of the unfortunate division, are well known. **Before the day when man separated what God had joined together, the name of the Apostolic See was held in Reverence by all the nations of the Christian world: and the East, like the West, agreed without hesitation in its obedience to the Pontiff of Rome, as the Legitimate Successor of St. Peter, and, therefore, the Vicar of Christ here on earth**.

And, accordingly, if we refer to the beginning of the dissension, we shall see that Photius himself was careful to send his advocates to Rome on the matters that concerned him; and Pope Nicholas I sent his Legates to Constantinople from the Eternal City, without the slightest opposition, "in order to examine the case of Ignatius the Patriarch with all diligence, and to bring back to the Apostolic See a full and accurate report"; so that the history of the whole negotiation is a manifest Confirmation of the Primacy of the Roman See with which the dissension then began. Finally, in two great Councils, the second of Lyons and that of Florence, Latins and Greeks, as is notorious, easily agreed, and all unanimously proclaimed as Dogma the Supreme Power of the Roman Pontiffs.

We have recalled those things intentionally, for they constitute an invitation to peace and reconciliation; and with all the more reason that in Our own days it would seem as if there were a more conciliatory spirit towards Catholics on the part of the Eastern Churches, and even some degree of kindly feeling. To mention an instance, those sentiments were lately made manifest when some of Our faithful travelled to the East on a Holy Enterprise, and received so many proofs of courtesy and good-will.

Therefore, Our mouth is open to you, to you all of Greek or other Oriental Rites who are separated from the Catholic Church, We earnestly desire that each and every one of you should meditate upon the words, so full of gravity and love, addressed by Bessarion to your forefathers: "What answer shall we give to God when He comes to ask why we have separated from our Brethren: to Him Who, to unite us and bring us into One Fold, came down from Heaven, was Incarnate, and was Crucified? What will our defense be in the eyes of posterity? Oh, my Venerable Fathers, we must not suffer this to be, we must not entertain this thought, we must not thus so ill provide for ourselves and for our Brethren."

Weigh carefully in your minds and before God the nature of Our request. It is not for any human motive, but impelled by Divine Charity and a desire for the salvation of all, that We advise the reconciliation and union with the Church of Rome; **and We mean a perfect and complete union, such as could not subsist in any way if nothing else was brought**

> **about but a certain kind of agreement in the Tenets of Belief and an intercourse of Fraternal love. The True Union between Christians is that which Jesus Christ, the Author of the Church, instituted and desired, and which consists in a Unity of Faith and Unity of Government.**
>
> Nor is there any reason for you to fear on that account that We or any of Our Successors will ever diminish your rights, the privileges of your Patriarchs, or the established Ritual of any one of your Churches. It has been and always will be the intent and Tradition of the Apostolic See, to make a large allowance, in all that is right and good, for the primitive Traditions and special customs of every nation. On the contrary, if you re-establish Union with Us, you will see how, by God's bounty, the glory and dignity of your Churches will be remarkably increased. May God, then, in His goodness, hear the Prayer that you yourselves address to Him: "Make the schisms of the Churches cease," and "Assemble those who are dispersed, bring back those who err, and unite them to Thy Holy Catholic and Apostolic Church." May you thus return to that one Holy Faith which has been handed down both to Us and to you from time immemorial; which your forefathers preserved untainted, and which was enhanced by the rival splendor of the Virtues, the great genius, and the sublime learning of St. Athanasius and St. Basil, St. Gregory of Nazianzum and St. John Chrysostom, the two Saints who bore the name of Cyril, and so many other great men whose glory belongs as a common inheritance to the East and to the West. (See also the excellent discussion of the the history of what led up to the Greek Schism that is contained in Fathers Francisco and Dominic Radecki's **Tumultuous Times**.)

Hegelian revisionists must deny history and Catholic doctrine both at the same time in an effort to build yet another story to the One World Ecumenical Church.

Yes, the conciliar "popes" have been whittling away at the last great Catholic bastion that they have sought to raze, a supposedly "triumphalistic" notion of Papal Primacy that does not correspond to the conciliar "orientation" in the direction of collegiality and service as opposed to monarchy and rule.

Bergoglio's whole style of carrying himself is completely egalitarian as he eschews any sign of "papal" regality or formality, which is one of the reasons he chose to live at the Casa Santa Marta rather than within the Apostolic Palace inside the walls of the Occupied Vatican on the West Bank of the Tiber River.

Bergoglio/Francis's stylistic changes did not go unnoticed by the cutting edge liturgical revolutionaries of the Order of Saint Benedict at Saint John's Abbey in Collegeville, Minnesota, during the first two weeks of Bergoglio's masquerade as "Pope Francis."

The revolutionaries at Saint John's Abbey control what is called "Liturgical Press," which publishes some of the most revolutionary books on the "liturgical reform" imaginable and also publishes missalettes for use in Catholic churches that are in the control of the counterfeit church of conciliarism. The musical settings for the ordinary parts of the Protestant and Masonic liturgical service contain some of most insipid, profane melodies that are in the style of the theme music of *The Brady Brunch*. The hymns contained in those missalettes are equally insipid, and many are simply without a shred of Catholic content. It is thus very reasonable for these revolutionaries to note with great satisfaction **Francis The Jansenist**'s stylistic changes:

- After his election, he came down from platform to greet the cardinal electors, rather than have them come up to his level to offer obedience. He appeared on the loggia without the red cape. (The BBC report, unconfirmed, is that he said to his aide, "No thank you, Monsignore. You put it on instead. Carnival time is over.")
- In his greeting he referred to himself only as "bishop," not as "pope."
- He referred to Benedict as "bishop emeritus," not "pope emeritus."
- He appeared without the stole, only putting it on to give the blessing. He then took it off in public (!), as if he couldn't wait to get it off.
- He asked for the people's blessing before he blessed them.
- He doesn't wear red shoes.
- Or white stockings. · Or cuff links.
- He rode the bus back to the residence with the cardinals rather than take the papal limousine.
- When he went to Mary Major to pray, he declined the papal Mercedes and took a Volkswagen Passat.
- On his way back from Mary Major, he stopped at his pre-conclave hotel to get his luggage and pay his own bill. · Though he has taken possession of the apostolic palace, he continued to receive guests at St. Martha's House rather than the palace.
- He drank Argentinian tea in public when receiving the Argentinian president – protocol is that popes are seen publicly consuming no food or drink except the Eucharist.
- His first Mass with cardinals was celebrated facing the people. (Pope Benedict started this way, but then did a "reform of the reform" and celebrated at the old high altar in the Sistine Chapel facing away from the congregation. Apparently this has been reversed.)
- He doesn't chant the prayers, he recites them – but this could be because of an impaired lung or his singing ability.
- The wall of candles between celebrant and congregation, another of Pope Benedict's "reform of the reform," was moved away with three candles on each side of the altar.
- At his inauguration Mass, photos show that the candles were originally set up across the front of the altar, but by Mass time they had been moved to the side.
- The crucifix on the altar was a small one at his first Mass.
- He wore his own simple miter from Argentina, not the papal miter.
- He preached from the ambo without miter – rather like a simple parish priest. (The concelebrating cardinals gradually realized what was going on and had to remove the miters they had started to put on after the Gospel reading.)
- He brushed aside the prepared Latin homily and preached in Italian without text.
- In general, less lace.
- His hands are folded during the liturgy, not the pious (some say prissy) way with palms together.

- He didn't genuflect at the Supper Narrative of the Eucharistic Prayer – is this really because of bad knees?
- He asked the cardinals not to wear their red cardinals' robes, but black. · He stood on the floor of the Clementine Hall to greet the cardinals rather than sit on the throne on the platform.
- He called them "brother cardinals" rather than "Lord cardinals."
- He bent to kiss the ring of a cardinal who kissed his ring.
- At his meeting with over 5,000 journalists, after Archbishop Celli introduced him, he got up to walk over to him (popes don't do that) and thanked him.
- He didn't bless the journalists like popes do, since not all of them are Catholic or believers. Instead he prayed for them in silence, then simply said "God bless you."
- After the meeting with journalists, he waved away the papal limousine and walked to the Vatican residence.
- When he saw the papal apartments he said, "There's room for 300 people here. I don't need all this space." He has yet to move into the apartments, and some wonder whether he will.
- At Mass Sunday at the Vatican parish Sunday morning, he gave the Kiss of Peace to the deacons and Master of Ceremonies, not just the concelebrants. This is breaking the rules – but perhaps also a nice show of support for MC Marini, who must be reeling from all the sudden changes.
- The deacon didn't kneel before Pope Francis for the blessing before the gospel (as they did for John Paul II and Benedict XVI).
- He doesn't wear the dalmatic. Pope Benedict revived the practice, not foreseen in the reformed liturgical books, of wearing this deacon's vestment under his papal vestments.
- He doesn't distribute Communion as the missal foresees of the celebrant, but is seated while others do so.
- He listened to the words of the Patriarch of Constantinople seated on an armchair rather than the throne that is customarily used in the Clementine Hall. When he thanked Bartholomew I, he called him "my brother Andrew."
- He has simplified his coat of arms, keeping the miter rather than tiara (as Benedict also did) but removing the pallium from it. · He is wearing a second-hand pallium.
- He has chosen a simple ring, re-using a ring once made for Paul VI's secretary.
- Pope Benedict recently began wearing a fanon under the pallium for big feasts, but Francis did not wear it as the inauguration Mass.
- He undid Pope Benedict's decision that all the cardinals would come up to pay obedience to the Pope at his inauguration, and decided that six representatives would be enough.
- Rather than being seated while they came up to pay him obedience, he stood and greeted them informally.
- Contrary to protocol, he has given a phone call to the Jesuit superior general, the people holding a prayer vigil outside the Buenos Aires cathedral, and the guy in Argentina who sold him his daily paper (to cancel his delivery).

- When he met the Jesuit general, he apologized for not keeping protocol and insisted on being treated like any other Jesuit with the "tu" informal address, rather than "Your Holiness" or "Holy Father."
- He is not celebrating Holy Thursday Mass of the Lord's Supper in St. Peter's Basilica (he hasn't yet taken possession of his cathedral, John Lateran), but in a juvenile prison.
- He celebrated an unannounced Mass at St. Martha's with hotel workers, Vatican gardeners, and people who clean St. Peter's square. He showed up before Mass and sat in the back row to pray a bit.
- In his official photograph, he signs his name simply "Franciscus" without "PP" ("pontifex pontificum") used by previous popes. (**Francis the Jansenist Is Our Hero, Our Dream Come True**.)

Sometimes it is the revolutionaries who provide the best, most comprehensive, incisive and concise summaries of why conciliarism is not Catholicism, which means that the "popes" or "Petrine Ministers" of the counterfeit church of conciliarism have no share whatsoever in the true communion of the Catholic Faith and are outside of the bosom of Holy Mother Church and thus in great peril of eternal loss. The way has been prepared for a revolutionary such as Jorge Mario Bergoglio/Francis after fifty-five years of **whittling away at one Catholic bastion after another**.

Bergoglio himself has expressed his desire for the exercise of the conciliar "Petrine Ministry" with what he terms as a "synodality" more in concert with the revisionist history of the papacy during the First Millennium:

> A fundamental contribution to the search for full communion between Catholics and Orthodox is offered by the Joint International Commission for Theological Dialogue, co-chaired by Your Eminence, Metropolitan Ioannis, and by my venerable brother Cardinal Kurt Koch. I sincerely thank you for your valuable and tireless commitment. **This Commission has already produced many common texts and is now studying the delicate issue of theological and ecclesiological relationship between primacy and synodality in the life of the Church. It is significant that today we are able to reflect together, in truth and love, on these issues, starting with what we have in common, but without hiding that which still separates us. This is not merely a theoretical exercise, but one of getting to know each other's traditions in order to understand, and sometimes also to learn from them. I refer for example to the reflection of the Catholic Church on the meaning of episcopal collegiality, and the tradition of synodality, so typical of the Orthodox Churches**. I am confident that the effort of shared reflection, so complex and laborious, will bear fruit in due time. I am comforted to know that Catholics and Orthodox share the same conception of dialogue that does not seek a theological minimalism on which to reach a compromise, but rather is based on the deepening of the one truth that Christ has given to His Church, which we never cease to understand better as we are moved by the Holy Spirit. For this, we should not be afraid of encounter and of true dialogue. It does not take us away from the truth, but rather, through an exchange of gifts, it leads us, under the guidance of the Spirit of truth, to the whole truth (cf. Jn 16:13). (**Francis the Flexible to Orthodox delegation from Ecumenical Patriarchate**.)

Ratzinger and Bergoglio have distorted history to suit their perverted purposes of effecting a false "communion" with the Orthodox. Those in the Motu world, especially those who believe in "resignationism," must suspend all pretense of rationality to contend that their man "Benedict" is more "orthodox" that the "bad" Bergoglio. Each man is more [Greek] Orthodox than Catholic. Indeed, neither man is a Catholic as they defect from numerous points of Catholic doctrine, placing them outside of the Catholic Faith.

Some, such as Joseph Alois Ratzinger/Benedict XVI, give lip-service to Purgatory without adhering to the defined doctrine of the Catholic Church on it, preferring the murkiness of Orthodoxy rather than the actual teaching of Holy Mother Church.

This is what the then "Petrine Minister" of the counterfeit church of conciliarism said about Purgatory in early-2011 as he misrepresented the teaching of Saint Catherine of Genoa:

> Catherine's thought on purgatory, for which she is particularly known, is condensed in the last two parts of the book mentioned at the beginning: "Treatise on Purgatory" and "Dialogues on the Soul and Body." It is important to observe that, in her mystical experience, Catherine never had specific revelations on purgatory or on souls that are being purified there. However, in the writings inspired by our saint purgatory is a central element, and the way of describing it has original characteristics in relation to her era.
>
> The first original feature refers to the "place" of the purification of souls. **In her time [purgatory] was presented primarily with recourse to images connected to space: There was thought of a certain space where purgatory would be found. For Catherine, instead, purgatory is not represented as an element of the landscape of the core of the earth; it is a fire that is not exterior but interior. This is purgatory, an interior fire.**
>
> The saint speaks of the soul's journey of purification to full communion with God, based on her own experience of profound sorrow for the sins committed, in contrast to the infinite love of God (cf. Vita Mirabile, 171v). We have heard about the moment of her conversion, when Catherine suddenly felt God's goodness, the infinite distance of her life from this goodness and a burning fire within her. And this is the fire that purifies, it is the interior fire of purgatory. Here also there is an original feature in relation to the thought of the era. She does not begin, in fact, from the beyond to narrate the torments of purgatory -- as was usual at that time and perhaps also today -- and then indicate the path for purification or conversion. Instead our saint begins from her own interior experience of her life on the path to eternity. The soul, says Catherine, appears before God still bound to the desires and the sorrow that derive from sin, and this makes it impossible for it to enjoy the Beatific Vision of God. Catherine affirms that God is so pure and holy that the soul with stains of sin cannot be in the presence of the Divine Majesty (cf. Vita Mirabile, 177r). And we also realize how far we are, how full we are of so many things, so that we cannot see God. The soul is conscious of the immense love and perfect justice of God and, in consequence, suffers for not having responded correctly and perfectly to that love, and that is why the love itself of God becomes a flame. Love itself purifies it from its dross of sin.

> Theological and mystical sources typical of the era can be found in Catherine's work. Particularly there is an image from Dionysius the Areopagite: that of the golden thread that unites the human heart with God himself. When God has purified man, he ties him with a very fine thread of gold, which is his love, and attracts him to himself with such strong affection that man remains as "overcome and conquered and altogether outside himself." Thus the human heart is invaded by the love of God, which becomes the only guide, the sole motor of his existence (cf. Vita Mirabile, 246rv). This situation of elevation to God and of abandonment to his will, expressed in the image of the thread, is used by Catherine to express the action of the divine light on souls in purgatory, light that purifies them and elevates them to the splendors of the shining rays of God (cf. Vita Mirabile, 179r).
>
> Dear friends, the saints, in their experience of union with God, reach such profound "knowledge" of the divine mysteries, in which love and knowledge are fused, that they are of help to theologians themselves in their task of study, of "intelligentia fidei," of "intelligentia" of the mysteries of the faith, of real deepening in the mysteries, for example, of what purgatory is. (**Text of Benedict/Ratzinger January 12, 2011, General Audience Address**.)

As readers of this site are aware, Ratzinger/Benedict has always taught that the entirety of Catholic teaching must be placed in the context of historical circumstances. He is a Modernist. He believes that images of souls burning in the fires of Purgatory are merely representations common to "the time" in which Saint Catherine of Genoa lived, using her own mystical experiences to cast doubt on the existence of Purgatory as an actual *state*. According to Ratzinger/Benedict, Purgatory is merely an "experience" of purification whereby the soul is made pure interiorly by the light of God's love. He believes that writings such as those of Saint Catherine of Genoa must guide "theologians" in their "deepening" of what Purgatory is.

While one could, quite understandably, be tempted to say that the retired false "pontiff" had contradicted Catholic teaching very clearly in this instance, it is far more accurate to state that he was undermining Catholic teaching by proposing something that had the "appearance of falsehood." He was careful not to deny the existence of Purgatory. It was his clear intention, however, to make Catholic teaching on it appear to be uncertain and in need of further "study" and "understanding." Such is the very *modus vivendi* (the mode of living) of Modernists. Ratzinger/Benedict was saying, yes, Purgatory exists. We simply don't know that much about it yet.

Yet it is that Pope Clement VI's *Super Quibusdam*, to the Consolator, the Cathicon of the Armenian Orthodox, made it clear that existence in Purgatory as a place, not a "state," is something that the Orthodox, whose murky theology is held is such high regard by both Ratzinger/Benedict and his successor, Cartoon Jorge Mario Bergoglio, must believe to be accepted back into the Catholic Church:

> We ask if you have believed and now believe that there is a purgatory to which depart the souls of those dying in grace who have not yet made complete satisfaction for their sins. Also, if you have believed and now believe that they will be tortured by fire for a time and that as soon as they are cleansed, even before the day of judgment, they may come to the

> true and eternal beatitude which consists in the vision of God face to face and in love. (Pope Clement VI, *Super Quibusdam*, To the Consolator, the Catholicon of the Armenians, September 20, 1351. As found in Henry Denzinger, *Enchirdion Symbolorum*, thirteenth edition, translated into English by Roy Deferrari and published in 1955 as *The Sources of Catholic Dogma*--referred to as "Denziger," by B. Herder Book Company of St. Louis, Missouri, and London, England, No. 570s, p. 206.)

Moreover, it was one hundred eight years later that the Council of Florence required belief in Purgatory as condition for all of the Greeks to be reunited with the Catholic Church:

> It has been likewise defined, that, if those truly penitent have departed in the love of God, before they have made satisfaction by worthy fruits of penance for sins of commission and omission, the souls of these are cleansed after death by purgatorial punishments and so that they may be released from punishments of this kind, the suffrages of the living faithful are of advantage to them, namely, the sacrifices of Masses, prayers, and almsgiving, and other works of piety, which are customarily performed by the faithful for other faithful according to the institutions of the Church. And that the souls of those, who after their reception of baptism have incurred no stain of sin whether in their bodies, or when released from the same bodies, as we have said before, are purged, are immediately received into heaven, and see clearly the one and triune God Himself, just as He is, yet according to the diversity of merits, one more perfectly than another. Moreover the souls of those who depart in actual mortal sin or in original sin only, descend immediately into hell but to undergo punishments of different kinds. (Pope Eugene IV, *Laetentur Coeli*, July 6, 1439, Decree for the Greeks, Council of Florence. As found in Henry Denzinger, *Enchirdion Symbolorum*, thirteenth edition, translated into English by Roy Deferrari and published in 1955 as *The Sources of Catholic Dogma*--referred to as "Denziger," by B. Herder Book Company of St. Louis, Missouri, and London, England, No. 693 p. 220.)

It is especially interesting that the next passage from the Decree for the Greeks demanded belief in Papal Primacy, putting the lie to the oft-expressed error of the likes of 'Saint John Paul II," Ratzinger/Benedict and Cartoon Jorge that said primacy can be "exercised" in a manner that would please Protestants and the Orthodox:

> We likewise defined that the holy Apostolic See, and the Roman Pontiff, hold the primacy throughout the entire world; and that the Roman Pontiff himself is the successor of blessed Peter, the chief of the Apostles, and the true vicar of Christ, and that he is the head of the entire Church, and the father and teacher of all Christians; and that full power was given to him in blessed Peter by our Lord Jesus Christ, the food, rule, and govern the universal Church; just as is contained in the acts of the ecumenical Councils and the sacred canons. (Pope Eugene IV, *Laetentur Coeli*, July 6, 1439, Decree for the Greeks, Council of Florence. As found in Henry Denzinger, *Enchirdion Symbolorum*, thirteenth edition, translated into English by Roy Deferrari and published in 1955 as *The Sources of Catholic Dogma*--referred to as "Denziger," by B. Herder Book Company of St. Louis, Missouri, and London, England, No. 694, p. 220.)

Jorge Mario Bergoglio continued to undermine Catholic doctrine on Papal Primacy and other matters of "difference" with the heretical and schismatic Greek Orthodox during he visted Constantinople on November 30, 2014, the Feast of Saint Andrew the Apostle. The currently reigning "Petrine Minister" demanded nothing of what Pope Eugene IV and the Council of Florence decreed five hundred seventy-five years ago now, including belief in Purgatory. That is all just "ancient history" that was "conditioned" by the circumstances of the time as the Greeks were, it is alleged, treated "unfairly" even though the Council of Florence met under the guidance of the Third Person of the Most Blessed Trinity, God the Holy Ghost, Who directed the Decree on the Greeks to be issued in the exact form that it was expressed by Pope Eugene and the Fathers of the Council of Florence.

Chapter Nine

Red China: Workshop for the New Theology

Joseph "Cardinal" Zen Ze-kiun, the former conciliar "bishop" of Hong Kong, was ordained as a priest for the Salesians of Saint John Bosco on February 11, 1961, the Feast of the Apparition of Our Lady of Lourdes. He has spent over sixty-five years of his eighty-two years of life living under the iron rule of the Red Chinese butchers. He is a firm opponent of Communism, about which Angelo Roncalli/John XXIII wanted nothing said at the "Second" Vatican Council (see the section below), and has manfully denounced the conciliar Vatican's appeasement of the Butchers of Beijing that has been ongoing for some decades now, especially since the issuance of the now retired Joseph Ratzinger/Benedict XVI's **Letter to Bishops, Priests, Consecrated Persons and Lay Faithful of Red China**, June 30, 2007, doing so with particular force in 2013:

> TORONTO - At 81 years old, the bishop who once led hundreds of thousands through the streets of Hong Kong — defying Beijing, demanding democracy and an accountable government — is not holding his tongue.
>
> Hong Kong's retired Cardinal Joseph Zen warns of an impending schism in the Chinese Catholic Church and blames the Vatican for allowing Communist Party officials to run roughshod over China's bishops.
>
> "For years they (the Communist Party of China) had everything their way. The Holy See adopted a policy of appeasement and compromise," Zen told The Catholic Register while in Toronto to deliver an early February address to Convivium magazine subscribers. "So they were happy that they could control more and more the Catholic Church, and they could make slaves of the bishops."
>
> Chinese Catholics on the mainland are split between the underground Church and officially registered churches, while the Chinese government interferes in the appointment of bishops. There is a serious risk of a Chinese schism, said the cardinal.
>
> "Do you know what I write to the Holy Father?" Zen asked. "I say it is only because of your kindness that the official Church is not called schismatic. It is actually schismatic without being named. It's risking being a schismatic Church with the blessing of the Holy See, because the Holy Father cannot command that Church. The whole command is in the hands of the government."
>
> Zen is aware his warnings lack prudence.
>
> "For a long time I have abstained from talking about the Holy See," he said. "But I think that is unfair. We must be fair to everybody. They (Vatican officials) should take the responsibility."
>
> The Catholic Church in both Shanghai and Wuhan have recently faced off with Chinese government officials.

In Shanghai the coadjutor Bishop Thaddeus Ma Daqin was relieved of all public ministry and had his episcopal appointment revoked by the Chinese episcopal conference — a body not recognized by the Vatican. At his ordination last July, Ma caused government panic when he announced he would step down from his position with the Chinese Patriotic Catholic Association to concentrate on his pastoral ministry as bishop of Shanghai. Faithful in Shanghai's cathedral greeted the announcement with extended applause, but Ma was immediately sent away on a retreat, sequestered in Shanghai's seminary. In December the Bishops' Conference of the Catholic Church of China revoked Ma's Shanghai appointment, which would have seen him eventually become bishop of Shanghai. The bishops' conference also let it be known that for all future appointments "a pledge of loyalty" would be required.

It's obvious that the bishop's conference is controlled by the State Administration for Religious Affairs, which also founded the Chinese Catholic Patriotic Association in 1957, said Zen.

"You can see all the presidents and vice presidents, both in the patriotic association and the so-called bishops' conference — they are all slaves of the government," said Zen. "There are some illegitimate, some legitimate (bishops), but they are all on the side of the government."

In Wuhan, State Administration for Religious Affairs officials have stepped in to cancel a pastoral plan that would have reorganized the diocese with priests shuffled among parishes. Zen warns that the next step will be for the government to impose a government-appointed bishop on Wuhan without Vatican approval. The Wuhan seminary has been closed and Chinese Catholic Patriotic Association officials are turning away seminary candidates, Zen said.

China and the Vatican have clashed over the appointment of bishops since shortly after Communist Party Chairman Mao Ze Dong declared the new People's Republic in 1949. In the mid-1950s China's new government discovered that the monarchy in Portugal retained the right to recommend bishops for China to the Holy Father. The new Chinese administration viewed this arrangement as clearly colonial interference in the internal affairs of China.

China's government declared it would henceforth exercise the powers of the Portuguese crown in appointing bishops. However, under Pope Pius XII the Holy See refused to acknowledge the communist government. For many years there were simply no appointments. Then during the Cultural Revolution of the 1960s and '70s, many Catholic bishops were accused to being counter-revolutionaries in league with foreign powers. The bishops found themselves in re-education camps and prisons.

Throughout this period the Communist Party of China promoted the "Three Self " principles in religious affairs. Rooted in Protestant missionary work in China before the turn of the 20th century, the Three Self movement promoted self-governance, self-support and self-propogation. It meant that Chinese churches should operate without financial support from outside China and that evangelization should be the work of Chinese themselves.

It's not the Three Self principles themselves that inhibit the Catholic Church in China, said Zen.

"You can practise the Three Self principles in a decent way," Zen said. "Now they practise in an indecent way. They impose an imperial command on the Church. They are treating the bishops as slaves. They just bring them here or there like dogs on a chain."

The principles presume the Church in China is independent enough to govern itself without government oversight.

"This is not possible without the internal witness in the Church. The Holy See has a long policy of compromise and in China there are weak people in the Church," Zen said.

Zen dismisses the Chinese government insistence on assuming the powers of the Portuguese crown as a mere pretext for communist control. When the king of Portugal proposed bishops for China it was a Catholic king of a Catholic country advising the pope, who was free to make his own choice.

"Under an atheist government, how can you accept bishops proposed by the government? It's ridiculous," said Zen. (**Vatican appeases Chinese government**.)

"Cardinal" Zen spoke the truth in 2013, doing so courageously. What he does not understand, however, is that appeasement of Communism has been a cornerstone of conciliarism, whose "popes" and "bishops" and priests/presbyters have suborned one error after another in matters of Faith, Worship and Morals. All manner of enemies of the Cross of the Divine Redeemer, Christ the King, have been appeased, starting most infamously with adherents of Talmud.

Protestants have been appeased.

Mohammedans have been appeased.

The Orthodox have been appeased.

Buddhists have been appeased.

Hindus have been appeased.

Practitioners of voodoo and other forms of animism have been appeased.

Catholics and non-Catholics in public life who support the chemical and surgical execution of innocent babies and who support special "rights," including "marriage," for those who are engaged in perverse sins against the Sixth and Ninth Commandments have been appeased.

Non-Communist statists have been appeased.

Environmentalists have been appeased.

Feminists have been appeased.

Actual practitioners of perversity have been appeased.

God has been profaned in formerly Catholic churches by hideous, abominable and sacramentally invalid liturgical rites.

In all of this, you see, the fomenters, propagators and institutionalizers of the "Second" Vatican Council have been appeasing the devil.

"Cardinal" Zen does not see this. Neither did I for far too many years.

It is important to see how Joseph Ratzinger/Benedict XVI used the terrible situation of the Catholic Church in Red China as a veritable workshop in his "new ecclesiology" as Jorge Mario Bergoglio, who has met Communists who are “good people,” intends to effect a final sellout of the underground Catholics in that enslaved country.

A Religion of Workshops

One of the banes of existence in the structures of the counterfeit church of concilairism is the use of the brainwashing tool called the "workshop," which is a device used to engage in "re-education,” "continuing education," and "theological and/or liturgical 'updating.'" Attendance at diocesan "workshops" is compulsory in many instances for priests and presbyters within a diocese. Although some of the more "conservative" or "traditionally-minded" priests and presbyters in the conciliar structures may grumble and grouse privately about these "workshops," most of them will attend these "workshops": in order to not to be sent to their diocesan equivalents of Siberia or to run the risk of losing a chance at promotion or appointment to or retention as the pastor of a parish in conciliar captivity.

Joseph Ratzinger/Benedict XVI used his false "pontificate" as a sort of universal "workshop" to institutionalize the conciliar revolution that he helped to plan in the years leading up to the "Second" Vatican Council. Ratzinger/Benedict has never retracted one word of anything he has ever written. He has never abjured any of his errors. He told us in his very own words that he is, at least in all essential things, same as "Benedict XVI" as he had been in the past:

> I've been taken apart various times: in my first phase as professor and in the intermediate phase, during my first phase as Cardinal and in the successive phase. Now comes a new division. Of course circumstances and situations and even people influence you because you take on different responsibilities. Let's say that my basic personality and even my basic vision have grown, **but in everything that is essential I have remained identical. I'm happy that certain aspects that weren't noticed at first are now coming into the open**.

(**Interview with Bayerische Rundfunk (ARD), ZDF, Deutsche Welle and Vatican Radio.)**

As I have noted in many articles, including **Singing the Old Songs** and **"Connecting" with Betrayal**, I know what it is to "project" one's own *sensus Catholicus* into the minds and hearts of the conciliar "popes." I did it for far too long with Karol Wojtyla/John Paul II, ignoring the plain evidence that was right in front of my face. This "projection" of Catholicism into the heart and mind of the former current conciliar "pontiff," Joseph Ratzinger/Benedict XVI took place even in spite of such frank admissions as he, Ratzinger/Benedict, gave in an interview to a reporter from a German television station in 2006. Ratzinger/Benedict has abjured nothing from his past.

Thus it is that "conservative" Catholics yet attached to the structures of the counterfeit church of concilairism are continuing to "project" Catholic thoughts and beliefs in the mind and heart of a man, Ratzinger/Benedict, who has been **at war with the Catholic Faith** throughout the course of his priesthood, even as he is in retirement.

Thus it is also that many traditionally-minded Catholics who had pinned their hopes on the "restoration" of the Church by means of Ratzinger/Benedict's *Summorum Pontificum*, July 7, 2007, had to pretend as though their past and most withering critiques of Joseph "Cardinal" Ratzinger never existed while others feigned righteous indignation when others drew the exact same conclusions about "Benedict XVI's" words and actions as they had done for years and years about "Cardinal" Ratzinger (and about the words and actions of Karol Wojtyla/John Paul II).

Ratzinger/Benedict, meanwhile, just went about his business of institutionalizing the conciliar revolution while he used his false "pontificate" as a sort of "workshop" to give a "papal" imprimatur, if you will, to the *corpus* of his writings over the decades.

This is something that ultra-progressivist revolutionaries in the conciliar structures do not understand, believing in the illusion of the former "pope" as a "conservative" because he had "liberalized" the offerings/stagings of the modernized version of the Immemorial Mass of Tradition, disregarding the fact that he, Ratzinger/Benedict, was only trying to patiently and methodically prepare the way for the introduction of more and more novelties into that modernized version of the Traditional Mass (changing the Good Friday Prayer for the Jews, seeking to have some of the new prefaces used in Motu venues, incorporating the "saints" "canonized" by the conciliar "popes," having readings done in the "vernacular" without being read in Latin at all, not forbidding the use of altar girls or the reception of what purports to be Holy Communion in the hand, to name just a few).

As **Weak In Mind, Weakest Yet In The Faith**, Ratzinger/Benedict told the ultra-progressive revolutionaries, that is, the conciliar "bishops" who were livid with him for "lifting" the "excommunications" of the four bishops of the Society of Saint Pius X on Wednesday, January 21, 2009, the Feast of Saint Agnes, that his intention was to blunt criticism of the conciliar revolution from the Society of Saint Pius X just as such criticism had been blunted (indeed, entirely muted) from the existing Motu communities by reforming "one-sided" positions:

So if the arduous task of working for faith, hope and love in the world is presently (and, in various ways, always) the Church's real priority, then part of this is also made up of acts of reconciliation, small and not so small. That the quiet gesture of extending a hand gave rise to a huge uproar, and thus became exactly the opposite of a gesture of reconciliation, is a fact which we must accept. But I ask now: Was it, and is it, truly wrong in this case to meet half-way the brother who 'has something against you' and to seek reconciliation? **Should not civil society also try to forestall forms of extremism and to incorporate their eventual adherents - to the extent possible - in the great currents shaping social life, and thus avoid their being segregated, with all its consequences? Can it be completely mistaken to work to break down obstinacy and narrowness, and to make space for what is positive and retrievable for the whole? I myself saw, in the years after 1988, how the return of communities which had been separated from Rome changed their interior attitudes; I saw how returning to the bigger and broader Church enabled them to move beyond one-sided positions and broke down rigidity so that positive energies could emerge for the whole**. Can we be totally indifferent about a community which has 491 priests, 215 seminarians, 6 seminaries, 88 schools, 2 university-level institutes, 117 religious brothers, 164 religious sisters and thousands of lay faithful? Should we casually let them drift farther from the Church? I think for example of the 491 priests. We cannot know how mixed their motives may be. All the same, I do not think that they would have chosen the priesthood if, alongside various distorted and unhealthy elements, they did not have a love for Christ and a desire to proclaim Him and, with Him, the living God. Can we simply exclude them, as representatives of a radical fringe, from our pursuit of reconciliation and unity? What would then become of them?

"Certainly, for some time now, and once again on this specific occasion, we have heard from some representatives of that community many unpleasant things - arrogance and presumptuousness, an obsession with one-sided positions, etc. Yet to tell the truth, I must add that I have also received a number of touching testimonials of gratitude which clearly showed an openness of heart. But should not the great Church also allow herself to be generous in the knowledge of her great breadth, in the knowledge of the promise made to her? **Should not we, as good educators, also be capable of overlooking various faults and making every effort to open up broader vistas**? And should we not admit that some unpleasant things have also emerged in Church circles? At times one gets the impression that our society needs to have at least one group to which no tolerance may be shown; which one can easily attack and hate. And should someone dare to approach them - in this case the Pope - he too loses any right to tolerance; he too can be treated hatefully, without misgiving or restraint. (**LETTER ON REMISSION OF EXCOMMUNICATION LEFEBVRE BISHOP**)

Any Catholic is very badly deceived if he believed, no less publicly asserted as being true, the absurd proposition that that Joseph Ratzinger/Benedict was a restorer of the Catholic Faith even though he, Ratzinger/Benedict, lacked the most rudimentary understanding of the First Commandment's direct and absolute prohibition against any esteem being paid to false religions, no less the public scandal he caused to Catholics and non-Catholics alike by calling "mosques" "sacred" places and "jewels" that stand out on the "face of the earth" and by agreeing to refrain from making any efforts at all to seek to convert those steeped in the false religion of Talmudic

Judaism. To refuse to rise to the defense of the honor and majesty and glory of God, as so many priests and presbyters in the conciliar structures, including the Motu communities and the Society of Saint Pius X, did during Ratzinger/Benedict's reign brings to mind once again these telling words of Pope Saint Leo the Great:

> **But it is vain for them to adopt the name of catholic, as they do not oppose these blasphemies: they must believe them, if they can listen so patiently to such words.** (Pope Saint Leo the Great, Epistle XIV, To Anastasius, Bishop of Thessalonica, **St. Leo the Great | Letters 1-59**)

I. The "Workshop" Against the Nature of Dogmatic Truth

As noted in Chapters Four and Five, Ratzinger/Benedict used his false "pontificate" to give "papal" expression to his lifelong warfare against the nature of dogmatic truth. There is no need to repeat again what was explained in those chapters.

II. The "Workshop" Against Scholasticism and the Church's Dogmatic Teachings

As noted in Chapter Five, Joseph Ratzinger/Benedict XVI believes that the Scholasticism of Saint Thomas Aquinas "corrupted" a "proper" reading of Sacred Scripture and of the Fathers of the Church, making "reconciliation" with Protestants and, quite particularly, the Orthodox, more "difficult" as a result. This means, of course, that the Fathers of the dogmatic councils and the popes who have relied upon Saint Thomas Aquinas and the Scholastic method were wrong to have done so. (Please see **Ratzinger's War Against Catholicism**.)

To this end, therefore, Ratzinger/Benedict tried to "correct" the "corruption" of Scholasticism by using his "general audience" addresses to make Saint Paul the Apostle and various Fathers of the Church serve as "witnesses" in behalf of conciliarism (see **Attempting to Coerce Perjury**).

Ratzinger/Benedict even tried to make Saint Augustine a witness in behalf of "religious liberty," which Saint Augustine, as Pope Pius VII noted in *Post Tam Diuturnas*, April 29, 1814, specifically condemned:

> For when the liberty of all "religions" is indiscriminately asserted, by this very fact truth is confounded with error and the holy and immaculate Spouse of Christ, the Church, outside of which there can be no salvation, is set on a par with the sects of heretics and with Judaic perfidy itself. **For when favour and patronage is promised even to the sects of heretics and their ministers, not only their persons, but also their very errors, are tolerated and fostered: a system of errors in which is contained that fatal and never sufficiently to be deplored HERESY which, as St. Augustine says (*de Haeresibus*, no.72), "asserts that all heretics proceed correctly and tell the truth: which is so absurd that it seems incredible to me.**" (Pope Pius VII, *Post Tam Diuturnas*, April 29, 1814.)

III. The "Workshop" in Behalf of False Ecumenism

Ratzinger/Benedict has tried to make Saint Paul a "witness" in behalf of a false ecumenism that the Apostle to the Gentiles specifically condemned in no uncertain terms:

> For know you this and understand, that no fornicator, or unclean, or covetous person (which is a serving of idols), hath inheritance in the kingdom of Christ and of God.
>
> Let no man deceive you with vain words. For because of these things cometh the anger of God upon the children of unbelief. Be ye not therefore partakers with them. For you were heretofore darkness, but now light in the Lord. Walk then as children of the light. For the fruit of the light is in all goodness, and justice, and truth; Proving what is well pleasing to God:
>
> And have no fellowship with the unfruitful works of darkness, but rather reprove them. For the things that are done by them in secret, it is a shame even to speak of. But all things that are reproved, are made manifest by the light; for all that is made manifest is light. Wherefore he saith: Rise thou that sleepest, and arise from the dead: and Christ shall enlighten thee. See therefore, brethren, how you walk circumspectly: not as unwise, But as wise: redeeming the time, because the days are evil. Wherefore become not unwise, but understanding what is the will of God. (Ephesians 5: 5-17.)

Joseph "Cardinal" Ratzinger wrote in *Principles of Catholic Theology* that the "unity" of the Church could not be effected by demanding the unconditional conversion of Protestants and the Orthodox to the Catholic Faith that would result in the destruction of their "structures" and a denial of their "history." One will see in the passage below Ratzinger's belief that "distinctions" must be made between what is true "in reality" and what has been "claimed" to be "true" as a result of contingent circumstances. In other words, Protestants and the Orthodox cannot be "forced" to accept the results of various dogmatic councils and/or papal pronouncements that are said to be the "products" of historical circumstances that have now changed:

> Against this background we can now weigh the possibilities that are open to Christian ecumenism. The maximum demands on which the search for unity must certainly founder are immediately clear. On the part of the West, the maximum demand would be that the East recognize the primacy of the bishop of Rome in the full scope of the definition of 1870 and in so doing submit in practice, to a primacy such as has been accepted by the Uniate churches. On the part of the East, the maximum demand would be that the West declare the 1870 doctrine of primacy erroneous and in so doing submit, in practice, to a primacy such as has been accepted with the removal of the Filioque from the Creed and including the Marian dogmas of the nineteenth and twentieth centuries. As regards Protestantism, the maximum demand of the Catholic Church would be that the Protestant ecclesiological ministers be regarded as totally invalid and that Protestants be converted to Catholicism; the maximum demand of Protestants, on the other hand, would be that the Catholic Church accept, along with the unconditional acknowledgement of all Protestant ministries, the Protestant concept of ministry and their understanding of the Church and thus, in practice, renounce the apostolic and sacramental structure of the Church, which would mean, in practice, the conversion of Catholics to Protestantism and their acceptance of a multiplicity of distinct community structures as the historical form of the Church. While the first three

maximum demands are today rather unanimously rejected by Christian consciousness, the fourth exercises a kind of fascination for it – as it were, a certain conclusiveness that makes it appear to be the real solution to the problem. This is all the more true since there is joined to it the expectation that a Parliament of Churches, a "truly ecumenical council', could then harmonize this pluralism and promote a Christian unity of action. That no real union would result from this, but that its very impossibility would become a single common dogma, should convince anyone who examines the suggestion closely that such a way would not bring Church unity but only a final renunciation of it. As a result, none of the maximum solutions offers any real hope of unity.

> **In any event, church unity is not a political problem that can be solved by means of compromise or the weighing of what is regarded as possible or acceptable. What is at stake here is unity of belief, that is, the question of truth, which cannot be the object of political maneuvering. As long as and to the extent that the maximum solution must be regarded as a requirement of truth itself, just so long and to just that extent there will be no other recourse than simply to strive to convert one's partner in the debate.** In other words, *the claim of truth ought not to be raised where there is not a compelling and indisputable reason for doing so. We may not interpret as truth that which is, in reality, a historical development with a more or less close relationship to truth.* Whenever, then, the weight of truth and its incontrovertibility are involved, they must be met by a corresponding sincerity that avoids laying claim to truth prematurely and is ready to search for the inner fullness of truth with the eyes of love. (Joseph Ratzinger, *Principles of Catholic Theology*, pp. 197-198)

This statement of utter apostasy was "ratified" by Ratzinger as "Benedict XVI" when he made the following statement to an "ecumenical" gathering in Cologne, Germany, on Friday, August 19, 2005:

> Benedict XVI: "We all know there are numerous models of unity and you know that the Catholic Church also has as her goal the full visible unity of the disciples of Christ, as defined by the Second Vatican Ecumenical Council in its various Documents (cf. Lumen Gentium, nn. 8, 13; Unitatis Redintegratio, nn. 2, 4, etc.). This unity, we are convinced, indeed subsists in the Catholic Church, without the possibility of ever being lost (cf. Unitatis Redintegratio, n. 4); the Church in fact has not totally disappeared from the world.
>
> **On the other hand, this unity does not mean what could be called ecumenism of the return: that is, to deny and to reject one's own faith history. Absolutely not!**
>
> It does not mean uniformity in all expressions of theology and spirituality, in liturgical forms and in discipline. Unity in multiplicity, and multiplicity in unity: in my Homily for the Solemnity of Sts Peter and Paul on 29 June last, I insisted that full unity and true catholicity in the original sense of the word go together. As a necessary condition for the achievement of this coexistence, the commitment to unity must be constantly purified and renewed; it must constantly grow and mature. **(Ecumenical meeting at the Archbishopric of Cologne English)**

It mattered not to Ratzinger/Benedict that his belief in the new ecclesiology's "partial communion" of non-Catholics with the Catholic Church has been condemned (see His Excellency Bishop Donald Sanborn in **The New Ecclesiology: An Overview** and **The New Ecclesiology: Documentation** and **Ratzinger's Dominus Jesus: A Critical Analysis** and **Communion: Ratzinger's Ecumenical One-World Church**) or that Pope Pius IX, *Iam Vos Omnes*, September 13, 1868, specifically called for the return of Protestants to the Catholic Church and that Popes Leo XIII and Pius XI called for the return of Protestants and the Orthodox to the true Church in, respectively, *Praeclara Gratulationis Publicae*, June 20, 1894, and *Mortalium Animos*, January 6, 1928,

No, what mattered to the Antipope Emeritus, Ratzinger/Benedict, was to deconstruct the nature of dogmatic truth so as to find what is "really" true in dogmatic pronouncements from what is an "historical development" so that "impediments" to "unity" may be overcome, which is why it is so necessary to understand Ratzinger/Benedict's warfare against the nature of dogmatic truth, which is really a warfare against the very nature of God as He has revealed Himself to be through His Catholic Church, in order to understand the entirety of his Modernist agenda.

Pope Pius XI specifically rejected "distinctions" between "fundamental" and "non-fundamental" truths as a condition of effecting the reunion of non-Catholics with the true Church:

> We know not; that unity can only arise from one teaching authority, one law of belief and one faith of Christians. But We do know that from this it is an easy step to the neglect of religion or *indifferentism* and to modernism, as they call it. **Those, who are unhappily infected with these errors, hold that dogmatic truth is not *absolute* but *relative*, that is, it agrees with the varying necessities of time and place and with the varying tendencies of the mind, since it is not contained in immutable revelation, but is capable of being accommodated to human life. Besides this, in connection with things which must be believed, it is nowise licit to use that distinction which some have seen fit to introduce between those articles of faith which are *fundamental* and those which are not fundamental, as they say, as if the former are to be accepted by all, while the latter may be left to the free assent of the faithful: for the supernatural virtue of faith has a formal cause, namely the authority of God revealing, and this is patient of no such distinction.** For this reason it is that all who are truly Christ's believe, for example, the Conception of the Mother of God without stain of original sin with the same faith as they believe the mystery of the August Trinity, and the Incarnation of our Lord just as they do the infallible teaching authority of the Roman Pontiff, according to the sense in which it was defined by the Ecumenical Council of the Vatican. Are these truths not equally certain, or not equally to be believed, because the Church has solemnly sanctioned and defined them, some in one age and some in another, even in those times immediately before our own? **Has not God revealed them all**? For the teaching authority of the Church, **which in the divine wisdom was constituted on earth in order that revealed doctrines might remain intact for ever, and that they might be brought with ease and security to the knowledge of men, and which is daily exercised through the Roman Pontiff and the Bishops who are in communion with him, has also the office of defining, when it sees fit, any truth with solemn rites and decrees, whenever this is necessary either to oppose the errors or the attacks of heretics, or more clearly and in greater detail to**

> **stamp the minds of the faithful with the articles of sacred doctrine which have been explained.** But in the use of this extraordinary teaching authority no newly invented matter is brought in, nor is anything new added to the number of those truths which are at least implicitly contained in the deposit of Revelation, divinely handed down to the Church: only those which are made clear which perhaps may still seem obscure to some, or that which some have previously called into question is declared to be of faith. (Pope Pius XI, *Mortalium Animos*, January 6, 1928.)

It is because of such pronouncements that Ratzinger/Benedict, like Karol Wojtyla/John Paul II before him and Jorge Mario Bergoglio/Francis after him, make few references to the encyclical letters of our true popes and the dogmatic pronouncements made at Holy Mother Church's true general councils. The only references that the conciliar "popes" have made have been, at least for the most part, gratuitous references in "cf" (confer) footnotes now and again.

The conciliar "popes," belonging to a false religion, must rely upon the documents of the counterfeit church of conciliarism and the statements of the conciliar "pontiffs" to justify their apostasies, including the "new ecclesiology" that can be used to place a Protestant syncretist, Roger Schutz, in "Heaven" even though he was a lifelong Protestant. And it is the new ecclesiology of effecting "unity" by means of "spiritual reconciliation," which is a variation on the theme of "spiritual ecumenism" of the late Abbe Paul Couturier, a direct disciple of the late Father Pierre Teilhard de Chardin, S.J., who believed that God Himself was in "the process of becoming" and that our "understanding" of Him must ever evolve as He "evolves," that Ratzinger/Benedict himself directly endorsed on numerous occasions, including explicitly in his August 19, 2005, address to "ecumenical" leaders in Cologne, Germany, that was the basis of his, Ratzinger/Benedict's efforts to forge "unity" between the heretical and schismatic rump "church" in Red China with the underground church of suffering Catholics there.

IV. Red China: "Workshop" for the New Ecclesiology

Joseph Ratzinger/Benedict XVI's **Letter to Bishops, Priests, Consecrated Persons and Lay Faithful of Red China**, June 30, 2007, used the situation facing Catholics in the "People's Republic of China" (hereinafter referred to as Red China)--the most elaborate "workshop"--of all as a means of making the "new ecclesiology" (bringing "full communion" out of "partial communion") a "workable" reality for relations with the Orthodox (as well as those Anglicans who might be interested in "converting" to what they think, albeit falsely, is the Catholic Church without having to "give up" their own structures and "traditions," each of which was born as a result of a rebellion against Papal Primacy by King Henry VIII in 1534 and then by Henry's daughter by Anne Boleyn, in 1558 and thereafter). There is only one little problem with the grand schema of this "workshop" in the new ecclesiology: many Catholics in Red China are confused about *how* it was supposed to work, thus the "need" for a **Compendium** to be issued in 2009 to make Ratzinger/Benedict's **Letter** more "comprehensible."

Ratzinger/Benedict's lifelong rejection of Scholasticism leads to all manner of internal contradictions in his writing that he does recognize. *The New Oxford Review*, whose editors reject sedevacantism, noted Ratzinger/Benedict's penchant in this regard, as did the anti-sedevacantist Tradition in Action site:

> In Cardinal Ratzinger's *Values in a Time of Upheaval*, he muddies up his phrase [the dictatorship of relativism]; indeed, he reverses his position. He says, "The modern concept of democracy seems indissolubly linked to that of relativism." Well, well! But then he backtracks: "**This means that a basic element of truth, namely, ethical truth, is indispensable to democracy**." But then he backtracks again: "**We do not want the State to impose one particular idea of the good on us. ... Truth is controversial, and the attempt to impose on all persons what one part of the citizenry holds to be true looks like enslavement of people's consciences." And he says this on the same page**!
>
> Yes, we know: Some of our readers feel that the Pope is above all criticism; he cannot make a mistake, even in his previous writings. **But what he has written here is contradictory and inscrutable**.
>
> Ratzinger says, "The relativists ...[are] flirting with totalitarianism even though they seek to establish the primacy of freedom ..." Huh?
>
> So, what is he saying? "The State is not itself the source of truth and morality.... Accordingly, the State must receive from outside itself the essential measure of knowledge and truth with regard to that which is good. ... The Church remains outside the State. ... The Church must exert itself with all its vigor so that in it there may shine forth moral truth ..."
>
> Then he says, "Conscience is the highest norm [italics in original] and ... and one must follow it even against authority. **When authority - in this case the Church's Magisterium - speaks on matters of morality, it supplies the material that helps the conscience form its own judgment, but ultimately it is only conscience that has the last word.**" (**A Contradictory Definition of Relativism**.)
>
> Cardinal Ratzinger's belief that the conscience can disobey the objective Moral teaching of the Church clearly admits, as did Descartes, that the soul comes first, and God only afterwards.
>
> The error is now within the Church. It is supported even by the highest Catholic authorities. Their current of thought, Progressivism, is nothing more than the exaltation of the self. Its most malicious ingredient is Immanentism, the error that the soul contains a divine immanence: "The principle of immanence essentially states that the first thing we know is ourselves and that all our knowledge of external reality is judged in light of it" (8). Because self has been placed first as "the last word," at the highest level of the Church, this should be a clarion call to Catholics to pray to Our Lady of Good Success for all who have succumbed to Progressivism, and also for all who are trying to maintain their Catholic faith in the increasingly more dominant Progressivist heresy. (**Cardinal Ratzinger's Subjectivism**)

Ratzinger/Benedict's writings also contain multiple contradictions of Catholic truth and of the most basic elements of logic as they cleave to condemned propositions of Modernism and the faulty non-Scholastic "reasoning" contained in the condemned methods of the "new theology."

Ratzinger/Benedict's Letter of June 30, 2007, contained the following basic contradictions, some of which conflict with Catholic truth and logic, others of which conflict with each other in the body of his Letter.

IV. 1. A conflict with Faith and with truth on the merely natural level:

> History remains indecipherable, incomprehensible. No one can read it. (Joseph Ratzinger/Benedict XVI, **Letter to Bishops, Priests, Consecrated Persons and Lay Faithful of Red China**, June 30, 2007.)

If this expression of Kantian immanentism was correct, then true pope after true pope who referred to the lessons of history dared to venture into the realm of the "indecipherable," the "incomprehensible." How can one claim to learn any lessons from history when it is alleged to be "indecipherable" and "incomprehensible"?

For Ratzinger/Benedict to be correct, therefore, Pope Gregory XVI, writing in *Mirari Vos*, August 15, 1832, had to be wrong when he taught us the lessons of history about the effects produced by "liberty of conscience" that is one of the prime constituent elements of Modernism and thus of the lords of the counterfeit church of conciliarism:

> This shameful font of indifferentism gives rise to that absurd and erroneous proposition which claims that **liberty of conscience** must be maintained for everyone. It spreads ruin in sacred and civil affairs, though some repeat over and over again with the greatest impudence that some advantage accrues to religion from it. "But the death of the soul is worse than freedom of error," as Augustine was wont to say. When all restraints are removed by which men are kept on the narrow path of truth, their nature, which is already inclined to evil, propels them to ruin. Then truly "the bottomless pit" is open from which John saw smoke ascending which obscured the sun, and out of which locusts flew forth to devastate the earth. Thence comes transformation of minds, corruption of youths, contempt of sacred things and holy laws -- in other words, a pestilence more deadly to the state than any other. **Experience shows, even from earliest times, that cities renowned for wealth, dominion, and glory perished as a result of this single evil, namely immoderate freedom of opinion, license of free speech, and desire for novelty**. (Pope Gregory XVI, *Mirari Vos*, August 15, 1832.)

Pope Pius IX himself must have been wrong when he used history in *Quanta Cura*, December 8, 1862, to condemn the falsehood that is "religious liberty:"

> For you well know, venerable brethren, that at this time men are found not a few who, applying to civil society the impious and absurd principle of "naturalism," as they call it, dare to teach that "the best constitution of public society and (also) civil progress altogether require that human society be conducted and governed without regard being had to religion

any more than if it did not exist; or, at least, without any distinction being made between the true religion and false ones." And, against the doctrine of Scripture, of the Church, and of the Holy Fathers, they do not hesitate to assert that "that is the best condition of civil society, in which no duty is recognized, as attached to the civil power, of restraining by enacted penalties, offenders against the Catholic religion, except so far as public peace may require." From which totally false idea of social government they do not fear to foster that erroneous opinion, most fatal in its effects on the Catholic Church and the salvation of souls, called by Our Predecessor, Gregory XVI, an "insanity," viz., that "liberty of conscience and worship is each man's personal right, which ought to be legally proclaimed and asserted in every rightly constituted society; and that a right resides in the citizens to an absolute liberty, which should be restrained by no authority whether ecclesiastical or civil, whereby they may be able openly and publicly to manifest and declare any of their ideas whatever, either by word of mouth, by the press, or in any other way." **But, while they rashly affirm this, they do not think and consider that they are preaching "liberty of perdition;" and that "if human arguments are always allowed free room for discussion, there will never be wanting men who will dare to resist truth, and to trust in the flowing speech of human wisdom; whereas we know, from the very teaching of our Lord Jesus Christ, how carefully Christian faith and wisdom should avoid this most injurious babbling**."

And, since where religion has been removed from civil society, and the doctrine and authority of divine revelation repudiated, the genuine notion itself of justice and human right is darkened and lost, and the place of true justice and legitimate right is supplied by material force, thence it appears why it is that some, utterly neglecting and disregarding the surest principles of sound reason, **dare to proclaim that "the people's will, manifested by what is called public opinion or in some other way, constitutes a supreme law, free from all divine and human control; and that in the political order accomplished facts, from the very circumstance that they are accomplished, have the force of right**." But who, does not see and clearly perceive that human society, when set loose from the bonds of religion and true justice, can have, in truth, no other end than the purpose of obtaining and amassing wealth, and that (society under such circumstances) follows no other law in its actions, except the unchastened desire of ministering to its own pleasure and interests? For this reason, men of the kind pursue with bitter hatred the Religious Orders, although these have deserved extremely well of Christendom, civilization and literature, and cry out that the same have no legitimate reason for being permitted to exist; and thus (these evil men) applaud the calumnies of heretics. For, as Pius VI, Our Predecessor, taught most wisely, "the abolition of regulars is injurious to that state in which the Evangelical counsels are openly professed; it is injurious to a method of life praised in the Church as agreeable to Apostolic doctrine; it is injurious to the illustrious founders, themselves, whom we venerate on our altars, who did not establish these societies but by God's inspiration." And (these wretches) also impiously declare that permission should be refused to citizens and to the Church, "whereby they may openly give alms for the sake of Christian charity"; and that the law should be abrogated "whereby on certain fixed days servile works are prohibited because of God's worship;" and on the most deceptive pretext that the said permission and law are opposed to the principles of the best public economy. Moreover, not content with removing religion from public society, they

> wish to banish it also from private families. For, teaching and professing the most fatal error of "Communism and Socialism," they assert that "domestic society or the family derives the whole principle of its existence from the civil law alone; and, consequently, that on civil law alone depend all rights of parents over their children, and especially that of providing for education." By which impious opinions and machinations these most deceitful men chiefly aim at this result, viz., that the salutary teaching and influence of the Catholic Church may be entirely banished from the instruction and education of youth, and that the tender and flexible minds of young men may be infected and depraved by every most pernicious error and vice. For all who have endeavored to throw into confusion things both sacred and secular, and to subvert the right order of society, and to abolish all rights, human and divine, have always (as we above hinted) devoted all their nefarious schemes, devices and efforts, to deceiving and depraving incautious youth and have placed all their hope in its corruption. **For which reason they never cease by every wicked method to assail the clergy, both secular and regular, from whom (as the surest monuments of history conspicuously attest), so many great advantages have abundantly flowed to Christianity, civilization and literature, and to proclaim that "the clergy, as being hostile to the true and beneficial advance of science and civilization, should be removed from the whole charge and duty of instructing and educating youth**." (Pope Pius IX, *Quanta Cura*, December 8, 1862.)

Moreover, if history is "indecipherable" and "incomprehensible," as Ratzinger/Benedict contended in his **Letter to Bishops, Priests, Consecrated Persons and Lay Faithful of Red China** of June 30, 2007, what business did *he* have a week later trying to "teach" us about alleged "missed opportunities" to prevent or heal schisms in the past?

> Looking back **over the past,** to the divisions which in the course of the centuries have rent the Body of Christ, **one continually has the impression that, at critical moments when divisions were coming about, not enough was done by the Church's leaders to maintain or regain reconciliation and unity. One has the impression that omissions on the part of the Church have had their share of blame for the fact that these divisions were able to harden. This glance at the past imposes an obligation on us today: to make every effort to unable for all those who truly desire unity to remain in that unity or to attain it anew.** I think of a sentence in the Second Letter to the Corinthians, where Paul writes: "Our mouth is open to you, Corinthians; our heart is wide. You are not restricted by us, but you are restricted in your own affections. In return ... widen your hearts also!" (2 Corinthians 6:11-13). Paul was certainly speaking in another context, but his exhortation can and must touch us too, precisely on this subject. Let us generously open our hearts and make room for everything that the faith itself allows. (**Explanatory Letter on "Summorum Pontificum"**)

If history is "indecipherable" and "incomprehensible, as Ratzinger/Benedict contended in his **Letter to Bishops, Priests, Consecrated Persons and Lay Faithful of Red China** on June 30, 2007, then how was it possible on July 7, 2007, to "decipher" that "not enough was done by the Church's leaders to maintain or regain reconciliation and unity?"

Remember, Ratzinger/Benedict wrote the following in his **Letter to Bishops, Priests, Consecrated Persons and Lay Faithful of Red China**:

> History remains indecipherable, incomprehensible. No one can read it. (Joseph Ratzinger/Benedict XVI, **Letter to Bishops, Priests, Consecrated Persons and Lay Faithful of Red China**, June 30, 2007.)

If "no one can read" history, then how could Ratzinger/Benedict have claimed to know that "not enough was done by the Church's leaders to maintain or regain reconciliation and unity"?

Obviously, the contention made on June 30, 2007, was completely contradictory of his own statement seven days later. Ratzinger/Benedict's statement about the "incomprehensible" and "indecipherable" nature of a history that "no one can read" also made it impossible for *him* to "know" the alleged "historical circumstances" that he contended, contrary to right reason and Catholic dogma, make specific dogma formulae and papal pronouncements "obsolete after having fulfilled their pastoral mission at their proper time."

Ratzinger/Benedict, a disciple of the late Father Hans Urs von Balthasar, an Hegelian who believed in the heresy of "universal salvation" that contradicts the plain words of Our Blessed Lord and Saviour Jesus Christ, daring to impute "ignorance" to Our Lord on the matter of the time of His Second Coming to judge the living and the dead on the Last Day (see Father Regis Scanlon, O.F.M., Cap., **The Inflated Reputation of Hans Urs von Balthasar**), remains as blithe to his contradictions as he was blithe to the fact that errors can in no way serve as the foundation of personal sanctity or of social order, as an article in *Si, Si, No, No* made clear:

> Up to the very end of his conference, Card. Ratzinger resolutely continues on this road of agnosticism and now logically comes to the most disastrous of conclusions. He writes:
>
> > In conclusion, as we contemplate our present-day religious situation, of which I have tried to throw some light on some of its elements, we may well marvel at the fact that, after all, people still continue believing in a Christian manner, not only according to Hick's, Knitter's as well as others' substitute ways or forms, but also according to that full and joyous Faith found in the New Testament of the Church of all time.
>
> So, there it is: For Card. Ratzinger, "Hick, Knitter, and others" who deny the divinity of our Lord Jesus Christ, His Church, His sacraments, and, in short, all of Christianity, **continue "despite everything" "believing in a Christian manner," even though they do so using "substitute forms of belief"! Here, the Cardinal Prefect of the Congregation for the Faith leaves us wondering indeed, just what it is he means by "believing in a Christian manner."**
>
> Moreover, once the "preambula fidei" have been eliminated, that "full and joyous Faith of the Church of all time" which seems [for Card. Ratzinger] to be no different from modern-day apostasies other than by its style and total character, is utterly lacking in any rational credibility in comparison with and in relation to what he refers to as "substitute ways or

forms" of faith. "How is it," Card. Ratzinger wonders, "in fact, that the Faith [the one of all time] still has a chance of success?" Answer:

> I would say that it is because it finds a correspondence in man's nature.....There is, in man, an insatiable desire for the infinite. None of the answers we have sought is sufficient [but must we take his own word for it, or must we go through the exercise of experiencing all religions?]. God alone [but Whom, according to Card. Ratzinger, human reason cannot prove to be truly God], Who made Himself finite in order to shatter the bonds of our own finitude and bring us to the dimension of His infinity [...and not to redeem us from the slavery of sin?] is able to meet all the needs of our human existence.

According to this, it is therefore not objective motives based on history and reason, and thus the truth of Christianity, but only a subjective appreciation which brings us to "see" that it [Christianity] is able to satisfy the profound needs of human nature and which would explain the "success" [modernists would say the "vitality"] of the "faith" ["of all time" or in its "substitute forms," it is of but little importance]. Such, however, is not at all Catholic doctrine: this is simply modernist apologetics (cf. Pope St. Pius X, Pascendi), based on their affirmed impossibility of grasping metaphysical knowledge (or agnosticism or skepticism), which Card. Ratzinger seemed to want to shun in the first part of his address.

Now we are in a position to better understand why Card. Ratzinger **has such a wide-open concept of "theology" and of "faith" that he includes everything: theology as well as heresies, faith and apostasy. On that road of denial of the human reason's ability of attaining metaphysical knowledge, a road which he continues to follow, he lacks the "means of discerning the difference between faith and non-faith" (R. Amerio, op. cit., p.340) and, consequently, theology from pseudo-theology, truth from heresy:**

> All theologies are nullified, because all are regarded as equivalent; the heart or kernel of religion is located in feelings or experiences, as the Modernists held at the beginning of this century (Amerio, op. cit., p.542).

We cannot see how this position of Card. Ratzinger can escape that solemn condemnation proclaimed at Vatican I: "**If anyone says...that men must be brought to the Faith solely by their own personal interior experience...let him be anathema**" (DB 1812). (Cardinal Ratzinger)

Actually, there is an explanation for Ratzinger's statement on June 30, 2007, that history is "indecipherable" and his exercise in *deciphering* history just seven days later by daring to state that true popes did not "do enough" "to maintain or regain reconciliation and unity." Ratzinger/Benedict did and said those things that he believed he "*had*" to do or say to accomplish a given end. As a pure subjectivist, Ratzinger/Benedict simply did and said what he wanted to do if he believed that he could "reconcile" his words and actions with "elements" of the Catholic Faith by means of his "hermeneutic of continuity."

Calling a mosque a "jewel" or "sacred" place? Well, he just *had* to do that to foster inter-religious dialogue and so as not to offend those who could be "instruments of peace" in the Middle East if only they could accept his appeal to them on the grounds of "reason."

Praying as a Jew at the Wailing Wall and refusing to invoke the Holy Name of the Divine Redeemer, Our Blessed Lord and Saviour Jesus Christ? Well, this was"justifiable" by making advertence to the crimes committed against Jews (and others) by the Third Reich. Ratzinger/Benedict himself told us that "things" have changed as a result of a "look" at that which he called on June 30, 2007, "indecipherable:" history!

> In particular, before the recent crimes of the Nazi regime and, in general, **with a retrospective look at a long and difficult history, it was necessary to evaluate and define in a new way the relationship between the Church and the faith of Israel.** **(Christmas greetings to the Members of the Roman Curia and Prelature, December 22, 2005**.)

It was expedient for Ratzinger/Benedict to appeal to the "indecipherability" of history on June 30, 2007, in order to overlook--or "purify the memory" about-- the crimes committed by the Red Chinese government and its Chinese Patriotic Catholic Association against the persecuted Catholics of the underground Church in Red China. Ratzinger/Benedict wants to forge a "unity" between the schismatic and heretical rump church that is a tool of the Communist Red Chinese government and the underground Church in China at the expense of truth, willing to jettison a complete adherence to principles of Faith and *any* discussion at all of Pope Pius XII's condemnation of the actions of the renegade bishops in Red China in ***Ad Sinarum Gentem***, October 7, 1954, and ***Ad Apostolorum Principis***, June 29, 1958, and Pope Pius XII's plea for prayers for the Church in Red China, ***Meminisse Iuvat***, June 14, 1958, none of which were referenced in Ratzinger/Benedict's **Letter to Bishops, Priests, Consecrated Persons and Lay Faithful of Red China**, of June 30, 2007. Indeed, there are no references at all in any of that letter's fifty-six footnotes to any "preconciliar" document. Talk about "purification of memory."

It was also expedient for Ratzinger/Benedict to appeal to his *own understanding* of history, that which he had termed "indecipherable" ("who can read it") on June 30, 2007, in his **Explanatory Letter on "Summorum Pontificum"** on July 7, 2007, as doing so made it appear to conciliar "bishops" opposed to any "liberation" of the modernized version of the Immemorial Mass of Tradition that was promulgated by Angelo Roncalli/John XXIII in 1961 and 1962 that he, Ratzinger/Benedict, wanted to prove himself better in the "eyes of history," shall we say, than Pope Leo IX, who did not "do enough" to prevent the Greek Schism in 1054, and better than Pope Leo X, who excommunicated the hideous drunkard named Martin Luther in the Papal Bull *Exsurge Domini*, June 15, 1520, and better than Pope Saint Pius V, who excommunicated the bloodthirsty Queen Elizabeth I in **Regnans in Excelsis**, March 5, 1570. Ratzinger/Benedict believed that his own understanding of dogmatic truth and of a "reconciled diversity" might have "saved the day" in the past, which is why it was necessary to make "reference" in his **Explanatory Letter on "Summorum Pontificum"** to a word that he called indecipherable in his **Letter to Bishops, Priests, Consecrated Persons and Lay Faithful of Red China**, namely, history.

Ratzinger/Benedict, of course, was not above rank deconstructing his own "history," which was on display in his **Explanatory Letter on "Summorum Pontificum**" when he claimed the following:

> **There is no contradiction between the two editions of the Roman Missal. In the history of the liturgy there is growth and progress, but no rupture**. What earlier generations held as sacred, remains sacred and great for us too, and it cannot be all of a sudden entirely forbidden or even considered harmful. It behooves all of us to preserve the riches which have developed in the Church's faith and prayer, and to give them their proper place. Needless to say, in order to experience full communion, the priests of the communities adhering to the former usage cannot, as a matter of principle, exclude celebrating according to the new books. The total exclusion of the new rite would not in fact be consistent with the recognition of its value and holiness (**Explanatory Letter on "Summorum Pontificum**".)

This is, of course, the exact opposite of what Ratzinger contended in his preface to the French language edition of the late Monsignor Klaus Gamber's T*he Reform of the Roman Liturgy*, in which Gamber wrote of the "destruction of the Roman Rite," and in his own memoirs, *Milestones*:

> What happened after the Council was something else entirely: in the place of liturgy as the fruit of development came **fabricated** liturgy. We abandoned the organic, living process of growth and development over centuries, and replaced it--**as in a manufacturing process--with a fabrication, a banal on-the-spot product. Gamber, with the vigilance of a true prophet and the courage of a true witness, oppose this falsification**, and thanks to his incredibly rich knowledge, indefatigably taught us about the living fullness of a true liturgy. As a man who knew and loved history, he showed us the multiple forms and paths of liturgical development; as a man who looked at history form the inside, he saw in this development and its fruit the intangible reflection of the eternal liturgy, that which is not the object of our action but which can continue marvelously to mature and blossom if we unite ourselves intimately with its mystery. (Joseph Ratzinger, Preface to the French language edition of Monsignor Klaus Gamber's *The Reform of the Roman Liturgy.)*
>
> **The prohibition of the missal that was now decreed, a missal that had known continuous growth over the centuries, starting with the sacramentaries of the ancient Church, introduced a breach into the history of the liturgy whose consequences could only be tragic**. It was reasonable and right of the Council to order a revision of the missal such as had often taken place before and which this time had to be more thorough than before, above all because of the introduction of the vernacular.
>
> **But more than this now happened: the old building was demolished, and another was built, to be sure largely using materials from the previous one and even using the old building plans. There is no doubt that this new missal in many respects brought with it a real improvement and enrichment; but setting it as a new construction over against what had grown historically, forbidding the results of this historical growth thereby makes the liturgy appear to be no longer living development but the produce of erudite work and juridical authority; this has caused an enormous harm.** For then

> the impress had to emerge that liturgy is something "made", not something given in advance but something lying without our own power of decision. (Joseph Ratzinger, *Milestones*.)

One will also note that Ratzinger/Benedict wrote in his **Explanatory Letter on "Summorum Pontificum"** that the 1962 Missal "was never judicially abrogated" even though he had written in *Milestones* the exact opposite:

> **The prohibition of the missal that was now decreed, a missal that had known continuous growth over the centuries, starting with the sacramentaries of the ancient Church, introduced a breach into the history of the liturgy whose consequences could only be tragic**. (Joseph Ratzinger, *Milestones*.)

Dizzying? To quote a former governor of Alaska who specializes in her own brand of illogic and contradiction, "You betcha."

A final point needs to be noted before moving on to discuss Ratzinger/Benedict's desire to "forge" a "spiritual reconciliation" in Red China that conceded authority to the Communist authorities there that Pope Pius VI refused to accord to the "Constitutional Church" of the revolutionary First Republic of France and that made no direct mention at all of the Chinese Patriotic Catholic Association's support for the Communist government's "population control" programs, including mandatory sterilizations and the policy of one-child-per-family (as well as the supposedly "former" policy of forced abortions in some regions of China).

If history is so "indecipherable" and so "incomprehensible" that no one "can read it," then how was Ratzinger/Benedict so very certain that Bishop Richard Williamson, formerly of the Society of Saint Pius X, had reached erroneous conclusions about the nature and extent of the crimes committed by the agents of the Third Reich upon Jews and others?

For Joseph Ratzinger/Benedict XVI, you see, "history" is, like the Faith itself, whatever it is he wants to make of it in light of the "needs" of the moment and/or the "historical circumstances" in which "modern man" finds himself. Such a view of the Faith and of the world is contrary to right reason and condemned dogmatically by the authority of the Catholic Church:

God cannot deny himself, nor can truth ever be in opposition to truth.

> **The appearance of this kind of specious contradiction is chiefly due to the fact that either:**
> **the dogmas of faith are not understood and explained in accordance with the mind of the church, or**
> **unsound views are mistaken for the conclusions of reason.**
> Therefore we **define** that every **assertion contrary to the truth of enlightened faith is totally false**. (Vatican Council, Session III, Dogmatic Constitution on the Catholic Faith, Chapter 4, On Faith and Reason, April 24, 1870. **SESSION 3 : 24 April 1870**.)

It is upon the false, gratuitous assertion that history is "indecipherable, incomprehensible," a proposition that, as noted above most extensively, Ratzinger/Benedict contradicted himself, sometimes in the most concrete of terms (see Williamson, Bishop Richard), upon which the entirety of Ratzinger/Benedict's **Letter to Bishops, Priests, Consecrated Persons and Lay Faithful of Red China** was founded, which is why, after having examined the falsity of this assertion, one can make short work of the letter and of the 2009 **Compendium** that was designed to "clarify" points made in 2007 that still had many Chinese Catholics in Red China or Americans of Chinese ancestry in the United States of America scratching their heads in utter mystification at how something so simple, the evil of a Communist effort to control the life of the Catholic Church, can be made so complex.

IV. 2: "Reconciliation" At the Price of Truth

One of the essential constituent elements of conciliarism's "new ecclesiology" of "partial" and "full communion" is that recognition of and adherence to a true and legitimate Successor of Saint Peter is not essential for salvation. If conciliarists such as Joseph Ratzinger/Benedict XVI and his successor, Jorge Mario Bergoglio, believed that recognition of and adherence to a true and legitimate Successor of Saint is indeed essential for salvation, you see, they would be seeking with urgency the unconditional conversion of all non-Catholics to the true Church, outside of which there is no salvation and without which there can be no true social order.

As noted above, Ratzinger/Benedict specifically rejected what he had referred to disparagingly as "the ecumenism of the return."

Ratzinger/Benedict held that a Jewish reading of the Bible is a "possible" one, meaning that God has revealed Himself so obscurely as to make it difficult for those to deny the Sacred Divinity of His Co-Equal and Co-Eternal Son made Flesh in Our Lady's Virginal and Immaculate Womb by the power of the Third Person of the Most Blessed Trinity, God the Holy Ghost, to recognize that everything in the Old Testament does indeed point unequivocally to Christ the King as Our Divine Redeemer.

It was in August of 2007 that Ratzinger/Benedict called Mount Hiei in Japan, where the Tendei sect of Buddhism established itself, as "sacred." He did not seek the conversion of Buddhists. Indeed, a symbol of Buddhism (along with symbols of Judaism, Mohammedanism, Jainism and Hinduism) was presented to him on Thursday, April 17, 2008, at the John Paul II Cultural Center in Washington, District of Columbia, and he received it with great admiration and joy.

All of this meant that Ratzinger/Benedict did not believe that anyone in these non-Catholic religions was in danger of losing their immortal souls for all eternity, which is, as I have noted before, a "back door" way of propagandizing in behalf of his mentor Von Balthasar's heresy of "universal salvation."

Indeed, the man who still serves as the "preacher" to the "papal household" under "Pope Francis," Father Raniero Cantalamessa, O.F.M., Cap., said the following on Good Friday in 2002 in the

Basilica of Saint Peter in the presence of then governing conciliar "pontiff," Karol Wojtyla/John Paul II, and, most likely, in the presence of the then Joseph "Cardinal" Ratzinger (if reasons of health did not preclude him from attending; I sat right behind "Cardinal" Ratzinger at the *Novus Ordo* Easter Vigil service in the Basilica of Saint Peter on Holy Saturday in 2005):

> "**It is more important that men and women become holy**," Cantalamessa said, standing in the center of a magnificent basilica erected to celebrate the earthly might of Catholicism and the papacy, "**than that they know the name of the one Savior**." (**National Catholic Reporter**)

Men and women cannot, however, become holy unless they know the Name of the one Saviour and adhere to everything He has entrusted exclusively to the Catholic Church and unless they submit to everything decreed by a true and legitimate Successor of Saint Peter, who, of course, can never do or say things that put the Church's perennial and immutable teaching in doubt or cast upon that teaching an interpretation that makes that teaching "obsolete" in light of the supposed "impossibility" of the human being's ability to know and to express the fullness of all truth with exactitude given the changing historical circumstances in which men find themselves.

Ratzinger/Benedict's successor, Jorge Mario Bergoglio, made it clear in his general audience remarks of Wednesday, November 26, 2014, that "all of us" go to Heaven, meaning that he believes in the heresy of universal salvation himself:

> 1. The Conciliar Constitution *Gaudium et Spes*, faced with these questions that forever resonate in the hearts of men and women, states: "We do not know the time for the consummation of the earth and of humanity, nor do we know how all things will be transformed. As deformed by sin, the shape of this world will pass away; but we are taught that God is preparing a new dwelling place and a new earth where justice will abide, and whose blessedness will answer and surpass all the longings for peace which spring up in the human heart" (n. 39). This is the Church's destination: it is, as the Bible says, the "new Jerusalem", "Paradise". More than a place, it is a "state" of soul in which our deepest hopes are fulfilled in superabundance and our being, as creatures and as children of God, reach their full maturity. We will finally be clothed in the joy, peace and love of God, completely, without any limit, and we will come face to face with Him! (cf. 1 Cor 13:12). **It is beautiful to think of this, to think of Heaven. We will all be there together. It is beautiful, it gives strength to the soul**. (General Audience, November 26, 2014.)

To believe that "we will all be there together" is to profess "universal salvation," which is nothing other than the sin of Presumption against the Third Person of the Most Blessed Trinity.

For his part, of course, Ratzinger/Benedict made it appear in his **Letter to Bishops, Priests, Consecrated Persons and Lay Faithful of Red China** that the "particular" churches in China are indeed united to the Roman Pontiff in the person of himself, which, he states, most correctly, is indeed a necessary element of the Catholic Faith, a necessity that he, of course, contradicted and vitiated later in his letter. However, this is not so. No such unity in Red China exists between the rump Church and the Catholic Church.

Quite specifically, many of the rump bishops in the Chinese Catholic Patriotic Association have *not* been in "communion" with the men who have claimed to be, albeit falsely, the Successors of Saint Peter since the death of Pope Pius IX on October 9, 1958, and many of these same bishops defect from the Catholic Faith in matters concerning the Fifth, Sixth and Ninth Commandments, a subject that was *never* raised directly by Ratzinger/Benedict in his June 30, 2007, letter, placing these bishops outside out of the Catholic Church (along, of course, with Ratzinger/Benedict himself because of his own multiple defections from the Faith long before his "election" on Tuesday, April 19, 2005).

Ratzinger/Benedict referred obliquely to these matters in the section of his letter that dealt with the situation facing the family in China:

> The above-mentioned values form part of the relevant Chinese cultural context, but also in your land there is no lack of forces that influence the family negatively in various ways. Therefore the Church which is in China, aware that the good of society and her own good are profoundly linked to the good of the family, must have a keener and more urgent sense of her mission to proclaim to all people God's plan for marriage and the family, ensuring the full vitality of each. (**Letter to Bishops, Priests, Consecrated Persons and Lay Faithful of Red China**.)

No lack of "forces that influence the family negatively in various ways"? Those forces are called Communism. And members of the true Church in Red China, the underground Church, *have* denounced Communism and its anti-family policies, which are state-sponsored and monitored, admitting regional variations in the enforcement of those policies, and have been persecuted mercilessly and relentlessly as a result. Referring to no "lack of forces that influence the family negatively" is somewhat akin to the then "Monsignor" Pietro Parolin, now serving as the Vatican's Secretariat of State under Bergoglio/Francis, having said in 2009 that the conciliar Vatican had "disagreements" with the administration on Barack Hussein Obama/Barry Soetoro on "bioethical matters." Such euphemisms are worthy of George Orwell's *1984* and Aldous Huxley's *Brave New World*. (See **Respect Those Who Break the First Commandment? Respect Those Who Break the Fifth Commandment**.)

Union with a true and legitimate Successor of Saint Peter must be real and without any reservation or qualification:

> Hence We teach and declare that by the appointment of Our Lord the Roman Church possesses a sovereignty of ordinary power over all other Churches, and that this power of jurisdiction of the Roman Pontiff which is truly episcopal, is immediate;...so that the Church of Christ may be one flock under one supreme pastor, **through the preservation of unity both of communion and of profession of the same faith, with the Roman Pontiff. This is the teaching of Catholic truth from which no one can deviate without**

> **loss of faith and of salvation**. (Pope Pius IX, *Pastor Aeternus*, July 18, 1870, cited in Bishop Donald Sanborn, **The New Ecclesiology: Documentation**.)

There is no such unity of "communion and of profession of the same faith" between the rump church in Red China and the Catholic Church.

Leaving aside the inconvenient little fact that the counterfeit church of conciliarism is *not* the Catholic Church, the rump church in Red China can never be reconciled to the Catholic Church until its bishops and priests publicly abjure their errors, among which is the concession that they need to "register" with the civil authorities to exercise their priestly duties and exercise them only according to the conditions outlined by the Communist authorities, and are then and only then received back into the Catholic Church. No such demand is being made of the clergy who belong to the rump church in Red China.

Indeed, public abjuration of error is *not* a requirement for most of those who are "reconciled" to the structures of the counterfeit church of conciliarism. It was in May of 2008 that I wrote in **Not Such a Triumph After All** about a bishop, Mar Bawai Soro, from the Assyrian Apostolic Church of the East, who, along with his clergy, were received into the conciliar structures by the Chaldean Rite Bishop of the Eparchy of Saint James the Apostle, the Most Reverend Yawsip Jammo, without making any public abjuration of errors. This prompted me to write to Bishop Jammo as follows:

> I want you to know this, Your Excellency, as it is important for me to be completely honest with you. My concern with the reception of His Excellency Bishop Mar Bawai Soro by the Eparchy of Saint Peter the Apostle goes to the heart of the problems with the conciliar notion of ecumenism that was condemned in no uncertain terms by His Holiness Pope Pius XI in *Mortalium Animos*, January 6, 1928. That conciliar notion of ecumenism is premised upon not insisting that those outside of the Catholic Church return to her maternal bosom unconditionally and without any preconditions whatsoever. No "negotiations" are needed to become Catholic. The only thing that one needs to do is to submit humbly and with docility to the entirety of the Deposit of Faith as It has been entrusted to the true Church by Our Blessed Lord and Saviour Jesus Christ Himself, assenting to all of its tenets as they have been defined by the magisterial authority of that same Catholic Church.
>
> It appears (and I place an emphasis on the word appears) that Bishop Mar Bawai Soro did not convert unconditionally to Chaldean Rite of the Catholic Church. This appearance is given by the fact that Bishop Soro's 2005 address to his brother Assyrian bishops accepted the primacy of Saint Peter as the head of the Universal Church because he had governed in Rome. There was no reference to the simple fact that Our Lord Himself founded that same Catholic Church upon Saint Peter, appointing Him and His Successors as the visible heads of the true Church, His own very Mystical Body. It is not clear that Bishop Soro believes in Papal Primacy as defined by the Catholic Church, especially by the First Vatican Council. Indeed, it is troubling to learn, as Father Michael Bazzi informed me today, that you, Your Excellency, engaged in "negotiations" with Bishop Soro.
>
> Thus, Your Excellency, my first question to you is this: What is there to negotiate with a potential convert to the Catholic Faith? What is negotiable about the truth?

My second question to you is this: Does Bishop Mar Bawai Soro believe in Papal Primacy and Papal Infallibility as taught solemnly by the First Vatican Council, which was presided over by His Holiness Pope Pius IX?

My third question to you is this: Does Bishop Mar Bawai Soro accept the Marian dogmas proclaimed by Pope Pius IX and Pope Pius XII in exactly the sense in which they were promulgated by the authority given them as Successors of Saint Peter? Does he accept the doctrine of Purgatory as taught solemnly by the Council of Trent?

My fourth question to you is this: Did Bishop Mar Bawai Soro and his priests and faithful have to make a formal, solemn and public Abjuration of Error before being received into the Chaldean Rite of the Catholic Church?

His Holiness Pope Leo XIII explained that there must be a perfect concord of Faith for there to be a true union between West and East. This is what he wrote in *Praeclara Gratulationis Publicae*, June 20, 1894:

> "Weigh carefully in your minds and before God the nature of Our request. It is not for any human motive, but impelled by Divine Charity and a desire for the salvation of all, that We advise the reconciliation and union with the Church of Rome; and We mean a perfect and complete union, such as could not subsist in any way if nothing else was brought about but a certain kind of agreement in the Tenets of Belief and an intercourse of Fraternal love. The True Union between Christians is that which Jesus Christ, the Author of the Church, instituted and desired, and which consists in a Unity of Faith and Unity of Government." (Pope Leo XIII, *Praeclara Gratulationis Publicae*, June 20, 1884.)

My fifth question to you is this: Was the Profession of Faith made by Bishop Mar Bawai Soro presaged or conditioned in way by the "nuancing" of language on various points, such as his notion of Papal Primacy and other doctrinal points, so that he could make "mental reservations" to hold him "harmless" for not assenting to every point of doctrine as it has been defined by the authority of the Catholic Church?

My sixth question to you is this: Did Walter Cardinal Kasper, the President of the Pontifical Council for Promoting Christian Unity, play any role in the negotiations between Bishop Mar Bawai Soro and you, Your Excellency?

The Ravenna Document, October 13, 2007, leaves open the possibility that some kind of union between the Catholic Church and the Orthdox confessions can be brought about if an agreement was reached to accept the Orthodox's misrepresentation (my characterization) of the "Petrine Ministry" in the First Millennium. This misrepresentation of true history was exploded by Pope Leo XIII in the aforementioned *Praeclara Gratulationis Publicae*, but has found itself expressed by none other than the then Joseph Cardinal Ratzinger in Principles of Catholic Theology in 1982 and in The Ravenna Document itself.

My seventh question to you is this: Was *The Ravenna Document* used as any kind of guideline or foundation to develop a mutually acceptable "understanding" about the doctrine of Papal Primacy between Bishop Mar Bawai Soro and you, Your Excellency?

My eighth question to you is this: Are the terms of the agreement you reached with Bishop Mar Bawai Soro "sensitive" because said terms might be used as the prototype for effecting a possible reconciliation of the entire Assyrian Apostolic Church of the East (and the Orthodox Churches) with the Catholic Church? Is there a fear that the questions being raised might undermine efforts to effect such future "reconciliations"?

A further concern held by many Catholics, Your Excellency, revolves around the Assyrian Anaphora of Addai and Mari without the words of consecration contained with its text. Although Father Michael Bazzi informed me on Friday, May 16, 2008, that Bishop Mar Bawai Soro and his priests will use the Assyrian anaphora *without the words of consecration for the time being*, there is no indication of how long "the time being" might be (other than until they "get used to" the Chaldean formula, which is identical to that of the traditional Roman Rite of the Catholic Church).

My ninth question to you is this: Was the Catholic Church wrong to have commanded the Chaldean Rite to use the proper form of consecration in the Sixteenth Century? Was the Catholic Church wrong to reaffirm this command in 1902 under the pontificate of Pope Leo XIII? How could the Catholic Church be wrong for 440 years before Joseph Cardinal Ratzinger finally "got it right" in 2001, thus affirming, for the first time in the history of the Catholic Church, a Canon of the Mass without any words of consecration?

My tenth and final question to you is this: Did Bishop Mar Bawai Soro, who has certainly suffered much injustice and excoriation at the hands of his former confreres of the Assyrian Apostolic Church of the East, take the initiative to commence discussions/negotiations with you, Your Excellency? Were Roman authorities involved prior to Bishop Soro's contacts with you?

The fear of many of us, Your Excellency, is that the recent agreement between the Bishop Mar Bawai Soro and the Chaldean Rite Eparchy of Saint Peter the Apostle is but another example of a false "reconciliation" that is presaged on preconditions that have nothing to do with a genuine conversion to and acceptance of the Catholic Faith.

Pope Saint Pius X put the matter this way in *Notre Charge Apostolique*, August 15, 1910:

> Alas! this organization [The Sillon, which had views identical to those expressed in Gaudium et Spes] which formerly afforded such promising expectations, this limpid and impetuous stream, has been harnessed in its course by the modern enemies of the Church, and is now no more than a miserable affluent of the great movement of apostasy being organized in every country for the establishment of a One-World Church which shall have neither dogmas, nor hierarchy, neither discipline for the mind, nor curb for the passions, and which, under the pretext of freedom and human dignity, would bring back to the world (if such a Church could

> overcome) the reign of legalized cunning and force, and the oppression of the weak, and of all those who toil and suffer." (Pope Saint Pius X, *Notre Charge Apostolique*, August 15, 1910.)

Pope Pius XI put the matter this way in *Mortalium Animos*, January 6, 1928:

> **Those, who are unhappily infected with these errors, hold that dogmatic truth is not absolute but relative, that is, it agrees with the varying necessities of time and place and with the varying tendencies of the mind, since it is not contained in immutable revelation, but is capable of being accommodated to human life.** Besides this, in connection with things which must be believed, it is nowise licit to use that distinction which some have seen fit to introduce between those articles of faith which are **fundamental and those which are not fundamental**, as they say, as if the former are to be accepted by all, while the latter may be left to the free assent of the faithful: for the supernatural virtue of faith has a formal cause, namely the authority of God revealing, and this is patient of no such distinction. **For this reason it is that all who are truly Christ's believe, for example, the Conception of the Mother of God without stain of original sin with the same faith as they believe the mystery of the August Trinity, and the Incarnation of our Lord just as they do the infallible teaching authority of the Roman Pontiff, according to the sense in which it was defined by the Ecumenical Council of the Vatican. Are these truths not equally certain, or not equally to be believed, because the Church has solemnly sanctioned and defined them, some in one age and some in another, even in those times immediately before our own? Has not God revealed them all? For the teaching authority of the Church, which in the divine wisdom was constituted on earth in order that revealed doctrines might remain intact for ever, and that they might be brought with ease and security to the knowledge of men, and which is daily exercised through the Roman Pontiff and the Bishops who are in communion with him, has also the office of defining, when it sees fit, any truth with solemn rites and decrees, whenever this is necessary either to oppose the errors or the attacks of heretics, or more clearly and in greater detail to stamp the minds of the faithful with the articles of sacred doctrine which have been explained.** But in the use of this extraordinary teaching authority no newly invented matter is brought in, nor is anything new added to the number of those truths which are at least implicitly contained in the deposit of Revelation, divinely handed down to the Church: only those which are made clear which perhaps may still seem obscure to some, or that which some have previously called into question is declared to be of faith." (Pope Pius XI, *Mortalium Animos*, January 6, 1928.)

Can it be said, Your Excellency, in all truth and without any reservations whatsoever, that Bishop Mar Bawai Soro accepts each of the doctrines enumerated by Pope Pius XI in exactly the sense that they have been taught by the authority of the Catholic Church without any degree of qualification or reservation, being willing to explicate and to defend these doctrines from his pulpit and in his apostolic work for souls? There is no such thing as "partial" communion with the Catholic Church.

> As I noted before, Your Excellency, I realize that you may not be willing to answer these questions. If that is the case, fiat voluntas tua. I would simply appreciate your indicating this to me, at which point I will proceed with my article, Your Excellency, including the questions that I have just asked you. (Bishop Jammo refused to respond to my questions. See **Not Such a Triumph After All** .)

True to his subjectivist self, the chief apostle of the "new ecclesiology", Ratzinger/Benedict, tried to use the situation in Red China as a grand "workshop" to "perfect" a "communion" among the "particular churches" in China without having required members of the rump church to renounce their errors publicly and while he strongly "encouraged" those who are still suffering in the underground Church to cooperate with the Communist officials there so that the "suffering" of the past can be overcome by means of the aforementioned "spiritual reconciliation," which must necessarily precede the "difficulties" of differences of Faith:

> Addressing the whole Church in his Apostolic Letter *Novo Millennio Ineunte*, my venerable predecessor Pope John Paul II, stated that an "important area in which there has to be commitment and planning on the part of the universal Church and the particular Churches [is] *the domain of communion (koinonia)*, which embodies and reveals the very essence of the mystery of the Church. Communion is the fruit and demonstration of that love which springs from the heart of the Eternal Father and is poured out upon us through the Spirit whom Jesus gives us (cf. *Rom* 5:5), to make us all 'one heart and one soul' (*Acts* 4:32). It is in building this communion of love that the Church appears as 'sacrament', as the 'sign and instrument of intimate union with God and of the unity of the human race.' The Lord's words on this point are too precise for us to diminish their import. Many things are necessary for the Church's journey through history, not least in this new century; but without charity (*agape*) all will be in vain. It is again the Apostle Paul who in his *hymn to love* reminds us: even if we speak the tongues of men and of angels, and if we have faith 'to move mountains', but are without love, all will come to 'nothing' (cf. 1 *Cor* 13:2). Love is truly the 'heart' of the Church".
>
> These matters, which concern the very nature of the universal Church, have a particular significance for the Church which is in China. **Indeed you are aware of the problems that she is seeking to overcome – within herself and in her relations with Chinese civil society – tensions, divisions and recriminations.**
>
> In this regard, last year, while speaking of the nascent Church, I had occasion to recall that "from the start the community of the disciples has known not only the joy of the Holy Spirit, the grace of truth and love, but also trials that are constituted above all by disagreements about the truths of faith, with the consequent wounds to communion. Just as the fellowship of love has existed since the outset and will continue to the end (cf. 1 *Jn* 1:1ff.), so also, from the start, division unfortunately arose. We should not be surprised that it still exists today ... Thus, in the events of the world but also in the weaknesses of the Church, there is always a risk of losing faith, hence, **also love and brotherhood**. Consequently it is a specific duty of those who believe in the Church of love and want to live in her to recognize this danger too".

> **The history of the Church teaches us, then, that authentic communion is not expressed without arduous efforts at reconciliation. Indeed, the purification of memory, the pardoning of wrong-doers, the forgetting of injustices suffered and the loving restoration to serenity of troubled hearts, all to be accomplished in the name of Jesus crucified and risen, can require moving beyond personal positions or viewpoints, born of painful or difficult experiences. These are urgent steps that must be taken if the bonds of communion between the faithful and the Pastors of the Church in China are to grow and be made visible.** (Letter to Bishops, Priests, Consecrated Persons and Lay Faithful of Red China.)

In other words, Ratzinger/Benedict was telling the members of the underground Church in Red China that it was up to *them* to make "visible" a "communion" with the "pastors" of a rump church that supports the Communist regime's "population control" policies. "Communion" depends upon *them*, the underground Catholics, being willing to forgive past--and *present*!--injustices as well as to forget the inconvenient truth that the most of the leaders of the rump church defect from several of the Church's defined teachings on Faith and Morals, placing them totally outside of the pale of the Catholic Church, as Pope Leo XIII noted in *Satis Cognitum,* June 29, 1896.

Ratzinger/Benedict was telling the long-suffering Catholics in the underground Church in Red China that their suffering is appreciated and noted. It was time, however, to "move on" and purify "memories" so that a "reconciliation" based on a deliberate and calculated overlooking of defections from Faith and Morals on the part of the rump church in China could take place, leaving to a later date--perhaps--"discussions" on the more "delicate" matters that might seem to the Communist authorities to be an "interference" in their "internal affairs." Just be quiet, therefore, don't complain about the government's "population control policies," be good citizens and be content that you have the sacraments and are in "communion" with your fellow Chinese Catholics.

An unfair reading of Ratzinger/Benedict's June 30, 2007 letter? Read this footnote from the text of the 2009 Compendium and decide for yourselves:

> We can see that the Holy Father is talking about a **spiritual reconciliation, which can and must take place now, even before a structural merger of official and unofficial Catholic communities takes place**. As a matter of fact, the Holy Father seems to make a distinction between "a spiritual reconciliation" and "a structural merger". He recognizes that the reconciliation is like a journey that "cannot be accomplished overnight" (6.6): however, he emphasizes that the steps to be taken on the way are necessary and urgent, and cannot therefore be postponed because - or on the pretext that - they are difficult since they require the overcoming of personal positions or views. Times and ways may vary according to local situations, but the commitment to reconciliation cannot be abandoned. This path of reconciliation, furthermore, cannot be limited to the spiritual realm of prayer alone but must also be expressed through practical steps of effective ecclesial communion (exchange of experiences, sharing of pastoral projects, common initiatives, etc.). Finally, it should not be forgotten that all without exception are invited to engage in these steps: Bishops, priests, religious and lay faithful. It is by means of practical steps that spiritual reconciliation, including visible reconciliation, will gradually occur, which will culminate one day in the complete structural unity of every diocesan community around its one Bishop and of every

> diocesan community with each other and with the universal Church. In this context, it is licit and fitting to encourage clergy and lay faithful to make gestures of forgiveness and reconciliation in this direction. (Footnote 2, **Compendium**, pp. 8-9.)

This footnote reflected entirely Joseph Ratzinger's abject rejection of the "ecumenism of the return." Ratzinger/Benedict believed that people are gradually "absorbed" into the Church by means of "perfecting" their "communion" with other Christians. This is heretical. This is condemned by the authority of the Catholic Church. Yet it remains of the essence of Ratzinger/Benedict's theology, which was reflected so completely in his June 30, 2007, **Letter to Bishops, Priests, Consecrated Persons and Lay Faithful of Red China** and in the **Compendium** released on May 24, 2009.

After all, it is "reconciliation" and "love" that matters the most, although Catholics understand that true love of God can never sanction anything that is offensive to Him, making, therefore, Ratzinger's appeal for a "reconciliation" with authorities of a rump church who support (or are silent about) government polices contrary to Faith and Morals nothing other than an exercise in pure subjectivism.

Ratzinger/Benedict's subjectivism was further displayed when he vitiated his earlier affirmation of Papal Primacy by excusing Catholics who seek out the sacraments from "pastors" who are not in "communion" with the Roman Pontiff, which is what he believed himself to be until 8:00 p.m., Rome time, on Thursday, February 28, 2014:

> In not a few situations, then, you have faced the problem of concelebration of the Eucharist. In this regard, I remind you that this presupposes, as conditions, profession of the same faith and hierarchical communion with the Pope and with the universal Church. Therefore it is licit to concelebrate with Bishops and with priests who are in communion with the Pope, **even if they are recognized by the civil authorities and maintain a relationship with entities desired by the State and extraneous to the structure of the Church, provided – as was said earlier (cf. section 7 above, paragraph 8) – that this recognition and this relationship do not entail the denial of unrenounceable principles of the faith and of ecclesiastical communion.**
>
> The lay faithful too, who are animated by a sincere love for Christ and for the Church, must not hesitate to participate in the Eucharist celebrated by Bishops and by priests who are in full communion with the Successor of Peter and are recognized by the civil authorities. The same applies for all the other sacraments.
>
> Concerning Bishops whose consecrations took place without the pontifical mandate yet respecting the Catholic rite of episcopal ordination, the resulting problems must always be resolved in the light of the principles of Catholic doctrine. Their ordination – as I have already said (cf. section 8 above, paragraph 12) – is illegitimate but valid, just as priestly ordinations conferred by them are valid, and sacraments administered by such Bishops and priests are likewise valid. **Therefore the faithful, taking this into account, where the eucharistic celebration and the other sacraments are concerned, must, within the limits of the possible, seek Bishops and priests who are in communion with the Pope:**

> **nevertheless, where this cannot be achieved without grave inconvenience, they may, for the sake of their spiritual good, turn also to those who are not in communion with the Pope.** (**Letter to Bishops, Priests, Consecrated Persons and Lay Faithful of Red China**.)

Never mind the fact that the rump church in Red China is a tool of the government. Never mind that there might be some "differences" between the teachings of the rump church in Red China and the Catholic Church. These differences do not matter to Ratzinger/Benedict unless they involve a "denial of unrenounceable principles of the faith and of ecclesiastical communion," although there is not one article of the Faith that is "renounceable." For if it is permissible to participate in the liturgical services of heretics who defect from the Catholic Faith, then Pope Saint Pius V was himself wrong when he told Catholics, many of whom did not look forward to heavy fines or the confiscation of their properties or imprisonment or martyrdom--or all of those things, in England not to assist at the liturgies of the heretical and schismatic Anglican Church.

Or, my friends, is *that* what Joseph Ratzinger/Benedict XVI was saying?

Was he saying, as he made reference to in his **Explanatory Letter on "Summorum Pontificum**, that he was doing then what others did not do in the past, that is, being willing to "bend" a little bit on some points in order to effect a "reconciliation" which comes at the price of truth itself?

What an affront to the witness of the martyrs over the history of the Church, including the martyrs of the underground Church in Red China in the past sixty-five years, who refused to make one compromise with error or heresy or any interference at all on the part of the civil state with the life and mission of the Catholic Church.

Then again, of course, the counterfeit church of conciliarism is "rife" with members in "good standing" who support some of the very evils promoted by the Communist regime in Red China. Others are in "good standing" despite supporting the promotion of perversity under cover of the civil law. Thus it is that the late Edward Moore Kennedy and John F. Kerry and Mario Matthew Cuomo and Andrew Mark Cuomo and David Paterson and Joseph Robinette Biden, Jr., and Arnold Schwarzenegger and Richard Durbin and Thomas Harkin and Jim Doyle and Kathleen Sebelius and Jennifer Granholm and Christopher Dodd, et al., can retain their "good standing" despite their open support for baby-killing and perversity under cover of the civil law.

Father John Jenkins is considered to be a "fit" president of an allegedly Catholic University after bestowing an award upon a man, Barack Hussein Obama, who is at war with God by means of supporting--and issuing Executive Orders permitting--the slaughter of the preborn under cover of the civil law.

Former Prime Minister of the United Kingdom Tony Blair was "received" into the counterfeit church of conciliarism without renouncing his support for baby-killing under cover of the civil law.

Conciliar "bishops" are permitted to renounce even those articles of the true Catholic Faith that are *supposed* to be part of the "official" doctrines of the counterfeit church of conciliarism. Robert

Zollitsch, now the former "archbishop" of Freising Germany, maintained his own "good standing" despite having denied that Our Blessed Lord and Saviour died on the wood of the Holy Cross on Good Friday in atonement for our sins.

There was, you see, quite a bit of logic involved in requesting the Catholics of the underground church in Red China to join up with the rump church that promotes some of the very evils that are support by "Catholics" in the counterfeit church of conciliarism without forfeiting their place in the One World Church of Ecumenism born of the new ecclesiology.

IV. 3 The New Ecclesiology Is Heretical

To seek to "perfect" a "communion" among Catholics who have suffered in the underground Church in Red China with the bishops and priests of the rump church without requiring an abjuration of errors, including a formal dissociation from the Communist authorities who have "licensed" that renegade church, was to attempt to put into practice on a large scale Ratzinger/Benedict's "new ecclesiology," which was summarized very succinctly by Bishop Donald Sanborn in **The New Ecclesiology: An Overview**:

> The new ecclesiology reduces the Church of Christ to an amalgam of many different churches with different and opposing doctrines, disciplines, and hierarchies. Membership in this great and broad Church of Christ is subject to degrees. The more elements you have, the better off you are, and the closer you are to the "fullness," which is found in the Roman Catholic Church.
>
> It is something like bingo. If your card has all the numbers, you have the "fullness" — you have bingo. But even if you miss bingo, your card could be half filled or a quarter filled. While you do not have bingo, your card nevertheless has value, since you have an imperfect collection of what makes up bingo.
>
> **Everything in this new ecclesiology is "partial" and "full." You are partially Church of Christ if you are non-Catholic, but fully if you are Catholic. Catholics are in "partial communion" with non-Catholics, but wait for the day when they can be in "full communion," i.e., when Modernism erodes the faith enough that people will not care anymore if they are Protestant, Orthodox, or Catholic.** Likewise these non-Catholic churches are means of salvation *to the extent that* they possess valid sacraments and true doctrines. **This is as silly as saying that an aircraft has the capacity to take you to Europe to the extent that it has a half a tank of fuel. The fact that it is lacking the other half of the fuel means that you and your fellow passengers are going to be food for the eyeless aquatic creatures that inhabit the dark depths of the Atlantic Ocean.**
>
> In other words, the true Church of Christ is not a collection of true elements, like a pile of rocks, but is a unified essence, a single thing, just as Christ, its head, is one Person. **What is outside of Christ cannot be "partially Christ." You cannot be partially a member of Christ, and partially not, any more than you could be partially someone's son, and partially not. Essence does not admit of degrees or separable parts. Either the whole essence (nature) is there, or none of it is there. Imagine a gas station that advertised**

that it sold a product "with elements of true gasoline." Imagine an airline that boasted of a fleet of aircraft which possessed "elements of true airplanes," or bragged that its pilots had "elements of true pilot training." Imagine if a waiter put a steak in front of you, and said that it came from an animal that had "elements of true cow." I think the point is made.

"Elements" of the true Church of Christ do not constitute any false sect as a partial member of the Church of Christ. The "elements" are stolen, like so much booty, from the Catholic Church. **They are false churches, sects, and their use of Catholic doctrine and Catholic sacraments is under false pretense and sacrilegious. They are involved in a shameful lie when they present themselves as true Christianity, and their lie should be exposed and condemned.**

But let the popes speak. I have prepared a triple-column comparison[1] of the new ecclesiology and the traditional ecclesiology. In the third column, I draw the conclusion from the comparison.

I have reduced the comparison of the two systems to four questions:

- Whether schismatic and/or heretical churches are part of the Church of Christ?
- Whether it is possible to be part of the Church of Christ without being submitted to the Roman Pontiff?
- Whether it is true that in every valid celebration of the Eucharist, the one, holy, catholic and apostolic Church becomes present?
- Whether the Holy Ghost uses schismatic and/or heretical sects as means of salvation?

Read it, and see if you can honestly say that Vatican II is not guilty of heresy. (**The New Ecclesiology: An Overview**.)

In other words, merge now for the sake "love" and "reconciliation." Other, presumably "renounceable" matters of Faith, can wait until people have become used to living in states of apostasy and betrayal. Sounds sort of familiar, doesn't it (see **Accustomed to Apostasy**)?

IV. 4 The Catholic Church Forbids the Civil State to Interfere with the Life of the Church and Forbids Cooperation with Communism

Showing his penchant for making one "pastoral" compromise after another, Ratzinger/Benedict XVI, after stating that the civil authorities cannot interfere with the life and the mission of the Catholic Church, "encouraged" Catholics in Red China to "register" with the Communist authorities, citing the "Second" Vatican Council's call to "respect" those who think "differently" than do Catholics:

Therefore the Second Vatican Council underlines that "**those also have a claim on our respect and charity who think and act differently from us in social, political, and religious matters.** In fact, the more deeply, through courtesy and love, **we come to**

understand their ways of thinking, the more easily will we be able to enter into dialogue with them". But, as the same Council admonishes us, "love and courtesy of this kind should not, of course, make us indifferent to truth and goodness."

Considering "Jesus' original plan", it is clear that the claim of some entities, desired by the State and extraneous to the structure of the Church, to place themselves above the Bishops and to guide the life of the ecclesial community, does not correspond to Catholic doctrine, according to which the Church is "apostolic", as the Second Vatican Council underlined. The Church is apostolic "in her *origin* because she has been built on 'the foundation of the Apostles' (*Eph* 2:20). She is apostolic in her *teaching* which is the same as that of the Apostles. She is apostolic by reason of her *structure* insofar as she is taught, sanctified, and guided until Christ returns by the Apostles through their successors who are the Bishops in communion with the Successor of Peter". Therefore, in every individual particular Church, "it is in the name of the Lord that the diocesan Bishop [and only he] leads the flock entrusted to him, and he does so as the proper, ordinary and immediate Pastor"; at a national level, moreover, only a legitimate Episcopal Conference can formulate pastoral guidelines, valid for the entire Catholic community of the country concerned.

Likewise, the declared purpose of the afore-mentioned entities to implement "the principles of independence and autonomy, self-management and democratic administration of the Church" is incompatible with Catholic doctrine, which from the time of the ancient Creeds professes the Church to be "one, holy, catholic and apostolic".

In the light of the principles here outlined, Pastors and lay faithful will recall that the preaching of the Gospel, catechesis and charitable activity, liturgical and cultic action, as well as all pastoral choices, are uniquely the competence of the Bishops together with their priests in the unbroken continuity of the faith handed down by the Apostles in the Sacred Scriptures and in Tradition, and therefore they cannot be subject to any external interference.

Given this difficult situation, not a few members of the Catholic community are asking whether recognition from the civil authorities – necessary in order to function publicly – somehow compromises communion with the universal Church. I am fully aware that this problem causes painful disquiet in the hearts of Pastors and faithful. **In this regard I maintain, in the first place, that the requisite and courageous safeguarding of the deposit of faith and of sacramental and hierarchical communion is not of itself opposed to dialogue with the authorities concerning those aspects of the life of the ecclesial community that fall within the civil sphere. There would not be any particular difficulties with acceptance of the recognition granted by civil authorities on condition that this does not entail the denial of unrenounceable principles of faith and of ecclesiastical communion. In not a few particular instances, however, indeed almost always, in the process of recognition the intervention of certain bodies obliges the people involved to adopt attitudes, make gestures and undertake commitments that are contrary to the dictates of their conscience as Catholics. I understand, therefore, how in such varied conditions and circumstances it is difficult to determine the correct choice to be made. For this reason the Holy See, after restating the**

> **principles, leaves the decision to the individual Bishop who, having consulted his presbyterate, is better able to know the local situation, to weigh the concrete possibilities of choice and to evaluate the possible consequences within the diocesan community. It could be that the final decision does not obtain the consensus of all the priests and faithful. I express the hope, however, that it will be accepted, albeit with suffering, and that the unity of the diocesan community with its own Pastor will be maintained.**
>
> It would be good, finally, if Bishops and priests, with truly pastoral hearts, were to take every possible step to avoid giving rise to situations of scandal, seizing opportunities to form the consciences of the faithful, **with particular attention to the weakest: all this should be lived out in communion and in fraternal understanding, avoiding judgements and mutual condemnations. In this case too, it must be kept in mind, especially where there is little room for freedom, that in order to evaluate the morality of an act it is necessary to devote particular care to establishing the real intentions of the person concerned, in addition to the objective shortcoming. Every case, then, will have to be pondered individually, taking account of the circumstances. .** (Letter to Bishops, Priests, Consecrated Persons and Lay Faithful of Red China.)

In other words, yes, the civil state cannot impose any external constraints on the Catholic Church. In practical terms, however, we just "have" to let the individual bishops make these decisions for themselves as they seek to re-educate the faithful about the fact that their resistance to registering with the Communist authorities over the years has been utterly in vain, which was exactly what Ratzinger/Benedict had sought to do with traditionally-minded Catholics attached to the structures of the counterfeit church of conciliarism by extending to them the "olive branch" of a "liberated" Mass of Tradition in exchange for their silence about the evil that is the Protestant and Judeo-Masonic *Novus Ordo* liturgical service and all of the other apostasies and blasphemies and sacrileges associated with the conciliar ethos.

Pope Pius XII, writing in *Ad Sinarum Gentem*, October 7, 1954, exhorted the bishops and priests and lay faithful in Red China who had defected to the Communist regime underground Church to recall the words of the first Pope, Saint Peter, who taught us to obey God rather than men:

> We earnestly exhort "in the heart of Christ" (Phil. 1. 8) those faithful of whom **We have mournfully written above to come back to the path of repentance and salvation. Let them remember that, when it is necessary, one must render to Caesar what is Caesar's, and with greater reason, one must render to God what is God's (Cf. Luke 20. 25). When men demand things contrary to the Divine Will, then it is necessary to put into practice the maxim of St. Peter: "We must obey God rather than men" (Acts 5. 29). Let them also remember that it is impossible to serve two masters, if these order things opposed to one another (Cf. Matt. 6. 24). Also at times it is impossible to please both Jesus Christ and men (Cf. Gal. 1. 10). But if it sometimes happens that he who wishes to remain faithful to the Divine Redeemer even unto death must suffer great harm, let him bear it with a strong and serene soul.**

> On the other hand, We wish to congratulate repeatedly those who, suffering severe difficulties, have been outstanding in their loyalty to God and to the Catholic Church, and so have been "counted worthy to suffer disgrace for the name of Jesus" (Acts 5. 41). **With a paternal heart We encourage them to continue brave and intrepid along the road they have taken, keeping in mind the words of Jesus Christ: "And do not be afraid of those who kill the body but cannot kill the soul. But rather be afraid of him who is able to destroy both soul and body in hell . . . But as for you, the very hairs of your head are all numbered. Therefore do not be afraid . . . Therefore everyone who acknowledges me before men, I will also acknowledge him before my Father in heaven. But whoever disowns me before men, I in turn will disown him before my Father in heaven**" (Matt. 10. 28, 30-33). (Pope Pius XII, *Ad Sinarum Gentem*, October 7, 1954.)

Pope Pius XII, writing in *Ad Apostolorum Principis* on June 29, 1958, just three months and ten days before his death, condemned the evils that were then--and are now to this day--propagated by the Chinese Patriotic Catholic Association:

> **Against methods of acting such as these, which violate the principal rights of the human person and trample on the sacred liberty of the sons of God, all Christians from every part of the world, indeed all men of good sense cannot refrain from raising their voices with Us in real horror and from uttering a protest deploring the deranged conscience of their fellow men.**
>
> And since these crimes are being committed under the guise of patriotism, We consider it Our duty to remind everyone once again of the Church's teaching on this subject.'
>
> For the Church exhorts and encourages Catholics to love their country with sincere and strong love, to give due obedience in accord with natural and positive divine law to those who hold public office, to give them active and ready assistance for the promotion of those undertakings by which their native land can in peace and order daily achieve greater prosperity and further true development.
>
> The Church has always impressed on the minds of her children that declaration of the Divine Redeemer: "Render therefore to Caesar the things that are Caesar's and to God the things that are God's."[5] We call it a declaration because these words make certain and incontestable the principle that Christianity never opposes or obstructs what is truly useful or advantageous to a country.
>
> However, if Christians are bound in conscience to render to Caesar (that is, to human authority) what belongs to Caesar, then Caesar likewise, or those who control the state, cannot exact obedience when they would be usurping God's rights or forcing Christians either to act at variance with their religious duties or to sever themselves from the unity of the Church and its lawful hierarchy.

Under such circumstances, every Christian should cast aside all doubt and calmly and firmly repeat the words with which Peter and the other Apostles answered the first persecutors of the Church: "We must obey God rather than men."

With emphatic insistence, those who promote the interests of this association which claims a monopoly on patriotism, speak over and over again of peace and admonish Catholics earnestly to exert all their efforts to establish it. On the surface these words are excellent and righteous, for who deserves greater praise than the man who prepares the way to introduce and establish peace?

But peace -- as you well know, Venerable Brethren and beloved sons -- does not consist of words alone and does not rely on changing formulas which are suitable for the moment but contradict one's real plans and practices, which do not conform with the meaning and way of true peace but with hatred, discord, and deceit.

Peace worthy of the name must be founded on the principles of charity and justice which He taught who is the "Prince of Peace," and who adopted this title as a kind of royal standard for Himself. True peace is that which the Church desires to be established: one that is stable, just, fair, and founded on right order; one which binds all together -- citizens, families, and peoples -- by the firm ties of the rights of the Supreme Lawgiver, and by the bonds of mutual fraternal love and cooperation.

As she looks forward to and hopes for this peaceful dwelling together of nations, the Church expects each nation to preserve that degree of dignity which becomes it. For the Church, which has ever kept a friendly attitude toward the various events in your country, long ago spoke through Our late Predecessor of happy memory and expressed the desire that "full recognition be given to the legitimate aspirations and rights of the nation, which is more populous than any other, whose civilization and culture go back to the earliest times, which has, in past ages, with the development of its resources, had periods of great prosperity, and which -- it may be reasonably conjectured -- will become even greater in the future ages, provided it pursues justice and honor." (Pope Pius XII, *Ad Apostolorum Principis*, June 29, 1858.)

Joseph Ratzinger/Benedict XVI, of course, made reference to none of these remarks made by our last true pope. How can he have done so? Pope Pius XII's words contradict his positivistic assertions that "progress" had been made in Red China that made possible the implementation of the new ecclesiology's program for a "spiritual reconciliation" as the means of "perfecting" a situation of "partial communion" into one of "full communion."

The one and only thing that has changed between June 29, 1958, and May 29, 2009, shortly after the Compedium has been released, was that we have had antipopes who have shown us over and over again they are willing to blaspheme God publicly and to sell out the interests of Catholic truth in the name of a "dialogue" that the enemies of the Church, such as Communists and other naturalists, do not want and will never accept until and unless a "concordat" is reached solely on their terms.

Joseph Ratzinger/Benedict XVI not only ignored the words that Pope Pius XII wrote about the situation of Catholics in Red China in 1954 and 1958 that are just as relevant today as they were, respectively, sixty and fifty-six years ago now. He ignored Pope Pius XI's absolute prohibition against any and all cooperation with Communist regimes whatsoever:

> **See to it, Venerable Brethren, that the Faithful do not allow themselves to be deceived! Communism is intrinsically wrong, and *no one who would save Christian civilization may collaborate with it in any undertaking whatsoever. Those who permit themselves to be deceived into lending their aid towards the triumph of Communism in their own country, will be the first to fall victims of their error.* And the greater the antiquity and grandeur of the Christian civilization in the regions where Communism successfully penetrates, so much more devastating will be the hatred displayed by the godless.** (Pope Pius XI, *Divini Redemptoris*, March 19, 1937.)

Joseph Ratzinger/Benedict XVI, believing in conciliarism's tolerant attitude about errors and the necessity of entering into "dialogue" with those who hold them so that we can "understand" them better, is one of the most deceived men on the face of this earth. His "new ecclesiology" is from Hell itself.

V. Renouncing the Social Reign of Christ the King and the Conversion of Red China

Joseph Ratzinger/Benedict XVI, who believes in the separation of Church and State that was called a "thesis absolutely false" by Pope Saint Pius X in *Vehementer Nos*, February 11, 1906, renounced all claims to the conversion of Red China and thus of the Social Reign of Christ the King when he wrote the following in his **Letter to Bishops, Priests, Consecrated Persons and Lay Faithful of Red China**:

> As far as relations between the political community and the Church in China are concerned, it is worth calling to mind the enlightening teaching of the Second Vatican Council, which states: "The Church, by reason of her role and competence, is not identified with any political community nor is she tied to any political system. She is at once the sign and the safeguard of the transcendental dimension of the human person". And the Council continues: "The political community and the Church are autonomous and independent of each other in their own fields. They are both at the service of the personal and social vocation of the same individuals, though under different titles. Their service will be more efficient and beneficial to all if both institutions develop better cooperation according to the circumstances of place and time,"
>
> Likewise, therefore, the Catholic Church which is in China does not have a mission to change the structure or administration of the State; rather, her mission is to proclaim Christ to men and women, as the Saviour of the world, basing herself – in carrying out her proper apostolate – on the power of God. As I recalled in my Encyclical *Deus Caritas Est*, "The Church cannot and must not take upon herself the political battle to bring about the most just society possible. She cannot and must not replace the State. Yet at the same time she cannot and must not remain on the sidelines in the fight for justice. She has to play her part through rational argument and she has to reawaken the spiritual energy without which

> justice, which always demands sacrifice, cannot prevail and prosper. A just society must be the achievement of politics, not of the Church. Yet the promotion of justice through efforts to bring about openness of mind and will to the demands of the common good is something which concerns the Church deeply. (**Letter to Bishops, Priests, Consecrated Persons and Lay Faithful of Red China**.)

Apostasy. The Catholic Church has a mission from her Divine Founder and Invisible Head to convert all men and all nations to the true Faith. The just society is the result of the growth of the Faith in a country, *not* of politics.

Ratzinger/Benedict categorized the murderous regime in Red China as nothing other than another kind of "structure" or "administration" of a civil state. It is nothing of the sort. It is an illegitimate regime that seized power by brute force, shedding the blood of millions upon millions of innocent human beings in the process, and it has maintained itself in power by those same means, enabled since 1971 by one American presidential administration after another and by large multinational corporations who have exploited the availability of cheap labor in Red China in many instances, to manufacture products, including food, replete with toxins that have actually killed people.

The government of the "People's" Republic of China is not based on "neutral" principles of garden-variety naturalism, not that those "ordinary" principles of naturalism are not offensive to God and harmful to social order, of course. The government of Red China is based on a specific and categorical rejection of God and upon the primacy of the civil state over its citizens. It is an evil regime from beginning to end, and it must be the duty of each Catholic in China to pray for an end to the reign of Communist terror there and to the conversion of this land to the true Faith.

The Catholic Church does not use "force" to effect such conversions. She uses the graces won for us on the wood of the Holy Cross by Our Blessed Lord and Saviour Jesus Christ and that flow into our hearts and souls through the loving hands of Our Lady, she who is the Mediatrix of All Graces, to effect such conversions, aided by the blood of the martyrs who refused to compromise one little bit with evil regimes. The Catholic Church seeks the establishment of the Social Reign of Christ the King in all nations as each civil government in the world recognizes her as the true religion and as its rulers stand ready to yield to her maternal intervention, exercised judiciously and rarely only after the exhausting of her Indirect Power of teaching and preaching and exhortation, when the good of souls demands such intervention.

Quite opposed to the apostate spirit of Joseph Ratzinger/Benedict XVI, Pope Saint Pius X wrote the following in *Notre Charge Apostolique*, August 15, 1910:

> But, on the contrary, by ignoring the laws governing human nature and by breaking the bounds within which they operate, the human person is lead, not toward progress, but towards death. This, nevertheless, is what they want to do with human society; they dream of changing its natural and traditional foundations; **they dream of a Future City built on different principles, and they dare to proclaim these more fruitful and more beneficial than the principles upon which the present Christian City rests**.
>
> No, Venerable Brethren, We must repeat with the utmost energy in these times of social

> and intellectual anarchy when everyone takes it upon himself to teach as a teacher and lawmaker - the City cannot be built otherwise than as God has built it; society cannot be setup unless the Church lays the foundations and supervises the work; **no, civilization is not something yet to be found, nor is the New City to be built on hazy notions; it has been in existence and still is: it is Christian civilization, it is the Catholic City. It has only to be set up and restored continually against the unremitting attacks of insane dreamers, rebels and miscreants. Omnia instaurare in Christo**. (Pope Saint Pius X, *Notre Charge Apostolique*, August 15, 1910.)

Joseph Ratzinger/Benedict XVI does not believe this. Neither does Jorge Mario Bergoglio. They are both apostates.

VI. Selling Out to Communists Over and Over Again

The counterfeit church of conciliarism has sold out to Communists over and over again, continuing in a much more overt manner a form of "diplomacy" that had its roots in the Vatican's Secretariat of State as early as the pontificate of Pope Saint Pius XI and continued during the pontificate of Pope Pius XII, especially by means of the machinations of one Monsignor Giovanni Battista Enrico Antonio Maria Montini, the future antipope Paul VI, also known as Paul the Sick.

A very good history of this legacy of compromise--and of a refusal to fulfill Our Lady's Fatima Message--can be find in an English language reprint of an article in *Si, Si, No, No*, "The Blindness of Catholics and the Social Kingship of Christ."

The counterfeit church of conciliarism wasted no time in turning a policy of failed diplomacy into one of outright surrender to the forces of Soviet Communism.

Angelo Roncalli/John XXIII, long a friend of Italian Communists and Socialists assisted by another friend of the Communists and Socialists, the Archbishop of Milan, the aforementioned Giovanni Montini, agreed to exchange absolute silence about evil of Communism at the "Second" Vatican Council in exchange for the presence of "observers" from the Russian Orthodox Church:

> In preparation for the Council, Catholic bishops around the world were polled by mail by the Office of the Secretariat to learn their opinions on topics to be considered at the Council. Communism topped the list.
>
> However, as documented in the previous chapter, at the instigation of Cardinal Montini, two months before the opening of the Council, Pope John XXIII approved the signing of the Metz Accord with Moscow officials, whereby the Soviets would permit two representatives from the Russian State Church to attend the Council in exchange for absolute and total silence at the Council on the subject of Communism/Marxism.
>
> With the exceptions of Cardinal Montini, who instructed Pope John to enter into negotiations with the Soviets, Cardinal Eugene Tisserant, who signed the Accord, and Bishop Jan Willebrands, who made the final contacts with the representatives of the Russian State Church, **the Church Fathers at the Council were ignorant of the existence**

and nature of the Metz Agreement and the horrendous betrayal that it represented. (Mrs. Randy Engel, *The Rite of Sodomy*, pp. 1135-1136)

Why didn't the last Ecumenical Council condemn Communism? A secret accord made at Metz supplies an answer.
Those who pass by the convent of the Little Sisters of the Poor in Borny - on the outskirts of the French city of Metz - never imagine that something of transcendental importance occurred in the residence of Fr. Lagarde, the convent's chaplain. In a hall of this religious residence in August 1962 - two months before Vatican Council II opened - a secret meeting of the greatest importance between two high-ranking personalities took place.

One dignitary was a Cardinal of the Curia, Eugène Tisserant, representing Pope John XXIII; the other was metropolitan Nikodin, who spoke in the name of the Russian Schismatic Church.

This encounter had consequences that changed the direction of Council, which was already prepared to open. In effect, the meeting at Metz determined a change in the trajectory of the very History of the Church in the 20th century.

What was the matter of such great importance that was resolved at his meeting? Based on the documents that are known today, there it was established that Communism would not be condemned by Vatican Council II. In 1962, The Vatican and the Schismatic Russian Church came to an agreement. According to its terms, the Russian "Orthodox Church" agreed to send observers to Vatican II under the condition that no condemnation whatsoever of communism should be made there (1). 1. Ulysses Floridi, Moscou et le Vatican, Paris: France-Empire, Paris, 1979, pp. 147-48; Romano Amerio, *Iota Unum*, K.C., MO: Sarto House, 1996, pp. 75-76; Ricardo de la Cierva, *Oscura rebelion en la Iglesia*, Barcelona: Plaza & Janes, 1987, pp. 580-81. And why were the consequences of such a pact so far-reaching and important?

Because in the 20th century a principal enemy of the Catholic Church was Communism. As such, until Vatican II it had been condemned numerous times by the Magisterium. Moreover, in the early '60s a new condemnation would have been quite damaging, since Communism was passing through a serious crisis, both internally and externally. On one hand, it was losing credibility inside the USSR since the people were becoming increasingly discontent with the horrendous administrative results of 45 years of Communist demagogy. On the other hand, outside the USSR Communism had not been able to persuade the workers and poor of free countries to take up its banner. In fact, up until that time it had never won a free election. Therefore, the leaders of international Communism decided that it was time to begin to change the appearances of the regime in order to retain the power they had and to experiment with new methods of conquest. So in the '60s President Nikita Khrushchev suddenly began to smile and talk about dialogue (2). 2. Plinio Correa de Oliveira, *Unperceived Ideological Transshipment and Dialogue*, New York: Crusade for a Christian Civilization, 1982, pp. 8-15. This would have been a particularly inopportune moment for the Pope or the Council to issue a formal condemnation, which could have either seriously damaged or possibly even destroyed the

Communist regime.

A half secret act

Speaking about the liberty at Vatican II to deal with diverse topics, Professor Romano Amerio revealed some previously unpublished facts. "The salient and half secret point that should be noted," he stated, "is the restriction on the Council's liberty to which John XXIII had agreed a few months earlier, in making an accord with the Orthodox Church by which the patriarchate of Moscow accepted the papal invitation to send observers to the Council, while the Pope for his part guaranteed the Council would refrain from condemning Communism. The negotiations took place at Metz in August 1962, and all the details of time and place were given at a press conference by Mgr. Paul Joseph Schmitt, the Bishop of that Diocese [newspaper *Le Lorrain*, 2/9/63]. The negotiations ended in an agreement signed by metropolitan Nikodim for the Orthodox Church and Cardinal Tisserant, the Dean of the Sacred College of Cardinals, for the Holy See.

"News of the agreement was given in the *France Nouvelle*, the central bulletin of the French communist party in the edition of January 16-22, 1963 in these terms: 'Because the world socialist system is showing its superiority in an uncontestable fashion, and is strong through the support of hundreds and hundreds of millions of men, the Church can no longer be content with a crude anti-communism. As part of its dialogue with the Russian Orthodox Church, it has even promised there will be no direct attack on the Communist system at the Council.' On the Catholic side, the daily *La Croix* of February 15, 1963 gave notice of the agreement, concluding: "'As a consequence of this conversation, Msgr. Nikodim agreed that someone should go to Moscow carrying an invitation, on condition that guarantees were given concerning the apolitical attitude of the Council.'

"Moscow's condition, namely that the Council should say nothing about Communism, was not, therefore, a secret, but the isolated publication of it made no impression on general opinion, as it was not taken up by the press at large and circulated, either because of the apathetic and anaesthetized attitude to Communism common in clerical circles or because the Pope took action to impose silence in the matter. Nonetheless, the agreement had a powerful, albeit silent, effect on the course of the Council when requests for a renewal of the condemnation of Communism were rejected in order to observe this agreement to say nothing about it" (3). 3. Romano Amerio, *Iota Unum*, pp. 65-66. Thus the Council, which made statements on capitalism and colonialism, said nothing specific about the greatest evil of the age, Communism. While the Vatican Monsignors were smiling at the Russian Schismatic representatives, many Bishops were in prison and innumerable faithful were either persecuted or driven underground for their fidelity to the Holy Roman Catholic Church.

The Kremlin-Vatican negotiations

This important information about Vatican-Kremlin negotiations is confirmed in an article 'The mystery of the Rome-Moscow pact' published in the October 1989 issue of *30 Dias*, which quotes statements made by the Bishop of Metz, Paul Joseph Schmitt. In a February 9, 1963 interview with the newspaper *Republicain Lorrain*, Mgr. Schmitt said:

"It was in our region that the 'secret' meeting of Cardinal Tisserant with archbishop Nikodin occurred. The exact place was the residence of Fr. Lagarde, chaplain for the *Little Sister of the Poor* in Borny [on the outskirts of Metz]. Here for the first time the arrival of the prelates of the Russian Church was mentioned. After this meeting, the conditions for the presence of the Russian church's observers were established by Cardinal Willebrands, an assistant of Cardinal Bea. Archbishop Nikodin agreed that an official invitation should be sent to Moscow, with the guarantee of the apolitical character of the Council" (4). 4. *30 Dias*, October 1988, pp. 55-56.

The same source also transcribed a letter of Bishop Georges Roches regarding the *Pact of Metz*:

"That accord was negotiated between the Kremlin and the Vatican at the highest level .... But I can assure you .... that the decision to invite Russian Orthodox observers to Vatican Council II was made personally by His Holiness John XXIII with the encouragement of Cardinal Montini, who was counselor to the Patriarch of Venice when he was Archbishop of Milan.... Cardinal Tisserant received formal orders to negotiate the accord and to make sure that it would be observed during the Council" (5). 5. *Ibid.* p. 57

In a book published some time after this, German theologian Fr. Bernard Häring - who was secretary-coordinator at the Council for the redaction of *Gaudium et Spes* - revealed the more profound reason for the 'pigeon-holing' of a petition that many conciliar Fathers signed asking Paul VI and the Council to condemn Communism: "When around two dozen Bishops requested a solemn condemnation of Communism," stated Fr. Häring, "Msgr. Glorieux .... and I were blamed like scapegoats. I have no reason to deny that I did everything possible to avoid this condemnation, which rang out clearly like a political condemnation. I knew that John XXIII had promised Moscow authorities that the Council would not condemn communism in order to assure the participation of observers of the Russian Orthodox church" (6). . . .

1. Catholic doctrine has always emphatically condemned Communism. It would be possible, should it be necessary, to publish a small book composed exclusively of anti-communist pontifical documents.

2. It would have been natural, therefore, for Vatican Council II, which met in Rome from 1962 to 1965, to have confirmed these condemnations against the greatest enemy of the Church and Christian Civilization in the 20th century.

3. In addition to this, 213 Cardinals, Archbishops, and Bishops solicited Paul VI to have the Council make such a condemnation. Later, 435 Conciliar Fathers repeated the same request. The two petitions were duly delivered within the time limits established by the *Internal Guidelines* of the Council. Nonetheless, inexplicably, neither petition ever came

up for debate. The first was not taken into consideration. As for the second, after the Council had closed, it was alleged that it had been "lost" by Mgr. Achille Glorieux, secretary of the commission that would have been entrusted with the request.

4. The Council closed without making any express censure of Communism. Why was no censure made? The matter seemed wrapped in an enigmatic fog. Only later did these significant facts on the topic appear. The point of my article is to gather and present information from several different sources for the consideration of my reader. How can the actions of the Catholic Prelates who inspired, ordered, followed and maintained the decisions of the Pact of Metz be explained? I leave the answer to my reader. (**The Council of Metz**)

The future Paul VI, Monsignor Giovanni Battista Enrico Antonio Maria Montini, directly betrayed Catholic priests sent behind the Iron Curtain by Pope Pius XII, effectively sentencing these priests to death or imprisonment:

> An elderly gentleman from Paris who worked as an official interpreter for high-level clerics at the Vatican in the early 1950s told this writer that the Soviets blackmailed Montini into revealing the names of priests whom the Vatican had clandestinely sent behind the Iron Curtain to minister to Catholics in the Soviet Union during the Cold War. The Soviet secret police were on hand as soon as the priests crossed over the Russian border and the priest infiltrators were either shot or sent to the gulag.
>
> The extent to which Pope Paul VI was subject to blackmail by the enemies of the Church will probably never be known. It may be that, in so far as the Communists and the Socialists were concerned, blackmail was entirely unnecessary given Montini's cradle to grave fascination and affinity for the Left. On the other hand, the Italian Freemasons, M16, the OSS and later the CIA and the Mafia were likely to have used blackmail and extortion against Montini beginning early in his career as a junior diplomat, then as Archbishop of Milan and finally as Pope Paul VI. (Randy Engel, *The Rite of Sodomy*, p. 1156.)

Giovanni Montini/Paul VI engaged in a policy of Communist surrender known as *Ostpolik* (East politics) wherein he appointed men as "bishops" in Communist countries behind the Iron Curtain who were friendly to, if not actual agents of, the Communist authorities in those countries. These "bishops" had a perverse "apostolic mandate," if you will, given then sub secreto by Montini: never criticize Communism or any Communist officials. In other words, be good stooges for various "people's" and "democratic" republics in exchange for promoting the false "gospel" of conciliarism.

It was also Montini/Paul VI who sold out the courageous Jozsef Cardinal Mindszenty, the Primate of Hungary and the Archbishop of Budapest, Josef Cardinal Mindszenty when the latter, after taking refuge in the American Embassy in Budapest for a decade following the Hungarian Revolution in October of 1956, was forced out of the American Embassy as a result of Vatican pressure and then, after being told by Montini/Paul VI that he remained as the Archbishop of Budapest, has his primatial see declared vacant by the theologically, liturgically and morally corrupt Montini.

This scenario is described by a sedeplenist, Dr. Steve O'Brien, in a review of two motion pictures about the life of Jozsef Cardinal Mindszenty:

> *The Prisoner*, as it happened, was wrapped too soon because Mindszenty's story, which had seemed to be *fini*, had scarcely begun. By 1956 Stalin was dead and Khrushchev was making some unusual noises. In October the Hungarians rose in revolt. Mindszenty had no clue of what was happening on the street; his guards told him that the rabble outside the prison was shouting for his blood. A few days later he was released and indeed a mob of locals set upon him. But instead of ripping his flesh they grabbed at the liberated hero to kiss his clothes. When he returned to Budapest the deposed Reds quivered over this ghost who would not stay buried, but in a radio broadcast he counseled against revenge. The Soviets were not so forgiving, and tanks rumbled to crush this unpleasant incident. A marked man, Mindszenty sought asylum in the American embassy as his last resort. Now a second long Purgatory had begun. Pius spoke out repeatedly against this latest example of Soviet terror but the West, heedless of its own liberation rhetoric, was deaf.
>
> When *The Prisoner* was released, the Church was still the implacable foe of communism. Frail Pius stood as a Colossus against both right and left totalitarianism. When Pius departed this world there ensued a moral void in the Vatican that has never been filled. By the early 1960s both the Western governments and the Novus Ordo popes decided that accommodation with the Communists was preferable to the archaic notions of Pius and Mindszenty. John XXIII and successor Paul VI welcomed a breath of fresh air into the Church, and that odor included cooperation with the Reds. **The new *Ostpolitik*, managed by Paul's Secretary of State Agostino Casaroli, hadn't room for Christian warriors of Mindszenty's stamp. The position of the Hungarian government was strengthened when Casaroli entered negotiations with the appalling regime of Janos Kadar. As the Cold War thawed, the freeze was put on Mindszenty. The American government made it understood that he was no longer welcome at the embassy. Worse still, Paul sent a functionary to persuade Mindszenty to leave, but only after signing a document full of stipulations that favored the Reds and essentially blaming himself for his ordeal. The confession that the Communists could not torture out of him was being forced on him by the Pope!**
>
> Driven from his native land against his wishes, Mindszenty celebrated Mass in Rome with Paul on October 23, 1971. The Pope told him, "You are and remain archbishop of Esztergom and primate of Hungary." It was the Judas kiss. For two years Mindszenty traveled, a living testament to truth, a man who had been scourged, humiliated, imprisoned and finally banished for the Church's sake. In the fall of 1973, as he prepared to publish his *Memoirs*, revealing the entire story to the world, he suffered the final betrayal. Paul, fearful that the truth would upset the new spirit of coexistence with the Marxists, "asked" Mindszenty to resign his office. When Mindszenty refused, Paul declared his See vacant, handing the Communists a smashing victory.
>
> If Mindszenty's story is that of the rise and fall of the West's resistance to communism it is also the chronicle of Catholicism's self-emasculation. In the 1950s a man such as Mindszenty could be portrayed as a hero of Western culture even though both American

> and English history is rife with hatred toward the Church. When the political mood changed to one of coexistence and *detente* rather than containment, Mindszenty became an albatross to the appeasers and so the Pilates of government were desperate to wash their hands of him. Still, politicians are not expected to act on principle, and therefore the Church's role in Mindszenty's agony is far more damning.
>
> Since movies, for good or ill, have a pervasive influence on American culture, perhaps a serious film that told Mindszenty's whole story could have some effect on the somnolent Catholics in the West. *Guilty of Treason* and *The Prisoner* are artifacts of their day. An updated film that follows the prelate through his embassy exile and his pathetic end would be a heart-wrenching drama. But knowing what we know now, the Communists, despicable as they are, would no longer be the primary villains. (**Shooting the Cardinal: Film and Betrayal in the Mindszenty Case**)

As we know, of course, no true pope of the Catholic Church sold out Jozsef Cardinal Mindszenty. A conciliar revolutionary did so.

Another conciliar revolutionary, one who was present at the "beginning" of the conciliar revolution and helped to chart its course, Joseph Ratzinger, sold out the faithful Catholics of the underground Church in Red China, justifying his June 30, 2007, **Letter to Bishops, Priests, Consecrated Persons and Lay Faithful of Red China** partially on the assertion that "progress" was being made in that country.

A report issued by another sedeplenist, Dr. Steven W. Mosher, the founder and President of the Population Research Institute, issued just nine days after Ratzinger/Benedict's **Letter to Bishops, Priests, Consecrated Persons and Lay Faithful of Red China** indicated the sort of "progress" that was taking place at that time in the southern part of Red China:

> The forced abortion campaign hit the southern Chinese province like a deadly hurricane. The provincial government decided that too many babies were being born. Local officials were warned that population control quotas had to be met or their heads would be on the chopping block. They reacted by hunting down and arresting hundreds of women for the crime of being pregnant. Taken by force to hospitals and clinics, these were aborted against their will. It did not matter whether the women were past the point of viability, or even whether they were already in labor. Their babies were killed all the same.
>
> The above could stand as an accurate description of what I witnessed in China's Guangdong province in 1979-80. In reality, it is what is happening right now in the neighboring province of Guangxi. And what has happened in county after county, province after province, over the past 27 years. The one-child terror campaign that started back in 1980 continues to the present day, violating women and tearing apart families throughout China.

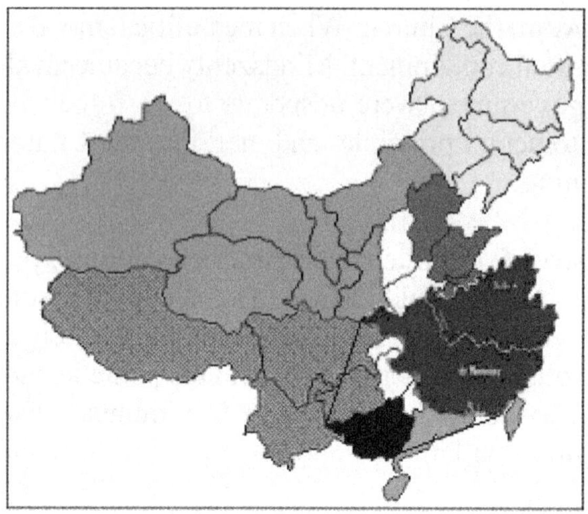

Guangxi's proximity to Hong Kong allowed word of the Communist crackdowns to leak out.

In fact, the only thing unusual about this latest campaign is how quickly news of these atrocities spread outside of China. Guangxi province is not far from Hong Kong. No sooner had the campaign begun in May of this year than word reached the former British colony and from there the outside world. Guangxi, like Guangdong and Hong Kong, is Cantonese speaking. It is also one of the more developed regions of China, where many people have cell phones and access to the Internet. It was by these means that the victims of the terror campaign communicated their suffering to the outside world.

National Public Radio, the taxpayer-funded alternative to Rush Limbaugh, actually ran a story on the campaign on its Morning Edition show. This described in harrowing detail the plight of Guangxi resident Wei Linrong. She and her husband, Liang Yage, already had one child but wanted a second. Mrs. Liang was arrested when she was seven months pregnant and forced to abort her child. The Liangs are Christian, NPR reported, and do not believe in abortion.

The Hong Kong and foreign press also reported how local officials were imposing punitive fines on those who had already given birth to second children. These fines were, in some cases, equivalent to several years' income.

In response to these heavy-handed tactics riots broke out in 28 towns throughout the region. Thousands went on the rampage, storming government buildings, breaking windows, smashing furniture and vandalizing vehicles. Some rioters even tried to set buildings on fire. To quell the unrest, the regional government called in hundreds of armed police.

Tian Congming, President of Xinhua News Agency. This Agency claimed that the Chinese who rioted against the one-child policy were only to be "re-educated."

The sympathy of the foreign press was obviously with the victims of forced abortions. NPR's Morning Edition told not just the Liang's story, but other tales of Chinese women whose babies were aborted weeks, sometimes days before they were due to be born. The Los Angeles Times published full-color photos of the riots and printed the stories of peasants who had "finally had enough." Even the New York Times finally got into the act with a long piece about the tragic inner-city abortion rates among young, unmarried Chinese women. (It apparently took the Times several days to figure out a pro-abortion slant.)

The official Xinhua News Agency, reacting to the foreign media coverage, went into damage control mode. Xinhua claimed that only 28 people were arrested in the aftermath of the riots, a number which seems ridiculously low under the circumstances. Xinhua also suggested that instead of jail terms the misguided villagers were to get counseling: 4,200 Communist Party cadres had been dispatched to the area to engage the villagers in dialogue about their complaints and ease tension in the 28 troubled towns. Xinhua did not reveal whether these cadres were armed.

Those arrested, whether 28 or, more likely, several hundred in number cannot expect to be treated well in jail. A blind attorney, who has been one of the leading activists in China against forced abortions, was recently severely beaten while in jail. Human rights groups say prison officials ordered fellow inmates to beat him after he resisted having his head shaved and insisted on his legal rights. This is unusual only in that the officials themselves did not administer the beating.

How many more millions of women will have to suffer forced abortion before China's leaders realize the bankruptcy of the policy they adopted so long ago? (Steven W. Mosher, **One-Child Terror Campaign Continues)**

Additionally, episodic persecution of Catholics in the underground Church in Red China continues in some parts of that country in spite of the call for "unity" that had been by Ratzinger/Benedict in 2007.

A policy of "reconciliation" based on misrepresentations and contradictions will result in one thing and one thing alone: the silencing of those Catholics in the underground Church who have heretofore been opposed to Communism and who will learn to do what many, although not all, Catholics convinced that *Summorum Pontificum* represented the start of the "restoration" of the Catholic Church, namely, how to be silent in the face of one outrage after another. Or to quote the words of the fictional John Ross Ewing, Jr., "Once you lose your integrity, the rest is easy."

VII. Caught In the Diabolical Grip of Two Revolutions

The Catholics who remained faithful to the Church in the years following the Maoist Revolution that took control of mainland China October 1, 1949, longed to cling to the Successor of Saint Peter, the Vicar of Christ on earth. Struggling to survive in the midst of terrible persecutions and to practice their Faith as faithfully as they could, Catholics in the underground Church in Red China looked to the Holy Father, Pope Pius XII, for support and consolation and encouragement in the midst of the terrible sufferings that were being visited upon them. They, like most other

Catholics in the world, believed that the men who "succeeded" Pope Pius XII were true and legitimate Successors of Saint Peter, which is why they accepted the conciliar changes.

After all, the devil's men in Peking (now rendered Beijing in English) told Catholics in Red China them that they could not adhere to the Vicar of Christ. These Catholics wanted to demonstrate their loyalty to the men whom they believed to be the Supreme Pastors during their respective false "pontificates." They went along with the changes without realizing that they had been trapped by the devil into believing that the changes he effected as a result of the "Second" Vatican Council and its "popes" thereafter were from God Himself, Who is immutable, and that it was necessary to oppose his, the devil's agents in Red China by going along with the conciliar revolution against the Catholic Faith in the name of "loyalty" to the Church.

Catholics in the underground Church in Red China have been struggling to survive. They have not had access to the information that most of us in other parts of the world have been able to access. We must pray to Our Lady, the Queen of the Apostles, that the truth of our ecclesiastical situation will be made manifest to the Catholics in Red China so that they can recognize that Ratzinger/Benedict is not a true Successor of Saint Peter, simply another kind of revolutionary, one who has made **war against Catholicism** throughout his priesthood, as demonstrated earlier in this article. We need to pray as well that these Catholics will be the beneficiaries of the Triumph of Our Lady's Sorrowful and Immaculate Heart sooner rather than later.

VIII. Answers to Questions

I posed a series of questions in October 2005, six months before I began to write about plausibility of sedevacantism and that it applied in our circumstances, concerning the invitation that Ratzinger/Benedict XVI had made to two bishops of the Chinese Patriotic Catholic Association to attend that year's "synod" of conciliar "bishops." These questions were answered by Ratzinger/Benedict's **Letter to Bishops, Priests, Consecrated Persons and Lay Faithful of Red China** in 2007 and by the **Compendium** that was released two years later:

> 1) Have the schismatic bishops been forced to abjure their support of the Red Chinese government's anti-life population policies?
> 2) Will the "reconciled" bishops who have served in the rump church be able to publicly oppose the evils of the Red Chinese government?
> 3) Will the Vatican demand the complete dissolution of the entire structure of the Chinese Patriotic Catholic Association?
> 4) If not, will "underground" bishops and priests be required to register with the Chinese Patriotic Catholic Association?
> 5) Is the Vatican going to require a cessation of the persecution and arrest of underground Catholics (bishops, priests, consecrated religious laity) in order to continue its "discussions" about the establishment of "diplomatic relations" with the "People's Republic" of China?
> 6) Will the Vatican require the marriages officiated by the bishops and the priests of the schismatic church in Red China to be regularized?

> 7) What will the Vatican do about the confessions heard by priests who were ordained by and associated with schismatic bishops nominated by the pro-abortion, pro-contraception, pro-sterilization, pro-torture, pro-slave-labor Red Chinese communist government?
> 8) Will the Red Chinese authorities be required by the Vatican to apologize for its torture, imprisonment, execution, and harassment of Catholics faithful to Rome? Will those authorities be forced by the Vatican to clear the names of all persons, living and deceased, who have been branded as "criminals" for adhering to an "illegal" religion?
> 9) Or will the the Vatican simply wave its bureaucratic hand and pretend, positivistically, that there has "always been one church in China" and seek to "educate" the Catholics who have been suffering in the underground church that they must accommodate themselves to the "actual reality" of the situation in their country and thus silence themselves about the evils being promoted by the government? (See **There is Schism and Then There is Schism, 2005**)

Question number nine was answered very clearly in the affirmative by Ratzinger/Benedict's **Letter to Bishops, Priests, Consecrated Persons and Lay Faithful of Red China** and the subsequent **Compendium**. If you want a nutshell summary of the meaning of Ratzinger/Benedict's **Letter to Bishops, Priests, Consecrated Persons and Lay Faithful of Red China** and the recently-released **Compendium**, good readers, just read question nine and you will understand everything you need to know about their contents without having to wade through all of the contradictions and errors.

Even those conditions, whose letter and spirit were violated most knowingly by the lords of the counterfeit church of conciliarism, that had been imposed in 1988 and 1998 by Karol Wojtyla/John Paul II concerning contacts between members of the underground Church in Red China were swept away by Ratzinger/Benedict in one fell swoop in his **Letter to Bishops, Priests, Consecrated Persons and Lay Faithful of Red China**:

> Considering in the first place some positive developments of the situation of the Church in China, and in the second place the increased opportunities and greater ease in communication, and finally the requests sent to Rome by various Bishops and priests, I hereby revoke all the faculties previously granted in order to address particular pastoral necessities that emerged in truly difficult times.
>
> Let the same be applied to all directives of a pastoral nature, past and recent. The doctrinal principles that inspired them now find a new application in the directives contained herein. (**Letter to Bishops, Priests, Consecrated Persons and Lay Faithful of Red China**.)

Positive developments?

There has been *positivism* in the mind of Joseph Ratzinger/Benedict XVI, reflected in the body of his **Letter to Bishops, Priests, Consecrated Persons and Lay Faithful of Red China**.

Positive developments?

Joseph Ratzinger's **Letter to Bishops, Priests, Consecrated Persons and Lay Faithful of Red China** was and remains a surrender of the faithful Catholics in the underground Church in Red China in a pathetic effort to advance the false premises of his "new ecclesiology."

All of the verbiage in Ratzinger/Benedict's **Letter to Bishops, Priests, Consecrated Persons and Lay Faithful of Red China** was simply a smokescreen to sweep away the "restrictions" of the past and to place the burden of "reconciliation" in Red China upon the very Catholics who have suffered so much and for so long, and the day will come when the ultimate sellout occurs on the occasion that Jorge Mario Bergoglio gets to visit Red China to urge "dialogue" and as he embraces his "brother" bishops in the rump church. Bergoglio would do this in a heartbeat now if he had his druthers. Only the suspicions of the murderous Communist dictators in Red China keep this from happening at the present time, although Pietro "Cardinal" Parolin, who has contacts aplenty in Beijing, is probably working behind the scenes to bring this about in the not-too-distant-future.

Obviously, we must, as always, spend time in prayer before Our Lord's Real Presence in the Most Blessed Sacrament and pray as many Rosaries each day as our states-in-life permit, using the shield of Our Lady's Brown Scapular of Mount Carmel and the weapon of her Rosary to protect us from the contagion of apostasy and betrayal that is all around us. We must also, of course, make reparation for our own many sins by offering up all of our prayers and sufferings and sacrifices and humiliations and penances and mortifications and fastings to the Most Sacred Heart of Jesus through the Sorrowful and Immaculate Heart of Mary.

Chapter Ten

The Problem Rests With A False Religion, Not the Identity of the Conciliar "Pope"

The insanity, yes, the total and complete insanity of "resignationism"--the delusional belief that the "defender" of doctrinal orthodoxy, Joseph Alois Ratzinger/Benedict XVI, was forced to "resign" from the conciliar "papacy" in 2013--is at a fever pitch, especially with the recent publication Italian journalist Antonio Socci's book on the subject, *Non E' Francesco: La Chisese Nella Grande Tempesta* (*It's Not Francis: The Church in a Great Tempest*).

The following insane letter to the antipope emeritus, Ratzinger/Benedict, was sent by some conciliar presbyters on January 23, 2014, the Feast of Saint Raymond of Pennafort and the Commemoration of Saint Emerentiana (and the Commemoration of the Espousal of Our Lady and Saint Joseph and the Commemoration of Saint Ildephonsus):

> Holy Father:
>
> The December 17, 2012 the Cardinals Herranz, Tomko and De Giorgi gave you the file of the results of research that asked them to do about leaks of confidential documents known as "Vatileaks" and about especially the threat of death that was against your person, leaked to the newspaper "Il Fatto Quotidiano", and which I had reported at the time Cardinal Darío Castrillón.
>
> In finding that, indeed, high prelates in the Vatican, belonging to the lodge of ecclesiastical Masonry, had decided to kill you, you resolved you to resign. A few days later you communicated to your brother, the priest Georg Ratzinger, that you would abandon the See of Peter, knowing he never imagined "that face of the Church." Before Christmas you had already decided to resign, but waited to publicly announce it until February 11, 2013.
>
> Not that you have been afraid of losing your life, knowing that you promised to be ready to give your life for Christ since your appointment as cardinal, but you did it for the good of the Church, considering that if they actually managed to kill you, your death would have caused an earthquake, triggering a hellish struggle for influence and shady maneuvers arising from internal antagonisms in the curia facing succession. Not fearing death, but for the damage it may have caused to the Church, you decided it was best to step aside to remove threats and advance a peaceful succession. And, here, yes you did.
>
> In a report that was prepared by the Jesuit priest Arnaldo Zenteno, posted on April 9, 2013 (ingrupobasesfys.blogspot.mx) noted that when the newly elected Pope Francis came to you to Castel Gandolfo, he trusted that same: that one of the causes that influenced your resignation threats were received, since you could find that they had already made the decision to kill.
>
> In this sense, Holy Father, if it is true that you expressed in your statement given "freely", the fact is that you were more or less forced by the pressure of a strong rush, so your freedom, according to the canonical doctrine was conditional "in radice". While it took the

decision to resign in accordance with the powers you grant the Code of Canon Law, took it under the duress of a moral violence, which, Holy Father, from the root invalidated your final decision and finally made invalid act you performed.

We must recognize that while the Church has always considered a sacred law that the election of a pope is ad vitam, it is good that canon law provides for the possibility of waiver in cases of extreme gravity, such as exile, persecution or other serious cause. In this sense, the waiver provided for in Canon 332 of the CDC is like a emergency exit door, and it is convenient to have both so that output helped you, Holy Father, to flee from the threat hanging over your person and the Church.

The fact is, Holy Father, that act being the vitiated at the root, a single moral violence, your waiver lacked canonical validity. Therefore, the seat was never vacant and the conclave that followed was completely invalid.

In this conclave, distorted and confused, not having you at any time ceasing to be the Vicar of Christ, an anti-pope, who took the name of Francis, emerged.

To say that Bergoglio is an antipope does not necessarily mean he is a bad person, or mean-spirited. In the history of the Church there have been 38 anti-popes. It only means that he is not the Vicar of Christ and, therefore, does not enjoy the charisma of inerrancy.

The proof that it has is that it has already fallen into various heresies and errors to Tradition, as the echo of Docetist heresy saying that Christ is not angry at all, but only pretended, or that the Mosaic covenant was not abrogated God, contradicting the Conciclio Florence and the teachings of several popes, or to apply, on a libearcionsita and marxistoide analysis, there must be a "poor Church for the poor," when our Lord taught that the Church should be for everyone, rich and poor, or to veto the Mass of St. Pius V, that you, Holy Father had approved various communities of religious and lay, or to wash the feet of two Muslims in the ceremony of the Last Supper on Holy Thursday, and not twelve priests, as you always did you and those before you, that tradition was founded by our Savior to wash the feet of his disciples. False inter-religious dialogue that threatens to reach dire consequences for the faith of God's people. This, not to mention the continuing transgressions in the liturgy and tradition, which reveal the meager appreciation Francis has for the papal investiture.

More and more priests have privately discussed the absurdities of Bergolio. Some, like Father Paul Kramer, an expert in the apparitions of Fatima, has dared to publicly demand the resignation of Francis, following the doctrine established by St. Robert Bellarmine, St. Alphonsus Liguori, San Anthony and Pope Innocent III, the which taught that when a pope is shown as a manifest heretic automatically ceases to be pope, it is not a Catholic: "He who is not a member, can not be head". And Saint Francis of Assisi, of whom Bergolio too his name, predicted that there would come a "non canonically elected" Pope, which would not be "a true Pastor, but a destroyer of the Church."

We know, Holy Father, who until now have preferred a prudent silence to many abuses, strengthening you spiritually as Christ was strengthened when he retired to the desert before his passion and death.

But you have to raise your voice the day seeking to adulterate the sacrament of the Eucharist to take the character of sacrifice and leave only the memorial, the Protestant style, so not to inconvenience other faiths. That day is not far off, no one will be outraged and resist and publicly condemn apostasy and sacrilege. Unfortunately, many have already been duped and have strayed from faith.

In this sense, Holy Father, will begin to be realized the situation predicted by saints and mystics, who predicted the painful schism in the Church, the division between the apostate church and the faithful Church.

The prophecies say that this schism is simultaneous to a sudden invasion of Russia on Europe, coinciding with the war described by the prophet Ezekiel (Ezekiel 38), the Third World War. Then, the legitimate Pope, you Holy Father, you will be betrayed and persecuted, and have to flee Rome for refuge hidden in a faraway place, while the antipope will rule the Church supporting the false peace, unification of religions sacrilegious. That false peace will support the religious world government of the Antichrist. That will be the last and greatest test will suffer the faithful Church.

At that time, the antipope betray faith accepting the coalition of all faiths and renouncing the Catholic identity. You Benedict XVI, you will be pursued to the end, and you will die a martyr of the Eucharist by a cruel death, according to his vision Pius X and Lucia had also narrated in the third secret of Fatima.
St. Francis of Assisi said: "There will be a pope canonically elected not to cause a great schism". And Blessed Anne Catherine Emmerich, Augustinian religious, said: "I saw a strong opposition between two popes, and saw how dire the consequences of the false church (...) This will cause the greatest schism that has been seen in the world ".

The Blessed Virgin said explicitly in the Salette: "Rome will lose the Faith and become the seat of the Antichrist."

And there are many private revelations and announcements of church leaders:

• Says P. Paul Kramer, "The antipope and his apostate collaborators will be like Lucy, supporters of the devil, those who work for evil without being afraid of anything Sister said."
• And the above, disclosed by Pope St. Pius X "I've had a terrible vision: I do not know if I or one of my successors, I will be, but I saw a Pope fleeing Rome among the corpses of his brothers he took refuge incognito somewhere and after a short time die a cruel death. "
• John Rocapartida: "Approaching the End Times, the Pope and his cardinals will have to flee Rome in tragic consequences to a place where they will not be recognized, and the Pope will suffer a cruel death in exile."

• Nicolas de Fluh: "The Pope with his cardinals will have to flee Rome in dire situation to a place where they will be unknown Pope die atrociously during his exile. The sufferings of the Church will be greater than any historical moment prior…"
• Venerable Bartholomew Holzhauser, founder societies secular clergy in the eighteenth century: "God will allow a great evil against His Church: come suddenly and unexpectedly bursting while bishops and priests are asleep will enter Italy and devastate Rome, burn churches. destroy everything ".
• The revelation received by Mother Elena Aiello, famous stigmatized it was often consulted by Pope Pius XII: "Italy will be shaken by a great revolution (…) Russia will be imposed on nations, especially on Italy, and raise the red flag on the dome of St. Peter. "
• John's words of Vitiguero: "When the world be disturbed, Pope change of residence".
• Elena Leonardi, power spiritual Padre Pio " The Vatican will be invaded by communist revolutionaries betrayed the pope Italy will suffer a major revolt and be cleansed by a great revolution Russia march on Rome and the Pope will be severely endangered…. "
• Enzo Alocci: "Pope temporarily disappear and this will happen when there is a revolution in Italy. "
Ana Maria • Blessed Taigi: "Religion is persecuted and massacred priests, the Holy Father will be forced to leave Rome.".
• Mystical Mary Steiner: "The Holy Church will be persecuted, Roma will be without a shepherd ".
• Revelations in Garabandal. "Pope may not be in Rome, you have to chase and hide"
• Al P. Stefano Gobbi, mystic and founder of the Marian Movement of Priests, Our Lady confided: "The Masonic forces have entered the church and hides in a disguised form, and established his headquarters in the same place where he lives and works the Vicar of my son Jesus is being carried as is contained in the third part of my message, which has not yet been revealed, but it has already become clear by the same events that are living".
• Your predecessor Pope Paul VI: "The smoke of Satan has entered through the cracks of the Church "(Homily of June 29, 1972).
• According to St. Paul, the Antichrist will be revealed just after the Pope be cast aside: "Just to put away means the one who holds it, then the wicked be revealed "(2 Thessalonians 2: 6-8).

Canon Rock wrote excommunicated Enlightenment who helped infiltration against the Church: "In its current form, the papacy will disappear, the new social order will be implemented from Rome but outside of Rome, not Rome, although Rome against Roma. And this new church though perhaps I should not keep anything of scholastic discipline and rudimentary form of the ancient Church of Rome however receive consecration and canonical jurisdiction. "
The new church, led by the antipope, support the unification of religions and false peace, fulfilled which was spoken by Jesus Christ in the sense that even the elect will be deceived.

Cardinal Karol Wojtyla was very clear when he declared, before the Eucharistic Congress in Pennsylvania in 1977. "We are facing the greatest historical confrontation humanity has ever had. We are at the final contest between the Church and the anti-Church, the Gospel

> and the anti-Gospel. This confrontation lies within the plans of Divine Providence and is a challenge that the whole Church has to accept. "
>
> In 1917 they were revealed to three shepherd children in Fatima, Portugal, the revelation that had Pope St. Pius X a few years ago, only in an even more precise: "We saw a bishop dressed in white, we had a feeling out the Holy Father, flee a city trembling unsteadily and ruins. "
>
> Fatima's version aims to further that it could be you, most blessed Father, and explain the phrase "We saw a bishop dressed in white, we had a feeling it was the Holy Father." If it had been evident that it was the reigning pope, they would have said so undeniable. Instead, they saw a "bishop dressed in white". They could never imagine your theme "waiver" so that they only had "a feeling".
>
> The second element is even more precise and revealing: they saw fleeing "trembling with halting step," which may be due to old age you already have.
> A third element is also revealing: of the same bishop dressed in white who are fleeing before Rome after state, when it is killed, yes it was the "Holy Father".
>
> Following the flight of the legitimate pope, antipope in Rome will lead the "new church", supporting the union apostate religions. It is the "abomination of desolation" foretold since ancient times by the prophet Daniel, established in the holy place, which will coincide with the installation of the antichrist in the temple of Jerusalem rebuilt for the third time.
>
> In the words of Cardinal Luigi Ciappi, personal theologian to Pope John Paul II: "The Third Secret refers to the loss of faith in the Church, i.e, apostasy, will enter the top of the Church."
>
> We want to tell you, Holy Father, we are continually praying for you, that your faith may not fail and God will give you the necessary to testify and be willing to embrace martyrdom for His sake forces always remember one of your last words while still in the See of Peter: "You will be with me, even though to the world remains hidden" (Address to the Roman Clergy, February 14, 2013). We, Holy Father, and will continue to be with you in the future which Providence throws at you. (**Letter to Ratzinger**.)

Here is news for the supposed "remnant clergy:" The last true pope to have sat on the Throne of Saint Peter was Eugenio Maria Giuseppe Giovanni Pacelli, Pope Pius XII, who died on October 9, 1958.

Angelo Roncalli was an antipope (see **Two For The Price Of One, part one** and **Francis: The Latest In A Long Line Of Ecclesiastical Tyrants**).

Giovanni Montini was an antipope (see **"Blessed" Paul The Sick**).

Albino Luciani was an antipope (see **Conciliarism's Weapons of Mass Destruction, part three**).

Karol Wojtyla/John Paul II was an antipope (see **Two For The Price Of One, part two**.)

And the supposed "restorer of Tradition," Joseph Alois Ratzinger/Benedict XVI, was an antipope. Only the intellectually dishonest can review the facts contained in **Mister Asteroid Is Looking Pretty Good Right About Now** and not conclude that the very same canonical precepts that you apply to Jorge Mario Bergoglio apply also to your man Ratzinger, a progenitor of the conciliar revolution who is a heretic to the core of his Modernist being. After all, a man who can make war upon the nature of dogmatic truth, which is nothing other than a direct warfare upon the very nature of God Himself, is not only a man unworthy of anyone's admiration, he is worthy of our condemnation as an enemy of Christ the King and the souls for whom He shed every single drop of His Most Precious Blood on the wood of the Holy Cross.

The close theological ties that bind Joseph Alois Ratzinger/Benedict XVI to his successor as the universal public face of apostasy, Jorge Mario Bergoglio/Francis, have been proved repeatedly on many websites, including, of course, **www.Christorchaos.com**.

Indeed, although much was made in early-2014 of Jorge Mario Bergoglio's document entitled "Communication at the Service of an Authentic Culture of Encounter," which merely rehashed the revolutionary tripe that he has repeated *ad nauseam, ad infinitum*, the willfully deluded who cling to the insanity that Joseph Ratzinger was truly "Pope Benedict XVI" and never "resigned" from an office he never held legitimately must come to understand that "Pope Francis's" remarks of early-2014 were indistinguishable from those of "Pope Benedict XVI."

Here is an excerpt of what Bergoglio released on January 24, 2014, the Feast of Saint Timothy:

> "Effective Christian witness is not about bombarding people with religious messages, but about our willingness to be available to others 'by patiently and respectfully engaging their questions and their doubts as they advance in their search for the truth and the meaning of human existence' (BENEDICT XVI, Message for the 47th World Communications Day, 2013). We need but recall the story of the disciples on the way to Emmaus. We have to be able to dialogue with the men and women of today, to understand their expectations, doubts and hopes, and to bring them the Gospel, Jesus Christ himself, God incarnate, who died and rose to free us from sin and death. We are challenged to be people of depth, attentive to what is happening around us and spiritually alert. **To dialogue means to believe that the 'other' has something worthwhile to say, and to entertain his or her point of view and perspective. Engaging in dialogue does not mean renouncing our own ideas and traditions, but the claim that they alone are valid or absolute**. (**"Communication at the Service of an Authentic Culture of Encounter"-Bergoglio's Message for World Communications Day**.)

This is pure Bergoglio. As will be shown shortly, however, it is also pure Ratzinger as well.

Bergoglio is a theological relativist. So is Ratzinger.

Here is a smattering of "Pope Francis's" belief that we can "learn" from those who believe in false religions and that Catholics must recognize that what he thinks is truth is "encountered," which is of the essence of one of the fundamental precepts of Modernism.

Attention is turned first to Jorge Mario Bergoglio's first encyclical letter, *Lumen Fidei*, July 5, 2013:

> Faith, in fact, needs a setting in which it can be witnessed to and communicated, a means which is suitable and proportionate to what is communicated. For transmitting a purely doctrinal content, an idea might suffice, or perhaps a book, or the repetition of a spoken message. But what is communicated in the Church, **what is handed down in her living Tradition**, is the new light born of an encounter with the true God, a light which touches us at the core of our being and engages our minds, wills and emotions, **opening us to relationships lived in communion**. There is a special means for passing down this fullness, a means capable of engaging the entire person, body and spirit, interior life and relationships with others. It is the sacraments, celebrated in the Church's liturgy. The sacraments communicate an incarnate memory, **linked to the times and places of our lives, linked to all our senses; in them the whole person is engaged as a member of a living subject and part of a network of communitarian relationships**. While the sacraments are indeed sacraments of faith, it can also be said that faith itself possesses a sacramental structure. The awakening of faith is linked to the dawning of a new sacramental sense in our lives as human beings and as Christians, in which visible and material realities are seen to point beyond themselves to the mystery of the eternal. (Jorge Mario Bergoglio/Francis, *Lumen Fidei*, July 5, 2013.)

In other words, the doctrinal content of the Faith is insufficient to transmit what God has revealed, which is why It must understood in light of a fluid "living tradition" that is "linked to the times and places of our lives" and "senses" as we grow, and row and mow and show together as "part of a network of communitarian relationships."

Alas, this is all a distortion and misrepresentation of the teaching of the Catholic Church.

You see, we are linked to other Catholics principally by means of the Communion of Saints, which is nowhere mentioned in the text of *Lumen Fidei*.

There is a reason for this.

Most of the conciliar revolutionaries do not believe in Purgatory, something that Ratzinger/Benedict, whose draft served as the foundation of *Lumen Fidei*, has made clear on a number of occasions, including thirty-six months ago now (see **From Sharp Focus to Fuzziness**). It is rather difficult for those who placed doubt upon the existence of Purgatory as a real place of punishment for the forgiven Mortal Sins, unforgiven Venial Sins and general attachment to sin and disordered self-love that the souls of those who have died in a State of Sanctifying Grace did not pay back here on earth by means of their joyful and loving acceptance of suffering as the consecrated slaves of Our Blessed Lord and Saviour Jesus Christ through the Sorrowful and Immaculate Heart of Mary.

At the root and throughout the essence of conciliarism's "theology of encounter" is an ethos evocative of the Modernist view of Faith that was condemned by Pope Saint Pius X in *Pascendi Dominci Gregis*, September 8, 1907:

> 14. Thus far, Venerable Brethren, We have considered the Modernist as a philosopher. Now if We proceed to consider him as a believer, and seek to know how the believer, according to Modernism, is marked off from the philosopher, it must be observed that, although the philosopher recognizes the reality of the divine as the object of faith, still this reality is not to be found by him but in the heart of the believer, as an object of feeling and affirmation, and therefore confined within the sphere of phenomena; but the question as to whether in itself it exists outside that feeling and affirmation is one which the philosopher passes over and neglects. For the Modernist believer, on the contrary, it is an established and certain fact that the reality of the divine does really exist in itself and quite independently of the person who believes in it. If you ask on what foundation this assertion of the believer rests, he answers: In the personal experience of the individual. On this head the Modernists differ from the Rationalists only to fall into the views of the Protestants and pseudo-mystics. The following is their manner of stating the question: **In the religious sense one must recognize a kind of intuition of the heart which puts man in immediate contact with the reality of God, and infuses such a persuasion of God's existence and His action both within and without man as far to exceed any scientific conviction. They assert, therefore, the existence of a real experience, and one of a kind that surpasses all rational experience. If this experience is denied by some, like the Rationalists, they say that this arises from the fact that such persons are unwilling to put themselves in the moral state necessary to produce it. It is this experience which makes the person who acquires it to be properly and truly a believer**.
>
> How far this position is removed from that of Catholic teaching! We have already seen how its fallacies have been condemned by the Vatican Council. Later on, we shall see how these errors, combined with those which we have already mentioned, open wide the way to Atheism. Here it is well to note at once that, given this doctrine of experience united with that of symbolism, every religion, even that of paganism, must be held to be true. What is to prevent such experiences from being found in any religion? In fact, that they are so is maintained by not a few. **On what grounds can Modernists deny the truth of an experience affirmed by a follower of Islam? Will they claim a monopoly of true experiences for Catholics alone?** Indeed, Modernists do not deny, but actually maintain, some confusedly, others frankly, that all religions are true. That they cannot feel otherwise is obvious. For on what ground, according to their theories, could falsity be predicated of any religion whatsoever? Certainly it would be either on account of the falsity of the religious sense or on account of the falsity of the formula pronounced by the mind. Now the religious sense, although it maybe more perfect or less perfect, is always one and the same; and the intellectual formula, in order to be true, has but to respond to the religious sense and to the believer, whatever be the intellectual capacity of the latter. In the conflict between different religions, the most that Modernists can maintain is that the Catholic has more truth because it is more vivid, and that it deserves with more reason the name of Christian because it corresponds more fully with the origins of Christianity. No one will find it unreasonable that these consequences flow from the premises. But what is most

> amazing is that there are Catholics and priests, who, We would fain believe, abhor such enormities, and yet act as if they fully approved of them. **For they lavish such praise and bestow such public honor on the teachers of these errors as to convey the belief that their admiration is not meant merely for the persons, who are perhaps not devoid of a certain merit, but rather for the sake of the errors which these persons openly profess and which they do all in their power to propagat**e.
>
> 15. There is yet another element in this part of their teaching which is absolutely contrary to Catholic truth. For what is laid down as to experience is also applied with destructive effect to tradition, which has always been maintained by the Catholic Church. **Tradition, as understood by the Modernists, is a communication with others of an original experience, through preaching by means of the intellectual formula. To this formula, in addition to its representative value they attribute a species of suggestive efficacy which acts firstly in the believer by stimulating the religious sense, should it happen to have grown sluggish, and by renewing the experience once acquired, and secondly, in those who do not yet believe by awakening in them for the first time the religious sense and producing the experience. In this way is religious experience spread abroad among the nations; and not merely among contemporaries by preaching, but among future generations both by books and by oral transmission from one to another. Sometimes this communication of religious experience takes root and thrives, at other times it withers at once and dies. For the Modernists, to live is a proof of truth, since for them life and truth are one and the same thing. Thus we are once more led to infer that all existing religions are equally true, for otherwise they would not survive**. (Pope Saint Pius X, *Pascendi Dominci Gregis,* September 8, 1907.)

In other words, Modernists believe that those who are steeped in error possess certain elements of truth that arise from within their own consciousness that can teach Catholics something about God and His Sacred Truths that they did not understood before, which is why it is necessary to be open to the "surprises" that God is said to have for us as we "encounter" the "other" with his own "beliefs" by laying aside our own "claim" to possess absolute truth. This is what both Joseph Ratzinger/Benedict XVI and Jorge Mario Bergoglio believe.

Two more examples from the collected "work," if it can be called that, of "Pope Francis" concerning the "theology of encounter" and absolute truth will be provided before providing documentation that there is no "space" between this Argentine Apostate and the German New Theologian, starting with the letter that Jorge Mario Bergoglio wrote to Eugenio Scalfari that provided the foundation for their infamous interview that was published in *La Repubblica* on October 1, 2013:

> As for the three questions you asked me in the article of August 7th. It would seem to me that in the first two, what you are most interested in is understanding the Church's attitude towards those who do not share faith in Jesus. **First of all, you ask if the God of the Christians forgives those who do not believe and do not seek faith. Given that - and this is fundamental - God's mercy has no limits if he who asks for mercy does so in contrition and with a sincere heart, the issue for those who do not believe in God is in obeying their own conscience. In fact, listening and obeying it, means deciding about**

> **what is perceived to be good or to be evil. The goodness or the wickedness of our behavior depends on this decision**.
>
> Second of all, you ask if the thought, according to which no absolute exists and therefore there is no absolute truth, but only a series of relative and subjective truths is a mistake or a sin. **To start, I would not speak about, not even for those who believe, an "absolute" truth, in the sense that absolute is something detached, something lacking any relationship. Now, the truth is a relationship! This is so true that each of us sees the truth and expresses it, starting from oneself: from one's history and culture, from the situation in which one lives, etc. This does not mean that the truth is variable and subjective. It means that it is given to us only as a way and a life**. Was it not Jesus himself who said: "I am the way, the truth, the life"? **In other words, the truth is one with love, it requires humbleness and the willingness to be sought, listened to and expressed. Therefore we must understand the terms well and perhaps, in order to avoid the oversemplification of absolute contraposition, reformulate the question. I think that today this is absolutely necessary in order to have a serene and constructive dialogue which I hoped for from the beginning**. (Full Text of Francis's letter to atheist Italian journalist Eugenio Scalfari.)

"God's mercy has no limits if he who asks for mercy does so in contrition and with a sincere heart, the issue for those who do not believe in God is obeying their own conscience"?

"The goodness of our behavior depends" on the "decision" about what is perceived to be good or to be evil"?

Refusing to speak about an absolute truth absent a "relationship"?

Jorge Mario Bergoglio/Francis is a dangerous, blaspheming, revolutionary heretic of the most vile and criminal sort imaginable. He does violence to both supernatural and natural truth as truths about God, His Revelation and morality exist in the nature of things and do not depend upon human acceptance or "relationship" for their binding force or validity.

Is the truth of the Natural Law unknowable to man, thus making acts of murder, including willful murder of the preborn, acceptable as long as one "decides" for what one perceives to be good?

Are the truths of the Ten Commandments not written on the very flesh of human hearts by the finger of God?

If this is so, then pagan writers such as Aristotle and Cicero had it all wrong about objective truth, admitting that Aristotle's understanding and application of the Natural Law in concrete circumstances was wanting in some instance.

Cicero must have been wrong when he wrote the following in *The Republic*:

> True law is right reason conformable to nature, universal, unchangeable, eternal, whose commands urge us to duty, and whose prohibitions restrain us from evil. Whether it enjoins

> or forbids, the good respect its injunctions, and the wicked treat them with indifference. This law cannot be contradicted by any other law, and is not liable either to derogation or abrogation. Neither the senate nor the people can give us any dispensation for not obeying this universal law of justice. It needs no other expositor and interpreter than our own conscience. It is not one thing at Rome, and another at Athens; one thing to-day, and another to-morrow; but in all times and nations this universal law must forever reign, eternal and imperishable. It is the sovereign master and emperor of all beings. God himself is its author, its promulgator, its enforcer. And he who does not obey it flies from himself, and does violence to the very nature of man. And by so doing he will endure the severest penalties even if he avoid the other evils which are usually accounted punishments. (Cicero, *The Republic*.)

Cicero had it almost entirely correct. Almost. He was wrong in asserting that the Natural Law does not need any "other expositor and interpreter than our own conscience." He lived before the Incarnation and before the founding of the true Church upon the Rock of Peter, the Pope. Cicero thus did not know that man does need an interpreter and expositor of the natural law, namely, the Catholic Church. Apart from this, however, Cicero understood that God's law does not admit of abrogations by a vote of the people or of a "representative" body, such as the Roman Senate in his day or the United States Congress or state legislatures, et al. in our own day.

Jorge Mario Bergoglio/Francis has it *entirely* wrong as he believes that conscience is king; but a man's conscience must be rightly formed, and it is thus the duty of Holy Mother Church to instruct the ignorant, starting with the simple fact that truth in the Order of Nature (Creation) exists independently of human acceptance of it. The physical laws of the universe, for example, do not depend upon our "perception" of them in order for them to be true and binding. One who defies a physical law by, say, jumping from a building while "perceiving" there is no law of gravity will suffer the consequences of such a mistaken perception with a variety of bruises and/or broken bones. Indeed, such a stupid person might wind up killing himself in an effort to "prove" his "perception" correct.

Jorge Mario Bergoglio/Francis is thus a pure subjectivist, unwilling to use the Five Proofs for the Existence of God as provided by Saint Thomas Aquinas in the *Summa Theologica* because they do not conform to the Modernist belief that truth is knowable only by "encounter" and not the very nature of things that exist in the Order of Nature and have been revealed definitively by God and entrusted to His Holy Catholic Church for their eternal safekeeping and infallible explication. This view of the human knowledge (epistemology) is really pretty identical with that of a philosophical progenitor of the French Revolution, Jean Jacques Rousseau himself:

> Rousseau carries on the revolution against the order of the world begun by Luther. Luther's revolt was that of our individuality and sense-life against the exigencies of the supernatural order instituted by God. It was an attempt to remain attached to Christ, while rejecting the order established by Christ for our return to God. Rousseau's revolt was against the order of natural morality, by the exaltation of the primacy of our sense-life.
>
> **The little world of each one of us, our individuality, is a divine person, supremely free and sovereignly independent of all order, natural and supernatural. The state of**

Liberty or of sovereign independence is the primitive state of man, and the nature of man demands the restoration of that state of liberty. It is to satisfy this so-called exigency that 'Father of modern thought' invented the famous myth of the Social Contract.

The Social Contract gives birth to a form of association in which each one, while forming a union with all the others, obeys only himself and remains as free as before. Each one is subject to the whole, but he is not subject to any man, there is no man above him. He is absorbed in the common Ego begotten in the pact, so that obeying the law, he obeys only himself. Each citizen votes in order, that by the addition of the number of votes, the general will, expressed by the vote of the majority, is, so to say, a manifestation of the 'deity' immanent in the multitude. **The People are God (no wonder we have gotten used to writing the word with a capital letter). The law imposed by this 'deity' does not need to be just in order to exact obedience. In fact, the majority vote makes or creates right and justice. An adverse majority vote can not only overthrow the directions and commands of the Heads of the Mystical Body on earth, the Pope and the Bishops, but can even deprive the Ten Commandments of all binding force.**

To the triumph of those ideals in the modern world, the Masonic denial of original sin and the Rousseauist dogma of the natural goodness of man have contributed not a little. The dogma of natural goodness signifies that man lived originally in a purely natural paradise of happiness and goodness and that, even in our present degraded state, all our instinctive movements are good. We do not need grace, for nature can do for what grace does. In addition, Rousseau holds that this state of happiness and goodness, of perfect justice and innocence, of exemption from servile work and suffering, is natural to man, that is, essentially demanded by our nature. Not only then is original sin nonexistent, not only do we not come into the world as fallen sons of the first Adam, bearing in us the wounds of our fallen nature, is radically anti-natural. Suffering and pain have been introduced by society, civilization and private property. Hence we must get rid of all these and set up a new form of society. We can bet back the state of the Garden of Eden by the efforts of our own nature, **without the help of grace**. For Rousseau, the introduction of the present form of society, and of private property constitute the real Fall. The setting up of a republic based on his principles will act as a sort of democratic grace which will restore in its entirety our lost heritage. In a world where the clear teaching of the faith of Christ about the supernatural order of the Life of Grace has become obscured, but where men are still vaguely conscious that human nature was once happy, Rousseau's appeal acts like an urge of homesickness. **We need not be astonished, then, apart from the question of Masonic-Revolutionary organization and propaganda, at the sort of delirious enthusiasm which takes possession of men at the thought of a renewal of society. Nor need we wonder that men work for the overthrow of existing government and existing order, in the belief that they are not legitimate forms of society. A State not constructed according to Rosseauist-Masonic principles is not a State ruled by laws. It is a monstrous tyranny, and must be overthrown in the name of "Progress" and of the "onward march of democracy.' All these influences must be borne in mind as we behold, since 1789, the triumph in one country after another of Rousseauist-Masonic democracy.** (Father Denis Fahey, *The Mystical Body of Christ in the Modern World*.)

Oscar Andres Maradiaga Rodriguez, Bergoglio's chief ideologist (see Commissar of Antichrist Speaks, part one, Commissar of Antichrist Speaks, part two, Commissar of Antichrist Speaks, part three and Commissar of Antichrist Speaks, part four), has said that it is necessary to have a "Congregation for the Laity" as they constitute the "majority" of the Church. Even though this arch-heretic contends that doctrine will be maintained, he continues to insist that pastoral adjustments need to made in light of "new" situations that are just old manifestations of sinful relationships under a new name in an era where it is believed that "the majority vote makes or creates right and justice" and that an "adverse majority vote can not only overthrow the directions and commands of the Heads of the Mystical Body on earth, the Pope and the Bishops, but can even deprive the Ten Commandments of all binding force." This is as applicable to the conciliar revolutionaries as it is to the the adherents of Judeo-Masonic sects as they are, after all, allies in Modernity and Modernism. (For a review of Maradiaga Rodriguez's recent call for "flexibility," see Maradiaga says Müller needs to "be a bit more flexible". A separate article will be written about this soon as Gerhard Ludwig Muller is very "flexible" when it comes to the Catholic Faith, including the way he denies the Perpetual Virginity of the Blessed Virgin Mary.)

One final quotation from "Pope Francis" on the "theology of encounter" will be offered to demonstrate that his comments of Thursday, January 23, 2014, were absolutely nothing new or out of the ordinary for him in his false "pontificate:"

> 250. **An attitude of openness in truth and in love must characterize the dialogue with the followers of non-Christian religions, in spite of various obstacles and difficulties, especially forms of fundamentalism on both sides. Interreligious dialogue is a necessary condition for peace in the world, and so it is a duty for Christians as well as other religious communities**. This dialogue is in first place a conversation about human existence or simply, as the bishops of India have put it, a matter of "**being open to them, sharing their joys and sorrows**".[194] In this way we learn to accept others and their different ways of living, thinking and speaking. We can then join one another in taking up the duty of serving justice and peace, which should become a basic principle of all our exchanges. **A dialogue which seeks social peace and justice is in itself, beyond all merely practical considerations, an ethical commitment which brings about a new social situation. Efforts made in dealing with a specific theme can become a process in which, by mutual listening, both parts can be purified and enriched. These efforts, therefore, can also express love for truth**.
>
> 251. **In this dialogue, ever friendly and sincere, attention must always be paid to the essential bond between dialogue and proclamation, which leads the Church to maintain and intensify her relationship with non-Christians.**[195] A facile syncretism would ultimately be a totalitarian gesture on the part of those who would ignore greater values of which they are not the masters. **True openness involves remaining steadfast in one's deepest convictions**, clear and joyful in one's own identity, while **at the same time being "open to understanding those of the other party" and "knowing that dialogue can enrich each side**".[196] What is not helpful is a diplomatic openness which says "yes" to everything in order to avoid problems, for this would be a way of deceiving others and denying them the good which we have been given to share generously with others. **Evangelization and interreligious dialogue, far from being opposed, mutually**

> **support and nourish one another.**[197] (Jorge Mario Bergoglio, *Evangelii Gaudium*, November 26, 2013.)

Jorge Mario Bergoglio believes that the "interreligious dialogue" that is an essential component of false ecumenism does not represent syncretism although it is nothing other than this. The Catholic Church does not need to "learn" about the evil beliefs of false religions as it is part of her Divine Constitution, a point that has been made on this site repeatedly.

No, nothing that Jorge Mario Bergoglio issued on January 24, 2014, in his "Communication at the Service of an Authentic Culture of Encounter" message was new for him or represents "originality" in any way as it is nothing other than boilerplate conciliarism of the sort that Joseph Ratzinger championed throughout his long career of theological destruction before he became "Pope Benedict XVI" of the counterfeit church of conciliarism on April 19, 2005.

In light of the madness of what can be called "Resignationism Rising," it is necessary to reprise some passages from the 1964 sermon of Ratzinger's that was highlighted in an earlier chapter of this book:

> **Everything we believe about God, and everything we know about man, prevents us from accepting that beyond the limits of the Church there is no more salvation, that up to the time of Christ all men were subject to the fate of eternal damnation. We are no longer ready and able to think that our neighbor, who is a decent and respectable man and in many ways better than we are, should be eternally damned simply because he is not a Catholic. We are no longer ready, no longer willing, to think that eternal corruption should be inflicted on people in Asia, in Africa, or wherever it may be, merely on account of their not having "Catholic" marked in their passport.**
>
> Actually, a great deal of thought had been devoted in theology, both before and after Ignatius, to the question of how people, without even knowing it, in some way belonged to the Church and to Christ and could thus be saved nevertheless. And still today, a great deal of perspicacity is used in such reflections.
>
> **Yet if we are honest, we will have to admit that this is not our problem at all. The question we have to face is not that of whether other people can be saved and how. We are convinced that God is able to do this with or without our theories, with or without our perspicacity, and that we do not need to help him do it with our cogitations. The question that really troubles us is not in the least concerned with whether and how God manages to save others.**
>
> **The question that torments us is, much rather, that of why it is still actually necessary for us to carry out the whole ministry of the Christian faith—why, if there are so many other ways to heaven and to salvation, should it still be demanded of us that we bear, day by day, the whole burden of ecclesiastical dogma and ecclesiastical ethics?**And with that, we are once more confronted, though from a different approach, with the same question we raised yesterday in conversation with God and with which we parted: What actually is the Christian reality, the real substance of Christianity that goes beyond

> mere moralism? What is that special thing in Christianity that not only justifies but compels us to be and live as Christians?
>
> **It became clear enough to us, yesterday, that there is no answer to this that will resolve every contradiction into incontrovertible, unambivalent truth with scientific clarity. Assent to the hiddenness of God is an essential part of the movement of the spirit that we call "faith."** And one more preliminary consideration is requisite. If we are raising the question of the basis and meaning of our life as Christians, as it emerged for us just now, then this can easily conceal a sidelong glance at what we suppose to be the easier and more comfortable life of other people, who will "also" get to heaven. We are too much like the workers taken on in the first hour whom the Lord talks about in his parable of the workers in the vineyard (Mt 20:1-6). When they realized that the day's wage of one denarius could be much more easily earned, they could no longer see why they had sweated all day. Yet how could they really have been certain that it was so much more comfortable to be out of work than to work? And why was it that they were happy with their wages only on the condition that other people were worse off than they were? But the parable is not there on account of those workers at that time; it is there for our sake. For in our raising questions about the "why" of Christianity, we are doing just what those workers did. We are assuming that spiritual "unemployment"—a life without faith or prayer—is more pleasant than spiritual service. Yet how do we know that?
>
> We are staring at the trials of everyday Christianity and forgetting on that account that faith is not just a burden that weighs us down; it is at the same time a light that brings us counsel, gives us a path to follow, and gives us meaning. We are seeing in the Church only the exterior order that limits our freedom and thereby overlooking the fact that she is our spiritual home, which shields us, keeps us safe in life and in death. We are seeing only our own burden and forgetting that other people also have burdens, even if we know nothing of them. And above all, what a strange attitude that actually is, when we no longer find Christian service worthwhile if the denarius of salvation may be obtained even without it! It seems as if we want to be rewarded, not just with our own salvation, but most especially with other people's damnation—just like the workers hired in the first hour. That is very human, but the Lord's parable is particularly meant to make us quite aware of how profoundly un-Christian it is at the same time. Anyone who looks on the loss of salvation for others as the condition, as it were, on which he serves Christ will in the end only be able to turn away grumbling, because that kind of reward is contrary to the loving-kindness of God. (**Catholic Church and Salvation**.)

Yes, Father Joseph Ratzinger, the "restorer of Tradition" who wore a jacket and tie while serving as a *peritus* at the "Second" Vatican Council, was rejecting the immutably binding character of dogmatic declarations and speaking against "moralism" to emphasize the "substance of Christianity" that cannot resolve "every contradiction into incontrovertible, unambivalent truth with scientific clarity." He believed then and he believes now in his late-eighties that "assent to the "hiddenness of God" is an essential part of the movement of the spirit that we call 'faith'" that will "save" non-Catholics in a way that we cannot understand or explain.

Acting out his fantasy as "Pope Benedict XVI" (remember, he signed his name in 2003 on a postcard to a friend in Spain as "Pope Benedict XVI" even though he was then just Joseph "Cardinal" Ratzinger), Ratzinger used the occasion of a 2010 musical concert in honor of the Russian Orthodox equivalent of Walter Kasper and his successor, Kurt Koch, to discuss the importance of music in the "theology of encounter:"

> VATICAN CITY, 21 MAY 2010 (VIS) - Yesterday evening in the Vatican's Paul VI Hall, Benedict XVI attended a concert in honour of his birthday and the anniversary of his election as Pope, offered by Kirill I, Patriarch of Moscow and All Russia. The concert, which included pieces by nineteenth- and twentieth-century Russian composers, was played by the National Orchestra of Russia conducted by Carlo Ponti, with the Synodal Choir of Moscow and the Horn Capella of St. Petersburg.
>
> At the end of the concert, which was part of the initiative "Days of Russian Culture and Spirituality in the Vatican", the Holy Father listened to a message sent by Patriarch Kirill and was greeted by Archbishop Hilarion of Volokolamsk, president of the Department for External Church Affairs of the Patriarchate of Moscow and composer of one of the pieces played during the concert. The Pope then pronounced a brief address.
>
> "Deep in these works," he said, "is the soul of the Russian people, and there with the Christian faith, both of which find extraordinary expression in divine liturgy and in the liturgical chants with which it is always accompanied. There is, in fact, a close and fundamental bond between Russian music and liturgical chant. It is in the liturgy and from the liturgy that a large part of the artistic creativity of Russian musicians is released and expressed, giving life to masterpieces which deserve to be better known in the West."
>
> Such nineteenth- and twentieth-century Russian composers as Mussorgsky, Rimsky-Korsakov, Tchaikovsky and Rachmaninov "treasured the rich musical-liturgical heritage of Russian tradition, re-modelling it and harmonising it with musical themes and experiences of the West. ...
>
> Music, then, anticipates and in some way creates encounter, dialogue and synergy between East and West, between tradition and modernity.
> "It was of just such a unified and harmonious vision of Europe that the Venerable John Paul II was thinking when, referring to the image of the 'two lungs' suggested by Vjaceslav Ivanovic Ivanov, he expressed his hope in a renewed awareness of the continent's profound and shared cultural and religious roots, without which today's Europe would be deprived of a soul or, at least, victim of a reduced and partial vision."
>
> "Modern culture, particularly in Europe, runs the risk of amnesia, of forgetting and thus abandoning the extraordinary heritage aroused and inspired by Christian faith, which is the essential framework of the culture of Europe, and not only of Europe. The Christian roots of the continent are, in fact, made up not only of religious life and the witness of so many generation of believers, but also of the priceless cultural and artistic heritage which is the pride and precious resource of the peoples and countries in which Christian faith, in its various expressions, has entered into dialogue with culture and the arts."

"**Today too these roots are alive and fruitful in East and West, and can in fact inspire a new humanism, a new season of authentic human progress in order to respond effectively to the numerous and sometimes crucial challenges that our Christian communities and societies have to fac**e: first among them that of secularism, which not only impels us to ignore God and His designs, but ends up by denying the very dignity of human beings, in view of a society regulated only by selfish interests".

The Holy Father concluded: "**Let us again let Europe breathe with both lungs, restore a soul not only to believers, but to all peoples of the continent, promote trust and hope, rooting them in the millennial experience of the Christian faith**. The coherent, generous and courageous **witness of believers must not now be lacking, so that together we may look to our shared future, a future in which the freedom and dignity of all men and women are recognised as a fundamental value, in which openness to the Transcendent, the experience of faith, is recognised as an essential element of the human being**". (MODERN CULTURE RISKS FORGETTING CHRISTIAN HERITAGE.)

Witness of believers?

Believers in what?

The Catholic Faith in Its holy integrity without qualification or reservation whatsoever?

Yes, *the Eastern Rites* of the Catholic Church are supposed to complement those of the Latin Rite of the Catholic Church. This is beyond question. Those in the Eastern Rites must, however, believe in everything taught by the Catholic Church or suffer from doctrinal emphysema in their lungs. The Eastern Rites and the Latin Rite of the Catholic Church (as well as the little used Ambrosian Rite and the Mozarabic Rite proper to parts of Spain) each must breathe the clear, unpolluted air of the totality of the Deposit of Faith exactly as Our Blessed Lord and Saviour Jesus Christ entrusted It to Holy Mother Church without any shadow of alteration, change, ambiguity or contradiction whatsoever. This is is not done in any Orthodox Church, whether Russian, Greek or Coptic, something that was pointed out in an earlier chapter of this book.

It was four months later that, on September 17 2010, the Feast of the Impression of the Stigmata on Saint Francis of Assisi, that Joseph Ratzinger/Benedict XVI, delivered the following remarks to "religious leaders" in Twickenham, England:

Ever since the Second Vatican Council, the Catholic Church has placed special emphasis on the importance of dialogue and cooperation with the followers of other religions. In order to be fruitful, this requires reciprocity on the part of all partners in dialogue and the followers of other religions. I am thinking in particular of situations in some parts of the world, where cooperation and dialogue between religions calls for mutual respect, the freedom to practise one's religion and to engage in acts of public worship, and the freedom to follow one's conscience without suffering ostracism or persecution, even after conversion from one religion to another. Once such a respect and openness has been

> established, peoples of all religions will work together effectively for peace and mutual understanding, and so give a convincing witness before the world.
>
> This kind of dialogue needs to take place on a number of different levels, and should not be limited to formal discussions. **The dialogue of life involves simply living alongside one another and learning from one another in such a way as to grow in mutual knowledge and respect. The dialogue of action brings us together in concrete forms of collaboration, as we apply our religious insights to the task of promoting integral human development, working for peace, justice and the stewardship of creatio**n. Such a dialogue may include exploring together how to defend human life at every stage and how to ensure the non-exclusion of the religious dimension of individuals and communities in the life of society. **Then at the level of formal conversations, there is a need not only for theological exchange, but also sharing our spiritual riches, speaking of our experience of prayer and contemplation, and expressing to one another the joy of our encounter with divine love**. In this context I am pleased to note the many positive initiatives undertaken in this country to promote such dialogue at a variety of levels. As the Catholic Bishops of England and Wales noted in their recent document Meeting God in Friend and Stranger, the effort to reach out in friendship to followers of other religions is becoming a familiar part of the mission of the local Church (n. 228), a characteristic feature of the religious landscape in this country. (**Meeting with Religious Leaders in the Waldegrave Drawing Room of St. Mary's University College in Twickenham, London Borough of Richmond, 17 September 2010**.)

Did Saint Francis Xavier engage in "dialogue" with the adherents of false religions in India? No, he sought with urgency to convert them unconditionally to the Catholic Faith, the one and only true Faith, outside of which there is no salvation and without which there can be no true social order. (See **Without Regard for Results**.)

The mania for "dialogue" to "discuss" matters of doctrine that we must accept on the authority of God Who has revealed them to us did not, however, begin with the lords of conciliarism, who are so wedded to this slogan that any thought of actively seeking the conversion of any non-Catholic is considered to be an "offense" against the conciliar falsehood of "religious liberty."

This is what Ratzinger said in his last Christmas address to the conciliar curia on December 21, 2012, the Feast of Saint Thomas the Apostle, although he would address the curia one final time before his free and voluntary "resignation" from the non-papacy took effect:

> At this point I would like to address the second major theme, which runs through the whole of the past year from Assisi to the Synod on the New Evangelization: the question of dialogue and proclamation. Let us speak firstly of dialogue. **For the Church in our day I see three principal areas of dialogue, in which she must be present in the struggle for man and his humanity: dialogue with states, dialogue with society – which includes dialogue with cultures and with science – and finally dialogue with religions**. In all these dialogues the Church speaks on the basis of the light given her by faith. But at the same time she incorporates the memory of mankind, which is a memory of man's experiences and sufferings from the beginnings and down the centuries, **in which she has**

> **learned about the human condition**, she has experienced its boundaries and its grandeur, its opportunities and its limitations. **Human culture, of which she is a guarantee, has developed from the encounter between divine revelation and human existence. The Church represents the memory of what it means to be human in the face of a civilization of forgetfulness**, which knows only itself and its own criteria. **Yet just as an individual without memory has lost his identity, so too a human race without memory would lose its identity. What the Church has learned from the encounter between revelation and human experience does indeed extend beyond the realm of pure reason, but it is not a separate world that has nothing to say to unbelievers. By entering into the thinking and understanding of mankind, this knowledge broadens the horizon of reason and thus it speaks also to those who are unable to share the faith of the Church**. In her dialogue with the state and with society, **the Church does not, of course, have ready answers for individual questions**. Along with other forces in society, **she will wrestle for the answers that best correspond to the truth of the human condition. The values that she recognizes as fundamental and non-negotiable for the human condition she must propose with all clarity**. She must do all she can to convince, and this can then stimulate political action. (**Apostate Provides Christmas greetings to the members of the Occupy Vatican Movement.**)

The Church must "be present in the struggle for man and his humanity"?

This is why Our Blessed Lord and Saviour Jesus Christ died on the wood of the Holy Cross?

Our Lord did not tell the Eleven before He Ascended to His Co-Equal an Co-Eternal Father's right hand in glory on Ascension Thursday that they were to engage in a "dialogue" with society or that the mission of His Catholic Church was to be "present in the struggle for man and his humanity." He told them to convert men and their nations to the true Church:

> And the eleven disciples went into Galilee, unto the mountain where Jesus had appointed them. And seeing him they adored: but some doubted. And Jesus coming, spoke to them, saying: All power is given to me in heaven and in earth. **Going therefore, teach ye all nations; baptizing them in the name of the Father, and of the Son, and of the Holy Ghost. Teaching them to observe all things whatsoever I have commanded you: and behold I am with you all days, even to the consummation of the world**. (Matthew 28: 16-20.)

No Catholic has to "search" for the "truth." This is something that many arch-conciliarists do not understand or accept.

The Catholic Church had to "learn" about the "human condition" over the centuries?

Apostasy.

As noted before in this commentary, Holy Mother Church is complete in her Divine Constitution. She lacks nothing to teach, govern and sanctify the flock entrusted to her pastoral care by her

Divine Founder and Invisible Head, Christ the King. She alone understands the true nature of man in light of Who has created him, Who redeemed him and Who sanctifies him.

"The Church represents the memory of what it means to be human in the face of a civilization of forgetfulness"?

"Yet just as an individual without memory has lost his identity, so too a human race without memory would lose its identity"?

Excuse me, Father Ratzinger, wherever you are out there in the twilight zone of the new theology on the grounds of the Occupied Vatican on the West Bank of the Tiber River. Excuse me. *You* helped to jettison the institutional memory of the Catholic Church, including the Social Reign of Christ the King, and thus have been part of a wholesale revolution that has robbed most Catholics of any understanding of the truth of what Our Lord revealed to us in His Sacred Deposit of Faith.

Ratzinger/Benedict's refusal to seek with urgency the conversion of all non-Catholics to the true Faith--indeed, his disparaging what he called the "ecumenism of the return" in Cologne, Germany, on August 19, 2005--is responsible for helping to keep men plunged deeper and deeper into the errors of Modernity. Many of these "modern men" are steeped in unrepentant sins of one sort or another. What has all of the conciliar church's "dialogue" with "modern man" and its "renewed liturgy," designed as it was to appeal to Protestants as it watered down or denied Catholic doctrine, especially that relating to the need for personal penance and the reality of a God Who judges us when we die, produced except a sea of lost Catholics?

Anyone in the "Resignationism Rising" crowd who does not recognize their beloved "pope" for what he is, a Modernist heretic, would be hard-pressed to reconcile the following passage from that December 21, 2012, curia address with the teaching of the Catholic Church:

> Two rules are generally regarded nowadays as fundamental for interreligious dialogue:
>
> > 1. Dialogue does not aim at conversion, but at understanding. In this respect it differs from evangelization, from mission;
> >
> > 2. Accordingly, both parties to the dialogue remain consciously within their identity, which the dialogue does not place in question either for themselves or for the other.
>
> These rules are correct, but in the way they are formulated here I still find them too superficial. **True, dialogue does not aim at conversion, but at better mutual understanding – that is correct. But all the same, the search for knowledge and understanding always has to involve drawing closer to the truth. Both sides in this piece-by-piece approach to truth are therefore on the path that leads forward and towards greater commonality, brought about by the oneness of the truth.** As far as preserving identity is concerned, it would be too little for the Christian, so to speak, to assert his identity in a such a way that he effectively blocks the path to truth. Then his

> Christianity would appear as something arbitrary, merely propositional. He would seem not to reckon with the possibility that religion has to do with truth. On the contrary, I would say that the Christian can afford to be supremely confident, yes, fundamentally certain that he can venture freely into the open sea of the truth, without having to fear for his Christian identity. **To be sure, we do not possess the truth, the truth possesses us: Christ, who is the truth, has taken us by the hand, and we know that his hand is holding us securely on the path of our quest for knowledge.** Being inwardly held by the hand of Christ makes us free and keeps us safe: free – because if we are held by him, **we can enter openly and fearlessly into any dialogue; safe – because he does not let go of us, unless we cut ourselves off from him. At one with him, we stand in the light of truth.** (Apostate Provides Christmas greetings to the members of the Occupy Vatican Movement.)

"True, dialogue does not aim at conversion, but better mutual understanding"?

Well, this may be true for the apostates of conciliarism as it invented the madness called "dialogue" and made it the "precondition" for "peace and justice" in the world, thereby flushing the true teaching of the Catholic Church down the Orwellian memory hole.

Jorge Mario Bergoglio believes in the exact same thing.

Consider the following report, written by Brian Stiller of the "Global Evangelical Alliance," on his meeting with Bergoglio in June of 2014 at the Casa Santa Marta inside the walls of the Occupied Vatican on the West Bank of the Tiber River: Bergoglio's meeting three weeks ago with Protestant evangelical "ministers" for the apostasy that anyone sixty years would have seen without any hestitation:

> I know some will wonder if we lack discernment, dining as we did with the head of a church many see as heretical. As an Evangelical, I'm clear in the importance of the Reformation and the role our community plays in announcing the Good News. I celebrate our understanding of the Scriptures as our only and final authority, the priesthood of every believer, the life-giving moment of rebirth and freedom for churches and ministries to spring up under the inspiration of the Spirit. **No one is interested in rewinding the clock. Also to construct a united church isn't doable and neither is it in our interest. Such plans do not lead us to fulfill Jesus' prayer in John 17 that we be one in Christ.**
>
> My counter argument to those who might dismiss friendship with the pope is this. For Evangelicals and Protestants, of all shapes and sizes, the state and condition of the Roman Catholic Church matters. Of the over 2 billion Christians, one-half are linked to the Vatican. About 600 million are Evangelicals and another 550 million members of the World Council of Churches, (which includes the Orthodox Churches). As a world body, it is our calling to have contact with other major Christian communities and faiths. **Conferencing with Rome no more compromises our doctrinal commitments than it would by meeting with the heads of other religions. We do that as a natural and important role of our calling. In places where Evangelicals are marginalized, having this official connection allows us to raise issues and ask for responses we would never otherwise get.**

In a worldwide community of faith, the work and role of each Christian community matters. Given that 50 percent of those who call themselves Christian affiliate with Rome, when its spiritual and ethical authority is diminished it affects the entire world. When Rome loses her way, when corruption characterizes her financial dealings, when sexual scandals rob her of moral influence, when she fades from view in strongly declaring the nature and salvation of Christ, secularism rules.

It's fair to ask what kind of Catholic Church we as Evangelicals want to see. At lunch I asked Pope Francis what his heart was for evangelism. **He smiled, knowing what was behind my question. His comment was, "I'm not interested in converting Evangelicals to Catholicism. I want people to find Jesus in their own community. There are so many doctrines we will never agree on. Let's not spend our time on those. Rather, let's be about showing the love of Jesus." (Of course Evangelicals do evangelize Catholics and Catholics do the same to us. However, that discussion we will raise another day.)**

We spoke about how in our diversity we might find unity and strength. Borrowing from Swiss Protestant theologian Oscar Cullman, we reflected how "reconciled diversity" allows us to stand within our own understandings of how Christ effects salvation. And then we press on to deal with global issues like religious freedom and justice and other matters, which affect our wellbeing.

We are in the middle of a major religious shakeup worldwide. The Middle East is on the edge of what we know not. Islam is on the rise. The Gospel witness permeates much of the global south. So what of the future?

A vibrant pope, spiritually vital, tough in ethical leadership and competent in overseeing his world communion is critical. What he says and does has a profound affect on us all. It matters to us that the Spirit rests upon him in wisdom and courage.

Evangelicals need not hide behind fear of engagement. Working on human suffering and matters of injustice with Christians who have a different tradition and read the biblical text differently does not violate who we are or what we believe.

Working on the world stage, it is evident there is respect for our distinctive evangelical message and regard for our responsibility and calling to represent our Christian community. International cooperation among Christians is built on that respect. (**Lunch with Jorge**. See also the post at **Novus Ordo Watch Wire**.)

So much for the work of so many martyrs who shed their blood seeking converts to the true Church.

So much for the mission that Our Lord Himself gave the Eleven as He asceneded into Heaven on Ascension Thursday.

For all the commotion about Jorge's comments as reported by Brian Stiller, however, it is important to remember that the Argentine Apostate has said very consistently that Catholics should not seek to convert anyone to what is thought to be the Catholic Church. This is what he said in a video presentation to Argentine youth on the Feast of Saint Cajetan on August 7, 2013:

> Thank you for listening to me. Thank you for coming here today. Thank you for all that you bear in your heart. Jesus loves you very much. Saint Cajetan loves you very much. He only asks one thing of you: that you come together! That you go out and seek and find one in greater need! But not alone - with Jesus, with Saint Cajetan! **Am I going to go out to convince someone to become a Catholic? No, no, no! You are going to meet with him, he is your brother! That's enough! And you are going to help him, the rest Jesus does, the Holy Spirit does it. Remember well: with Saint Cajetan, we the needy go to meet with those who are in greater need. And, hopefully, Jesus will direct your way so that you will meet with one in greater need.** (**Francis the Insane Dreamer, Rebel and Miscreant's Message for the Feast of Saint Cajetan**.)

Meet one in greater need?

There is no greater need for a soul than who is outside of the bosom of Holy Mother Church to be invited with urgency to convert to the true Faith.

Yet it is that Jorge Mario Bergolio equates seeking the conversion of non-Catholics to the true Faith with what he disparages as "proselytizing." This is one of his first such visceral denunciations of "proselytizing" in favor of the "new evangelization" of conciliarism, which means preaching the corrupted version of the Gospel of Our Blessed Lord and Saviour Jesus Christ that is nothing other than pure, unadulterated Modernism:

> (Vatican Radio) **Evangelization is not proselytizing.** This was the focus of Pope Francis' remarks to faithful gathered for Mass on Wednesday morning in the Chapel of the Domus Sanctae Marthae residence in the Vatican. **The Pope reiterated that the Christian who wants to proclaim the Gospel must dialogue with everyone, knowing that no one owns the truth, because the truth is received by the encounter with Jesus**.
>
> Pope Francis stressed the courageous attitude of Paul St Paul at the Areopagus, when, in speaking to the Athenian crowd, he sought to build bridges to proclaim the Gospel. The Pope called Paul's attitude one that "seeks dialogue" and is "closer to the heart" of the listener. The Pope said that this is the reason why St Paul was a real pontifex: a "builder of bridges" and not of walls. The Pope went on to say that this makes us think of the attitude that a Christian ought always to have.
>
> "A Christian," said Pope Francis, "must proclaim Jesus Christ in such a way that He be accepted: received, not refused – and Paul knows that he has to sow the Gospel message. He knows that the proclamation of Jesus Christ is not easy, but that it does not depend on him. He must do everything possible, but the proclamation of Jesus Christ, the proclamation of the truth, depends on the Holy Spirit. Jesus tells us in today's Gospel: 'When He shall come, the Spirit of truth, shall guide you into all the truth.' Paul does not say to the Athenians: 'This is the encyclopedia of truth. Study this and you have the truth, the truth.' No! The truth does not enter into an encyclopedia. The truth is an encounter - it is a meeting with Supreme

> Truth: **Jesus, the great truth. No one owns the truth. The we receive the truth when we meet** [it]. (**Miss Frances at Wednesday Liturgical Travesty: build bridges, not walls**.)

No one owns the truth?

The Catholic Church is the sole repository of every jot and tittle of what her Divine Founder, Invisible Head and Mystical Bridegroom entrusted to her exclusively for Its infallible explication and eternal safekeeping.

Jorge Mario Bergoglio does not believe this, which is why he believes that Protestants and the Orthodox have a "mission" to proclaim their versions of the Gospel. This hideous apostate believes that one can "learn" something about Our Lord that is lacking within the Divine Constitution of Holy Mother Church. He is a heretic in the mode of his immediate predecessor, Joseph Ratzinger/Benedict XVI (where is the Antipope Emeritus these days?), who quoted Protestant "theologians" with great admiration in his "unofficial" books.

For the *Catholic* Church, however, conversion has been her mission from the beginning. Just two quick examples out of so many that could be provided:

> "It is for this reason that so many who do not share 'the communion and the truth of the Catholic Church' must make use of the occasion of the Council, by the means of the Catholic Church, which received in Her bosom their ancestors, proposes [further] demonstration of profound unity and of firm vital force; hear the requirements [demands] of her heart, t**hey must engage themselves to leave this state that does not guarantee for them the security of salvation. She does not hesitate to raise to the Lord of mercy most fervent prayers to tear down of the walls of division, to dissipate the haze of errors, and lead them back within holy Mother Church, where their Ancestors found salutary pastures of life; where, in an exclusive way, is conserved and transmitted whole the doctrine of Jesus Christ and wherein is dispensed the mysteries of heavenly grace**.
>
> "It is therefore by force of the right of Our supreme Apostolic ministry, entrusted to us by the same Christ the Lord, which, having to carry out with [supreme] participation all the duties of the good Shepherd and to follow and embrace with paternal love all the men of the world, we send this Letter of Ours to all the Christians from whom We are separated, with which **we exhort them warmly and beseech them with insistence to hasten to return to the one fold of Christ; we desire in fact from the depths of the heart their salvation in Christ Jesus, and we fear having to render an account one day to Him, Our Judge, if, through some possibility, we have not pointed out and prepared the way for them to attain eternal salvation. In all Our prayers and supplications, with thankfulness, day and night we never omit to ask for them, with humble insistence, from the eternal Shepherd of souls the abundance of goods and heavenly graces**. And since, if also, we fulfill in the earth the office of vicar, with all our heart we await with open arms the return of the wayward sons to the Catholic Church, in order to receive them with infinite fondness into the house of the Heavenly Father and to enrich them with its inexhaustible treasures. **By our greatest wish for the return to the truth and the**

communion with the Catholic Church, upon which depends not only the salvation of all of them, but above all also of the whole Christian society: the entire world in fact cannot enjoy true peace if it is not of one fold and one shepherd." (Pope Pius IX, *Iam Vos Omnes*, September 13, 1868.)

"So, Venerable Brethren, it is clear why this Apostolic See has never allowed its subjects to take part in the assemblies of non-Catholics: for the union of Christians can only be promoted by promoting the return to the one true Church of Christ of those who are separated from it, for in the past they have unhappily left it. To the one true Church of Christ, we say, which is visible to all, and which is to remain, according to the will of its Author, *exactly the same as He instituted it*. . . . Let, therefore, the separated children draw nigh to the Apostolic See, set up in the City which Peter and Paul, the Princes of the Apostles, consecrated by their blood; to that See, We repeat, which is 'the root and womb whence the Church of God springs,' not with the intention and the hope that 'the Church of the living God, the pillar and ground of the truth' will cast aside the integrity of the faith and tolerate their errors, but, on the contrary, that they themselves submit to its teaching and government. Would that it were Our happy lot to do that which so many of Our predecessors could not, to embrace with fatherly affection those children, whose unhappy separation from Us We now bewail. Would that God our Savior, "Who will have all men to be saved and to come to the knowledge of the truth," would hear us when We humbly beg that He would deign to recall all who stray to the unity of the Church! In this most important undertaking We ask and wish that others should ask the prayers of Blessed Mary the Virgin, Mother of divine grace, victorious over all heresies and Help of Christians, that She may implore for Us the speedy coming of the much hoped-for day, when all men shall hear the voice of Her divine Son, and shall be 'careful to keep the unity of the Spirit in the bond of peace.'" (Pope Pius XI, *Mortalium Animos*, January 6, 1928.)

Not enough? How about testimony from the Mother of God herself?

"Do you think that I do not know that you are the heretic? Realize that your end is at hand. If you do not return to the True Faith, you will be cast into Hell! But if you change your beliefs, I shall protect you before God. Tell people to pray that they may gain the good graces which, God in His mercy has offered to them." (See: **If You Do Not Return to the True Faith, You Will Be Cast Into Hell!**)

No, there is no space whatsoever between Joseph Alois Ratzinger and Jorge Mario Bergoglio. Both are believers in the "theology of encounter." Both are insidious heretics. They differ only in matters of style and emphasis, not in substance. Only the wilfully blind refuse to see this, accept this and to act on it decisively by fleeing from them and everything to do with their false church that is but a counterfeit ape of the spotless, virginal Mystical Spouse of Christ the King, the Catholic Church.

Father Charles Arminjon related the attitude that Catholics have in the midst of the storms of the present world, a world that will pass away soon enough, by contrasting the worldly man with the man of Faith:

One thing is certain: there has never been, and never will be, moral sublimity, heroic holiness, or virtue worthy of the name that does not have its principle or draw its growth and strength in suffering freely accepted or dauntlessly undergone.

How is it that our will is often wavering and undecided, that our life is strewn with such strange fluctuations and such unhappy fickleness, that we are so dejected by insignificant things, that an inconsiderate word is said to us, or a change in the serenity of the sky, is enough to make us go from the height of joy to the depths of gloom? The cause of these fluctuations and changes is simply the repugnance and instinctive horror we feel toward suffering.

By the assiduous care we take to refuse the slightest hardship and the least injury, and to keep away from us anything that seems even in the smallest degree demanding, we create for ourselves a state of abject bondage. Our heart falls under the sway of as many tyrants as there are impressions, each of which in turn grips us in its influence. No virtue can subsist in such fickle souls, no high position is compatible with a character that drifts along with every current and turn of fortune.

Thus, the man in this state turns aside from stern duties and becomes a slave to the most futile fantasies. Forgetting that human life is a reality and not fiction, he seeks diversion in frivolous amusements, squanders his best years in pleasures and idleness and boredom, and consumes fruitlessly the talent that God had entrusted to him. In this enfeebling frame of mind, a man need only come before him with threatening words and the power to interfere with his repose, interests, or pleasures, and that man will at once be his master, will have full power to subject him to a degrading bondage or to unspeakable tortures.

How far removed from the inexhaustible pettiness of these flabby, effeminate souls is the firm, high-minded attitude of him who, by dint of doing battle with suffering, has become, as it were, insensitive to its wounds and blows? How fine it is to see him serene and majestic amidst storms and the agitation of passions, fulfilling the words of the wise man: "Whatsoever shall befall the just man, it shall not make him sad."

Calmly he [the man of Faith] hears the noise of revolutions, and sees republics and dynasties pass; it is as if the scene of men's vain and conflicting interests lay in the nether regions beneath his feet. No disturbance on this earth moves him, because he had learned to see events in the infinite wisdom that governs all things by its providence, and which permits evil only in order to draw good from it by a striking manifestation. He carries within himself a kind of sanctuary of peace and happiness. Mankind and the elements combined are powerless to offend or harm him. Is he sent into exile? He will reply with a great bishop: "For me, the whole earth is my native land and my exile." Is he stripped of his goods? He has learned how to possess them without permitting them to enthrall his heart. Is he put to death? Death, for him, is the transfiguration to a better life, emancipation from his sufferings.

Such was the serenity and heroic constancy of St. John Chrysostom, banished by Eudoxia, Empress of Constantinople:

> When I was fleeing the town, I did not feel my misfortune at all, and I was interiorly inundated with the most indescribable consolations. If he Empress sends me into exile--I said to myself--I shall consider that the earth and all that it contains is the Lord's. If she has me thrown into the sea, I shall remember Jonah. If she orders me to be stoned, I shall be the companion of St. Stephen. If she has me beheaded, I shall have the glory of St. John the Baptist. If she strips me of what I possess, I shall reflect that I came forth naked from the bowels of the earth, and must return to it naked and stripped of everything. (Father Charles Arminjon, *The End of the Present World and the Mysteries of the Future Life*, translated by Susan Conroy and Peter McEnerny. Manchester, New Hampshire: Sophia Institute Press, 2008, pp. 282-284.)

Let us, therefore, trust in Our Lady, whose Immaculate Heart was pierced by Seven Swords of Sorrow, to help us to promote Catholic dogmatism over the madness of "dialogue" and its "theology of encounter," remaining perfectly calm in the storms around us as we pray as many Rosaries each day as our state-in-life permits, eager to suffer and to suffer even some more as the consecrated slaves of Christ the King through that same Sorrowful and Immaculate Heart of Mary, she who is Our Immaculate Queen.

Chapter Eleven
Seeking to Indemnify One Heretic to Condemn Another

Those who are part of the "Resignationism Rising" movement and others in the fantasy-land that is the Motu world where well-meaning Catholics think that they are being "loyal" while having a beautiful liturgy staged mostly by men who are not truly ordained priests of the Catholic Church have shown a decided tendency to ignore actual facts by resorting constantly to shopworn slogans that prove only one thing: their willingness to overlook what they know to be grave offenses to the Catholic Faith that harm the souls for whom Our Blessed Lord and Saviour Jesus Christ shed every single drop of His Most Precious Blood to Redeem.

Thus it is that a few points to emphasize and reiterate the work done in the previous chapters of this book will be made in the hope that a few disinterested readers who have yet to realize that the spotless, mystical bride of Our Blessed Lord and Saviour Jesus Christ can never give us any ambiguity in her doctrine, no less to contradict or to deconstruct articles contained in the Sacred Deposit of Faith, will come to see the truth of our ecclesiastical situation in this time of apostasy and betrayal.

First, Joseph Ratzinger has always rejected what Jorge Mario Bergoglio continues to reject: the belief that it is necessary to seek with urgency the unconditional conversion of non-Catholics to the true Church, outside of which there is no salvation and without which there can be no true social order.

This is what the then Joseph "Cardinal" Ratzinger wrote in the very misnamed book, *Principles of Catholic Theology*, that is really a compendium of his lectures rather than a text he wrote at one time from cover to cover:

> "As regards Protestantism, the maximum demand of the Catholic Church would be that the Protestant ecclesiological ministers be regarded as totally invalid and that Protestants be converted to Catholicism; the maximum demand of Protestants, on the other hand, would be that the Catholic Church accept, along with the unconditional acknowledgement of all Protestant ministries, the Protestant concept of ministry and their understanding of the Church and thus, in practice, renounce the apostolic and sacramental structure of the Church, which would mean, in practice, the conversion of Catholics to Protestantism and their acceptance of a multiplicity of distinct community structures as the historical form of the Church. While the first three maximum demands are today rather unanimously rejected by Christian consciousness, the fourth exercises a kind of fascination for it – as it were, a certain conclusiveness that makes it appear to be the real solution to the problem. This is all the more true since there is joined to it the expectation that a Parliament of Churches, a "truly ecumenical council', could then harmonize this pluralism and promote a Christian unity of action. That no real union would result from this, but that its very impossibility

would become a single common dogma, should convince anyone who examines the suggestion closely that such a way would not bring Church unity but only a final renunciation of it. As a result, none of the maximum solutions offers any real hope of unity.

> "In any event, church unity is not a political problem that can be solved by means of compromise or the weighing of what is regarded as possible or acceptable. What is at stake here is unity of belief, that is, the question of truth, which cannot be the object of political maneuvering. As long as and to the extent that the maximum solution must be regarded as a requirement of truth itself, just so long and to just that extent there will be no other recourse than simply to strive to convert one's partner in the debate. In other words, the claim of truth ought not to be raised where there is not a compelling and indisputable reason for doing so. We may not interpret as truth that which is, in reality, a historical development with a more or less close relationship to truth. Whenever, then, the weight of truth and its incontrovertibility are involved, they must be met by a corresponding sincerity that avoids laying claim to truth prematurely and is ready to search for the inner fullness of truth with the eyes of love." (Joseph "Cardinal" Ratzinger, *Principles of Catholic Theology*, pp. 197-198.)

"None of the maximum solutions offers any real hope of unity," not even the immutable teaching of the Catholic Church that all non-Catholics, including Protestants, must convert unconditionally to the Catholic Faith in order to be save?

No, this is not "Pope" Benedict XVI's "vision" of "unity," something that he noted in 2010 in an address to the "Pontifical" Council for Promoting Christian Unity in terms that were almost identical to the apostasy he published twenty-eight years beforehand:

> "Dear friends, despite the presence of new problematic situations or difficult points for the dialogue, the aim of the ecumenical path remains unchanged, as does the firm commitment in pursuing it. It is not, however, a commitment according to political categories, so to speak, in which the ability to negotiate or the greater capacity to find compromises come into play, from which could be expected, as good mediators, that, after a certain time, one will arrive at agreements acceptable to all. Ecumenical action has a twofold movement. On one hand there is the convinced, passionate and tenacious search to find full unity in truth, to excogitate models of unity, to illumine oppositions and dark points in order to reach unity. And this in the necessary theological dialogue, but above all in prayer and in penance, in that spiritual ecumenism which constitutes the throbbing heart of the whole path: The unity of Christians is and remains prayer, it resides in prayer. On the other hand, another operative movement, which arises from the firm awareness that we do not know the hour of the realization of the unity among all the disciples of Christ and we cannot know it, because unity is not "made by us," God "makes" it: it comes from above, from the unity of the Father with the Son in the dialogue of love which is the Holy Spirit; it is a taking part in the divine unity. And this should not make our commitment diminish, rather, it should make us ever more attentive to receive the signs of the times of the Lord, knowing how to recognize with gratitude that which already unites us and working to consolidate it and make it grow. In the end, also in the ecumenical path, it is about leaving to God what

> is only his and of exploring, with seriousness, constancy and dedication, what is our task, being aware that to our commitment belongs the binomial of acting and suffering, of activity and patience, of effort and joy.
>
> "We confidently invoke the Holy Spirit, so that he will guide our way and that each one will feel with renewed vigor the appeal to work for the ecumenical cause. I encourage all of you to continue your work; it is a help that you render to the Bishop of Rome in fulfilling his mission at the service of unity. As a sign of affection and gratitude, I impart to you my heartfelt apostolic blessing." (Antipapal Words to Members of Christian Unity Council.)

"Excogitate models of unity"? This is the talk of an insane man. This is craziness. This is absurdity.

Yet it is that the supposedly more revolutionary Jorge Mario Bergoglio has taught the exact same thing since Wednesday, March 13, 2013, including during an "ecumenical" vespers service at the Basilica of Saint Paul Outside the Walls on January 25, 2014, the Feast of the Conversion of Saint Paul the Apostle, as he participated in an "ecumenical" vespers service along with a Greek Orthodox bishop and an Anglican non-bishop, David Moxon. The parallels between Bergoglio's heresy and that of Ratzinger's are striking in their similarity, proving yet again to those who have the honesty to see and to accept the truth that there is no space between these two heretics on matters of theological substance:

> "'Has Christ been divided?' (1 Cor 1:13). The urgent appeal which Saint Paul makes at the beginning of his First Letter to the Corinthians, and which has been proclaimed at this evening's liturgy, was chosen **by a group of our fellow Christians in Canada** as the theme for our meditation during this year's Week of Prayer.
>
> "The Apostle was grieved to learn that the Christians of Corinth had split into different factions. Some claimed: "I belong to Paul"; while others claimed: "I belong to Apollos" or "I belong to Cephas", and others yet claimed: "I belong to Christ" (cf. v. 12). Paul could not even praise those who claimed to belong to Christ, since they were using the name of the one Saviour to set themselves apart from their other brothers and sisters within the community. In other words, the particular experience of each individual, or an attachment to certain significant persons in the community, had become a yardstick for judging the faith of others.
>
> "Amid this divisiveness, Paul appeals to the Christians of Corinth "by the name of our Lord Jesus Christ" to be in agreement, so that divisions will not reign among them, but rather a perfect union of mind and purpose (cf. v. 10). **The communion for which the Apostle pleads, however, cannot be the fruit of human strategies.** Perfect union among brothers and sisters can only come from looking to the mind and heart of Christ Jesus (cf. Phil 2:5). This evening, as we gather here in prayer, may we realize that Christ, who cannot be divided, wants to draw us to himself, to the sentiments of his heart, to his complete and

confident surrender into the hands of the Father, to his radical self-emptying for love of humanity. Christ alone can be the principle, the cause and the driving force behind our unity.

"As we find ourselves in his presence, we realize all the more that we may not regard divisions in the Church as something natural, inevitable in any form of human association. Our divisions wound Christ's body, they impair the witness which we are called to give to him before the world. The Second Vatican Council's Decree on Ecumenism, appealing to the text of Saint Paul which we have reflected on, significantly states: "**Christ the Lord founded one Church and one Church only. However, many Christian communities present themselves to people as the true inheritance of Jesus Christ; all indeed profess to be followers of the Lord but they differ in outlook and go their different ways, as if Christ were divided". And the Council continues: "Such division openly contradicts the will of Christ, scandalizes the world, and damages the sacred cause of preaching the Gospel to every creature**" (Unitatis Redintegratio, 1).

"Christ, dear friends, cannot be divided! This conviction must sustain and encourage us to persevere with humility and trust on the way to the restoration of full visible unity among all believers in Christ. **Tonight I think of the work of two great Popes: Blessed John XXIII and Blessed John Paul II. In the course of their own lives, both came to realize the urgency of the cause of unity and, once elected to the See of Peter, they guided the entire Catholic flock decisively on the paths of ecumenism. Pope John blazed new trails which earlier would have been almost unthinkable. Pope John Paul held up ecumenical dialogue as an ordinary and indispensable aspect of the life of each Particular Church**. With them, I think too of Pope Paul VI, another great promoter of dialogue; in these very days we are commemorating the fiftieth anniversary of his historic embrace with the Patriarch Athenagoras of Constantinople.

"The work of these, my predecessors, enabled ecumenical dialogue to become an essential dimension of the ministry of the Bishop of Rome, **so that today the Petrine ministry cannot be fully understood without this openness to dialogue with all believers in Christ. We can say also that the journey of ecumenism has allowed us to come to a deeper understanding of the ministry of the Successor of Peter, and we must be confident that it will continue to do so in the future**. As we look with gratitude to the progress which the Lord has enabled us to make, and without ignoring the difficulties which ecumenical dialogue is presently experiencing, let us all pray that we may put on the mind of Christ and thus progress towards the unity which he wills.

"In this climate of prayer for the gift of unity, I address a cordial and fraternal greeting to His Eminence Metropolitan Gennadios, the representative of the Ecumenical Patriarch, and to His Grace David Moxon, the personal representative in Rome of the Archbishop of Canterbury, and to all the representatives of the various Churches and Ecclesial Communities gathered here this evening.

"Dear brothers and sisters, let us ask the Lord Jesus, who has made us living members of his body, to keep us deeply united to him, to help us overcome our conflicts, our divisions

> and our self-seeking, and to be united to one another by one force, by the power of love which the Holy Spirit pours into our hearts (cf. Rom 5:5)."
>
> http://w2.vatican.va/content/francesco/en/homilies/2014/documents/papa-francesco_20140125_vespri-conversione-san-paolo.html

Yes, what Angelo Roncalli/John XXIII started would have been unthinkable in the *Catholic Church* as she has consistently condemned any fellowship with false religions, each of which is hated by God and is an agent of the devil.

It is useful once again to make reference to what the Catholic Church has taught concerning false ecumenism of the sort preached and practiced by the likes of Joseph Alois Ratzinger/Benedict XVI and Jorge Mario Bergoglio/Francis:

> "It is for this reason that so many who do not share 'the communion and the truth of the Catholic Church' must make use of the occasion of the Council, by the means of the Catholic Church, which received in Her bosom their ancestors, proposes [further] demonstration of profound unity and of firm vital force; hear the requirements [demands] of her heart, they must engage themselves to leave this state that does not guarantee for them the security of salvation. **She does not hesitate to raise to the Lord of mercy most fervent prayers to tear down of the walls of division, to dissipate the haze of errors, and lead them back within holy Mother Church, where their Ancestors found salutary pastures of life; where, in an exclusive way, is conserved and transmitted whole the doctrine of Jesus Christ and wherein is dispensed the mysteries of heavenly grace**.
>
> "It is therefore by force of the right of Our supreme Apostolic ministry, entrusted to us by the same Christ the Lord, which, having to carry out with [supreme] participation all the duties of the good Shepherd and to follow and embrace with paternal love all the men of the world, we send this Letter of Ours to all the Christians from whom **We are separated, with which we exhort them warmly and beseech them with insistence to hasten to return to the one fold of Christ; we desire in fact from the depths of the heart their salvation in Christ Jesus, and we fear having to render an account one day to Him, Our Judge, if, through some possibility, we have not pointed out and prepared the way for them to attain eternal salvation. In all Our prayers and supplications, with thankfulness, day and night we never omit to ask for them, with humble insistence, from the eternal Shepherd of souls the abundance of goods and heavenly graces**. And since, if also, we fulfill in the earth the office of vicar, with all our heart we await with open arms the return of the wayward sons to the Catholic Church, in order to receive them with infinite fondness into the house of the Heavenly Father and to enrich them with its inexhaustible treasures. **By our greatest wish for the return to the truth and the communion with the Catholic Church, upon which depends not only the salvation of all of them, but above all also of the whole Christian society: the entire world in fact cannot enjoy true peace if it is not of one fold and one shepherd**. (Pope Pius IX, *Iam Vos Omnes*, September 13, 1868.)

> **"So, Venerable Brethren, it is clear why this Apostolic See has never allowed its subjects to take part in the assemblies of non-Catholics: for the union of Christians can only be promoted by promoting the return to the one true Church of Christ of those who are separated from it, for in the past they have unhappily left it**. To the one true Church of Christ, we say, which is visible to all, and which is to remain, according to the will of its Author, exactly the same as He instituted it. **During the lapse of centuries, the mystical Spouse of Christ has never been contaminated, nor can she ever in the future be contaminated**, as Cyprian bears witness: **'The Bride of Christ cannot be made false to her Spouse: she is incorrupt and modest**. She knows but one dwelling, she guards the sanctity of the nuptial chamber chastely and modestly.' The same holy Martyr with good reason marveled exceedingly that anyone could believe that 'this unity in the Church which arises from a divine foundation, and which is knit together by heavenly sacraments, could be rent and torn asunder by the force of contrary wills.' For since the mystical body of Christ, in the same manner as His physical body, is one, compacted and fitly joined together, it were foolish and out of place to say that the mystical body is made up of members which are disunited and scattered abroad: whosoever therefore is not united with the body is no member of it, neither is he in communion with Christ its head." (Pope Pius XI, *Mortalium Animos*, January 6, 1928.)

It was on August 19, 2005, that Joseph Ratzinger proved, as "Pope Benedict XVI," his absolute "papal" rejection of this consistent teaching of the Catholic Church, which dates back to the command that Our Blessed Lord and Saviour Jesus Christ gave to the Eleven before He Ascended to His Co-Equal and Co-Eternal God the Father's right hand in Heaven on Ascension Thursday, that began with Saint Peter's first *Urbi et Orbi* address on Pentecost Sunday that resulted in the conversion of over three thousand Jews from all over the Mediterranean (an address that Ratzinger/Benedict does not believe that Saint Peter delivered–see **Coloring Everything He Says and Does, part two)**:

> "We all know there are numerous models of unity and you know that the Catholic Church also has as her goal the full visible unity of the disciples of Christ, as defined by the Second Vatican Ecumenical Council in its various Documents (cf. **Lumen Gentium**, nn. 8, 13; **Unitatis Redintegratio**, nn. 2, 4, etc.). This unity, we are convinced, indeed subsists in the Catholic Church, without the possibility of ever being lost (cf. **Unitatis Redintegratio**, n. 4); the Church in fact has not totally disappeared from the world.
>
> "On the other hand, this unity does not mean what could be called ecumenism of the return: that is, to deny and to reject one's own faith history. Absolutely not!

> "It does not mean uniformity in all expressions of theology and spirituality, in liturgical forms and in discipline. **Unity in multiplicity, and multiplicity in unity**: in my **Homily for the Solemnity of Sts Peter and Paul on 29 June last**, I insisted that full unity and true catholicity in the original sense of the word go together. As a necessary condition for the achievement of this coexistence, the commitment to unity must be constantly purified and renewed; it must constantly grow and mature." (**Ecumenical meeting at the Archbishopric of Cologne English**.)

Why is this wrong? Permit a man who has been exasperated by three straight days of dealing with the devils within Adobe Contribute and must now adjust to WordPress on a permanent basis a moment to sigh. Oh, I'm back. Here is why:

> **"To characterize the relation between Catholics and Protestants as 'unity-in-diversity' is misleading, inasmuch as it implies that essentially Catholics are one with heretics, and that their diversities are only accidental. Actually, the very opposite is the true situation. For, however near an heretical sect may seem to be to the Catholic Church in its particular beliefs, a wide gulf separates them, insofar as the divinely established means whereby the message of God is to be communicated to souls–the infallible Magisterium of the Church–is rejected by every heretical sect**. By telling Protestants that they are one with us in certain beliefs, in such wise as to give the impression that we regard this unity as the predominant feature of our relation with them, we are actually misleading them regarding the true attitude of the Catholic Church toward those who do not acknowledge Her teaching authority." (Father Francis Connell, Father Connell Answers Moral Questions, published in 1959 by Catholic University of America Press, p. 11; quoted in Fathers Dominic and Francisco Radecki, CMRI, **TUMULTUOUS TIMES**, p. 348.)

There is no space on the matter of false ecumenism between Ratzinger and Bergoglio. I defy anyone in the the "Resignationism Rising" movement to report accurately on their "pope's" rejection of the Divine Constitution of the Catholic Church, including the teaching found in one of the very dogmatic statements cited in the letter to Ratzinger that was quoted in Chapter Seven of this book, *Cantate Domino*, February 4, 1442, which was issued by Pope Eugene IV at the Council of Florence.

Indeed, as noted in Chapter One of this book, Ratzinger and Bergoglio are as one in their false teaching about the supposedly perpetually binding nature of the Mosaic Covenant and in their rejection of these words of Saint John Chrystostom, whose feast is celebrated on January 27, 2014:

> **"Let that be your judgment about the synagogue, too. For they brought the books of Moses and the prophets along with them into the synagogue, not to honor them but to outrage them with dishonor. When they say that Moses and the prophets knew not Christ and said nothing about his coming, what greater outrage could they do to those holy men than to accuse them of failing to recognize their Master, than to say that those saintly prophets are partners of their impiety**? And so it is that we must hate both them and their synagogue all the more because of their offensive treatment of those holy men." (Saint John Chrysostom, Fourth Century, A.D., **Saint John Chrysostom: Eight Homilies Against the Jews.**)
>
> **"Many, I know, respect the Jews and think that their present way of life is a venerable one. This is why I hasten to uproot and tear out this deadly opinion. I said that the synagogue is no better than a theater and I bring forward a prophet as my witness. Surely the Jews are not more deserving of belief than their prophets. 'You had a harlot's brow; you became shameless before all'. Where a harlot has set herself up, that place is a brothel. But the synagogue is not only a brothel and a theater; it also is a den of robbers and a lodging for wild beasts**. Jeremiah said: 'Your house has become for me the den of a hyena'. He does not simply say 'of wild beast', but 'of a filthy wild beast', and again: 'I have abandoned my house, I have cast off my inheritance'. **But when God forsakes a people, what hope of salvation is left? When God forsakes a place, that place becomes the dwelling of demons**.
>
> "(2) **But at any rate the Jews say that they, too, adore God. God forbid that I say that. No Jew adores God! Who says so? The Son of God says so. For he said: 'If you were to know my Father, you would also know me. But you neither know me nor do you know my Father'. Could I produce a witness more trustworthy than the Son of God**?
>
> "(3) If, then, the Jews fail to know the Father, if they crucified the Son, if they thrust off the help of the Spirit, who should not make bold to declare plainly that the synagogue is a dwelling of demons? **God is not worshipped there. Heaven forbid! From now on it**

remains a place of idolatry. But still some people pay it honor as a holy place." **(Saint John Chrysostom: Eight Homilies Against the Jews)**

Neither Joseph Alois Ratzinger or Jorge Mario Bergoglio believe that this is so. Each has shown himself ready, willing and able to enter into synagogues and to give the appearance of validating the false religion of Talmudism while participating, whether passively by listening or actively while praying aloud, in prayers that deny the Sacred Divinity of the Second Person of the Most Blessed Trinity made Man in the Virginal and Immaculate Womb of the Blessed Virgin Mary by the power of the Third Person of the Most Blessed Trinity, God the Holy Ghost, at the Annunciation.

Additionally, there is no space between Ratzinger and Bergoglio when it comes to esteeming the symbols, rites and blasphemous teachings of Mohammedanism found in the Koran.

Here are several visual reminders of Ratzinger/Benedict's gestures of esteem shown to Mohammedanism:

November 30, 2006: Joseph Ratzinger/Benedict XVI entered into the Blue Mosque in Istanbul, Turkey, taking off his shoes so as to symbolize that he was in a "holy place" and then turned in the direction of Mecca at the behest of his Mohammedan "host," who instructed him to assume the Mohammedan prayer position as they "prayed" together. God is offended by honor being given to such a false religion as the souls of His faithful Catholics are scandalized and bewildered and confused as a consequence.

Ratzinger at the Blue Mosque

Ratzinger/Benedict receiving a copy of the Koran, "John Paul II Cultural Center," Washington, District of Columbia, Thursday, April 17, 2008. Would Our Lord receive a copy of this blasphemous document, no less with a smile on his face? See the video of this exercise in apostasy, (**See for yourself, April 17, 2008 – 6:15 p.m. – Interreligious Gathering.**) It was a few weeks later that Ratzinger/Benedict received yet another copy of the Koran in the Vatican, referring to it as "this dear, precious book." A book of blasphemy is "dear" and "precious"? Yes, to an apostate, absolutely.

May 9, 2008: Joseph Ratzinger/Benedict XVI visited Amman, Jordan, making the following incredible statement while there:

> **"Places of worship, like this splendid Al-Hussein Bin Talal mosque named after the revered late King, stand out like jewels across the earth's surface. From the ancient to the modern, the magnificent to the humble, they all point to the divine, to the Transcendent One, to the Almighty. And through the centuries these sanctuaries have drawn men and women into their sacred space to pause, to pray, to acknowledge the presence of the Almighty, and to recognize that we are all his creatures.**" **(Speech to**

Muslim religious leaders, members of the Diplomatic Corps and Rectors of universities in Jordan in front of the mosque al-Hussein bin Talal in Amman)

Ratzinger/Benedict at the Mosque Al-Hussein bin Talal, Amman, Jordan, Saturday, May 9, 2009.

Three days later, that is, on May 12, 2009, Ratzinger/Benedict yet again called another Mohammedan mosque, the Dome of the Rock in Jerusalem, "sacred," proving himself to be bereft of any understanding of the precepts contained in the First and Second Commandments:

> "I cordially thank the Grand Mufti, Muhammad Ahmad Hussein, together with the Director of the Jerusalem Islamic Waqf, Sheikh Mohammed Azzam al-Khatib al-Tamimi, and the Head of the Awquaf Council, Sheikh Abdel Azim Salhab, for the welcome they have extended to me on your behalf. **I am deeply grateful for the invitation to visit this sacred place,** and I willingly pay my respects to you and the leaders of the Islamic community in Jerusalem." (**Courtesy visit to the Grand Mufti of Jerusalem at the Mount of the Temple**, since when is a place of false worship "sacred" to the true God of Divine Revelation?)

Joseph Ratzinger/Benedict XVI entering the Dome of the Rock in Jerusalem, Wednesday, May 12, 2009. The false "pontiff" took off his shoes once again.

Saints gave up their lives rather than to give even the appearance of such apostasy.

There was hardly a word of protest in 2006, 2008 and 2009 from those who now constitute the "Resignationism Rising" movement and/or those in the Disneyland of the World of Motumania concerning these grave offenses given by the supposed "restorer of tradition" to the honor and glory and majesty of the Most Blessed Trinity. Most of these individuals kept their mouths shut in an exercise of the prudence of the flesh in order to seek and then to preserve their beloved *Summorum Pontificum*, July 5, 2007, that was issued precisely to keep their mouths shut and their spirits "pacified" in the wake of apostasies such as the ones depicted and documented above.

How is it, therefore, that anyone in the "Resignationism Rising" movement and or those in the Disneyland of the World of Motumania can be upset by the following words of Jorge Mario Bergoglio that reaffirmed Mohammedans in the "value" of the Koran that has been called "dear" and "precious" by a "pope" who has taken off his shoes, turned in the direction of Mecca, assumed the Mohammedan prayer position and called mosques, which are dens of the devil himself, "sacred"?

> "Sharing our experience in carrying that cross, to expel the illness within our hearts, which embitters our life: it is important that you do this in your meetings. Those that are Christian, with the Bible, **and those that are Muslim, with the Quran. The faith that your parents instilled in you will always help you move on**." (Antipope Francis, **Address to Refugees at Sacred Heart Basilica,** Rome, Jan. 19, 2014. As found at The "Gospel" according to Bergoglio at Novus Ordo Watch Wire Blog.)

A blasphemous book of a false prophet, Mohammed, has no ability to help people "move" anywhere but Hell, whose minions were the inspiration for the false prophet's false religion, which is violent of its own bloody nature.

Yet it is that Jorge Mario Bergoglio continued to show great respect for Mohammedanism when he visited Ankara, Turkey, on Friday, November 28, 2014, the Feast of Saint Catherine Laboure, and Istanbul, Turkey, on Saturday, November 29, 2014, the Vigil of the Feast of Saint Andrew and the Commemoration of Saint Saturninus, and on Sunday, November 30, 2014, the First Sunday of Advent. Bergoglio's visit to Turkey at the end of November, 2014, placed him in perfect "continuity with the "tradition" of his predecessors, including "Saint John Paul II," who kissed the blasphemous Koran, and Joseph Ratzinger/Benedict XVI, who turned in the direction of Mecca and assumed the Mohammedan prayer position when touring the Blue Mosque in Istanbul, Turkey, on November 30, 2006, the Feast of Saint Andrew the Apostle.

Here is part of what Bergoglio said to civic leaders of Turkey on Friday, November 29, 2014;

> Sadly, to date, we are still witnessing grave conflicts. In Syria and Iraq, particularly, terrorist violence shows no signs of abating. Prisoners and entire ethnic populations are experiencing the violation of the most basic humanitarian laws. Grave persecutions have taken place in the past and still continue today to the detriment of minorities, especially – though not only – Christians and Yazidis. Hundreds of thousands of persons have been

forced to abandon their homes and countries in order to survive and remain faithful to their religious beliefs.

Turkey, which has generously welcomed a great number of refugees, is directly affected by this tragic situation on its borders; the international community has the moral obligation to assist Turkey in taking care of these refugees. In addition to providing much needed assistance and humanitarian aid, we cannot remain indifferent to the causes of these tragedies. In reaffirming that it is licit, while always respecting international law, to stop an unjust aggressor, I wish to reiterate, moreover, that the problem cannot be resolved solely through a military response.

What is required is a concerted commitment on the part of all, based on mutual trust, which can pave the way to lasting peace, and enable resources to be directed, not to weaponry, but to the other noble battles worthy of man: the fight against hunger and sickness, the promotion of sustainable development and the protection of creation, and the relief of the many forms of poverty and marginalization of which there is no shortage in the world today.

Turkey, by virtue of its history, geographical position and regional influence, has a great responsibility: the choices which Turkey makes and its example are especially significant and can be of considerable help in promoting an encounter of civilizations and in identifying viable paths of peace and authentic progress.

May the Most High bless and protect Turkey, and help the nation to be a strong and fervent peacemaker! Thank you! (**Meeting with the President, Prime Minister and Civil Authorities**.)

May the "Most High bless and protect Turkey"?

Jorge Mario Bergoglio is an apostate.

Frank M. Rega's book, *Saint Francis of Assisi and the Conversion of the Muslims*, contains some very poignant episodes in Saint Francis's efforts to convert Sultan al-Kamil. Here is one such passage:

An early font presents the following account of the discourse of the Franciscans: "If you do not wish to believe," said the two friars, "we will commend your soul to God because we declare **that if you die while holding to your law, you will be lost**; **God will not accept your soul**. For this reason we have come to you." They added that they would demonstrate to the Sultan's wisest counselors the truth of Christianity, **before which Mohammed's law counted for nothing**. In answer to this challenge, and in order to confute the teaching of the two missionaries, the Sultan called in the religious advisers, the imams. However, they refused to dispute with the Christians and instead insisted that they be killed, in accordance with Islamic law.

> But the Sultan, captivated by the speech of the two Franciscans, and by their sincere concern for his own salvation, ignored the demand of his courtiers. Instead, al-Kamil listened willingly to Francis, permitting him great liberty in his preaching. He told his imams that beheading the friars would be an unjust recompense for their efforts, since they had arrived with the praiseworthy intention of seeking his personal salvation. To Francis he said: "I am going to go counter to what my religious advisers demand and will not cut off your heads . . . you have risked you own lives in order to save my soul." (Frank M. Rega, *St. Francis of Assisi and the Conversion of the Muslims*, TAN Books and Publishers, 2007, pp. 60-61.)

Saint Francis, a Catholic, spoke in a slightly different manner than the ecumenist, the retired Joseph Ratzinger/Benedict XVI, who spoke as follows: in Amman, Jordan, on May 8, 2009:

> Places of worship, like this splendid Al-Hussein Bin Talal mosque named after the revered late King, **stand out like jewels** across the earth's surface. From the ancient to the modern, the magnificent to the humble, they all point to the divine, to the Transcendent One, to the Almighty. And through the centuries these sanctuaries have drawn men and women into their sacred space to pause, to pray, to acknowledge the presence of the Almighty, and to recognize that we are all his creatures. (**Muslim religious leaders, members of the Diplomatic Corps and Rectors of universities in Jordan in front of the mosque al-Hussein bin Talal in Amman**)

As Mr. Rega noted in his fine book, Saint Francis of Assisi made no compromises whatsoever with the Holy Integrity of the Catholic Faith.

To believe that the leaders of ISIS are going to engage in "dialogue" is madness writ large. It is a madness that Bergoglio believes as insanity is his religion. As if his remarks to the civil authorities were not enough apostasy for one day, Bergoglio reiterated his pleas for "understanding" and "dialogue" when he addressed Turkey's President of Religious Affairs, who is a Turkish equivalent of Kurt "Cardinal" Koch, who, of course, carries on the work of the retired but nontheless busy apostate named Walter "Cardinal" Kasper:

> **As religious leaders, we are obliged to denounce all violations against human dignity and human rights. Human life, a gift of God the Creator, possesses a sacred character. As such, any violence which seeks religious justification warrants the strongest condemnation because the Omnipotent is the God of life and peace. The world expects those who claim to adore God to be men and women of peace who are capable of living as brothers and sisters, regardless of ethnic, religious, cultural or ideological differences.**
>
> As well as denouncing such violations, we must also work together to find adequate solutions. This requires the cooperation of all: governments, political and religious leaders, representatives of civil society, and all men and women of goodwill. In a unique way, religious leaders can offer a vital contribution by expressing the values of their respective traditions. **We, Muslims and Christians, are the bearers of spiritual treasures of inestimable worth. Among these we recognize some shared elements, though lived according to the traditions of each, such as the adoration of the All-Merciful God,**

reference to the Patriarch Abraham, prayer, almsgiving, fasting... elements which, when lived sincerely, can transform life and provide a sure foundation for dignity and fraternity. Recognizing and developing our common spiritual heritage – through interreligious dialogue – helps us to promote and to uphold moral values, peace and freedom in society (cf. John Paul II, *Address to the Catholic Community in Ankara*, 29 November 1979). The shared recognition of the sanctity of each human life is the basis of joint initiatives of solidarity, compassion, and effective help directed to those who suffer most. In this regard, I wish to express my appreciation for everything that the Turkish people, Muslims and Christians alike, are doing to help the hundreds of thousands of people who are fleeing their countries due to conflicts. There are two million of them. This is a clear example of how we can work together to serve others, an example to be encouraged and maintained.

> I wish also to express my satisfaction at the good relations which exist between the *Diyanet* and the Pontifical Council for Interreligious Dialogue. It is my earnest desire that these relations will continue and be strengthened for the good of all, so that every initiative which promotes authentic dialogue will offer a sign of hope to a world which so deeply needs peace, security and prosperity. Following my meeting with the President, I am also hopeful that this interreligious dialogue will take on creative new forms.

> Mr President, I renew my gratitude to you and your colleagues for this meeting, which fills my heart with joy. I am grateful also to each one of you, for your presence and for your prayers which, in your kindness, you offer for me and my ministry. For my part, I assure you of my prayers. May the Lord grant us all his blessing. (**Visit to the President of Religious Affairs**.)

Religious leaders?

Well, including Jorge himself, there were no "religious leaders" present when Jorge spoke on Friday, November 28, 2014, in Ankara, Turkey, about the madness of "dialogue," only representatives of false religions. Nothing else.

Bergoglio, once again following the "traditions" of "Saint John Paul II" and Ratzinger/Benedict, entered into the "Blue Mosque" on Saturday, November 29, 2014, and "prayed" while there, turning in the direction of Mecca just as Ratzinger had done one day shy of eight years previously.

Vatican spokesflack "Father" Federico Lombardi, S.J., explained that Bergoglio had done exactly what Ratzinger had done in 2006:

> Vatican City, Nov 29, 2014 / 06:04 am (CNA/EWTN News).- During Pope Francis' visit to Istanbul's Blue Mosque, he paused for a moment of prayer alongside Ankara's Grand Mufti – **a moment of "interreligious dialogue" which mirrored that of his predecessor**.

> **"When they were under the Dome, the Pope insisted: 'not only must we praise and glorify him, but we must adore him,'"** Vatican spokesman Fr. Federico Lombardi S.J.

told journalists Nov. 29. "**Therefore it is reasonable to qualify this moment of silence a moment of silent adoration.**"

"(It was) a beautiful moment of interreligious dialogue, and it the exact same thing happened in 2006 with Pope Benedict, it was exactly the same."

Fr. Lombardi offered his statement to the head of the Holy See Press Office association of journalists by telephone. The message was then relayed to the journalists present in the press center in Istanbul.

Pope Francis' visit to the historic Sultan Ahmet Mosque, known as the "Blue Mosque" due to the blue tiles covering the inside, marks the third time a Pope has ever gone inside, the first being St. John Paul II in 1979.

In his statement, Fr. Lombardi said that upon his arrival, the Roman Pontiff was greeted in the Mosque's garden by a group of 50-60 people coming from different Christian communities – including Latin, Coptic, Syro and Armenian – as well as their bishops.

President of the Turkish Episcopal Conference Bishop Smirme Franceschini offered a welcoming address before the Pope went inside.

The Bishop of Rome was accompanied into the mosque by Ankara's Grand Mufti Mehmet Görmez and two imam. After entering, the Grand Mufti explained to the Pope some verses from the Quran in which Niqab spoke of Zachariah, the birth of John the Baptist, of Elizabeth and Mary.

Once the Grand Mufti finished speaking, he and the Pope "took a moment of silence, a silent adoration (and) **the Pope said twice to the Muftì: we must adore God**," Fr. Lombardi said.

It was a true moment of interreligious dialogue, he observed, noting that afterward the Grand Mufti cited more verses of the Quran which refer to God as a God of love and justice.

Fr. Lombardi recalled how the Mufti said to Pope Francis that "**'on that we are agreed.' And the Pope said: 'Yes, on that we are agreed.' It was also a beautiful moment of dialogue.**"

After leaving the Mosque the Roman Pontiff went to visit the nearby Hagia Sofia, which is a former Greek Orthodox patriarchal basilica that was later turned into an imperial mosque, and is now a museum.

While inside Pope Francis signed the museum's Golden Book, writing in Greek "St. Sofia, Holy Wisdom of God," and cited a passage in Latin from psalm 84 that says "How lovely is thy dwelling place, O LORD of hosts!" (**Bergoglio's prayer at Blue Mosque 'exactly the same' as Ratzinger's.** Also see the post at **Novus Ordo Watch Wire**.)

As noted in August of 2010 on www.Christorchaos.com, the conciliar revolutions have created "**Ever More "Traditions" That Come From Hell**." What happened at the Blue Mosque on Saturday, November 29, 2014, was simply one of those "traditions" that "Pope Francis" was more than happy to continue in perfect "continuity" with his predecessor.

Bergoglio explained his visit to the "Blue Mosque" and the "prayer" he said there during a press conference that he held on Sunday, November 30, 2014, on the plane that was taking the "papal" entourage back to Rome:

> "I sincerely believe that you cannot say that all Muslims are terrorists just as you cannot say that all Christians are fundamentalists; every religion has these little groups," the pope said. (**Jorge's Press Confab**.)

To equate faithful Catholics with the killers of the Islamic State of Iraq and Syria is obscene. It is perverse.

Ah, what can one expect from a man who does not believe that Mohammedanism is a religion of terror, first of all against the honor and glory of God and His Sacred Deposit of Faith, which He has revealed and entrusted to the Catholic Church exclusively, and secondly against infidels who will not convert to the worship of its false gods?

Bergoglio even boasted of having prayed inside the "Blue Mosque," which is a den of the devil, on Saturday, November 29, 2014, the Feast of the Vigil of Saint Andrew and the Commemoration of Saint Saturninus:

> During a televised moment of silent prayer in Istanbul's Blue Mosque Nov. 29, alongside the city's grand mufti, "I prayed for Turkey, I prayed for the mufti, I prayed for myself because I need it, and I prayed above all for the peace and an end to war." (**Jorge's Press Confab**.)

It was in 1948 that The Holy Office, which was headed at the time by none other than Pope Pius XII, reiterated the Catholic Church's complete ban on Catholics participating in the services of false religions or "praying" within their temples that had been reaffirmed by Pope Pius XI *Mortalium Animos*, January 6, 1928:

> Mixed gatherings of non-Catholics with Catholics have been reportedly held in various places, where things pertaining to the Faith have been discussed against the prescriptions of the Sacred Canons and without previous permission of the Holy See. Therefore all are reminded that according to the norm of Canon 1325 § 3 laypeople as well as clerics both secular and regular are forbidden to attend these gatherings without the aforesaid permission. It is however much less licit for Catholics to summon and institute such kind of gatherings. Let therefore Ordinaries urge all to serve these prescriptions accurately.
>
> These are to be observed with even stronger force of law when it comes to gatherings called "ecumenical", which laypeople and clerics may not attend at all without previous consent of the Holy See.

Moreover, since acts of mixed worship have also been posed not rarely both within and without the aforesaid gatherings, all are once more warned that any communication in sacred affairs is totally forbidden according to the norm of Canons 1258 and 731, § 2.

Given at Rome, at the premises of the Holy Office, on June 5th 1948. (This was translated by those who run *Novus Ordo Watch*. **See The Holy Office's 1948 Canonical Warning against Ecumenical Gatherings**.)

Jorge Mario Bergoglio, acting in complete "continuity" with his conciliar predecessors, believes that such statements were erroneous because men sought to "cage" God the Holy Ghost. We know that the origins of Jorge's "spirits are diabolical as he projects into God his own imaginings of what He *really* teaches in spite of all past "errors." Bergoglio placed himself outside of the pale of Holy Mother Church long before his "election" six hundred twenty-nine days ago, that is, on Wednesday, March 13, 2013.

What Catholics need to do is to pray Rosaries for the conversion of all infidels, including those who follow the false religion of the false, lecherous "prophet" named Mohammed, who had twelve "wives."

Pope Saint Pius V urged Christendom to pray Our Lady's Most Holy Rosary prior to the Battle of Lepanto on October 7, 1571, resulting in a triumph of the outnumbered Christian naval fleet under the command of John of Austria over the *Turkish* Mohammedans, and it was Our Lady's Most Holy Rosary that helped King John Sobieski of Poland to defeat the Turkish Mohammedans once again in the Battle of the Gates of Vienna on September 12, 1683. Ah, yes, those "peace-building" Turks.

We need to have recourse as never before to Our Lady's Most Holy Rosary, offering up the sufferings of this present moment as the consecrated slaves of her Divine Son, Our Blessed Lord and Saviour Jesus Christ, through her own Sorrowful and Immaculate Heart.

Consider the following meditation of Saint Louis de Montfort on the power of the Most Holy Rosary, contained in the Twenty-sixth Rose of *The Secret of the Rosary*:

"Whatever you do, do not be like a certain pious but self-willed lady in Rome, so often referred to by speakers on the Rosary. She was so devout and fervent that she put to shame by her holy life even the strictest religious in the church.

"Having decided to ask St. Dominic's advice about her spiritual life, she made her confession to him. For penance he gave her one Rosary to say and advised her to say it every day. She excused herself, saying that she had her regular exercises, that she made the Stations of Rome every day, that she wore sackcloth as well as a hair-shirt, that she gave herself the discipline several times a week, that she often fasted and did other penances. Saint Dominic urged her over and over again to take his advice and say the Rosary, but she would not hear of it. She left the confessional, horrified at the methods of this new spiritual director who had tried so hard to persuade her to take up a devotion for which she had no taste.

"Later on, when she was at prayer she fell into ecstasy and had a vision of her soul appearing before the Supreme Judge. Saint Michael put all her penances and to her prayers on one side of the scale and all her sins and imperfections on the other. The tray of her good works were greatly outweighed by that of her sins and imperfections.

"Filled with alarm, she cried out for mercy, imploring the help of the Blessed Virgin, her gracious advocate, who took the one and only Rosary she had said for her penance and dropped it on the tray of her good works. This one Rosary was so heavy that it weighed more than all her sins as well as her good works. Our Lady then reproved her for having refused to follow the counsel of her servant Dominic and for not saying the Rosary every day.

"As soon as she came to herself she rushed and threw herself at the feet of Saint Dominic and told him all that had happened, begged his forgiveness and promised to say the Rosary faithfully every day. By this means she rose to Christian perfection and finally to the glory of everlasting life.

"You who are people of prayer, learn from this the power, the value and importance of this devotion of the holy Rosary when it is said with meditation on the mysteries.

"Few saints have reached the same heights of prayer as Saint Mary Magdalen, who was lifted up to heaven by angels each day, and who had the privilege of learning at the feet of Jesus and his holy Mother. Yet one day, when she asked God to show her a sure way of advancing in his love and arriving at the heights of perfection, he sent the archangel St. Michael to tell her, on his behalf, that there was no other way to reach perfection than to meditate on our Lord's passion. So he placed a cross in the front of her cave and told her to pray before it, contemplating the sorrowful mysteries which she had seen take place with her own eyes.

"The example of Saint Francis de Sales, the great spiritual director of his time, should spur you on to join the holy confraternity of the Rosary, since, great saint though he was, he bound himself by vow to say the whole Rosary every day as long as he lived.

"Saint Charles Borromeo also said it every day and strongly recommended this devotion to his priests and clerics in seminaries and to all his people.

"Blessed Pius V, one of the greatest popes who have ever ruled the Church, used to say the Rosary every day. Saint Thomas of Villanova, Archbishop of Valencia, Saint Ignatius, Saint Francis Xavier, Saint Francis Borgia, Saint Teresa, and Saint Philip Neri, as well as many other great men whom I do not mention, were greatly devoted to the Rosary.

> "Follow their example; your spiritual directors will be very pleased, and if they are aware of the benefits which you can derive from this devotion, they will be the first to urge you to adopt it." (**The Secret of the Rosary.**)

Let us continue to trust in the power of Our Lady's Most Holy Rosary as we await in confidence the Triumph of her Immaculate Heart when a true pope fulfills her Fatima Message.

These days of chastisement will come to an end. We just need to bear the difficulties of the moment with joy and gratitude as we seek to make reparation for our sins and those of the whole world as the consecrated slaves of Christ the King through the Sorrowful and Immaculate Heart of Mary.

Chapter Twelve
Believing in "Peace" While Making War Upon Christ the King

Pope Saint Pius X told us what the agents of Antichrist would do to corrupt the Catholic Faith: they would seek to build the One World Ecumenical Church:

And now, overwhelmed with the deepest sadness, We ask Ourselves, Venerable Brethren, what has become of the Catholicism of the Sillon? **Alas! this organization which formerly afforded such promising expectations, this limpid and impetuous stream, has been harnessed in its course by the modern enemies of the Church, and is now no more than a miserable affluent of the great movement of apostasy being organized in every country for the establishment of a One-World Church which shall have neither dogmas, nor hierarchy, neither discipline for the mind, nor curb for the passions, and which, under the pretext of freedom and human dignity, would bring back to the world (if such a Church could overcome) the reign of legalized cunning and force, and the oppression of the weak, and of all those who toil and suffer**. (Pope Saint Pius X, *Notre Charge Apostolique*, August 15, 1910.)

Almost everything that one can say about the blasphemous outrage against the honor and glory and majesty of the true God of Divine Revelation, the Most Blessed Trinity, in the Vatican Gardens where prayers were offered to the devils worshiped by adherents of Talmudists and Mohmmedans was said in Antichrist and His Anti-Pentecost, which had been written before the outrage took place.

I, for one, have run out of ways to explain that Jorge Mario Bergoglio, a true son of the conciliar revolution just as much as his predecessor, Joseph Ratzinger/Benedict XVI, was of its progenitors, apologists and guiding forces, lacks the Catholic Faith.

No believing Catholic can react with passivity while adherents of false religions utter prayers to their devils at the invitation of a putative "pope," who listens to those prayers with attentiveness and, at times, a bowed head.

No faithful Catholic believes that prayers of false religion addressed to their false gods are pleasing to God, less yet that they can produce "peace" in the world.

Writing in *Mit Brennender Sorge*, March 17, 1937, Pope Pius XI explained that the souls of men must be a peace with God by means of Sanctifying Grace in order for there to be order within nations and peace among them:

> **Every true and lasting reform has ultimately sprung from the sanctity of men who were driven by the love of God and of men**. Generous, ready to stand to attention to any call from God, yet confident in themselves because confident in their vocation, they grew to the size of beacons and reformers. No doubt "the Spirit breatheth where he will" (John iii. 8): "of stones He is able to raise men to prepare the way to his designs" (Matt. iii. 9). He chooses the instruments of His will according to His own plans, not those of men. **But the Founder of the Church, who breathed her into existence at Pentecost, cannot disown the foundations as He laid them. Whoever is moved by the spirit of God,**

> **spontaneously adopts both outwardly and inwardly, the true attitude toward the Church, this sacred fruit from the tree of the cross, this gift from the Spirit of God, bestowed on Pentecost day to an erratic world**. (Pope Pius XI, *Mit Brennender Sorge*, March 17, 1937.)

Jorge Mario Bergoglio did the work of Antichrist once again on Pentecost Sunday, June 8, 2014, as he engaged in behavior that was Anti-Pentecost. Saint Peter sought to convert the Jews. Countless numbers of Catholic missionaries sought to convert the Mohammedans, never shrinking from the task of having to fight them on the battlefield as they sought to spread their false religion at the point of the sword and the scimitar.

Saint Anthony of Padua left the Canons Regular of Saint Augustine to seek to follow the path of the Protomartyrs of the Order of Friars Minor on January 16, 1220, whose martyrdom is recounted in The Roman Martyrology:

> At Morocco, in Africa, the martyrdom of the holy martyrs of the Order of Friars Minor, Berard, Peter, Accursius, Adjutus, and Otto. **The Roman Martyrology, January 16**.)

Saint Anthony, who had distinguished himself in the Augustinian order, did not realize his desire to die a martyr's death. A shipwreck in 1221 en route back to Portugal from Morocco, where he had taken seriously ill, placed Saint Anthony on the shores of Sicily.

Saint Francis of Assisi himself, however, was able to preach the Cross of the Divine Redeemer, Christ the King, to the Mohammedans, something that Mr. Frank Rega recounted in *Saint Francis of Assisi and the Conversion of the Muslims*:

> An early font presents the following account of the discourse of the Franciscans: "If you do not wish to believe," said the two friars, "we will commend your soul to God because we declare **that if you die while holding to your law, you will be lost**; **God will not accept your soul**. For this reason we have come to you." They added that they would demonstrate to the Sultan's wisest counselors the truth of Christianity, **before which Mohammed's law counted for nothing**. In answer to this challenge, and in order to confute the teaching of the two missionaries, the Sultan called in the religious advisers, the imams. However, they refused to dispute with the Christians and instead insisted that they be killed, in accordance with Islamic law.
>
> But the Sultan, captivated by the speech of the two Franciscans, and by their sincere concern for his own salvation, ignored the demand of his courtiers. Instead, al-Kamil listened willingly to Francis, permitting him great liberty in his preaching. He told his imams that beheading the friars would be an unjust recompense for their efforts, since they had arrived with the praiseworthy intention of seeking his personal salvation. To Francis he said: "I am going to go counter to what my religious advisers demand and will not cut off your heads . . . you have risked you own lives in order to save my soul." (Frank M. Rega, *St. Francis of Assisi and the Conversion of the Muslims*, TAN Books and Publishers, 2007, pp. 60-61.)

Conciliar revolutionaries have attempted to claim that Saint Francis of Assisi was engaged in "ecumenical dialogue." He was not. He wanted to convert the Sultan and those around him out of their false religion, something that the Sultan al-Kamil appreciated as he knew men of integrity when saw them.

Certainly, Jorge Mario Bergoglio has integrity of faith. Unfortunately for him, however, his faith, conciliarism, is just as false as Talmudism and Mohammedanism. His faith is counter to the true Faith, the Catholic Faith, which is why he must misrepresent the very life's work and blaspheme the person of the great Saint of Assisi who bore the brand marks of Our Blessed Lord and Saviour Jesus Christ's stigmata on his holy body for the final year of his life (although he had borne the stigmata in his heart for a long time before).

Unlike "Pope Francis," who listened attentively on June 8, 2014, to the Talmudic and Mohammedan "prayers" and to the remarks made by Israeli President **Shimon Peres** and Palestinian Authority President **Mahmoud Abbas**, Saint Francis of Assisi defended with honor and glory of the Most Blessed Trinity with manly courage. He was not the effeminate enabler of falsehoods in the name of a false charity for "fellow believers."

Pope Pius XI explained the true character of Saint Francis of Assisi in Rite Expiatis, April 13, 1926:

> **What evil they do and how far from a true appreciation of the Man of Assisi are they who, in order to bolster up their fantastic and erroneous ideas about him, imagine such an incredible thing as that Francis was an opponent of the discipline of the Church, that he did not accept the dogmas of the Faith, that he was the precursor and prophet of that false liberty which began to manifest itself at the beginning of modern times and which has caused so many disturbances both in the Church and in civil society**! That he was in a special manner obedient and faithful in all things to the hierarchy of the Church, to this Apostolic See, and to the teachings of Christ, the Herald of the Great King proved both to Catholics and nonCatholics by the admirable example of obedience which he always gave. It is a fact proven by contemporary documents, which are worthy of all credence, "that he held in veneration the clergy, and loved with a great affection all who were in holy orders." (Thomas of Celano, Legenda, Chap. I, No. 62) "As a man who was truly Catholic and apostolic, he insisted above all things in his sermons that the faith of the Holy Roman Church should always be preserved and inviolably, and that the priests who by their ministry bring into being the sublime Sacrament of the Lord, should therefore be held in the highest reverence. He also taught that the doctors of the law of God and all the orders of clergy should be shown the utmost respect at all times." (Julian a Spira, Life of St. Francis, No. 28) That which he taught to the people from the pulpit he insisted on much more strongly among his friars. We may read of this in his famous last testament and, again, at the very point of death he admonished them about this with great insistence, namely, that in the exercise of the sacred ministry they should always obey the bishops and the clergy and should live together with them as it behooves children of peace. (**Pius XI, Rite expiatis**)

Pope Leo XIII had pointed out the same thing about Saint Francis of Assisi forty-three and one-half years before in *Auspicato Concessum*, September 17, 1882:

> **Thenceforth, amidst the effeminacy and over-fastidiousness of the time, he is seen to go about careless and roughly clad, begging his food from door to door, not only enduring what is generally deemed most hard to bear, the senseless ridicule of the crowd, but even to welcome it with a wondrous readiness and pleasure. And this because he had embraced the folly of the cross of Jesus Christ, and because he deemed it the highest wisdom. Having penetrated and understood its awful mysteries, he plainly saw that nowhere else could his glory be better placed**. (Pope Leo XIII, *Auspicato Concessum*, September 17, 1882.)

The man who placed a non-denominational "Christian" prayer on an equal footing with prayers from Talmudism and Mohammedanism, Jorge Mario Bergoglio, believes that he did the work of Saint Francis of Assisi by having convened his "prayer meeting" in June of 2014. He did not. Just as Bergoglio is a figure of Anti-Christ and an Anti-Saint Peter as an Antipope, he is an Anti-Saint Francis of Assisi who, though mentioning Our Lord and His Most Blessed near the end of his own remarks on Pentecost Sunday in 2014, never once urged Peres or Abbas to convert to the true Faith nor point out that Christ the King has appointed the path of true peace to run through the Sorrowful and Immaculate Heart of Mary:

> I greet you with immense joy and I wish to offer you, and the eminent delegations accompanying you, the same warm welcome which you gave to me during my recent pilgrimage to the Holy Land.
>
> I am profoundly grateful to you for accepting my invitation to come here and to join in imploring from God the gift of peace. It is my hope that this meeting will mark the beginning of a new journey where we seek the things that unite, so as to overcome the things that divide.
>
> I also **thank Your Holiness, my venerable Brother Bartholomaios, for joining me in welcoming these illustrious guests. Your presence here is a great gift, a much-appreciated sign of support, and a testimony to the pilgrimage which we Christians are making towards full unity**.
>
> Your presence, dear Presidents, **is a great sign of brotherhood which you offer as children of Abraham**. It is also a concrete expression of trust in God, the Lord of history, who today looks upon all of us as brothers and who desires to guide us in his ways.
>
> This meeting of prayer for peace in the Holy Land, in the Middle East and in the entire world **is accompanied by the prayers of countless people of different cultures, nations, languages and religions: they have prayed for this meeting and even now they are united with us in the same supplication. It is a meeting which responds to the fervent desire of all who long for peace and dream of a world in which men and women can live as brothers and sisters and no longer as adversaries and enemies**.

Dear Presidents, our world is a legacy bequeathed to us from past generations, but it is also on loan to us from our children: our children who are weary, worn out by conflicts and yearning for the dawn of peace, our children who plead with us to tear down the walls of enmity and to set out on the path of dialogue and peace, so that love and friendship will prevail.

Many, all too many, of those children have been innocent victims of war and violence, saplings cut down at the height of their promise. It is our duty to ensure that their sacrifice is not in vain. The memory of these children instils in us the courage of peace, the strength to persevere undaunted in dialogue, the patience to weave, day by day, an ever more robust fabric of respectful and peaceful coexistence, for the glory of God and the good of all.

Peacemaking calls for courage, much more so than warfare. It calls for the courage to say yes to encounter and no to conflict: yes to dialogue and no to violence; yes to negotiations and no to hostilities; yes to respect for agreements and no to acts of provocation; yes to sincerity and no to duplicity. All of this takes courage, it takes strength and tenacity.

History teaches that our strength alone does not suffice. More than once we have been on the verge of peace, but the evil one, employing a variety of means, has succeeded in blocking it. That is why we are here, because we know and we believe that we need the help of God. We do not renounce our responsibilities, but we do call upon God in an act of supreme responsibility before our consciences and before our peoples. We have heard a summons, and we must respond. It is the summons to break the spiral of hatred and violence, and to break it by one word alone: the word "brother". But to be able to utter this word we have to lift our eyes to heaven and acknowledge one another as children of one Father.

To him, the Father, in the Spirit of Jesus Christ, I now turn, begging the intercession of the Virgin Mary, a daughter of the Holy Land and our Mother.

Lord God of peace, hear our prayer!

We have tried so many times and over so many years to resolve our conflicts by our own powers and by the force of our arms. How many moments of hostility and darkness have we experienced; how much blood has been shed; how many lives have been shattered; how many hopes have been buried... But our efforts have been in vain.

Now, Lord, come to our aid! Grant us peace, teach us peace; guide our steps in the way of peace. Open our eyes and our hearts, and give us the courage to say: "Never again war!"; "With war everything is lost". Instil in our hearts the courage to take concrete steps to achieve peace.

Lord, God of Abraham, God of the Prophets, God of Love, you created us and you call us to live as brothers and sisters. Give us the strength daily to be instruments of peace; enable us to see everyone who crosses our path as our brother or sister. Make us sensitive to the plea of our citizens who entreat us to turn our weapons of war into implements of peace, our trepidation into confident trust, and our quarreling into forgiveness.

Keep alive within us the flame of hope, so that with patience and perseverance we may opt for dialogue and reconciliation. In this way may peace triumph at last, and may the words "division", "hatred" and "war" be banished from the heart of every man and woman. Lord, defuse the violence of our tongues and our hands. Renew our hearts and minds, so that the word which always brings us together will be "brother", and our way of life will always be that of: Shalom, Peace, Salaam! Amen. (**Jorge's prayer for peace**.)

Brief Comment Number One:

Once again, Talmudists and Mohammedans do not pray to the true God of Divine Revelation.

Brief Comment Number Two:

Talmudists and Mohammedans are not the children of Abraham. Catholics alone are the true spiritual descendants of Abraham today.

Brief Comment Number Three:

The souls of Shimon Peres and Mahmoud Abbas are captive to the devil by means of Original Sin. They are thus incapable of serving as instruments of a true peace, that of Christ the King Himself, something that has been pointed out on this site scores upon scores of times by citing the following passage from Pope Pius XI's *Ubi Arcano Dei Consilio*, December 23 1922:

> **Since the Church is the safe and sure guide to conscience, for to her safe-keeping alone there has been confided the doctrines and the promise of the assistance of Christ, she is able not only to bring about at the present hour a peace that is truly the peace of Christ, but can, better than any other agency which We know of, contribute greatly to the securing of the same peace for the future, to the making impossible of war in the future. For the Church teaches (she alone has been given by God the mandate and the right to teach with authority) that not only our acts as individuals but also as groups and as nations must conform to the eternal law of God. In fact, it is much more important that the acts of a nation follow God's law, since on the nation rests a much greater responsibility for the consequences of its acts than on the individual.**
>
> When, therefore, governments and nations follow in all their activities, whether they be national or international, the dictates of conscience grounded in the teachings, precepts, and example of Jesus Christ, and which are binding on each and every individual, then only can we have faith in one another's word and trust in the peaceful solution of the difficulties and controversies which may grow out of differences in point of view or from clash of interests. An attempt in this direction has already and is now being made; its results, however, are almost negligible and, especially so, as far as they can be said to affect those major questions which divide seriously and serve to arouse nations one against the other. **No merely human institution of today can be as successful in devising a set of**

international laws which will be in harmony with world conditions as the Middle Ages were in the possession of that true League of Nations, Christianity. It cannot be denied that in the Middle Ages this law was often violated; still it always existed as an ideal, according to which one might judge the acts of nations, and a beacon light calling those who had lost their way back to the safe road.

There exists an institution able to safeguard the sanctity of the law of nations. This institution is a part of every nation; at the same time it is above all nations. She enjoys, too, the highest authority, the fullness of the teaching power of the Apostles. **Such an institution is the Church of Christ. She alone is adapted to do this great work, for she is not only divinely commissioned to lead mankind, but moreover, because of her very make-up and the constitution which she possesses, by reason of her age-old traditions and her great prestige, which has not been lessened but has been greatly increased since the close of the War, cannot but succeed in such a venture where others assuredly will fail.**

It is apparent from these considerations that true peace, the peace of Christ, is impossible unless we are willing and ready to accept the fundamental principles of Christianity, unless we are willing to observe the teachings and obey the law of Christ, **both in public and private life. If this were done, then society being placed at last on a sound foundation, the Church would be able, in the exercise of its divinely given ministry and by means of the teaching authority which results therefrom, to protect all the rights of God over men and nations.**

It is possible to sum up all We have said in one word, "the Kingdom of Christ." For Jesus Christ reigns over the minds of individuals by His teachings, in their hearts by His love, in each one's life by the living according to His law and the imitating of His example. Jesus reigns over the family when it, modeled after the holy ideals of the sacrament of matrimony instituted by Christ, maintains unspotted its true character of sanctuary. In such a sanctuary of love, parental authority is fashioned after the authority of God, the Father, from Whom, as a matter of fact, it originates and after which even it is named. (Ephesians iii, 15) The obedience of the children imitates that of the Divine Child of Nazareth, and the whole family life is inspired by the sacred ideals of the Holy Family. **Finally, Jesus Christ reigns over society when men recognize and reverence the sovereignty of Christ, when they accept the divine origin and control over all social forces, a recognition which is the basis of the right to command for those in authority and of the duty to obey for those who are subjects, a duty which cannot but ennoble all who live up to its demands. Christ reigns where the position in society which He Himself has assigned to His Church is recognized, for He bestowed on the Church the status and the constitution of a society which, by reason of the perfect ends which it is called upon to attain, must be held to be supreme in its own sphere; He also made her the depository and interpreter of His divine teachings, and, by consequence, the teacher and guide of every other society whatsoever, not of course in the sense that she should abstract in the least from their authority, each in its own sphere supreme, but that she should really perfect their authority, just as divine grace perfects human nature, and should give to them the assistance necessary for men to attain their true final end, eternal**

happiness, and by that very fact make them the more deserving and certain promoters of their happiness here below.

> 49. **It is, therefore, a fact which cannot be questioned that the true peace of Christ can only exist in the Kingdom of Christ — "the peace of Christ in the Kingdom of Christ." It is no less unquestionable that, in doing all we can to bring about the re-establishment of Christ's kingdom, we will be working most effectively toward a lasting world peace.** (Pope Pius XI, *Ubi Arcano Dei Consilio*, December 23, 1922.)

Brief Comment Number Four:

Bartholomew, the Greek Orthodox patriarch of Constantinople, may be Jorge's "brother" in heresy. However, Greek Orthodox bishops have no mandate from God to sanctify and serve souls. They adhere to doctrines that are heretical, including a denial of Papal Primacy and Infallibility. The true patriarchs of Constantinople were obedient of the Successor of Saint Peter in the First Millennium, something that Pope Leo XIII pointed out in *Praeclara Gratulationis Publicae,* June 29, 1894, which has been cited in this book previously. Each of the three men who spoke in the Vatican Gardens on June 8, 2014, did so as non-Catholics.

Shimon Peres spoke as a Zionist and a Talmudist.

Mahmound Abbas spoke as a Mohmmedan and Palestinian advocate.

Jorge Mario Bergoglio spoke as a Sillonist, which means he spoke in the language of Judeo-Masonry, yes, even with the gratuitous reference to Our Lord and Our Lady as he focused on purely secular, natural means to obtain "peace" between the Zionists and those whom they displaced with brute force from their homes while despoiling them of their property and confining many of them to "refugee" centers." The mere mention of Our Lord and Our Lady can never redeem acts which place the Catholic Faith on a level of equality any false religion, especially those false religions that go so far as to deny the Sacred Divinity of Our Blessed Lord and Saviour Jesus Christ.

Obviously, Joseph Alois Ratzinger had spoken and written in much the same manner. His Assisi III event, mentioned earlier in this book, on October 27, 2011, was the rotten fruit of his 2011 "World Day of Peace" message, which contained the following telling passages in behalf of his erroneous view that the heresy of "religious liberty" is the foundation of "peace" among nations:

> 8. The same determination that condemns every form of fanaticism and religious fundamentalism must also oppose every form of hostility to religion that would restrict the public role of believers in civil and political life.
>
> It should be clear that *religious fundamentalism and secularism are alike in that both represent extreme forms of a rejection of legitimate pluralism and the principle of secularity.* Both absolutize a reductive and partial vision of the human person, favouring in the one case forms of religious integralism and, in the other, of rationalism. *A society that would violently impose or, on the contrary, reject religion is not only unjust to*

> *individuals and to God, but also to itself. God beckons humanity with a loving plan that, while engaging the whole person in his or her natural and spiritual dimensions, calls for a free and responsible answer which engages the whole heart and being, individual and communitarian.* Society too, as an expression of the person and of all his or her constitutive dimensions, must live and organize itself in a way that favours openness to transcendence. Precisely for this reason, the laws and institutions of a society cannot be shaped in such a way as to ignore the religious dimension of its citizens or to prescind completely from it. Through the democratic activity of citizens conscious of their lofty calling, those laws and institutions must adequately reflect the authentic nature of the person and support its religious dimension. Since the latter is not a creation of the state, it cannot be manipulated by the state, but must rather be acknowledged and respected by it.
>
> Whenever the legal system at any level, national or international, allows or tolerates religious or antireligious fanaticism, it fails in its mission, which is to protect and promote justice and the rights of all. These matters cannot be left to the discretion of the legislator or the majority since, as Cicero once pointed out, justice is something more than a mere act which produces and applies law. It entails *acknowledging the dignity of each person,* which, unless religious freedom is guaranteed and lived in its essence, ends up being curtailed and offended, exposed to the risk of falling under the sway of idols, of relative goods which then become absolute. All this exposes society to the risk of forms of political and ideological totalitarianism which emphasize public power while demeaning and restricting freedom of conscience, thought and religion as potential competitors. (**44th World Day of Peace 2011, Religious Freedom, the Path to Peace**.)

Joseph Ratzinger/Benedict XVI believes what Jorge Mario Bergoglio/Francis continues to profess on an almost daily basis. Fidelity to the immutable truths of the Holy Faith must be equated with the "fantacism" and "fundamentalism" of the supposed "distortions" of the great "religion of peace," Mohammedanism.

Catholicism was never violently imposed upon any nation. The Catholic Faith grew organically amongst the former barbaric tribes and pagan peoples of Europe in the First Millennium, resulting in the establishment of the era we know as Christendom, that Christ-centered world that was distinguished by many holy civil rulers who understood that they had to rule according to the mind of Christ the King as He had discharged It in Holy Mother Church. Sure, there were stinkers in the Middle Ages who ruled for their themselves and their corrupt courtiers, enabled all too frequently by bishops who betrayed Christ the King by selling out the Faith and even the demands of natural justice in order to live lives of empty pleasure at the court. There were also, however, the likes of Saint Louis IX, King of France, and Saint Edward the Confessor in England and Saint Wenceslaus in Bohemia and Saint Casimir in Poland and Saint Canute in Denmark. These exemplars of the Social Reign of Christ the King did not "impose" their rule upon anyone. They simply attempted to pursue the common temporal good in light of man's Last End, the possession of the glory of the Beatific Vision of God the Father, God the Son, and God the Holy Ghost for all eternity in Heaven.

Ratzinger/Benedict believes, incredibly enough, that the rise of political and ideological totalitarianism is the result of the lack of the "guarantee" of "religious freedom," not the overthrow of the Social Reign of Christ the King wrought by the Protestant Revolution and institutionalized by the rise of the revolutionary naturalistic forces associated with the phrase Judeo-Masonry.

It is the madness of "freedom of conscience" that leads to such social abyss in "democratic" nations that provides naturalists with one opportunity to impose statism, whether all or once, as happened in Russia and other Communist nations, or incrementally, as has been happening for decades now right here in the United States of America.

Pope Gregory XVI, who was nowhere quoted in any of the documents of the "Second" Vatican Council and who, quite of course, was not quoted in Ratzinger/Benedict's new "World Day of Peace Message," explained in very succinct terms what happens to nations that permit unrestricted liberty of conscience of the sort favored by Ratzinger/Benedict that permits people of every religion or of no religion to express their views publicly in the "marketplace of ideas:"

> "This shameful font of indifferentism gives rise to that absurd and erroneous proposition which claims that liberty of conscience must be maintained for everyone. It spreads ruin in sacred and civil affairs, though some repeat over and over again with the greatest impudence that some advantage accrues to religion from it. "**But the death of the soul is worse than freedom of error**," as Augustine was wont to say. **When all restraints are removed by which men are kept on the narrow path of truth, their nature, which is already inclined to evil, propels them to ruin. Then truly "the bottomless pit" is open from which John saw smoke ascending which obscured the sun, and out of which locusts flew forth to devastate the earth. Thence comes transformation of minds, corruption of youths, contempt of sacred things and holy laws -- in other words, a pestilence more deadly to the state than any other. Experience shows, even from earliest times, that cities renowned for wealth, dominion, and glory perished as a result of this single evil, namely immoderate freedom of opinion, license of free speech, and desire for novelty**.
>
> Here We must include that harmful and never sufficiently denounced freedom to publish any writings whatever and disseminate them to the people, which some dare to demand and promote with so great a clamor. We are horrified to see what monstrous doctrines and prodigious errors are disseminated far and wide in countless books, pamphlets, and other writings which, though small in weight, are very great in malice. We are in tears at the abuse which proceeds from them over the face of the earth. Some are so carried away that they contentiously assert that the flock of errors arising from them is sufficiently compensated by the publication of some book which defends religion and truth. **Every law condemns deliberately doing evil simply because there is some hope that good may result. Is there any sane man who would say poison ought to be distributed, sold publicly, stored, and even drunk because some antidote is available and those who use it may be snatched from death again and again?**(Pope Gregory XVI, *Mirari Vos*, August 15, 1832.)

As is noted earlier in this book, Pope Pius VII condemned Ratzinger/Benedict's vision of "religious liberty" as a heresy in 1814 and Pope Pius IX did so fifty years years later, that is, in 1864.

Ratzinger/Benedict knows this, which is why there was not one single, solitary reference in the footnotes of his "World Day of Peace Message" to the teaching of any true pope of the Catholic Church. Not one. There is no true pope of the Catholic Church for the now retired false “pontiff” to cite in support of this massive work of apostasy that was contained in the "2011 World Day of Peace Message." Not one. That is why the Antipope Emeritus conciliar "pontiff" invented his absurd "hermeneutic of continuity and discontinuity" as he taught the *exact opposite* of what has been taught by the Catholic Church from time immemorial. His has been the teaching of Antichrist, that is, of the opposite of Our Blessed Lord and Saviour Jesus Christ. Ratzinger/Benedict's invented "hermeneutic of continuity and discontinuity," however, is premised on the blasphemous proposition that God the Holy Ghost not only kept knowledge about the joys of "religious freedom" until the "Second" Vatican Council but permitted our true popes to condemn something that the false "pope" wants to believe is a basic "human right," the very foundation of world peace. This is both blasphemous and utterly absurd.

Obviously, Jorge Mario Bergoglio simply ignores the “past” as everything he believes is premised upon a false religion that sprung forth above ground at the “Second” Vatican Council after germinating underground for several hundred years, although demonic forces attempted to make Modernism’s volcanic eruption occur at the beginning of the Twentieth Century. The courage of Pope Saint Pius X forced Modernism underground until the dawning of the age of conciliarism with the “election” of Angelo Roncalli/”Saint John XXIII” on October 28, 1958, the Feast of Saints Simon and Jude.

Where has this pluralism gotten the Catholic Faith?

Mohammedans and Hindus and Buddhists and downright atheists continue to attack Catholics worldwide. Indeed, Ratzinger/Benedict noted the suffering of Catholics in Iraq at the beginning of his "message" and the suffering of Catholics in Asia, Africa and elsewhere in the Middle East near the end of the "message." In perfect concert with his successor, Bergoglio, Ratzinger/Benedict really believed however, that the "solution" to this suffering is not to seek with urgency the unconditional conversion of all men and their nations to the Catholic Faith but for all peoples in the world to join together in an expression of inter-religious harmony as we learn to accept our differences and work together for the common brotherhood of humanity. This man is stuck in the delusions of the 1960s. Those who hate the Sacred Divinity of Our Blessed Lord and Saviour Jesus Christ Whose Kingship was honored by the Three Kings from the East on the Feast of the Epiphany have no intention of ceasing their warfare against Catholics by joining the conciliarists in the madness of "inter-religious dialogue" and "freedom of religion."

Where has this pluralism gotten the Catholic Faith in the very nation of pluralism that the conciliar “popes” have told us the "model" for the rest of the world?

The United States of America?

It is pluralism that has led to the sort of subtle persecutions against Catholics that the false "pope" noted in his "message." He does not see that this is the case. Pope Leo XIII, however, did:

> To hold, therefore, that there is no difference in matters of religion between forms that are unlike each other, and even contrary to each other, most clearly leads in the end to the rejection of all religion in both theory and practice. **And this is the same thing as atheism, however it may differ from it in name. Men who really believe in the existence of God must, in order to be consistent with themselves and to avoid absurd conclusions, understand that differing modes of divine worship involving dissimilarity and conflict even on most important points cannot all be equally probable, equally good, and equally acceptable to God**. (Pope Leo XIII, *Immortale Dei,* November 1, 1885.)

The pluralism that has been extolled by the conciliar "popes," including Ratzinger/Benedict and Bergoglio/Francis, is what has cowed Catholics into saying "happy holidays" in their places of business and that prevents even the secular music associated with the "holiday season," no less actual Christmas music, from being played in public places.

Indeed, I was told at Bear Mountain State Park in Bear Mountain, New York, on Saturday, January 1, 2011, the Feast of the Circumcision, that even secular music connoting Christmas in any way could not be played on an outdoor loudspeaker as too many people had registered complaints that they were "offended" by such music. It is also the fear of "offending" others that causes many Catholic businessmen to avoid posting signs wishing their customers a "Merry Christmas."

This fear of human respect is but the natural, logical, inexorable end-result of pluralism, which makes Catholics believe that they are somehow exempt from the example provided us by the Apostles about the willingness to suffer for the sake of the Holy Name of Jesus:

> Then went the officer with the ministers, and brought them without violence; for they feared the people, lest they should be stoned. And when they had brought them, they set them before the council. And the high priest asked them, Saying: Commanding we commanded you, that you should not teach in this name; and behold, you have filled Jerusalem with your doctrine, and you have a mind to bring the blood of this man upon us. But Peter and the apostles answering, said: We ought to obey God, rather than men. The God of our fathers hath raised up Jesus, whom you put to death, hanging him upon a tree.
>
> Him hath God exalted with his right hand, to be Prince and Saviour, to give repentance to Israel, and remission of sins. And we are witnesses of these things and the Holy Ghost, whom God hath given to all that obey him. When they had heard these things, they were cut to the heart, and they thought to put them to death. But one in the council rising up, a Pharisee, named Gamaliel, a doctor of the law, respected by all the people, commanded the men to be put forth a little while. And he said to them: Ye men of Israel, take heed to yourselves what you intend to do, as touching these men.
>
> For before these days rose up Theodas, affirming himself to be somebody, to whom a number of men, about four hundred, joined themselves: who was slain; and all that believed him were scattered, and brought to nothing. After this man, rose up Judas of Galilee, in the days of the enrolling, and drew away the people after him: he also perished; and all, even as many as consented to him, were dispersed. And now, therefore, I say to you, refrain from these men, and let them alone; for if this council or this work be of men, it will come

to nought; But if it be of God, you cannot overthrow it, lest perhaps you be found even to fight against God. And they consented to him. And calling in the apostles, after they had scourged them, they charged them that they should not speak at all in the name of Jesus; and they dismissed them.

And they indeed went from the presence of the council, rejoicing that they were accounted worthy to suffer reproach for the name of Jesus. And every day they ceased not in the temple, and from house to house, to teach and preach Christ Jesus. (Acts 5: 26-42)

Pluralism is of the devil.

So is the separation of Church and State that Ratzinger/Benedict and Bergoglio/Francis have praised time and time again. Ratzinger/Benedict and Bergoglio/Francis believe that it is "enough" for what they think is the Catholic Church to engage in a "dialogue" with civil leaders as leaders of other religions do the same to fight the influences of irreligion in the world:

9. The patrimony of principles and values expressed by an authentic religiosity is a source of enrichment for peoples and their *ethos*. It speaks directly to the conscience and mind of men and women, it recalls the need for moral conversion, and it encourages the practice of the virtues and a loving approach to others as brothers and sisters, as members of the larger human family.

With due respect for the positive secularity of state institutions, the public dimension of religion must always be acknowledged. *A healthy dialogue between civil and religious institutions* is fundamental for the integral development of the human person and social harmony. (**44th World Day of Peace 2011, Religious Freedom, the Path to Peace**.)

Authentic religiosity?

This is the talk of Judeo-Masonry. The civil state is duty bound to recognize the true religion as its leaders seek to foster those conditions in which citizens may better sanctify and save their souls as members of the Catholic Church.

Who says so?

Pope after true pope.

One such papal condemnation that has been referenced in this book thus far will be enough for present purposes to demonstrate the falsity of what the conciliar "popes" have professed concerning the separation of Church and State:

20. **Nor can We predict happier times for religion and government from the plans of those who desire vehemently to separate the Church from the state, and to break the**

mutual concord between temporal authority and the priesthood. It is certain that that concord which always was favorable and beneficial for the sacred and the civil order is feared by the shameless lovers of liberty.

21. But for the other painful causes We are concerned about, you should recall that certain societies and assemblages **seem to draw up a battle line together with the followers of every false religion and cult. They feign piety for religion; but they are driven by a passion for promoting novelties and sedition everywhere. They preach liberty of every sort; they stir up disturbances in sacred and civil affairs, and pluck authority to pieces**.

22. We write these things to you with grieving mind but trusting in Him who commands the winds and makes them still. Take up the shield of faith and fight the battles of the Lord vigorously. You especially must stand as a wall against every height which raises itself against the knowledge of God. Unsheath the sword of the spirit, which is the word of God, and may those who hunger after justice receive bread from you. Having been called so that you might be diligent cultivators in the vineyard of the Lord, do this one thing, and labor in it together, so that every root of bitterness may be removed from your field, all seeds of vice destroyed, and a happy crop of virtues may take root and grow. The first to be embraced with paternal affection are those who apply themselves to the sacred sciences and to philosophical studies. For them may you be exhorter and supporter, lest trusting only in their own talents and strength, they may imprudently wander away from the path of truth onto the road of the impious. Let them remember that God is the guide to wisdom and the director of the wise.[31] It is impossible to know God without God who teaches men to know Himself by His word.[32] It is the proud, or rather foolish, men who examine the mysteries of faith which surpass all understanding with the faculties of the human mind, and rely on human reason which by the condition of man's nature, is weak and infirm.

23. May Our dear sons in Christ, the princes, support these Our desires for the welfare of Church and State with their resources and authority. May they understand that they received their authority not only for the government of the world, but especially for the defense of the Church. **They should diligently consider that whatever work they do for the welfare of the Church accrues to their rule and peace. Indeed let them persuade themselves that they owe more to the cause of the faith than to their kingdom. Let them consider it something very great for themselves as We say with Pope St. Leo, "if in addition to their royal diadem the crown of faith may be added." Placed as if they were parents and teachers of the people, they will bring them true peace and tranquility, if they take special care that religion and piety remain safe. God, after all, calls Himself "*King of kings and Lord of lords*."** (Pope Gregory XVI, *Mirari Vos*, August 15, 1832.)

Pope Gregory XVI's condemnation of secret societies and assemblages, that is, the sect of the Freemasons and their allies in Talmudism, applies equally as much to the conciliar "popes" who, allied as they have been and continue to be with the forces of Judeo-Masonry, are men who have drawn up a "**battle line together with the followers of every false religion and cult**" as they have feigned "**piety for religion**." In truth, however, the conciliar "popes" have been "**driven by**

a passion for promoting novelties and sedition everywhere." They have preached "**liberty of every sort**" and they have stirred "**up disturbances in sacred and civil affairs,** and have plucked **authority to pieces**."

Let those who have eyes accept the fact that these words, written over one hundred eighty years ago now, apply to the conciliar "popes," including the supposedly "traditional" or "conservative" Ratzinger/Benedict and his more visceral, vulgar successor, Bergoglio/Francis.

Antichrist has shown us his calling card.

Do you care?

Chapter Thirteen
Antichrist Has His Own Hierarchy

The adversary has his own perverse hierarchy that apes and mocks the hierarchy of the Holy Catholic Church. This perverse hierarchy has manifested itself more and more in the course of the past six hundred fifty years since the onset of the early phases of the Renaissance and has come more into full public view in the past five hundred years since the beginning of the Protestant Revolution October 31, 1517, that overthrew the Social Reign of Christ the King and as the welter of Judeo-Masonic "philosophies" and ideologies arose in its wake.

Today, of course, figures of Antichrist have established a very visible, if yet to be fully congealed, hierarchy that can be listed as follows:

1. International agencies of global governance (e.g. United Masonic Nations Organization, World Trade Organization, World Health Organization, International Court of Justice, International Bank for Reconstruction and Development (IBRD/World Bank), International Monetary Fund, European Union, North American Free Trade Association (NAFTA) Secretariat, Group of Eight/Group of Twenty, International Labor Organization, etc.)
2. The permanent civil servants of civil governments in the nations of the world to whom national legislatures have delegated legislative powers that regulate national economies and restrict the legitimate liberties of citizens.
3. Members of the judiciary of nation-states and their subordinate units (e.g. states, provinces, departments, administrative districts, regions, etc.)
4. Political party leaders and their campaign donors, that is, those who control the strings of the elected officials.
5. The international banking community.
6. The corporate world.
7. The mainslime media and what passes for entertainment.
8. The high priests and priestesses of popular culture (i.e., education, law, journalism, psychology/psychiatry, sociology, feminists, environmentalists, the homosexual collective, actors, actresses, professional celebrities, professional sports).
9. Public opinion surveys designed to "ratify" decisions made by the elite leadership levels.
10. Religious institutions.

If you want an easier way to understand this hierarchy, perhaps it should be called to mind that Joseph Robinette Biden, Jr., told us last year that it is, after all, all about the fact that the **Synagogue's Risen**.

Demonstrating their complete subservience to this *de facto*, if not *de jure*, hierarchy of Antichrist, the lords of conciliarism are ever ready to submit "reports" to those who are above them in the Judeo-Masonic pecking order (and we are experts in the Droleskey household on the pecking order as we have ten parakeets who live according to a very exact pecking order). This is what "Archbishop" Silvano Tomasi, representing the Secretariat of the Holy See in conciliar captivity, did on Thursday, January 16, 2014, the Feast of Pope Saint Marcellus I, as he made a report in John Calvin's former stronghold of Geneva, Switzerland, to the United Nations Committee on the Convention on the Rights of the Child.

Here is an excerpt from the report that "Archbishop" Tomasi gave to his false church's superiors at the United Masonic Nations Organization's committee in Geneva in early 2014:

> At the time of the ratification in 1990, the Holy See made the following declaration.
>
> "The Holy See regards the present Convention as a proper and laudable instrument aimed at protecting the rights and interests of children, who are that precious treasure given to each generation as a challenge to its wisdom and humanity."
>
> "By acceding to the Convention on the Rights of the Child, the Holy See intends to give renewed expression to its constant concern for the well-being of children and families. In consideration of its singular nature and position, the Holy See, in acceding to this Convention, does not intend to prescind in any way from its specific mission which is of a religious and moral character."
>
> The protection of children remains a major concern for contemporary society and for the Holy See. The UN report on Violence Against Children, issued in 2006, cited shocking WHO estimates that 150 million girls and 73 million boys under 18 "experienced forced sexual intercourse and other forms of sexual violence involving physical contact".[1] Even if they contain a significant margin of error, these estimates should never be ignored nor overshadowed by other priorities or interests on the part of the international community. Moreover, this estimate does not include projections on the number of victims of child labour and child trafficking, whether for sexual exploitation, forced work, sale of organs, and other shameful reasons. Although little is known about the magnitude of the problem, the International Labor Organization, in 2002, estimated that there were 1.2 million children being trafficked each year.[2]
>
> Abusers are found among members of the world's most respected professions, most regrettably, including members of the clergy and other church personnel.[3] This fact is particularly serious since these persons are in positions of great trust and they are called to levels of service that are to promote and protect all elements of the human person, including physical, emotional, and spiritual health. This relationship of trust is critical and demands a higher sense of responsibility and respect for the persons served.
>
> Confronted with this reality, the Holy See has carefully delineated policies and procedures designed to help eliminate such abuse and to collaborate with respective State authorities to fight against this crime. The Holy See is also committed to listen[ing] carefully to victims of abuse and to address the impact such situations have on survivors of abuse and on their families. The vast majority of church personnel and institutions on the local level have provided, and continue to provide, a wide variety of services to children by educating them, and by supporting their families, and by responding to their physical, emotional, and spiritual needs. Egregious crimes of abuse committed against children have rightly been adjudicated and punished by the competent civil authorities in the respective countries.

Therefore, the response of the Holy See to the sad phenomenon of the sexual abuse of minors has been articulated in different ambits.

On the level of the Holy See, as the Sovereign of Vatican City State, the response to sexual abuse has been in accord with its direct responsibility over the territory of Vatican City State. In this regard, special legislation has been enacted to implement international legal obligations, and covers the State, and its tiny population.[4]

On the international level, the Holy See has taken concrete action by the ratification of the Convention on the Rights of the Child in 1990. In 2000, the Holy See acceded to the Optional Protocol on the Sale of Children, Child Prostitution, and Child Pornography, as well as the Optional Protocol on the Involvement of Children in Armed Conflict. The Holy See then promotes and encourages these international instruments.

At the same time, the Holy See as the central organ of the Catholic Church has formulated guidelines to facilitate the work of the local Churches to develop effective measures within their jurisdiction and in conformity with canonical legislation.

Local Churches, taking into account the domestic law in their respective countries, have developed guidelines and monitored their implementation with the aim of preventing any additional abuse and dealing promptly with it, in accordance with national law whenever it occurs. Reference to examples of such measures by local Churches are cited in paragraph 99 of the Holy See Periodic Report. For example, the Catholic Church in the United States adopted a Charter for the Protection of Children and Young People and a series of related measures.[5] Other practical initiatives have been undertaken, for example the production of e-courses by the Pontifical Gregorian University in Rome together with the University of Munich and the promotion of good practices by Catholic-inspired NGO's, and these have a transnational accessibility.

The result of the combined action taken by local Churches and by the Holy See presents a framework that, when properly applied, will help eliminate the occurrence of child sexual abuse by clergy and other church personnel. Given the unique standing of the Holy See within the international community, and the presence of the local Churches in so many parts of the world, the Catholic Church is keen to become an example of best practice in this important endeavour as required by the high values and ideals incorporated in the Convention and its Protocols.

The Holy See's Periodic Report on the CRC is divided into four Parts: Part I deals with general considerations, including the nature of the Holy See as a subject of international law. Part II responds to the concluding observations of the Committee to the Holy See's Initial Report, and, in particular, questions concerning reservations; the Committee's four principles and the duties and rights of parents, the education of girls, education about health, and education on the CRC. The Holy See also discusses the principles it promotes concerning the rights and duties of the child within the context of the family. Part III presents the international contributions of the Holy See in advancing and promoting basic principles recognized in the CRC on a full range of issues pertaining to children (e.g., the family, adoption, children with disabilities; health and welfare; leisure and culture; and special measures to protect children, including questions pertaining to sexual abuse, drug addiction, children living on the streets and minority groups). Finally, Part IV addresses the implementation of the Convention in Vatican City State. (**Presentation of the Periodic Reports of the Holy See by H.E. Msgr. Silvano Tomasi to the Committee on the Convention of the Rights of the Child, 16 January 2014**.)

Suffice it to say that Silvano Tomasi's report is a farce from beginning to end.

First, the Catholic Church is subservient to no civil body on the face of this earth.

Second, no official of the Catholic Church makes "reports" to a civil body. Indeed, Saint Thomas a Becket was martyred because he sought to uphold the liberties of Holy Mother Church in England to prosecute clergy accused of civil crimes in her own courts (see **A Martyr for the Church's Liberties**).

Third, officials of the counterfeit church of conciliarism have placed themselves in a position of reporting to the civil authorities on the matter of the clerical abuse of children precisely because they have refused to punish such clergy until the systematic and sustained program of protecting and enabling them became a matter of international headlines twelve years ago even though some of us had been reporting on these crimes in the previous decade and before.

Fourth, even though it was confirmed in early-2014 that Joseph Ratzinger/Benedict XVI approved the laicization of three hundred eighty-four priest/presbyter abusers in calendar years 2011 and 2012, the fact remains that the proverbial "barn door" remains wide open to future abuse as no one, starting with Joseph Ratzinger/Benedict and his successor, Jorge Mario Bergoglio, in the counterfeit church of conciliarism has yet to admit that the problem of clerical abuse has been caused principally by the systematic recruitment and retention of homosexual and/or effeminate men into seminaries and communities of religious men while candidates exhibiting any traits of firmness and masculinity have been weeded out as "psychologically unfit" and/or "rigid," "insensitive," "judgmental" and "Pharisaical."

Fifth, the following empirical proof can be given that Jorge Mario Bergoglio will never rid himself of what he once called a "gay lobby": Bergoglio continues to maintain "Monsignor" Battista Ricca, a proven pervert and abuser, as the head of the Vatican Institute for Religious Works, known more commonly as the Vatican Bank (see **Dispensing With The Last Pretenses Of Catholicism**). Remember, it was in reference to Ricca's record as an abuser that Bergoglio responded "Who am I to judge?" when questioned by reporters aboard his flight back to Rome on Monday, July 29, 2013, the Feast of Saint Martha, following the conclusion of the travesty known as World Youth Day in Rio de Janiero, Brazil (see **Francis Says ¡Viva la Revolución!, part three**)

Sixth, all one needs to do to demonstrate the purely symbolic nature of the laicization of three hundred eighty-four priests/presbyters in 2011 and 2012 is to point to the fact that very few conciliar 'bishops" have been forced to resign or take early "retirement" for their own roles in protecting these abusers.

Seventh, Vatican support for the United Nations Convention on the Rights of the Child, which dates back to 1990 and hence to the time of the false pontificate of the Karol Wojtyla/John Paul II, is in and of itself manifest proof that, all of their protestations to the contrary notwithstanding, the conciliar revolutionaries truly do not support the Natural Law principle of Subsidiarity and are willing to subordinate their own policies to the "mandates" of international organizations that are universally headed and staffed by those who support the chemical and surgical execution of the innocent preborn in their mothers' wombs and who support feminism, the agenda of the homosexual collective and every bit of pantheism that represents itself under the aegis of the slogan of "environmentalism."

Dr. Stephen M. Krason, who is the chairman of the Department of Politics at the Franciscan University of Steubenville and a co-founder, along with Dr. Joseph Varacalli of Nassau Community College, of the Society of Catholic Social Scientists, has written extensively on the odious provisions of "child abuse" laws in the fifty states of the United States of America, many of which have been used against home schooling parents. It was in a 2007 article of his that Dr. Krason mentioned the United Nations Convention on the Rights of the Child, making detailed reference to a letter that he co-wrote with this writer in 1995 that was sent to every member of the United States Senate at that time to convince them not to ratify this Marxist "convention:"

> While all of these legal problems are caused by the nature of both our federal and state laws, a new threat to the family has loomed on the international horizon which, if not approached properly by the U.S. Government, may render fruitless any efforts to correct our laws--and may have the effect of extending the threat to families throughout the world. This is the United Nations Convention on the Rights of the Child, which was motivated by the thinking of, and drafted by, Western and Western-oriented "child-savers" and has now been widely ratified by nations around the world, some with reservations, although the U.S. Senate has not yet done so. A detailed discussion of the Convention is not possible here. We will merely quote from a letter the Society of Catholic Social Scientists sent to all the members of the Senate, urging a vote not to ratify. The letter was primarily drafted by political scientist and journalist Dr. Thomas A. Droleskey and contributed to by this writer:
>
> It is clear that the Convention on the Rights of the Child seeks to subject parents to close bureaucratic supervision. Parents who do not educate or raise their children according to the dictates of the prevailing cultural trends will be subject to all kinds of civil and criminal penalties, if not the seizure of their children. This is a form of ideological totalitarianism.
>
> Article 12 of the Convention states that children have the "right" to express their own views freely in all matters. All matters? Child-rearing? Discipline? The fact there are some self-appointed child advocates, such as Hillary Clinton, who believe that children as young as *seven* years of age can assert legal rights indicates that it would be possible under the Convention for grammar school students to sue their parents in order to express their views. This is absurd. Children are children. They need to *learn* about life. They need to *respect* their parents. They need to understand the virtues of humility and obedience, of submission to lawful authority. Also, of course, they will not be able to sue or otherwise oppose their parents on their own. The state will do it for them, with "child advocates" supplanting parents and deciding what is best for children.

Article 13 asserts that children have the right to receive all kinds of information through the "media of the child's choice." Parents concerned about protecting the purity and innocence of their children would be legally barred from censoring the television watched in the home, the movies their children choose to watch, and the books they choose to read. And those parents who do not have a television in their homes might be forced to secure one in order to respect their children's "right" to receive information. Is it overkill to point out that child pornography laws would be invalidated by this article of the Convention? Article 17 extends this "right" to national and international sources in the media.

Article 14 discusses the right of each child to freedom of religion. This appears, at first glance, to be praiseworthy. The article, however, contains an implicit threat to the rights of parents to raise their children. Can a child who does not want to receive religious education sue his parents for abuse because the parents refuse to honor the child's wishes? Can parents who tell their children to engage in family prayers be judged guilty of not respecting a child's freedom *from* religion? This is an attempt on the part of the secularists to free children from the influence of parents who desire to pass along transcendent truths to their children.

Article 16 immunizes children from any degree of parental censorship insofar as correspondence is concerned. While confidentiality is an important part of correspondence, parents nevertheless have to monitor the activities of their children, particularly those in the adolescent years. Can one seriously suggest that a parent has no right to determine if his child is being solicited by a pornographer or child molester? Does a parent have no right to determine if his child is receiving contraband drugs through the mail? This is absurd.

Article 18 seems likely to encourage the displacement of parents in raising their children by the state as it calls for the expansion in the state role in providing facilities to care for children.

Article 19 provides the basis for the establishment of dangerous, coercive state structures to track and pressure parents who violate the *Convention's* notion of their children's "rights." In fact, Article 43 establishes perhaps the ultimate in distant, arrogant bureaucratic structures--an international committee of ten "experts" to oversee the progress of the *Convention's* implementation. In other words, ten individuals will dictate to the hundreds of millions of parents in the world how to raise their children.

It appears as though Article 30, which guarantees a child the right to use his own language, might sanction the use of profanity. A parent would be powerless to tell his child to speak clearly and nobly, never using any vile language. And Article 31, giving children the "right to rest and leisure," would make it difficult for parents to command their children to do anything. All a child would have to do to avoid chores or assignments is to say that he is entitled to rest and leisure.
(http://www.catholicsocialscientists.org/Content/Organization/PDFs/chap9Krason.pdf)

How ironic it is that I helped to draft the points above while being oblivious to the fact that the man I believed to be the "pope," Karol Wojtyla/John Paul II, had legally bound the Holy See to the very United Nations Convention on the Rights of the Child whose passages I had critiqued. To be honest, it is pretty shameful to have been reasonably clear about the dangers in the "convention" while ignoring the fact that the "pope" supported the very thing I was opposing. No, it more than "pretty shameful." It is very shameful. Yes, I have much for which to make reparation before I die. Much.

Eighth and finally, it is absurd for any conciliar official, including Silvano Tomasi, to speak of the "protection" of children when the counterfeit church of conciliarism exposes children to the liturgical abuse par excellence, the Protestant and Judeo-Masonic *Novus Ordo* liturgical service, and as its officials abuse children by means of the rot of explicit classroom instruction in matters pertaining to the Sixth and Ninth Commandment while filling their immortal souls with the junk of conciliarism's numerous false doctrines and odious pastoral practices. These are the greatest child abuses of all, something that so few people, including traditionally-minded Catholics who are attached as of yet to the counterfeit ape of the Catholic Church despite all of the evidence proving the heretical nature of conciliarism and its lords to be Modernists, seem to want to understand and accept.

These words of Pope Leo XIII, contained in *Sapientiae Christianae*, January 10, 1890, should give us pause before we continue to rush into the insanity of considering the conciliar officials as anything other than outside the pale of the Catholic Church as they embrace naturalism while rejecting the fact that Catholicism is the one and only foundation of personal and social order:

> **Nor can such misgivings be removed by *any mere human effort,* especially as a vast number of men, having rejected the Christian faith, are on *that account justly incurring the penalty of their pride,* since blinded by their passions *they search in vain for truth, laying hold on the false for the true*, and thinking themselves wise when they call "evil good, and good evil, and "put darkness in the place of light, and light in the place of darkness." It is therefore necessary that God come to the rescue, and that, mindful of His mercy, He turn an eye of compassion on human society.** (Pope Leo XIII, *Sapientiae Christianae*, January 10, 1890.)

The late Louis-Edouard-François-Desiré Cardinal Pie, as can be see in this passage from *Selected Writings of Cardinal Pie of Poitiers* (which is available from Mr. Hugh Akin's Catholic Action Resource Center), explained in the most basic terms the simple truth that the conciliar revolutionaries reject so boldly even though they keep being bitten by the snake whose allurements they simply cannot resist:

> "**If Jesus Christ**," proclaims Msgr. Pie in a magnificent pastoral instruction, "**if Jesus Christ Who is our light whereby we are drawn out of the seat of darkness and from the shadow of death, and Who has given to the world the treasure of truth and grace, if He has not enriched the world, I mean to say the social and political world itself, from the great evils which prevail in the heart of paganism, then it is to say that the work of Jesus Christ is not a divine work**. Even more so: if the Gospel which would save men is incapable of procuring the actual progress of peoples, if the revealed light which is

> profitable to individuals is detrimental to society at large, if the scepter of Christ, sweet and beneficial to souls, and perhaps to families, is harmful and unacceptable for cities and empires; in other words, if Jesus Christ to whom the Prophets had promised and to Whom His Father had given the nations as a heritage, is not able to exercise His authority over them for it would be to their detriment and temporal disadvantage, **it would have to be concluded that Jesus Christ is not God**". . . .
>
> **"To say Jesus Christ is the God of individuals and of families, but not the God of peoples and of societies, is to say that He is not God. To say that Christianity is the law of individual man and is not the law of collective man, is to say that Christianity is not divine. To say that the Church is the judge of private morality, but has nothing to do with public and political morality, is to say that the Church is not divine**."
>
> In fine, Cardinal Pie insists:
>
> **"Christianity would not be divine if it were to have existence within individuals but not with regard to societies**."
>
> Fr. de St. Just asks, in conclusion:
>
> **"Could it be proven in clearer terms that social atheism conduces to individualistic atheism**?"

The conciliar revolutionaries do not see or accept this because they have rejected the Catholic Faith in favor of another: the New World Order of Judeo-Masonry.

It is that simple.

Pope Leo XIII explained the agenda of Freemasonry in *Humanum Genus*, April 20, 1884:

> 18. When this greatest fundamental truth has been overturned or weakened, it follows that those truths, also, which are known by the teaching of nature must begin to fall -- namely, that all things were made by the free will of God the Creator; that the world is governed by Providence; that souls do not die; that to this life of men upon the earth there will succeed another and an everlasting life.
>
> 19. When these truths are done away with, which are as the principles of nature and important for knowledge and for practical use, **it is easy to see what will become of both public and private morality. We say nothing of those more heavenly virtues, which no one can exercise or even acquire without a special gift and grace of God; of which necessarily no trace can be found in those who reject as unknown the redemption of mankind, the grace of God, the sacraments, and the happiness to be obtained in heaven**. We speak now of the duties which have their origin in natural probity. That God is the Creator of the world and its provident Ruler; that the eternal law commands the natural order to be maintained, and forbids that it be disturbed; that the last end of men is

a destiny far above human things and beyond this sojourning upon the earth: these are the sources and these the principles of all justice and morality.

If these be taken away, as the naturalists and Freemasons desire, there will immediately be no knowledge as to what constitutes justice and injustice, or upon what principle morality is founded. **And, in truth, the teaching of morality which alone finds favor with the sect of Freemasons, and in which they contend that youth should be instructed, is that which they call "civil," and "independent," and "free," namely, that which does not contain any religious belief. But, how insufficient such teaching is, how wanting in soundness, and how easily moved by every impulse of passion, is sufficiently proved by its sad fruits, which have already begun to appear. For, wherever, by removing Christian education, this teaching has begun more completely to rule, there goodness and integrity of morals have begun quickly to perish, monstrous and shameful opinions have grown up, and the audacity of evil deeds has risen to a high degree**. All this is commonly complained of and deplored; and not a few of those who by no means wish to do so are compelled by abundant evidence to give not infrequently the same testimony.

20. **Moreover, human nature was stained by original sin, and is therefore more disposed to vice than to virtue**. For a virtuous life it is absolutely necessary to restrain the disorderly movements of the soul, and to make the passions obedient to reason. In this conflict human things must very often be despised, and the greatest labors and hardships must be undergone, in order that reason may always hold its sway. **But the naturalists and Freemasons, having no faith in those things which we have learned by the revelation of God, deny that our first parents sinned, and consequently think that free will is not at all weakened and inclined to evil**.[13] On the contrary, exaggerating rather the power and the excellence of nature, and placing therein alone the principle and rule of justice, they cannot even imagine that there is any need at all of a constant struggle and a perfect steadfastness to overcome the violence and rule of our passions.

Wherefore we see that men are publicly tempted by the many allurements of pleasure; that there are journals and pamphlets with neither moderation nor shame; that stage-plays are remarkable for license; that designs for works of art are shamelessly sought in the laws of a so-called verism; that the contrivances of a soft and delicate life are most carefully devised; and that all the blandishments of pleasure are diligently sought out by which virtue may be lulled to sleep. Wickedly, also, but at the same time quite consistently, do those act who do away with the expectation of the joys of heaven, and bring down all happiness to the level of mortality, and, as it were, sink it in the earth. Of what We have said the following fact, astonishing not so much in itself as in its open expression, may serve as a confirmation. **For, since generally no one is accustomed to obey crafty and clever men so submissively as those whose soul is weakened and broken down by the domination of the passions, there have been in the sect of the Freemasons some who have plainly determined and proposed that, artfully and of set purpose, the multitude should be satiated with a boundless license of vice, as, when this had been done, it would easily come under their power and authority for any acts of daring.**

21. What refers to domestic life in the teaching of the naturalists is almost all contained in the following declarations: that marriage belongs to the genus of commercial contracts, which can rightly be revoked by the will of those who made them, and that the civil rulers of the State have power over the matrimonial bond; **that in the education of youth nothing is to be taught in the matter of religion as of certain and fixed opinion; and each one must be left at liberty to follow, when he comes of age, whatever he may prefer. To these things the Freemasons fully assent; and not only assent, but have long endeavored to make them into a law and institution**. For in many countries, and those nominally Catholic, it is enacted that no marriages shall be considered lawful except those contracted by the civil rite; in other places the law permits divorce; and in others every effort is used to make it lawful as soon as may be. **Thus, the time is quickly coming when marriages will be turned into another kind of contract -- that is into changeable and uncertain unions which fancy may join together, and which the same when changed may disunite.**

With the greatest unanimity the sect of the Freemasons also endeavors to take to itself the education of youth. They think that they can easily mold to their opinions that soft and pliant age, and bend it whither they will; and that nothing can be more fitted than this to enable them to bring up the youth of the State after their own plan. Therefore, in the education and instruction of children they allow no share, either of teaching or of discipline, to the ministers of the Church; and in many places they have procured that the education of youth shall be exclusively in the hands of laymen, and that nothing which treats of the most important and most holy duties of men to God shall be introduced into the instructions on morals.

22. Then come their doctrines of politics, in which the naturalists lay down that all men have the same right, and are in every respect of equal and like condition; that each one is naturally free; that no one has the right to command another; that it is an act of violence to require men to obey any authority other than that which is obtained from themselves. According to this, therefore, all things belong to the free people; power is held by the command or permission of the people, so that, when the popular will changes, rulers may lawfully be deposed and the source of all rights and civil duties is either in the multitude or in the governing authority when this is constituted according to the latest doctrines. It is held also that the State should be without God; that in the various forms of religion there is no reason why one should have precedence of another; and that they are all to occupy the same place.

23. That these doctrines are equally acceptable to the Freemasons, and that they would wish to constitute States according to this example and model, is too well known to require proof. For some time past they have openly endeavored to bring this about with all their strength and resources; and in this they prepare the way for not a few bolder men who are hurrying on even to worse things, in their endeavor to obtain equality and community of all goods by the destruction of every distinction of rank and property. (Pope Leo XIII, *Humanum Genus*, April 20, 1884.)

Pope Leo XIII prophetically described the shape of a world founded upon false, naturalistic principles, which have served as the foundation of the counterfeit church of conciliarism's attempt at an official reconciliation with the new era inaugurated in 1789. (Joseph Ratzinger, *Principles of Catholic Theology*, p. 382.)

What happened in 1789? Wasn't there some kind of anti-Theistic revolution in France, the elder daughter of the Church? What did Pope Leo XIII write about such reconciling with the principles of the revolution just a year before he promoted the Bishop of Mantua, Giuseppe Melchiorre Sarto, to be the Patriarch of Venice?

> Every familiarity should be avoided, not only with those impious libertines who openly promote the character of the sect**, but also with those who hide under the mask of universal tolerance, respect for all religions, and the craving to reconcile the maxims of the Gospel with those of the revolution. These men seek to reconcile Christ and Belial, the Church of God and the state without God**. (Pope Leo XIII, *Custodi Di Quella Fede*, December 8, 1892.)

The caesars of the civil state see themselves as the masters of all, including those who are believed to be officials of the Catholic Church. Not even the domestic cell of the Church Militant on earth, the family, is outside the scope of the caesars' tyrannical dominance.

To bow down before the United Nations is to submit oneself to its Judeo-Masonic principles, which is what the conciliar "popes" have done time and time and time again, starting with Giovanni Enrico Antonio Maria Montini/Paul VI's address to the General Assembly in New York, New York, on October 4, 1965, continuing with Karol Josef Wojtyla/John Paul II in 1979 and 1995 and with Joseph Alois Ratzinger/Benedict XVI in 2008:

> Our message is meant to be, first of all, a moral and solemn ratification of this lofty institution. This message comes from Our historical experience. It is as an "expert in humanity" that We bring to this Organization the suffrage of Our recent Predecessors, that of the entire Catholic Episcopate, and Our own, convinced as We are that this Organization represents the obligatory path of modern civilization and of world peace.
>
> In saying this, We feel We are speaking with the voice of the dead as well as of the living: of the dead who have fallen in the terrible wars of the past, dreaming of concord and world peace; of the living who have survived those wars, bearing in their hearts a condemnation of those who seek to renew them; and of those rightful expectation of a better humanity. And We also make Our own, the voice of the poor, the disinherited, the suffering; of those who long for justice for the dignity of life, for freedom, for well being and for progress. **The peoples of the earth turn to the United Nations as the last hope of concord and peace.** We presume to present here, together with Our own, their tribute to honour and of hope. That is why this moment is a great one for you also. We know that you are fully aware of this. Now for the continuation of Our message. It looks entirely towards the future. **The edifice which you have constructed must never collapse; it must be continually perfected and adapted to the needs which the history of the world will present. You mark a stage in the development of mankind; from now on retreat is impossible; you**

must go forward. (Giovanni Montini/Paul VI's Address to the United Nations, October 4, 1965.)

I come before you today with the desire to be able to contribute to that thoughtful meditation on the history and role of this Organization which should accompany and give substance to the anniversary celebrations. The Holy See, in virtue of its specifically spiritual mission, which makes it concerned for the integral good of every human being, has supported the ideals and goals of the United Nations Organization from the very beginning. Although their respective purposes and operative approaches are obviously different, the Church and the United Nations constantly find wide areas of cooperation on the basis of their common concern for the human family. It is this awareness which inspires my thoughts today; they will not dwell on any particular social, political, or economic question; rather, I would like to reflect with you on what the extraordinary changes of the last few years imply, not simply for the present, but for the future of the whole human family. **(Karol Wojtyla/John Paul II's Address to the United Nations Organization, New York, October 5, 1995)**

As I begin my address to this Assembly, I would like first of all to express to you, Mr President, my sincere gratitude for your kind words. My thanks go also to the Secretary-General, Mr Ban Ki-moon, for inviting me to visit the headquarters of this Organization and for the welcome that he has extended to me. I greet the Ambassadors and Diplomats from the Member States, and all those present. Through you, I greet the peoples who are represented here. They look to this institution to carry forward the founding inspiration to establish a "centre for harmonizing the actions of nations in the attainment of these common ends" of peace and development (cf. *Charter of the United Nations,* article 1.2-1.4). As Pope John Paul II expressed it in 1995, the Organization should be "a moral centre where all the nations of the world feel at home and develop a shared awareness of being, as it were, a 'family of nations'" *(Address to the General Assembly of the United Nations on the 50th Anniversary of its Foundation, New York,* 5 October 1995, 14).

Through the United Nations, States have established universal objectives which, even if they do not coincide with the total common good of the human family, undoubtedly represent a fundamental part of that good. **The founding principles of the Organization - the desire for peace, the quest for justice, respect for the dignity of the person, humanitarian cooperation and assistance - express the just aspirations of the human spirit, and constitute the ideals which should underpin international relations. As my predecessors Paul VI and John Paul II have observed from this very podium, all this is something that the Catholic Church and the Holy See follow attentively and with interest, seeing in your activity an example of how issues and conflicts concerning the world community can be subject to common regulation.** The United Nations embodies the aspiration for a "greater degree of international ordering" (John Paul II, *Sollicitudo Rei Socialis,* 43), inspired and governed by the principle of subsidiarity, and therefore capable of responding to the demands of the human family through binding international rules and through structures capable of harmonizing the day-to-day unfolding of the lives of peoples. This is all the more necessary at a time when we experience the obvious paradox of a multilateral consensus that continues to be in crisis because it is still subordinated to the

> decisions of a few, whereas the world's problems call for interventions in the form of collective action by the international community. (**Joseph Ratzinger/Benedict XVI's Address to the United Nations General Assembly, April 18. 2005 English**.)

The conciliar "popes" have endorsed the "work" of the United Nations, a thoroughly Masonic organization, as a means to ensure "peace" in the world when it funds and promotes abject moral evils such as contraception, sterilization, abortion and perversity that are open acts of war against the Most Blessed Trinity and wind up making conflict among men and among nations more possible as a result of the proliferation of unrepented sins in the world.

Jorge Mario Bergoglio is even *more* disposed to the naturalism of the United Nations and other related groups than any of his Judeo-Masonic predecessors who have headed the counterfeit church of conciliarism. Bergoglio's worldview is entirely naturalistic, something that he made clear when he addressed both the European Parliament and the Council of Europe on Tuesday, November 25, 2014:

> The second challenge which I would like to mention is *transversality*. Here I would begin with my own experience: in my meetings with political leaders from various European countries, I have observed that the younger politicians view reality differently than their older colleagues. They may appear to be saying the same things, but their approach is different. The lyrics are the same but the music is different. This is evident in younger politicians from various parties. This empirical fact points to a reality of present-day Europe which cannot be overlooked in efforts to unite the continent and to guide its future: we need to take into account this *transversality* encountered in every sector. To do so requires engaging in dialogue, including *intergenerational* dialogue. Were we to define the continent today, we should speak of a Europe in dialogue, one which puts a transversality of opinions and reflections at the service of a harmonious union of peoples.
>
> To embark upon this path of transversal communication requires not only generational empathy, but also an historic methodology of growth. In Europe's present political situation, merely internal dialogue between the organizations (whether political, religious or cultural) to which one belongs, ends up being unproductive. Our times demand the ability to break out of the structures which "contain" our identity and to encounter others, for the sake of making that identity more solid and fruitful in the fraternal exchange of transversality. A Europe which can only dialogue with limited groups stops halfway; it needs that youthful spirit which can rise to the challenge of transversality.
>
> In light of all this, I am gratified by the desire of the Council of Europe to invest in intercultural dialogue, including its religious dimension, through the *Exchange on the Religious Dimension of Intercultural Dialogue*. **Here is a valuable opportunity for open, respectful and enriching exchange between persons and groups of different origins and ethnic, linguistic and religious traditions, in a spirit of understanding and mutual respect**.
>
> These meetings appear particularly important in the current multicultural and multipolar context, for finding a distinctive physiognomy capable of skilfully linking the European

> identity forged over the course of centuries to the expectations and aspirations of other peoples who are now making their appearance on the continent.
>
> **This way of thinking also casts light on the contribution which *Christianity* can offer to the cultural and social development of Europe today within the context of a correct relationship between religion and society. In the Christian vision, faith and reason, religion and society, are called to enlighten and support one another, and, whenever necessary, to purify one another from ideological extremes**. European society as a whole cannot fail to benefit from a renewed interplay between these two sectors, whether to confront a form of religious fundamentalism which is above all inimical to God, or to remedy a reductive rationality which does no honour to man. (**Antipope's Address to Eurosocialist Plutocrats, known as the Council of Europe**.)

The heretics of Modernism in the counterfeit church of conciliarism do as much violence to language as they have done to doctrine, worship, moral and pastoral praxis. A false religion that emanates from a counterfeit church with a false liturgy has had to give rise to a revolutionary vocabulary to speak to the "modern world," which is itself the product of the diabolical lies of Protestantism and Judeo-Masonry. I mean, what in the world is "transversality"? "Inter-generational dialogue"?

Moreover, to believe that the Catholic Church can be "purified" from "ideological extremes" by the world is to assert that she can be misled into various errors, which is yet another denial of her Divine Constitution on the part of the Argentine Apostate.

Jorge Mario Bergoglio told the pro-abortion, pro-perversity stronghold of statism and one world governance, the European Parliament, which is a different parliamentary body than the Council of Europe, that contrary to all truth, the Catholic Church has committed errors, which he believes have been "purified" by the world, whose "secularity" is not threatened by the Catholic Church:

> Taking as a starting point this opening to the transcendent, I would like to reaffirm the centrality of the human person, which otherwise is at the mercy of the whims and the powers of the moment. I consider to be fundamental not only the legacy that Christianity has offered in the past to the social and cultural formation of the continent, but above all the contribution which it desires to offer today, and in the future, to Europe's growth. **This contribution does not represent a threat to the secularity of states or to the independence of the institutions of the European Union, but rather an enrichment**. This is clear from the ideals which shaped Europe from the beginning, such as peace, subsidiarity and **reciprocal solidarity, and a humanism centred on respect for the dignity of the human person**. (**Address to the European Union**.)

Behold Jorge Mario Bergoglio in his capacity as an historical revisionist.

Most of Europe was in a state of barbarism "at the beginning" while other parts served as homes to paganism of one sort or another. It was Catholicism that transformed Europe, which has returned to its barbaric, pagan ways precisely because its countries have abandoned the Catholic Faith, outside of which there is no salvation and without which there can be no true social order.

Pope Pius XII made this point very clear in his first encyclical letter, *Summi Pontificatus*, October 10, 1939:

> **The denial of the fundamentals of morality had its origin, in Europe, in the abandonment of that Christian teaching of which the Chair of Peter is the depository and exponent. That teaching had once given spiritual cohesion to a Europe which, educated, ennobled and civilized by the Cross, had reached such a degree of civil progress as to become the teacher of other peoples, of other continents. But, cut off from the infallible teaching authority of the Church, not a few separated brethren have gone so far as to overthrow the central dogma of Christianity, the Divinity of the Savior, and have hastened thereby the progress of spiritual decay.**
>
> **The Holy Gospel narrates that when Jesus was crucified "there was darkness over the whole earth" (Matthew xxvii. 45); a terrifying symbol of what happened and what still happens spiritually wherever incredulity, blind and proud of itself, has succeeded in excluding Christ from modern life, especially from public life, and has undermined faith in God as well as faith in Christ. The consequence is that the moral values by which in other times public and private conduct was gauged have fallen into disuse; and the much vaunted civilization of society, which has made ever more rapid progress, withdrawing man, the family and the State from the beneficent and regenerating effects of the idea of God and the teaching of the Church, has caused to reappear, in regions in which for many centuries shone the splendors of Christian civilization, in a manner ever clearer, ever more distinct, ever more distressing, the signs of a corrupt and corrupting paganism**: "There was darkness when they crucified Jesus" (Roman Breviary, Good Friday, Response Five).
>
> Many perhaps, while abandoning the teaching of Christ, were not fully conscious of being led astray by a mirage of glittering phrases, which proclaimed such estrangement as an escape from the slavery in which they were before held; nor did they then foresee the bitter consequences of bartering the truth that sets free, for error which enslaves. They did not realize that, in renouncing the infinitely wise and paternal laws of God, and the unifying and elevating doctrines of Christ's love, they were resigning themselves to the whim of a poor, fickle human wisdom; they spoke of progress, when they were going back; of being raised, when they groveled; of arriving at man's estate, when they stooped to servility. **They did not perceive the inability of all human effort to replace the law of Christ by anything equal to it; "they became vain in their thoughts**" (Romans i. 21).
>
> With the weakening of faith in God and in Jesus Christ, and the darkening in men's minds of the light of moral principles, there disappeared the indispensable foundation of the stability and quiet of that internal and external, private and public order, which alone can support and safeguard the prosperity of States.
>
> **It is true that even when Europe had a cohesion of brotherhood through identical ideals gathered from Christian preaching, she was not free from divisions, convulsions and wars which laid her waste; but perhaps they never felt the intense pessimism of today as to the possibility of settling them, for they had then an effective moral sense of the**

> **just and of the unjust, of the lawful and of the unlawful, which, by restraining outbreaks of passion, left the way open to an honorable settlement**. In Our days, on the contrary, dissensions come not only from the surge of rebellious passion, but also from a deep spiritual crisis which has overthrown the sound principles of private and public morality. (Pope Pius XII, *Summi Pontificatus*, October 10, 1939.)

Yes, as has been stated on this site so many times, Catholicism is the one and only foundation of personal and social order. Nothing else.

Each of the conciliar "popes" have preached the "dignity of man, "not the glory of God" or the fact that there is only one true means for men to be united: the Catholic Faith. What Jorge Mario Bergoglio said on Tuesday, November 25, 2014, in Strasbourg, France, it should be noted, was simply yet another manifestation of the conciliar commitment to the principles of The Sillon that were condemned by Pope Saint Pius X in *Notre Charge Apostolique*, August 15, 1910:

> **Further, whilst Jesus was kind to sinners and to those who went astray, He did not respect their false ideas, however sincere they might have appeared. He loved them all, but He instructed them in order to convert them and save them. Whilst He called to Himself in order to comfort them, those who toiled and suffered, it was not to preach to them the jealousy of a chimerical equality.** Whilst He lifted up the lowly, it was not to instill in them the sentiment of a dignity independent from, and rebellious against, the duty of obedience. Whilst His heart overflowed with gentleness for the souls of good-will, **He could also arm Himself with holy indignation against the profaners of the House of God, against the wretched men who scandalized the little ones, against the authorities who crush the people with the weight of heavy burdens without putting out a hand to lift them. He was as strong as he was gentle. He reproved, threatened, chastised, knowing, and teaching us that fear is the beginning of wisdom, and that it is sometimes proper for a man to cut off an offending limb to save his body**. Finally, He did not announce for future society the reign of an ideal happiness from which suffering would be banished; but, by His lessons and by His example, He traced the path of the happiness which is possible on earth and of the perfect happiness in heaven: the royal way of the Cross. **These are teachings that it would be wrong to apply only to one's personal life in order to win eternal salvation; these are eminently social teachings, and they show in Our Lord Jesus Christ something quite different from an inconsistent and impotent humanitarianism**. (Pope Saint Pius X, *Notre Charge Apostolique*, August 15, 1910.)

It was as the Patriarch of Venice in 1896 that Giuseppe Melchiorre Sarto, the future Pope Saint Pius X, condemned the Modernist view of the civil state and its penchant for providing cradle-to-grave entitlements, which he termed "welfarism," that Jorge Mario Bergoglio believes are nothing other than fundamental "human rights":

> In August 1896 in Padua, the second Congress of the Catholic Union for Social Studies took place. We have already seen that this organization had been created seven years before by Professor Giuseppe Toniolo, in the presence of the Bishop of Mantua [Giuseppe Melchiorre Sarto]. This time, eight bishops were present and several directors of the *Opera del Congressi* took part. All the eminent representatives of the Italian Catholic Movement were

present (Medolago Pagnuzzi, Alessi and others). Cardinal Sarto's address attracted considerable notice. Faced with "**ardent enemies**" (unbelief and revolution) "...menacing and trying to destroy the social fabric," the Patriarch of Venice invited the participants to make Jesus Christ the foundation of their work: "**the only peace treaty is the Gospel.**" He warned them against what is now called the "**welfare state**," the state which provides everything and provides all socialization: **"substituting public almsgiving for private almsgiving involves the complete destruction of Christianity and it is a terrible attack on the principle of ownership. Christianity cannot exist without charity, and the difference between charity and justice is that justice may have recourse to laws and even to force, depending on the circumstances, whereas charity can only be imposed by the tribunal of God and of conscience**." If public assistance and the redistribution of wealth are institutionalized, "**poverty becomes a function, a way of life, a public trade**..." (Yves Chiron, *Saint Pius X: Restorer of the Church*. Translated by Graham Harrison. Angelus Press, 2002, p. 100.)

This is all one really needs to know about Jorge Mario Bergoglio's view of the world, which he does the bidding of Antichrist in repeating one boilerplate conciliar cliché after another as the world applauds him for his supposed "wisdom."

Where does one begin to explain to the unconvinced that none of the errors being promoted by the conciliar revolutionaries come from the Catholic Church?

> As for the rest, We greatly deplore the fact that, where the ravings of human reason extend, there is somebody who studies new things and strives to know more than is necessary, against the advice of the apostle. **There you will find someone who is overconfident in seeking the truth outside the Catholic Church, in which it can be found without even a light tarnish of error**. Therefore, the Church is called, and is indeed, a pillar and foundation of truth. You correctly understand, venerable brothers, that We speak here also of that erroneous philosophical system which was recently brought in and is clearly to be condemned. **This system, which comes from the contemptible and unrestrained desire for innovation, does not seek truth where it stands in the received and holy apostolic inheritance. Rather, other empty doctrines, futile and uncertain doctrines not approved by the Church, are adopted. Only the most conceited men wrongly think that these teachings can sustain and support that truth**. (Pope Gregory XVI, *Singulari Nos*, May 25, 1834.)

> In the Catholic Church Christianity is Incarnate. It identifies Itself with that perfect, spiritual, and, in its own order, sovereign society, which is the Mystical Body of Jesus Christ and which has for Its visible head the Roman Pontiff, successor of the Prince of the Apostles. It is the continuation of the mission of the Savior, the daughter and the heiress of His Redemption. It has preached the Gospel, and has defended it at the price of Its blood, and strong in the Divine assistance and of that immortality which has been promised it, **It makes no terms with error but remains faithful to the commands which it has received, to carry the doctrine of Jesus Christ to the uttermost limits of the world and to the end of time, and to protect it in its inviolable integrity**. (Pope Leo XIII, *A Review of His Pontificate*, March 19, 1902.)

> For the teaching authority of the Church, which in the divine wisdom was constituted on earth **in order that revealed doctrines might remain intact for ever, and that they might be brought with ease and security to the knowledge of men**, and which is daily exercised through the Roman Pontiff and the Bishops who are in communion with him, has also the office of defining, when it sees fit, any truth with solemn rites and decrees, whenever this is necessary either to oppose the errors or the attacks of heretics, or more clearly and in greater detail to stamp the minds of the faithful with the articles of sacred doctrine which have been explained. (Pope Pius XI, *Mortalium Animos*, January 6, 1928.)

> Let, therefore, the separated children draw nigh to the Apostolic See, set up in the City which Peter and Paul, the Princes of the Apostles, consecrated by their blood; to that See, We repeat, which is 'the root and womb whence the Church of God springs,' **not with the intention and the hope that 'the Church of the living God, the pillar and ground of the truth' will cast aside the integrity of the faith and tolerate their errors, but, on the contrary, that they themselves submit to its teaching and government**. (Pope Pius XI, *Mortalium Animos*, January 6, 1928.)

Yes, **The Chair is Still Empty**, which is why we need to pray for the restoration of a true pope on the Throne of Saint Peter, something that will occur in a truly miraculous manner.

Far, far from the mind and heart of the conciliar revolutionaries, including Jorge Mario Bergoglio/Francis and minions such as Silvano Tomasi, is the following expression of Catholic truth found in Pope Saint Pius X's *Notre Charge Apostolique*, August 15, 1910:

> This, nevertheless, is what they want to do with human society; they dream of changing its natural and traditional foundations; they dream of a Future City **built on different principles, and they dare to proclaim these more fruitful and more beneficial than the principles upon which the present Christian City rests**.

> No, Venerable Brethren, We must repeat with the utmost energy in these times of social and intellectual anarchy when everyone takes it upon himself to teach as a teacher and lawmaker - the City cannot be built otherwise than as God has built it; society cannot be setup unless the Church lays the foundations and supervises the work; no, civilization is not something yet to be found, **nor is the New City to be built on hazy notions**; it has been in existence and still is: **it is Christian civilization, it is the Catholic City. It has only** to be set up and restored continually against the unremitting attacks of insane dreamers, rebels and miscreants. Omnia instaurare in Christo. (Pope Saint Pius X, *Notre Charge Apostolique*, August 15, 1910.)

May we believe in this exhortation with all of our hearts as we give unto the Most Sacred Heart of Jesus and the Immaculate Heart of Mary all of our efforts to plant a few seeds for the time when all men everywhere will exclaim "*Viva Cristo Rey*!" as the fruit of the Triumph of the Immaculate Heart of Mary when the only peace plan that matters, Heaven's Peace Plan, Our Lady's Fatima Peace Plan, is fulfilled.

We need to pray as many Rosaries each day as our states-in-life permit and make much reparation for our sins and those of the whole world as clients of those twin Hearts of matchless love that suffered as one during our Redemption and beat now as they have always beat, as one Heart that wills our salvation and the right ordering of men in states that are subordinate at all times to the Social Reign of Christ the King.

Chapter Fourteen

A New Sense for a New Faith

Although the number of people who will ever read the International Theological Commission's *Sensus Fidei: In the Life of the Church* will probably wind up being lower than those who read this book, it is important to include a discussion of it in this text as it served as a prelude to Jorge Mario Bergoglio's "extraordinary synod on the family" that met in October of 2014. This "unofficial" document provided a compendium of theological justifications for their Modernist presuppositions and prescriptions that would come to the forefront at the "extraordinary synod."

Joseph Ratzinger/Benedict XVI spent a good deal of time during his false "pontificate" seeking to "stabilize" the conciliar revolution by his infamous, philosophically absurd and dogmatically condemned "hermeneutic of continuity," which was nothing more and nothing less than Modernism's "evolution of dogma" that had been presented to us by Wojtyla/John Paul II as "living tradition" (**Deft? Daft Is More Like It, part two**). Ratzinger/Benedict gave his "papal" imprimatur to supposedly "unofficial" documents issued by the International Theological Commission and the Joint International Commission for the Theological Dialogue Between the Conciliar Church and the Orthodox Church while using his general audience addresses to deconstruct and misrepresent the teachings and the lives of very Saints and Doctors to make them **perjured witnesses in behalf of conciliarism**. And this is to say nothing of his "unofficial" books issued during the time he served as the head of the counterfeit church of conciliarism.

It is only natural for the conciliar revolutionaries to seek to provide some kind of theological justification for their revolution by misrepresenting, deconstructing and corrupting the true meaning of the *sensus fidei*, that supernatural sense of the Holy Faith by which members of the Church Militant are able to distinguish that which is in accord with the Holy Faith from that which is not.

The theological justification found in ***Sensus fidei* in the life of the Church** represents nothing other than a transparent effort, no matter how "unofficial" (although it was signed by the conciliar prefect of the Congregation of the Doctrine of the Faith, the arch-heretic named Gerhard Ludwig Muller), to prepare the way for the *Instrumentum Laboris* that was released on Thursday, June 26, 2014, the Octave of the Solemnity of Corpus Christi and the Commemoration of Saints John and Paul, and its revolutionary program for the "Extraordinary Synod on the Family."

As noted in **Jorge Cooks the Books** in April of 2014, the hootenanny that met in in Rome in October of 2014 set the stage very carefully for the future sanctioning of the administration of what purports to be Holy Communion to civilly divorced and remarried Catholics who lack even the fig leaf of a conciliar decree of nullity and to provide a foundation for providing the liturgical invalid sacramental rites of the counterfeit church of conciliarism to "couples" who are engaged in unrepentant acts of perversity.

***Sensus fidei* in the life of the Church** aims to make the case, albeit indirectly in its final passages, that the "non-reception" of Catholic doctrine on the part of the lay faithful might represent a need to reconsider how the doctrine is formulated. Translation: do you hear the people sing, singing the song of wanting to be reaffirmed in their sins.

The conciliar revolutionaries have long sought to destroy the *sensus Catholicus*, the sense of the Catholic Faith, and they have been so successful in this regard that most Catholics alive today regard as alien to the Holy Faith teaching and pastoral practices that have been passed down to us from time immemorial. Those who cleave to the unchanging truths of the Holy Faith are said to be "disobedient" and "schismatic" and "disloyal" and "out of the church" altogether.

The principal means by which the conciliar revolutionaries sought to create a new *sensus fidei* was the Protestant and Judeo-Masonic *Novus Ordo* liturgical service. The revolution against Catholic Worship that resulted in the overthrow of the Roman Rite of the Catholic Church as a synthetic concoction, designed to appeal to Protestants and unbelievers, replaced it as a means to propagandize a new and false religion, conciliarism, with such lightning speed so as to break down the supernatural resistance of ordinary Catholics to un-Catholic and anti-Catholic "innovations" by calling upon them to be "obedient" and by helping to disseminate propaganda designed to "erase" true memories of the glories of the Catholic past in order to create "artificial" memories that would justify their efforts to "restore" liturgical rites that either never existed or that were used by heretical sects. Most Catholics were so convinced by the revolutionaries that the "past" had been bad that they came to accept the innovations in what was said to be the Catholic liturgy in the name of a "renewal" that was nothing other than a revival of the spirit of antiquarianism (claiming to "restore" ancient rites that never existed or that were used by heretics) that was condemned by Pope Pius VI in *Auctorem Fidei* on August 28, 1794, and condemned as well by Pope Pius XII in *Mediator Dei*, November 20, 1947:

> The Church is without question a living organism, and as an organism, in respect of the sacred liturgy also, she grows, matures, develops, adapts and accommodates herself to temporal needs and circumstances, provided only that the integrity of her doctrine be safeguarded. This notwithstanding, **the temerity and daring of those who introduce novel liturgical practices, or call for the revival of obsolete rites out of harmony with prevailing laws and rubrics, deserve severe reproof. It has pained Us grievously to note, Venerable Brethren, that such innovations are actually being introduced, not merely in minor details but in matters of major importance as well. We instance, in point of fact, those who make use of the vernacular in the celebration of the august eucharistic sacrifice; those who transfer certain feast-days — which have been appointed and established after mature deliberation — to other dates; those, finally, who delete from the prayer books approved for public use the sacred texts of the Old Testament, deeming them little suited and inopportune for modern times**.
>
> The use of the Latin language, customary in a considerable portion of the Church, is a manifest and beautiful sign of unity, as well as an effective antidote for any corruption of doctrinal truth. In spite of this, the use of the mother tongue in connection with several of the rites may be of much advantage to the people. But the Apostolic See alone is empowered to grant this permission. It is forbidden, therefore, to take any action whatever of this nature without having requested and obtained such consent, since the sacred liturgy, as We have said, is entirely subject to the discretion and approval of the Holy See.

> **The same reasoning holds in the case of some persons who are bent on the restoration of all the ancient rites and ceremonies indiscriminately. The liturgy of the early ages is most certainly worthy of all veneration. But ancient usage must not be esteemed more suitable and proper, either in its own right or in its significance for later times and new situations, on the simple ground that it carries the savor and aroma of antiquity. The more recent liturgical rites likewise deserve reverence and respect.** They, too, owe their inspiration to the Holy Spirit, who assists the Church in every age even to the consummation of the world. They are equally the resources used by the majestic Spouse of Jesus Christ to promote and procure the sanctity of man.
>
> Assuredly it is a wise and most laudable thing to return in spirit and affection to the sources of the sacred liturgy. For research in this field of study, by tracing it back to its origins, contributes valuable assistance towards a more thorough and careful investigation of the significance of feast-days, and of the meaning of the texts and sacred ceremonies employed on their occasion. But it is neither wise nor laudable to reduce everything to antiquity by every possible device. **Thus, to cite some instances, one would be straying from the straight path were he to wish the altar restored to its primitive table form; were he to want black excluded as a color for the liturgical vestments; were he to forbid the use of sacred images and statues in Churches; were he to order the crucifix so designed that the divine Redeemer's body shows no trace of His cruel sufferings; and lastly were he to disdain and reject polyphonic music or singing in parts, even where it conforms to regulations issued by the Holy See**.
>
> Clearly no sincere Catholic can refuse to accept the formulation of Christian doctrine more recently elaborated and proclaimed as dogmas by the Church, under the inspiration and guidance of the Holy Spirit with abundant fruit for souls, because it pleases him to hark back to the old formulas. No more can any Catholic in his right senses repudiate existing legislation of the Church to revert to prescriptions based on the earliest sources of canon law. Just as obviously unwise and mistaken is the zeal of one who in matters liturgical would go back to the rites and usage of antiquity, discarding the new patterns introduced by disposition of divine Providence to meet the changes of circumstances and situation.
>
> **This way of acting bids fair to revive the exaggerated and senseless antiquarianism to which the illegal Council of Pistoia gave rise. It likewise attempts to reinstate a series of errors which were responsible for the calling of that meeting as well as for those resulting from it, with grievous harm to souls, and which the Church, the ever watchful guardian of the "deposit of faith" committed to her charge by her divine Founder, had every right and reason to condemn. For perverse designs and ventures of this sort tend to paralyze and weaken that process of sanctification by which the sacred liturgy directs the sons of adoption to their Heavenly Father of their souls' salvation**. (Pope Pius XII, *Mediator Dei*, November 20, 1947.)

"For perverse designs and ventures of this sort tend to paralyze and weaken that process of sanctification by which the sacred liturgy directs the sons of adoption to their Heavenly Father of their souls' salvation." Anyone who cannot see that this one sentence describes the effects of the innovations of the abomination that is the Protestant and Judeo-Masonic *Novus Ordo* service is not being intellectually honest. The *Novus Ordo* service is of its very nature as much a revolution against Catholic Faith and Worship as that represented by the liturgies of Protestant sects.

The true sense of the Catholic Faith that should be possessed by baptized Catholics has been replaced by a diabolically-inspired sense that has paralyzed and weakened the processes by which they can sanctify and thus save their immortal souls. Although ***Sensus fidei* in the life of the Church** seeks to make a distinction between a "healthy democracy" in the world and the *sensus fidei*, the document actually endorses a sense of public opinion in the false church of conciliarism founded on the false theology of the "people as the Church of God" that is an essential component of the new ecclesiology propagated by *Lumen Gentium*, November 21, 1964.

The "people" have come to accept all manner of heretical teachings and aberrant, deviant practices as just part of a natural "evolution." Most Catholics in the conciliar structures today do not get shocked when a false "pontiff" hides his pectoral cross in the presence of Talmudic rabbis in Jerusalem or speak of the Old Covenant as having never been revoked or personally esteem the symbols of false religions with their hands. Joseph Ratzinger/Benedict XVI did the latter with his own priestly hands on Thursday, April 17, 2009, at the John Paul II Cultural Center in Washington, District of Columbia, without a word of protest from those who maintained a studied silence about his outrages against the honor and glory and majesty of the Most Blessed Trinity because they had too much to "lose" by pointing out the sins against the First and Second Commandments committed by their supposed "pope of Tradition."

The "people" are not shocked by any kind of ecumenical "dialogue" or "inter-religious prayer" service as this is this is all that those born after 1965 or so have known and it is what many others born before that time have come to accept as part of being "open" to the "goodness" of other "faith traditions."

The "people" have simply come to accept what those who have the true *sensus Catholicus* now are apostasies, blasphemies, sacrileges and heresies as integral parts of what they think is the Catholic Faith. They look to Jorge Mario Bergoglio as the man who will do away with any remaining vestiges of the past, and the new document from the International Theological Commission means to empower them all the more, giving the false "pontiff" the false theology that he needs to justify change and novelty in the name of responding to the "sense" of the faithful.

Yes, the same folks who produced **The Hope of Salvation for Infants Who Die Without Being Baptised**, April 19, 2007, that in essence, swept away Catholic belief in the existence of Limbo as a place of natural happiness for infants made a similar effort to represent its text as being in keeping with the teaching of the Catholic Church by making references to historical examples of how the *sensus fidei* has guided Holy Mother Church in the past. The examples given do not prove what the conciliar revolutionaries desire.

To cite one such example, ***Sensus fidei* in the life of the Church** *attempts* to use Pope Pius IX's request to the bishops of the world to ascertain whether he should proclaim the doctrine of the Immaculate Conception of the Blessed Virgin Mary as similar to its own revolutionary redefinition and application of the *sensus fidei*:

38. The influence of Perrone's research on Pope Pius IX's decision to proceed with the definition of the Immaculate Conception is evident from the fact that before he defined it the Pope asked the bishops of the world to report to him in writing regarding the devotion of their clergy and faithful people to the conception of the Immaculate Virgin.[37] In the apostolic constitution containing the definition, *Ineffabilis Deus* (1854), Pope Pius IX said that although he already knew the mind of the bishops on this matter, he had particularly asked the bishops to inform him of the piety and devotion of their faithful in this regard, and he concluded that 'Holy Scripture, venerable Tradition, the constant mind of the Church [*perpetuus Ecclesiae sensus*], the remarkable agreement of Catholic bishops and the faithful [*singularis catholicorum Antistitum ac fidelium conspiratio*], and the memorable Acts and Constitutions of our predecessors' all wonderfully illustrated and proclaimed the doctrine.[38] He thus used the language of Perrone's treatise to describe the combined testimony of the bishops and the faithful. Newman highlighted the word, *conspiratio*, and commented: 'the two, the Church teaching and the Church taught, are put together, as one twofold testimony, illustrating each other, and never to be divided'.[39] (***Sensus fidei* in the life of the Church**.)

There is quite an essential difference between what Pope Pius IX did before proclaiming the doctrine of Our Lady's Immaculate Conception and what has been done by the revolutionaries who have jettisoned the Catholic past in order to "return" to what they claim are the "sources" of the Faith without any "corrupting filter" provided by the Scholastics of the High Middle Ages.

Devotion to Our Lady as conceived without stain of Original Sin can be traced to the time after the Council of Ephesus in 431 A.D. as bishops in Syria authorized the Feast of the Conception of the Most Holy and All Pure Mother of God that was celebrated on December 9, the date on which Our Lady appeared for the first time to the devout Indian named Juan Diego atop Tepayec Hill exactly eleven hundred years later. And Pope Alexander VII, largely as a result of the influence of Venerable Mary of Agreda, who was, after all, a member of the Conceptionist sisters, and of King Philip IV of Spain, issued the first decree in 1661 on the doctrine. It should also be noted that the Venerable Mary of Agreda had a primary source for her devotion to the Immaculate Conception of the Blessed Virgin Mary: Our Lady herself.

Pope Pius IX explained the consistent testimony in favor of the doctrine of Our Lady's Immaculate Conception as follows in *Ineffabilus Deus*, December 8, 1854:

Supreme Reason for the Privilege: The Divine Maternity

And indeed it was wholly fitting that so wonderful a mother should be ever resplendent with the glory of most sublime holiness and so completely free from all taint of original sin that she would triumph utterly over the ancient serpent. To her did the Father will to give his only-begotten Son — the Son whom, equal to the Father and begotten by him, the Father loves from his heart — and to give this Son in such a way that he would be the one and the same common Son of God the Father and of the Blessed Virgin Mary. It was she whom the Son himself chose to make his Mother and it was from her that the Holy Spirit willed and brought it about that he should be conceived and born from whom he himself proceeds.[1]

Liturgical Argument

The Catholic Church, directed by the Holy Spirit of God, is the pillar and base of truth and has ever held as divinely revealed and as contained in the deposit of heavenly revelation this doctrine concerning the original innocence of the august Virgin — a doctrine which is so perfectly in harmony with her wonderful sanctity and preeminent dignity as Mother of God — and thus has never ceased to explain, to teach and to foster this doctrine age after age in many ways and by solemn acts. **From this very doctrine, flourishing and wondrously propagated in the Catholic world through the efforts and zeal of the bishops, was made very clear by the Church when she did not hesitate to present for the public devotion and veneration of the faithful the Feast of the Conception of the Blessed Virgin.[2] By this most significant fact, the Church made it clear indeed that the conception of Mary is to be venerated as something extraordinary, wonderful, eminently holy, and different from the conception of all other human beings — for the Church celebrates only the feast days of the saints**.

And hence the very words with which the Sacred Scriptures speak of Uncreated Wisdom and set forth his eternal origin, the Church, both in its ecclesiastical offices and in its liturgy, has been wont to apply likewise to the origin of the Blessed Virgin, inasmuch as God, by one and the same decree, had established the origin of Mary and the Incarnation of Divine Wisdom.

Ordinary Teaching of the Roman Church

These truths, so generally accepted and put into practice by the faithful, indicate how zealously the Roman Church, mother and teacher of all Churches, has continued to teach this doctrine of the Immaculate Conception of the Virgin. Yet the more important actions of the Church deserve to be mentioned in detail. For such dignity and authority belong to the Church that she alone is the center of truth and of Catholic unity. It is the Church in which alone religion has been inviolably preserved and from which all other Churches must receive the tradition of the Faith.[3]

The same Roman Church, therefore, desired nothing more than by the most persuasive means to state, to protect, to promote and to defend the doctrine of the Immaculate Conception. **This fact is most clearly shown to the whole world by numerous and significant acts of the Roman Pontiffs, our predecessors. To them, in the person of the Prince of the Apostles, were divinely entrusted by Christ our Lord, the charge and supreme care and the power of feeding the lambs and sheep; in particular, of confirming their brethren, and of ruling and governing the universal Church**.

Veneration of the Immaculate

Our predecessors, indeed, by virtue of their apostolic authority, gloried in instituting the Feast of the Conception in the Roman Church. They did so to enhance its importance and dignity by a suitable Office and Mass, whereby the prerogative of the Virgin, her exception from the hereditary taint, was most distinctly affirmed. As to the homage already instituted, they spared no effort to promote and to extend it either by the granting of indulgences, or by allowing cities, provinces and kingdoms to choose as their patroness God's own Mother, under the title of "The Immaculate Conception." **Again, our predecessors approved confraternities, congregations and religious communities founded in honor of the Immaculate Conception, monasteries, hospitals, altars, or churches; they praised persons who vowed to uphold with all their ability the doctrine of the Immaculate Conception of the Mother of God. Besides, it afforded the greatest joy to our predecessors to ordain that the Feast of the Conception should be celebrated in every church with the very same honor as the Feast of the Nativity; that it should be celebrated with an octave by the whole Church; that it should be reverently and generally observed as a holy day of obligation; and that a pontifical Capella should be held in our Liberian pontifical basilica on the day dedicated to the conception of the Virgin. Finally, in their desire to impress this doctrine of the Immaculate Conception of the Mother of God upon the hearts of the faithful, and to intensify the people's piety and enthusiasm for the homage and the veneration of the Virgin conceived without the stain of original sin, they delighted to grant, with the greatest pleasure, permission to proclaim the Immaculate Conception of the Virgin in the Litany of Loreto, and in the Preface of the Mass, so that the rule of prayer might thus serve to illustrate the rule of belief. Therefore, we ourselves, following the procedure of our predecessors, have not only approved and accepted what had already been established, but bearing in mind, moreover, the decree of Sixtus IV,** [4] have confirmed by our authority a proper Office in honor of the Immaculate Conception, and have with exceeding joy extended its use to the universal Church.[5]

The Roman Doctrine

Now inasmuch as whatever pertains to sacred worship is intimately connected with its object and cannot have either consistency or durability if this object is vague or uncertain, our predecessors, the Roman Pontiffs, therefore, while directing all their efforts toward an increase of the devotion to the conception, made it their aim not only to emphasize the object with the utmost zeal, but also to enunciate the exact doctrine.[6] Definitely and clearly they taught that the feast was held in honor of the conception of the Virgin. They denounced as false and absolutely foreign to the mind of the Church the opinion of those who held and affirmed that it was not the conception of the Virgin but her sanctification that was honored by the Church. They never thought that greater leniency should be extended toward those who, attempting to disprove the doctrine of the Immaculate Conception of the Virgin, devised a distinction between the first and second instance of conception and inferred that the conception which the Church celebrates was not that of the first instance of conception but the second. In fact, they held it was their duty not only to uphold and defend with all their power the Feast of the Conception of the Blessed Virgin but also to assert that the true object of this veneration was her conception considered in its first instant. Hence the words of one of our predecessors, **Alexander VII, who authoritatively and decisively declared the mind of the Church: "Concerning the most Blessed Virgin Mary, Mother of God, ancient indeed is that devotion of the faithful based on the belief that her soul, in the first instant of its creation and in the first instant of the soul's infusion into the body, was, by a special grace and privilege**

of God, in view of the merits of Jesus Christ, her Son and the Redeemer of the human race, preserved free from all stain of original sin. And in this sense have the faithful ever solemnized and celebrated the Feast of the Conception."[7]

Moreover, our predecessors considered it their special solemn duty with all diligence, zeal, and effort to preserve intact the doctrine of the Immaculate Conception of the Mother of God. **For, not only have they in no way ever allowed this doctrine to be censured or changed, but they have gone much further and by clear statements repeatedly asserted that the doctrine by which we profess the Immaculate Conception of the Virgin is on its own merits entirely in harmony with the ecclesiastical veneration; that it is ancient and widespread, and of the same nature as that which the Roman Church has undertaken to promote and to protect, and that it is entirely worthy to be used in the Sacred Liturgy and solemn prayers. Not content with this they most strictly prohibited any opinion contrary to this doctrine to be defended in public or private in order that the doctrine of the Immaculate Conception of the Virgin might remain inviolate. By repeated blows they wished to put an end to such an opinion. And lest these oft-repeated and clearest statements seem useless, they added a sanction to them.**

Papal Sanctions

All these things our illustrious predecessor, Alexander VII, summed up in these words: "**We have in mind the fact that the Holy Roman Church solemnly celebrated the Feast of the Conception of the undefiled and ever-Virgin Mary, and has long ago appointed for this a special and proper Office according to the pious, devout, and laudable instruction which was given by our predecessor, Sixtus IV. Likewise, we were desirous, after the example of our predecessors, to favor this praiseworthy piety, devotion, feast and veneration — a veneration which is in keeping with the piety unchanged in the Roman Church from the day it was instituted. We also desired to protect this piety and devotion of venerating and extolling the most Blessed Virgin preserved from original sin by the grace of the Holy Spirit. Moreover, we were anxious to preserve the unity of the Spirit in the bond of peace in the flock of Christ by putting down arguments and controversies and by removing scandals. So at the instance and request of the bishops mentioned above, with the chapters of the churches, and of King Philip and his kingdoms, we renew the Constitutions and Decrees issued by the Roman Pontiffs, our predecessors, especially Sixtus IV,[8] Paul V,[9] and Gregory XV,[10] in favor of the doctrine asserting that the soul of the Blessed Virgin, in its creation and infusion into the body, was endowed with the grace of the Holy Spirit and preserved from original sin; and also in favor of the feast and veneration of the conception of the Virgin Mother of God, which, as is manifest, was instituted in keeping with that pious belief. So we command this feast to be observed under the censures and penalties contained in the same Constitutions.**

"And therefore, against all and everyone of those who shall continue to construe the said Constitutions and Decrees in a manner apt to frustrate the favor which is thereby given to the said doctrine, and to the feast and relative veneration, or who shall dare to call into question the said sentence, feast and worship, or in any way whatever, directly or indirectly, shall declare themselves opposed to it under any pretext whatsoever, were it but only to the extent of examining the possibilities of effecting the definition, or who shall comment upon and interpret the Sacred Scripture, or the Fathers or Doctors in connection therewith, or finally, for any reason, or on any occasion, shall dare, either in writing or verbally, to speak, preach, treat, dispute or determine upon, or assert whatsoever against the foregoing matters, or who shall adduce any arguments against them, while leaving them unresolved, or who shall disagree therewith in any other conceivable manner, we hereby declare that in addition to the penalties and censures contained in the Constitutions issued by Sixtus IV to which we want them to be subjected and to which we subject them by the present Constitution, we hereby decree that they be deprived of the authority of preaching, reading in public, that is to say teaching and interpreting; and that they be also deprived ipso facto of the power of voting, either actively or passively, in all elections, without the need for any further declaration; and that also, ipso facto, without any further declaration, they shall incur the penalty of perpetual disability from preaching, reading in public, teaching and interpreting, and that it shall not be possible to absolve them from such penalty, or remove it, save through ourselves, or the Roman Pontiffs who shall succeed us.

"We also require that the same shall remain subject to any other penalties which by us, of our own free will — or by the Roman Pontiffs, our successors (according as they may decree) — shall be deemed advisable to establish, and by the present Constitution we declare them subject thereto, and hereby renew the above Decrees and Constitutions of Paul V and Gregory XV.

"Moreover, as regards those books in which the said sentence, feast and relative veneration are called into question or are contradicted in any way whatsoever, according to what has already been stated, either in writing or verbally, in discourses, sermons, lectures, treatises and debates — that may have been printed after the above-praised Decree of Paul V, or may be printed hereafter we hereby prohibit them, subject to the penalties and censures established by the Index of prohibited books, and ipso facto, without any further declaration, we desire and command that they be held as expressly prohibited."[11]

Testimonies of the Catholic World

All are aware with how much diligence this doctrine of the Immaculate Conception of the Mother of God has been handed down, proposed and defended by the most outstanding religious orders, by the more celebrated theological academies, and by very eminent doctors in the sciences of theology. All know, likewise, how eager the bishops have been to profess openly and publicly, even in ecclesiastical assemblies, that Mary, the most holy Mother of God, by virtue of the foreseen merits of Christ, our Lord and Redeemer, was never subject to original sin, but was completely preserved from the original taint, and hence she was redeemed in a manner more sublime.

The Council of Trent

Besides, we must note a fact of the greatest importance indeed. Even the Council of Trent itself, when it promulgated the dogmatic decree concerning original sin, following the testimonies of the Sacred Scriptures, of the Holy Fathers and of the renowned Council, **decreed and defined that all men are born infected by original sin; nevertheless, it solemnly declared that it had no intention of including the blessed and immaculate Virgin Mary, the Mother of God, in this decree and in the general extension of its definition. Indeed, considering the times and circumstances, the Fathers of Trent sufficiently intimated by this declaration that the Blessed Virgin Mary was free from the original stain; and thus they clearly signified that nothing could be reasonably cited from the Sacred Scriptures, from Tradition, or from the authority of the Fathers, which would in any way be opposed to so great a prerogative of the Blessed Virgin.**[12]

Testimonies of Tradition

And indeed, illustrious documents of venerable antiquity, of both the Eastern and the Western Church, very forcibly testify that this doctrine of the Immaculate Conception of the most Blessed Virgin, which was daily more and more splendidly explained, stated and confirmed by the highest authority, teaching, zeal, knowledge, and wisdom of the Church, and which was disseminated among all peoples and nations of the Catholic world in a marvelous manner — this doctrine always existed in the Church as a doctrine that has been received from our ancestors, and that has been stamped with the character of revealed doctrine. **For the Church of Christ, watchful guardian that she is, and defender of the dogmas deposited with her, never changes anything, never diminishes anything, never adds anything to them; but with all diligence she treats the ancient documents faithfully and wisely; if they really are of ancient origin and if the faith of the Fathers has transmitted them, she strives to investigate and explain them in such a way that the ancient dogmas of heavenly doctrine will be made evident and clear, but will retain their full, integral, and proper nature, and will grown only within their own genus — that is, within the same dogma, in the same sense and the same meaning**. (Pope Pius IX, *Ineffabilus Deus*, December 8, 1854.)

Veneration of the Most Blessed Virgin Mary under her title of her Immaculate Conception, a doctrine that was ratified by Our Lady herself on March 25, 1858, when she said "I am the Immaculate Conception" to Saint Bernadette Soubirous in the Grotto of Massabielle near Lourdes, France, is of ancient origin. Pope Pius IX invented nothing new. Neither did the faithful of the Nineteenth Century. The proclamation of the doctrine was a merely an infallible statement of the fact itself.

What ancient sources can the conciliar revolutionaries produce to justify the new ecclesiology's "the church as communion" and false ecumenism and inter-religious "dialogue" and inter-religious "prayer" and episcopal collegiality and religious liberty and separation of Church and State and their embrace of the condemned and philosophically absurd Modernist concept known as the "evolution of doctrine"?

None.

None whatsoever.

Moreover, can anyone with a shred of intellectual honesty assert that the conciliar revolutionaries and their novelties have "grown within their own genus, within the same dogma, in the same sense and the same meaning"?

Indeed, the conciliar "doctrines," such as they are, represent wholesale contradictions of the defined teaching of the Catholic Church, and the fact that most of the lay faithful today have no sense of this is because they have been exposed to false doctrines, false liturgical rites and false pastoral practices that have helped to create, foster and sustain a false *sensus Catholicus*.

Sensus fidei in the life of the Church goes so far as to state that the *sensus fidei* has an "ecumenical dimension," meaning that non-Catholics have a role to play in the development of what is said to be Catholic doctrine. No, I am not making this up.

See for yourselves:

> **The notions, *sensus fidei*, *sensus fidelium*, and *consensus fidelium*, have all been treated, or at least mentioned, in various international dialogues between the Catholic Church and other churches and ecclesial communities. Broadly speaking, there has been agreement in these dialogues that the whole body of the faithful, lay as well as ordained, bears responsibility for maintaining the Church's apostolic faith and witness, and that each of the baptised, by reason of a divine anointing (1Jn 2:20, 27), has the capacity to discern the truth in matters of faith**. There is also general agreement that certain members of the Church exercise a special responsibility of teaching and oversight, but always in collaboration with the rest of the faithful.[106]
>
> 86. Two particular questions related to the *sensus fidelium* arise in the context of the ecumenical dialogue to which the Catholic Church is irrevocably committed:[107]
>
> i) Should only those doctrines which gain the common consent of all Christians be regarded as expressing the *sensus fidelium* and therefore as true and binding? This proposal goes counter to the Catholic Church's faith and practice. By means of dialogue, Catholic theologians and those of other traditions seek to secure agreement on Church-dividing questions, but the Catholic participants cannot suspend their commitment to the Catholic Church's own established doctrines.
>
> ii) **Should separated Christians be understood as participating in and contributing to the *sensus fidelium* in some manner? The answer here is undoubtedly in the affirmative.[108] The Catholic Church acknowledges that 'many elements of sanctification and truth' are to be found outside her own visible bounds,[109] that 'certain features of the Christian mystery have at times been more effectively emphasised' in other communities,[110] and that ecumenical dialogue helps her to deepen and clarify her own understanding of the Gospel**. (*Sensus fidei* in the life of the Church.)

Complete and total heresy.

The Divine Constitution of Holy Mother Church is complete in and of itself. There is no need to gather the "*sensus fidelium*" of the Protestants and the Orthodox as they are outside her maternal bosom and cleave to heresies of one sort or another. The Catholic Church alone is the guardian of truth and the sole means of human sanctification. None other.

This has sprung from within the "same dogma, in the same sense and the same meaning"?

Hardly.

There must be a new sense for a new faith, a faith that is the counterfeit ape of the Catholic Faith.

The entire goal of ***Sensus fidei* in the life of the Church** is to provide a theological justification for Jorge Mario Bergoglio's plans to expedite the evolutionary processes, if you will, of the counterfeit church of conciliarism's logical path of degeneration to the point of complete paganism. Although the point has been made several times before in my writing, the counterfeit church of conciliarism is rapidly matching the heretical and schismatic Anglican sect's complete abandonment of any semblance of even a generic sense of Christianity in order to assuage the consciences of those steeped in lives of unrepentant sins, whether those sins be of the natural or unnatural variety.

The authors of ***Sensus fidei* in the life of the Church** attempted to explain that the conciliar religion's concept of the sense of their false faith must be distinguished from public opinion as found in the realm of civil "democracies," which are, of course, actually republics in that a pure democracy is a form of government in which the whole number of citizens meeting eligibility requirement gather in assembly to directly decide matters of public policy (e.g. ancient Athens and the "town meeting" form of government that exists to this very day in some New England communities), before proceeding to extol the role of public opinion in the gathering of the sense of the faithful. Such must ever be the fate of minds who reject what Joseph Ratzinger/Benedict XVI considered the "crystal-clear logic" of Saint Thomas Aquinas's Scholasticism that is disparaged by Jorge Mario Bergoglio as producing a "church that is closed-in-on-itself" and thus incapable of letting what he thinks is the Third Person of Most Blessed Trinity "blow freely" without being "caged in" by the "filter" of a dogmatically "rigid" past.

Here is the supposed rejection of public opinion as the foundation of the sense of the faithful while admitting that it does have a "proper role in the Church":

> One of the most delicate topics is the relationship between the *sensus fidei* and public or majority opinion both inside and outside the Church. **Public opinion is a sociological concept, which applies first of all to political societies. The emergence of public opinion is linked to the birth and development of the political model of representative democracy. In so far as political power gains its legitimacy from the people, the latter must make known their thoughts, and political power must take account of them in the exercise of government. Public opinion is therefore essential to the healthy functioning of democratic life, and it is important that it be enlightened and informed**

in a competent and honest manner. That is the role of the mass media, which thus contribute greatly to the common good of society, as long as they do not seek to manipulate opinion in favour of particular interests.

114. The Church appreciates the high human and moral values espoused by democracy, but she herself is not structured according to the principles of a secular political society. The Church, the mystery of the communion of humanity with God, receives her constitution from Christ. It is from him that she receives her internal structure and her principles of government. Public opinion cannot, therefore, play in the Church **the determinative role that it legitimately plays in the political societies that rely on the principle of popular sovereignty, though it does have a proper role in the Church, as we shall seek to clarify below**. (***Sensus fidei* in the life of the Church.**)

Extensive and Protracted Comments:

There is a great deal of error in this one paragraph. Much time has to be taken to examine the matter in depth as the conciliar revolutionaries must by their very reprobate nature distort the meaning, history and application in concrete circumstances of Holy Mother Church's Social Teaching.

First, it is false that political power derives its legitimacy from the people. Although it will be explained below that the people may choose to adopt any particular form of government as befits the pursuit of the common good in accord with the binding precepts of the Divine Positive Law and the Natural Law, the source of all sovereignty is God, not the people.

Pope Leo XIII made this eminently clear in *Immortale Dei*, November 1, 1885:

30. Now, natural reason itself proves convincingly that such concepts of the government of a State are wholly at variance with the truth. Nature itself bears witness **that all power, of every kind, has its origin from God, who is its chief and most august source.**

31. **The sovereignty of the people, however, and this without any reference to God, is held to reside in the multitude; which is doubtless a doctrine exceedingly well calculated to flatter and to inflame many passions, but which lacks all reasonable proof, and all power of insuring public safety and preserving order. Indeed, from the prevalence of this teaching, things have come to such a pass that may hold as an axiom of civil jurisprudence that seditions may be rightfully fostered. For the opinion prevails that princes are nothing more than delegates chosen to carry out the will of the people; whence it necessarily follows that all things are as changeable as the will of the people, so that risk of public disturbance is ever hanging over our heads.**

To hold, therefore, that there is no difference in matters of religion between forms that are unlike each other, and even contrary to each other, most clearly leads in the end to the rejection of all religion in both theory and practice. And this is the same thing as atheism, however it may differ from it in name. Men who really believe in the existence of God must, in order to be consistent with themselves and to avoid absurd

conclusions, understand that differing modes of divine worship involving dissimilarity and conflict even on most important points cannot all be equally probable, equally good, and equally acceptable to God.

32. So, too, the liberty of thinking, and of publishing, whatsoever each one likes, without any hindrance, is not in itself an advantage over which society can wisely rejoice. On the contrary, it is the fountain-head and origin of many evils. Liberty is a power perfecting man, and hence should have truth and goodness for its object. But the character of goodness and truth cannot be changed at option. These remain ever one and the same, and are no less unchangeable than nature itself. If the mind assents to false opinions, and the will chooses and follows after what is wrong, neither can attain its native fullness, but both must fall from their native dignity into an abyss of corruption. **Whatever, therefore, is opposed to virtue and truth may not rightly be brought temptingly before the eye of man, much less sanctioned by the favor and protection of the law. A well-spent life is the only way to heaven, whither all are bound, and on this account the State is acting against the laws and dictates of nature whenever it permits the license of opinion and of action to lead minds astray from truth and souls away from the practice of virtue. To exclude the Church, founded by God Himself, from life, from laws, from the education of youth, from domestic society is a grave and fatal error.** A State from which religion is banished can never be well regulated; and already perhaps more than is desirable is known of the nature and tendency of the so-called civil philosophy of life and morals. **The Church of Christ is the true and sole teacher of virtue and guardian of morals. She it is who preserves in their purity the principles from which duties flow, and, by setting forth most urgent reasons for virtuous life, bids us not only to turn away from wicked deeds, but even to curb all movements of the mind that are opposed to reason, even though they be not carried out in action.**

33. To wish the Church to be subject to the civil power in the exercise of her duty is a great folly and a sheer injustice. Whenever this is the case, order is disturbed, for things natural are put above things supernatural; the many benefits which the Church, if free to act, would confer on society are either prevented or at least lessened in number; and a way is prepared for enmities and contentions between the two powers, with how evil result to both the issue of events has taught us only too frequently.

34. Doctrines such as these, which cannot be approved by human reason, and most seriously affect the whole civil order, Our predecessors the Roman Pontiffs (well aware of what their apostolic office required of them) have never allowed to pass uncondemned. **Thus, Gregory XVI in his encyclical letter "Mirari Vos," dated August 15, 1832, inveighed with weighty words against the sophisms which even at his time were being publicly inculcated-namely, that no preference should be shown for any particular form of worship; that it is right for individuals to form their own personal judgments about religion; that each man's conscience is his sole and allsufficing guide; and that it is lawful for every man to publish his own views, whatever they may be, and even to conspire against the State. On the question of the separation of Church and State the same Pontiff writes as follows: "Nor can We hope for happier results either for religion or for the civil government from the wishes of those who desire that the**

> **Church be separated from the State, and the concord between the secular and ecclesiastical authority be dissolved. It is clear that these men, who yearn for a shameless liberty, live in dread of an agreement which has always been fraught with good, and advantageous alike to sacred and civil interests." To the like effect, also, as occasion presented itself, did Pius IX brand publicly many false opinions which were gaining ground, and afterwards ordered them to be condensed in summary form in order that in this sea of error Catholics might have a light which they might safely follow**. (Pope Leo XIII, *Immortale Dei*, November 1, 1885.)

The conciliar revolutionaries celebrated the "joys" of Modernity as "good" in and of themselves even though they are contrary to Divine Revelation and to right reason. Again, one must face the plain reality that these revolutionaries profess a false religion and thus are not members of the Catholic Church, no less officials within her.

Second, yes, the Catholic Church can adapt herself to any legitimate form of government, including the republican form of democratic governance, as long as those governments are directed toward their proper end by pursuing the common temporal good in light of man's Last End, the possession of God the Father, God the Son and God the Holy Ghost for all eternity in Heaven. Our true popes have urged children of Holy Mother Church to obey just laws and to resist those that are repugnant to the binding precepts of the Divine Positive Law and the Natural Law by making use of the liberties accorded them by the civil law. Holy Mother Church does *not*, however, esteem "democracy's" supposed "high human and moral values.)

Writing in his encyclical letter on the French Third Republic, which came into existence in 1871 following the overthrow of Emperor Napoleon III (Louis Bonaparte) and then had proceeded to institute gravely anti-Catholic legislation that caused many Catholics in France to protest its legitimacy, Pope Leo XIII wrote that Holy Mother Church accepts as legitimate all forms of government that aim to promote the common good, noting that she is not blind to the inherent defects, such as the separation of Church and State, found in that same Third Republic:

> 12. We have expressly recalled some features of the past that Catholics might not be dismayed by the present. Substantially the struggle is ever the same: **Jesus Christ is always exposed to the contradictions of the world, and the same means are always used by modern enemies of Christianity, means old in principle and scarcely modified in form; but the same means of defense are also clearly indicated to Christians of the present day by our apologists, our doctors and our martyrs.** What they have done it is incumbent upon us to do in our turn. Let us therefore place above all else the glory of God and of His Church; let us work for her with an assiduity at once constant and effective, and leave all care of success to Jesus Christ, who tells us: "In the world you shall have distress: but have confidence, I have overcome the world."[5]
>
> 13. To attain this We have already remarked that a great union is necessary, and if it is to be realized, it is indispensable that all preoccupation capable of diminishing its strength and efficacy must be abandoned. **Here We intend alluding principally to the political differences among the French in regard to the actual republic — a question We would**

> **treat with the clearness which the gravity of the subject demands, beginning with the principles and descending thence to practical results.**
>
> 14. Various political governments have succeeded one another in France during the last century, each having its own distinctive form: the Empire, the Monarchy, and the Republic. **By giving one's self up to abstractions, one could at length conclude which is the best of these forms, considered in themselves; and in all truth it may be affirmed that each of them is good, provided it lead straight to its end — that is to say, to the common good for which social authority is constituted; and finally, it may be added that, from a relative point of view, such and such a form of government may be preferable because of being better adapted to the character and customs of such or such a nation. In this order of speculative ideas, Catholics, like all other citizens, are free to prefer one form of government to another precisely because no one of these social forms is, in itself, opposed to the principles of sound reason nor to the maxims of Christian doctrine**. What amply justifies the wisdom of the Church is that in her relations with political powers she makes abstraction of the forms which differentiate them and treats with them concerning the great religious interests of nations, knowing that hers is the duty to undertake their tutelage above all other interests. Our preceding Encyclicals have already exposed these principles, but it was nevertheless necessary to recall them for the development of the subject which occupies us to-day.
>
> 15. In descending from the domain of abstractions to that of facts, we must beware of denying the principles just established: they remain fixed. However, becoming incarnated in facts, they are clothed with a contingent character, determined by the center in which their application is produced. **Otherwise said, if every political form is good by itself and may be applied to the government of nations, the fact still remains that political power is not found in all nations under the same form; each has its own. This form springs from a combination of historical or national, though always human, circumstances which, in a nation, give rise to its traditional and even fundamental laws, and by these is determined the particular form of government, the basis of transmission of supreme power.** (Pope Leo XIII, *Au Milieu Des Sollicitudes*, February 16, 1892.)

Pope Leo XIII was not praising the French Third Republic. He was only stating that it was possible for Catholics to work within it for the common good, noting that the sovereign of all states is God Himself, not the people. Christ the King is sovereign. His language was measured and diplomatic as he endeavored to give the Concordat between the Church and the Third Republic a chance to work.

Pope Leo XIII, however, went on to reiterate Holy Mother Church's absolute condemnation of the separation of Church and State in France that had been condemned consistently by his predecessors dating back to Pope Pius VII's *Post Tam Diuturnas*, April 29, 1814. While Holy Mother Church will adapt herself to the particular circumstances in which her children live and tolerate the existence of such a situation, she never yields anything to the the anti-Incarnational errors of the modern civil state that is but the misbegotten issue of Protestantism and Judeo-Masonry:

28. **We shall not hold to the same language on another point, concerning the principle of the separation of the State and Church, which is equivalent to the separation of human legislation from Christian and divine legislation. We do not care to interrupt Ourselves here in order to demonstrate the absurdity of such a separation; each one will understand for himself. As soon as the State refuses to give to God what belongs to God, by a necessary consequence it refuses to give to citizens that to which, as men, they have a right; as, whether agreeable or not to accept, it cannot be denied that man's rights spring from his duty toward God. Whence if follows that the State, by missing in this connection the principal object of its institution, finally becomes false to itself by denying that which is the reason of its own existence. These superior truths are so clearly proclaimed by the voice of even natural reason, that they force themselves upon all who are not blinded by the violence of passion; therefore Catholics cannot be too careful in defending themselves against such a separation. In fact, to wish that the State would separate itself from the Church would be to wish, by a logical sequence, that the Church be reduced to the liberty of living according to the law common to all citizens....**It is true that in certain countries this state of affairs exists. It is a condition which, if it have numerous and serious inconveniences, also offers some advantages — above all when, by a fortunate inconsistency, the legislator is inspired by Christian principles — and, though these advantages cannot justify the false principle of separation nor authorize its defense, they nevertheless render worthy of toleration a situation which, practically, might be worse.

29. But in France, a nation Catholic in her traditions and by the present faith of the great majority of her sons, the Church should not be placed in the precarious position to which she must submit among other peoples; and the better that Catholics understand the aim of the enemies who desire this separation, the less will they favor it. To these enemies, and they say it clearly enough, this separation means that political legislation be entirely independent of religious legislation; **nay, more, that Power be absolutely indifferent to the interests of Christian society, that is to say, of the Church; in fact, that it deny her very existence.** But they make a reservation formulated thus: As soon as the Church, utilizing the resources which common law accords to the least among Frenchmen, will, by redoubling her native activity, cause her work to prosper, then the State intervening, can and will put French Catholics outside the common law itself. . . **In a word: the ideal of these men would be a return to paganism: the State would recognize the Church only when it would be pleased to persecute her.** (Pope Leo XIII, *Au Milieu Des Sollicitudes*, February 16, 1892.)

This is what was happening in France at that time. This is what happening all over the world today. Yet it is that the conciliar revolutionaries have long praised the ethos of "pluralism" and "religious liberty" and "separation of Church and State" and "freedom of the press" and "freedom of speech" despite all of the objective evidence testifying to the prophetic statements made by our true popes in the Nineteenth and early Twentieth Centuries. Then again, of course, the conciliar revolutionaries are busy celebrating those who are said to "live on the existential peripheries" as a result of the tide of evils that have been let loose by Modernity and that Modernism has enabled by its heresies, apostasies, errors and by its every celebration of the world in its liturgically abominable and sacramentally barren Protestant and Judeo-Masonic liturgical service.

Insofar as the case of France, a country where so-called "gay marriage" was approved in 2013 without a word of protest from Jorge Mario Bergoglio, it is well known that the leaders of the French Third Republic responded to Pope Leo XIII's careful explication and application of Catholic principles with even more anti-Catholic legislation than before, which is what prompted Pope Saint Pius X, who had the inestimable benefit of not having had any experience in the diplomatic service of the Holy See, wrote the following forceful and completely unequivocal words in *Vehementer Nos* almost exactly fourteen years later, that is, on February 11, 1906.

> Our soul is full of sorrowful solicitude and Our heart overflows with grief, when Our thoughts dwell upon you. How, indeed, could it be otherwise, immediately after the promulgation of that law which, by sundering violently the old ties that linked your nation with the Apostolic See, creates for the Catholic Church in France a situation unworthy of her and ever to be lamented? That is, beyond question, an event of the gravest import, and one that must be deplored by all the right-minded, for it is as disastrous to society as it is to religion; but it is an event which can have surprised nobody who has paid any attention to the religious policy followed in France of late years. For you, Venerable Brethren, it will certainly have been nothing new or strange, witnesses as you have been of the many dreadful blows aimed from time to time by the public authority at religion. **You have seen the sanctity and the inviolability of Christian marriage outraged by legislative acts in formal contradiction with them; the schools and hospitals laicized; clerics torn from their studies and from ecclesiastical discipline to be subjected to military service; the religious congregations dispersed and despoiled, and their members for the most part reduced to the last stage of destitution. Other legal measures which you all know have followed: the law ordaining public prayers at the beginning of each Parliamentary Session and of the assizes has been abolished; the signs of mourning traditionally observed on board the ships on Good Friday suppressed; the religious character effaced from the judicial oath; all actions and emblems serving in any way to recall the idea of religion banished from the courts, the schools, the army, the navy, and in a word from all public establishments. These measures and others still which, one after another really separated the Church from the State, were but so many steps designedly made to arrive at complete and official separation, as the authors of them have publicly and frequently admitted**.
>
> 2. On the other hand the Holy See has spared absolutely no means to avert this great calamity. While it was untiring in warning those who were at the head of affairs in France, and in conjuring them over and over again to weigh well the immensity of the evils that would infallibly result from their separatist policy, it at the same time lavished upon France the most striking proofs of indulgent affection. It has then reason to hope that gratitude would have stayed those politicians on their downward path, and brought them at last to relinquish their designs. **But all has been in vain-the attentions, good offices, and efforts of Our Predecessor and Ourself. The enemies of religion have succeeded at last in effecting by violence what they have long desired, in defiance of your rights as a Catholic nation and of the wishes of all who think rightly. At a moment of such gravity for the Church, therefore, filled with the sense of Our Apostolic responsibility, We have considered it Our duty to raise Our voice and to open Our heart to you, Venerable Brethren, and to your clergy and people-to all of you whom We have ever**

cherished with special affection but whom We now, as is only right, love more tenderly than ever.

3. **That the State must be separated from the Church is a thesis absolutely false, a most pernicious error. Based, as it is, on the principle that the State must not recognize any religious cult, it is in the first place guilty of a great injustice to God; for the Creator of man is also the Founder of human societies, and preserves their existence as He preserves our own**. We owe Him, therefore, not only a private cult, but a public and social worship to honor Him. Besides, this thesis is an obvious negation of the supernatural order. I**t limits the action of the State to the pursuit of public prosperity during this life only, which is but the proximate object of political societies; and it occupies itself in no fashion (on the plea that this is foreign to it) with their ultimate object which is man's eternal happiness after this short life shall have run its course. But as the present order of things is temporary and subordinated to the conquest of man's supreme and absolute welfare, it follows that the civil power must not only place no obstacle in the way of this conquest, but must aid us in effecting i**t. The same thesis also upsets the order providentially established by God in the world, which demands a harmonious agreement between the two societies. Both of them, the civil and the religious society, although each exercises in its own sphere its authority over them. It follows necessarily that there are many things belonging to them in common in which both societies must have relations with one another. **Remove the agreement between Church and State, and the result will be that from these common matters will spring the seeds of disputes which will become acute on both sides; it will become more difficult to see where the truth lies, and great confusion is certain to arise. Finally, this thesis inflicts great injury on society itself, for it cannot either prosper or last long when due place is not left for religion, which is the supreme rule and the sovereign mistress in all questions touching the rights and the duties of men. Hence the Roman Pontiffs have never ceased, as circumstances required, to refute and condemn the doctrine of the separation of Church and State**. Our illustrious predecessor, Leo XIII, especially, has frequently and magnificently expounded Catholic teaching on the relations which should subsist between the two societies. "Between them," he says, "there must necessarily be a suitable union, which may not improperly be compared with that existing between body and soul.-"Quaedam intercedat necesse est ordinata colligatio (inter illas) quae quidem conjunctioni non immerito comparatur, per quam anima et corpus in homine copulantur." He proceeds: "Human societies cannot, without becoming criminal, act as if God did not exist or refuse to concern themselves with religion, as though it were something foreign to them, or of no purpose to them.... As for the Church, which has God Himself for its author, to exclude her from the active life of the nation, from the laws, the education of the young, the family, is to commit a great and pernicious error. — "Civitates non possunt, citra scellus, gerere se tamquam si Deus omnino non esset, aut curam religionis velut alienam nihilque profuturam abjicere.... Ecclesiam vero, quam Deus ipse constituit, ab actione vitae excludere, a legibus, ab institutione adolescentium, a societate domestica, magnus et perniciousus est error."[1]

4. And if it is true that any Christian State does something eminently disastrous and reprehensible in separating itself from the Church, how much more deplorable is it that

> France, of all nations in the world, would have entered on this policy; France which has been during the course of centuries the object of such great and special predilection on the part of the Apostolic See whose fortunes and glories have ever been closely bound up with the practice of Christian virtue and respect for religion. Leo XIII had truly good reason to say: "France cannot forget that Providence has united its destiny with the Holy See by ties too strong and too old that she should ever wish to break them. And it is this union that has been the source of her real greatness and her purest glories.... **To disturb this traditional union would be to deprive the nation of part of her moral force and great influence in the world.**"[2] (Pope Saint Pius X, *Vehementer Nos*, February 11, 1906.)

Although this quotation is very familiar to longtime readers of my writing, I do want to emphasize yet again this one sentence: "**Hence the Roman Pontiffs have never ceased, as circumstances required, to refute and condemn the doctrine of the separation of Church and State**." The conciliar "popes" have never ceased praising the separation of the Church and State, which should help to convince the unconvinced that they have not been true and legitimate Successors of Saint Peter and that the "church" they head is but the counterfeit ape of the Catholic Church.

The modern civil state with its reliance on the falsehoods of "popular sovereignty," "freedom of religion," "separation of Church and State" and maintained by "public opinion," each of which is praised, celebrated and exalted by the conciliar revolutionaries has done away with the truth contained in the following statement: God (as He has revealed Himself to us through His true Church) is a majority of One.

Paragraphs 113 and 114 from ***Sensus fidei* in the life of the Church** were meant to set up the reader for a very revolutionary discussion of how public opinion, although it is not part of the Catholic Church's Divine Constitution, nevertheless plays a role in the development of pastoral approaches, something that will be discussed below in the context of the ***Instrumentum Laboris*** that was issued issued in preparation for Jorge's g "extraordinary synod on the family" that took place between October 5, 2014, and October 19, 2010, within the walls of the Occupied Vatican on the West Banks of the Tiber River.

Here are the next pertinent passages from ***Sensus fidei* in the life of the Church**:

> 115. The mass media comment frequently on religious affairs. Public interest in matters of faith is a good sign, and the freedom of the press is a basic human right. **The Catholic Church is not afraid of discussion or controversy regarding her teaching. On the contrary, she welcomes debate as a manifestation of religious freedom**. Everyone is free either to criticise or to support her. Indeed, she recognises that fair and constructive critique can help her to see problems more clearly and to find better solutions. She herself, in turn, is free to criticise unfair attacks, and needs access to the media in order to defend the faith if necessary. She values invitations from independent media to contribute to public debates. **She does not want a monopoly of information, but appreciates the plurality and interchange of opinions. She also, however, knows the importance of informing society about the true meaning and content both of her faith and of her moral teaching**.

116. **The voices of lay people are heard much more frequently now in the Church, sometimes with conservative and sometimes with progressive positions, but generally participating constructively in the life and the mission of the Church. The huge development of society by education has had considerable impact on relations within the Church**. The Church herself is engaged worldwide in educational programmes aimed at giving people their own voice and their own rights. It is therefore a good sign if many people today are interested in the teaching, the liturgy and the service of the Church. Many members of the Church want to exercise their own competence, and to participate in their own proper way in the life of the Church. They organise themselves within parishes and in various groups and movements to build up the Church and to influence society at large, and they seek contact via social media with other believers and with people of good will.

117. The new networks of communication both inside and outside the Church call for new forms of attention and critique, and the renewal of skills of discernment. There are influences from special interest groups which are not compatible, or not fully so, with the Catholic faith; there are convictions which are only applicable to a certain place or time; and there are pressures to lessen the role of faith in public debate or to accommodate traditional Christian doctrine to modern concerns and opinions. (***Sensus fidei* in the life of the Church**.)

Fatigued Man's Bleary-Eyed Commentary:

First, While Holy Mother Church will always defend her doctrine, which she has received from her Divine Founder, Invisible Head and Mystical Bridegroom, Christ the King and has maintained inviolate by the infallible guidance and protection of God the Holy Ghost, she has never "welcomed debate as a manifestation of religious freedom." The Catholic Church is the true and only teacher of Christianity and thus it is that she jealously safeguards her Divinely appointed role as the the only true teacher and the only sanctifier of men in the whole world.

For the sake of the one person who has never read these articles before or for the sake of a reader or two who may have read them but has forgotten the quotes below soon after reading them, here are healthy antidotes to the poison contained in the papal quotations below:

> This shameful font of indifferentism gives rise to that absurd and erroneous proposition which claims that **liberty of conscience** must be maintained for everyone. It spreads ruin in sacred and civil affairs, though some repeat over and over again with the greatest impudence that some advantage accrues to religion from it. "**But the death of the soul is worse than freedom of error,"** as Augustine was wont to say. When all restraints are removed by which men are kept on the narrow path of truth, their nature, which is already inclined to evil, propels them to ruin. **Then truly "the bottomless pit" is open from which John saw smoke ascending which obscured the sun, and out of which locusts flew forth to devastate the earth. Thence comes transformation of minds, corruption of youths, contempt of sacred things and holy laws — in other words, a pestilence more deadly to the state than any other. Experience shows, even from earliest times, that cities renowned for wealth, dominion, and glory perished as a result of this single evil, namely immoderate freedom of opinion, license of free speech, and desire for novelty.**

Here We must include that harmful and never sufficiently denounced **freedom to publish** any writings whatever and disseminate them to the people, which some dare to demand and promote with so great a clamor. We are horrified to see what monstrous doctrines and prodigious errors are disseminated far and wide in countless books, pamphlets, and other writings which, though small in weight, are very great in malice. We are in tears at the abuse which proceeds from them over the face of the earth. Some are so carried away that they contentiously assert that the flock of errors arising from them is sufficiently compensated by the publication of some book which defends religion and truth. Every law condemns deliberately doing evil simply because there is some hope that good may result. Is there any sane man who would say poison ought to be distributed, sold publicly, stored, and even drunk because some antidote is available and those who use it may be snatched from death again and again? (Pope Gregory XVI, *Mirari Vos*, August 15, 1832.)

"For you well know, venerable brethren, that at this time men are found not a few who, applying to civil society the impious and absurd principle of "naturalism," as they call it, dare to teach that "the best constitution of public society and (also) civil progress altogether require that human society be conducted and governed without regard being had to religion any more than if it did not exist; or, at least, without any distinction being made between the true religion and false ones." And, against the doctrine of Scripture, of the Church, and of the Holy Fathers, they do not hesitate to assert that "that is the best condition of civil society, in which no duty is recognized, as attached to the civil power, of restraining by enacted penalties, offenders against the Catholic religion, except so far as public peace may require." From which totally false idea of social government they do not fear to foster that erroneous opinion, most fatal in its effects on the Catholic Church and the salvation of souls, called by Our Predecessor, Gregory XVI, an "insanity," viz., that "liberty of conscience and worship is each man's personal right, which ought to be legally proclaimed and asserted in every rightly constituted society; and that a right resides in the citizens to an absolute liberty, which should be restrained by no authority whether ecclesiastical or civil, whereby they may be able openly and publicly to manifest and declare any of their ideas whatever, either by word of mouth, by the press, or in any other way." But, while they rashly affirm this, they do not think and consider that they are preaching "liberty of perdition;" and that "if human arguments are always allowed free room for discussion, there will never be wanting men who will dare to resist truth, and to trust in the flowing speech of human wisdom; whereas we know, from the very teaching of our Lord Jesus Christ, how carefully Christian faith and wisdom should avoid this most injurious babbling."

And, since where religion has been removed from civil society, and the doctrine and authority of divine revelation repudiated, the genuine notion itself of justice and human right is darkened and lost, and the place of true justice and legitimate right is supplied by material force, thence it appears why it is that some, utterly neglecting and disregarding the surest principles of sound reason, dare to proclaim that "the people's will, manifested by what is called public opinion or in some other way, constitutes a supreme law, free from all divine and human control; and that in the political order accomplished facts, from the very circumstance that they are

> **accomplished, have the force of right."** But who, does not see and clearly perceive that human society, when set loose from the bonds of religion and true justice, can have, in truth, no other end than the purpose of obtaining and amassing wealth, and that (society under such circumstances) follows no other law in its actions, except the unchastened desire of ministering to its own pleasure and interests? (Pope Pius IX, *Quanta Cura*, December 8, 1864.)

This is so clear as to obliterate the sophistic praise of the very diabolical instruments that have been used to convert Catholics from the Holy Faith into a ready acceptance of everything presented by lords of Modernity as being true and good even though they are repugnant to the peace and happiness of eternity. We live in age of insanity and injurious babbling that suits the insane babblers of conciliarism so very well.

The conciliar masters of contradiction attempted to explain the distinctions between public opinion and the *sensus fidei* before going on to embrace "consultation" as a means of deciding what they think is the Catholic Church's pastoral practices as an effort is made to "renew" the Church's doctrine. The translation of this is most simple: The conciliar revolutionaries use the word "renew" to signify a change in what the true sense of the Holy Faith informs us is repugnant to the honor and glory of the Most Holy Trinity and to the good of the souls for whom Our Blessed Lord and Saviour Jesus Christ shed every single drop of His Most Precious Blood during His Passion and His Death on the wood of the Holy Cross to redeem.

After all, of course, the conciliar revolutionaries have been attempting to peddle the Protestant and Judeo-Masonic *Novus Ordo* liturgical service as a "liturgical renewal" when it is nothing other than a wholesale overthrow of the Roman Rite of the Catholic Church in favor of the errors of conciiarism and its "reconciliation" with the principles of Modernity.

Second, there is no such thing as a "conservative" or a "progressive" Catholic. Such are the misapplication of the labels used to identify the false opposites of naturalism to the realm of the Holy Faith, where one and all are bound to be united to everything contained in the Sacred Deposit of Faith without any reservation and qualification whatsoever, admitting that, as Pope Leo XIII tried to address in *Au Milieu Sollicitudes*, February 16, 1892, Catholics might and do disagree at times over the application of the principles of Holy Mother Church's Social Teaching in concrete circumstances.

As pertains to the doctrine of the Holy Faith, we are simply Catholic, nothing else.

Pope Leo XIII made this very clear in *Satis Cognitum*, June 29, 1896:

> **Agreement and union of minds is the necessary foundation of this perfect concord amongst men, from which concurrence of wills and similarity of action are the natural results**. Wherefore, in His divine wisdom, He ordained in His Church Unity of Faith; a virtue which is the first of those bonds which unite man to God, and whence we receive the name of the faithful – "one Lord, one faith, one baptism" (Eph. iv., 5). That is, as there is one Lord and one baptism, so should all Christians, without exception, have but one faith. And so the Apostle **St. Paul not merely begs, but entreats and implores Christians**

> **to be all of the same mind, and to avoid difference of opinions: "I beseech you, brethren, by the name of our Lord Jesus Christ, that you all speak the same thing, and that there be no schisms amongst you, and that you be perfect in the same mind and in the same judgment**" (I Cor. i., 10). ***Such passages certainly need no interpreter; they speak clearly enough for themselves.*** Besides, all who profess Christianity allow that there can be but one faith. **It is of the greatest importance and indeed of absolute necessity, as to which many are deceived, that the nature and character of this unity should be recognized. And, as We have already stated, this is not to be ascertained by conjecture, but by the certain knowledge of what was done; that is by seeking for and ascertaining what kind of unity in faith has been commanded by Jesus Christ.** (Pope Leo XIII, *Satis Cognitum*, June 29, 1896.)

To speak in terms of "conservative" and "progressive" Catholics is to divide that which is indivisible, the Mystical Body of Christ that is the Catholic Church. The divisions that exist between Catholics in the past fifty years have been caused by conciliarism, not by the Holy Faith.

The expression of the Catholic Faith is meant to be clear, not foggy. The expression of the dogmas of the Catholic Faith is precise, not ambiguous or subject to a variety of different interpretations. While it is certainly the case that many theological questions (such as the coexistence of God's Divine foreknowledge of human events with human free will, a matter that divided the Thomists and the Dun Scotists and is still a matter of active debate among orthodox Catholic theologians) are subject to legitimate interpretations and explanations, the dogmas of the Faith are meant to be grasped clearly by the human mind and accepted on the authority of the One Who has revealed them and caused them to be expressed in precise terms by legitimate popes and councils of the Catholic Church. While it is certainly true that the application of certain theological principles in concrete circumstances can be fraught with subjective considerations and other difficulties of the practical order, solemnly defined dogmatic truths demand the assent of the mind and the will without any degree of dissent or deviation whatsoever.

The Scholasticism of Saint Thomas Aquinas has been a major protection against the imprecise expression of the doctrines of the Church and a sure guide to their definitive explication. One true pope after another has recognized this to be the case. Pope Saint Pius X did so in a tribute to Saint Thomas Aquinas, *Doctoris Angelici*:

> For just as the opinion of certain ancients is to be rejected which maintains that it makes no difference to the truth of the Faith what any man thinks about the nature of creation, provided his opinions on the nature of God be sound, because error with regard to the nature of creation begets a false knowledge of God; **so the principles of philosophy laid down by St. Thomas Aquinas are to be religiously and inviolably observed, because they are the means of acquiring such a knowledge of creation as is most congruent with the Faith; of refuting all the errors of all the ages, and of enabling man to distinguish clearly what things are to be attributed to God and to God alone**....
>
> St. Thomas perfected and augmented still further by the almost angelic quality of his intellect all this superb patrimony of wisdom which he inherited from his predecessors and

> applied it to prepare, illustrate and protect sacred doctrine in the minds of men. **Sound reason suggests that it would be foolish to neglect it and religion will not suffer it to be in any way attenuated. And rightly, because, if Catholic doctrine is once deprived of this strong bulwark, it is useless to seek the slightest assistance for its defense in a philosophy whose principles are either common to the errors of materialism, monism, pantheism, socialism and modernism, or certainly not opposed to such systems. The reason is that the capital theses in the philosophy of St Thomas are not to be placed in the category of opinions capable of being debated one way or another, but are to be considered as the foundations upon which the science of natural and divine things is based; if such principles are once removed or in any way impaired, it must necessarily follow that students of the sacred sciences will ultimately fail to perceive so much as the meaning of the words in which the dogmas of divine revelation are proposed by the magistracy of the Church. . . .** (Pope Saint Pius X, *Doctoris Angelici*, quoted in James Larson's **Article 11: A Confusion of Loves**.)

This is why it is so important for the conciliar revolutionaries to have made war upon the Scholasticism of Saint Thomas Aquinas and to have recourse to "meeting the people where they are" that is nothing other than a descent into sentimentality and emotionalism in order to tickle the itching ears of unrepentant sinners. Those who get in the way of theological "renewal" are said to be without "mercy" or "love" even though it is they, believing Catholics, who are showing forth their true love of God as He has revealed Himself to us through His true Church and for souls by refusing to make any concessions to the errors and the diabolical agenda of the conciliar revolutionaries.

Having extolled the possible role of public opinion in the "development" of the *sensus fidei,* the apostates who wrote ***Sensus fidei* in the life of the Church**, attempted once again to prove that the two are not the same thing explaining the "proper" role of public opinion in the life of their false church.

Got all that?

It *is* fatiguing.

Why delay?

Be fatigued:

> 118. It is clear that there can be no simple identification between the *sensus fidei* and public or majority opinion. These are by no means the same thing.
>
> i) First of all, the *sensus fidei* is obviously related to faith, and faith is a gift not necessarily possessed by all people, so the *sensus fidei* can certainly not be likened to public opinion in society at large. Then also, while Christian faith is, of course, the primary factor uniting members of the Church, many different influences combine to shape the views of Christians living in the modern world. As the above discussion of dispositions implicitly shows, the *sensus fidei* cannot simply be identified, therefore, with public or majority

> opinion in the Church, either. Faith, not opinion, is the necessary focus of attention. **Opinion is often just an expression, frequently changeable and transient, of the mood or desires of a certain group or culture, whereas faith is the echo of the one Gospel which is valid for all places and times**. (*Sensus fidei* in the life of the Church.)

Quick Comment:

There has been nothing more changeable and transient than the ever-changing doctrines, liturgies and pastoral practices of the counterfeit church of conciliarism, which is degenerating to the point of self-caricature.

Back to those who specializing in giving believing Catholics a case of exhaustion (hey, I get a little funny when I am tired):

> ii) In the history of the people of God, it has often been not the majority but rather a minority which has truly lived and witnessed to the faith. The Old Testament knew the 'holy remnant' of believers, sometimes very few in number, over against the kings and priests and most of the Israelites. Christianity itself started as a small minority, **blamed and persecuted by public authorities. In the history of the Church, evangelical movements such as the Franciscans and Dominicans, or later the Jesuits, started as small groups treated with suspicion by various bishops and theologians**. In many countries today, Christians are under strong pressure from other religions or secular ideologies to neglect the truth of faith and weaken the boundaries of ecclesial community. It is therefore particularly important to discern and listen to the voices of the 'little ones who believe' (Mk 9:42). (*Sensus fidei* in the life of the Church.)

Another Quick Comment or Two:

First, curious, is it not, that the authors of do not name that among the "public authorities" who persecuted Catholics in Holy Mother Church's infancy were the Jews. They did so with great fury prior to the chastisement that Christ the King visited upon them in 70 A.D. as he used the pagan Romans to punish them for their unbelief as they were dispersed into the quarters of the known world.

Second, the Franciscans, Dominicans and Jesuits may have been viewed with suspicions by many at first. Each, however, received the favor of true Successors of Saint Peter. Pope Innocent III was particularly solicitous of the Franciscans and the Dominicans as he knew that their respective founders, Saint Francis of Assisi and Saint Dominic de Guzman, were true sons of Holy Mother Church. The Jesuits, for their part, were meant by Saint Ignatius of Loyola to be the Pope's Army in defense of the Holy Faith.

The "lay movements" spawned by conciliarism may have had the favor of the conciliar "popes" and the approval of a large number of the "bishops." Each of these "movements," however, have enjoyed the favor of the conciliar "popes" precisely because their religious sentiments are those of conciliarism, not Catholicism. Moreover, Jorge Mario Bergoglio, despite his recent meeting with a delegation from the Franciscan Friars of the Immaculate, has authorized a major warfare upon them because they have held to a great deal of the Catholic Faith, including the devotion that large numbers of them have for the modernized version of the Immemorial Mass of Tradition that is "approved" for use under the Motu proprio of Joseph Ratzinger/Benedict XVI, *Summorum Pontificum*, July 7, 2007.

Although very tired by this all, there are eight more sections of this bilge to plow through before connecting this all to the agenda of the new ***Instrumentum Laboris*** in part three:

> 119. It is undoubtedly necessary to distinguish between the *sensus fidei* and public or majority opinion, hence the need to identify dispositions necessary for participation in the *sensus fidei*, such as those elaborated above. Nevertheless, it is the whole people of God which, in its inner unity, confesses and lives the true faith. **The magisterium and theology must work constantly to renew the presentation of the faith in different situations, confronting if necessary dominant notions of Christian truth with the actual truth of the Gospel, but it must be recalled that the experience of the Church shows that sometimes the truth of the faith has been conserved not by the efforts of theologians or the teaching of the majority of bishops but in the hearts of believers.** (***Sensus fidei* in the life of the Church.**)

Pointed Comment:

There's that word "renew" again as the suggestion is made "to renew the presentation of the faith in different situations, confronting dominant notions of Christian truth with the actual truth of the Gospel." In other words, the apostates are saying that it is necessary to rethink the "message" as "dominant notions of Christian truth" held by some stuffy theologians yield to the "hearts of believers." This means that there can be a conflict between "dominant notions of Christian truth" and the "actual truth of Gospel, meaning the "actual truth" has been obscured by Holy Mother Church's true popes and true councils and those of her Fathers and Doctors whose writings "corrupted" this "actual truth." There is a word for this: Gnosticism.

Actually, of course, the Third Person of the Most Blessed Trinity, God the Holy Ghost, has conserved the teaching of the Catholic Church, which never changes her manner of speaking:

> [The Ancient Doctors] **knew the capacity of innovators in the art of deception. In order not to shock the ears of Catholics, they sought to hide the subtleties of their tortuous maneuvers by the use of seemingly innocuous words such as would allow them to insinuate error into souls in the most gentle manner. Once the truth had been compromised, they could, by means of slight changes or additions in phraseology, distort the confession of the faith which is necessary for our salvation, and lead the faithful by subtle errors to their eternal damnation. This manner of dissimulating and lying is vicious, regardless of the circumstances under which it is used. For very good reasons it can never be tolerated in a synod of which the principal glory consists above all in teaching the truth with clarity and excluding all danger of error.**

"Moreover, if all this is sinful, it cannot be excused in the way that one sees it being done, **under the erroneous pretext that the seemingly shocking affirmations in one place are further developed along orthodox lines in other places, and even in yet other places corrected; as if allowing for the possibility of either affirming or denying the statement, or of leaving it up the personal inclinations of the individual – such has always been the fraudulent and daring method used by innovators to establish error. It allows for both the possibility of promoting error and of excusing it.**

"**It is as if the innovators pretended that they always intended to present the alternative passages, especially to those of simple faith who eventually come to know only some part of the conclusions of such discussions which are published in the common language for everyone's use. Or again, as if the same faithful had the ability on examining such documents to judge such matters for themselves without getting confused and avoiding all risk of error. It is a most reprehensible technique for the insinuation of doctrinal errors and one condemned long ago by our predecessor Saint Celestine who found it used in the writings of Nestorius, Bishop of Constantinople, and which he exposed in order to condemn it with the greatest possible severity. Once these texts were examined carefully, the impostor was exposed and confounded, for he expressed himself in a plethora of words, mixing true things with others that were obscure; mixing at times one with the other in such a way that he was also able to confess those things which were denied while at the same time possessing a basis for denying those very sentences which he confessed.**

"In order to expose such snares, something which becomes necessary with a certain frequency in every century, no other method is required than the following: **Whenever it becomes necessary to expose statements which disguise some suspected error or danger under the veil of ambiguity, one must denounce the perverse meaning under which the error opposed to Catholic truth is camouflaged.**" (Pope Pius VI, *Auctorem Fidei*, August 28, 1794.)

These firings, therefore, with all diligence and care having been formulated by us, **we define that it be permitted to no one to bring forward, or to write, or to compose, or to think, or to teach a different faith. Whosoever shall presume to compose a different faith, or to propose, or teach, or hand to those wishing to be converted to the knowledge of the truth, from the Gentiles or Jews, or from any heresy, any different Creed; or to introduce a new voice or invention of speech to subvert these things which now have been determined by us, all these, if they be Bishops or clerics let them be deposed, the Bishops from the Episcopate, the clerics from the clergy; but if they be monks or laymen: let them be anathematized.** (**Constantinople III**).

These and many other serious things, which at present would take too long to list, but which you know well, cause Our intense grief. It is not enough for Us to deplore these innumerable evils **unless We strive to uproot them**. We take refuge in your faith and call upon your concern for the salvation of the Catholic flock. Your singular prudence and diligent spirit give Us courage and console Us, afflicted as We are with so many trials. We must raise Our voice and attempt all things lest a wild boar from the woods should destroy the vineyard or wolves kill the flock. **It is Our duty to lead the flock only to the food which is healthful. In these evil and dangerous times, the shepherds must never neglect their duty; they must never be so overcome by fear that they abandon the sheep**. Let them never neglect the flock and become sluggish from idleness and apathy. Therefore, united in spirit, let us promote our common cause, or more truly the cause of God; let our vigilance be one and our effort united against the common enemies.

Indeed you will accomplish this perfectly if, as the duty of your office demands, you attend to yourselves and to doctrine and meditate on these words: **"the universal Church is affected by any and every novelty" and the admonition of Pope Agatho: "nothing of the things appointed ought to be diminished; nothing changed; nothing added; but they must be preserved both as regards expression and meaning." Therefore may the unity which is built upon the See of Peter as on a sure foundation stand firm. May it be for all a wall and a security, a safe port, and a treasury of countless blessings.** To check the audacity of those who attempt to infringe upon the rights of this Holy See or to sever the union of the churches with the See of Peter, instill in your people a zealous confidence in the papacy and sincere veneration for it. As St. Cyprian wrote: "He who abandons the See of Peter on which the Church was founded, falsely believes himself to be a part of the Church . . . .

But for the other painful causes We are concerned about, you should recall that certain societies and assemblages seem to draw up a battle line together with the followers of every false religion and cult. **They feign piety for religion; but they are driven by a passion for promoting *novelties* and sedition everywhere. They preach liberty of every sort; they stir up disturbances in sacred and civil affairs, and pluck authority to pieces.** (Pope Gregory XVI, *Mirari Vos*, August 15, 1832.)

Would that they had but displayed less zeal and energy in propagating it! But such is their activity and such their unwearying labor on behalf of their cause, that one cannot but be pained to see them waste such energy in endeavoring to ruin the Church when they might have been of such service to her had their efforts been better directed. **Their artifices to delude men's minds are of two kinds, the first to remove obstacles from their path, the second to devise and apply actively and patiently every resource that can serve their purpose**. They recognize that the three chief difficulties which stand in their way are the scholastic method of philosophy, the authority and tradition of the Fathers, and the magisterium of the Church, and on these they wage unrelenting war. Against scholastic philosophy and theology they use the weapons of ridicule and contempt. Whether it is ignorance or fear, or both, that inspires this conduct in them, certain it is that the passion for novelty is always united in them with hatred of scholasticism, and there is no surer sign that a man is tending to Modernism than when he begins to show his dislike for the scholastic method. Let the Modernists and their admirers remember the proposition condemned by Pius IX: "The method and principles which have served the ancient doctors of scholasticism when treating of theology no longer correspond with the exigencies of our time or the progress of science." **They exercise all their ingenuity in an effort to weaken the force and falsify the character of tradition, so as to rob it of all its weight and authority. But for Catholics nothing will remove the authority of the second Council**

> **of Nicea, where it condemns those "*who dare, after the impious fashion of heretics, to deride the ecclesiastical traditions, to invent novelties of some kind...or endeavor by malice or craft to overthrow any one of the legitimate traditions of the Catholic Church*";** nor that of the declaration of the fourth Council of Constantinople: "**We therefore profess to preserve and guard the rules bequeathed to the Holy Catholic and Apostolic Church, by the Holy and most illustrious Apostles, by the orthodox Councils, both general and local, and by everyone of those divine interpreters, the Fathers and Doctors of the Church**." Wherefore the Roman Pontiffs, Pius IV and Pius IX, ordered the insertion in the profession of faith of the following declaration: "**I most firmly admit and embrace the apostolic and ecclesiastical traditions and other observances and constitutions of the Church**." (Pope Saint Pius X, *Pascendi Dominici Gregis*, September 8, 1907.)

There is a special irony, however, found in Paragraph 119 of *Sensus Fidei in the Life of the Church* as the true Catholic Faith today is found in the hearts of believing Catholics in the underground, not in the structures of the counterfeit church of conciliarism.

Back to the brutal apostates and their tortuous schemes:

> c) Ways of consulting the faithful
>
> 120. There is a genuine equality of dignity among all the faithful, because through their baptism they are all reborn in Christ. 'Because of this equality they all contribute, each according to his or her own condition and office, to the building up of the Body of Christ.'[133] **Therefore, all the faithful 'have the right, indeed at times the duty, in keeping with their knowledge, competence and position, to manifest to the sacred Pastors their views on matters which concern the good of the Church'. 'They have the right to make their views known to others of Christ's faithful, but in doing so they must always respect the integrity of faith and morals, show due reference to the Pastors and take into account both the common good and the dignity of individuals.'**[134] Accordingly, the faithful, and specifically the lay people, should be treated by the Church's pastors with respect and consideration, and consulted in an appropriate way for the good of the Church. (*Sensus fidei* in the life of the Church.)
>
> 121. The word 'consult' includes the idea of seeking a judgment or advice as well as inquiring into a matter of fact. **On the one hand, in matters of governance and pastoral issues, the pastors of the Church can and should consult the faithful in certain cases in the sense of asking for their advice or their judgment. On the other hand, when the magisterium is defining a doctrine, it is appropriate to consult the faithful in the sense of inquiring into a matter of fact, 'because the body of the faithful is one of the witnesses to the fact of the tradition of revealed doctrine, and because their consensus through Christendom is the voice of the Infallible Church'**.[135] (*Sensus fidei* in the life of the Church.)

A Comment that will require a moment or two of your time:

Insofar as instances of pastoral abuse or immoral conduct or heterodox teaching heard from the pulpit or taught in a school, then, yes, of course, the faithful have a right and duty to make their concerns known privately, although there might be occasions when serious abuse might have to be rebuked publicly according to the teaching of Saint Thomas Aquinas on the matter if all private entreaties fail to rectify the abuse.

Begging a thousand pardons here, but how respectful have the conciliar authorities been to members of the laity who brought instances of grave clerical immorality to the attention of their "bishops" and various chancery factotums? In most cases, of course, the members of the laity–not a few members of the conciliar clergy, have been treated with contempt as they were browbeaten, intimidated by diocesan attorneys or attorneys for the diocese's insurance companies and castigated for daring to call abuse by its proper name.

The only recourse that victims of clerical immorality had was to threaten or to actually file lawsuits and to take matters into the public domain, whereupon the conciliar officials, at least at first, castigated them all over again and engaged in all manner of delaying tactics that were designed to keep their protection of the sodomites that they had recruited and promoted completely under wraps as though it was but the figments of the imaginations of "gold-digging" Catholics. I suggest that those who have any doubt about this fact should consider the massive amount of documented evidence that Mrs. Randy Engel amassed in ***The Rite of Sodomy***. Remember, "Monsignor" Batista Ricca is *still* the head of the Vatican Institute for Religious Works (the Vatican Bank) despite his own proven perversity.

Begging yet another thousand pardons, but how respectful have the conciliar authorities in many places shown themselves to believing Catholics who have complained about "liturgical abuses" and aberrant teachings and practices that they know are abhorrent to the Most Blessed Trinity and harmful to souls and to the common good as well? These Catholics have also been treated with great cruelty, especially by the first generation of Catholic revolutionaries appointed by Paul the Sick and promoted by "Saint John Paul II," men whose apostate minds believe and lips spoke exactly as Jorge Mario Bergoglio has been doing since his masquerade of as "Pope Francis" began on Wednesday, March 13, 2013.

Yes, yes, yes, power to the "people" with the little exception of those who are considered not part of the "people" by the lords of the conciliar revolution. There is no "consultation" with believing Catholics, only castigation, scorn, mockery and ridicule from the lips of Jorge Mario Bergoglio, who is always inveighing against "judging others," at the Casa Santa Marta.

Talk about hypocrisy, Jorge.

As to the teaching of Faith and Morals and the discipline meted out by Holy Mother Church, however, the faithful have only to be concerned about following the teaching of Pope Leo XIII, contained in *Sapientiae Christianae*, January 10, 1890, to be living echoes of their shepherds, warding off error, imagine that, as much as it is within their power, ability and competence to do:

> No one, however, must entertain the notion that private individuals are prevented from taking some active part in this duty of teaching, especially those on whom God has

> bestowed gifts of mind with the strong wish of rendering themselves useful. **These, so often as circumstances demand, may take upon themselves, not, indeed, the office of the pastor, but the task of communicating to others what they have themselves received, becoming, as it were, living echoes of their masters in the faith. Such co-operation on the part of the laity has seemed to the Fathers of the Vatican Council so opportune and fruitful of good that they thought well to invite it. "All faithful Christians, but those chiefly who are in a prominent position, or engaged in teaching, we entreat, by the compassion of Jesus Christ, and enjoin by the authority of the same God and Savior, that they bring aid to ward off and eliminate these errors from holy Church, and contribute their zealous help in spreading abroad the light of undefiled faith." Let each one, therefore, bear in mind that he both can and should, so far as may be, preach the Catholic faith by the authority of his example, and by open and constant profession of the obligations it imposes. In respect, consequently, to the duties that bind us to God and the Church, it should be borne earnestly in mind that in propagating Christian truth and warding off errors the zeal of the laity should, as far as possible, be brought actively into play.**
>
> The faithful would not, however, so completely and advantageously satisfy these duties as is fitting they should were they to enter the field as isolated champions of the faith. Jesus Christ, indeed, has clearly intimated that the hostility and hatred of men, which He first and foremost experienced, would be shown in like degree toward the work founded by Him, so that many would be barred from profiting by the salvation for which all are indebted to His loving kindness. **Wherefore, He willed not only to train disciples in His doctrine, but to unite them into one society, and closely conjoin them in one body, "which is the Church," whereof He would be the head. The life of Jesus Christ pervades, therefore, the entire framework of this body, cherishes and nourishes its every member, uniting each with each, and making all work together to the same end, albeit the action of each be not the same. Hence it follows that not only is the Church a perfect society far excelling every other, but it is enjoined by her Founder that for the salvation of mankind she is to contend "as an army drawn up in battle array." The organization and constitution of Christian society can in no wise be changed, neither can any one of its members live as he may choose, nor elect that mode of fighting which best pleases him. For, in effect, he scatters and gathers not who gathers not with the Church and with Jesus Christ, and all who fight not jointly with him and with the Church are in very truth contending against God.** (Pope Leo XIII, *Sapientiae Christianae*, January 10, 1890.)

A final comment on Paragraphs 120 and 121, which is also relevant to Paragraph 122 below, should be made for your thoughtful consideration.

How can Catholics in the conciliar stuctures today, having been fed a steady diet of heresy, apostasy and blasphemy and exposed to all manner of unspeakable sacrilege, serve as "**witnesses to the fact of the tradition of revealed doctrine**" when they have been taught to revile that tradition and/or are entirely ignorant of it?

To the next two paragraphs of *Sensus Fidei in the Life of the Church*:

> 122. The practice of consulting the faithful is not new in the life of the Church. In the medieval Church a principle of Roman law was used: *Quod omnes tangit, ab omnibus tractari et approbari debet* (what affects everyone, should be discussed and approved by all). In the three domains of the life of the Church (faith, sacraments, governance), 'tradition combined a hierarchical structure with a concrete regime of association and agreement', and this was considered to be an 'apostolic practice' or an 'apostolic tradition'.[136] (***Sensus fidei* in the life of the Church.**)

> 123. Problems arise when the majority of the faithful remain indifferent to doctrinal or moral decisions taken by the magisterium or when they positively reject them. This lack of reception may indicate a weakness or a lack of faith on the part of the people of God, caused by an insufficiently critical embrace of contemporary culture. **But in some cases it may indicate that certain decisions have been taken by those in authority without due consideration of the experience and the *sensus fidei* of the faithful, or without sufficient consultation of the faithful by the magisterium.**[137] (***Sensus fidei* in the life of the Church.**)

A Mercifully Short Observation:

What was noted above is apropos yet again concerning the inability of most Catholics in the conciliar structures to serve as "witnesses" to anything other than the false "traditions" of the false conciliar religion.

It is, though, in Paragraph 123 that the framework is being established for the acceptance of "same-sex couples" and public fornicators, adulterers, mutants (transvestites) and other unrepentant sinners as outlined in not-so-subtle terms in the *Instrumentum Laboris* issued in preparation for Jorge's embrace of "pastoral outreach" to those who find themselves in the "existential peripheries" that are called in the world "alternative living arrangements" that really are ancient paths to personal and social ruin and to Hell itself.

Moreover, to say that "**that certain decisions have been taken by those in authority without due consideration of the experience and the *sensus fidei* of the faithful, or without sufficient consultation of the faithful by the magisterium**" is to blaspheme the Third Person of the Most Blessed Trinity, God the Holy Ghost, Who has always guided the magisterium infallibly. It is to exalt the role of the "people"–and a people who are misinformed about the true teachings of the Catholic Church–even while contending that "public opinion" is not the same as the *sensus fidei.*

Hubris writ large.

To the final three sections of ***Sensus fidei* in the life of the Church** that will be reviewed for present purposes and for the sanity of the readers and of this writer himself (obviously, what, if any, I ever had to begin with):

> 124. **It is only natural that there should be a constant communication and regular dialogue on practical issues and matters of faith and morals between members of the Church. *Public opinion is an important form of that communication in the Church.***

> **'Since the Church is a living body, she needs** ***public opinion in order to sustain a giving and taking between her members. Without this, she cannot advance in thought and action.'[138] This endorsement of a public exchange of thought and opinions in the Church was given soon after Vatican II, precisely on the basis of the council's teaching on the sensus fidei and on Christian love, and the faithful were strongly encouraged to take an active part in that public exchange. 'Catholics should be fully aware of the real freedom to speak their minds which stems from a "feeling for the faith" [i.e. the sensus fidei] and from love***. It stems from that feeling for the faith which is aroused and nourished by the spirit of truth in order that, under the guidance of the teaching Church which they accept with reverence, the People of God may cling unswervingly to the faith given to the early Church, with true judgement penetrate its meaning more deeply, and apply it more fully in their lives [*Lumen Gentium*, 12]. This freedom also stems from love. For it is with love that ... the People of God are raised to an intimate sharing in the freedom of Christ Himself, who cleansed us from our sins, in order that we might be able freely to make judgements in accordance with the will of God. Those who exercise authority in the Church will take care to ensure that there is responsible exchange of freely held and expressed opinion among the People of God. More than this, they will set up norms and conditions for this to take place.'[139] (***Sensus fidei*** **in the life of the Church.**)

Hermeneutic of Self-Contradiction Comment:

Who wrote this?

Georg Wilhelm Friedrich Hegel?

Someone on the drafting committee that produced *Sensus Fidei in the Life of the Church* wrote the following in Paragraph 118:

> First of all, the *sensus fidei* is obviously related to faith, and faith is a gift not necessarily possessed by all people, so the *sensus fidei* can certainly not be likened to public opinion in society at large. (***Sensus fidei*** **in the life of the Church.**)

Did that same person draft the following words in Paragraph 124 above?

> ***Public opinion is an important form of that communication in the Church.*** **'Since the Church is a living body, she needs** ***public opinion in order to sustain a giving and taking between her members. Without this, she cannot advance in thought and action. (Sensus fidei in the life of the Church.)***

Which is it?

Well, I suppose that we just are supposed to forget Aristotle's principle of non-contradiction. That went out the conciliar window with the Scholasticism of Saint Thomas Aquinas.

As to what is thought to be the Catholic Church's "advancing" in "thought and action," there is need only to have recourse to Pope Saint Pius X:

It remains for Us now to say a few words about the Modernist as reformer. **From all that has preceded, it is abundantly clear how great and how eager is the passion of such men for innovation. In all Catholicism there is absolutely nothing on which it does not fasten. They wish philosophy to be reformed, especially in the ecclesiastical seminaries. They wish the scholastic philosophy to be relegated to the history of philosophy and to be classed among absolute systems, and the young men to be taught modern philosophy which alone is true and suited to the times in which we live**. They desire the reform of theology: rational theology is to have modern philosophy for its foundation, and positive theology is to be founded on the history of dogma. As for history, it must be written and taught only according to their methods and modern principles. **Dogmas and their evolution, they affirm, are to be harmonized with science and history. In the Catechism no dogmas are to be inserted except those that have been reformed and are within the capacity of the people**. (Pope Saint Pius X, *Pascendi Dominci Gregis*, September 8, 1907.)

Those who do not see by now that the conciliar ecclesiology of "power to the people" is false and can never come from any instrumentality of the Catholic Church, no matter how "unofficial" it is alleged to be, do not want to make the sacrifices of human respect necessary to do so. I mean, Paragraph 124 admits that the conciliar concept of "public opinion" as part of the "normal" processes of what they allege to be the Catholic Church was unknown until after the "Second" Vatican Council. So much for "rooted in tradition."

Ah, I digressed, as I meant to cover three paragraphs at once. Paragraph 124, however, cried out for individualized attention.

Now, at long last, to the final two paragraphs of this "unofficial" "official" document before connecting to the *Instrumentum Laboris* for Jorge's Oktoberfest on the Tiber that has set the stage of a "final" product in 2015:

125. Such public exchange of opinion is a prime means by which, in a normal way, the *sensus fidelium* can be gauged. Since the Second Vatican Council, however, various institutional instruments by which the faithful may more formally be heard and consulted have been established, such as particular councils, to which priests and others of Christ's faithful may be invited,[140] diocesan synods, to which the diocesan bishop may also invite lay people as members,[141] the pastoral council of each diocese, which is 'composed of members of Christ's faithful who are in full communion with the Catholic Church: clerics, members of institutes of consecrated life, and especially lay people',[142] and pastoral councils in parishes, in which 'Christ's faithful, together with those who by virtue of their office are engaged in pastoral care in the parish, give their help in fostering pastoral action'.[143]

126. Structures of consultation such as those mentioned above can be greatly beneficial to the Church, **but only if pastors and lay people are mutually respectful of one another's charisms and if they carefully and continually listen to one another's experiences and concerns. Humble listening at all levels and proper consultation of those concerned**

are integral aspects of a living and lively Church. ([*Sensus fidei* in the life of the Church.]())

Final Commentary on This Particular Madness Before Drawing Matters to a Conclusion:

Endless committees doing endless things to destroy the actual *sensus Catholicus*. These revolutionaries and their committees and "consultations," albeit with the theologically and liturgically and morally "correct" kind of conciliar Catholics, have been very successful in helping to brainwash the average Catholic into looking at the actual teaching of Holy Mother Church with scorn and disdain. The result has been a new sense for a new faith, one that is as loathsome in the sight of the true God of Divine Revelation, the Most Blessed Trinity, as every other false religion.

Where is this all leading?

I will let the ***Instrumentum Laboris*** explain it all to you:

> 31. The family is acknowledged in the People of God to be an invaluable asset, the natural setting in which life grows and develops and a school of humanity, love and hope for society. The family continues to be the privileged place in which Christ reveals the mystery and vocation of the person. In addition to commonly affirming these basic facts, the great majority of respondents agree that the family has the potential of being this privileged place, **despite their indicating, and often explicitly recounting, the worrisome difference between the forms of the family in today's world and Church's teaching in this regard. Real-life situations, stories and multiple trials demonstrate that the family is experiencing very difficult times, requiring the Church's compassion and understanding in offering guidance to families "as they are" and, from this point of departure, proclaim the Gospel of the Family in response to their specific needs**. (***Instrumentum Laboris***.)

Saint Anthony Mary Claret found families in irregular situations in Cuba in the Nineteenth Century, meeting them "where they were" to bring them out of lives of sin so that those involved therein could save their immortal souls as members of the Catholic Church:

> Here he was met by disturbing news. In this town of pilgrimage [Cobre] where the island's most famous shrine was located, his missionaries had found hardly a dozen legitimately married couples! He praised their diligence in having substantially raised this figure prior to his arrival but–even so! This shocking situation required a strong hand–the hand of a patient but uncompromising prelate. The unhappy fact was that the Spanish-descended Cubans rarely condescended to marry their Negro and mulatto concubines, even when their half-caste progeny might number as many as nine or ten. Rightly suspecting that this intolerable state of affairs might prove typical, he attacked the problem vigorously. A committee was appointed to study each case individually. On its recommendations, he let it be known, all such unions must be regularized or, where impediments existed, dissolved!
>
> It was a most trying undertaking, fraught with complications, both tragic and absurd. Persons who expressed their willingness, even eagerness, to legalize their unions were

> frequently not free to receive the Sacrament of marriage. Others, without the excuse of impediments under Church law were sometimes overcome with indignation to hear that they were expected to make wives of their colored concubines. There were emphatic affirmations that Spain prohibited mixed marriages, a fallacy the archbishop had no need to consider. In all her colonial history Spain had never forced any such regulation. However, for any who persisted in this persuasion in spite of Padre Claret's assurances, his command was clear. They must immediately terminate their illicit unions. It would be a painful problem–the provision for their innocent children–but it would have to be faced. Although he praised God that many of these easy-going folk accepted their prelate's reprimands contritely and docilely obeyed his injunctions to amend their lives, Cobre had certainly given him a first-hand acquaintance with the repugnant moral deterioration that had engulfed a traditionally Christian nation. (Fanchon Royer, *The Life of St. Anthony Mary Claret*, published originally by Farrar, Straus and Cudahy in 1957 and republished in 1985 by TAN Books and Publishers, pp. 130-131.)

Countless are the examples of Catholic bishops and priests, many of them raised to the altars of Holy Mother Church, who worked to reform the morals of the people who had been entrusted to their pastoral care.

Another Spaniard, Saint Francis Solano, for example, preached a sermon in the public square in Lima, Peru, in 1610 during which he prophesied of the great earthquake that God would visit upon Lima to chastise the people there for their ingratitude and immorality:

> By the time Francis had reached the market, the theme of his sermon was clear. God was love, yet man was constantly thwarting that love. Many times this was because of thoughtlessness, but there were also countless times when it was because of sheer selfishness, and even malice. Well, atonement for sin must be made by means of penance.
>
> "Unless you do penance, you shall likewise perish," Our Lord had said to his disciples.
>
> "I will say these words, too," Francis thought. "Oh, Heavenly Father, may they help some souls tonight to turn away from sin!"
>
> Naturally many at the market were astonished when they saw the Father Guardian of Saint Mary of the Angels making his way through their midst. Since his return from Trujillo he had appeared in the streets only rarely, and certainly never in the evenings. Then in a little while there was even more astonishment. Father Francis had come not to buy for his friars, or even to beg. He had come to preach!
>
> At first, however, since business was brisk, not much heed was paid to his words. Merchants vied with one another in calling out the merits of their wares while customers argued noisily for a lower price. Beggars whined for alms. Babies cried. Dogs barked. Donkeys brayed. Older children ran in and out of the crowd intent upon their games. Music was everywhere–weird tunes played by Indian musicians on their wooden flutes, gay Spanish rhythms played on guitar and tambourine. At the various food students succulent

rounds of meat sizzled and sputtered as they turned over slow fires. Then suddenly a thunderous voice rang about above the noisy and carefree scene:

"For all that is in the world is the concupiscence of the flesh, and the concupiscence of the eyes, and the pride of life, which is not of the Father but is in the world."

It was as though a bombshell had fallen. At once the hubbub died away, and hundreds of Lima's startled citizens turned to where a grey-clad friar, cross in hand, had mounted an elevation in the center of the marketplace and now stood gazing down upon them with eyes of burning coals. But before anyone could wonder about the text from Saint John's first epistle, Francis began to explain the meaning of concupiscence: that, because of Original Sin, it is the tendency within each person to do evil instead of good; that this hidden warfare will end only when we have drawn our last breath.

"If we were to die tonight, would good or evil be the victor within our hearts" he cried. "Oh, my friends! Think about this question. *Think hard*!

Within just a few minutes Lima's marketplace was as hushed and solemn as a cathedral. All eyes were riveted upon the Father Guardian and all ears were filled with his words as he described God's destruction of the ancient cities of Sodom and Gomorrha because of the sins committed within them.

"Who is to say that here in Lima we do not deserve a like fate?" he demanded in ringing tones. "Look into your hearts now, my children. Are they clean? Are they pure? Are they filled with love of God?"

As the minutes passed and twilight deepened into darkness, the giant torches of the marketplace cast their flickering radiance over a moving scene. As usual, crowds of people were on hand, but now no one was interested in buying or selling. Instead, faces were bewildered, agonized and fearful. Tears were streaming from many eyes as Francis' words continued to pour out in torrents, urging repentance while there was still time.

"Can we say that we shall ever see tomorrow?" he cried, fervently brandishing his missionary cross. "Can we say that this night is not the last we shall have in which to return to God's friendship?"

As these and still more terrifying thoughts struck home one after another, the speaker stretched out both arms, bowed his head, and in heartrending tones began the Fifth Psalm. At once the crowd was filled with fresh sorrow and made the contrite phrases their own:

"*Have mercy on me, O God, according to Thy great mercy.*

"And according to the multitude of Thy tender mercies, blot out my iniquity.

"Wash me yet more from my iniquity, and cleanse me from my sin.

"For I know my iniquity, and my sin is always before me.

"To Thee only have I sinned, and have done evil before Thee: that Thou mayest be justified in Thy words, and mayest overcome when Thou art judged . . ."

Soon wave upon wave of sound was filling the torch lit marketplace as priest and people prayed together. Then Francis preached again, doing his best to implant a greater sorrow for sin and an even firmer purpose of amendment in the hearts of his hearers. Finally, looking neither to right nor left, he prepared to depart for Saint Mary of the Angels. But on all sides men and women pressed about him, sobbing and begging for his blessing.

"Father, please pray for me!" cried one young girl. "I've deserved to go to Hell a thousand times!"

"Last year, I robbed a poor widow of ten pounds of gold!" declared a swarthy-faced Spaniard. "May God forgive me!"

"'I'm worse than anyone," moaned a wild-eyed black man. "Tonight, I was going to kill a man . . . *and for money*!"

So it was that first one, then another, cried out his fault and expressed a desire to go to Confession at once. But Francis had to refuse all such requests. Yes, he was a priest. It was his privilege and duty to administer the Sacraments. But he was also a religious, and bound by rule to various observances. One of them was that he must be in his cell at Saint Mary of the Angels by a certain hour each night.

"There are other priests in the city who can help you, though," he said kindly. "Go then now, my children. And may the Holy Virgin bring you back to her Son without delay." (Mary Fabyan Windeatt, *Saint Francis of Solano: Wonderworker of the New World and Apostle of Argentina and Peru*, published originally by Sheed and Ward in 1946 and republished by TAN Books and Publishers in 1994, pp. 167-172.)

This is just a slight contrast with the approach taken by Jorge Mario Bergoglio and his band of revolutionaries, who doubt the ability of the truths of the Divine Positive Law and the Natural Law, when preached with conviction for love of Christ the King and for the souls for whom He shed every single drop of His Most Precious Blood on the wood of the Holy Cross to redeem, to touch hearts and to reform lives in an instant.

Wait a minute!

The problem is more basic than that: Jorge Mario Bergoglio and his band of conciliar revolutionaries do not believe in the binding truths of the Divine Positive Law as they have been explicated by the Catholic Church from time immemorial and they scoff at the ability of the "people" to understand the Natural Law:

> 30. The language traditionally **used in explaining the term "natural law" should be improved so that the values of the Gospel can be communicated to people today in a more intelligible manner. In particular, the vast majority of responses and an even greater part of the observations request that more emphasis be placed on the role of the Word of God as a privileged instrument in the conception of married life and the family, and recommend greater reference to the Bible, its language and narratives. In this regard, respondents propose bringing the issue to public discussion and developing the idea of biblical inspiration and the "order in creation," which could permit a re-reading of the concept of the natural law in a more meaningful manner in today's world** (cf. the idea of the law written in the human heart in *Rm* 1:19-21; 2:14-15). Moreover, this proposal insists on using language which is accessible to all, such as the language of symbols utilized during the liturgy. The recommendation was also made to engage young people directly in these matters. (***Instrumentum Laboris***.)

Yes, They Go After the Natural Law Comment:

Nothing is beyond the reach of these revolutionaries. This makes sense, though, when you consider the fact that the lords of conciliarism have made short work of the binding precepts of the Ten Commandments, especially the First through Third Commandments, as a result of false ecumenism and inter-religious "prayer services" and by their words and actions praising the beliefs and esteeming the symbols of one false religion after another. Why not try to re-read the Natural Law, therefore?

A pagan, Cicero, had a very good, although not perfect, grasp of the Natural Law which he defined as follows in his Republic:

> True law is right reason conformable to nature, universal, unchangeable, eternal, whose commands urge us to duty, and whose prohibitions restrain us from evil. Whether it enjoins or forbids, the good respect its injunctions, and the wicked treat them with indifference. This law cannot be contradicted by any other law, and is not liable either to derogation or abrogation. Neither the senate nor the people can give us any dispensation for not obeying this universal law of justice. It needs no other expositor and interpreter than our own conscience. It is not one thing at Rome, and another at Athens; one thing to-day, and another to-morrow; but in all times and nations this universal law must forever reign, eternal and imperishable. It is the sovereign master and emperor of all beings. God himself is its author, its promulgator, its enforcer. And he who does not obey it flies from himself, and does violence to the very nature of man. And by so doing he will endure the severest penalties even if he avoid the other evils which are usually accounted punishments. (Cicero, *The Republic*.)

Cicero had it almost entirely correct. Almost. He was wrong in asserting that the natural law does not need any "other expositor and interpreter than our own conscience." He lived before the Incarnation and before the founding of the true Church upon the Rock of Peter, the Pope. Cicero thus did not know that man does need an interpreter and expositor of the natural law, namely, the Catholic Church. Apart from this, however, Cicero understood that God's law does not admit of abrogations by a vote of the people or of a "representative" body, such as the Roman Senate in his day or the United States Congress or state legislatures, et al. in our own day.

Pope Leo XIII explained in *Tametsi Futura Prospicientibus*, November 1, 1900, that the Catholic Church is the guardian of the Natural Law and that men need her guidance to hep them to know it fully and to keep it as befits redeemed creatures:

> Consequently Jesus Christ, the creator and preserver of faith, also preserves and nourishes our moral life. This He does chiefly by the ministry of His Church. To Her, in His wise and merciful counsel, He has entrusted certain agencies which engender the supernatural life, protect it, and revive it if it should fail. This generative and conservative power of the virtues that make for salvation is therefore lost, whenever morality is dissociated from divine faith. A system of morality based exclusively on human reason robs man of his highest dignity and lowers him from the supernatural to the merely natural life. Not but that man is able by the right use of reason to know and to obey certain principles of the natural law. But though he should know them all and keep them inviolate through life-and even this is impossible without the aid of the grace of our Redeemer-still it is vain for anyone without faith to promise himself eternal salvation. "If anyone abide not in Me, he shall be cast forth as a branch, and shall wither, and they shall gather him up and cast him into the fire, and he burneth" (John xv., 6). "He that believeth not shall be condemned" (Mark xvi., 16). We have but too much evidence of the value and result of a morality divorced from divine faith. How is it that, in spite of all the zeal for the welfare of the masses, nations are in such straits and even distress, and that the evil is daily on the increase? We are told that society is quite able to help itself; that it can flourish without the assistance of Christianity, and attain its end by its own unaided efforts. Public administrators prefer a purely secular system of government. **All traces of the religion of our forefathers are daily disappearing from political life and administration. What blindness! Once the idea of the authority of God as the Judge of right and wrong is forgotten, law must necessarily lose its primary authority and justice must perish: and these are the two most powerful and most necessary bonds of society. Similarly, once the hope and expectation of eternal happiness is taken away, temporal goods will be greedily sought after. Every man will strive to secure the largest share for himself. Hence arise envy, jealousy, hatred. The consequences are conspiracy, anarchy, nihilism. There is neither peace abroad nor security at home. Public life is stained with crime**. (Pope Leo XIII, *Tametsi Futura Prospicientibus*, November 1, 1900.)

Although much more time could be spent examining the *Instrumentum Laboris* in the detail that has been given to *Sensus Fidei in the Life of the Church*, there is really no need to do so as the results of the "extraordinary synod on the family" have been **cooked for a long time now**. The *Instrumentum Laboris* is the result of the answers to questions that were sent to the world's conciliar "bishops" in October of 2013 and were the subject of extensive commentary in **Always Asking All The Wrong Questions, part one** and **Always Asking All the Wrong Questions, part two**.

It is important to remember that Joseph Ratzinger/Benedict XVI helped to set the stage for the events that are unfolding before us at this time:

In like manner, those who want to live in a Manichean world have convinced themselves that a man who has long lived in a world of paradox and contradiction born of his rejection of Scholasticism in favor of Modernism's precept of the "evolution of dogma," Joseph Ratzinger/Benedict XVI, is a "defender" of the absolute indissolubility of a valid, ratified and consummated marriage. He is, of course, no such thing.

Ever the Hegelian, the then Father Joseph Ratzinger wrote a now-infamous article in 1972 that was mentioned favorably by Walter "Cardinal" Kasper in the address that he gave to the conciliar conclave of "cardinals" on Friday, February 21, 2014:

> **One notification was given to us by the congregation for the doctrine of the faith in 1994 when it established - and Pope Benedict XVI reiterated this during the world meeting of families in Milan in 2012 - that the divorce and remarried cannot receive sacramental communion but can receive spiritual communion.** [. . .]
>
> Many will be grateful for this response, which is an instance of true openness. But it also brings up a number of questions. In fact, someone who receives spiritual communion is one with Jesus Christ. [. . .] Why, then, can he not also receive sacramental communion? [. . .] Some maintain that non-participation in communion is itself a sign of the sanctity of the sacrament. The question that is posed in response is: is it not perhaps an exploitation of the person who is suffering and asking for help if we make him a sign and a warning for others? Are we going to let him die of hunger sacramentally in order that others may live?
>
> **The early Church gives us an indication that can serve as a means of escape from the dilemma, to which Professor Joseph Ratzinger referred in 1972. [. . .] In the individual local Churches there existed the customary law on the basis of which Christians who, although their first partner was still alive, were living in a second relationship, after a time of penance had available [. . .] not a second marriage, but rather through participation in communion a table of salvation.** [. . .] (**Kasper Uses Ratzinger Against Benedict**.)

Heretics can be very clever. Walter Kasper was attempting to use an article written by Father Joseph Ratzinger in 1972 against the work of Joseph "Cardinal" Ratzinger in 1994 and "Pope" Benedict XVI in 2012.

Ratzinger, however, is unfazed by little things such as intellectual consistency as his "hermeneutic of continuity" can be employed to justify whatever apparent contradictions in his work just as he has used this hermeneutic to dispense with "past" teachings that he believes have become "obsolete" in their "particulars."

In this instance, though, there is little "inconsistency" in the thought of Ratzinger/Benedict, such as it may be, as he, acting as "Cardinal" Ratzinger, issued a "clarification" on January 1, 1998, in response to his September 14, 1994, "notification" on the inadmissibility of divorced and civilly "remarried" Catholics for the reception of what purports to be "Holy Communion" in the Protestant and Judeo-Masonic *Novus Ordo* liturgical service. The 1998 "clarification" contained "true elements," which was republished in *L'Osservatore Romano* on November 30,

2011, borrowed heavily from a 1972 article of his that has been published recently, albeit with an entirely different conclusion than the one he had been offered originally, in a book of his collected works that is under the editorial supervision of that other great "defender" of the indissolubility of a ratified and consummated marriage, the heretic named Gerhard Ludwig Muller (see the post on this matter as found at **Novus Ordo Watch Wire**).

What has missed the eye of Vaticanologists thus far, however, is that the 1998 "clarification" of the 1994 "notification" was revolutionary in its own right as it both defended the ban of the divorced and civilly "remarried" Catholics from the sacraments and undermined that ban at the very same time. It was, in other words, pure, unadulterated Ratzinger.

Two excerpts from the January 1, 1998, "clarification" will be provided below.

The first excerpt demonstrates Ratzinger's pride in boasting of the overthrow of the primary end of marriage, the propagation and education of children, in favor of the personalist view of marriage that had been condemned by the Holy Office in 1944 and would serve as the basis of Giovanni Battista Enrico Antonio Maria Montini/Paul the Sick's *Humane Vitae*'s endorsement of "natural family planning" as a means to engage in "responsible parenthood" (see **Forty-Three Years After *Humanae Vitae***):

> Some theologians claim that at the new magisterial documents having to do with questions of marriage are based on a naturalistic, legalistic concept of marriage. Attention is given to the contract between the spouses and to the *ius in corpus.* It is claimed that the Council overturned this static understanding and described marriage in a more personalistic way as a covenant of love and life. Thus it would have opened up possibilities for resolving difficult situations more humanely. Thinking further along this line, some scholars pose the question of whether or not one could speak of the death of the marriage, if the personal bond of love between the spouses no longer exists. Others resurrect the old question of whether or not the Pope would have the capability of dissolving marriage in such cases.
>
> **Yet anyone who attentively reads the more recent statements of the Church will note that their central assertions are based on *Gaudium et spes* and that they further develop the teaching contained therein in a thoroughly personalist line, in the direction indicated by the Council**. However, it is inappropriate to set up a contradiction between the personalist and juridical views of marriage. **The Council did not break with the traditional concept of marriage, but on the contrary developed it further**. When, for example, it is continually pointed out that the Council substituted the broader and theologically more profound concept of covenant for the strictly legal concept of contract, one must not forget that within covenant, the element of contract is also contained and indeed placed within a broader perspective. The fact that marriage reaches well beyond the purely juridical realm into the depths of humanity and into the mystery of the divine, has always been indicated by the word "sacrament," although often it has not been pondered with the same clarity which the Council gave to these aspects. Law is not everything, but it is an indispensable part, one dimension of the whole. Marriage without a juridical dimension which integrates it into the whole fabric of society and the Church simply does not exist. If

> the post-Conciliar revision of canon law included the realm of marriage, this is not a betrayal of the Council, but the implementation of its mandate.
>
> If the Church were to accept the theory that a marriage is dead when the two spouses no longer love one another, then she would thereby sanction divorce and would uphold the indissolubility of marriage only in word, and no longer in fact. Therefore, the opinion that the Pope could potentially dissolve a consummated sacramental marriage, which has been irrevocably broken, must be considered erroneous. Such a marriage cannot be dissolved by anyone. At their wedding, the spouses promise to be faithful to each other until death. (Joseph "Cardinal" Ratzinger, **Reception of Holy Communion by divorced and remarried Catholics**.)

Personalism, however, directly leads to the undermining of marriage as it is premised first of all on the spouses and not on the honor and glory of God by bringing forth as many (or as few) children as He chooses them to have, and it was condemned by Pope Pius XII in a decree issued by the Holy Office on April 1, 1944:

> Certain publications concerning the purposes of matrimony, and their interrelationship and order, have come forth within these last years which either assert that the primary purpose of matrimony is not the generation of offspring, or that the secondary purposes are not subordinate to the primary purpose, but are independent of it.
>
> In these works, different primary purposes of marriage are designated by other writers, as for example: the complement and personal perfection of the spouses through a complete mutual participation in life and action; mutual love and union of spouses to be nurtured and perfected the psychic and bodily surrender of one's own person; and many other such things.
>
> In the same writings a sense is sometimes attributed to words in the current documents of the Church (as for example, primary, secondary purpose), which does not agree with these words according to the common usage by theologians.
>
> This revolutionary way of thinking and speaking aims to foster errors and uncertainties, to avoid which the Eminent and Very Fathers of this supreme Sacred Congregation, charged with the guarding of faith and morals, in a plenary session on Wednesday, the 29th of March, 1944, when the question was proposed to them: "Whether the opinion of certain writers can be admitted, who either deny that the primary purpose of matrimony is the generation of children and raising offspring, or teach that the secondary purposes are not essentially subordinate to the primary purpose, but are equally first and independent," have decreed that the answer must be: In the negative. (As found in Henry Denzinger, *Enchirdion Symbolorum*, thirteenth edition, translated into English by Roy Deferrari and published in 1955 as *The Sources of Catholic Dogma*–referred to as "Denziger," by B. Herder Book Company of St. Louis, Missouri, and London, England, No. 2295, pp. 624-625.)

Pope Pius XII amplified this condemnation when he delivered his Address to Italian Midwives on the Nature of their Profession, October 29, 1951:

"Personal values" and the need to respect such are a theme which, over the last twenty years or so, has been considered more and more by writers. In many of their works, even the specifically sexual act has its place assigned, that of serving the "person" of the married couple. The proper and most profound sense of the exercise of conjugal rights would consist in this, that the union of bodies is the expression and the realization of personal and affective union.

Articles, chapters, entire books, conferences, especially dealing with the "technique" of love, are composed to spread these ideas, to illustrate them with advice to the newly married as a guide in matrimony, in order that they may not neglect, through stupidity or a false sense of shame or unfounded scruples, that which God, Who also created natural inclinations, offers them. **If from their complete reciprocal gift of husband and wife there results a new life, it is a result which remains outside, or, at the most, on the border of "personal values"; a result which is not denied, but neither is it desired as the center of marital relations.**

According to these theories, your dedication for the welfare of the still hidden life in the womb of the mother, and your assisting its happy birth, would only have but a minor and secondary importance.

Now, if this relative evaluation were merely to place the emphasis on the personal values of husband and wife rather than on that of the offspring, it would be possible, strictly speaking, to put such a problem aside. **But, however, it is a matter of a grave inversion of the order of values and of the ends imposed by the Creator Himself. We find Ourselves faced with the propagation of a number of ideas and sentiments directly opposed to the clarity, profundity, and seriousness of Christian thought. Here, once again, the need for your apostolate. It may happen that you receive the confidences of the mother and wife and are questioned on the more secret desires and intimacies of married life. How, then, will you be able, aware of your mission, to give weight to truth and right order in the appreciation and action of the married couple, if you yourselves are not furnished with the strength of character needed to uphold what you know to be true and just**?

The primary end of marriage

Now, the truth is that matrimony, as an institution of nature, in virtue of the Creator's will, **has not as a primary and intimate end the personal perfection of the married couple but the procreation and upbringing of a new life. The other ends, inasmuch as they are intended by nature, are not equally primary, much less superior to the primary end, but are essentially subordinated to it. This is true of every marriage, even if no offspring result, just as of every eye it can be said that it is destined and formed to see, even if, in abnormal cases arising from special internal or external conditions, it will never be possible to achieve visual perception.**

It was precisely to end the uncertainties and deviations which threatened to diffuse errors regarding the scale of values of the purposes of matrimony and of their reciprocal relations, that a few years ago (March 10, 1944), **We Ourselves drew up a declaration on the order**

of those ends, pointing out what the very internal structure of the natural disposition reveals. We showed what has been handed down by Christian tradition, what the Supreme Pontiffs have repeatedly taught, and what was then in due measure promulgated by the Code of Canon Law. Not long afterwards, to correct opposing opinions, the Holy See, by a public decree, proclaimed that *it could not admit the opinion of some recent authors who denied that the primary end of marriage is the procreation and education of the offspring, or teach that the secondary ends are not essentially subordinated to the primary end, but are on an equal footing and independent of it*.

Would this lead, perhaps, to Our denying or diminishing what is good and just in personal values resulting from matrimony and its realization? Certainly not, because the Creator has designed that for the procreation of a new life human beings made of flesh and blood, gifted with soul and heart, shall be called upon as men and not as animals deprived of reason to be the authors of their posterity. It is for this end that the Lord desires the union of husband and wife. Indeed, the Holy Scripture says of God that He created man to His image and He created him male and female, and willed—as is repeatedly affirmed in Holy Writ—that "a man shall leave mother and father, and shall cleave to his wife: and they shall be two in one flesh".

All this is therefore true and desired by God. **But, on the other hand, it must not be divorced completely from the primary function of matrimony—the procreation of offspring. Not only the common work of external life, but even all personal enrichment—spiritual and intellectual—all that in married love as such is most spiritual and profound, has been placed by the will of the Creator and of nature at the service of posterity. The perfect married life, of its very nature, also signifies the total devotion of parents to the well-being of their children, and married love in its power and tenderness is itself a condition of the sincerest care of the offspring and the guarantee of its realization**.

To reduce the common life of husband and wife and the conjugal act to a mere organic function for the transmission of seed would be but to convert the domestic hearth, the family sanctuary, into a biological laboratory. Therefore, in Our allocution of September 29, 1949, to the International Congress of Catholic Doctors, We expressly excluded artificial insemination in marriage. The conjugal act, in its natural structure, is a personal action, a simultaneous and immediate cooperation of husband and wife, which by the very nature of the agents and the propriety of the act, is the expression of the reciprocal gift, which, according to Holy Writ, effects the union "in one flesh".

That is much more than the union of two genes, which can be effected even by artificial means, that is, without the natural action of husband and wife. The conjugal act, ordained and desired by nature, is a personal cooperation, to which husband and wife, when contracting marriage, exchange the right.

Therefore, when this act in its natural form is from the beginning perpetually impossible, the object of the matrimonial contract is essentially vitiated. This is what we said on that occasion: "Let it not be forgotten: only the procreation of a new life according to the will and the design of the Creator carries with it in a stupendous degree of perfection the intended ends. It is at the same time in conformity with the spiritual and bodily nature and the dignity of the married couple, in conformity with the happy and normal development of the child".

> **Advise the fiancée or the young married woman who comes to seek your advice about the values of matrimonial life that these personal values, both in the sphere of the body and the senses and in the sphere of the spirit, are truly genuine, but that the Creator has placed them not in the first, but in the second degree of the scale of values.** (Pope Pius XII, Address to Midwives on the Nature of Their Profession, October 29, 1951.)

This was a ringing condemnation of the very philosophical and theological foundations of the indiscriminate, institutionalized teaching and practice of "natural family planning" in the lives of Catholic married couples. It is also yet another papal condemnation of conciliarism's view of marriage.

One cannot overemphasize the importance of Pope Pius XII's condemnation of the very personalist ideology that is at the root of what is called today "natural family planning" as it came just a little over seven years and one-half years *after* the Holy Office's condemnation of the work, which was *identical* to that of Dietrich von Hildebrand's, of Father Herbert Doms, who had inverted the end of marriage. The condemnation of Father Doms' work was alluded to in a passage from the October 29, 1951, address just cited above. Here it is once again for the sake of emphasis:

> It was precisely to end the uncertainties and deviations which threatened to diffuse errors regarding the scale of values of the purposes of matrimony and of their reciprocal relations, that a few years ago (March 10, 1944), **We Ourselves drew up a declaration on the order of those ends, pointing out what the very internal structure of the natural disposition reveals. We showed what has been handed down by Christian tradition, what the Supreme Pontiffs have repeatedly taught, and what was then in due measure promulgated by the Code of Canon Law. Not long afterwards, to correct opposing opinions, the Holy See, by a public decree, proclaimed that *it could not admit the opinion of some recent authors who denied that the primary end of marriage is the procreation and education of the offspring, or teach that the secondary ends are not essentially subordinated to the primary end, but are on an equal footing and independent of it*.** (Pope Pius XII, Address to Midwives on the Nature of Their Profession, October 29, 1951.)

Yet is that Joseph "Cardinal" Ratzinger *boasted* in his "clarification" on January 1, 1998, that his September 14, 1994, "notification" did not reverse the "Second" Vatican Council's commitment to "personalism," which he endorsed very enthusiastically. Pope Pius XII's condemnation of the personalist view of marriage, which he wrote himself, was one of those things that could be dispensed with by means of the "hermeneutic of continuity," of course. And it is this "personalist" view of marriage that has led to the triumph of the naturalist sentimentality of Jorge Mario Bergoglio, Walter Kasper, Bruno Forte, Lorenzo Baldiserri, Sean O'Malley, et al.

Importantly, though, Ratzinger noted on January 1, 1998, that the definition of what constituted a true indissoluble marriage was "open" to further study and clarification, meaning that the grounds for obtaining a conciliar decree of nullity could be expanded and the process streamlined. There is thus no inconsistency whatsoever between the revision that Ratzinger made in the conclusion of his 1972 article on the subject and what he had written in 1998:

> a. *Epikeia* and *aequitas canonica* exist in the sphere of human and purely ecclesiastical norms of great significance, but cannot be applied to those norms over which the Church has no discretionary authority. The indissoluble nature of marriage is one of these norms which goes back to Christ Himself and is thus identified as a norm of divine law. The Church cannot sanction pastoral practices - for example, sacramental pastoral practices - which contradict the clear instruction of the Lord.
>
> In other words, if the prior marriage of two divorced and remarried members of the faithful was valid, under no circumstances can their new union be considered lawful and therefore reception of the sacraments is intrinsically impossible. The conscience of the individual is bound to this norm without exception.[2]
>
> b. **However the Church has the authority to clarify those conditions which must be fulfilled for a marriage to be considered indissoluble according to the sense of Jesus' teaching**. In line with the Pauline assertion in 1 Cor. 7, she established that only two baptized Christians can enter into a sacramental marriage. She developed the legal concept of the Pauline privilege and the Petrine privilege. With reference to the *porneia* clauses in Matthew and in Acts 15:20, the impediments to marriage were established. **Furthermore, grounds for the nullity of marriage were identified with ever greater clarity, and the procedural system was developed in greater detail. All of this contributed to delineating and articulating more precisely the concept of the indissolubility of marriage. One can say that, in this way, the Western Church also made allowance for the principle of *oikonomia*, but without touching the indissolubility of marriage as such. The further juridical development of the 1983 *Code of Canon Law* was in this same direction, granting probative force to the declarations of the parties. Therefore, according to experts in this area, it seems that cases in which an invalid marriage cannot be shown to be such by the procedural are practically excluded**.
>
> Since marriage has a fundamental public ecclesial character and the axiom applies that *nemo iudex in propria causa* (no one is judge in his own case), marital cases must be resolved in the external forum. If divorced and remarried members of the faithful believe that their prior marriage was invalid, they are thereby obligated to appeal to the competent marriage tribunal so that the question will be examined objectively and under all available juridical possibilities.
>
> c. Admittedly, it cannot be excluded that mistakes occur in marriage cases. In some parts of the Church, well-functioning marriage tribunals still do not exist. Occasionally, such cases last an excessive amount of time. Once in a while they conclude with questionable decisions. **Here it seems that the application of *epikeia* in the internal forum is not automatically excluded from the outset**. This is implied in the 1994 letter of the Congregation for the

> Doctrine of the Faith, in which it was stated that new canonical ways of demonstrating nullity should exclude "as far as possible" every divergence from the truth verifiable in the judicial process (cf. No. 9). **Some theologians are of the opinion that the faithful ought to adhere strictly even in the internal forum to juridical decisions which they believe to be false. Others maintain that exceptions are possible here in the internal forum, because the juridical forum does not deal with norms of divine law, but rather with norms of ecclesiastical law. This question, however, demands further study and clarification. Admittedly, the conditions for asserting an exception would need to be clarified very precisely, in order to avoid arbitrariness and to safeguard the public character of marriage, removing it from subjective decisions**. (Joseph "Cardinal" Ratzinger, **Reception of Holy Communion by divorced and remarried Catholics**.)

The gist of this Ratzingerspeak can be translated as follows: Ratzinger was applying his "hermeneutic of continuity" to the "discovery" of new grounds for conciliar marriage tribunals to issue decrees of nullity, stating that what has been happening in recent years is simply part of a process of "clarification" that has been ongoing through the history of the Catholic Church. If this is so, one wonders if Jorge Mario Bergoglio is going to issue a posthumous decree of nullity to King Henry VIII to "clarify" Pope Urban VII's firm defense of the validity of the lecherous monarch's marriage to his devoted wife, Catherine of Aragon, who forgave her husband everything in a letter she wrote to him shortly before her death:

> My most dear lord, King and husband,
>
> The hour of my death now drawing on, the tender love I owe you forceth me, my case being such, to commend myself to you, and to put you in remembrance with a few words of the health and safeguard of your soul which you ought to prefer before all worldly matters, and before the care and pampering of your body, for the which you have cast me into many calamities and yourself into many troubles. For my part, I pardon you everything, and I wish to devoutly pray God that He will pardon you also. For the rest, I commend unto you our daughter Mary, beseeching you to be a good father unto her, as I have heretofore desired. I entreat you also, on behalf of my maids, to give them marriage portions, which is not much, they being but three. For all my other servants I solicit the wages due them, and a year more, lest they be unprovided for. Lastly, I make this vow, that mine eyes desire you above all things.
>
> Katharine the Queen (January 7, 1536.) (**Letter of Katharine of Aragon to her husband**)

Catherine of Aragon did not seek to get "remarried" as her husband had done away with her in favor of his mistress, Anne Boleyn. Catherine of Aragon offered up her suffering for the salvation of the soul of her faithless husband, a concept that is foreign to men such as Ratzinger, the supposed "defender of marriage," and Bergoglio, the supposed "revolutionary" who is attacking it. The former is just as much a revolutionary as the latter by embracing a personalist view of marriage that was condemned by Pope Pius XII and by stating that "clarifications" can find newer grounds and "reformed" legal processes to help couples while not, significantly, ruling out the use of the "internal forum" solution in some cases.

Indeed, Vaticanologist Sandro Magister reported on the publication of the 1998 article in *L'Osservatore Romano* on November 30, 2011, to this very same effect:

> ROME, December 5, 2011 – During Benedict XVI's recent visit to Germany, many were expecting "openness" from the pope to divorced and remarried Catholics: with the attenuation, if not the revocation, of the ban on receiving communion.
>
> This expectation was expressed by the president of the German federal republic himself, Christian Wulff, Catholic and remarried, in the official welcome he extended to the pope at his arrival in Berlin.
>
> Neither during the four days of his voyage to Germany, however, nor afterward, did pope Joseph Ratzinger say anything on this issue.
>
> But it is well known that this question is very close to his heart. He has spoken of it repeatedly in the past, and has said that "**the problem is very difficult and must be explored further**."
>
> Last November 30, Benedict XVI returned to the issue in indirect form: with the republication in "L'Osservatore Romano" of a "little-known" essay of his from 1998, supplemented with a footnote presenting his remark on this issue to the clergy of the diocese of Aosta on July 25, 2005.
>
> An important footnote, because it concerns precisely one of the points on **which Benedict XVI maintains that an exception could be opened in the general ban on communion**. (**No Communion for Outlaws. But Benedict Is Studying Two Exceptions**.)
>
> In the third part of his essay, Pope Benedict replies to those who demand that the Catholic Church respect the choice of the divorced and remarried when "in conscience" they believe it just to receive communion, in contrast with the juridical norm that bans it.
>
> Benedict XVI begins with a consideration that seems to close any sort of loophole:
>
> "If the prior marriage of two divorced and remarried members of the faithful was valid, under no circumstances can their new union be considered lawful and therefore reception of the sacraments is intrinsically impossible. The conscience of the individual is bound to this norm without exception." A norm, the indissolubility of marriage, that is of "divine law" and "over which the Church has no discretionary authority."
>
> But immediately afterward, he adds:
>
> "However, the Church has the authority to clarify those conditions which must be fulfilled for a marriage to be considered indissoluble according to the **sense of Jesus' teaching**."
>
> And, he writes, the ecclesiastical tribunals that should ascertain whether or not a marriage is valid do not always function well. Sometimes the processes "last an excessive amount of

time." In some cases "they conclude with questionable decisions."In still others "mistakes occur."

In these cases, therefore – the pope recognizes –, "**it seems that the application of 'epikeia' in the internal forum is not automatically excluded**," meaning a decision of conscience:

"Some theologians are of the opinion that the faithful ought to adhere strictly even in the internal forum to juridical decisions which they believe to be false. Others maintain that exceptions are possible here in the internal forum, because the juridical forum does not deal with norms of divine law, but rather with norms of ecclesiastical law. This question, however, demands further study and clarification. Admittedly, the conditions for asserting an exception would need to be clarified very precisely, in order to avoid arbitrariness and to safeguard the public character of marriage, removing it from subjective decisions". (No Communion for Outlaws. But Benedict Is Studying Two Exceptions.)

As noted before, this was vintage Ratzinger doublespeak.

The false "pontiff emeritus" was trying to *appear* to maintain the Catholic doctrine of the indissolubility of marriage while at the same time "rediscovering" the "sense" of a teaching that is very clear. This is just another manifestation of Ratzinger/Benedict's lack of understanding of the nature of the immutability of God, Who is immutable. Ratzinger/Benedict must analyze almost every point of Catholic doctrine and pastoral praxis on the basis of the agnosticism critiqued by Pope Saint Pius X in *Pascendi Dominici Gregis*. That is, Ratzinger/Benedict does not believe that anything about the Catholic Faith is *ever* truly settled once and for all, something that Pope Saint Pius X noted in *Pascendi Domínci Gregis*, September 8, 1907:

It remains for Us now to say a few words about the Modernist as reformer. **From all that has preceded, it is abundantly clear how great and how eager is the passion of such men for innovation. In all Catholicism there is absolutely nothing on which it does not fasten. They wish philosophy to be reformed, especially in the ecclesiastical seminaries. They wish the scholastic philosophy to be relegated to the history of philosophy and to be classed among absolute systems, and the young men to be taught modern philosophy which alone is true and suited to the times in which we live**. They desire the reform of theology: rational theology is to have modern philosophy for its foundation, and positive theology is to be founded on the history of dogma. As for history, it must be written and taught only according to their methods and modern principles. Dogmas and their evolution, they affirm, are to be harmonized with science and history. In the Catechism no dogmas are to be inserted except those that have been reformed and are within the capacity of the people. Regarding worship, they say, the number of external devotions is to be reduced, and steps must be taken to prevent their further increase, though, indeed, some of the admirers of symbolism are disposed to be more indulgent on this head. They cry out that ecclesiastical government requires to be reformed in all its branches, but especially in its disciplinary and dogmatic departments. They insist that both outwardly and inwardly it must be brought into harmony with the modern conscience which now wholly tends towards democracy; a share in ecclesiastical government should therefore be given to the lower ranks of the clergy and

> even to the laity and authority which is too much concentrated should be decentralized. The Roman Congregations and especially the index and the Holy Office, must be likewise modified The ecclesiastical authority must alter its line of conduct in the social and political world; while keeping outside political organizations it must adapt itself to them in order to penetrate them with its spirit. **With regard to morals, they adopt the principle of the Americanists, that the active virtues are more important than the passive, and are to be more encouraged in practice**. They ask that the clergy should return to their primitive humility and poverty, and that in their ideas and action they should admit the principles of Modernism; and there are some who, gladly listening to the teaching of their Protestant masters, would desire the suppression of the celibacy of the clergy. What is there left in the Church which is not to be reformed by them and according to their principles? (Pope Saint Pius X, *Pascendi Dominici Gregis*, September 8, 1907.)

Everything must be "discovered" and expressed anew.

Therefore, what Ratzinger/Benedict has written on the issue of giving what he thinks is Holy Communion to those engaged in adulterous marriages can be summarized as follows: "We will uphold the teaching on the indissolubility of marriage by changing the meaning of what constitutes an indissoluble marriage, thereby making it possible for those who are divorced and civilly remarried to resort to a 'solution' within the confessional that is pastorally sensitive to their 'difficult' circumstances."

This is similar to the conciliar protestations that the Assisi events have not been exercises in religious syncretism when, of course, they have been precisely this. Simply saying that something is not so does nothing to change the reality of what an event actually is in the eyes of God. Joseph Ratzinger/Benedict XVI "prayed" with ministers of false religions. He entered into their places of false worship. He esteemed the symbols of false religions. He extolled the nonexistent ability of false religions to "contribute" to the common good and the building of a just world order and world peace. Masquerading as a "true pope," Joseph Ratzinger/Benedict XVI even gave "joint blessings" with the likes of Rowan Williams, the layman then masquerading as the "archbishop" of Canterbury. None of this is from the Catholic Church. All of this represents efforts to destroy the Catholic Faith.

Jorge Mario Bergoglio has done like things, obviously, which should tell everyone who is looking for "good guys" and "bad guys" in what can be called "Communion Wars, 2014," that such a search is delusional. There are no "good guys" to be found, only different shades of revolutionaries.

Joseph Ratzinger/Benedict XVI's revised conclusion to his 1972 article was really nothing new whatsoever. Rather, it was simply an incorporation of his comments from 1998 into the context of his earlier article, demonstrating yet again that he uses the "hermeneutic of continuity" even in his own work.

Although any kind of speculation as to why Ratzinger/Benedict acted as he has did in late-2014 is simply that, it is highly unlikely that the Antipope Emeritus did not inform the currently reigning Antipope of the publication of the new article. It is quite possible that the two apostates are playing "good cop, bad cop" to each other to give the appearance of a "conflict" between the two when none may exist as a matter of fact. Then again, it really does not matter as this is but a sideshow to keep Catholics diverted from an understanding that the problem with conciliarism is not trying to maintain particular doctrines that have been undermined, if not contradicted in their entirety. The problem with conciliarism is that it is *in se* a "defection" from the Catholic Faith. Conciliarism is the antithesis of Catholicism. It is that simple.

Jorge Mario Bergoglio is a good politician. He is going to make use of the coming year to condition Catholics for a "clarification" on a "pastoral" matter in the name of "mercy," and it would not be at all surprising if a supposedly "moderate" solution along the lines suggested by Ratzinger/Benedict is the one that he winds up adopting, thus appearing to have saved the "doctrine of marriage" that the conciliar revolutionaries undermined by the "Second" Vatican Council and by the "magisterium" of the conciliar "popes," especially by means of Giovanni Battista Enrico Antonio Maria/Paul the Sick's *Humanae Vitae*, July 25, 1968, which created a means of "Catholic contraception" that has become the norm in the structures of the counterfeit church of concilairism, and Karol Joseph Wojtyla/John Paul II's personalist approach to marriage that gave rise to the hideous "theology of the body."

Bergoglio will be, at least humanly speaking, an unstoppable force after his visit to the United States of America in September of 2015, which will probably include an address to the United Nations General Assembly. He will get what he wants at his 2015 synod a month later, making it appear to be "democratically" determined as he does so.

Lost in all of this, of course, is Catholic truth.

Although Pope Pius XII was addressing the situation of Catholic spouses who had to abstain from that which is proper to the married state for grave reasons, his words reminding Catholics that it is not impossible for married couples to live in a Josephite manner are as applicable to those who Catholics today who do not live in true marriages but must stay together for the good of their children:

> Perhaps you will now press the point, however, observing that in the exercise of your profession you find yourselves sometimes faced with delicate cases, in which, that is, there cannot be a demand that the risk of maternity be run, **a risk which in certain cases must be absolutely avoided, and in which as well the observance of the agenesic periods either does not give sufficient security, or must be rejected for other reasons. Now, you ask, how can one still speak of an apostolate in the service of maternity**?
>
> If, in your sure and experienced judgment, the circumstances require an absolute "no," that is to say, the exclusion of motherhood, it would be a mistake and a wrong to impose or advise a "yes." Here it is a question of basic facts and therefore not a theological but a medical question; and thus it is in your competence. However, in such cases, the married couple does not desire a medical answer, of necessity a negative one, but seeks an approval of a "technique" of conjugal activity which will not give rise to maternity. And so you are again called to exercise your apostolate inasmuch as you leave no doubt whatsoever that even in these extreme cases every preventive practice and every direct attack upon the life and the development of the seed is, in conscience, forbidden and excluded, and that there is

only one way open, namely, to abstain from every complete performance of the natural faculty. Your apostolate in this matter requires that you have a clear and certain judgment and a calm firmness.

It will be objected that such an abstention is impossible, that such a heroism is asking too much. You will hear this objection raised; you will read it everywhere. Even those who should be in a position to judge very differently, either by reason of their duties or qualifications, are ever ready to bring forward the following argument: "No one is obliged to do what is impossible, and it may be presumed that no reasonable legislator can will his law to oblige to the point of impossibility. But for husbands and wives long periods of abstention are impossible. Therefore they are not obliged to abstain; divine law cannot have this meaning."

In such a manner, from partially true premises, one arrives at a false conclusion. To convince oneself of this it suffices to invert the terms of the argument: "God does not oblige anyone to do what is impossible. But God obliges husband and wife to abstinence if their union cannot be completed according to the laws of nature. Therefore in this case abstinence is possible." To confirm this argument, there can be brought forward the doctrine of the Council of Trent, which, in the chapter on the observance necessary and possible of referring to a passage of St. Augustine, teaches: "God does not command the impossible but while He commands, He warns you to do what you can and to ask for the grace for what you cannot do and He helps you so that you may be able".

Do not be disturbed, therefore, in the practice of your profession and apostolate, by this great talk of impossibility. Do not be disturbed in your internal judgment nor in your external conduct. Never lend yourselves to anything which is contrary to the law of God and to your Christian conscience! **It would be a wrong towards men and women of our age to judge them incapable of continuous heroism. Nowadays, for many a reason,—perhaps constrained by dire necessity or even at times oppressed by injustice—heroism is exercised to a degree and to an extent that in the past would have been thought impossible. Why, then, if circumstances truly demand it, should this heroism stop at the limits prescribed by the passions and the inclinations of nature? It is clear: he who does not want to master himself is not able to do so, and he who wishes to master himself relying only upon his own powers, without sincerely and perseveringly seeking divine help, will be miserably deceived.**

Here is what concerns your apostolate for winning married people over to a service of motherhood, not in the sense of an utter servitude under the promptings of nature, but to the exercise of the rights and duties of married life, governed by the principles of reason and faith. (Pope Pius XII, **Address to Midwives on the Nature of Their Profession**, October 29, 1951.)

For anyone to assert that it is "impossible" for a married couple to maintain complete marital abstinence by mutual consent if truly extraordinary circumstances require it, whether for reasons of being remarried invalidly after having received a decree of nullity from a conciliar tribunal or for the reasons outlined by Pope Pius XII in 1951, that it is "too tough" for them to do so, perhaps it would be more than a little wise to become familiar with these words of Pope Pius XII cited just above:

> **In such a manner, from partially true premises, one arrives at a false conclusion. To convince oneself of this it suffices to invert the terms of the argument: "God does not oblige anyone to do what is impossible. But God obliges husband and wife to abstinence if their union cannot be completed according to the laws of nature. Therefore in this case abstinence is possible." To confirm this argument, there can be brought forward the doctrine of the Council of Trent, which, in the chapter on the observance necessary and possible of referring to a passage of St. Augustine, teaches: "God does not command the impossible but while He commands, He warns you to do what you can and to ask for the grace for what you cannot do and He helps you so that you may be able**". (Pope Pius XII, **Address to Midwives on the Nature of Their Profession**, October 29, 1951.)

Neither Joseph Ratzinger/Benedict nor Jorge Mario Bergoglio/Francis believe such a thing. Ratzinger/Benedict is a rationalist who uses his intellect to come up with fallacious arguments to deny articles of the Catholic Faith. Bergoglio/Francis is a naturalist who lives and moves and breathes by the viscera of emotion and sentimentality. They are just different shades of revolutionaries. Nothing more, nothing less. Neither man has the Catholic Faith.

Thus it is that the “extraordinary synod on the family” that concluded on October 19, 2014, has set the stage for the following “developments of doctrine” in 2015 and the years to follow:

1. Following the practice of the heretical and schismatic Greek Orthodox, divorced and civilly remarried Catholics without a decree of nullity from the conciliar officials, not that it is worth anything, will be permitted to receive what is purported to be Holy Communion in the Protestant and Judeo-Masonic *Novus Ordo* liturgical service on a case-by-case basis handled by means of the interior forum of the conciliar “reconciliation room.” In other words, everybody gets to stick their paws out to receive what they think is the Body, Blood, Soul and Divinity of Our Blessed Lord and Saviour Jesus Christ.

2. The nullity process itself will be “streamlined” even further, making it possible for “decisions” in a matter of months, if not sooner.

3. “Pastoral outreach” to “unmarried couples” will be enlarged and expanded.

4. The “internal forum” solution, which has been used for decades now by cooperative priests and presbyters, will be adopted to assuage the consciences of married couples who find it “too difficult” to avoid the use of contraceptives. “Education” in methods of “natural family planning” will be recommended as the way to “plan” the number of children a married couple desires to have. For the refutation of “natural family planning,” please see **Forty-Three Years After *Humanae Vitae***, **Always Trying To Find A Way** and **Planting Seeds of Revolutionary Change**.

5. "Ministries" to those engaged in the commission of perverse sins against nature will be expanded and found more universally than they have been up until to now, confined in some dioceses to a few well-known dens of iniquity (e.g. Saint Francis Xavier Church in New York, Most Holy Redeemer Church in San Francisco, California, Saint Brigid's Church in Westbury, New York, Saints Cyril and Methodius Church in Deer Park, New York, Saint Joan of Arc Church in Minneapolis, Minnesota, among so many, many others). The children who are unfortunate to be in the care of unrepentant practitioners of perversity with be baptized and welcomed into conciliar schools, thereby mainstreaming acceptance of perverse behavior and overthrowing any lingering concept of a detestation of personal sin that might be lurking in the hearts of Catholics who are as of yet attached to the conciliar structures.

Here is proof from *Instrumentum Laboris* itself:

> **b) Concerning Unions of Persons of the Same Sex**
>
> *Civil Recognition*
>
> 110. On unions of persons of the same sex, the responses of the bishops' conferences refer to Church teaching. "There are absolutely no grounds for considering homosexual unions to be in any way similar or even remotely analogous to God's plan for marriage and family. [...] Nonetheless, according to the teaching of the Church, men and women with homosexual tendencies 'must be accepted with respect, compassion and sensitivity. Every sign of unjust discrimination in their regard should be avoided'" (*CDF*, *Considerations regarding Proposals to Give Legal Recognition to Unions between Homosexual Persons*, 4). The responses indicate that the recognition in civil law of unions between persons of the same sex largely depends on the socio-cultural, religious and political context. In this regard, the episcopal conferences describe three instances: **the first exists when repressive and punitive measures are taken in reaction to the phenomenon of homosexuality in all its aspects, especially when the public manifestation of homosexuality is prohibited by civil law. Some responses indicate that, in this context, the Church provides different forms of spiritual care for single, homosexual people who seek the Church's assistance.** (*Instrumentum Laboris*)

Reality Checks Provided by Saint Paul the Apostle and Pope Saint Pius V:

Here is the sort of "pastoral care" recommended by Saint Paul the Apostle:

> **Wherefore God gave them up to the desires of their heart, unto uncleanness, to dishonour their own bodies among themselves. Who changed the truth of God into a lie**; and worshipped and served the creature rather than the Creator, who is blessed for ever. Amen.
>
> **For this cause God delivered them up to shameful affections. For their women have changed the natural use into that use against which is their nature.**

And in like manner, the men also, leaving the natural use of the women, have burned in their lusts one towards another, men with men working that which is filthy, and receiving in themselves the recompense which was due to their error.

And as they liked not to have God in their knowledge, God delivered them up to a reprobate sense, to do those things which are not convenient; being filled with all iniquity, malice, fornication, avarice, wickedness, full of envy, murder, contention, deceit, malignity, whisperers, detractors, hateful to God, contumelious, proud, haughty, inventors of evil things, disobedient to parents, foolish, dissolute, without affection, without fidelity, without mercy.

Who, having known the justice of God, did not understand that they who do such things are worthy of death; and not only they that do them, but they also that consent to them that do them. (Romans 1: 24-32)

Writing under the Divine inspiration of the Third Person of the Most Blessed Trinity, God the Holy Ghost, Saint Paul the Apostle, condemned "shameful affections." Jorge Mario Bergoglio/Francis and others in the counterfeit church of conciliarism, speak of a "gay orientation."

It is telling that the misnamed conciliar *Catechism of the Catholic Church* speaks of a "homosexual orientation" while Saint Paul the Apostle wrote about shameful affections. And it is because at least one of those who served as a peritus under the liturgical revolutionary Annibale Bugnini, C.M., on the *Consilium* that planned the Protestant and Judeo-Masonic *Novus Ordo* service, which boasts of containing almost every passage of Sacred Scripture in its triennial cycle of Sunday readings and its biennial cycle of weekday readings, excludes verses twenty-four to thirty-two of the first chapter of Saint Paul the Apostle's Epistle to the Romans.

Oh, the name of that one person? Yes, sure, thanks for asking. Rembert George Weakland, O.S.B. (see **Weak In Mind, Weakest Yet In Faith** and **Just A Matter of Forgiveness?**)

Pope Saint Pius V offered his own version of "pastoral care" to those who persist in crimes against nature:

That horrible crime, on account of which corrupt and obscene cities were destroyed by fire through divine condemnation, causes us most bitter sorrow and shocks our mind, impelling us to repress such a crime with the greatest possible zeal.

Quite opportunely the Fifth Lateran Council [1512-1517] issued this decree: "Let any member of the clergy caught in that vice against nature . . . **be removed from the clerical order or forced to do penance in a monastery**" (chap. 4, X, V, 31). So that the contagion of such a grave offense may not advance with greater audacity by taking advantage of impunity, which is the greatest incitement to sin, and so as to more severely punish the clerics who are guilty of this nefarious crime and who are not frightened by the death of their souls, we determine that they should be handed over to the severity of the secular authority, which enforces civil law.

> Therefore, wishing to pursue with the greatest rigor that which we have decreed since the beginning of our pontificate, we establish that any priest or member of the clergy, either secular or regular, who commits such an execrable crime, by force of the present law be deprived of every clerical privilege, of every post, dignity and ecclesiastical benefit, **and having been degraded by an ecclesiastical judge, let him be immediately delivered to the secular authority to be put to death, as mandated by law as the fitting punishment for laymen who have sunk into this abyss**. (Pope Saint Pius V, *Horrendum illud scelus*, August 30, 1568.)

Just a slightly different approach, wouldn't you say? A true pope understood the horror of such a detestable sin on the part of the clergy and sought to administer punishment to serve as a medicinal corrective for other priests and to demonstrate to the laity the horrific nature of such a moral crime. A false "bishop" seeks to protect his "institution" and the "clerical club." Quite a different approach.

Mind you, I am not suggesting the revival of this penalty in a world where it would not be understood and where the offender would be made a "martyr" for the cause of perversity, only pointing out the fact that the *Catholic* Church teaches that clerics and others in ecclesiastical authority who are guilty of serious moral crimes are deserving of punishment, not protection, by their bishops. Such is the difference yet again between Catholicism and conciliarism.

Moreover, the *Instrumentum Laboris* called for a "non-judgmental" approach to be taken toward those living perversely sinful lives by means, whether or not with the "blessing" of the civil authorities by means of "civil unions" and "same-sex marriages":

> 113. Every bishops' conference voiced opposition to "redefining" marriage between a man and a woman through the introduction of legislation permitting a union between two people of the same sex. **The episcopal conferences amply demonstrate that they are trying to find a balance between the Church's teaching on the family and a respectful, non-judgmental attitude towards people living in such unions. On the whole, the extreme reactions to these unions, whether compromising or uncompromising, do not seem to have facilitated the development of an effective pastoral programme which is consistent with the Magisterium and compassionate towards the persons concerned**.
>
> 114. A factor which clearly has an impact on the Church's pastoral care and one which complicates the search for a balanced attitude in this situation is the promotion of a gender ideology. In some places, this ideology tends to exert its influence even at the elementary level, spreading a mentality which, **intending to eliminate homophobia**, proposes, in fact, to undermine sexual identity. (***Instrumentum Laboris***)

The midterm report of the "extraordinary synod of bishops on the family" contained the following passages that caused some of the "conservatives" present at the soiree to rend their garments and gnash their teeth:

> **Homosexuals have gifts and qualities to offer to the Christian community: are we capable of welcoming these people, guaranteeing to them a fraternal space in our**

> **communities? Often they wish to encounter a Church that offers them a welcoming home. Are our communities capable of providing that, accepting and valuing their sexual orientation, without compromising Catholic doctrine on the family and matrimony**?
>
> The question of homosexuality leads to a serious reflection on how to elaborate realistic paths of affective growth and human and evangelical maturity integrating the sexual dimension: it appears therefore as an important educative challenge. The Church furthermore affirms that unions between people of the same sex cannot be considered on the same footing as matrimony between man and woman. Nor is it acceptable that pressure be brought to bear on pastors or that international bodies make financial aid dependent on the introduction of regulations inspired by gender ideology.
>
> Without denying the moral problems connected to homosexual unions it **has to be noted that there are cases in which mutual aid to the point of sacrifice constitutes a precious support in the life of the partners. Furthermore, the Church pays special attention to the children who live with couples of the same sex, emphasizing that the needs and rights of the little ones must always be given priority**. (**Synod on Family: Midterm report presented, 2015 Synod announced**.)

This reflected the apostate mind of Jorge Mario Bergoglio perfectly. Even though the final report of the 2014 "extraordinary synod" changed the language of the "midterm report," Bergoglio made it clear in a press conference while en route back from Turkey on Sunday, November 30, 2014, the First Sunday of Advent, that he expects that something close to the language of the "midterm report" will be reflected in the 2015 synod of conciliar "bishops." Bergoglio has said that what he thinks is the Catholic Church has a year to "mature" as the "bishops" listen to the "people" in a "dialogue of encounter":

> The "substance" of controversial language on "welcoming homosexuals" in the midterm report at the October 2014 extraordinary Synod of Bishops on the family survived in the corresponding section of the final document, even though the latter was widely considered more conservative. He said the synod was not a parliament but an "ecclesial space where the Holy Spirit can work" and was just part of a process to be continued through the coming year of preparation for an October 2015 worldwide synod on the same subject. (**Jorge's Press Confab**)

Yes, **Jorge Cooked the Books** from the very beginning of his false "pontificate" on Wednesday, March 13, 2013. He is a patient man, who may engage in a few more "purges" of conciliar non-bishops that have sought, he believes, to "cage" or to "tame" God the Holy Ghost from leading what he thinks is the Catholic Church into a less "closed-in-on-itself" and "unwelcoming" position about those who practice the sin of Sodom, one of the four sins that out to Heaven for vengeance.

Indeed, the conciliar revolution that was spawned at least in part by those inclined to the commission of perverse sins against nature, something that can be demonstrated in the art, architecture and music of the conciliar liturgy as well as by its orations, most of which mention nothing about a God who judges or about the possibility of eternal damnation or even the necessity of doing penance for one's sins, has created given diocesans and schools and hospitals in the control of the conciliar officials of a decidedly lavender slant, if you will.

As the conciliar church is "all inclusive," except to those who reject its blasphemies, outrages and sacrileges without agreeing to silence as a price of "admission" and tolerance, it is not surprising to find clerics and lavender activists in the conciliar structures who justify their support for unrepentant sins against nature to as to justify themselves before men. They are as militant and as "in your face" as they are because their mission is to convince everyone, including God Himself, that they are right, that anyone who opposes them is "hateful" and opposed to "human rights."

Only those who do not believe that homosexuality is seriously disordered and that the acts associated therewith cry out to Heaven for vengeance can claim that there is such a thing as "homophobia." It is not to hate anyone or to judge the subjective state of his soul, which is known to God alone, to judge and condemn sinful actions.

Pastors of the Catholic Church have an obligation to judge sinful actions for what they are and to tell sinners in clear, unmistakable terms: Quit your lives of sin. You risk the fires of Hell if you do not.

Our Blessed Lord and Saviour Jesus Christ never reaffirmed anyone in a life of sin. While he dissuaded those who were about to stone his friend, Saint Mary Magdalene, when she was caught in adultery, he told his friend the following:

> Go, and now sin no more. (John 8: 11.)

The conciliar revolutionaries are bereft of the Catholic Faith.

Why is this so hard to understand and accept?

The *Instrumentum Laboris* devoted an entire ten paragraphs to the care of those steeped in unrepentant sins of perversity that cry out to Heaven for vengeance even though there is one way to care for them, to discharge the Spiritual Works of Mercy to them, including admonishing the sinner in no uncertain terms, to quit his sins lest he be condemned to Hell for all eternity. In no small measure, of course, the sin of Sodom has spread like wildfire in the world because of the indifference and/or complacency shown by the conciliar officials, to say nothing of the active support, approval and glorification of this sin against nature by conciliar "bishops," priests/presbyters, religious and laity.

Laughably, the *Instrumentum Laboris* recommends not using the word "gay" to describe those who have shameful affections:

> 116. When considering the possibility of a ministry to these people, a distinction must be made between those who have made a personal, and often painful, choice and live that choice discreetly so as not to give scandal to others, and those whose behaviour promotes and actively — often aggressively — calls attention to it. Many conferences emphasize that, due to the fact that these unions are a relatively recent phenomenon, no pastoral

> programs exist in their regard. **Others admit a certain unease at the challenge of accepting these people with a merciful spirit and, at the same time, holding to the moral teaching of the Church, all the while attempting to provide appropriate pastoral care which takes every aspect of the person into consideration. Some responses recommend not using phrases such as "gay," "lesbian" or "homosexual" to define a person's identity. (*Instrumentum Laboris*)**

Go tell this to Jorge Mario Bergoglio:

> Speaking of other problems within the administration of the Holy See, including rumours of a 'gay lobby' within the Vatican, Pope Francis said there are many saintly people working in the Curia but also those who are not so saintly and cause scandals which harm the Church. Quoting from the Catechism of the Catholic Church, **he said that people with homosexual tendencies must not be excluded but should be integrated into society**. "**If a person is gay and seeks God and has good will, who am I to judge him**?" he asked. (**Francis the Revolutionary holds press conference on flight back from Brazil**.)

A human being's identity is based upon the fact that he has a rational, immortal soul made in the image and likeness of God that has been redeemed by the shedding of the Most Precious Blood of Our Blessed Lord and Saviour Jesus Christ on the wood of the Holy Cross whether or not the person knows or accepts this fact. Period.

Jorge Mario Bergoglio has done more to advance the agenda of what Mrs. Randy Engel terms the "homosexual collective" than anyone else before him in the counterfeit church of conciliarism and even in the secular world-at-large. **Call Me Jorge** detailed how the Franciscans, one of many strongholds of the homosexual agenda within the structures of the conciliar church, in the Archdiocese of Boston featured "Who Am I To Judge" t-shirts, buttons and banners for those walking in the annual "pride" parade in this month of the Most Sacred Heart of Jesus.

Sensus fidei, anyone?

> 117. **Many responses and observations call for theological study in dialogue with the human sciences to develop a multi-faceted look at the phenomenon of homosexuality. Others recommend collaborating with specific entities, e.g., the Pontifical Academy of the Social Sciences and the Pontifical Academy for Life, in thoroughly examining the anthropological and theological aspects of human sexuality and the sexual difference between man and woman in order to address the issue of *gender* ideology**.
>
> 118. **The great challenge will be to develop a ministry which can maintain the proper balance between accepting persons in a spirit of compassion and gradually guiding them to authentic human and Christian maturity**. In this regard, some conferences refer to certain organizations as successful models for such a ministry. (***Instrumentum Laboris***)

Preaching from the pulpits of Catholic churches must be firm in the denunciation of sin and clear about the compassion that awaits *repentant* sinners in the Sacred Tribunal of Penance. Unreprentant sinners can never be affirmed, coddled or in any way congratulated for their entirely free-will choice to place themselves, objectively speaking, on the path to Hell. There is nothing to "understand" about perverse behavior. Holy Mother Church has all of the gifts given unto her by God the Holy Ghost to effect their conversion. The counterfeit church of conciliarism lacks those gifts and lacks even the desire to effect a true conversion to personal sancity.

Only one more passage from the *Instrumentum Laboris* will be cited:

> 119. Sex education in families and educational institutions is an increasingly urgent challenge, especially in countries where the State tends to propose in schools a one-sided view and a *gender* ideology. Formation programmes ought to be established in schools or parish communities which offer young people an adequate idea of Christian and emotional maturity to allow them to face even the phenomenon of homosexuality. At the same time, the observations show that there is still no consensus in the Church on the specific way of receiving persons in these unions. The first step would be a slow process of gathering information and distinguishing criteria of discernment for not only ministers and pastoral workers but also groups and ecclesial movements. (***Instrumentum Laboris***)

Conciliar programs of explicit classroom instruction in matters pertaining to the Sixth and Ninth Commandments have done as much as, if not more than, similar programs in secular brainwashing and detention centers (sometimes referred to as "schools") to propagate promiscuity among the young and acceptance of sodomy as a practice that is expressive of "love."

Pope Pius IX warned us about such programs in the following passages contained in *Divini Illius Magistri*, December 31, 1929:

> 65. Another very grave danger is that naturalism which nowadays invades the field of education in that most delicate matter of purity of morals. **Far too common is the error of those who with dangerous assurance and under an ugly term propagate a so-called sex-education, falsely imagining they can forearm youths against the dangers of sensuality by means purely natural, such as a foolhardy initiation and precautionary instruction for all indiscriminately, even in public; and, worse still, by exposing them at an early age to the occasions, in order to accustom them, so it is argued, and as it were to harden them against such dangers**.
>
> 66. **Such persons grievously err in refusing to recognize the inborn weakness of human nature, and the law of which the Apostle speaks, fighting against the law of the mind**;[43] and also in ignoring the experience of facts, from which it is clear that, particularly in young people, evil practices are the effect not so much of ignorance of intellect as of weakness of a will exposed to dangerous occasions, and unsupported by the means of grace.
>
> 67. In this extremely delicate matter, if, all things considered, some private instruction is found necessary and opportune, from those who hold from God the commission to teach and who have the grace of state, every precaution must be taken. Such precautions are well known in traditional Christian education, and are adequately described by Antoniano cited above, when he says:

> Such is our misery and inclination to sin, that often in the very things considered to be remedies against sin, we find occasions for and inducements to sin itself. Hence it is of the highest importance that a good father, while discussing with his son a matter so delicate, **should be well on his guard and not descend to details, nor refer to the various ways in which this infernal hydra destroys with its poison so large a portion of the world; otherwise it may happen that instead of extinguishing this fire, he unwittingly stirs or kindles it in the simple and tender heart of the child. Speaking generally, during the period of childhood it suffices to employ those remedies which produce the double effect of opening the door to the virtue of purity and closing the door upon vice**. [44]

Thus is condemned all classroom instruction in matters pertaining to the Sixth and Ninth Commandments.

Prohibited also, of course, is the graphically explicit speech of the conciliar "popes" and their disciples who promote the "theology of the body" that engages in the most vile, vulgar forms of speech that would never issue forth from the mouth of the Divine Redeemer, Our Blessed Lord and Saviour Jesus Christ, or that of His Most Blessed Mother. Such vile, vulgar forms of speech have never issued forth from the lips of our saints, who maintained custody of their eyes and who shunned all immodest speech at all times.

The 2014 "extraordinary synod on the family" was just another step in the conciliar revolution of placing it on the fact track to a complete, seamless merger with the Anglican sect, which has long since made its "official peace" with "moral issues."

Indeed, among the other heresies spouted incessantly by his mouth that is an engine of heresy, blasphemy, apostasy and sacrilege, Jorge Mario Bergoglio has dared to blaspheme Our Blessed Lord and Saviour Jesus Christ by saying that He was not a "moralist":

> "And this is why the people followed Jesus, because He was the Good Shepherd. He wasn't a moralistic, quibbling Pharisee, or a Sadducee who made political deals with the powerful, or a guerrilla who sought the political liberation of his people, or a contemplative in a monastery. He was a pastor! A pastor who spoke the language of His people, Who understood, Who spoke the truth, the things of God: He never trafficked in the things of God! But He spoke in such a way that the people loved the things of God. That's why they followed Him." (**Whom do I like to follow?**.)

Blasphemer.

At the root of the entire conciliar agenda, including its agenda for the family, is the lack of any sense of the horror of personal sin, including Mortal Sin itself.

While it is true that many who are steeped today in what are Mortal Sins in the objective order of things may not understand or accept this to be so and/or may seek to minimize, it is the case nevertheless that each Mortal Sin wounds the soul, making it a captive to the devil and thus making it an instrument of chaos, disorder, anger, oftentimes displaced at those who seek to admonish it, and perhaps even violence in their own lives and that of those around them and the world-at-large.

The family and the world are in the mess that they are because of the commission of unrepentant sins, most of which are protected under cover of the civil law and celebrated in every single aspect of what passes for "popular culture." Saint Alphonsus de Liguori's taught us about the malice of Mortal Sin in a sermon, "On the Malice of Mortal Sin," that serves as a sober antidote to what the conciliar revolutionaries believe are nothing more than "irregular" situations:

> "**Hence Hell and a thousand Hells are not sufficient chastisement for a single mortal sin**." (Saint Alphonsus de Liguori, "On the Malice of Mortal Sin.)

The path to personal ruin and social chaos that we see all around us at this time was charted as a direct, inevitable result of the Protestant Revolution against the Social Reign of Christ the King and the rise of the multifaceted, interrelated maze of naturalistic ideologies and "philosophies" that can be termed collectively by the name of Judeo-Masonry (see **To Blot Out the Holy Name Forever, part one** and **To Blot Out the Holy Name Forever, part two**.)

Jorge Mario Bergoglio and his band of conciliar revolutionaries do not believe that each of the problems in the world is caused by Original Sin and the Actual Sins of men, thus showing themselves to be utterly ignorant of the truths of the Catholic Faith concerning the offense that sin is in the eyes of God, how it wounded Our Lord once in time and how it wounds His Mystical Body, the Church Militant on earth, today. These truths were summarized so very clearly by Silvio Cardinal Antoniano (and quoted by Pope Pius XI in the aforementioned *Divini Illius Magistri,* December 31, 1929, by Pope Saint Pius X and by Pope Pius XI directly:

> The more closely the temporal power of a nation aligns itself with the spiritual, and the more it fosters and promotes the latter, by so much the more it contributes to the conservation of the commonwealth. For it is the aim of the ecclesiastical authority by the use of spiritual means, to form good Christians in accordance with its own particular end and object; and in doing this it helps at the same time to form good citizens, and prepares them to meet their obligations as members of a civil society. This follows of necessity because in the City of God, the Holy Roman Catholic Church, a good citizen and an upright man are absolutely one and the same thing. How grave therefore is the error of those who separate things so closely united, and who think that they can produce good citizens by ways and methods other than those which make for the formation of good Christians. **For, let human prudence say what it likes and reason as it pleases, it is impossible to produce true temporal peace and tranquillity by things repugnant or opposed to the peace and happiness of eternity**. (Silvio Cardinal Antoniano, quoted by Pope Pius XI in *Divini Illius Magistri*, December 31, 1929.)
>
> Here we have, founded by Catholics, an inter-denominational association that is to work for the reform of civilization, an undertaking which is above all religious in character; **for there is no true civilization without a moral civilization, and no true moral civilization without the true religion: it is a proven truth, a historical fact**. The new Sillonists cannot pretend t**hat they are merely working on "the ground of practical realities" where differences of belief do not matter**. Their leader is so conscious of the influence which the convictions of the mind have upon the result of the action, that he invites them, **whatever religion they may belong to, "to provide on the ground of practical realities,**

> **the proof of the excellence of their personal convictions.**" And with good reason: indeed, all practical results reflect the nature of one's religious convictions, just as the limbs of a man down to his finger-tips, owe their very shape to the principle of life that dwells in his body. (Pope Saint Pius X, *Notre Charge Apostolique*, August 15, 1910.)

> **Every true and lasting reform has ultimately sprung from the sanctity of men who were driven by the love of God and of men**. Generous, ready to stand to attention to any call from God, yet confident in themselves because confident in their vocation, they grew to the size of beacons and reformers. . . No doubt "the Spirit breatheth where he will" (John iii. 8): "of stones He is able to raise men to prepare the way to his designs" (Matt. iii. 9). He chooses the instruments of His will according to His own plans, not those of men. **But the Founder of the Church, who breathed her into existence at Pentecost, cannot disown the foundations as He laid them. Whoever is moved by the spirit of God, spontaneously adopts both outwardly and inwardly, the true attitude toward the Church, this sacred fruit from the tree of the cross, this gift from the Spirit of God, bestowed on Pentecost day to an erratic world**. (Pope Pius XI, *Mit Brennender Sorge*, March 17, 1937.)

Saint Irenaeus explained the nature of the conciliar approach of a supposed "love" for sinners as he analyzed and condemned the heresies of Carpocrates:

> 5. **And thus, if ungodly, unlawful, and forbidden actions are committed among them, I can no longer find ground for believing them to be such**. And in their writings we read as follows, the interpretation which they give [of their views], declaring that Jesus spoke in a mystery to His disciples and apostles privately, and that they requested and obtained permission to hand down the things thus taught them, to others who should be worthy and believing. We are saved, indeed, **by means of faith and love; but all other things, while in their nature indifferent, are reckoned by the opinion of men-some good and some evil, there being nothing really evil by nature**. (Against Heresies, Book I.)

Saint Irenaeus simply made no concessions at all to the heretics of his own day, the gnostics, whose false religion does indeed play an important role in shaping the Modernist mind of Jorge Mario Bergoglio, who desires to jettison the Fathers and the Doctors of the Church as presented to us by Holy Mother Church under the infallible guidance of God the Holy Ghost in order to "re-read" the Scriptures and to re-read even the Natural Law. Jorge has the "secret" ability to do this. We simply have to "trust" him. How did the "trust me" slogan work out with the thirty-ninth President of the United States of America, James Earl Carter, Jr?

While Saint Irenaeus urged the Vicar of Christ to be gentle with those who returned to the Faith after being involved in heresy, he was firm in his denunciation *of* heresy as he sought the conversion of those steeped within its grip. We can no do no less in our own day as we rely upon the intercessory help of the Mother of God and of the Apostles Saints Peter and Paul, who gave up their lives rather than to compromise the integrity of the Faith.

Chapter Fifteen

Nothing of Conciliarism Comes from the Catholic Church

There is a sentence in Pope Pius XI's *Quas Primas*, December 11, 1925, that, though merely reiterating the constant teaching of Holy Mother Church about her Divine Constitution, puts the lie to the schismatic mentality represented by the "resist while recognize" movement."

> **Not least among the blessings which have resulted from the public and legitimate honor paid to the Blessed Virgin and the saints is the perfect and perpetual immunity of the Church from error and heresy**. (Pope Pius XI, *Quas Primas*, December 11, 1925.)

The Catholic Church is incapable of being touched by any kind of error, no less heresy, yes, even in her Universal Ordinary Magisterium.

Who says so?

None other than the late Alfred Cardinal Ottaviani, who was the Pro-Secretary of the Holy Office under Pope Pius XII from January 15, 1953, to the time of the last true pontiff's death on October 9, 1958.

Yes, that's who, well at least that's one who taught us this fact.

Using the teaching of Pope Pius XII about the binding nature of papal encyclical letters as the starting point for his treatise, Cardinal Ottaviani explained that no Catholic may put into question, no less reject, a pronouncement of a true and legitimate Successor of Saint Peter.

The principal target of Cardinal Ottaviani's treatise was, of course, none other than Father John Courtney Murray, S.J., the infamous proponent of the heresy of "religious liberty" that wound up being enshrined in the "Second" Vatican Council's *Dignitatis Humanae*, December 7, 1965.

Father Murray argued that papal pronouncements on matters pertaining to the Social Teaching of the Catholic Church, especially condemnations of religious liberty and separation of Church and State, were merely "transitory" or, more accurately, had "transitory elements" and were thus subject to be "reformed." Murray's boldness in this regard was so open that Alfred Cardinal Ottaviani, saw fit to confront Murray's assertions without any kind of equivocation:

> Here the problem presents itself of how the Church and the lay state are to live together. Some Catholics are propagating ideas with regard to this point which are not quite correct. Many of these Catholics undoubtedly love the Church and rightly intend to find a mode of possible adaptation to the circumstances of the times. **But it is none the less true that their position reminds one of that of the faint-hearted soldier who wants to conquer without fighting, or of that of the simple, unsuspecting person who accepts a hand, treacherously held out to him, without taking account of the fact that this hand will subsequently pull him across the Rubicon towards error and injustice**.

The first mistake of these people is precisely that of not accepting fully the "arms of truth" and the teaching which the Roman Pontiffs, in the course of this last century, and in particular the reigning Pontiff, Pius XII, by means of encyclicals, allocutions and instructions of all kinds, have given to Catholics on this subject.

To justify themselves, these people affirm that, in the body of teaching given in the Church, a distinction must be made between what is permanent and what is transitory, this latter being due to the influence of particular passing conditions. Unfortunately, however, they include in this second zone the principles laid down in the Pontifical documents, principles on which the teaching of the Church has remained constant, as they form part of the patrimony of Catholic doctrine.

In this matter, the pendulum theory, elaborated by certain writers in an attempt to sift the teaching set forth in Encyclical Letters at different times, cannot be applied. "The Church," it has been written, "takes account of the rhythm of the world's history after the fashion of a swinging pendulum which, desirous of keeping the proper measure, maintains its movement by reversing it when it judges that it has gone as far as it should.... From this point of view a whole history of the Encyclicals could be written. Thus in the field of Biblical studies, the Encyclical, Divino Afflante Spiritu, comes after the Encyclicals Spiritus Paraclitus and Providentissimus. In the field of Theology or Politics, the Encyclicals, Summi Pontificatus, Non abbiamo bisogno and Ubi Arcano Deo, come after the Encyclical, Immortale Dei."

Now if this were to be understood in the sense that the general and fundamental principles of public Ecclesiastical Law, solemnly affirmed in the Encyclical Letter, Immortale Dei, are merely the reflection of historic moments of the past, while the swing of the pendulum of the doctrinal Encyclicals of Pope Pius XI and Pope Pius XII has passed in the opposite direction to different positions, **the statement would have to be qualified as completely erroneous, not only because it misrepresents the teaching of the Encyclicals themselves, but also because it is theoretically inadmissible. In the Encyclical Letter, Humani Generis, the reigning Pontiff teaches us that we must recognize in the Encyclicals the ordinary magisterium of the Church: "Nor must it be thought that what is expounded in Encyclical Letters does not of itself demand assent, in that, when writing such Letters, the Popes do not exercise the supreme power of their teaching authority. For these matters are taught with the ordinary teaching authority, of which it is true to say "He who heareth you heareth Me" (St. Luke 10:16); and generally what is expounded and inculcated in Encyclical Letters already belongs for other reasons to Catholic doctrine.**"

Because they are afraid of being accused of wanting to return to the Middle Ages, **some of our writers no longer dare to maintain the doctrinal positions that are constantly affirmed in the Encyclicals as belonging to the life and legislation of the Church in all ages. For them is meant the warning of Pope Leo XIII who, recommending concord and unity in the combat against error, adds that "care must be taken never to connive, in anyway, at false opinions, never to withstand them less strenuously than truth allows.**" (**Duties of the Catholic State in Regard to Religion**.)

Father John Courtney Murray was trying to "historicize" Catholic Social Teaching even though our true popes had condemned "religious liberty" and "separation of Church and State" as heretical *in se* as matters of principle while, of course, conceding the existence of those heresies as a *fait accompli* in the pluralist, religious indifferentist state of Modernity. Our true popes never ceased *condemning* these heresies while making allowance for Holy Mother Church's childen in such countries to make use of the constitutional and legal structures under which they lived to practice their Faith and to profess It openly without inteference or molestation from the civil authorities.

Father Murray sought to "historicize" Catholic Social Teaching even though such "historicization," which asserts that part of a particular teaching was applicable only to the situation that existed at a certain time and thus was not binding upon the Church in perpetuity, had been condemned by Pope Pius XII in *Humani Generis*, August 12, 1950, which was, of course, simply a reiteration of the condemnations of the "evolution of dogma" promulgated at the [First] Vatican Council by Pope Pius IX and contained in the teaching of Pope Saint Pius X, most particularly in *Pascendi Dominici Gregis*, September 8, 1907.

Father Murray's efforts to "historicize" Catholic Social Teaching did not escape the notice of a young priest who had been ordained on June 29, 1951, the Solemnity of Saints Peter and Paul, in Munich, Germany, named Father Joseph Alois Ratzinger, who had been trained in his seminary years by the "new theologians" in this exact same methodology.

Father Joseph Alois Ratzinger has been perfectly consistent on this "historicization" throughout the course of his priestly career, including his time as "Cardinal" Ratzinger and as "Pope Benedict XVI:"

> **1971**: "In theses 10-12, the difficult problem of the relationship between language and thought is debated, which in post-conciliar discussions was the immediate departure point of the dispute.
>
> **The identity of the Christian substance as such, the Christian 'thing' was not directly ... censured, but it was pointed out that no formula, no matter how valid and indispensable it may have been in its time, can fully express the thought mentioned in it and declare it unequivocally forever, since language is constantly in movement and the content of its meaning changes.** (Fr. Ratzinger: Dogmatic formulas must always change.)
>
> **1990**: The text [of the document Instruction on the Theologian's Ecclesial Vocation] also presents the various types of bonds that rise from the different degrees of magisterial teaching. **It affirms - perhaps for the first time with this clarity - that there are decisions of the magisterium that cannot be the last word on the matter as such, but are, in a substantial fixation of the problem, above all an expression of pastoral prudence, a kind of provisional disposition. The nucleus remains valid, but the particulars, which the circumstances of the times influenced, may need further correction.**
>
> **In this regard, one may think of the declarations of Popes in the last century [19th century] about religious liberty, as well as the anti-Modernist decisions at the**

> **beginning of this century, above all, the decisions of the Biblical Commission of the time [on evolutionism]. As a cry of alarm in the face of hasty and superficial adaptations, they will remain fully justified. A personage such as Johann Baptist Metz said, for example, that the Church's anti-Modernist decisions render the great service of preserving her from falling into the liberal-bourgeois world. But in the details of the determinations they contain, they became obsolete after having fulfilled their pastoral mission at their proper time.**
>
> (Joseph Ratzinger, "Instruction on the Theologian's Ecclesial Vocation," published with the title "Rinnovato dialogo fra Magistero e Teologia," in L'Osservatore Romano, June 27, 1990, p. 6, cited at Card. Ratzinger: The teachings of the Popes against Modernism are obsolete)
>
> It is precisely in this combination of continuity and discontinuity at different levels that the very nature of true reform consists. **In this process of innovation in continuity we must learn to understand more practically than before that the Church's decisions on contingent matters - for example, certain practical forms of liberalism or a free interpretation of the Bible - should necessarily be contingent themselves, precisely because they refer to a specific reality that is changeable in itself. *It was necessary to learn* to recognize that in these decisions it is only the principles that express the permanent aspect, since they remain as an undercurrent, motivating decisions from within.**
>
> **On the other hand, not so permanent are the practical forms that depend on the historical situation and are therefore subject to change.** (Christmas greetings to the Members of the Roman Curia and Prelature, December 22, 2005.)

The very foundation of what Ratzinger/Benedict came to term the "heremeneutic of continuity" is both philosophically absurd and stands as dogmatically condemned, representing also, of course, utter blasphemy against the Third Person of the Most Blessed Trinity, God the Holy Ghost, by not only "hiding" a "discovery" of the impermanence of dogmatic formulations but had actually permitted direct condemnations of this very proposition by a dogmatic council and various true popes.

As noted earlier in this book, Pope Saint Pius X condemned the thesis of "separation of Church and State" as "absolutely false" in Paragraph Three of *Vehementer Nos*, February 11, 1906, which was nothing other than a reiteration of a truth that had been stated at numerous times by his predecessors:

> **That the State must be separated from the Church is a thesis absolutely false, a most pernicious error. . . . Hence the Roman Pontiffs have never ceased, as circumstances required, to refute and condemn the doctrine of the separation of Church and State.** (Pope Saint Pius X, *Vehementer Nos*, Feburary 11, 1906.)

How does something that was declared to be absoluely false in 1906 become "true" a century later, a "truth" that must be celebrated by the "popes" of the counterfeit church of conciliarism?

This is impossible.

Cardinal Ottaviani's treatise against the contentions of Father John Cardinal Murray, S.J., was written at about the same time that the great Monsignor Joseph Clifford Fenton of the *American Ecclesiastical Review* examined the binding nature of all pronouncements of the Sovereign Pontiff as recorded in the *Acta Apostolicae Sedis* and of fact that all decisions of the Roman congregations must be "religiously observed."

Using the teaching of Pope Pius XII about the binding nature of papal encyclical letters as the starting point for his treatise, Monsignor Fenton explained that no Catholic may put into question, no less reject, a pronouncement of a true and legitimate Successor of Saint Peter.

As was the case with Alfredo Cardinal Ottaviani's own treatise, the principal target, albeit unnamed, of Monsignor Fenton's treatise was, of course, none other than Father John Courtney Murray, S.J. Monsignor Fenton discussed a "tendency towards an unhealthy minimism" in the United States of America concerning whether papal allocutions and "other vehicles of the Holy Father's ordinary magisterium" should be acceped as authoritative:

> Despite the fact that there is nothing like an adequate treatment of the papal allocutions in existing theological literature, every priest, and particularly every professor of sacred theology, should know whether and under what circumstances these allocutions addressed by the Sovereign Pontiffs to private groups are to be regarded as authoritative, as actual expressions of the Roman Pontiff's **ordinary magisterium**. **And, especially because of the tendency towards an unhealthy *minimism* current in this country and elsewhere in the world today, they should also know how doctrine is to be set forth in the allocutions and the other vehicles of the Holy Father's ordinary magisterium if it is to be accepted as authoritative**. The present brief paper will attempt to consider and to answer these questions.
>
> The first question to be considered is this: Can a speech addressed by the Roman Pontiff to a private group, a group which cannot in any sense be taken as representing either the Roman Church or the universal Church, contain doctrinal teaching authoritative for the universal Church?
>
> The clear and unequivocal answer to this question is contained in the Holy Father's encyclical letter *Humani generis*, issued Aug. 12, 1950. According to this document: "**if, in their '*Acta*' the Supreme Pontiffs take care to render a decision on a point that has hitherto been controverted, it is obvious to all that this point, according to the mind and will of these same Pontiffs, can no longer be regarded as a question theologians may freely debate among themselves**."[6]
>
> Thus, in the teaching of the *Humani generis*, **any doctrinal decision made by the Pope and included in his "*Acta*" are authoritative. Now many of the allocutions made by the Sovereign Pontiff to private groups are included in the "*Acta*" of the Sovereign Pontiff himself, as a section of the *Acta apostolicae sedis*. Hence, any doctrinal decision**

made in one of these allocutions that is published in the Holy Father's "*Acta*" is authoritative and binding on all the members of the universal Church.

There is, according to the words of the *Humani generis*, an authoritative doctrinal decision whenever the Roman Pontiffs, in their "*Acta*," "*de re hactenus controversa data opera sententiam ferunt*." **When this condition is fulfilled, even in an allocution originally delivered to a private group, but subsequently published as part of the Holy Father's "*Acta*," an authoritative doctrinal judgment has been proposed to the universal Church. All of those within the Church are obliged, under penalty of serious sin, to accept this decision.** . . .

Now the questions may arise: is there any particular form which the Roman Pontiff is obliged to follow in setting forth a doctrinal decision in either the positive or the negative manner? Does the Pope have to state specifically and explicitly that he intends to issue a doctrinal decision on this particular point? Is it at all necessary that he should refer explicitly to the fact that there has hitherto been a debate among theologians on the question he is going to decide?

There is certainly nothing in the divinely established constitutional law of the Catholic Church which would in any way justify an affirmative response to any of these inquiries. The Holy Father's doctrinal authority stems from the tremendous responsibility Our Lord laid upon him in St. Peter, whose successor he is. Our Lord charged the Prince of the Apostles, and through him, all of his successors until the end of time, with the commission of feeding, of acting as a shepherd for, of taking care of, His lambs and His sheep.[7] Included in that responsibility was the obligation, and, of course, the power, to confirm the faith of his fellow Christians.

And the Lord said: "Simon, Simon, behold Satan hath desired to have you, that he may sift you as wheat. But I have prayed for thee, that thy faith fail not: and thou, being once converted, confirm thy brethren."[8]

St. Peter had, and has in his successor, the duty and the power to confirm his brethren in their faith, to take care of their doctrinal needs. Included in his responsibility is an obvious obligation to select and to employ the means he judges most effective and apt for the accomplishment of the end God has commissioned him to attain. **And in this era, when the printed word possesses a manifest primacy in the field of the dissemination of ideas, the Sovereign Pontiffs have chosen to bring their authoritative teaching, the doctrine in which they accomplish the work of instruction God has commanded them to do, to the people of Christ through the medium of the printed word in the published "*Acta*."**

The *Humani generis* reminds us that the doctrinal decisions set forth in the Holy Father's "*Acta*" manifestly are authoritative "according to the mind and will" of the Pontiffs who have issued these decisions. Thus, wherever there is a doctrinal judgment expressed in the "*Acta*" of a Sovereign Pontiff, it is clear that the Pontiff understands that decision to be authoritative and wills that it be so.

Now when the Pope, in his "*Acta*," sets forth as a part of Catholic doctrine or as a genuine teaching of the Catholic Church some thesis which has hitherto been opposed, even legitimately, in the schools of sacred theology, **he is manifestly making a doctrinal decision. This certainly holds true even when, in making his statement, the Pope does not explicitly assert that he is issuing a doctrinal judgment and, of course, even when he does not refer to the existence of a controversy or debate on the subject among theologians up until the time of his own pronouncement. All that is necessary is that this teaching, hitherto opposed in the theological schools, be now set forth as the teaching of the Sovereign Pontiff, or as "*doctrina catholica*.**"

Private theologians have no right whatsoever to establish what they believe to be the conditions under which the teaching presented in the "*Acta*" of the Roman Pontiff may be accepted as authoritative. This is, on the contrary, the duty and the prerogative of the Roman Pontiff himself. The present Holy Father has exercised that right and has done his duty in stating clearly that any doctrinal decision which the Bishop of Rome has taken the trouble to make and insert into his "*Acta*" is to be received as genuinely authoritative.

In line with the teaching of the *Humani generis*, then, it seems unquestionably clear that any doctrinal decision expressed by the Sovereign Pontiff in the course of an allocution delivered to a private group is to be accepted as authoritative when and if that allocution is published by the Sovereign Pontiff as a part of his own "*Acta*." Now we must consider this final question: What obligation is incumbent upon a Catholic by reason of an authoritative doctrinal decision made by the Sovereign Pontiff and communicated to the universal Church in this manner?

The text of the *Humani generis* itself supplies us with a minimum answer. This is found in the sentence we have already quoted: "And if, in their '*Acta*,' the Supreme Pontiffs take care to render a decision on a point that has hitherto been controverted, it is obvious to all that this point, according to the mind and will of these same Pontiffs, can no longer be regarded as a question theologians may freely debate among themselves."

Theologians legitimately discuss and dispute among themselves doctrinal questions which the authoritative magisterium of the Catholic Church has not as yet resolved. Once that magisterium has expressed a decision and communicated that decision to the Church universal, the first and the most obvious result of its declaration must be the cessation of debate on the point it has decided. **A man definitely is not acting and could not act as a theologian, as a teacher of Catholic truth, by disputing against a decision made by the competent doctrinal authority of the Mystical Body of Christ on earth**.

In line with the teaching of the *Humani generis*, then, it seems unquestionably clear that any doctrinal decision expressed by the Sovereign Pontiff in the course of an allocution delivered to a private group is to be accepted as authoritative when and if that allocution is published by the Sovereign Pontiff as a part of his own "*Acta*." Now we must consider this final question: What obligation is incumbent upon a Catholic by reason of an authoritative doctrinal decision made by the Sovereign Pontiff and

communicated to the universal Church in this manner? (**The doctrinal Authority of Papal allocutions**.)

Monsignor Fenton answered the question he posted with a ringing condemnation of the false proposition that one can "ignore," no less seek to "refute," anything contained in the *Acta Apostolicae Sedis*:

> The text of the *Humani generis* itself supplies us with a minimum answer. This is found in the sentence we have already quoted: "And if, in their '*Acta*,' the Supreme Pontiffs take care to render a decision on a point that has hitherto been controverted, it is obvious to all that this point, according to the mind and will of these same Pontiffs, can no longer be regarded as a question theologians may freely debate among themselves."
>
> Theologians legitimately discuss and dispute among themselves doctrinal questions which the authoritative magisterium of the Catholic Church has not as yet resolved. **Once that magisterium has expressed a decision and communicated that decision to the Church universal, the first and the most obvious result of its declaration must be the cessation of debate on the point it has decided. A man definitely is not acting and could not act as a theologian, as a teacher of Catholic truth, by disputing against a decision made by the competent doctrinal authority of the Mystical Body of Christ on earth.**
>
> **Thus, according to the clear teaching of the *Humani generis*, it is morally wrong for any individual subject to the Roman Pontiff to defend a thesis contradicting a teaching which the Pope, in his "*Acta*," has set forth as a part of Catholic doctrine. It is, in other words, wrong to attack a teaching which, in a genuine doctrinal decision, the Sovereign Pontiff has taught officially as the visible head of the universal Church. This holds true always and everywhere, even in those cases in which the Pope, in making his decision, did not exercise the plenitude of his apostolic teaching power by making an infallible doctrinal definition.**
>
> **The *Humani generis* must not be taken to imply that a Catholic theologian has completed his obligation with respect to an authoritative doctrinal decision made by the Holy Father and presented in his published "*Acta*" when he has merely refrained from arguing or debating against it. The *Humani generis* reminded its readers that "this sacred magisterium ought to be the immediate and universal norm of truth for any theologian in matters of faith and morals."[9] Furthermore, it insisted that the faithful are obligated to shun errors which more or less approach heresy, and "to follow the constitutions and decrees by which evil opinions of this sort have been proscribed and forbidden by the Holy See."[10] In other words, the *Humani generis* claimed the same internal assent for declarations of the magisterium on matters of faith and morals which previous documents of the Holy See had stressed.**
>
> We may well ask why the *Humani generis* went to the trouble of mentioning something as fundamental and rudimentary as the duty of abstaining from further debate on a point where the Roman Pontiff has already issued a doctrinal decision, and has communicated that decision to the Church universal by publishing it in his "*Acta*." The reason is to be found in

the context of the encyclical itself. The Holy Father has told us something of the existing situation which called for the issuance of the "Humani generis." This information is contained in the text of that document. The following two sentences show us the sort of condition the *Humani generis* was written to meet and to remedy:

"And although this sacred magisterium ought to be the immediate and universal norm of truth on matters of faith and morals for any theologian, as the agency to which Christ the Lord has entrusted the entire deposit of faith - that is, the Sacred Scriptures and divine Tradition - to be guarded and defended and explained, still, **the duty by which the faithful are obligated also to shun those errors which approach more or less to heresy, and therefore 'to follow the constitutions and decrees by which evil opinions of this sort have been proscribed and forbidden by the Holy See,' is sometimes ignored as if it did not exist. What is said in encyclical letters of the Roman Pontiffs about the nature and constitution of the Church is habitually and deliberately neglected by some with the idea of giving force to a certain vague notion which they claim to have found in the ancient Fathers, especially the Greeks.**"[11]

Six years ago, then, Pope Pius XII was faced with a situation in which some of the men who were privileged and obligated to teach the truths of sacred theology had perverted their position and their influence and had deliberately flouted the teachings of the Holy See about the nature and the constitution of the Catholic Church. **And, when he declared that it is wrong to debate a point already decided by the Holy Father after that decision has been published in his "*Acta*," he was taking cognizance of and condemning an existent practice. There actually were individuals who were contradicting papal teachings. They were so numerous and influential that they rendered the composition of the *Humani generis* necessary to counteract their activities. These individuals were continuing to propose teachings repudiated by the Sovereign Pontiff in previous pronouncements. The Holy Father, then, was compelled by these circumstances to call for the cessation of debate among theologians on subjects which had already been decided by pontifical decisions published in the "*Acta*."**

The kind of theological teaching and writing against which the encyclical *Humani generis* was directed was definitely not remarkable for its scientific excellence. It was, as a matter of fact, exceptionally poor from the scientific point of view. The men who were responsible for it showed very clearly that they did not understand the basic nature and purpose of sacred theology. For the true theologian the magisterium of the Church remains, as the *Humani generis* says, the immediate and universal norm of truth. And the teaching set forth by Pope Pius IX in his *Tuas libenter* is as true today as it always has been.

But when we treat of that subjection by which all Catholic students of speculative sciences are obligated in conscience so that they bring new aids to the Church by their writings, the men of this assembly ought to realize that it is not enough for Catholic scholars to receive and venerate the above-mentioned dogmas of the Church, but [they ought also to realize] that they must submit to the doctrinal decisions issued by the Pontifical Congregations and also to those points of doctrine which are held by the common and constant agreement of Catholics as theological truths and conclusions which are so certain that, even though the opinions opposed to them cannot be called heretical, they still deserve some other theological censure.[12]

It is definitely the business of the writer in the field of sacred theology to benefit the Church by what he writes. It is likewise the duty of the teacher of this science to help the Church by his teaching. **The man who uses the shoddy tricks of minimism to oppose or to ignore the doctrinal decisions made by the Sovereign Pontiff and set down in his "*Acta*" is, in the last analysis, stultifying his position as a theologian**. (The doctrinal Authority of Papal allocutions.)

Are there any further questions about the binding nature of what a true and legitimate Successor of Saint Peter places in the *Acta Apostolicae Sedis*?

Monsignor Joseph Clifford Fenton denounced "**the shoddy tricks of minimism to ignore the doctrinal decisions made by the Sovereign Pontiff and set down his his 'Acta'**."

The same shoddy tricks of minimism that were being used by the likes of Father John Courtney Murray, S.J., and the "new theologians," including Father Joseph Ratzinger, in the 1950s that prompted Pope Pius XII to issue *Humani Generis*, August 12, 1950, have been employed for the past forty years or more by those seeking to claim the absolutely nonexistent ability to ignore and/or refute the teaching of men they have recognized to be a true and legitimate Successor of Saint Peter. I know. I contributed to that literature for a while. I was wrong. So are those who persist in their willful, stubborn rejection of the binding nature of all that is contained in the Universal Ordinary Magisterium of the Catholic Church even though if not declared infallible in a solemn manner.

Writing in 1949, a year before Pope Pius XII issued *Humani Generis* and seven years before his commentary on the binding authority of papal allocutions, Monsignor Fenton explained that what is contained in the Universal Ordinal Magisterium of Holy Mother Church is to be believed with religious assent, which means that no one has the authority to dissent therefrom:

[Theologians] Vacant and Scheeben make it clear that in speaking of the *Decreta* (as distinct from the Constitutiones), the Vatican Council definitely included the pronouncements of the various Roman Congregations among those teachings which Catholics are bound in conscience to accept perseveringly. [62] These pronouncements are unquestionably non-infallible statements. They have obviously less authority than those documents which emanate directly from the Holy Father, even when the Vicar of Christ does not intend to use the fullness of his apostolic teaching power. If these decrees of the Roman Congregations are mentioned as doctrinal pronouncements "to be observed" by all of the faithful, then it is perfectly clear that the Vatican Council, speaking as the voice of the entire *ecclesia docens*, insists that the teachings set forth in papal encyclicals must be accepted sincerely.

The Vatican Council's exhortation has reference, immediately and directly, to those *Constitutiones et Decreta* which appeared prior to the promulgation of the *Dei Filius* and which dealt with doctrine closely connected with the teachings set forth in the *Dei Filius*.

> Indirectly however, by reason of the Council's mode of procedure, **it most certainly affirmed the obligation incumbent upon all Catholics of accepting and assenting to the teachings presented to the City of God on earth, even in a non-infallible manner, by the Roman Pontiff. It must be remembered that the Council did not intend to oblige the faithful to accept these pontifical statements by reason of any command contained in the *Dei Filius*. It simply warned them to be faithful to the obligation already incumbent upon them by reason of the pontifical authority itself. The encyclicals which have appeared since the year 1870 have manifestly just as much claim to be accepted and believed by all the faithful as had the pontifical documents issued prior to that date**.
>
> The internal acceptance which Catholics are bound to give to that portion of the Church's teaching not presented absolutely as infallible is described as a "religious assent." It is truly religious by reason of its object and of its motives. The Vatican Councl's conclusion to its Constitution *Dei Filius* stresses the religious object of this assent. The faithful are reminded of their obligation to believe the doctrinal pronouncements of the Roman Congregations because these statements denounce and forbid definite errors which are closely connected with "heretical wickedness" and which thus are opposed to the purity of the faith. Teachings that contradict errors of this sort are obviously religious in character since they deal more or less directly with the content of divine revelation, the body of truth which guides and directs the Church of God in its worship.
>
> The letter *Tuas libentur*, sent on Dec. 21, 1863 by Pope Pius IX to the Archbishop of Munich, stresses in a singularly effective way the religious motivation of the assent Catholics are bound to give to those teachings presented in a non-infallible manner in the Church's ordinary *magisterium*. After reminding his readers that the dogma itself can be set forth by the Church's ordinary *magisterium* as well as in its solemn judgments, the great Pontiff made the following statement.
>
> Sed cum agatur de illa subiectione, qua ex conscientia ii omnes catholici obstringuntur, qui in contemplatrices scientias incumbunt, ut novas suis scriptis Ecclesiae afferant utilitates, idcirco eiusdem conventus viri recognoscere debent, sapientibus catholicis haud satis esse, ut praefata Ecclesiae dogmata recipiant ac venerentur, verum etiam opus esse, ut se subiciant decisionibus, quae ad doctrinam pertinentes a Pontificiis Congregationibus proferuntur, tum iis doctrinae capitibus, quae communi et constanti Catholicorum consensu retinentur ut theologicae veritates et conclusiones ita certae, ut opiniones eisdem doctrinae capitibus adversae quamquam haereticae dici nequant, tamen aliam theologicam mereantur censuram. [63] (**Authority of Papal Encyclicals**.)

The passage from Pope Pius IX's *Tuas Liberantur* that was cited by Monsignor Fenton in 1949, a year before the issuance of *Humani Generis* by Pope Pius XII that prompted him, Monsignor Fenton, to explicate once again on the matter as he applied the teaching of *Human Generis* to papal allocutions and all other pronouncements recorded in the *Acta Apostolicae Sedis*, was preceded by another paragraph that is just as important to demonstrate the fallacy of "rejecting" the teaching of the Universal Ordinary Magisterium while claiming to "recognize" a man to be a true and legitimate Successor of Saint Peter:

> While, in truth, We laud these men with due praise because they professed the truth, which necessarily arises from their obligation to the Catholic faith. We wish to persuade Ourselves **that they did not wish to confine the obligation, by which Catholic teachers and writers are absolutely bound, only to those decrees which are set forth by the infallible judgment of the Church as dogmas of faith, to be believed by all. And We persuade Ourselves, also, that they did not wish to declare that that perfect adhesion to revealed truths, which they recognized as absolutely necessary to attain true progress in the sciences and to refute errors, could be obtained if faith and obedience were only given to the dogmas expessly defined by the Church**. For, even if it were a matter concerning that subjection which is to be manifested by an act of divine faith, nevertheless, it would not have to be limited to those matters which have been defined by express decrees of the ecumenical Councils, or of the Roman Pontiffs and of this See, **but would have to be extended also to those matters which are handed down as divinely revealed by the ordinary teaching power of the whole Church spread throughout the world, and therefore, by universal and common consent are held by Catholic theologians to belong to faith**.
>
> But since it is a matter of subjection by which in conscience all those Catholics are bound who work in the speculative sciences, in order that they may bring new advantages to the Church by their writings, on that account, then, the men of the same convention should recognize that it is not sufficient for learned Catholics to accept and revere the aforesaid dogmas of the Church, **but that it is also necessary to subject themselves to the decisions pertaining to doctrine which are issued by the Pontifical Congregations, and also to those forms of doctrine which are held by the common and constant consent of Catholics as theological truths and conclusions, so certain that opinions opposed to these same forms of doctrine, although they cannot be called heretical, nevertheless deserve some theological censure**. (Pope Pius IX, "The Conventions of the Theologians of Germany," from the letter *Tuas Libenter*, to the Archbishop of Munich-Freising, December 21, 1863. As found in Henry Denzinger, *Enchirdion Symbolorum*, thirteenth edition, translated into English by Roy Deferrari and published in 1955 as *The Sources of Catholic Dogma*--referred to as "Denziger," by B. Herder Book Company of St. Louis, Missouri, and London, England, Nos. 1683-1684, pp. 427-428.)

Remember, it was a priest of the Archdiocese of Munich-Freising who wrote the following twenty-four years ago during his time as the "prefect" of the countefeit church of conciliarism's misnamed Congregation for the Doctrine of the Faith:

> **1990**: The text [of the document Instruction on the Theologian's Ecclesial Vocation] also presents the various types of bonds that rise from the different degrees of magisterial teaching. **It affirms - perhaps for the first time with this clarity - that there are decisions of the magisterium that cannot be the last word on the matter as such, but are, in a substantial fixation of the problem, above all an expression of pastoral prudence, a kind of provisional disposition. The nucleus remains valid, but the particulars, which the circumstances of the times influenced, may need further correction.**
>
> **In this regard, one may think of the declarations of Popes in the last century [19th**

century] about religious liberty, as well as the anti-Modernist decisions at the beginning of this century, above all, the decisions of the Biblical Commission of the time [on evolutionism]. As a cry of alarm in the face of hasty and superficial adaptations, they will remain fully justified. A personage such as Johann Baptist Metz said, for example, that the Church's anti-Modernist decisions render the great service of preserving her from falling into the liberal-bourgeois world. But in the details of the determinations they contain, they became obsolete after having fulfilled their pastoral mission at their proper time.

(Joseph Ratzinger, "Instruction on the Theologian's Ecclesial Vocation," published with the title "Rinnovato dialogo fra Magistero e Teologia," in L'Osservatore Romano, June 27, 1990, p. 6, cited at **Card. Ratzinger: The teachings of the Popes against Modernism are obsolete**.)

Alas, condemnations of "religious liberty" and "separation of Church and State" that Ratzinger rejected in complete conformity to what Father John Courtney Murray had been doing in his, Ratzinger's, seminary days and first decade as a priest were made by our true popes, not merely by the Roman Congregations. Murray believed what Ratzinger still holds, namely, that no dogmatic pronouncement of the Catholic Church is ever free from reformulation as it is never possible to adequately express the many-fold aspects of dogma within the confines of human language, which must, it is contended, be the prisoner of subjective circumstances and the imperfection of those who choose the language.

Unfortunately for those who believe this, the One responsible for the formulation of dogma is the Third Person of the Most Blessed Trinity, under Whose infallible protection popes teach the truths of the Catholic at all times, yes, even when not proclaiming something solemnly *ex cathedra.* Catholics are bound to obey everything proposed by a true and legitimate Successor of Saint Peter without any degree of dissent, reservation or qualification. Monsignor Joseph Clifford Fenton proved that this is so in his scholary treatises cited above.

As this is indeed the case, therefore, Catholics who recognize Jorge Mario Bergoglio to be "Pope Francis" must accept everything he chooses to have published in the *Acta Apostolicae Sedis* as binding upon their consciences without any public crticism whatsoever, including the following two passages from *Evangelii Gaudium*, November 26, 2013, that were cited in paragraph one of this book:

247. **We hold the Jewish people in special regard because their covenant with God has never been revoked, for "the gifts and the call of God are irrevocable" (*Rom* 11:29). The Church, which shares with Jews an important part of the sacred Scriptures, looks upon the people of the covenant and their faith as one of the sacred roots of her own Christian identity (cf. *Rom* 11:16-18). As Christians, we cannot consider Judaism as a foreign religion; nor do we include the Jews among those called to turn from idols and to serve the true God (cf. *1 Thes* 1:9). With them, we believe in the one God who acts in history, and with them we accept his revealed word.**

> 248. Dialogue and friendship with the children of Israel are part of the life of Jesus' disciples. The friendship which has grown between us makes us bitterly and sincerely regret the terrible persecutions which they have endured, and continue to endure, especially those that have involved Christians.
>
> 249. **God continues to work among the people of the Old Covenant and to bring forth treasures of wisdom which flow from their encounter with his word. For this reason, the Church also is enriched when she receives the values of Judaism. While it is true that certain Christian beliefs are unacceptable to Judaism, and that the Church cannot refrain from proclaiming Jesus as Lord and Messiah, there exists as well a rich complementarity which allows us to read the texts of the Hebrew Scriptures together and to help one another to mine the riches of God's word. We can also share many ethical convictions and a common concern for justice and the development of peoples.** (Jorge Mario Bergoglio, *Evangelii Gaudium*, November 26, 2013.)

"Pope Francis" chose to have this "apostolic exhortation" published in the December, 2013, edition of the *Acta Apostolicae Sedis*.

Here are the three passages as found in the Italian language (not Latin, by the way!) in the *Acta Apostolicae Sedis* as it is published in its conciliar captivity:

> 247. Uno sguardo molto speciale si rivolge al popolo ebreo, la cui Alleanza con Dio non è mai stata revocata, perché "i doni e la chiamata di Dio sono irrevocabili" (Rm 11, 29). La Chiesa, che condivide con l'Ebraismo una parte importante delle Sacre Scritture, considera il popolo dell'Alleanza e la sua fede come una radice sacra della propria identità cristiana (cfr Rm 11, 16-18). Come cristiani non possiamo considerare l'Ebraismo come una religione estranea, né includiamo gliebrei tra quanti sono chiamati ad abbandonare gli idoli per convertirsi al vero Dio (cfr 1 Ts 1, 9). Crediamo insieme con loro nell'unico Dio che agisce nella storia, e accogliamo con loro la comune Parola rivelata.
>
> 248. Il dialogo e l'amicizia con i figli d'Israele sono parte della vita dei discepoli di Gesù. L'affetto che si è sviluppato ci porta sinceramene ed amaramente a dispiacerci per le terribili persecuzioni di cui furono e sono oggetto, particolarmente per quelle che coinvolgono o hanno coinvolto cristiani.
>
> 249. Dio continua ad operare nel popolo dell'Antica Alleanza e fa nascere tesori di saggezza che scaturiscono dal suo incontro con la Parola divina. Per questo anche la Chiesa si arricchisce quando raccoglie i valori dell'Ebraismo. Sebbene alcune convinzioni cristiane siano inaccettabili per l'Ebraismo, e la Chiesa non possa rinunciare ad annunciare Gesù come Signore e Messia, esiste una ricca complementarietà che ci permette di leggere insieme i testi della Bibbia ebraica e aiutarci vicendevolmente a scerare le ricchezze della Parola, come pure di condividere molte convinzioni etiche e la comune preoccupazione per la giustizia e lo sviluppo dei popoli. (Data presso San Pietro, alla chiusura dell'Anno della fede, il 24 novembre, Solennità i i. S. Gesù Cristo Re dell'Universo, dell'anno 2013, primo del mio Pontificato. **Acta Apostolicae Sedis, December, 2013**.)

If one professes belief that a particular claimant to the Throne of Saint Peter is legitimate and is indeed the Vicar of Christ on earth, a matter about which no Catholic is free to err or to profess indifference, then one must accept as binding upon his conscience and beyond all criticism even *Evangelii Gaudium* as part of the Universal Ordinary Magisterium of the Catholic Church without complaint, reservation or qulification of any kind.

Obviously, Jorge Mario Bergoglio's "teaching" on the Jews is heretical, and it is in this and in so many other ways that he shows himself to be a perfect disciple of the falsehoods promulgated by the authority of his predecessors since the death of Pope Pius XII on October 9, 1958. Jorge Mario Bergolio lacks the Catholic Faith. He has openly denied Catholic doctrine on this subject with great boldness. Although his style is more vulgar, visceral and profane than those who have perceded him, he is, of course, merely following those before him who have denied, whether implicitly or explicitly, the Catholic truth about the Old Covenant that was summarized so clearly by Pope Pius XII in *Mystici Corporis*, June 29, 1943:

> 28. That He completed His work on the gibbet of the Cross is the unanimous teaching of the holy Fathers who assert that the Church was born from the side of our Savior on the Cross like a new Eve, mother of all the living. [28] "And it is now," says the great St. Ambrose, speaking of the pierced side of Christ, "that it is built, it is now that it is formed, it is now that is .... molded, it is now that it is created . . . Now it is that arises a spiritual house, a holy priesthood." [29] One who reverently examines this venerable teaching will easily discover the reasons on which it is based.
>
> 29. **And first of all, by the death of our Redeemer, the New Testament took the place of the Old Law which had been abolished; then the Law of Christ together with its mysteries, enactments, institutions, and sacred rites was ratified for the whole world in the blood of Jesus Christ**. For, while our Divine Savior was preaching in a restricted area -- He was not sent but to the sheep that were lost of the house of Israel [30] -the Law and the Gospel were together in force; [31] **but on the gibbet of his death Jesus made void the Law with its decrees, [32] fastened the handwriting of the Old Testament to the Cross, [33] establishing the New Testament in His blood shed for the whole human race. [34] "To such an extent, then," says St. Leo the Great, speaking of the Cross of our Lord, "was there effected a transfer from the Law to the Gospel, from the Synagogue to the Church, from many sacrifices to one Victim, that, as our Lord expired, that mystical veil which shut off the innermost part of the temple and its sacred secret was rent violently from top to bottom**." [35]
>
> 30. **On the Cross then the Old Law died, soon to be buried and to be a bearer of death, [36] in order to give way to the New Testament of which Christ had chosen the Apostles as qualified ministers**; [37] and although He had been constituted the Head of the whole human family in the womb of the Blessed Virgin, it is by the power of the Cross that our Savior exercises fully the office itself of Head in His Church. "For it was through His triumph on the Cross," according to the teaching of the Angelic and Common Doctor, "that He won power and dominion over the gentiles"; [38] by that same victory He increased the immense treasure of graces, which, as He reigns in glory in heaven, He lavishes continually on His mortal members it was by His blood shed on the Cross that God's anger was averted

and that all the heavenly gifts, especially the spiritual graces of the New and Eternal Testament, could then flow from the fountains of our Savior for the salvation of men, of the faithful above all; it was on the tree of the Cross, finally, that He entered into possession of His Church, that is, of all the members of His Mystical Body; for they would not have been united to this Mystical Body. (Pope Pius XII, *Mystici Corporis*, June 29, 1943.)

Pope Pius XII's *Mystici Corporis* was inserted into the *Acta Apostolicae Sedis* in 1943. Although it was nothing new whatsoever, Pope Pius XII reaffirmed an irreformable teaching that is part of the Sacred Deposit of Faith. The fact that Jorge Mario Bergoglio chose to insert a contrary teaching into the *Acta Apostlicae Sedis* shows that he is in perfect communion of mind and heart with his conciliar predecessors, a heretic who is outside of the bosom of the Catholic Church, an imposter on the Throne of Saint Peter.

Although the apologists of the schismatic "resist while recognize" movement keep making caricatures of themselves by engaging in the same kind of minimism that was condemned by Monsignor Joseph Clifford Fenton in 1956 in his treatise on the binding authority of papal allocutions, the fact remains that, yes, despite their best efforts to refuse to admit the reality that is plainly before their eyes, **The Chair is Still Empty**.

Indeed, the apologists of the "resist while recognize" movement keep *expanding the scope of that minimism* to reduce into meaninglessness Jorge Mario Bergoglio's claim to the papacy as if human salvation had nothing to do with the identity of the Roman Pontiff and/or that one can "ignore" a true Sovereign Pontiff with absolute impunity yet save his soul.

This is not so.

Pope Leo XIII chose to insert two apostolical letters into the *Acta Apostlicae Sedis* in 1885 and 1888, respectively, that condemned all efforts on the part of writers to arrogate unto themselves public criticisms of bishops who had been duly appointed by and are submissive to a true and legitimate Successor of Saint Peter, no less criticism of the pope himself:

> To the shepherds alone was given all power to teach, to judge, to direct; on the faithful was imposed the duty of following their teaching, of submitting with docility to their judgment, and of allowing themselves to be governed, corrected, and guided by them in the way of salvation. Thus, it is an absolute necessity for the simple faithful to submit in mind and heart to their own pastors, and for the latter to submit with them to the Head and Supreme Pastor. In this subordination and dependence lie the order and life of the Church; in it is to be found the indispensable condition of well-being and good government. **On the contrary, if it should happen that those who have no right to do so should attribute authority to themselves, if they presume to become judges and teachers, if inferiors in the government of the universal Church attempt or try to exert an influence different from that of the supreme authority, there follows a reversal of the true order, many minds are thrown into confusion, and souls leave the right path** . . . .
>
> On this point what must be remembered is that in the government of the Church, except for the essential duties imposed on all Pontiffs by their apostolic office, each of them can adopt

the attitude which he judges best according to times and circumstances. ***Of this he alone is the judge. It is true that for this he has not only special lights, but still more the knowledge of the needs and conditions of the whole of Christendom, for which, it is fitting, his apostolic care must provide. He has the charge of the universal welfare of the Church, to which is subordinate any particular need, and all others who are subject to this order must second the action of the supreme director and serve the end which he has in view.*** **Since the Church is one and her head is one, so, too, her government is one, and all must conform to this.**

When these principles are forgotten there is noticed among Catholics a diminution of respect, of veneration, and of confidence in the one given them for a guide; then there is a loosening of that bond of love and submission which ought to bind all the faithful to their pastors, the faithful and the pastors to the Supreme Pastor, the bond in which is principally to be found security and common salvation.

In the same way, by forgetting or neglecting these principles, the door is opened wide to divisions and dissensions among Catholics, to the grave detriment of union which is the distinctive mark of the faithful of Christ, and which, in every age, but particularly today by reason of the combined forces of the enemy, should be of supreme and universal interest, in favor of which every feeling of personal preference or individual advantage ought to be laid aside.

That obligation, if it is generally incumbent on all, is, you may indeed say, especially pressing upon journalists. If they have not been imbued with the docile and submissive spirit so necessary to each Catholic, they would assist in spreading more widely those deplorable matters and in making them more burdensome. The task pertaining to them in all the things that concern religion and that are closely connected to the action of the Church in human society is this: to be subject completely in mind and will, just as all the other faithful are, to their own bishops and to the Roman Pontiff; to follow and make known their teachings; to be fully and willingly subservient to their influence; and to reverence their precepts and assure that they are respected. He who would act otherwise in such a way that he would serve the aims and interests of those whose spirit and intentions We have reproved in this letter would fail the noble mission he has undertaken. So doing, in vain would he boast of attending to the good of the Church and helping her cause, no less than someone who would strive to weaken or diminish Catholic truth, or indeed someone who would show himself to be her overly fearful friend. *(Pope Leo XIII, Epistola Tua*, June 17, 1885.)

Not only must those be held to fail in their duty who openly and brazenly repudiate the authority of their leaders, but those, too, who give evidence of a hostile and contrary disposition by their clever tergiversations and their oblique and devious dealings. The true and sincere virtue of obedience is not satisfied with words; it consists above all in submission of mind and heart.

But since We are here dealing with the lapse of a newspaper, it is absolutely necessary for Us once more to enjoin upon the editors of Catholic journals to respect as sacred

laws the teaching and the ordinances mentioned above and never to deviate from them. Moreover, let them be well persuaded and let this be engraved in their minds, that if they dare to violate these prescriptions and abandon themselves to their personal appreciations, whether in prejudging questions which the Holy See has not yet pronounced on, or in wounding the authority of the Bishops by arrogating to themselves an authority which can never be theirs, let them be convinced that it is all in vain for them to pretend to keep the honor of the name of Catholic and to serve the interests of the very holy and very noble cause which they have undertaken to defend and to render glorious.

Now, We, exceedingly desirous that any who have strayed return to soundness of mind and that deference to the sacred Bishops inhere deeply in the hearts of all men, in the Lord We bestow an Apostolic Blessing upon you, Venerable Brother, and to all your clergy and people, as a token of Our fatherly good will and charity. (Pope Leo XIII, *Est Sane Molestum*, December 17, 1888. The complete text may be found at: *Est Sane Molestum*, December 17, 1888. See also **Pope Leo XIII Quashes Popular "Resist-And-Recognize Position**.)

According to the explication provided by Monsignor Fenton, this is all binding upon the consciences of every Catholic around the world and cannot be questioned by any serious Catholic who loves the Holy Faith.

Yet it is that those in the "resist while recognize" movement continue to refuse to admit that these apostolic letters even exist or that they are applicable to their own false view of papal infallibility and the due submission we must give to a true Roman Pontiff. No amount of ignoring them, however, can make them or their authority go away.

Catholic teaching, though, remains what it is despite the vast multitude of those who refuse even to look seriously at what a conciliar "cardinal," the late Mario Francesco Pompedda, who had been head of the conciliar Apostolic Signatura, said as "Saint John Paul II" was dying of Stage III Parkinson's disease in February of 2005:

> **It is true that the canonical doctrine states that the see would be vacant in the case of heresy**. ... But in regard to all else, I think what is applicable is what judgment regulates human acts. And the act of will, namely a resignation or capacity to govern or not govern, is a human act. (**Cardinal Says Pope Could Govern Even If Unable to Speak**, Zenit, February 8, 2005.)

It does not take one with a doctorate in sacred theology to see that Jorge Mario Bergoglio and each of his predecessors have been heretics. The evidence to prove that this is so is overwhelming.

Indeed, a recently published article in Germany provides telling proof that a thirty-seven year-old German priest, who had shaken up one of his students in a sermon that he gave on December 13, 1964, the Feast of Saint Lucy, was preaching heresy publicly thirteen years after his ordination on June 29, 1951, the Feast of Saints Peter and Paul:

> On the night of December 13, almost exactly 50 years ago to the day, a student named Franz wandered through the streets of Münster. He could not sleep. He was too upset by the homily he had heard in the cathedral earlier that evening, **delivered by a young priest and professor only a few years older than himself, which interpreted Advent and Christmas in an entirely different, even revolutionary way: the old doctrine, according to which human history falls into a time of darkness and a time of salvation - namely, into the time before and the time after the birth of Christ - is one which no one today can take seriously, said the young theologian. Who, after the World Wars, after Auschwitz and Hiroshima, could still speak of the 'Time of Grace' which began 2000 years ago in Bethlehem? No, the dividing line between the darkness and the light, between captivity and salvation, does not divide history, but rather our own soul. Advent is not an event which takes place in the calendar, but rather in our hearts - or it founders there fruitlessly. That's strong stuff, and one can easily understand why the young student had trouble finding sleep after this homily, and instead wanted to be alone to think it all through**.
>
> **Today, both the student and the priest of this memorable evening in Münster are old men: Franz Kamphaus, who suffered that sleepless night, and Joseph Ratzinger, the 37-year-old academic rising star who was shaking up students of theology**. It is remarkable how the lives of these two men crossed paths for the first time. In retrospect, these two names - Ratzinger and Kamphaus - stand for two paths in Germany which, though they need not be labelled as 'right' and 'left,' were nonetheless quite divergent. Both attempted to preach Christianity under a different set of circumstances and to somehow translate it safely into the modern world - and they fought bitterly over the true and false compromises being made in the relationship between Christ and the World. And now, at the end of life and despite the distances separating them, the two men remain connected through a shared result of failure: Christianity in Germany is ideologically bankrupt. (**http://theradicalcatholic.blogspot.hu/2014/12/church-in-crisis-diaspora-germany.html**.)

The conciliar "popes" have been and remain heretics because they profess a false religion, one that is the counterfeit ape of Catholicism. It simply takes courage to recognize the truth of the state of the Church Militant in this time of apostasy and betrayal as we are reminded once again by the words of Pope Pius XI that were cited at the beginning of this commentary:

> **Not least among the blessings which have resulted from the public and legitimate honor paid to the Blessed Virgin and the saints is the perfect and perpetual immunity of the Church from error and heresy**. (Pope Pius XI, *Quas Primas*, December 11, 1925.)

We must pray for the restoration of a true pope on the Throne of Saint Peter.

The twin pillars of the Church of Rome, Saints Peter and Paul, were steadfast in their proclamation of the truths of the true Faith.

Saint Peter, our first pope, had denied Our Lord three times before repenting.

Saint Paul had persecuted the true Church before he, a Jew, was converted by Our Lord Himself, thus showing Himself, the God-Man, to cast His disapproval upon the "Second" Vatican Council's *Nostra Aetate*, October 28, 1965.

Here is the account of the apostolic labors and martyrdom of our beloved Saints Peter and Paul as found from the readings for Matins in the Divine Office for the Solemnity of Saints Peter and Paul, which is observed each year on June 29:

> Dearly beloved brethren, in the joy of all the holy Feast-days the whole world is partaker. There is but one love of God, and whatsoever is solemnly called to memory, if it hath been done for the salvation of all, must needs be worth the honour of a joyful memorial at the hands of all. Nevertheless, this feast which we are keeping to-day, besides that world-wide worship which it doth of right get throughout all the earth, doth deserve from this city of ours an outburst of gladness altogether special and our own. In this place it was that the two chiefest of the Apostles did so right gloriously finish their race. And upon this day whereon they lifted up that their last testimony, let it be in this place that the memory thereof receiveth the chiefest of jubilant celebrations. **O Rome these twain are the men who brought the light of the Gospel of Christ to shine upon thee These are they by whom thou, from being the teacher of lies, wast turned into a learner of the truth**.
>
> These twain be thy fathers, these be in good sooth thy shepherds, these twain be they who laid for thee, as touching the kingdom of heaven, better and happier foundations, than did they that first planned thine earthly ramparts, wherefrom he that gave thee thy name took occasion to pollute thee with a brother's blood. These are they who have set on thine head this thy glorious crown, that thou art become an holy nation, a chosen people, a city both Priestly and Kingly, whom the Sacred Throne of blessed Peter hath exalted till thou art become the Lady of the world, unto whom the world-wide love for God hath conceded a broader lordship than is the possession of any mere earthly empire. Thou wast once waxen great by victories, until thy power was spread haughtily over land and sea, but thy power was narrower then which the toils of war had won for thee, than that thou now hast which hath been laid at thy feet by the peace of Christ.
>
> It is well suited for the doing of the work which God had decreed that the multitude of kingdoms should be bound together under one rule, and that so the universal preaching of the Gospel should find easier entry into all peoples, since all were governed by the empire of one city. But this city, knowing not Him, Who had been pleased to make her great, used her lordship over almost all nations to make herself the minister of all their falsehoods and seemed to herself exceeding godly because there was no false god whom she rejected. But the tighter that Satan had bound her, the more wondrous was the work of Christ in setting her free. (From Matins, Divine Office, June 29.)

The lesson for Holy Mass on the Solemnity of Saints Peter and Paul, which is read also during Holy Mass on the Feast of Saint Peter's Chains on August 1 each year, described how an angel of Lord freed our first pope from his bondage at the hands of Herod as he, Saint Peter, slept so soundly that the angel had to wake him up:

> In those days, Herod the king set hands on certain members of the Church to persecute them. He killed James the brother of John with the sword, and seeing that it pleased the Jews, he proceeded to arrest Peter also, during the days of the Unleavened Bread. After arresting him he cast him into prison, committing the custody of him to four guards of soldiers, four in each guard, intending to bring him forth to the people after the Passover. So Peter was being kept in the prison; but prayer was being made to God for him by the Church without ceasing. **Now when Herod was about to bring him forth, that same night Peter was sleeping between two soldiers, bound with two chains, and outside the door sentries guarded the prison. And behold, an angel of the Lord stood beside him, and a light shone in the room; and he struck Peter on the side and woke him, saying, Get up quickly. The chains dropped from his hands. And the angel said to him, Gird yourself and put on your sandals. And he did so; and he said to him, Wrap your cloak about you and follow me. And he followed him out, without knowing that what was being done by the angel was real, for he thought he was having a vision. They passed through the first and second guard and came to the iron gate that leads into the city; and this opened to them of its own accord. And they went out, and passed on through one street, and straightway the angel left him. Then Peter came to himself, and he said, Now I know for certain that the Lord has sent His angel and rescued me from the power of Herod and from all that the Jewish people were expecting.** (Acts 12: 1-11.)

Do not be agitated by the events of the moment as each of the events unfolding quickly before our eyes is simply part of the Great Apostasy. More and more chastisements are to be visited upon us, and we must accept each with joy and gratitude because God has so ordained it that we would be alive in these challenging times.

Saint Peter was freed by no "movement," traditional or otherwise.

Saint Peter was freed by no "strategy" to keep silent about the truths of Our Blessed Lord and Saviour Jesus Christ in order to curry favor with the officials of the day.

Saint Peter was freed by the hand of Christ the King Himself through the work of His angel.

Do not be concerned about how a true pope will be restored to the Throne of Saint Peter. This will happen in God's good time, which is not quite, by the way, the same as "our" time. We must be patient and endure suffering with joy and gratitude, something that comes hard to many Americans, who want tangible "solutions" now and without any kind of delay.

Christ the King will release the chains that fetter the Chair of Peter today in His good time and by means so miraculous that each of the warring tribes in the underground Church at present will recognize the miracle for what it is without any murmuring. This is because such a miracle will occur, most likely, after a terrible chastisement that will make the ones we are experiencing at present to seem like so much child's play.

Writing in *Mirari Vos*, August 15, 1832, Pope Gregory XVI, reminded us that Our Lady crushes all heresies:

> 24. That all of this may come to pass prosperously and happily, let Us raise Our eyes and hands to the most holy Virgin Mary**, who alone crushes all heresies, and is Our greatest reliance and the whole reason for Our hope.**[33] May she implore by her patronage a successful outcome for Our plans and actions. Let Us humbly ask of the Prince of the Apostles, Peter and his co-apostle Paul that all of you may stand as a wall lest a foundation be laid other than that which has already been laid. Relying on this happy hope, We trust that the Author and Crown of Our faith Jesus Christ will console Us in all these Our tribulations. We lovingly impart the apostolic benediction to you, venerable brothers, and to the sheep committed to your care as a sign of heavenly aid. (Pope Gregory XVI, *Mirari Vos*, August 15, 1832.)

In the end, you see, we know that Our Lady's Sorrowful and Immaculate Heart will triumph. She promised that this would be so when she appeared to Jacinta and Francisco Marto and their cousin Lucia dos Santos in the Cova da Iria near Fatima, Portugal, ninety-seven years ago.

Our Lady simply asks us to pray her Most Holy Rosary and to do penance for the conversion of sinners as we offer up all to the Throne of the Most Blessed Trinity through her own Sorrowful and Immaculate Heart.

All we must do is to be faithful to Our Lady as the servants of her Divine Son, Christ the King, through her Immaculate Heart, which is united in such a matchless communion of love with His Most Sacred Heart.

What are we waiting for?

Vivat Christus Rex!

Viva Cristo Rey!

Appendix A
Reminding Catholics That They Cannot "Resist" The Teaching of A Man They Consider to be the Vicar of Our Lord Jesus Christ on Earth

Mr. Michael Creighton's List of the Errors of the Society of Saint Pius X

Mr. Michael Creighton has catalogued the principle errors of the Society of Saint Pius X and the ways in which those who assist at Society chapels justify these errors by way of responding to an article that appeared a few years ago on the *Tradition in Action* website:

To briefly enumerate some of the problems in the SSPX, they are:

1. A rejection of the ordinary magisterium (Vatican I; Session III - Dz1792) which must be divinely revealed. For instance Paul VI claimed that the new mass and Vatican II were his "Supreme Ordinary Magisterium" and John Paul II promulgated his catechism which contains heresies and errors in Fide Depositum by his "apostolic authority" as "the sure norm of faith and doctrine" and bound everyone by saying who believes what was contained therein is in "ecclesial communion", that is, in the Church.

2. A rejection of the divinely revealed teaching expressed in Vatican I , Session IV, that the faith of Peter [the Pope] cannot fail. Three ancient councils are quoted to support this claim. (2nd Lyons, 4th Constantinople & Florence). Pope Paul IV's bull Cum Ex Apostolatus Officio teaches the same in the negative sense of this definition.

3. A distortion of canon law opposed to virtually all the canonists of the Church prior to Vatican II which tell us a heretical pope ipso facto loses his office by the operation of the law itself and without any declaration. This is expressed in Canon 188.4 which deals with the divine law and footnotes Pope Paul IV's bull, Cum ex Apostolatus Officio. The SSPX pretends that sections of the code on penalties somehow apply to the pope which is flatly contradicted by the law itself. The SSPX pretends that jurisdiction remains in force when the code clearly says jurisdiction is lost and only 'acts' of jurisdiction are declared valid until the person is found out (canons 2264-2265). This is simply to protect the faithful from invalid sacraments, not to help heretics retain office and destroy the Church. Charisms of the office, unlike indelible sacraments, require real jurisdiction. The SSPX pretends that penalties of the censure of ipso facto excommunication cannot apply to cardinals since it is reserved to the Holy See (canon 2227). This is another fabrication since the law does not refer to automatic (latae sententiae) penalties but only to penalties in which a competent judge is needed to inflict or declare penalties on offenders. Therefore it only refers to condemnatory and declaratory sentences but not automatic sentences. To say that ipso facto does not mean what it says is also condemned by Pope Pius VI in Auctorem Fidei.

4. The SSPX holds a form of the Gallican heresy that falsely proposes a council can depose a true pope. This was already tried by the Council of Basle and just as history condemned those schismatics, so it will condemn your Lordship. This belief also denies canon 1556: "The First See is Judged by no one." This of course means in a juridical sense of judgment, not remaining blind to apostasy, heresy and crime which automatically takes effect.

5. The SSPX denies the visible Church must manifest the Catholic faith. They claim that somehow these men who teach heresy can't know truth. This is a notion that has been condemned by Vatican I, Session III, Chapter 2. It is also condemned by canon 16 of the 1917 code of canon law. Clearly La Salette has been fulfilled. Rome is the seat of anti-Christ & the Church is eclipsed. Clearly, our Lord's words to Sr. Lucy at Rianjo in 1931 have come to pass. His "Ministers [Popes] have followed the kings of France into misfortune".

6. The SSPX reject every doctor of the Church and every Church father who are unanimous in stating a heretic ipso facto is outside the Church and therefore cannot possess jurisdiction & pretends that is only their opinion when St. Robert states "... it is proven, with arguments from authority and from reason, that the manifest heretic is ipso facto deposed." The authority he refers to is the magisterium of the Church, not his own opinion.

7. Pope Pius XII's Vacantis Apostolicae Sedis is misinterpreted by the SSPX to validly elect a heretic to office against the divine law. A public heretic cannot be a cardinal because he automatically loses his office. This decree only refers to cardinals and hence it does not apply to ex-cardinals who automatically lost their offices because they had publicly defected from the Catholic faith. The cardinals mentioned in this decree who have been excommunicated are still Catholic and still cardinals; hence their excommunication does not cause them to become non-Catholics and lose their offices, as does excommunication for heresy and public defection from the Catholic faith. This is what the Church used to call a minor excommunication. All post 1945 canonists concur that Vacantis Apostolicae Sedis does not remove ipso facto excommunication: Eduardus F. Regatillo (1956), Matthaeus Conte a Coronata (1950), Serapius Iragui (1959), A. Vermeersch - I. Creusen (1949), Udalricus Beste (1946) teach that a pope or cardinal or bishop who becomes a public heretic automatically loses his office and a public heretic cannot legally or validly obtain an office. Even supposing this papal statement could apply to non-Catholics (heretics), Pope Pius XII goes on to say "at other times they [the censures] are to remain in vigor" Does this mean the Pope intends that a notorious heretic will take office and then immediately lose his office? It is an absurd conclusion, hence we must respect the interpretation of the Church in her canonists.

Errors/Heresies typical of an SSPX chapel attendees & priests:

1) We are free to reject rites promulgated by the Church. [Condemned by Trent Session VII, Canon XIII/Vatican I, Session II]

2) The Pope can't be trusted to make judgments on faith and morals. We have to sift what is Catholic. [Condemned by Vatican I, Session IV, Chapter III.]

3) We are free to reject or accept ordinary magisterial teachings from a pope since they can be in error. This rejection may include either the conciliar 'popes' when teach heresy or the pre-conciliar popes in order to justify the validity of the conciliar popes' jurisdiction, sacraments, etc. [Condemned by Vatican I (Dz1792)/Satis Cognitum #15 of Leo XIII]

4) The Kantian doctrine of unknowability of reality. **We can't know what is heresy, therefore we can't judge**. [Condemned by Vatican I, Session III, Chapter 2: On Revelation, Jn7:24].

5) The faith of the Pope can fail. Frequently this is expressed as "we work for" or "we pray for the Pope's conversion to the Catholic faith". [condemned by Vatican I and at least 3 earlier councils mentioned above].

6) Universal salvation, ecumenism, religious liberty, validity of the Old Covenant, etc. can be interpreted in a Catholic sense. [Condemned by every saint, every doctor of the Church and every Pope who comments on such issues; for instance Pope Eugene IV (*Cantate* Domino – Council of Florence)]

7) Contraries can be true. [Hegelian doctrine against Thomistic Philosophy]. If these positions appear to be contradictory, they are.

When I point out these positions are against the Faith, frequently the Hegelian doctrine is employed by those in attendance at the SSPX chapel.

Appendix B

Pope Saint Pius X's Allocution on True Love of a True Pope

Distracted with so many occupations, it is easy to forget the things that lead to perfection in priestly life; it is easy [for the priest] to delude himself and to believe that, by busying himself with the salvation of the souls of others, he consequently works for his own sanctification. Alas, let not this delusion lead you to error, because nemo dat quod nemo habet [no one gives what he does not have]; and, in order to sanctify others, it is necessary not to neglect any of the ways proposed for the sanctification of our own selves....

The Pope is the guardian of dogma and of morals; he is the custodian of the principles that make families sound, nations great, souls holy; he is the counsellor of princes and of peoples; he is the head under whom no one feels tyrannized because he represents God Himself; he is the supreme father who unites in himself all that may exist that is loving, tender, divine.

It seems incredible, and is even painful, that there be priests to whom this recommendation must be made, but we are regrettably in our age in this hard, unhappy, situation of having to tell priests: love the Pope!

And how must the Pope be loved? Non verbo neque lingua, sed opere et veritate. **[Not in word, nor in tongue, but in deed, and in truth** - 1 Jn iii, 18] When one loves a person, one tries to adhere in everything to his thoughts, to fulfill his will, to perform his wishes. And if Our Lord Jesus Christ said of Himself, "si quis diligit me, sermonem meum servabit," [if any one love me, he will keep my word - Jn xiv, 23] **therefore, in order to demonstrate our love for the Pope, it is necessary to obey him**.

Therefore, when we love the Pope, there are no discussions regarding what he orders or demands, or up to what point obedience must go, and in what things he is to be obeyed; when

we love the Pope, we do not say that he has not spoken clearly enough, almost as if he were forced to repeat to the ear of each one the will clearly expressed so many times not only in person, but with letters and other public documents; we do not place his orders in doubt, adding the facile pretext of those unwilling to obey – that it is not the Pope who commands, but those who surround him; we do not limit the field in which he might and must exercise his authority; we do not set above the authority of the Pope that of other persons, however learned, who dissent from the Pope, who, even though learned, are not holy, because whoever is holy cannot dissent from the Pope.

This is the cry of a heart filled with pain, that with deep sadness I express, not for your sake, dear brothers, but to deplore, with you, the conduct of so many priests, who not only allow themselves to debate and criticize the wishes of the Pope, but are not embarrassed to reach shameless and blatant disobedience, with so much scandal for the good and with so great damage to souls. (Pope Saint Pius X, *Allocution* Vi ringrazio to priests on the 50th anniversary of the Apostolic Union, November 18, 1912, as found at: **RORATE CÆLI: "Love the Pope!" – no ifs, and no buts: For Bishops, priests, and faithful, Saint Pius X explains what loving the Pope really entails**.)

Appendix C
Catholic Antidotes to the Ratzinger-Bergoglio Heresies About the Jews

It [the Holy Roman Church] **firmly believes, professes, and teaches that the matter pertaining to the law of the Old Testament, of the Mosaic law, which are divided into ceremonies, sacred rites, sacrifices, and sacraments, because they were established to signify something in the future, although they were suited to the divine worship at that time, after our Lord's coming had been signified by them, ceased, and the sacraments of the New Testament began; and that whoever, even after the passion, placed hope in these matters of the law and submitted himself to them as necessary for salvation, as if faith in Christ could not save without them, sinned mortally. Yet it does not deny that after the passion of Christ up to the promulgation of the Gospel they could have been observed until they were believed to be in no way necessary for salvation; but after the promulgation of the Gospel it asserts that they cannot be observed without the loss of eternal salvation. All, therefore, who after that time observe circumcision and the Sabbath and the other requirements of the law, it declares alien to the Christian faith and not in the least fit to participate in eternal salvation, unless someday they recover from these errors**. Therefore, it commands all who glory in the name of Christian, at whatever time, before or after baptism, to cease entirely from circumcision, since, whether or not one places hope in it, it cannot be observed at all without the loss of eternal salvation. Regarding children, indeed, because of danger of death, which can often take place, when no help can be brought to them by another remedy than through the sacrament of baptism, through which they are snatched from the domination of the Devil and adopted among the sons of God, it advises that holy baptism ought not to be deferred for forty or eighty days, or any time according to the observance of certain people, but it should be conferred as soon as it can be done conveniently, but so that, when danger of death is imminent, they be baptized in the form of the Church, early without delay, even by a layman or woman, if a priest should be lacking, just as is contained more fully in the decree of the Armenians. . . .

It firmly believes, professes, and proclaims that those not living within the Catholic Church, not only pagans, but also Jews and heretics and schismatics cannot become participants in eternal life, but will depart "into everlasting fire which was prepared for the devil and his angels" [Matt. 25:41], unless before the end of life the same have been added to the flock; and that the unity of the ecclesiastical body is so strong that only to those remaining in it are the sacraments of the Church of benefit for salvation, and do fastings, almsgiving, and other functions of piety and exercises of Christian service produce eternal reward, and that no one, whatever almsgiving he has practiced, even if he has shed blood for the name of Christ, can be saved, unless he has remained in the bosom and unity of the Catholic Church. (Pope Eugene IV, *Cantate Domino*, Council of Florence, February 4, 1442.)

POPE: We are unable to favor this movement [of Zionism]. We cannot prevent the Jews from going to Jerusalem—but we could never sanction it. The ground of Jerusalem, if it were not always sacred, has been sanctified by the life of Jesus Christ. As the head of the Church I cannot answer you otherwise. **The Jews have not recognized our Lord, therefore we cannot recognize the Jewish people**.

HERZL: [The conflict between Rome and Jerusalem, represented by the one and the other of us, was once again under way. At the outset I tried to be conciliatory. I said my little piece. . . . It didn't greatly impress him. Jerusalem was not to be placed in Jewish hands.] And its present status, Holy Father?

POPE: I know, it is disagreeable to see the Turks in possession of our Holy Places. We simply have to put up with it. But to sanction the Jewish wish to occupy these sites, that we cannot do.

HERZL: [I said that we based our movement solely on the sufferings of the Jews, and wished to put aside all religious issues].

POPE: Yes, but we, but I as the head of the Catholic Church, cannot do this. One of two things will likely happen. **Either the Jews will retain their ancient faith and continue to await the Messiah whom we believe has already appeared—in which case they are denying the divinity of Jesus and we cannot assist them. Or else they will go there with no religion whatever, and then we can have nothing at all to do with them. The Jewish faith was the foundation of our own, but it has been superceded by the teachings of Christ, and we cannot admit that it still enjoys any validity. The Jews who should have been the first to acknowledge Jesus Christ have not done so to this day**.

HERZL: [It was on the tip of my tongue to remark, "It happens in every family: no one believes in his own relative." But, instead, I said:] Terror and persecution were not precisely the best means for converting the Jews. [His reply had an element of grandeur in its simplicity:]

POPE: Our Lord came without power. He came in peace. He persecuted no one. He was abandoned even by his apostles. It was only later that he attained stature. It took three centuries for the Church to evolve. **The Jews therefore had plenty of time in which to accept his divinity without duress or pressure. But they chose not to do so, and they have not done it yet**.

HERZL: But, Holy Father, the Jews are in a terrible plight. I do not know if Your Holiness is aware of the full extent of their tragedy. We need a land for these harried people.

POPE: Must it be Jerusalem?

HERZL: We are not asking for Jerusalem, but for Palestine—for only the secular land.

POPE: We cannot be in favor of it.

[Editor Lowenthal interjects here] Here unrelenting replacement theology is plainly upheld as the norm of the Roman Catholic Church. Further, this confession, along with the whole tone of the Pope in his meeting with Herzl, indicates the perpetuation of a doctrinal emphasis that has resulted in centuries of degrading behavior toward the Jews. However, this response has the "grandeur" of total avoidance of that which Herzl had intimated, namely that the abusive reputation of Roman Catholicism toward the Jews was unlikely to foster conversion. Further, if, "It took three centuries for the Church to evolve," it was that very same period of time that it took for the Church to consolidate and launch its thrust of anti-Semitism through the following centuries.

HERZL: Does Your Holiness know the situation of the Jews?

POPE: Yes, from my days in Mantua, where there are Jews. I have always been in friendly relations with Jews. Only the other evening two Jews were here to see me. There are other bonds than those of religion: social intercourse, for example, and philanthropy. Such bonds we do not refuse to maintain with the Jews. Indeed we also pray for them, that their spirit see the light. This very day the Church is celebrating the feast of an unbeliever who became converted in a miraculous manner—on the road to Damascus. **And so if you come to Palestine and settle your people there, we will be ready with churches and priests to baptize all of you.** (Marvin Lowenthal, *The Diaries of Theodore Herzl.*)

28. That He completed His work on the gibbet of the Cross is the unanimous teaching of the holy Fathers who assert that the Church was born from the side of our Savior on the Cross like a new Eve, mother of all the living. [28] "And it is now," says the great St. Ambrose, speaking of the pierced side of Christ, "that it is built, it is now that it is formed, it is now that is .... molded, it is now that it is created . . . Now it is that arises a spiritual house, a holy priesthood." [29] One who reverently examines this venerable teaching will easily discover the reasons on which it is based.

29. **And first of all, by the death of our Redeemer, the New Testament took the place of the Old Law which had been abolished; then the Law of Christ together with its mysteries, enactments, institutions, and sacred rites was ratified for the whole world in the blood of Jesus Christ**. For, while our Divine Savior was preaching in a restricted area - He was not sent but to the sheep that were lost of the house of Israel [30] -the Law and the Gospel were together in force; [31] **but on the gibbet of his death Jesus made void the Law with its decrees, [32] fastened the handwriting of the Old Testament to the Cross, [33] establishing the New Testament in His blood shed for the whole human race. [34] "To such an extent, then," says St. Leo the Great, speaking of the Cross of our Lord, "was there effected a transfer from the Law to the Gospel, from the Synagogue to the Church, from many sacrifices to one Victim,**

that, as our Lord expired, that mystical veil which shut off the innermost part of the temple and its sacred secret was rent violently from top to bottom." [35]

30. **On the Cross then the Old Law died, soon to be buried and to be a bearer of death, [36] in order to give way to the New Testament of which Christ had chosen the Apostles as qualified ministers**; [37] and although He had been constituted the Head of the whole human family in the womb of the Blessed Virgin, it is by the power of the Cross that our Savior exercises fully the office itself of Head in His Church. "For it was through His triumph on the Cross," according to the teaching of the Angelic and Common Doctor, "that He won power and dominion over the gentiles"; [38] by that same victory He increased the immense treasure of graces, which, as He reigns in glory in heaven, He lavishes continually on His mortal members it was by His blood shed on the Cross that God's anger was averted and that all the heavenly gifts, especially the spiritual graces of the New and Eternal Testament, could then flow from the fountains of our Savior for the salvation of men, of the faithful above all; it was on the tree of the Cross, finally, that He entered into possession of His Church, that is, of all the members of His Mystical Body; for they would not have been united to this Mystical Body. (Pope Pius XII, *Mystici Corporis*, June 29, 1943.)

Let that be your judgment about the synagogue, too. For they brought the books of Moses and the prophets along with them into the synagogue, not to honor them but to outrage them with dishonor. When they say that Moses and the prophets knew not Christ and said nothing about his coming, what greater outrage could they do to those holy men than to accuse them of failing to recognize their Master, than to say that those saintly prophets are partners of their impiety? And so it is that we must hate both them and their synagogue all the more because of their offensive treatment of those holy men." (Saint John Chrysostom, Fourth Century, A.D., **Saint John Chrysostom: Eight Homilies Against the Jews**.)

Many, I know, respect the Jews and think that their present way of life is a venerable one. This is why I hasten to uproot and tear out this deadly opinion. I said that the synagogue is no better than a theater and I bring forward a prophet as my witness. Surely the Jews are not more deserving of belief than their prophets. "You had a harlot's brow; you became shameless before all". Where a harlot has set herself up, that place is a brothel. But the synagogue is not only a brothel and a theater; it also is a den of robbers and a lodging for wild beasts. Jeremiah said: "Your house has become for me the den of a hyena". He does not simply say "of wild beast", but "of a filthy wild beast", and again: "I have abandoned my house, I have cast off my inheritance". **But when God forsakes a people, what hope of salvation is left? When God forsakes a place, that place becomes the dwelling of demons**.

(2) **But at any rate the Jews say that they, too, adore God. God forbid that I say that. No Jew adores God! Who says so? The Son of God says so. For he said: "If you were to know my Father, you would also know me. But you neither know me nor do you know my Father". Could I produce a witness more trustworthy than the Son of God**?

(3) If, then, the Jews fail to know the Father, if they crucified the Son, if they thrust off the help of the Spirit, who should not make bold to declare plainly that the synagogue is a dwelling of demons? **God is not worshipped there. Heaven forbid! From now on it remains a place of**

idolatry. But still some people pay it honor as a holy place. (Saint John Chrysostom: Eight Homilies Against the Jews)

From this passage the learned translators of the Rheims New Testament, in their note, justly observe, "**That, in matters of religion, in praying, hearing their sermons, presence at their service, partaking of their sacraments, and all other communicating with them in spiritual things, it is a great and damnable sin to deal with them.**" And if this be the case with all in general, how much more with **those who are well instructed and better versed in their religion than others**? **For their doing any of these things must be a much greater crime than in ignorant people, because they know their duty better**. (Bishop George Hay, The Laws of God Forbidding All Communication in Religion With Those of a False Religion.)

The spirit of Christ, which dictated the Holy Scriptures, and the spirit which animates and guides the Church of Christ, and teaches her all truth, **is the same; and therefore in all ages her conduct on this point has been uniformly the same as what the Holy Scripture teaches**. **She has constantly forbidden her children to hold any communication, in religious matters, with those who are separated from her communion; and this she has sometimes done under the most severe penalties. In the apostolical canons, which are of very ancient standing, and for the most part handed down from the apostolical age, it is thus decreed: "If any bishop, or priest, or deacon, shall join in prayers with heretics, let him be suspended from Communion"**. (Can. 44)

Also, "**If any clergyman or laic shall go into the synagogue of the Jews, or the meetings of heretics, to join in prayer with them, let him be deposed, and deprived of communion**". (Can. 63) (Bishop George Hay, (The Laws of God Forbidding All Communication in Religion With Those of a False Religion.)

ABOUT THE AUTHOR

Dr. Thomas A. Droleskey, who was born on November 24, 1951, in Jamaica, Queens, New York, received a Bachelor of Arts, *cum laude*, from Saint Saint's Univeristy, Jamaica New York, on January 31, 1973, a Master of Arts degree from the Univeristy of Notre Dame, Notre Dame, Indiana, on January 10, 1974, and a Doctor of Philosophy degree in political science from the State University of New York at Albany, Albany, New York, on August 5, 1977. Droleskey also studied theology at Mount Saint Mary's Seminary, Emittsburg, Maryland, and at Holy Apostles Seminary, Cromwell, Connecticut.

Droleskey taught as a full-time faculty member at numerous colleges and universities (Mohawk Valley Community College, Utica, New York, 1976-1977; Illinois State University, Normal, Illinois, 1977-1979; Allentown College of Saint Francis de Sales, Center Valley, Pennsylvania, 1979-1980; Nassau Coummnity College, Garden City, New York, 1980-1983; Saint Francis College, Brooklyn, New York, 1985-1986; Illinois State University, 1986-1987; Morningside College, Sioux City, Iowa, 1992-1993;and the C. W. Post Campus of Long Island University, 1994-1995) and as an adjunct professor of political science (Saint John's University, Jamaica, New York, 1982-1992; C. W. Post Campus of Long Island University, Greenvale, New York, 1991-2007; and New York Institue of Technology (1991-1992 and 1993-1994) between September of 1976 and January of 2007. He also worked in the Office of Consumer Affairs for the County of Nassau, New York (1987-1988) and as the Director of Communications for the Diocese of Fargo, North Dakota (1988-1989).

Formerly a pro-life activist and candidate for public office, Dr. Droleskey was nominated by the Right to Life Party of the State of New York as its candidate for lieutenant governor in 1986 and as its candidate for Supervisor of the Town of Oyster Bay, New York in 1987. Droleskey was asked by some Right to Life Party members to challenge incumbent United States Senator Alphose M. D'Amato for the party's senatorial nomination in 1998, receiving enough delegate votes to qualify for a primary, which he lost to D'Amato after garnering over thirty-seven percent of the primary vote on September 14, 1998. He also served as a volunteer surrogate speaker for presidential candidate Patrick Joseph Buchanan from December of 1995 through March of 1996.

Committed to the restoration of the Social Reign of Christ the King and of His Most Blessed Mother, she who is Our Immaculate Queen, hundreds of Drolesky's articles appeared in *The Wanderer* (1992-2001) and later *The Remnant* (2002-2006) and *Catholic Family News* (2004-2006). A few of his articles appeared in *Celebrate Life* and *The Latin Mass: A Journal of Catholic Culture*. This writing led to numerous invitations to speak to groups of Catholics across the nation in the 1990s into the latter part of the first decade of the Twenty-first Century.

Droleskey's online publication, www.Christorchaos.com, is the continuation of a printed journal that began in September 1996 and continued until June of 2003. Over two thousand articles have appeared online since the debut of the website on February 20, 2004.

Married since June 7, 2001, to the former Sharon Collins, Droleskey and his wife live with their daughter, Lucy Mary Therese Norma, who was born on March 27, 2002, within the United States of America.

Made in United States
Orlando, FL
10 July 2024